Management

Management

Ricky W. Griffin

TEXAS A & M UNIVERSITY

Houghton Mifflin Company **BOSTON**

Dallas   **Geneva, Illinois**   **Lawrenceville, New Jersey**   **Palo Alto**

Cover Photo by: David F. Hughes/The Picture Cube
Alterations by: Color Response, Inc.

Printed in the U.S.A.

Library of Congress Catalog Card Number: 83-80786

ISBN: 0-395-34280-5

DEFGHIJ-M-898765

For Glenda, Dustin, and Ashley
The Lights of My Life

CONTENTS

ix

P A R T T H R E E
THE ORGANIZING PROCESS   257

P A R T   F O U R
LEADING   381

P R E F A C E

E ach day millions of us go to work in organizations, are educated or healed in organizations, while others of us are born or die within organizations. The individuals who guide the fortunes of these organizations are managers, and it is about them, their skills, roles, and responsibilities, that I have written *Management*. The actions and decisions of managers, whether they be in large or small, profit or not-for-profit organizations, have a profound impact on all of us. My hope is that readers of *Management* will be better able to execute the crucial responsibility of managing.

When I first began writing this book, I had several objectives in mind. I wanted to write a book that summarizes contemporary management literature in order to convey to the reader the nature of the management process. Further, I wanted this book to enhance student skills in understanding the managerial role and how the managerial role influences organizational performance. Finally, I wanted the book to facilitate the reader's understanding of the importance of management vis-à-vis other organizational functions and the broader social context. Overall, the objectives of the book are perhaps best characterized by the old folk saying "you can give people fish and they'll eat for a day, but if you teach them how to fish, they'll eat for a lifetime." Rather than simply summarizing various studies and theories, the book will describe *how* and *why* the management process operates and *how* managers can better understand, facilitate, and more effectively manage the various functional activities inherent in their jobs.

Organization

Management is organized around the traditional management functions of planning, leading, organizing, and controlling; a framework that effectively captures the essence of the manager's job. In Part 1, the reader is introduced to the field of management, to the development of theory, and to the external environment of management and its impact on managers. The five chapters of Part 2 discuss planning and decision making in organizations. The chapters in this section deal with such topics as organizational goals, strategic planning, development and implementation of plans, and managerial decision making. The final chapter in this part introduces the major quantitative techniques used in making managerial decisions. Part 3 focuses on the organizing process and includes chapters on the structure of organizations, staffing and conflict in organizations, organizational design processes, and organizational change and development. Part 4, Leading, contains chapters on motivation, leadership, groups and group processes, and communication in organizations. The controlling function is dealt with in Part 5, which includes chapters on the nature of organizational control, control techniques and methods, and organizational effectiveness, performance, and productivity.

Part 6, which deals with management in special contexts, concludes the book. Because a discussion of operations, personnel, small business, and international management does not always blend into a comprehensive survey of the field, I have included them in a separate part in order to highlight their importance and so they can provide a forum for an in-depth study.

Features

Contemporary

Though *Management* is organized around the traditional framework, it is clearly not an old-fashioned book. The field of management is changing rapidly and an effective new text in management must offer a balanced presentation of both the old and the new. In this case, while tradition is embodied in the structure of the book, every effort has been made to include a complete discussion of the newest concepts, models, and applications that are having an impact on the field.

This text is the first to present all three of the most popular contemporary approaches to strategic planning: the Hofer and Schendel perspective, the adaptation model, and the business portfolio matrix approach. It is the first introductory text to present Mintzberg's view of strategy and organization design. Contemporary behavioral concepts such as reward systems and organizational politics are covered in the section on leading and the chapters on controlling provide in-depth coverage of such current topics as productivity and organizational effectiveness. The timeliness of the text is reinforced by its myriad references, approximately half of which date from the 1980s.

Management applications

In preparing the book, I have made a major effort to relate abstract management concepts and ideas to management as it is actually practiced. Throughout this text are examples of how management concepts are being applied by well-known organizations such as General Electric, Chase Manhattan Bank, Resorts International, Texas Instruments, Volvo, 3 M, U.S. Civil Service, and numerous others. Each chapter opens with a critical incident focusing on a particular management issue and ends with a case based on a real organization and tied to the opening incident. The case expands upon the incident, identifies the company, explains what the company did, and raises additional issues for consideration. Among the organizations described in these cases are Westinghouse, Boeing, Levi Strauss, K mart, Columbia Pictures, Philip Morris, the Dallas Cowboys, Revlon, Burger King, British Steel, Tandem Computers, and ITT. My hope is that readers of *Management* will clearly see the dynamic nature of management in action and, at the same time, gain some experience in managerial decision making.

International management

Over the past few years, it has become abundantly clear that the study of management must include more than the study of management in a strictly American context. In this book, the importance of international management has received greater attention than has been accorded in earlier texts. Chapter 23 provides in-depth treatment of the topic and the dimension of international management is covered throughout the book where appropriate. In addition, many of the organizations cited are multinational or international in scope.

Pedagogical aids

Several features of the book are designed to aid in the learning process. Each chapter begins with a set of chapter objectives and a chapter outline and closes with a summary of key points and a set of thought-provoking questions designed to promote discussion. Each chapter is followed by two cases. Of the 46 cases in the book, half are based on real-world companies; the remainder are hypothetical cases written to illustrate particular points.

Supplementary materials

A complete instructional package is available to reinforce and enhance readers' mastery of management concepts and skills. The *Study Guide,* prepared by Dr. Joe G. Thomas, includes worksheets for annotating the chapter objectives, a pretest, a posttest, a list of the key terms used in the chapter, a completion summary for each chapter, and other learning aids.

Another component of the package, *Practicing Management,* offers 23 experiential exercises designed to develop and exercise key management skills. *Practicing Management* also includes 26 cases for further practice in analyzing management situations, and 21 recent readings drawn from leading management publications.

The third instructional aid is a computerized management game called *Manager: A Simulation* prepared by Dr. Jerald R. Smith. This game simulates a business environment in which students act as management teams to produce and market a product. Players experience both positive and negative outcomes of various management decisions.

A C K N O W L E D G M E N T S

$\mathbf{A}$s any author can attest, far more people are involved in the creation of a book than the person whose name appears on the cover. This book is certainly no exception.

I owe a large intellectual debt to several colleagues who played important roles in shaping my early and ongoing intellectual development. This book would not be what it is had I not had the good fortune to work with Skip Szilagyi, Jack Ivancevich, Bob Keller, Art Jago, Ron Ebert, Everett Adam, Jim Patterson, Allen Slusher, Bob Monroe, Don Hellriegel, Dick Daft, Carl Zeithaml, Bob Albanese, Dave Van Fleet, and Dick Woodman.

Many reviewers played a very active role in developing this book. They were asked to take an especially detailed and critical approach to the manuscript, and their positive imprint can be found on many parts of the finished product. Of course, any and all errors of omission, interpretation, and emphasis remain the responsibility of the author. A special note of appreciation is extended to the following colleagues who played such an important role in bringing this project to fruition:

Mary Lippitt Nichols
University of Minnesota

Allen Bluedorn
University of Missouri

Charles W. Cole
University of Oregon

Robert L. Taylor
University of Wisconsin — Stevens Point

J. Malcolm Walker
San Jose State University

Paul Preston
University of Texas — San Antonio

Carl P. Zeithaml
Texas A & M University

Thomas L. Keon
University of Missouri

Gregory G. Dess
University of South Carolina

J. G. Hunt
Texas Tech University

Ramon J. Aldag
University of Wisconsin

Thomas J. Dougherty
University of Missouri

Arthur G. Jago
University of Houston

J. P. Miller
University of Minnesota

Gunther S. Boroschek
*University of Massachusetts —
Harbor Campus*

John Drexler, Jr.
Oregon State University

Robert D. Van Auken
University of Oklahoma

John P. Van Gigch
California State University — Sacramento

Ralph Roberts
University of West Florida

George J. Gore
University of Cincinnati

Douglas A. Elvers
University of North Carolina

Gary N. Dicer
University of Tennessee

Ben L. Kedia
Louisiana State University

Paul Harmon
University of Utah

Neil W. Jacobs
University of Denver

Winston Oberg
Michigan State University

John M. Purcell
*State University of New York —
Farmingdale*

Stanley D. Guzell, Jr.
Youngstown State University

Nicholas Siropolis
Cuyahoga Community College

H. Schollhammer
University of California — Los Angeles

John Byrne
St. John's University

Dale A. Level, Jr.
University of Arkansas

Wayne A. Meinhart
Oklahoma State University

George R. Carnahan
Northern Michigan University

Mark A. Hammer
Washington State University

The book would never have been completed without the fine support available at Texas A & M University. Lyle Schoenfeldt, Head of the Department of Management, and Bill Mobley, Dean of the College of Business Administration, maintain an environment that encourages and facilitates professional endeavors. The bulk of the typing was ably handled by Pam Ross, Necia Mueller, Aurelia Jimenez, and Barbara Bishop. Tony Cataliotti, Beth Carnahan, and Roger Pollack assisted with many of the administrative details.

Special thanks are due to those who helped with the special-context chapters. Ron Ebert of the University of Missouri at Columbia prepared the discussion of operations management in Chapter 20. Cynthia Fisher of Texas A & M wrote Chapter 21 on personnel management. Nicholas Siropolis of Polychem Spartan Industries contributed much of the material on small business management in Chapter 22. Finally, Jack Reynolds of Texas A & M drafted Chapter 23 on international management while consulting and teaching in Scotland and Indonesia.

Thanks are also due to three very special friends. Greg Moorhead of Arizona State University, Bruce Johnson of Marquette University, and Jim Quick of the University of Texas at Arlington have individually and collectively shared many highs and lows with me during and since our years together in graduate school.

Robert Frost wrote about two roads diverging in a wood; we may not all have taken the same road, but at least our paths cross along the way.

Finally, there is my family. My father, James Griffin, and my mother, Ione Griffin, each helped point me in the right direction. My wife, Glenda, and our children, Dustin and Ashley, are the foundation of my professional and private life. They do a remarkable job of persuading me to work if I'm playing too much and play if I'm working too much. Without them, I would have become an idler or a basket case. It is with all my love that I dedicate this book to them.

Management

An Introduction To Management

P A R T   C O N T E N T S

1

1

MANAGING AND
THE MANAGER'S JOB

CHAPTER OBJECTIVES

1. Define *management* and *managers*.

2. Identify and briefly explain the four basic management functions.

3. Describe different kinds of managers from both horizontal and vertical perspectives and provide examples.

4. List and discuss the main kinds of managerial roles, giving examples of each.

5. Identify and describe the five basic skills required for effective management.

6. Discuss the advantages and relative merits of education and experience as sources of management skills.

7. Demonstrate the scope of management by identifying several kinds of management settings.

CHAPTER OUTLINE

Management and managers defined

The management process: An overview of the book
Planning: Determining courses of action
Organizing: Coordinating activities and resources
Leading: Motivating and managing employees
Controlling: Monitoring and evaluating activities

Kinds of managers
The horizontal perspective
The vertical perspective

Roles and skills of managers
Managerial roles
Managerial skills

Sources of management skills
Education as a source of management skills
Experience as a source of management skills

The scope of management
Profit-seeking organizations
Not-for-profit organizations

Summary of key points

OPENING INCIDENT

Suppose you are the chief executive officer of a major retail company and are responsible for its overall management. For decades, the company operated a chain of five-and-dime stores, but it was not a dominant factor in that kind of business. About twenty years ago, however, your company moved into discounting and achieved an unparalleled growth rate. The company became the number two nonfood retailer in the country, with nearly two thousand stores and annual sales in excess of $14 billion. In recent years, however, troublesome problems have developed. In 1980, despite record sales, the company's net profits dropped by 27 percent. Regional discounters and specialty discount stores are encroaching on your share of the market. Indicators point to failure to keep pace with changing consumer tastes. What would you do to revitalize the company?

Consider the following names: Clifton Garvin, Tom Landry, Maurice Tuchman, Barbara Uehling, Lewis Preston, Joan D. Manley, Bill Oglevee, and John Paul II. Who are these people and what do they have in common? Answer: They are all managers. Garvin manages Exxon, the largest industrial corporation in the world; Landry manages the Dallas Cowboys; Tuchman manages the Los Angeles County Museum of Art as its senior curator; Uehling manages the University of Missouri, Columbia, as its chancellor; Preston manages J. P. Morgan & Company, the fifth largest commercial bank in the United States; Manley manages Time-Life Books; Bill Oglevee owns and manages Bill's Nursery in College Station, Texas; and John Paul II manages the Catholic Church as its pope. As diverse as they and their organizations are, these managers are all confronted by many of the same challenges, strive to achieve many of the same goals, and apply many of the same principles of effective management in their work.

For better or worse, our society is strongly influenced by managers and their organizations.[1] We can define an *organization* as a group of two or more people working together in predetermined fashion to attain a set of goals. These goals may include such things as profit (General Motors), spreading of knowledge (your university), national defense (the U.S. Army), or social satisfaction (a college fraternity). So thoroughly do organizations pervade our society that we couldn't escape their influence even if we wanted to. A good way to dispel any doubt you may have about the impact of organizations on our daily lives is to spend a few minutes drawing up a list of organizations you come into contact with in a typical day. After you have made your list, com-

---

1. See William G. Scott and David K. Hart, *Organizational America* (Boston: Houghton Mifflin, 1979).

Table 1.1 Organizations that influence the life of a typical college student

6:30 A.M.	Awaken to sound of Panasonic clock-radio.
6:40 A.M.	Finally get up . . . Shower with Dial soap, wash hair with Suave shampoo, dry hair with Schick hair dryer.
7:10 A.M.	Dress (T-shirt with local FM station logo, Levi's jeans, Nike sneakers).
7:15 A.M.	Breakfast (Minute Maid orange juice, Taster's Choice coffee, cereal from General Foods).
7:40 A.M.	Ride Raleigh bike to eight o'clock class (on rainy days drive '75 Toyota Celica).
12:00	Lunch (local hamburger joint by campus).
2:00 P.M.	Go to part-time job at local clothing store.
5:00 P.M.	Quick meal at McDonald's.
7:00 P.M.	Go to play performance by college repertory company.
10:00 P.M.	Stop for refreshment at local pub.
11:00 P.M.	Turn on RCA television at home and watch rerun of M*A*S*H.
11:30 P.M.	Read local paper.
12:00 P.M.	Go to bed between Cannon sheets.

pare it to the list shown in Table 1.1, which was drawn up by another college student. You may be surprised to see just how many organizations appear. Because they dominate our lives, it is important to understand how organizations operate and how they are managed.

This book is about managers and the work they do. Here in Chapter 1, we will examine the general nature of management, its pressures, and its challenges. We will define the term *management*, discuss the management process, and identify various kinds of managers. We will describe the different roles and skills of managers, discuss various ways of acquiring management skills, and examine the scope of management in contemporary organizations. Chapters 2 and 3 deal with management theory and the external environment of management. As a unit, then, these first three chapters provide an introduction to management.

Management and managers defined

There are probably as many definitions of management as there are books on the subject, and most of these definitions are relatively simple and concise. For example, management was once defined as "knowing exactly what you want men to do, and then seeing that they do it in the best and cheapest way."[2] As we will see throughout this book, however, management is actually a very complex process—much more complex than this definition would lead us to believe. We need to develop a definition of management that better captures

2. Frederick W. Taylor, *Shop Management* (New York: Harper & Row, 1903), p. 21.

Table 1.2 Examples of resources used by organizations

Organization	Human resources	Financial resources	Physical resources	Information resources
Mobil Corp.	Drilling platform workers Corporate executives	Profits Stockholder investments	Refineries Office buildings	Sales forecasts OPEC proclamations
University of Michigan	Faculty Secretarial staff	Alumni contributions Government grants	Computers Campus facilities	Research reports Government publications
City of New York	Police officers Municipal employees	Tax revenue Government grants	Sanitation equipment Municipal buildings	Economic forecasts Crime statistics
Joe's Corner Grocery Store	Grocery clerks Bookkeeper	Profits Owner investment	Building Display shelving	Price lists from suppliers Newspaper ads for competitors

the true nature of the process. (And, of course, we should recognize that managers can be women as well as men!)

Management is perhaps best understood from the viewpoint of systems theory. (Systems theory will be described in depth in Chapter 2; at this point, we will consider only those components of it that are appropriate for our definition.) Systems theory suggests that systems such as organizations utilize four basic kinds of inputs or resources from the environment: human resources, monetary resources, physical resources, and information resources. Human resources include managerial talent, labor, and so forth. Monetary resources are the financial capital the organization uses to finance both ongoing and long-term operations. Physical resources include raw materials, office and production facilities, and equipment. Information resources are data and other kinds of information utilized by the organization. Examples of the resources used by four different kinds of organizations are provided in Table 1.2.

The manager's job involves combining and coordinating these various resources to achieve the organization's goals. For Mobil Corporation, a major goal may be a certain profit margin or return on investment. For the University of Michigan, the manager (president) may try to improve the balance between teaching, research, and service. New York City's manager (mayor) may attempt to achieve a higher level of police and fire protection. The manager of Joe's Corner Grocery Store (Joe) is trying to provide an adequate standard of living for the organization's owner (also Joe).

How do these and other managers combine and coordinate various kinds of resources? They do so by carrying out four basic managerial functions: planning and decision making, organizing, leading, and controlling. Management, then, as shown in Figure 1.1, can be defined as follows:

Figure 1.1
A schematic
diagram of
management in
organizations

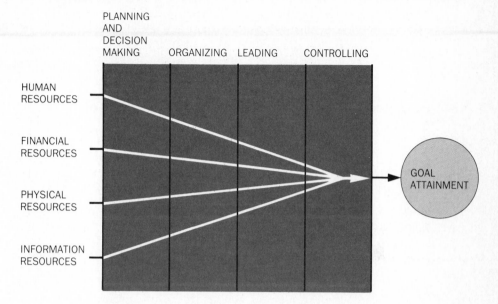

THE MANAGEMENT PROCESS

> *Management* is the process of planning, organizing, leading, and
> controlling an organization's human, financial, physical, and infor-
> mation resources to achieve organizational goals in an efficient and
> effective manner.

Management involves taking the various resources an organization has at its
disposal and combining them in such a way that the organization's goals are
attained. By efficient, we mean doing things in a systematic fashion without
waste. For example, a firm that produces its products at the lowest possible
costs and then sells them for premium prices is efficient. By effective, we mean
doing the right things. A firm could produce slide rules and buggy whips very
efficiently but still not succeed. In general, successful management involves
being *both* efficient and effective.

With this basic understanding of management, defining the term *manager*
becomes relatively simple:

> A *manager* is someone whose primary activities are a part of the
> management process. In particular, a manager is someone who
> plans, organizes, leads, and controls human, financial, physical, and
> information resources.

A manager faces a variety of interesting and challenging situations. Bill
Simon, former secretary of the treasury, is now an active corporate executive.
He is up every morning by 5:45, commutes 40 miles to Manhattan, and works
10 to 12 hours each day. At California-based Tandem Computers, Jim Treybig

has contended with an extremely low supply of qualified employees by throwing Friday afternoon beer busts and building a company swimming pool. Irwin Jacobs, a Minneapolis businessman, has made millions of dollars by buying losing businesses and turning them into winners.[3] It is clear from these examples that the various managerial functions and organizational resources can be combined in many different ways to achieve organizational goals.

The management process: An overview of the book

A useful way to illustrate the various aspects of the management process is to describe how it works in an actual organization. In 1975 Jim Treybig entered the computer business and began planning to build a dual computer system designed to eliminate garbled or lost data. Along the way, he made many crucial decisions about the components of the system and designed a special organization consisting of designers, production specialists, and distribution experts. Treybig maintained a strong leadership role in first selecting the right kinds of people for his organization and then in motivating them to get their jobs done. And, throughout the entire process, he imposed a unique control system in order to optimize human, financial, and material resources.[4]

The four stages that we have identified in the management process are apparent in this sketch of Treybig's activities. Treybig *planned* what his company would do and made *decisions* about how to do it. He set up an *organization* to carry out his decisions and took the *leadership* role in selecting and hiring organization members. Finally, he developed a *control* system to maximize resources. But, remember that the management process does not really exhibit these functions in a step-by-step fashion. That is, managers do not plan on Monday, make decisions on Tuesday, organize on Wednesday, lead on Thursday, and control on Friday. At any given time, a manager is likely to be engaged in several different activities simultaneously. This is part of what makes management an interesting and demanding task. Now let us see what each aspect of the management process really consists of.

Planning: Determining courses of action

In a nutshell, *planning* means determining what the organization's position and situation should be at some time in the future and deciding how best to bring that situation about. Planning helps maintain managerial effectiveness by guiding future activities. Upper management at Litton Industries, for example, might decide that by 1995 it wants to double its share of the microwave oven market, and that to attain that share it must increase its advertising budget,

---

3. See Irwin Ross, "Bill Simon's Out of the Limelight and in the Money," *Fortune*, May 3, 1982, pp. 122–127; Myron Magnet, "Managing by Mystique at Tandem Computers," *Fortune*, June 28, 1982, pp. 84–91; and Peter W. Bernstein, "Who Buys Corporate Losers," *Fortune*, January 26, 1981, pp. 60–66.

4. Magnet, pp. 84–91.

expand its product line, and improve the mix of dealer incentives. These goals and methods would then serve as the planning framework for that part of the company.

Five chapters in this text deal with the planning function. A logical first step in planning is to establish goals that define an expected or desired future situation. The manager also establishes a number of subgoals, or objectives. If Litton's market share goal for microwave ovens is 45 percent by 1995, it might target a 41 percent share by 1988 and a 43 percent share by 1991. The concepts of organizational goals and objectives are discussed in Chapter 4.

Knowing where he or she wants the organization to be at a given time in the future, the manager next develops a strategy for getting there. This development process is referred to as *strategic planning*. Chapter 5 addresses the topics of management strategy and strategic planning. Once the strategic plans are developed, the next step is to implement them—to put the plans into effect. This topic is discussed in Chapter 6. Specifying where the organization is to go and how it is to get there involves making many decisions, and many more will have to be made along the way. Managerial decision making is covered in Chapter 7. In the final chapter in the planning section, Chapter 8, we discuss a number of quantitative tools and techniques that managers can use for both planning and decision making.

Organizing: Coordinating activities and resources

Once a manager has developed a workable plan, the next phase of management is to organize the people and other resources necessary to carry out the plan. At a very basic level, consider the following scenario. You have a $90,000 budget and three subordinates to carry out a plan. One approach might involve giving each subordinate a $30,000 budget and having each one report to you. A different method might establish one of them as supervisor of the other two, who would have budgets of $45,000 each. Determining the best method of grouping your activities and resources is the *organizing* process.

Chapter 9 introduces basic concepts of organizing, such as departmentalization, spans of control, coordination, authority relationships, and specialization. Chapter 10 discusses different ways of getting work done in organizations; it treats such topics as line and staff roles, committees, work design and work schedules, managing conflict, and staffing. Chapter 11 explains how all these various components fit together to form an overall organization structure or design. Finally, organizational change and development—various strategies, approaches, and techniques for changing organizational components and processes—are the focus of Chapter 12.

Leading: Motivating and managing employees

Once the organizing process is complete, all management has to do is plug people into the various "slots" and everything will take care of itself, right? Wrong. It is at this point that managers must engage in what some people consider the hardest part of the management process: *leading,* which means getting members of the organization to work together to achieve the organization's goals and plans.

The leading function consists of four different activities. One is motivating employees to expend effort. This activity involves giving employees the opportunity to attain individual goals and rewards through their performance on the job. Motivation is discussed in Chapter 13. A second aspect of leading, covered in Chapter 14, is leadership. Leadership focuses on what the manager does to encourage organizational performance (rather than on management activities geared to employee needs and expectations).

The third part of leading is dealing with groups and group processes. The initial creation of groups in a company is part of the organizing process. However, the manager must then deal with group members and activities, on an ongoing basis, from an interpersonal perspective. This perspective on groups in organizations is the subject of Chapter 15. Communication, a fourth component of leading, is addressed in Chapter 16.

Controlling: Monitoring and evaluating activities

The final phase of the management process is controlling. As the organization moves toward its goals, management must monitor its progress. It must make sure the organization is performing in such a way as to arrive at its "destination" at the appointed time. A useful analogy is that of a space mission to Jupiter. NASA doesn't simply shoot a rocket in the general direction of the planet and then look again in six months to see whether it hit the mark. NASA monitors the spacecraft almost continuously and makes whatever course corrections are needed to keep the projectile on track. This monitoring and correcting cycle, discussed in three chapters of the text, is the *controlling* function. Controlling helps assure the effectiveness and efficiency needed for successful management.

Chapter 17 explores the nature of the control process. It discusses control systems, how such systems are created, and why some people resist organizational control. Specific methods and techniques for organizational control are described in Chapter 18. Finally, Chapter 19 takes a broad look at organizational effectiveness, performance, and productivity.

These, then, are the four primary functions of management: planning and decision making, organizing, leading, and controlling. An expanded view of these functions is shown in Figure 1.2, which provides the framework for most of the chapters in this book.

The remaining chapters explore areas of management that are of special interest to certain kinds of managers. Chapter 20 describes operations management. Personnel management and the staffing process are treated in Chapter 21. Entrepreneurship and small business management are the subject of Chapter 22. Managing in the international sector is discussed in Chapter 23 (international management will also be treated where appropriate throughout the text, but this chapter covers international management in more detail).

Figure 1.2
An expanded view of
the management
process

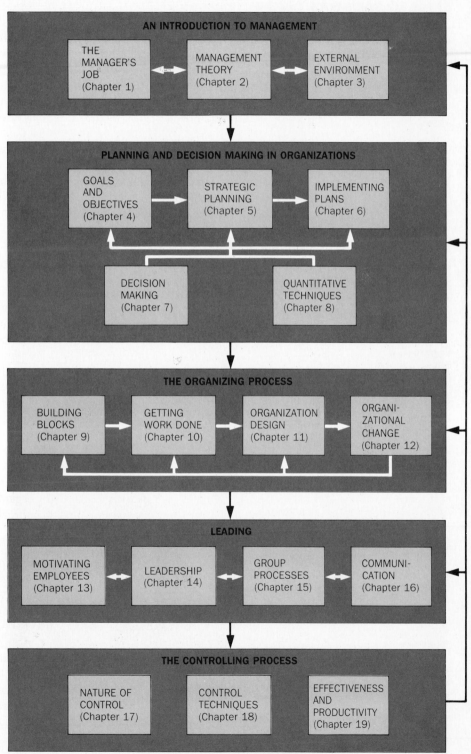

Kinds of managers

The people cited at the beginning of this chapter highlight the diversity that characterizes much of management. There are many ways to describe these different kinds of managers. One useful approach takes a horizontal perspective, and another takes a vertical perspective. That is, different kinds of managers can be identified by imagining horizontal and vertical lines drawn through the organization, as shown in Figure 1.3.

The horizontal perspective

The horizontal perspective for identifying different kinds of managers focuses on levels within the organization. Most people think of three basic levels of management: top, middle, and first-line managers.

Top managers. *Top managers* make up the relatively small group of executives who control the organization. Titles found in this group include "president," "vice president," and "chief executive officer" (CEO). Top management establishes the organization's goals, overall strategy, and operating policies.

Figure 1.3
Horizontal and vertical perspectives on kinds of managers

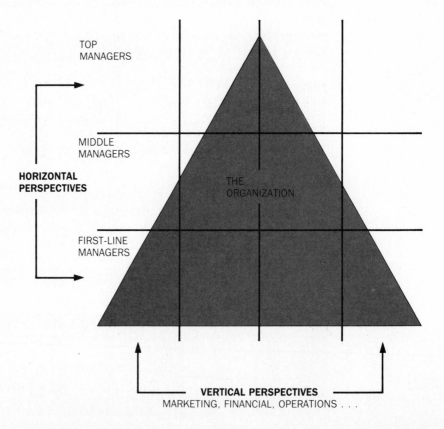

TOP
MANAGERS

MIDDLE
MANAGERS

**HORIZONTAL
PERSPECTIVES**

THE
ORGANIZATION

FIRST-LINE
MANAGERS

VERTICAL PERSPECTIVES
MARKETING, FINANCIAL, OPERATIONS . . .

Top executives also officially represent the organization to the external environment by meeting with government officials, other executives, and so forth. The job of a top manager is likely to be complex and varied. Top managers make decisions about such activities as acquiring other companies, investing in research and development, entering or abandoning various markets, and building new plants and offices. They often work long hours and spend much of their time in meetings and on the phone.

Middle managers. Middle management is probably the largest group of managers in most organizations. Common middle management titles include "plant manager," "operations manager," and "division head." *Middle managers* are primarily responsible for implementing the policies and plans developed by top management. Another major responsibility of many middle managers is to supervise and coordinate the activities of first-line managers. Plant managers, for example, handle inventory management, quality control, equipment failures, and minor union problems; they also supervise the first-line managers in the plant. In recent years, the middle manager has been called on to play the role of innovator in many organizations. A recent study has shown that, when middle managers are given freedom and resources to explore different opportunities for the organization, innovation and productivity improve.[5]

First-line managers. *First-line managers* supervise and coordinate the activities of operating employees. Common titles for first-line managers include "foreman," "supervisor," and "office manager." This is often the first position held by employees who enter management from the ranks of operating personnel. In contrast to top and middle managers, first-line managers typically spend a large proportion of their time directly supervising the work of subordinates.

Later in this chapter, we will return to these three levels of management when we discuss managerial skills. Now, however, let us develop the vertical perspective on different kinds of managers.

The vertical perspective

The vertical perspective focuses on a manager's function within the organization, whatever the level. An accountant may head a cost-accounting team (first-line management), run an internal auditing department (middle management), or serve as corporate vice president for finance (top management). But in all cases he or she performs the function of a financial manager.

Marketing managers. Marketing managers are those whose primary duties are related to the marketing function, which involves getting whatever the organization produces (be it Ford automobiles, *Newsweek* magazines, or

5. Rosabeth Moss Kanter, "The Middle Manager as Innovator," *Harvard Business Review*, July–August 1982, pp. 95–105.

United Press International news reports) into the hands of customers and clients. The marketing function includes several specific activities: market research, advertising and promotion, sales, distribution, and the study of consumer psychology.

One recent survey has shown that approximately 13.7 percent of the CEOs of the largest U.S. corporations had a primary career emphasis in marketing.[6] Clearly, marketing is one well-trod path to the top.

In recent years, many successful firms (such as Procter & Gamble and IBM) have adopted what is termed the "marketing concept." This approach to management is based on the premise that everything the organization does should be geared toward enhancing customer satisfaction. Marketing managers are important in all organizations, but their function is of particular importance in organizations that subscribe to the marketing concept.

Financial managers. Financial managers deal primarily with an organization's financial resources. Areas of financial management include accounting and investments. In some businesses, such as banking, financial managers are found in especially large numbers. Almost 20 percent of the CEOs of large U.S. corporations come from the ranks of financial managers.[7] Hence this area is also a good training ground for top management.

Operations managers. Operations managers are primarily concerned with establishing the systems that create an organization's products and services; they also plan and control the day-to-day activities within these systems. Typical tasks dealt with by the operations manager include production control, inventory control, quality control, plant layout, site selection, and work design. Although operations management originated as a means of solving problems in manufacturing facilities, the principles and tools of this speciality are now widely applied to all kinds of organizations. The current concern for improving productivity and conserving scarce resources makes operations managers vital to many organizations, and roughly 10.7 percent of the CEOs of U.S. corporations have a background in operations management.[8] We will concentrate on operations management in Chapter 20.

Personnel managers. Personnel managers are involved with hiring, maintaining, and discharging employees. Personnel managers are typically involved in human resource planning, recruiting, selection, training and development, designing compensation and benefit systems, designing performance appraisal systems, and discharging low-performing and/or problem employees. In large organizations like Exxon, these activities may be specialized, with in-

6. Louis E. Boone and James C. Johnson, "The 801 Men (and 1 Woman) at the Top: A Profile of the CEOs of the Largest U.S. Corporations," *Business Horizons*, February 1980, pp. 47–52.

7. Boone and Johnson, pp. 47–52.

8. Boone and Johnson, pp. 47–52.

dividual departments handling only a few activities. Smaller organizations are more likely to have a few people performing all personnel functions.

At one time, personnel departments in many organizations were small in size and low in status. However, because of the complexity of recent government legislation concerning personnel practices (for example, Title VII of the Civil Rights Act of 1964 and the Occupational Safety and Health Act of 1970), the importance of personnel managers has increased substantially in the last two decades. Because of this relatively recent growth in importance, few CEOs come from personnel. However, some organizations have appointed CEOs with personnel backgrounds, and many others are now requiring prospective CEOs to spend some time in personnel. The personnel management process will be treated in more depth in Chapter 21.

Administrative managers. Administrative or general managers are not associated with any particular management specialty. Their importance to organizations, however, is demonstrated by their presence (about 16.4 percent) in the ranks of American CEOs.[9] Probably the best example of an administrative management position is that of a hospital or clinic administrator. Administrative managers tend to be generalists; they have some basic familiarity with all functional areas of management rather than specialized training in any one area.

Other kinds of managers. Many organizations have specialized management positions in addition to those already described. Public relations managers, for example, interface with the public and the media to protect and enhance the image of the organization. Research and development (R&D) managers coordinate the activities of scientists and/or engineers working on scientific projects in such organizations as Monsanto and NASA. Internal consultants are specialists who provide expert advice to other managers in the organization, as at Prudential. Many areas of international management are also coordinated by specialized managers. The number, nature, and importance of these specialized managers vary tremendously from one organization to another, and as the complexity and size of contemporary organizations continue to grow, their number and importance are likely to increase.

Roles and skills of managers

Certain roles and skills are usually required of all managers, no matter what their specialty. The concept of role, in this sense, is similar to the role an actor plays in a theatrical production. A person does certain things, meets certain needs in the system, and has certain responsibilities. Management skills are the talents necessary for effective performance.

9. Boone and Johnson, pp. 47–52.

Figure 1.4
Managerial roles

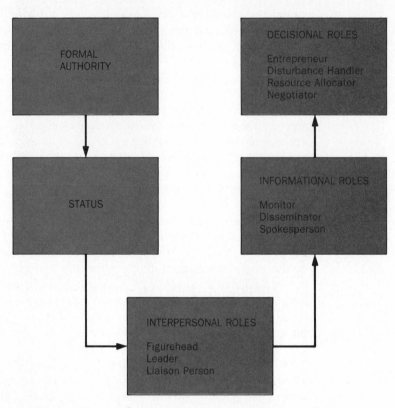

Source: Reprinted by permission of the *Harvard Business Review.* An exhibit from "The Manager's Job: Folklore and Fact" by Henry Mintzberg (July–August 1975), p. 55. Copyright © 1975 by the President and Fellows of Harvard College; all rights reserved.

Managerial roles

Henry Mintzberg affords us a great deal of insight into the nature of managerial roles.[10] In the mid-1970s he closely observed the day-to-day activities of a group of CEOs. From his observations, Mintzberg suggested that the formal authority granted to managers by the organization is accompanied by a certain degree of status. This status facilitates interpersonal relationships with superiors, peers, and subordinates. These individuals, in turn, provide managers with the information they need to make decisions. From this analysis, he concluded that managers play several different roles and that these roles fall into three basic categories: interpersonal, informational, and decisional. As suggested by Figure 1.4, there are three interpersonal roles, three informational roles, and four decisional roles.

10. Henry Mintzberg, "The Manager's Job: Folklore and Fact," *Harvard Business Review,* July–August 1975, pp. 49–61. See also Cynthia M. Pavett and Alan W. Lau, "Managerial Work: The Influence of Hierarchical Level and Functional Speciality," *Academy of Management Journal,* March 1983, pp. 170–177.

Interpersonal roles. There are three *interpersonal roles* inherent in the manager's job. First, the manager is often asked to serve as a *figurehead*—taking visitors to dinner, attending ribbon-cutting ceremonies, and the like. The manager is also asked to serve as a *leader*—hiring, training, and motivating employees. A manager who formally or informally shows subordinates how to do things, how to perform under pressure, and what hours a company person should work is engaged in leading. Finally, managers have a *liaison* role—dealing with people outside of the organization on an ongoing basis. For example, the manager may establish a good working relationship with a manager who works for a key supplier. When the manager is able to get supplies during a time of shortage or arrange a special delivery to meet a deadline by calling the "contact" at the supplier, he or she has successfully performed one facet of the liaison role.

Informational roles. The three *informational roles* identified by Mintzberg flow naturally from the interpersonal roles we have just discussed. That is, the process of carrying out the roles of figurehead, leader, and liaison person place the manager at a strategic point to gather and disseminate information.

The first informational role is that of *monitor*, one who actively seeks information that may be of value. The manager queries subordinates, is receptive to unsolicited information, and attempts to be as well-informed as possible. The manager is also a *disseminator* of information, transmitting relevant information back to others in the workplace. When the roles of monitor and disseminator are viewed together, the manager emerges as a vital link in the organization's chain of communication.

The third informational role focuses on external communication. This role, that of the *spokesperson*, involves dealing with people outside the unit or outside the organization. For example, the manager of a unit may transmit information to superiors so that they will be better informed about the unit's activities. Or the manager may represent the organization before a Chamber of Commerce or consumer group. Although the roles of figurehead and spokesperson are similar, there is one basic difference between the two. When a manager acts as a figurehead, the manager's presence as a symbol of the organization is what is of interest. In the spokesperson role, however, the manager carries information and communicates it to others in a formal sense.

Decisional roles. The manager's informational roles typically lead to the *decisional roles,* as indicated earlier in Figure 1.4. That is, the information the manager acquires as a result of performing the informational roles has a significant bearing on important decisions that he or she makes. Mintzberg identified four decisional roles.

First, the manager fills the role of *entrepreneur,* the voluntary initiator of change. For example, the manager may recognize a problem or spot an opportunity to be exploited. As the next step, he or she may initiate a change to deal with the situation. A second decisional role is initiated not by the manager, but by some other individual or group. The manager responds in his or her role as *disturbance handler*. Disturbances may include such problems as strikes, copyright infringements, and energy shortages.

The third decisional role is that of *resource allocator*. In this role the manager decides who in the unit will be given various parts of the unit's resources and who will have access to the manager's time. For example, the manager allocates the funds in the unit's operating budget among the unit's members and projects. The final decisional role is that of *negotiator*. In this role the manager enters into negotiations as a representative of the company. For example, managers may negotiate a union contract, an agreement with a consultant, or a long-term relationship with a supplier. Negotiations may also be internal to the organization. The manager may, for instance, mediate a dispute between two subordinates or negotiate a certain level of support from another department.

Mintzberg's research provides us with a number of important insights into the manager's job. First, simply being aware of the various roles inherent in the job helps us understand what a manager does. Second, by observing actual behavior, Mintzberg was able to describe how managers at the upper levels of the organization allocate their time. In a typical day, CEOs are likely to spend 59 percent of their time in scheduled meetings, 22 percent doing "desk work," 10 percent in unscheduled meetings, 6 percent on the telephone, and the remaining 3 percent on tours. The proportions are different for managers at lower levels.

Finally, the role framework helps us understand why managers do not move from planning to organizing to leading to controlling in a neat, systematic fashion. The turbulence of their surroundings demands a more flexible style. Their schedule is seldom compatible with a logical, ordered progression of activities. For example, if managers typically spend about 10 percent of their time in unscheduled meetings, it is no wonder that a successful manager needs to have mastered a variety of skills.

Managerial skills

A particular manager may need a number of specific skills. Key managerial skills are commonly described as technical skills, interpersonal skills, and conceptual skills.[11] Diagnostic skills and analytic skills are also prerequisites to managerial success.

Technical skills. Technical skills are the skills necessary to accomplish specialized activities. Project engineers, physicians, and accountants all have the technical skills necessary for their respective professions. Most managers, especially at the middle and lower levels, need technical skills for effective task performance.

Later in this chapter, we will discuss how managers acquire various skills through some combination of education and experience. The project engineer,

11. See Robert L. Katz, "Skills of an Effective Administrator," *Harvard Business Review*, September–October 1974, pp. 90–102.

physician, and accountant must all complete recognized programs of study at colleges and universities. Then they gain experience in actual work situations, honing their skills before eventually becoming, say R&D manager, chief of surgery, or partner in a CPA firm.

Similarly, the top marketing executive of any large firm probably started as a sales representative or sales manager, whereas the production vice president was probably a plant manager at one time. Technical skills are especially important for first-line managers. These managers spend much of their time training subordinates and answering questions about work-related problems. They must know how to perform the tasks assigned to those they supervise if they are to be effective managers who enjoy the respect of their subordinates.

Interpersonal skills. Managers spend considerable time interacting with people both inside and outside the organization. Recall Mintzberg's description of how top managers spend their time: 59 percent in meetings, 6 percent on the phone, and 3 percent on tours. All these activities involve other people. For obvious reasons, the manager needs interpersonal skills: the ability to communicate with, understand, and motivate both individuals and groups.

Mintzberg again offers useful insights: The roles of liaison person, monitor, disseminator, spokesperson, and negotiator relate quite specifically to communication. The ability to understand others is of special importance to one who is called on to handle disturbances, allocate resources, and negotiate. Finally, the roles of leader, disseminator, and resource allocator require skill in motivating.

It is interesting to note that not all successful managers exhibit good interpersonal skills. Harold Geneen, former chief executive of International Telephone and Telegraph Corporation, had a reputation for humiliating managers who failed to live up to his expectations. Other managers were afraid of Geneen and many left ITT to seek employment elsewhere.[12] In the long run, harsh treatment tends to increase personnel turnover; moreover, it becomes increasingly difficult to replace those who leave. Other things being equal, a manager who has good interpersonal skills is likely to be more successful than a manager with poor interpersonal skills.

Conceptual skills. Conceptual skills depend on the manager's ability to think in the abstract. Managers need the mental capacity to understand various cause-and-effect relationships in the organization, to grasp how all the parts of the organization fit together, and to view the organization in a holistic manner.

Consider, for example, a pure production perspective versus a pure marketing perspective within an organization. A production manager might argue for a limited product line to minimize production costs and for a limited inventory to minimize warehouse costs. The focus is on minimizing costs. A marketing manager in the same organization might argue for an expanded product line to appeal to more customers and for a large inventory to guarantee prompt delivery. The objective here is sales maximization.

12. See Hugh D. Menzies, "The Ten Toughest Bosses," *Fortune*, April 21, 1980, pp. 62–72.

"... and give me good abstract-reasoning ability, interpersonal skills, cultural perspective, linguistic comprehension, and a high sociodynamic potential."

Drawing by Ed Fisher; © 1981 The New Yorker Magazine, Inc.

A manager with conceptual skills, however, would see the problems that would arise from both extremes. Decreased product lines would cut costs but would also cut sales; expanded lines would increase both. Taking a larger view, production and marketing should be seen as complementary rather than antagonistic processes. Conceptual skills enable the manager to understand that the objective should not be simply to minimize costs *or* to maximize sales; a better objective would be to maximize profit as a result of *optimizing* costs *and* sales.

Charles Wilson very effectively used his conceptual skills in the early 1950s. While traveling with his family on vacation in 1951, he was amazed at the high prices that hotels charged for mediocre accommodations. Wilson reasoned that a chain of good-quality, medium-priced, roadside hotels would be successful. His unique conceptualizing of a business opportunity while on vacation led to the founding of a $1 billion chain of motels. Its name? Holiday Inn.[13]

Another example of conceptual thinking comes from the railroad industry. From about 1920 well into the 1940s, the railroads made the mistake of assuming they were in the railroad business. The result? Trucking and air

13. See Arthur M. Louis, ''The Hall of Fame for U.S. Business Leadership,'' *Fortune,* March 22, 1982, pp. 101–107.

freight companies captured large portions of their market, crippling the rail-roads. Finally the railroads realized they were in the transportation business. Today General Motors recognizes that it too is in the transportation business, not just the automobile business. It has learned to view its competitors as not only Ford, Honda, and Toyota, but also Schwinn, Kawasaki, public transportation systems, and automobile repair companies. Conceptual skills are required to visualize these connections.

Diagnostic skills. Successful managers also possess diagnostic skills. A physician diagnoses a patient's illness by analyzing a number of symptoms and determining their probable cause. Similarly, a manager can diagnose a problem in the organization by studying its symptoms. For example, a particular unit may be suffering from high turnover. The manager who can diagnose the situation may discover that the unit's supervisor has poor interpersonal skills. The problem might then be solved by training or transferring the supervisor to a post that demands less interaction.

Diagnostic skills are also useful in favorable situations. The company may find that its sales are increasing at a much higher rate than anticipated. Possible causes might include low price, greater demand than predicted, high prices charged by a competitor, and other factors. Diagnostic skills would enable the manager to determine what was causing the sales explosion and how best to take advantage of it.

Analytic skills. In a sense, analytic skills are similar to decision-making skills, and they complement diagnostic skills. By analytic skills we mean the manager's ability to identify the key variables in a situation, see how they are interrelated, and decide which ones should receive the most attention.

In discussing diagnostic skills, we used the example of a unit supervisor who lacked interpersonal skills and so caused turnover. The manager whose diagnostic skill achieved that insight, however, was then faced with the problem of what action to take. Analytic skills enable managers to determine possible strategies (firing the supervisor, training the supervisor, transferring the supervisor, and so on) and to select the most appropriate strategy for the situation. Diagnostic skills, in short, enable managers to *understand* a situation, whereas analytic skills enable managers to determine *what to do* in the situation.

Analytic skills are similar to decision-making skills, but analysis may not involve an actual decision. When selecting a site for a new plant, for example, a manager may analyze the advantages and disadvantages of several sites and make a recommendation to a site-selection committee. The committee then makes the decision, but the manager clearly enlisted analytic skills to arrive at the recommendation.

In summary, successful managers are likely to have five basic types of skills: technical, interpersonal, conceptual, diagnostic, and analytic. Figure 1.5 suggests the extent to which managers at different levels in the organization need different kinds of skills. As one progresses up the organization, fewer technical skills are needed, because top managers spend less time in actual operating situations and are concerned with broader aspects of the organiza-

Figure 1.5
The managerial
skills necessary at
different
organizational levels

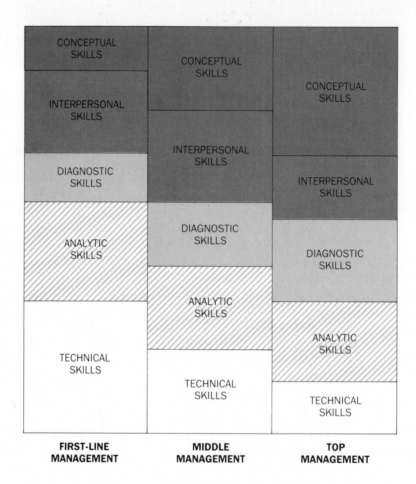

tion. Similarly, interpersonal skills may not play a large part in the role of a top manager. Figure 1.5 suggests that conceptual, diagnostic, and analytic skills become more important at higher levels.

Sources of management skills

How does one acquire the skills necessary for successful management? Donald Wills Douglas, founder of Douglas Aircraft (now a part of McDonnell Douglas Corporation), studied at MIT and then spent several years working himself up in the aviation industry. Joseph Irwin Miller graduated from Yale and attended Oxford. He later combined his formal education with a background in mechanics to become the driving force behind the success of Cummins Engine Company.[14]

14. See Max Ways, "The Hall of Fame for Business Leadership," *Fortune*, January 30, 1978, pp. 91–97.

Douglas and Miller, like most successful managers, acquired their technical, interpersonal, conceptual, diagnostic, and analytic skills from two primary sources: education and experience. Some managers draw largely from one source or the other, whereas others rely on a combination of the two.

Education as a source of management skills

Many of you reading this book right now are doing so because you are enrolled in a management course at a college or university. You are acquiring management skills in an educational setting. When you complete the course (and the book), you will have a foundation for developing your management skills in more advanced courses.

Enrollments in business schools and colleges have mushroomed in recent years. More and more students are seeking undergraduate degrees in business and management. M.B.A. programs (conferring Master's degrees in business administration) have also experienced rapid growth, and they often attract students whose undergraduate majors were in other fields.

Even after obtaining the degree, most prospective managers have not seen the end of their management education. Many middle and top managers periodically return to campus to participate in executive or management development programs (MDPs) ranging in duration from a few days to several weeks. First-line managers also take advantage of extension and continuing education programs offered by institutions of higher education. A recent innovation in extended management education is the Executive M.B.A. program offered by many top business schools. Under this system, middle and top managers with several years of experience complete an accelerated program of study on weekends. Finally, many large companies have in-house training programs for furthering the education of managers.

We should note that formal programs of study in business and management are relatively new. During the first several decades of this century, few successful managers attended college, and those who did usually majored in the humanities or liberal arts. About the closest a person could get to a business degree was to study economics. Even today, some successful executives lack college degrees.

The current trend, however, is clearly toward formal education as a prerequisite to business success. Nonbusiness undergraduates have recently begun to take more and more business courses in an effort to increase their job opportunities. Engineers frequently return to school for M.B.A. degrees. In 1977, 12 percent of the chief executives of the 1,300 largest U.S. companies did not have a degree. By 1980 this figure had fallen to 10.8 percent and 46 of the 50 largest companies were headed by college graduates.[15] American companies are spending tens of millions of dollars annually for seminars and other executive education programs.[16]

The primary advantage of education as a source of management skills is

15. See Walter Kiechel III, "Executives Without Degrees," *Fortune*, June 28, 1982, pp. 119–120.

16. See Jeremy Main, "The Executive Yearn to Learn," *Fortune*, May 3, 1982, pp. 234–248. See also Roy Rowan, "Executive Ed. at Computer U.," *Fortune*, March 7, 1983, pp. 58–64.

that a student can follow a well-developed program of study, becoming familiar with current research and thinking on management. And many college students can devote full-time energy and attention to learning. On the negative side, management education may be so general, in order to meet the needs of a wide variety of students, that specific know-how is hard to obtain. Further, many aspects of the manager's job can be discussed in a book but cannot really be appreciated and understood until they are experienced.

Experience as a source of management skills

This book will help provide you with a solid foundation for enhancing your management skills. However, even if you were to memorize every word in every management book ever written, you could not automatically step into a top management position and be effective. The reason? Management skills must also be learned through experience. Most managers advanced to their present position from other jobs. By experiencing the day-to-day pressures a manager is subject to and by meeting a variety of managerial challenges, the individual develops insights that cannot be learned from a book.

For this reason most large companies, and many smaller ones as well, have management training programs developed for their prospective managers. People are hired from college campuses, from other organizations, or from the ranks of the organization's first-line managers and/or operating employees. These people are systematically assigned to a variety of different jobs. Over time, the individual is exposed to most, if not all, of the major aspects of the organization. In this way the manager learns by experience.

The training programs at certain companies, such as Procter & Gamble, General Foods, and General Mills, are so good that some recruiters think of them as second M.B.A.'s. About half of the people who make it through the General Mills program, for example, use this experience to secure good jobs with other companies.[17]

Even without formal training programs, it is possible for managers to achieve success as they profit from varied experiences. For example, David Ogilvy used his experiences as a store salesman, a Paris chef, a tobacco farmer, and an intelligence agent to found one of the largest advertising agencies in the country, Ogilvy & Mather.[18] And, of course, natural ability, drive, and self-motivation all play a role in acquiring experience and developing management skills.

Most effective managers learn their skills through a combination of education and experience. Some type of college degree, even if it is not in business administration, usually provides a foundation. The individual then participates in a variety of management situations as her or his career progresses. During the manager's rise in the organization, occasional educational "up-dates" such

17. Ann M. Morrison, "The General Mills Brand of Managers," *Fortune*, January 12, 1981, pp. 98–107.
18. Max Ways, "The Hall of Fame for Business Leadership," *Fortune*, March 26, 1979, pp. 43–48.

as management development programs may supplement on-the-job experience. The next section explores the wide variety of organizations in which modern managers gain the experience they need.

The scope of management

When most people think of managers and management, they think of profit-seeking organizations. At the beginning of this chapter, we considered Clifton Garvin of Exxon, Joan Manley of Time-Life Books, and Lewis Preston of J. P. Morgan as examples of managers. But we also used examples from sports, education, and religion—fields in which managers are also essential. In fact, any group of two or more people working to achieve a goal (our definition of an organization) and having human, material, financial, and/or informational resources at its disposal is engaged in management. The following brief section is an overview of the wide scope of management in a diverse group of organizations.

Profit-seeking organizations

Most of what we know about management comes from profit-seeking organizations, because their survival has long depended on efficiency and effectiveness. Examples of profit-seeking organizations include industrial firms (General Motors, Tenneco, Procter & Gamble, Xerox, Levi Strauss), commercial banks (Citicorp, Wells Fargo, Chase Manhattan), insurance companies (Prudential, Metropolitan), retailers (Sears, Safeway, K mart), transportation companies (Pan American World Airways, Consolidated Freightways, Sohio Pipe Line), utilities (AT&T, Consolidated Edison), communication companies (CBS, The New York Times Company), and service organizations (the local pizza parlor and laundromat).

Small businesses. Many people associate management just as much with large businesses as with profit-seeking businesses. But good management is also essential for small businesses, which play an important role in the country's economy. Almost 97 percent of all businesses in the United States qualify as small businesses and about 77 percent employ 9 or fewer employees. In some respects, effective management in a small business is particularly important: A large firm like Exxon can afford to lose several thousand dollars on an incorrect decision, whereas a small business may ill afford a much smaller loss. We will focus on small business management in Chapter 22.

International management. In recent years, the importance of international management has increased dramatically. The list of American firms doing business in other countries is staggering. Boeing, for example, did over $5.5 *billion* in export trade in 1980.[19] Other major exporters include General

---

19. "The 50 Leading Exporters," *Fortune,* August 24, 1981, p. 85.

Motors, General Electric, Ford, and Caterpillar Tractor. Two-thirds of Exxon's business is done outside the United States. Moreover, a number of major firms that do business in the United States have their headquarters in other countries. Firms in this category include Shell (Holland), Fiat (Italy), Nestle (Switzerland), and Massey-Ferguson (Canada). Essays on Japanese management dominated the pages of business publications in the early 1980s; indeed, a book on the subject spent several weeks on best-seller lists across the country in 1981.[20] Moreover, international management is not confined to profit-seeking organizations. There are several international sports federations (such as Little League baseball); the federal government has branches (embassies) in most countries; and the Roman Catholic Church is established in most countries too. In some respects, the military was one of the first multinational organizations. International management will be covered in more depth in Chapter 23.

Not-for-profit organizations

Intangible goals such as education, social services, public protection, and recreation are often the primary aim of not-for-profit organizations. Examples include the United Fund, the U.S. Postal Service, Boy Scouts of America, Little League baseball, art galleries, museums, and the Public Broadcasting Service. Although these and similar organizations may not have to be profitable in order to attract investors, they must still employ sound management practices if they are to survive and work toward their goals. And money must be handled in an efficient and effective way. For example, if the United Fund were to begin to spend large portions of its contributions on administration, contributors would lose confidence in the organization and make their charitable donations elsewhere.

Governmental organizations. The management of governmental organizations and agencies is often regarded as a separate specialty: public administration. Governmental organizations include the Federal Trade Commission, the Environmental Protection Agency, the National Science Foundation, all branches of the military, state highway departments, federal and state prison systems, and other government units familiar to all of us. Tax dollars support governmental organizations, so politicians and citizens groups are acutely sensitive to the possibility of mismanagement.

Educational organizations. Public and private schools, colleges, and universities all stand to benefit from the efficient use of resources. Taxpayer "revolts" in states like California and Massachusetts have drastically cut back the tax money available for education, forcing administrators to make tough decisions about allocating the resources that remain.

---

20. William Ouchi, *Theory Z—How American Business Can Meet the Japanese Challenge* (Reading, Mass.: Addison-Wesley, 1981).

Health care facilities. Managing health care facilities such as clinics, hospitals, and HMOs (health maintenance organizations) is now considered a separate field of management. Here, as in other organizations, scarce resources dictate an efficient and effective approach. In recent years many universities have established health care administration programs to train managers as specialists in this field.

Nontraditional settings. Finally, good management is required in several nontraditional settings to meet established goals. To one extent or another, management is practiced in religious organizations, terrorist groups, fraternities and sororities, organized crime, street gangs, neighborhood associations, and households. In short, as we noted at the beginning of this chapter, management and managers have a profound influence on all of us.

Summary of key points

Management is the process of planning, organizing, leading, and controlling an organization's human, financial, physical, and information resources to achieve organizational goals in an efficient and effective manner. A manager is someone whose primary activities are a part of the management process.

Organizations, and therefore management and managers, play a significant role in most of our daily activities. Managers face a variety of interesting and challenging situations. The basic activities within the management process are planning and decision making (determining courses of action), organizing (coordinating activities and resources), leading (motivating and managing employees), and controlling (monitoring and evaluating activities).

Managers can be studied from either a horizontal or a vertical perspective. From a horizontal perspective, we can identify top, middle, and first-line managers. From a vertical perspective, the kinds of managers include marketing, financial, operations, personnel, administrative, and specialized managers.

Most managers have ten basic roles to play, including three interpersonal roles (figurehead, leader, and liaison), three informational roles (monitor, disseminator, and spokesperson), and four decisional roles (entrepreneur, disturbance handler, resource allocator, and negotiator). Effective managers tend to have technical, interpersonal, conceptual, diagnostic, and analytic skills.

Management skills may be acquired through education (formal coursework and continuing education) or experience (training programs and previous jobs). Increasingly, successful managers are drawing on both experience and education as a means of acquiring and developing the skills they need.

Management processes are applicable in a wide variety of settings, including profit-seeking organizations (large and small businesses and international businesses) and not-for-profit organizations (governmental organizations, educational organizations, health care organizations, and nontraditional organizations).

QUESTIONS FOR DISCUSSION

1. Can you think of other ways of defining management besides the definition developed in this chapter?
2. Is it possible to be involved in the management process and not be a manager? Is it possible to be a manager and not have any subordinates? Why or why not?
3. What are the strengths and limitations of describing the management process in terms of planning, organizing, leading, and controlling?
4. Describe a hypothetical manager whose activities reflect the four basic functions but exhibit them in a different sequence.
5. Why is it useful to describe kinds of managers from both vertical and horizontal perspectives?
6. Do you think that, as one moves up the organization (from one horizontal level to another), he or she should also move across different functional areas (from one vertical level to another)? Why or why not?
7. Can you identify any managerial activity that is *not* reflected in one or more of Mintzberg's ten roles?
8. Which kinds of managerial skills do you think you are strongest in now? Which ones are you weakest in?
9. In the past, there were many people who started at the bottom and worked themselves up to become head of a large company. Is this still possible? Why or why not?
10. On the basis of your educational experiences to date, do you think that a formal college education is necessary for a successful career? Why or why not?
11. Can you think of any group situation in which managerial processes, roles, and/or skills are *not* relevant?
12. In what ways are the jobs of bank manager, college president, and football coach alike? In what ways are they different?

C A S E   1.1

At the beginning of the chapter, you read a scenario about a large retailer. The company had experienced a period of phenomenal growth but had recently fallen on hard times. You were asked what you would do to revitalize the company. The retailer being described was K mart (formerly Kresge). The case that follows tells what K mart is doing and then raises some other issues about the future for your consideration.

  Up until 1959 the Kresge company was a nondescript chain of five-and-dime stores. The new company president, Harry B. Cunningham, felt that a change of direction was needed. Specifically, he believed that the company should move heavily into discounting. Rather than simply announcing that decision, though, he used

Revitalizing K mart

management teams to research the problem. The consensus that emerged, and the one he had expected all along, was that discounting was indeed the future of the company. Plans were developed for stores of standard size and layout, and the name chosen for the discount stores was K mart.

The first K mart opened in Michigan in 1962. Before the doors to that first store swung open, however, the company had already committed $80 million in leases and merchandise for 33 projected stores. Kresge would have folded if the gamble had failed. Fortunately, however, the risks paid off. By 1981 the company, now officially named K mart Corporation, was operating 1,968 stores and was the second largest nonfood retailer in the United States. Throughout the 1960s and most of the 1970s, K mart clearly led the field. For example, by 1975 the company had increased its sales to 21 times their level in 1961 and its earnings per share to 27 times their 1961 level. For comparison, Woolco, a division of F. W. Woolworth Company, increased its sales by 5 times and its earnings per share by 2 times during this same period. (Woolco eventually folded in 1983.)

Beginning in the mid-1970s, however, K mart began to develop problems. Regional discount chains such as Wal-Mart Stores and Target Stores, carrying more fashionable merchandise in more attractive stores, began to skim off customers. Specialty discounters such as Toys "Я" Us were making big inroads. K mart was also failing to keep pace with changes in customer tastes; its stores were perceived as being out-of-date and tacky. In 1980 the problem was brought home on the bottom line: Despite a record $14.2 billion in sales, profits dropped 27 percent to $261 million.

Recognizing these problems, K mart management has undertaken a number of programs to regain the company's leadership position in the industry. First, future expansion has been curtailed. The goal of 2,400 K marts by 1984 has been cut somewhat and more emphasis has been placed on remodeling and restocking existing stores. Refurbishing efforts at a rate of 450 stores per year were undertaken beginning about 1981. This refurbishing included new paint treatments and better counters and display racks.

Restocking efforts have focused primarily on the provision of more prestigious name-brand items. For example, K mart now carries designer jeans such as Calvin Klein, Jordache, and Sasson; Seiko watches; Puma running shoes; and Izod sports shirts. In short, the company is trying to attract more middle- and upper-income customers while maintaining its strong base of lower-income customers.

K mart has opened ten huge distribution centers covering about a million square feet each. The highly automated centers get merchandise to the stores about a week after orders have been sent and with half the previous labor costs. The resulting smaller inventory needs have enabled the company to cut short-term borrowing by millions of dollars.

Finally, the company has also begun to diversify. It presently owns Furr's Cafeterias and has a large stake in Astra, a Mexican discount chain. K mart has also provided assistance to a large Japanese retailer, Daiei, in return for a share of future profits from that company's discount operations.

While developing these programs, K mart has attempted to maintain many of its basic operating procedures. Store managers, for example, still have control over their own inventories and may cut prices at their own discretion to remain competitive. The company will also attempt to retain its image as the most inexpensive place to shop. Of course, the question of how successful K mart is at revitalizing itself will not be answered for several years to come.

CASE QUESTIONS	**1.** Can you identify examples of planning, organizing, leading, and controlling in this case?
	2. What differences and similarities can you suggest between the roles and skills inherent in the job of a K mart manager and the jobs of managing a manufacturing plant, a hospital, and a university?
	3. In your opinion, how successful will K mart be with its new program?
	4. Can you suggest any other things K mart should do to revitalize itself?

CASE REFERENCES

"Bargains with Few Frills." *Time,* August 25, 1980, p. 43.

Main, Jeremy. "K mart's Plans to Be Born Again, Again." *Fortune,* September 21, 1981, pp. 74–85.

Stevens, Charles W. "K mart, Beset by Steady Drop in Earnings, Tries to Attract Higher-Income Shoppers." *Wall Street Journal,* August 10, 1982, p. 29.

"Where K mart Goes Next Now That It's No. 2." *Business Week,* June 2, 1980, pp. 109–111.

C A S E   1.2

Hank Keller is the midwestern sales manager for Butler Manufacturing, a medium-sized firm producing and marketing a line of office and desk accessories. Butler Manufacturing was founded in 1957 by William Butler. From 1957 through 1977, Butler grew at a fairly consistent rate of 10 percent per year and established itself as a respected firm in the industry. William Butler retired in 1977 and the presidency was assumed by Sarah Henderson, who had previously been vice president of marketing for Butler. In consultation with William Butler, Sarah promoted Art Jacobs from the position of midwestern sales manager to her old position as vice president, and Hank Keller, the district's top sales representative, became the new sales manager.

One of the first things Hank did was to set up some structured training activities for his sales representatives. Twice a year (one weekend in January and one weekend in July), all the sales

Do training programs really pay off?

representatives assemble at a plush hotel or conference center and hear lectures and presentations on current sales techniques. One or more consultants are usually brought in for these seminars. The bill for each of these training weekends generally runs about $5,000.

In the last year, Butler Manufacturing has encountered some financial problems. Poor economic conditions and increased competition have combined to slow the company's growth rate. In the last fiscal year, for example, Butler's sales increased only 1.5 percent over the previous year and profits declined by 3 percent. Sarah Henderson has ordered all vice presidents to develop cost-cutting programs in their respective areas of responsibility.

Art Jacobs and Hank Keller recently had a meeting to discuss Hank's training programs. Art had suggested that Hank drop one of the two weekend sessions in order to cut marketing expenses. In particular, Art had noted, "You know, Hank, we're hiring only college graduates for our sales program now. These people have already studied the new sales techniques in school. I know some of them look at these weekend excursions as just a free vacation. I think it's an unnecessary expense, and you're going to have to convince me otherwise if you want to continue having them."

Hank responded, "I know all of our reps have degrees, Art, but the stuff they memorized in college doesn't mean anything to them until they've been on the firing line for a while. Under my program they come in from college, spend time working with a senior rep, make some low-risk calls on their own, and then attend one of our seminars. That way, the sales education program builds on their experiences in the field. Since I developed this program, our sales volume per rep has increased and we're getting fewer customer complaints about the reps. We just can't cut it out now."

"I'm sorry, Hank, but my hands are tied," said Art. "Henderson told me I have to cut expenses. I can't eliminate jobs, because we have barely enough reps now. I can't eliminate our offices or our support staff. Our travel expenses are already at the bottom of the industry. No, Hank, I'm really sorry, but your training programs are the only real fat we can get rid of. You're down to one program next year, and it may have to go later, too."

CASE
QUESTIONS

1. Do you agree or disagree with Hank's approach to combining education and experience?

2. Are training programs like Butler's really fat that can be cut during hard times?

3. Is this situation complicated by the fact that Art previously held the position that Hank now occupies?

4. Can you suggest compromises that might satisfy *both* managers?

2

THE DEVELOPMENT OF MANAGEMENT THEORY

1. Justify the use of history and theory in management.

2. Briefly trace the historical development of management thought.

3. Summarize and critique classical management theory.

4. Summarize and critique behavioral management theory.

5. Summarize and critique quantitative management theory.

6. Discuss the systems perspective and the contingency perspective on management, and explain their potential to integrate other areas of management.

7. Describe Theory Z management and compare it to other forms of management in the United States and Japan.

CHAPTER OUTLINE

Why study history and theory?
Why theory?
Why history?

The historical context

Classical management theory
Scientific management
Classical organization theory
Contributions and limitations of classical management theory

Behavioral management theory
The Hawthorne studies
The human relations movement
Organizational behavior
Contributions and limitations of behavioral management theory

Quantitative management theory
Management science and quantitative decision making
Operations management
Management information systems
Contributions and limitations of quantitative management theory

Integrating perspectives for management
Systems theory
Contingency theory
An integrative framework

Theory Z management

Summary of key points

OPENING INCIDENT

Your company, a large electrical equipment firm, has what might be termed a bureaucratic structure characterized by an established chain of command and a large staff of tradition-minded engineers. During the 1970s the company had a rough time. It made a number of bad acquisitions, was involved in more than one bribery case, lost money on a consumer appliances division before finally disposing of it, and entered into what turned out to be a series of disastrous contracts (to supply uranium at fixed prices) that resulted in more than $1 billion in losses. To counteract these setbacks, your company has decided it must increase productivity much faster than other companies in the industry. How would you proceed?

The history of management is somewhat paradoxical. On the one hand, society has been concerned with the effective practice of management for thousands of years. On the other hand, the scientific study of management dates only from around the turn of this century. Because of the relative newness of management as an area of study, no unified and generally accepted theory of management has yet emerged.

In this chapter we discuss the historical development and major theories of management. We set the stage by establishing the historical context of management. We then discuss the three major schools of management thought: classical, behavioral, and quantitative. Next we describe the systems approach and the contingency approach, which help integrate these three schools of thought. Finally we discuss Theory Z, a relatively new approach to management that has recently attracted much attention and stirred up considerable controversy.

Why study history and theory?

Some people question the value of history and theory. Their arguments are usually based on the assumptions that history has no relevance to contemporary society and that theory is abstract and of no practical value. This introductory section proposes to demonstrate that both theory and history *are* useful to the practicing manager.

Why theory?

Karl E. Weick provides a good example of the usefulness of theory in our everyday experiences and observations.[1] The next time you are in a building

---

1. Karl E. Weick, "Amendments to Organizational Theorizing," *Academy of Management Journal,* September 1974, pp. 487–502.

with an escalator, Weick suggests, spend a few minutes observing the behavior of the people who ride it. Quite commonly, as an individual gets close to the next floor, he or she starts to walk in order to get there faster. More formal research also suggests that, as people get closer to their goals, they are increasingly motivated to work harder to reach them. Here an everyday observation provides a framework or theory to explain behavior in certain situations.

Almost by definition, management is practiced in the real world, so useful management theories must always be grounded in reality. It is easy to identify organizations that have explicitly applied different theories of management. Practically any organization that uses assembly lines (such as Ford and General Motors) is drawing on what we will describe later in this chapter as scientific management theory. Numerous organizations, including AT&T and Texas Instruments, have adopted some aspect of organizational behavior theory to improve employee satisfaction and motivation. It would be difficult to name a *Fortune* 500 company (or a *Fortune* 5,000 company, if such a list existed) that did not use one or more techniques from quantitative management theory. Oil companies such as Shell and Texaco, which manage everything from oil fields to gasoline stations while coping with shrinking natural resources, are drawing on systems theory. Universities often use management science models and theories in registration and course scheduling. Firms such as General Foods that structure plants in a nonuniform fashion are using contingency theory. And many organizations, including Dayton-Hudson, Eli Lilly, and Rockwell International, have adopted Theory Z.

Theories help us by organizing information and providing a systematic framework for action. A firm might be just as successful using contingency theory as using Theory Z, but *either* approach is likely to be more successful than applying no theory at all. A theory is simply a blueprint or road map to guide the manager toward achievement of the organization's goals.

Why history?

Awareness and understanding of important historical developments are also important to contemporary managers. Indeed, most courses in American history devote substantial amounts of time to business and economic developments in this country, including the industrial revolution, the early labor movement, the Great Depression, and such captains of American industry as Commodore Cornelius Vanderbilt (railroads), John D. Rockefeller (oil), and Andrew Carnegie (steel). The contributions of these and other industrialists left a profound imprint on contemporary culture.[2]

Many organizations have recently recognized that they, too, can learn from their past. Corporations such as Polaroid, Consolidated Edison, AT&T, Wells Fargo, and International Harvester have all employed corporate historians to help them develop a long-term perspective on their roots.

Polaroid, for example, was troubled because one of its plants had evolved from a good place to work into one plagued by poor productivity and low morale. The corporate historian reviewed a fifteen-year period and found evi-

2. See Daniel A. Wren, *The Evolution of Management Theory*, 2nd ed. (New York: Wiley, 1979).

dence that increased management control had caused the decline in the plant. Because such a long time had passed and because a variety of managers had been involved, company officials had been unable to solve the problem themselves. But the historian was able to put all the pieces together and suggest a workable solution.[3]

The historical context

Interest in management can be traced back thousands of years. Imagine the monumental task of building an Egyptian pyramid with only primitive tools. Think of conducting a military campaign the scope of Alexander the Great's with no mechanisms for coordination or leadership. Consider the intricacies of establishing and controlling the vast Roman Empire with no elaborate communications network. Obviously, management practices *had* to have been used in order for these activities to have played such a significant role in world history.

The Egyptians applied the management functions of planning, organizing, and controlling to construct the pyramids. Alexander the Great employed staff organization to coordinate activities during his military campaigns. The Roman Empire developed a well-defined organizational structure that greatly facilitated communication and control. Accounts of some of these issues also appear in early literature. Management was discussed by Socrates in 400 B.C., Plato described specialization in 350 B.C., and Alfarabi listed several leadership traits in A.D. 900.[4]

Yet business management was not considered a serious field of study for several centuries. The reasons for this lack of interest are many. Organizations such as the Roman Empire were essentially governmental and had unlimited powers of taxation. Because they were not interested in "maximizing sales" or "minimizing costs," there was little need for them to be concerned with "proper" management. They were interested in coordinating and controlling their empires, but efficiency was not a primary consideration.

A second reason for the lack of attention to business management was that the first discipline devoted to commerce was economics. Economists generally *assumed* that managerial practice was efficient and focused instead on national policy and other nonmanagerial aspects of business. Finally, the simple fact that there were essentially no large business organizations until the 1800s served to delay interest in business management. When family businesses first emerged, their goal was not growth or expansion, but simply survival. If a family could produce and sell enough to sustain itself, nothing else was needed.

During the eighteenth and nineteenth centuries, however, a few people began to concern themselves with business management problems. Two prominent men in this category were Robert Owen and Charles Babbage.

---

3. See "Profiting From the Past," *Newsweek*, May 10, 1982, pp. 73–74.

4. Claude S. George, Jr., *The History of Management Thought* (Englewood Cliffs, N.J.: Prentice-Hall, 1968).

Robert Owen. Robert Owen (1771–1858), British industrialist and re-
former, was one of the first managers to recognize the importance of an organization's human resources. Until then, factory workers were generally
regarded and discussed in much the same terms as machinery and equipment.
As a factory owner himself, Owen recognized that people deserved more respect and dignity. Accordingly, he incorporated such "radical" innovations as
better working conditions, a higher minimum working age for children, meals
for employees, and reduced working hours. Of course, he also assumed that
giving more attention to workers would pay off in increased output. Owen
was a pioneer in humane business practice. Although no one followed his lead
at the time, his ideas were later developed in behavioral management theory.

Charles Babbage. Whereas Owen was primarily interested in employee
welfare, Charles Babbage (1792–1871), an English mathematician, focused his
attention on efficiencies of production. His primary contribution is his book *On
the Economy of Machinery and Manufactures.*[5] Babbage placed great faith in division of labor and advocated the application of mathematics to such problems
as the efficient use of facilities and materials. In a sense, he was a forerunner
of both classical management theory and quantitative management theory. Nor
did he overlook the human element. He understood that a harmonious relationship between management and labor could serve to benefit both, and he
favored such devices as profit-sharing plans. In many ways, then, Babbage was
a pioneer of modern management theory and practice.[6]

Classical management theory

Classical management theory is a label applied to the beliefs about management that emerged during the early years of this century—ideas that represent
the first well-developed framework of management. Classical management theory actually includes two different approaches to management: scientific management and classical organization theory.

Scientific management

Scientific management, which is concerned with the management of work and
workers, grew from the pioneering work of five people: Frederick W. Taylor
(1856–1915), Frank Gilbreth (1868–1924), Lillian Gilbreth (1878–1972), Henry
Gantt (1861–1919), and Harrington Emerson (1853–1931). Taylor played the
dominant role.

Frederick W. Taylor. At the beginning of the twentieth century, there
was considerable concern about productivity. Business was expanding and
capital was readily available, but labor was in short supply. Hence a primary

Frederick W. Taylor
(1856–1915)
Source: THE
BETTMAN ARCHIVE,
INC.

5. Charles Babbage, *On the Economy of Machinery and Manufactures* (London: Charles Knight,
1832).

6. See Wren, *The Evolution of Management Theory.*

goal of management was to use existing labor more efficiently. Frederick Taylor was very much interested in developing solutions to this problem.

One of Taylor's first jobs was as a foreman at the Midvale Steel Company in Philadelphia, where he developed a strong dislike for waste and inefficiency. At Midvale he observed what he called "soldiering": working at less than a normal pace. The reason the employees worked at a reduced pace was that they feared the consequences of working harder; all the work might be completed and they might be laid off. Management was unaware of this practice because it had never analyzed the jobs closely enough to determine what the employees *should* be producing.

Taylor observed and timed each element of the steel workers' jobs. First he determined what each worker should be producing, and then he designed the most efficient way of doing each part of the overall task. Next he implemented an early form of a piece-rate pay system. Rather than paying all employees the same wage, he began increasing the pay of workers who met and exceeded the target level of output set for each job.

Taylor left Midvale and worked for several years as an independent consultant for Simonds Rolling Machine Company and Bethlehem Steel, among others. At Simonds he studied and redesigned jobs, introduced rest periods to reduce fatigue, and converted to a differential pay scale. The results were higher quality and quantity of output and improved morale. At Bethlehem Steel, Taylor studied efficient ways of loading and unloading railcars and applied his conclusions with equally impressive results.

The essence of Taylor's scientific management can be summarized in the following four steps ("they" are the managers who are implementing his philosophy in a particular situation).

First. They develop a science for each element of a man's work, which replaces the old rule-of-thumb method.

Second. They scientifically select and then train, teach, and develop the workman, whereas in the past he chose his own work and trained himself as best he could.

Third. They heartily cooperate with the men so as to insure all of the work being done in accordance with the principles of the science which has been developed.

Fourth. There is an almost equal division of the work and the responsibility between the management and the workmen. The management takes over all work for which they are better fitted than the workmen, while in the past almost all of the work and the greater part of the responsibility were thrown upon the men.[7]

This process is illustrated more fully in Figure 2.1. In discussing the figure, we begin with analysis of the work situation and then go on to three additional phases.

Phase 1: The work situation. In any work situation there are three elements: a job to be done, a pool of workers, and a manager. In the situation

7. Frederick W. Taylor, *Principles of Scientific Management* (New York: Harper and Brothers, 1911).

Figure 2.1
The phases of
scientific
management

PHASE 1: THE WORK SITUATION
A TASK TO BE PERFORMED, A POOL OF WORKERS, AND MANAGEMENT

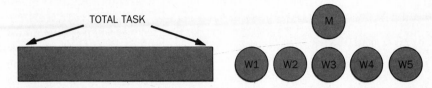

TOTAL TASK

PHASE 2: TASK ANALYSIS
MANAGEMENT SCIENTIFICALLY STUDIES, SPECIALIZES, AND STANDARDIZES TASKS

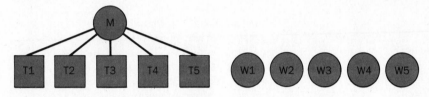

PHASE 3: MATCHING TASKS WITH WORKERS
MANAGEMENT SELECTS, TRAINS, AND ASSIGNS WORKERS TO TASKS

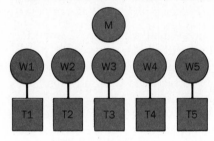

PHASE 4: CONTINUED MANAGEMENT
MANAGEMENT SUPERVISES AND MAINTAINS PLANNING RESPONSIBILITIES

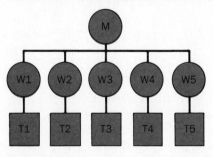

KEY:
M = MANAGEMENT
W = WORKER
T = TASK

Source: Ricky W. Griffin, *Task Design—An Integrative Approach* (Glenview, Illinois: Scott, Foresman, 1982), pp. 18–19. Used with permission.

shown in Figure 2.1, the total task might consist of coordinating a vending machine territory, and the company might assign a route manager and five workers to handle the territory.

Phase 2: Task analysis.   Phase 2 in Figure 2.1 represents management's scientific study of the task wherein it is determined what elements the task consists of, what skills each aspect demands, and how many workers should be assigned to each. The route manager may decide that two people should carry merchandise from the storage area and load it on the trucks, that two people should drive the trucks and stock the machinery, and that one person should keep records of all expenses and income. Next the manager decides how the tasks are to be performed and enumerates the skills needed to carry out these requirements.

Phase 3: Matching tasks with workers.   As shown in Phase 3 of Figure 2.1, the manager then matches the available personnel with the skills required for each task. The two strongest people are probably assigned the loading jobs, the two people who know the area best and have the best driving records become the drivers, and the person with some bookkeeping skills maintains the records.

Phase 4: Continued management.   Finally, as indicated in Phase 4, the manager continues to cooperate with the workers by supervising the work and serving as primary planner for the work group.

Frank Gilbreth
(1868–1924)
Source: THE
BETTMAN ARCHIVE,
INC.

The work of Taylor had a significant impact on American society. By applying his principles and similar approaches to job specialization, manufacturing organizations came to rely heavily on mass-production techniques. Taylor was not without his detractors, however. Labor argued that scientific management was just a device to get more work from each employee and to reduce the total number of workers a firm needed. There was even a congressional investigation into Taylor's methods. On a more damaging note, fairly convincing evidence suggests that Taylor falsified some of his findings and that some of his writing was actually done by someone else.[8] Nevertheless, Taylor's mark on American society can still be seen today.

The Gilbreths.   Frank and Lillian Gilbreth were a husband–wife team of industrial engineers. They were primarily interested in time-and-motion study and job simplification, although Lillian Gilbreth was also concerned with the welfare of the worker. Her doctoral dissertation, dealing with human factors in business, was published in *Industrial Engineering Magazine* in 1912 (the publisher listed her name as L. M. Gilbreth to hide the fact that she was a woman).

One of Frank Gilbreth's more interesting contributions was to the craft of bricklaying. Gilbreth was surprised to find that, even though bricklaying dated back thousands of years, there was no generally accepted technique for doing it. After carefully studying bricklayers at work, he developed procedures for

Lillian Gilbreth
(1878–1972)
Source: THE
BETTMAN ARCHIVE,
INC.

8. Charles D. Wrege and Amedeo G. Perroni, "Taylor's Pig-Tale: A Historical Analysis of Frederick W. Taylor's Pig-Iron Experiment," *Academy of Management Journal,* March 1974, pp. 6–27; and Charles D. Wrege and Ann Marie Stotka, "Cooke Creates a Classic: The Story Behind F. W. Taylor's Principles of Scientific Management," *Academy of Management Review,* October 1978, pp. 736–749.

doing the job more efficiently. He specified standard materials and techniques, including the positioning of the bricklayers themselves. He designed a new type of scaffold that held the bricklayer, the bricks, and the mortar at different levels. He assigned to less expensive laborers the job of carrying bricks to the scaffold and stacking them "best edge up" (something the bricklayers had formerly done themselves). Finally, Gilbreth developed a standard mortar formula to ensure consistency. The results of these changes were a reduction in movements from 18 to 5 and an increase in output of about 200 percent!

Working individually and together, Frank and Lillian Gilbreth developed numerous techniques and strategies for eliminating inefficiency. They also applied many of their ideas to their family: their experiences in raising twelve children have been documented in a book and movie called *Cheaper by the Dozen*.

Henry Gantt
(1861–1919)
Source: Historical
Picture Service,
Chicago

Henry Gantt. Henry Gantt was an associate of Taylor's at Midvale, Simonds, and Bethlehem Steel. Later, working alone, he developed two specific techniques for improving worker output. First he developed the *Gantt chart*. Essentially, a Gantt chart schedules work over a time span. A Gantt chart can be generated for each worker or for a complex project as a whole. The method is still used today.

Gantt's second major contribution dealt with pay systems. Under Taylor's differential rate system, a worker's pay was tied entirely to output. If workers produced a lot, they made a reasonable wage; if nothing was produced during the day, no wage was earned. Gantt believed that workers should be entitled to some minimum wage, and this belief was reflected in his pay system. If workers produced at the minimum level or below, a certain fixed wage was paid. Workers who exceeded the minimum were paid a bonus on top of the fixed wage. Gantt also extended the system to reward supervisors whose employees exceeded the minimum levels.

Harrington Emerson. Like Taylor, the Gilbreths, and Gantt, Harrington Emerson was one of the first management consultants. He made quite a stir when he appeared before the Interstate Commerce Commission in 1910 to testify concerning a rate increase request by the railroads. As an expert witness, Emerson asserted that the railroads could save $1 million per day by practicing scientific management. Emerson was also a strong advocate of making a strict distinction between line and staff roles in organizations. (As we will learn in Chapter 10, line managers are directly responsible for doing the work of the organization. Staff managers generally provide support.) This argument was derived from his observations of the efficiency of military organizations.

Classical organization theory

Whereas scientific management deals with the jobs of individual employees, *classical organization theory* focuses on managing the total organization. Classical organization theory was the precursor of contemporary organization theory. The primary contributors to classical organization theory were Henri Fayol

(1841–1925), Lyndall Urwick (1891–   ), Max Weber (1864–1920), and Chester Barnard (1886–1961).

Henry Fayol
(1841–1925)
Source: Courtesy of
Ronald Greenwood

Henri Fayol. Fayol was the Frederick Taylor of classical organization theory. That is, he offered the most definitive statement and made the greatest contribution to this area of management thought. A French industrialist, Fayol was unknown to American managers and scholars until his most significant work, *General and Industrial Management,*[9] was translated into English in 1930.

Drawing on over 50 years of his own managerial experience, he attempted to systematize the practice of management to provide guidance and direction to other managers. Part of his thinking was expressed in fourteen principles, or guidelines, for effective management.

1. **Division of labor.** A high degree of specialization should result in efficiency. Both managerial and technical work are amenable to specialization.
2. **Authority.** Authority is needed to carry out managerial responsibilities. This includes the formal authority to command and also personal authority deriving from intelligence and experience.
3. **Discipline.** People in the organization must respect the rules that govern the organization.
4. **Unity of command.** Each subordinate should report to one and only one superior.
5. **Unity of direction.** Similar activities in an organization should be grouped together under one manager.
6. **Subordination of individual to the common good.** Interests of individuals should not be placed before the goals of the overall organization.
7. **Remuneration.** Compensation should be fair to both employees and the organization.
8. **Centralization.** Power and authority should be concentrated at the upper levels of the organization to the extent possible.
9. **Scalar chain.** A chain of authority should extend from the top to the bottom of the organization and should be followed at all times.
10. **Order.** Human and material resources should be coordinated so as to be in the required place at the required time.
11. **Equity.** Managers should be kind and fair when dealing with subordinates.
12. **Stability.** High turnover of employees should be avoided.
13. **Initiative.** Subordinates should have the freedom to take initiative.
14. **Esprit de corps.** Teamwork, team spirit, and a sense of unity and togetherness should be fostered and maintained.[10]

Fayol did not intend this list to be exhaustive; the principles simply reflect procedures that he found useful. Other managers before Fayol had probably

9. Henri Fayol, *Industrial and General Management,* translated by J. A. Coubrough (Geneva, Switzerland: International Management Institute, 1930).

10. Fayol, *Industrial and General Management.*

practiced many of these principles, but Fayol has the distinction of being the first to formalize them.

Fayol also was the first to identify the specific managerial functions of planning, organizing, leading, and controlling. He felt that these functions accurately reflect the core of the management process. Most contemporary management books (including this one) still use this framework, and most practicing managers are familiar with this description of their jobs.

Lyndall Urwick. After a career as a British army officer, Lyndall Urwick became a noted management theorist and consultant. He tried to synthesize and integrate scientific management with the work of Fayol and other classical organization theorists. He further advanced modern thinking about the management functions of planning, organizing, and controlling. Like Fayol, he developed a list of general guidelines for improving managerial effectiveness. Urwick is noted not so much for his own contributions as for his synthesis and integration of the work of others.

Max Weber. Another influential classical organization theorist was Max Weber. Weber lived and worked at the same time as Fayol and Taylor, but his contributions were not recognized until some years had passed. Weber was a German sociologist, and his most significant work was not translated into English until 1947.[11] Weber's work on bureaucracy laid the foundation for contemporary organization theory and will be discussed in more detail in Chapter 11. The concept of bureaucracy, as we shall see, is based on a rational set of guidelines for structuring organizations in the most efficient manner.

Chester Barnard. Chester Barnard, former president of New Jersey Bell Telephone Company, made significant contributions to management in his classic book, *The Functions of the Executive.*[12] In it he proposed a well-known theory about the acceptance of authority. This theory holds that subordinates weigh the legitimacy of a supervisor's directives and *then* decide whether to accept them. An order is accepted if the subordinate understands it, is able to comply with it, and views it as appropriate given the goals of the organization. The importance of Barnard's work is enhanced by the fact that he drew from his experience as a top manager.

Max Weber
(1864–1920)
Source: BROWN
BROTHERS

Chester Barnard
(1886–1961)
Source: Historical
Picture Service,
Chicago

Contributions and limitations of classical management theory

The contributions and limitations of classical management theory are summarized in Table 2.1. Classical management theory is the framework from which later theorists have worked, and many insights derived from it still hold true today. Several aspects of classical management theory will be apparent when we consider planning (Chapters 4–8), organizing (Chapters 9–12), and controlling (Chapters 17–19). Another important contribution is the fact that early

11. Max Weber, *Theory of Social and Economic Organizations,* translated by T. Parsons (New York: Free Press, 1947).

12. Chester Barnard, *The Functions of the Executive* (Cambridge, Mass.: Harvard University Press, 1938).

Table 2.1 Classical management theory

General summary	Classical management theory had two primary thrusts. Scientific management focused on employees within organizations and on ways to improve their productivity. Noted pioneers of scientific management included Frederick Taylor, Frank and Lillian Gilbreth, Henry Gantt, and Harrington Emerson. Classical organization theory focused on the total organization and on ways to make it more efficient and effective. Prominent classical organization theorists were Henri Fayol, Lyndall Urwick, Max Weber, and Chester Barnard.
Period of greatest interest	1895–mid 1930s; renewed interest in recent years as a means of cutting costs, increasing productivity, and so on.
Contributions	Laid the foundation for later developments in management theory. Identified key management processes, functions, and skills that are still recognized as such today. Focused attention on management as a valid subject of scientific inquiry.
Limitations	More appropriate for stable and simple organizations than for today's dynamic and complex organizations. Often prescribed universal procedures that are not really appropriate in some settings. Even though some writers (such as Lillian Gilbreth and Chester Barnard) were concerned with the human element, many viewed employees as tools rather than resources.

management theorists were the first to focus attention on management as a meaningful field of study.

However, the limitations of classical management theory should not be overlooked. The theory dealt best with stable, simple organizations, whereas many organizations today are changing and complex. It proposed universal guidelines that don't fit every organization. These drawbacks have been countered by recent developments in quantitative methods, systems theory, and contingency theory. A third limitation of classical management theory is that it slighted the role of the individual in organizations. This role was much more fully developed by behavioral management theory.

Behavioral management theory

To one degree or another, the developers of classical management theory viewed organizations and jobs from a mechanistic point of view. That is, organizations were thought of as machines and workers as cogs within those machines. Even though most classical management theorists recognized the role of individuals, they focused on controlling and standardizing the behavior of these individuals. By contrast, behavioral management theory placed much more emphasis on individual attitudes and behaviors and on group processes.

Behavioral management theory was stimulated by a number of writers and theoretical movements. One of those movements was industrial psychology, the practice of applying psychological concepts to industrial settings. Hugo Munsterberg (1863–1916), a noted German psychologist, is recognized as the father of industrial psychology. He established a psychological laboratory at Harvard in 1892, and his pioneering book *Psychology and Industrial Efficiency*[13] was translated into English in 1913. Munsterberg suggested that psychologists could make empirically valuable contributions to managers in the areas of selection and motivation. Industrial psychology is still a major course of study at many colleges and universities.

Another early advocate of the behavioral school of thought was Mary Parker Follett.[14] Follett worked and wrote during the scientific management era, but she anticipated behavioral management theory and appreciated the need to understand the role of behavior in organizations. In particular, she was interested in adult education and vocational guidance, and she felt that organizations should become more democratic in accommodating employees and managers.

The Hawthorne studies

Elton Mayo
(1880–1949)
Baker Library, Harvard
Business School

Munsterberg and Follett made significant contributions to the development of behavioral management theory, but the primary catalyst for this movement was a series of studies conducted near Chicago at the Hawthorne Plant of Western Electric by Elton Mayo and his associates between 1927 and 1932.[15] Mayo was a faculty member and consultant at Harvard. The first experiment in what have come to be known as the *Hawthorne studies* involved manipulating illumination for one group of workers and comparing subsequent productivity in that group with productivity in another group whose illumination was not changed. Surprisingly, when illumination was increased for the experimental group, productivity went up in *both* groups. Productivity continued to increase in both groups, even when the lighting for the experimental group was decreased. It wasn't until the lighting was reduced to the level of moonlight that productivity began to decline.

Another experiment established a piecework incentive pay plan for a group of nine men assembling terminal banks for telephone exchanges. According to classical management theory, each man should try to maximize his pay by producing as many units as possible. Mayo and his associates found otherwise. They found that the social group informally established an acceptable level of output for its members. Workers who overproduced were branded as "rate busters" and underproducers were labeled "chiselers." To be accepted by the group, workers had to produce at the accepted level. As they approached this level, workers slacked off to avoid overproducing.

Other studies (and an interview program involving several thousand

13. Hugo Munsterberg, *Psychology and Industrial Efficiency* (Boston: Houghton Mifflin, 1913).

14. See Wren, *The Evolution of Management Theory*, pp. 324–335.

15. See Elton Mayo, *The Human Problems of an Industrial Civilization* (New York: MacMillan, 1933); and Fritz J. Roethlisberger and William J. Dickson, *Management and the Worker* (Cambridge, Mass.: Harvard University Press, 1939).

workers) led Mayo and his associates to conclude that the human element was much more important in the workplace than previous theorists had realized. In the lighting experiment, for example, the peculiar results were attributed to the fact that the participants were receiving special attention and sympathetic supervision for perhaps the first time. The incentive pay plans didn't work because wage incentives were less important than social acceptance in determining output. In short, individual and social processes played a major role in shaping worker attitudes and behavior.

The human relations movement

The human relations movement grew from the Hawthorne studies and was a popular approach to management for many years. Classical management theory in general and scientific management in particular assumed a simple stimulus–response relationship in the workplace. If jobs were properly designed and appropriate incentives established, predictable results would follow. Workers would perform their jobs as they were told and would maximize output to increase their pay.

Human relations theory, however, suggested a more complex process (see Figure 2.2). It proposed that workers respond primarily to the social context, including social conditioning, sentiments, and the interpersonal situation at work. An underlying assumption of the human relations movement was that management concern for the worker would lead to increased satisfaction, which would, in turn, result in better performance. Two early writers who helped advance the human relations movement were Abraham Maslow and Douglas McGregor.

Figure 2.2
Scientific
management versus
human relations

THE SCIENTIFIC MANAGEMENT PERSPECTIVE

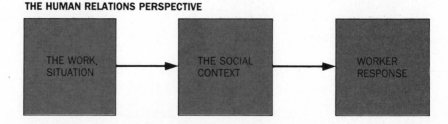

THE HUMAN RELATIONS PERSPECTIVE

Table 2.2 Theory X and Theory Y

Theory X assumptions	1. People do not like work and try to avoid it. 2. People do not like work, so managers have to control, direct, coerce, and threaten employees to get them to work toward organizational goals. 3. People prefer to be directed, to avoid responsibility, to want security; they have little ambition.
Theory Y assumptions	1. People do not naturally dislike work; work is a natural part of their lives. 2. People are internally motivated to reach objectives to which they are committed. 3. People are committed to goals to the degree that they receive personal rewards when they reach their objectives. 4. People will both seek and accept responsibility under favorable conditions. 5. People have the capacity to be innovative in solving organizational problems. 6. People are bright, but under most organizational conditions their potentials are underutilized.

Source: Douglas McGregor, *The Human Side of Enterprise* (New York: McGraw-Hill, 1960), pp. 33–34, 47–48. Used with permission of the publisher.

Abraham Maslow
(1908–1970)
Source: THE
BETTMAN ARCHIVE,
INC.

Douglas McGregor
(1906–1964)
Source: THE MIT
MUSEUM

Abraham Maslow. One of the earliest theoretical contributions to human relations was made by Abraham Maslow.[16] In 1943 he advanced a theory suggesting that people are motivated by a sequence of needs, including monetary incentives, social acceptance, and others. Maslow's theory of "hierarchical needs" was a primary factor in the increased attention that managers began to give to the work of academic theorists. Maslow's theory will be described in more detail in Chapter 13.

Douglas McGregor. Whereas Maslow's theory was one of the first in the emerging area of human relations, Douglas McGregor's Theory X and Theory Y[17] perhaps best represent the essence of the human relations movement (see Table 2.2). *Theory X* takes a relatively pessimistic and negative view of workers; it is quite compatible with scientific management. *Theory Y,* on the other hand, is more positive; it represents the assumptions that human relations advocates make. In McGregor's view, Theory Y was a more appropriate foundation for management. Both Maslow and McGregor significantly influenced the thinking of many practicing managers.

Organizational behavior

The work of Munsterberg, Mayo, Maslow, McGregor, and others has made valuable contributions to management. Contemporary theorists, however, have noted that many assertions of the human relationists were simplistic, inadequate descriptions of work behavior. For example, the assumption that

16. Abraham Maslow, "A Theory of Human Motivation," *Psychological Review*, July 1943, pp. 370–396.

17. Douglas McGregor, *The Human Side of Enterprise* (New York: McGraw-Hill, 1960).

worker satisfaction leads to improved performance has been shown to have little if any validity.[18] If anything, satisfaction follows good performance rather than preceding it (these issues will be addressed in Chapter 13).

Contemporary behavioral management theory, generally referred to as *organizational behavior,* acknowledges that behavior is much more complex than the human relationists realized. The field of organizational behavior draws from a broad, interdisciplinary base of psychology, sociology, anthropology, economics, and medicine. Organizational behavior theorists take a holistic view of behavior by considering individual, group, *and* organization processes.

Organizational behavior is an important element in contemporary management theory. Topics of current interest to people in this field include job satisfaction, stress, motivation, leadership, group dynamics, communication, organizational politics, interpersonal conflict, and organization structure and design. A contingency orientation (discussed more fully later in this chapter) also characterizes the field. Finally, it emphasizes the potential application of research findings. Our discussions of organizing (Chapters 9–12) and leading (Chapters 13–16) are heavily influenced by concepts of organizational behavior.

Contributions and limitations of behavioral management theory

Table 2.3 summarizes the contributions and limitations of behavioral management theory. The primary contributions relate to ways in which this theory has changed managerial thinking. Managers are now more likely to recognize the importance of behavioral processes and to view employees as valuable resources rather than mere tools. On the other hand, organizational behavior is still very imprecise in its predictions. It is not always accepted and/or understood by practicing managers, partly because behavioral scholars tend to use technical terms and unfamiliar "buzz-words." Hence the contributions of the behavioral school have yet to be fully realized.

Quantitative management theory

Of the three major schools of thought, quantitative management theory is the newest. Classical management theory was born in the early years of this century, and behavioral management theory began to emerge in the 1920s and 1930s. Quantitative management theory did not fully develop until early in World War II. After the war, industrial firms such as Du Pont began to use techniques that were developed by the military for moving troops and equipment and deploying submarines. Essentially, quantitative management theory applies quantitative techniques to problem solving and decision making. More specifically, quantitative management focuses on decision making, economic effectiveness, formal mathematical models, and the use of electronic comput-

18. See Cynthia D. Fisher, "On the Dubious Wisdom of Expecting Job Satisfaction to Correlate with Performance," *Academy of Management Review,* October, 1980, pp. 607–812.

TABLE 2.3 Behavioral management theory

General summary	Behavioral management theory focuses on employee behavior in an organizational context. Stimulated by the birth of industrial psychology, the human relations movement supplanted scientific management as the dominant approach to management in the 1930s and 1940s. Prominent contributors to this movement were Elton Mayo, Abraham Maslow, and Douglas McGregor. Organizational behavior, the contemporary perspective on behavioral management theory, draws from an interdisciplinary base and recognizes the complexities of human behavior in organizational settings.
Period of greatest interest	Human relations enjoyed its peak of acceptance from 1931 to the late 1940s. Organizational behavior emerged in the late 1950s and is presently of great interest to researchers and managers.
Contributions	Provided important insights into motivation, group dynamics, and other interpersonal processes in organizations. Focused managerial attention on these same processes. Challenged the view that employees are tools and furthered the belief that employees are valuable resources.
Limitations	The complexity of individual behavior makes prediction of that behavior difficult. Many behavioral concepts have not yet been put to use because some managers are reluctant to adopt them. Contemporary research findings by behavioral scientists are often not communicated to practicing managers in an understandable form.

ers.[19] For our purposes, quantitative management theory will be broken down into three dimensions: management science, operations management, and management information systems.

Management science and quantitative decision making

Unfortunately, the term *management science* sounds very much like *scientific management*, the approach developed by Taylor and others early in this century. But the two have little in common and should not be confused. The *management science* approach focuses specifically on the development of mathematical models. A mathematical model is a simplified representation of a system, process, or relationship. Consider the following simple model as an illustration.

In a manufacturing setting, it may take 3 units of raw material X and 2 units of raw material Y to produce 1 unit of Z, the final product. Further, the costs of X and Y may fluctuate due to erratic demand. A cost model for producing Z may then be established as follows:

$$3X + 2Y = Z$$

19. See Harvey M. Wagner, *Principles of Management Science* (Englewood Cliffs, N.J.: Prentice-Hall, 1970) and Robert Markland, *Topics in Management Science*, 2nd ed. (New York: Wiley, 1983).

A manager can easily compute the cost of Z at any particular time by inserting the costs of X and Y into the model. For example, if X costs \$2 today and Y costs \$4, the cost of producing Z will be $3(2) + 2(4) = \$14$. Of course, most mathematical models used in real organizations are much more complex than this example. A complete model may consist of several equations, each with a large number of variables, which must be solved simultaneously.

The purpose of a management science model is usually to provide a solution to a problem or to indicate the best of several alternatives in a decision-making process. We will learn more about management science models and their uses in Chapter 8.

Operations management

Operations management involves somewhat less mathematical and statistical sophistication than management science dictates, and it can be applied more directly to managerial situations. In fact, we can think of operations management as a form of applied management science. It refers to almost all aspects of the on-going activities of an organization, whether or not a product is manufactured.

There are a wide variety of activities, processes, and problems for which operations management is appropriate. Inventory management and linear programming, for example, are both widely used. Inventory management is concerned with specific inventory problems such as balancing carrying costs and ordering costs and determining the optimal order quantity. Linear programming, which involves computing simultaneous solutions to a set of linear equations, helps managers solve problems of product mix and production scheduling.

Other techniques of operations management include network modeling, queuing theory, break-even analysis, and simulation. All of these techniques and procedures apply directly to production, but they are also helpful in such areas as finance, marketing, and personnel. We touch on these techniques in Chapters 8 and 18. The material will then be more fully integrated in our in-depth discussion of operations management in Chapter 20.

Management information systems

The third dimension of quantitative management theory is the concept of *management information systems* (MIS). As the term implies, MIS is a system designed to provide information to managers. It entails an integrated data base (usually in a computer), a hierarchical information structure, and an orientation toward decision support.

An example of how MIS might function appears in Figure 2.3. Without MIS, each manager in each functional area maintains a body of information relevant to that area. If Jones in marketing wants to know something about current inventory levels, she or he must obtain the information from the production area by going through White. After the MIS is installed, however, Jones can get the information from the MIS without having to go through other people in the organization.

Figure 2.3
The results of
installing a
management
information system

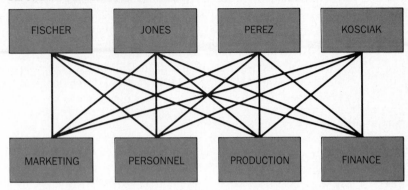

BEFORE IMPLEMENTATION OF MIS

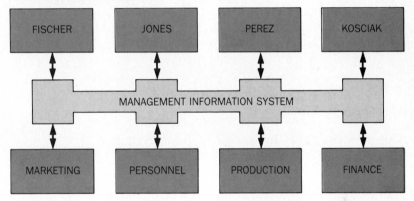

AFTER IMPLEMENTATION OF MIS

The purpose of MIS is to provide managers with the information they need to make informed decisions. A fully developed MIS contains data about the organization itself and about its external environment. It is set up to satisfy the needs of managers at each level (first-line, middle, and top management) and in each functional area (marketing, production, finance, personnel, and so on). It is able to supply reports on demand and allows the manager to query the system's data base. Not least important, it provides management science models that the manager can use in arriving at decisions. We will discuss MIS further in Chapter 16.

Contributions and limitations of quantitative management theory

Like other management theories, quantitative management theory has made significant contributions and has certain limitations. Both are summarized in Table 2.4.

Quantitative management theory has provided the manager with an

Table 2.4 Quantitative management theory

General summary	Quantitative management theory focuses on applying mathematical models and processes to management situations. Management science specifically deals with the development of mathematical models to aid in decision making and problem solving. Operations management focuses more directly on the application of management science to organizations. Management information systems are systems developed to provide information to managers.
Period of greatest interest	1940s to present.
Contributions	The development of sophisticated quantitative techniques to assist in decision making.
	Application of models has increased our awareness and understanding of complex organizational processes and situations.
	Has been very useful in the planning and controlling processes.
Limitations	Cannot fully explain or predict the behavior of people in organizations.
	Mathematical sophistication may come at the expense of other important skills.
	Models may require unrealistic or unfounded assumptions.

abundance of decision making tools and techniques and has increased our understanding of overall organizational processes. It has been particularly useful in the areas of planning and controlling. On the other hand, mathematical models cannot fully account for individual behaviors and attitudes. Moreover, some believe that the time needed to develop competence in quantitative techniques retards the development of other managerial skills. Finally, mathematical models typically require a set of assumptions that may not be realistic.

An important point to keep in mind is that the classical, behavioral, and quantitative schools of thought are not competing or mutually exclusive approaches. Even though some contradictory and inconsistent assumptions and predictions are made by the three schools, they can actually complement each other. Indeed, a complete understanding of management requires an appreciation of the basic tenets of all three schools.

Integrating perspectives for management

Systems theory and contingency theory are relative newcomers to the field of management. These theories are not yet supported by enough research, practice, and acceptance to qualify as distinct schools of thought, but they can help us integrate the classical, behavioral, and quantitative management theories and can enlarge our understanding of all three.

Figure 2.4
A systems model of
organizations

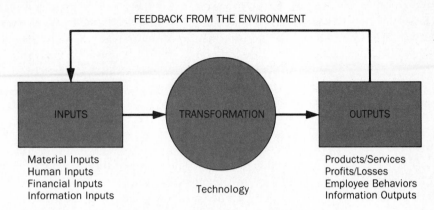

Source: Ricky W. Griffin, *Task Design—An Integrative Approach* (Glenview, Illinois: Scott, Foresman, 1982), p. 101. Used with permission.

Systems theory

We briefly introduced systems theory in Chapter 1 in our discussion of the definition of management. A *system* can be defined as an interrelated set of elements functioning as a whole.[20] As shown in Figure 2.4, an organizational system consists of four basic elements. First, inputs enter the system from the environment. Material, human, financial, and information inputs are the most important for organizations. Next, through technological and managerial processes, the inputs undergo a transformation. Outputs are then produced in the form of a product or service (note that an abstract "product" such as aesthetic pleasure in an art gallery is just as meaningful from a managerial viewpoint as an automobile or a tube of toothpaste), profits or losses (even not-for-profit organizations such as hospitals and universities must operate within their budgets), employee behaviors (relevant to their jobs), and information. Finally, the environment reacts to these outputs and provides feedback to the system.

Four especially useful ideas that managers can glean from systems theory are the concepts of open versus closed systems, subsystems and interdependencies, synergy, and entropy.

Open versus closed systems. *Open systems* interact with their environment whereas *closed systems* do not. All organizations are open systems, although the degree of interaction may vary. A potentially costly mistake that some organizations make is to assume that they are closed systems and can afford to ignore the environment. The railroads were guilty of making that

20. For more information on systems theory in general, see Ludwig von Bertalanffy, C. G. Hempel, R. E. Bass, and H. Jonas, "General Systems Theory: A New Approach to Unity of Science," I–VI *Human Biology*, Vol. 23, 1951, pp. 302–361. For systems theory as applied to organizations, see Fremont E. Kast and James E. Rosenzweig, "General Systems Theory: Applications for Organization and Management," *Academy of Management Journal*, December 1972, pp. 447–465.

mistake earlier in this century; the consequences of their error are readily apparent. They assumed, for example, that they were invulnerable to environmental shifts in the nature of the transportation industry and eventually were replaced by trucks as the dominant form of materials transportation in this country. Similarly, passengers moved first to buses and then to planes. Managers must recognize that conditions outside the company can dramatically affect their organization.

Subsystems. A primary assumption of systems theory is that the elements, or subsystems, of the system are interdependent. A *subsystem* is a system within a system. For example, the marketing, production, and finance functions can be thought of as subsystems within the organizational system. From another perspective, subsystems are also systems in their own right. A change in one subsystem affects other subsystems as well. If production lowers quality, for example, the effects are felt in finance (improved cash flow in the short run due to lower costs), marketing (decreased sales in the long run due to customer dissatisfaction), and perhaps personnel (increased turnover due to workers' loss of pride in work). Organizational subsystems can be managed with some degree of autonomy, but their interdependence should not be overlooked.

Synergy. The term *synergy* suggests that the whole is greater than the sum of its parts. Two people, each working alone, may be unable to lift a weight. Together, however, they may find that lifting the weight is easy. Similarly, organizational units tend to be more successful working together than working alone. Synergy is an important concept for managers in that it reinforces the need to work together in a cooperative fashion.

Entropy. *Entropy* is the process by which systems decay. When any system, including an organizational system, does not monitor feedback from the environment and make appropriate adjustments, the system may fail. Witness the problems of Studebaker, W. T. Grant, and Penn Central Railroad. Each of these organizations went bankrupt because it failed to revitalize itself and keep pace with its environment.[21] A primary objective of management, from a systems perspective, is to avoid entropy.

Systems theory offers the manager a useful perspective. The manager who grasps the nature of open systems can recognize and assess the importance of the environment and understand how the organization operates within it. The concept of subsystems highlights the importance of interdependencies among units of an organization. Synergy points to the value of cooperation within the organization. And the manager must take appropriate steps to avoid entropy.

---

21. See John Clark, *Business Today—Successes and Failures* (New York: Random House, 1979).

Contingency theory

The other recent addition to management theory is the contingency approach. Essentially, *contingency theory* suggests that appropriate managerial behavior in a given situation depends on, or is contingent on, a wide variety of elements.[22] Appropriate behavior cannot always be generalized or extrapolated from other situations. Recall Taylor's assumptions about the effect of financial incentives on worker behavior. He assumed that all workers would generate the highest possible level of output in order to maximize their own personal economic gain. We can imagine some people being motivated primarily by money; but we can just as easily imagine other people being motivated by leisure time, status, and/or social acceptance (as Mayo found at Hawthorne).

The classical, behavioral, and quantitative schools of thought originally tried to find the "one best way" to approach all problems. These schools were thus universal in scope.[23] The contingency perspective holds that universal solutions and principles cannot be applied to social systems such as organizations. When a chemist combines specified quantities of certain chemicals in a test tube, the results can be predicted with certainty. When a manager with unique characteristics applies a management solution in a unique organizational context populated by a group of unique individuals, the results are much less predictable. Hence the manager must consider as many relevant elements (contingencies) as possible in every new situation. Contingency relationships are considered throughout this book; areas where contingency models have been especially useful are organization design (Chapter 11) and leadership (Chapter 14).

An integrative framework

We have said that the classical, behavioral, and quantitative schools of management thought are complementary rather than contradictory and that the systems and contingency perspectives can help integrate the three schools. Our framework for relating the various approaches to management is shown in Figure 2.5.

The initial premise of the framework is that, before attempting to apply any concepts or ideas from the three schools of management thought, the manager must recognize the interdependence of units within the organization, the effect of environmental influences, and the need to respond to each situation that arises in terms of its unique characteristics. The ideas of system and subsystem interdependencies and environmental influences foreshadow the importance of a systems perspective, whereas the situational view of management is a prelude to a contingency orientation.

With these ideas as basic assumptions, the manager has at his or her

22. See Fremont E. Kast and James E. Rosenzweig, *Contingency Views of Organization and Management* (Chicago: Science Research Associates, 1973).

23. The contemporary views developed from these schools of thought (for example, contemporary organizational theory and organizational behavior) recognize the limitations of universal approaches and now embrace the contingency philosophy.

Figure 2.5
An integrative
framework of
management
theories

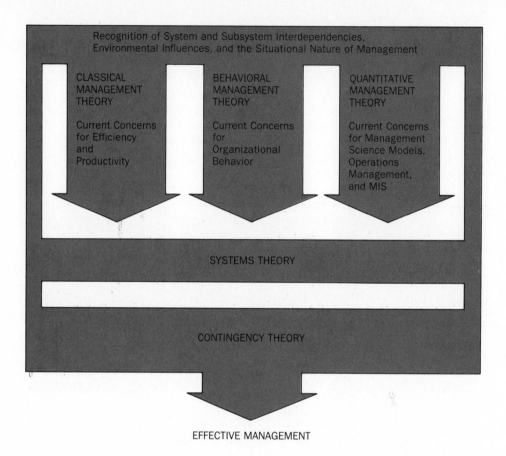

disposal all the valid tools, techniques, concepts, and theories of the classical, behavioral, and quantitative schools of thought. Armed with classical management theory, organizations can profit from a scientific approach to management. Of course, they should not fall victim to the pitfalls and problems associated with a strict and narrow interpretation of these early ideas. In many contemporary settings, the scientific study of jobs and production techniques can be used to enhance efficiency and production.

Behavioral management theory is also of use to modern managers. By drawing on the contemporary ideas of organizational behavior, the manager can better appreciate the importance of employee needs and behaviors in the workplace. Motivation, leadership, communication, and group processes are especially important.

Quantitative management theory also provides the manager with useful tools and techniques. The development and use of management science models, the application of operations management methods, and the use of management information systems are all ways in which a manager can increase her or his efficiency and effectiveness.

In choosing and applying ideas from any of these areas, however, the manager must use both a systems and a contingency orientation. Systems theory tells the manager that environmental influences must be considered. Similarly, the manager must recognize the concept of interdependencies: a change in one part of the organizational system may change other parts of the system as well. Finally, the contingency orientation reminds the manager that a tool, technique, concept, or theory that works perfectly in one setting or situation may not be appropriate under different circumstances.

Consider the new distribution manager of a large wholesaling firm. His job is to manage 100 truck drivers and to coordinate standard truck routes in the most efficient fashion. This new manager, with little relevant experience, might attempt to increase efficiency and productivity by employing strict time-and-motion analysis, work specialization, and close supervision (as suggested by scientific management). But doing so may cause decreased satisfaction and morale and increased turnover (as suggested by organizational behavior). Similarly, our manager might develop a management science model to use route driver time more efficiently (from the quantitative school). But this new system could disrupt existing work groups and social patterns (from organizational behavior). The manager may create even more problems by trying to impose programs and practices derived from her or his previous job. The incentive programs welcomed by retail clerks, for example, might not work for truck drivers.

Such a manager should soon realize that a broader perspective is needed. Systems and contingency orientation help provide this breadth. To solve a problem of declining productivity, the manager might look to the classical school (perhaps jobs are inefficiently designed or workers improperly trained), the behavioral school (worker motivation may be low or group norms may be restricting output), and/or the quantitative school (facilities may be improperly laid out or material stock-outs may be resulting from poor inventory management). Of course, before implementing any plans for improvement, the manager should try to assess their effect on other areas of the organization.

Now suppose that this manager is involved in planning a new warehouse. He or she will probably consider how to structure the management team and whether to use an incentive system (classical school), what kinds of leaders and work-group arrangements to develop (behavioral school), and how to develop and apply a network model for designing and operating the facility itself (quantitative school).

As a final example, if employee turnover is too high, the manager might consider an incentive system (classical school), plan a motivational enhancement program (behavioral school), or use a model to discover that turnover costs may actually be lower than the cost of making any changes at all!

Theory Z management

During the 1970s and on into the 1980s, productivity in the United States failed to keep pace with that of other industrial countries.[24] At the same time many

---

24. See Jerome A. Mark, ''Productivity Travels and Prospects,'' in Clark Kerr and Jerome M. Rosow (eds.), *Work in America—The Decade Ahead* (New York: Van Nostrand, 1979), pp. 188–203.

foreign firms, especially Japanese companies, began to carve out substantial niches for themselves in U.S. markets. Prominent examples include Nissan, Toyota, Sanyo, and Sony. Worried about declining productivity rates and faced with challenges from abroad, U.S. managers became aware that Japanese organizations were managed differently from their own. Some managers may have considered transplanting Japanese management practices directly into U.S. organizations, but differing sociocultural, economic, and technological settings made the wholesale transfer of managerial philosophies impossible.

Theory Z, as expounded by William Ouchi in 1981, is an attempt to integrate common business practices in the United States and Japan into one middle-ground framework.[25] Figure 2.6 summarizes what are termed Types A, J, and Z organizations. It shows that American and Japanese firms are essentially different along seven important dimensions: (1) length of employment, (2) mode of decision making, (3) location of responsibility, (4) speed of evaluation and promotion, (5) mechanisms of control, (6) specialization of career path, and (7) nature of concern for the employee. For example, Japanese firms are usually characterized by lifetime employment opportunities and collective decision making, whereas their American counterparts exhibit short-term employment prospects and usually rely on individual decision making.

Ouchi also observed that a few particularly successful American firms (such as IBM, Hewlett-Packard, Eastman Kodak, and Procter & Gamble) did not follow the typical American Type A model. Years of research and investigation led him to conclude that a middle course could be charted between the extreme Types A and J and that this course was especially appropriate for U.S. organizations. As shown in Figure 2.6, this middle course is found in Type Z organizations. They borrow one characteristic (individual responsibility) from Type A, incorporate three characteristics (collective decision making, slow evaluation and promotion, and holistic concern) from Type J, and assume an intermediate stance with respect to the other three dimensions (for instance, they postulate long-term employment—as opposed to short-term employment in Type A and lifetime employment in Type J).

Ouchi's ideas have been well received by practicing managers. His book was on most best-seller lists for several weeks in 1981, and many organizations are trying to implement his suggestions. On the other hand, controversy has arisen about whether some of Ouchi's research was conducted as scientifically as it should have been.[26] Whether Theory Z will emerge as a major theoretical perspective for management or fall by the wayside still remains to be seen. From all indications, the former possibility seems more likely.

Summary of key points

Theories are important as organizers of knowledge and road maps for action. Understanding the historical context of management and organizations pro-

25. See William Ouchi, *Theory Z—How American Business Can Meet the Japanese Challenge* (Reading, Mass.: Addison-Wesley, 1981). For a recent analysis of Theory Z, see Jeremiah J. Sullivan, "A Critique of Theory Z," *Academy of Management Review,* January 1983, pp. 132–142.

26. See William Bowen, "Lessons from Behind the Kimono," *Fortune,* June 15, 1981, pp. 247–250.

Figure 2.6
Comparison of
American,
Japanese, and
Theory Z
organizations

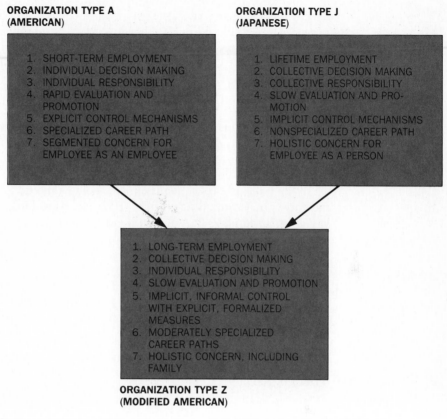

ORGANIZATION TYPE A
(AMERICAN)

1. SHORT-TERM EMPLOYMENT
2. INDIVIDUAL DECISION MAKING
3. INDIVIDUAL RESPONSIBILITY
4. RAPID EVALUATION AND
   PROMOTION
5. EXPLICIT CONTROL MECHANISMS
6. SPECIALIZED CAREER PATH
7. SEGMENTED CONCERN FOR
   EMPLOYEE AS AN EMPLOYEE

ORGANIZATION TYPE J
(JAPANESE)

1. LIFETIME EMPLOYMENT
2. COLLECTIVE DECISION MAKING
3. COLLECTIVE RESPONSIBILITY
4. SLOW EVALUATION AND PRO-
   MOTION
5. IMPLICIT CONTROL MECHANISMS
6. NONSPECIALIZED CAREER PATH
7. HOLISTIC CONCERN FOR
   EMPLOYEE AS A PERSON

1. LONG-TERM EMPLOYMENT
2. COLLECTIVE DECISION MAKING
3. INDIVIDUAL RESPONSIBILITY
4. SLOW EVALUATION AND PROMOTION
5. IMPLICIT, INFORMAL CONTROL
   WITH EXPLICIT, FORMALIZED
   MEASURES
6. MODERATELY SPECIALIZED
   CAREER PATHS
7. HOLISTIC CONCERN, INCLUDING
   FAMILY

ORGANIZATION TYPE Z
(MODIFIED AMERICAN)

Source: Adapted from William Ouchi, *Theory Z*, © 1981, Addison-Wesley, Reading, Mass., p. 58. Reprinted with permission of the publisher.

vides a sense of heritage and can also help managers avoid repeating the mistakes of others.

Isolated pieces of evidence date interest in management back thousands
of years, but a scientific approach to management has emerged only in the last
hundred years. The work of Robert Owen and Charles Babbage played a key
role in the beginnings of management theory. Over the course of the development of management thought, three primary schools or theories of management emerged. The earliest of these was classical management theory. The
other two schools of thought are referred to as behavioral management theory
and quantitative management theory.

The two areas of classical management theory, scientific management and
classical organization theory, focused on effective management at the level of
the worker and at the level of the total organization, respectively. Scientific
management was concerned with improving efficiency and work methods.
Key contributors to scientific management included Frederick Taylor, Frank
and Lillian Gilbreth, Henry Gantt, and Harrington Emerson. Key contributors
to classical organization theory included Henri Fayol, Max Weber, Lyndall Urwick, and Chester Barnard.

Behavioral management theory, characterized by a concern for individual and group behavior, had its roots in industrial psychology, but it emerged primarily as a result of the Hawthorne studies. The human relations movement assumed that improved employee satisfaction would lead to improved performance; today, we know this is not the case. Organizational behavior, an outgrowth of behavioral management theory, is of interest to many contemporary managers.

Quantitative management theory and its three components, management science, operations management, and management information systems, attempt to apply quantitative techniques to decision making and problem solving. These areas are also of considerable importance to contemporary managers.

The three schools of management thought should be viewed in a complementary, not a contradictory, light. Each has something of value to offer. The key is understanding how to use them effectively. Two relatively recent additions to management theory, the systems and contingency perspectives, seem to have great potential both as approaches to management and as frameworks for integrating other schools of thought.

Theory Z combines elements of Type A (American) and Type J (Japanese) organizations into a form appropriate for many contemporary American organizations. Theory Z management may become increasingly popular in the years ahead.

QUESTIONS FOR DISCUSSION

1. Do you think it would be possible to understand contemporary management fully without looking at past developments?
2. Do management techniques from "the old days" have any value today? Why or why not?
3. In what ways are the three schools of management thought contradictory and inconsistent with each other? In what ways are they complementary?
4. If you had to "sell" a manager on using a theory discussed in this chapter, how would you proceed?
5. In your opinion, which management theory holds the most promise for the future? Why?
6. If a manager said to you, "What we need is some good scientific management," what would you think he or she meant?
7. Taylor has recently been criticized for stretching the truth about his research. Others have argued that we shouldn't worry about this, because he played such a key role in stimulating interest in management and because we have progressed far beyond his ideas anyway. What do you think? Should different standards of accuracy and objectivity be upheld in research into management than are adhered to in the sciences?
8. Do you think management theory will ever be as precise and objective as, say, chemistry or physics? Why or why not?
9. Some people view systems theory as a part of contingency theory,

whereas others think of them as different approaches. Which view do you think is correct?

10. Is Theory Z likely to become as important as the other theories discussed in this chapter, or is it just a fad?

C A S E   2.1

At the beginning of the chapter, you read a scenario about an electrical equipment firm. The company had encountered a number of problems and had decided to embark on an ambitious plan to increase productivity faster than its competitors. The company being described was Westinghouse. The case that follows tells how Westinghouse proceeded and then raises some other issues for your consideration.

Westinghouse Electric Corporation, long a leader in the electronics industry, did not fare well in the 1970s. The company made a number of bad acquisitions, was involved in a nasty bribery incident, and lost large sums of money in consumer appliances before eventually selling that division. The company's worst mistake, however, was to agree to supply uranium under a series of fixed-price contracts. This decision may eventually cost the firm nearly $1.5 billion. Westinghouse also faces a mounting challenge from Japanese manufacturers.

Every year the senior executives of Westinghouse convene to discuss future activities. At the 1979 meeting, declining productivity was a major issue. Thomas J. Murrin, president of the Public Systems Company of Westinghouse, was appointed head of an *ad hoc* committee to increase productivity. A number of alternatives were explored, including price and/or volume increases and changes in the company's product mix. The solution eventually adopted, however, was Theory Z.

Over the years, Westinghouse had developed a rigid, bureaucratic hierarchy. It had a strict chain of command and tended to be somewhat centralized. Theory Z, however, stresses the importance of participative decision making. This approach was selected after numerous trips to Japan to observe the work force there. Preliminary efforts were directed at the firm's construction group, which represents 7 percent of Westinghouse's work force.

At first Westinghouse encountered some problems in its attempts to use Theory Z. Preliminary efforts centered on operating employees rather than on management. And philosophical problems arose when managers resisted participation because they viewed Theory Z as a personal loss of power and control. Surprisingly, some operating employees also opposed the new system. For the most part, however, these problems were ironed out with minimal disruption.

Two examples illustrate the issues and problems addressed by the new management system. One group of managers attacked the problem of unexpected interruptions, such as phone calls, that

Theory Z at Westinghouse

disrupt a manager's schedule. Computers were programmed to hold all messages until it was convenient for the manager to handle them. In another location, workers and supervisors established a company cafeteria and developed a plan for discouraging vandalism in the plant restrooms.

Despite the problems, Westinghouse reports favorable results to date with Theory Z. One plant reported big drops in absenteeism and grievances. In another plant, long-term hostility between labor and management has begun to ease. Other significant improvements have been introduced in the company's communication system. Most significantly, Westinghouse has begun to meet its target goal of a 6.1 percent increase in productivity every year.

CASE
QUESTIONS

1. Which, if any, of the other management theories could Westinghouse have chosen? Do you think the results would have been the same? Why or why not?
2. What characteristics of Westinghouse made its use of Theory Z so successful?
3. What additional benefits and problems do you think Westinghouse might face in the future as a result of Theory Z?
4. If you were advising an organization to adopt Theory Z, how would you recommend that it begin?

CASE
REFERENCES

"Catch-Up Time." *Forbes,* February 18, 1980, pp. 164–165.
Main, Jeremy. "Westinghouse's Cultural Revolution." *Fortune,* June 15, 1981, pp. 74–93.

C A S E   2.2

Helen Winthrup, Hank Pride, Joe Garcia, and Sally Moorhead are all middle managers for Johnson Fabricating, a Southwestern metalworking company. Helen and Joe are in sales; Hank and Sally are in manufacturing. They are en route home after a two-day management development program at a nearby university. The program had covered a wide variety of subjects, but the most important topics were contingency theory, systems theory, and employee motivation. The four participants disagreed among themselves about which topic was most useful and valid.

"Personally, I think systems theory has a lot to offer a company like ours," Joe commented. "I can see lots of ways that we are interdependent. For example, if your people in production change product specs, or if your prices for materials go up, I can see the effects on my sales right away. That environmental influence stuff also fits us. I mean, right now, with the economy the way it is, the effects are really obvious. Back when the oil boom was on, we had all the business we could handle. Look at us now,

Does theory apply in the real world?

though; we're having to hustle and fight for every sale we get. You guys in production are probably feeling the pinch, too."

"I know what you mean," agreed Sally. "We have to really try to hold down the scrappage in times like these, and it just makes it harder on all of us. I don't see what it has to do with systems theory, however. Sure, you can argue that we're getting hurt by the economy, and that's consistent with systems theory, but I don't see how we can use it. I mean, if everything is a system, and all systems affect all other systems, how can we predict what those effects are going to be? It's just like contingency theory. If you argue that 'it all depends' or that 'everything depends on everything else,' how does that help us?"

Helen, the other sales manager, disagrees. She says, "I haven't thought enough yet about systems theory to have an opinion. I do think that contingency theory has some value, though. In fact, I've been using it for some time now without realizing it. For example, I've got one customer who is really family-oriented. We spend lots of time talking about our kids and what we do on weekends. I've learned that he already knows what he is going to order before I arrive, and he doesn't want me to push him. If I just spend a couple of hours chatting with him, he'll place a big order. But I have another customer who is just the opposite. He wants me to take charge, tell him what he currently has in stock and on order, and suggest a new order. He almost always goes along—he's no nonsense, all business. So you see, I use contingency theory every day: I adjust my selling style to match the situation. The sales representatives in any territory who handle new and small accounts use the same approach."

"As for me," chimed in Hank, "I don't understand what all the hoopla is about. As for this systems and contingency theory, I agree with Sally. They sound good when some professor is talking about them, but they don't apply to the real world. What I really didn't go for, though, was that motivation stuff. I think Frederick Taylor had the right idea about that all along. To motivate people, you pay them for what they do. If they don't do anything, don't pay them anything. You all know as well as I do that the only reason people work is for money. And the main motivator is a good swift kick in the tail."

CASE
QUESTIONS

1. Do you agree with Joe and Helen or with Sally and Hank?

2. If you were Joe or Helen, how could you try to convince Sally of the usefulness of systems theory and contingency theory?

3. What do you think of Hank's ideas about motivation? Which theory or theories of management does he subscribe to?

4. What factors might explain the differences of opinion expressed by the members of this group?

3

THE MANAGER AND THE EXTERNAL ENVIRONMENT

CHAPTER OBJECTIVES

1. Distinguish among the general, task, and internal environments of organizations.

2. Cite and describe the five dimensions of the general environment.

3. Identify and provide examples of the six dimensions of the task environment.

4. Explain how organizations are influenced by their general and task environments.

5. Explain how organizations influence their general and task environments.

6. Describe the roles of boundary spanners.

7. Discuss the organizations' social responsibility, the meaning of ethics in the business setting, and the social audit.

OPENING INCIDENT

You are a member of the board of directors of a major film company. The president of the company is paid $4,500 a week plus bonuses and enjoys elaborate fringe benefits. Recent allegations of "unauthorized financial transactions" on his part, however, led to his suspension (with full pay) until the problem could be investigated. As it turns out, the president has stolen $84,208 from the company by forging checks and padding expense accounts. What would you do?

P rocter & Gamble, television's biggest advertiser, recently announced that the company would not sponsor programs of objectionable moral content. Examining another situation entirely, we see that the market for trucks is somewhat confusing: domestic manufacturers such as Ford, GM, and International Harvester are losing money in what they say is a shrinking market, yet overseas manufacturers such as Volvo and Renault are eager to enter that same market. In one of the biggest financial deals in history, Seagram, Du Pont, Texaco, and Mobil all attempted to buy Conoco; Du Pont eventually acquired the nation's ninth largest oil company for $7.6 billion. AT&T, long a conservative, low-profile company operating as a public utility, has become an aggressive marketer, and it has changed its image to that of a communications and data processing concern. A few years ago, Union Carbide brought its air pollution under control and began to publicize its role as a socially responsible corporation. Due to excess capacity and small profits in the aluminum can industry in the early 1960s, the two industry leaders, Continental Can and American Can, both recognized the need to diversify. Continental moved into insurance and natural gas while American entered the aluminum recycling, record distribution, and forest products markets. Continental is presently flourishing, but American's acquisitions have not done as well.

What do these examples have in common? They all illustrate the importance of an organization's environments. *Environment,* in the sense used here, means the set of forces and conditions that surround and permeate an organization. Procter & Gamble is responding to pressure from interest groups like the Moral Majority and the Coalition for Better Television. Domestic and foreign truck manufacturers have evidently looked at the same market and predicted quite different future business environments. A distiller, a chemical company, and two other oil companies wanted Conoco; Du Pont, the winner, acquired a guaranteed source of petroleum for its chemical and plastic products. AT&T was forced to change its position because numerous court settlements had jeopardized its status as a monopoly. Union Carbide, like many other large companies, realized it was acquiring a negative public image and took steps to change its reputation. Continental Can and American Can faced the same environmental outlook and came to the same conclusions regarding the proper course of action, but they embarked on that course of action with different approaches and achieved different results.

Environmental factors clearly play a major role in determining an organization's success or failure. As we discussed in Chapter 2, organizations that take a closed-system perspective and ignore or do not respond to the environment are asking for trouble. This chapter discusses the organization's relationship with its environment in more depth. It briefly describes the three kinds of organizational environments—general, task, and internal—and then devotes considerable attention to general and task environments and how they interact with the organization. Subsequent sections focus on boundary spanning processes and social responsibility.

The nature of organizational environments

It would be simple to define an organization's environment as everything outside the organization, but this definition has at least three shortcomings. It is too broad. Local business transactions in, say, Hong Kong are not likely to affect a small retailer in Ohio. Furthermore, the boundary of the organization is not as obvious as we might think. In one sense, stockholders and part-time workers are part of the organization, while in another sense they are part of its environment. Finally, this definition ignores the manager. When we focus on an individual manager, the organization itself can be considered part of the environment. What, then, is an acceptable definition of an organization's environment? Actually, we need to define three organizational environments: a general environment,[1] a task environment,[2] and an internal environment.[3] The relationship of these environments to the organization is indicated in Figure 3.1.

The general environment

An organization's *general environment* consists of those nonspecific dimensions in the organization's surroundings that might affect the organization's activities. These elements are not necessarily associated with other specific organizations. The general environment of most organizations consists of the economic, technological, sociocultural, political–legal, and international dimensions.[4]

---

1. See Richard N. Osborn, James G. Hunt, and Lawrence R. Jauch, *Organization Theory: An Integrated Approach* (New York: Wiley, 1980), especially Chapter 5.

2. See James D. Thompson, *Organizations in Action* (New York: McGraw-Hill, 1967).

3. See G. Litwin and R. Stringer, *Motivation and Organization Climate* (Cambridge, Mass.: Harvard University Press, 1968).

4. See Osborn, Hunt, and Jauch, *Organization Theory;* and Richard H. Hall, *Organizations: Structure and Process,* 2nd ed. (Englewood Cliffs, N.J.: Prentice-Hall, 1977).

Figure 3.1
The organization
and its environment

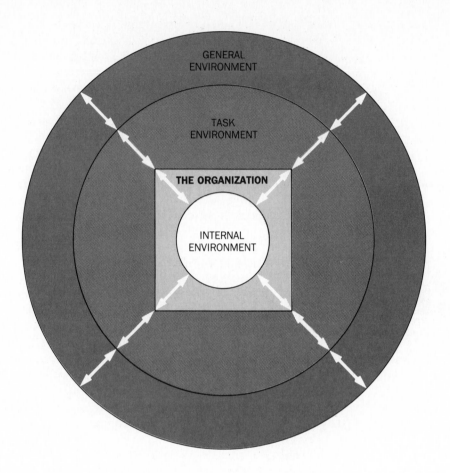

The task environment

The *task environment* of an organization consists of other specific organizations that are likely to influence that organization. The task environment typically includes competitors, customers, suppliers, regulators, unions, and associates.[5] The task environment will be discussed in the third section of this chapter. Taken together, the general and task environments represent the organization's external environment.

The internal environment

An organization's *internal environment,* also called its climate, consists of the perceptions that the members of the organization share regarding its nature, style, and character. We will discuss the internal environment in Chapter 11.

5. See Thompson, *Organizations in Action;* and Hall, *Organizations: Structure and Process.*

The general environment

The general environment of an organization, as noted earlier, consists of five dimensions: economic, technological, sociocultural, political–legal, and international. As is illustrated in Figure 3.2, the dimensions of the general environment are typically not considered individual units. They are general factors or processes that interact among themselves and also affect the organization. Each dimension embodies conditions and events that have the potential to influence organizations in significant ways.

The economic dimension

The economic dimension of the general environment depends on the economic system of the country in which the organization functions.[6] In the United

Figure 3.2
The general
environment

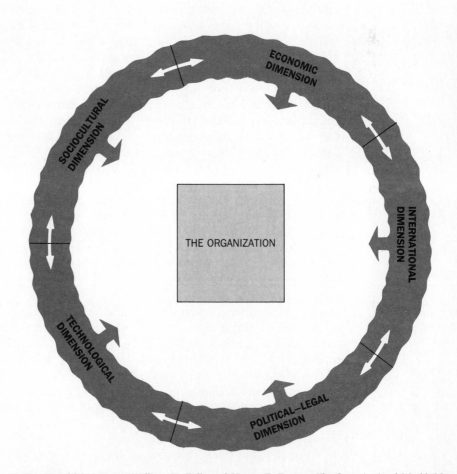

6. See Harold J. Leavitt, William R. Dill, and Henry E. Eyring, *The Organizational World* (New York: Harcourt, 1973). Chapter 15 offers an overview of how economic conditions influence organizations.

States, our economic system is based on the tenets of capitalism (private ownership of the assets that produce goods and services). Major economic systems that prevail in other countries include socialism and communism.

Under capitalism, an organization may find itself operating in one of four conditions: monopoly, oligopoly, imperfect competition, and perfect competition. A monopoly exists when one organization provides almost all of a particular good or service to the market. Traditionally, regulated utilities are viewed as monopolies. A similar form of monopoly that has recently come into being is the franchised cable television company that offers service in a particular area. Many professional sports teams and some newspapers are also monopolies.

In an oligopoly, relatively few organizations (perhaps three or four) provide most of the goods or services to the market. Examples of oligopolistic industries include the automobile, tire, steel, and chemical industries.

Under conditions of imperfect competition, a large number of competitors exist. They serve specialized markets, and their customers perceive few differences among the goods and services offered because of incomplete information and the barriers of time and distance. Consider two dry-cleaning establishments in a community. When a man stops by one dry cleaner and finds that the price for cleaning a pair of slacks is $1.00, he probably has the work done and doesn't worry about whether the other dry cleaner may be a little cheaper. Even if he found out that the other cleaner charged only $.90 for cleaning a pair of slacks, he might still decide that the drive across town wasn't worth $.10 savings. The organizations that operate under conditions of imperfect competition include most retail outlets, restaurants, and barbers and beauty salons.

Finally, with perfect competition, many firms offer essentially the same goods or services. Moreover, all customers and potential customers are presumed to be fully familiar with each firm's offerings. Hence price is an important factor. Conditions of perfect competition seldom exist. The concept is useful, however, because it provides a theoretical counterpart to monopoly; oligopolies and imperfect competition fall in between.

The economic conditions in which an organization operates clearly have a significant impact on managers' actions. For the monopoly, a fundamental goal of management is typically to maintain the monopolistic status of the organization. A manager in an oligopolistic organization, on the other hand, must anticipate environmental activity and attempt to manage the firm's environments by monitoring, pricing, and negotiating. The manager who faces imperfect competition attempts to justify price differentials by maintaining the image (either real or illusory) that the relevant goods or services really are different. Under conditions of perfect competition, the manager attempts to understand the prevailing market situation fully and tries to stay as close as possible to acceptable and prevailing price, quality, and quantity levels.

For all organizations, general economic conditions directly influence labor and raw materials costs, as do the monetary and fiscal policies of the government. During times of high inflation, for example, several forces affect organizations. On the one hand, many firms are forced to pay higher prices to acquire the raw materials they need. They also must pay rising maintenance costs, utility bills, and so forth. Yet they are also subject to external pressures to hold the line on the prices *they* charge consumers.

Unemployment rates also affect managerial actions. If unemployment is high, the organization can usually choose employees from a large labor pool and does not have to pay premium wages. When unemployment is low, however, skilled employees are in short supply and it may take high wages to attract them.

Interest rates, which are strongly influenced by federal monetary and fiscal policies, clearly affect an organization's ability to borrow money, and they affect the buying power of consumers. For example, in the early 1980s mortgage interest rates skyrocketed. As more and more potential home buyers were forced out of the market, not only did the housing industry suffer, but effects were also felt in related industries such as carpet and appliance manufacturing. The economic dimension of an organization's general environment, then, is of great importance.

The technological dimension

Another major component of the general environment is the technological dimension.[7] Although technological processes may be carried out within the organization, the nature and availability of that technology usually comes from the general environment. The rate of technological breakthroughs in recent years has been spectacular. In just the last four decades we have seen the advent of computers, lasers, integrated circuits, semiconductors, xerography, and other wonders. Presently, computer-assisted manufacturing and design are paving the way for even more significant strides. Computer techniques, for example, allow aircraft manufacturers such as McDonnell Douglas to simulate the three miles of hydraulic tubing running through a DC-10. The results include decreased warehouse needs, higher-quality tube fittings, fewer employees, and significant time savings.[8] Another important technological innovation is robots. In some automobile plants in Japan, for example, entire automated shifts run with little or no human intervention![9]

Obviously, management must be concerned with technology and technological innovations if an organization is to keep pace with its competitors. And, on a national scale, failure to support research and development adequately is often cited as a cause of declines in the growth rate of productivity in the United States.[10] Managers must pay careful attention to the technology dimension of their general environment, monitoring current developments in order to make informed decisions about investing in new technological breakthroughs.

7. See John B. Miner, *Theories of Organizational Structure and Process* (Chicago: Dryden, 1982). Chapter 8 offers an overview of technology and its impact on organizations.

8. See Gene Bylinsky, "A New Industrial Revolution Is on the Way," *Fortune*, October 5, 1981, pp. 106–114.

9. See "Robots: Japan Takes the Lead," *Newsweek*, September 21, 1981.

10. See Burton G. Malkiel, "Productivity—The Problem Behind the Headlines," *Harvard Business Review*, May–June 1979.

The sociocultural dimension

The sociocultural dimension of the general environment is made up of the customs, mores, and values that characterize the society in which the organization functions.[11] Sociocultural processes are important to organizations because they indicate the products, services, and standards of conduct that the society is likely to value.

In the United States, for example, status is important to many people, and they may be willing to pay premium prices for designer jeans. In other countries such merchandise would have no market; consumers there put more emphasis on function. Appropriate standards of business conduct also vary across cultures. In the United States, accepting bribes and bestowing political favors are considered immoral. In other countries the standards are different; side payments to local politicians may be openly expected in return for a favorable response to common business transactions such as applications for zoning and operating permits.

Another aspect of the sociocultural dimension is that it influences how employees feel about their organizations. Japanese workers, for example, often evince more commitment and attachment to their organization than American workers.

There is a strong tendency to equate cultures with countries, but many countries exhibit a variety of cultures. Many people would agree that New York, Nebraska, and California have different cultures. In Canada, the culture in Quebec is probably more similar to France than to the rest of Canada.

The impact of sociocultural changes on organizations can perhaps best be demonstrated by noting recent changes that have obvious implications for management: (1) social and geographic mobility have increased dramatically over the last decade, (2) the costs of refusing various kinds of jobs have been reduced due to increased welfare support, dual-career families, and so forth. (3) the demand for more job options, such as part-time work and flexible working hours, has increased, and (4) a better-educated work force is demanding more interesting jobs and more control over those jobs.[12]

The shape of the market, the ethics of political influence, and attitudes in the work force are only a few of the many ways in which culture can affect an organization. The important point is that managers should be alert to such effects and to sociocultural variations from place to place.

The political–legal dimension

The political–legal dimension of the general environment is important for three basic reasons. It imposes certain legal constraints on an organization; the extent

11. See John Child, "Culture, Contingency and Capitalism in the Cross-National Study of Organizations," in L. L. Cummings and Barry M. Staw (eds.), *Research in Organizational Behavior*, Vol. 3 (Greenwich, Conn.: JAI Press, 1981), pp. 303–356 for a recent review of culture and its effects on organizations.

12. See Clark Kerr and Jerome M. Rosow (eds.), *Work in America—The Decade Ahead* (New York: Van Nostrand, 1979).

to which it is pro- or anti-business significantly influences management policy; and its stability is an important element in long-range planning.[13]

First, the legal system partially defines what an organization can and cannot do. When we were discussing the economic dimension, we noted that a primary goal of managers in a monopolistic organization is to maintain the monopolistic status of that organization. Yet many monopolies are subject to government control. If the organization is a utility, for example, regulatory agencies define acceptable levels of profit; management is not allowed to maximize profits or to invest excess funds in other businesses. State and federal laws require all firms to provide safe working conditions, to hire and promote with no discrimination, to protect the environment, and so on. Organizations that rely heavily on government funding, such as state universities and defense contractors, are especially susceptible to government constraints.

Second, pro- or anti-business sentiment in government influences business activity. The acquisition of Conoco by Du Pont was possible partly because of the pro-business stance of the Reagan administration. If an anti-business attitude had prevailed, the acquisition might have been blocked on grounds of anti-trust regulations.

Finally, the stability of the political–legal dimension has ramifications for long-range planning activities. No company wants to set up shop in another country unless our trade relationship with that country is relatively well defined and stable. Hence, organizations are much more likely to do business with England, Mexico, and Canada than with Iran and El Salvador. This same kind of process also occurs with local and state governments as well. A change in the mayor's or the governor's position can affect many organizations, especially smaller firms that do business in only one location and are susceptible to deed and zoning restrictions, property and school taxes, and the like.

The international dimension

A final component of the general environment for many organizations is the international dimension.[14] International commerce and other activities can take a variety of forms. Most obvious are the giant multinationals like Boeing, IBM, Monsanto, and Exxon. These and similar organizations have production facilities and/or marketing units in a large number of foreign countries.

At a more modest level, a growing number of companies are just beginning to export their products and are experimenting with using a foreign agent or a few foreign sales offices. Even firms that do business in only one country may face foreign competition at home, and they may use materials and/or production equipment imported from abroad. Or a magazine publisher using photographs taken in another country may have to deal in foreign exchange in order to pay the photographer.

13. See Mayer N. Zald, "Political Economy: A Framework for Comparative Analysis," in Mary Zey-Ferrell and Michael Aiken (eds.), *Complex Organizations: Critical Perspectives* (Glenview, Il.: Scott, Foresman, 1981), pp. 237–262 for a discussion of political influences on organizations.

14. See J. Daniels, E. Ogram, Jr., and L. Radebaugh, *International Business: Environments and Operations,* 2nd ed. (Reading, Mass.: Addison-Wesley, 1979) for a discussion of the international dimension of business.

The international dimension also has implications for not-for-profit organizations. For example, the Peace Corps and the Methodist Church send representatives to underdeveloped countries. Medical breakthroughs achieved in one country spread rapidly to others, and cultural exchanges of all kinds take place between countries. Conditions as diverse as war, immigration, and educational exchange programs all contribute to this process.

With the tremendous advances in transportation and communication technology in the past century, almost no part of the world is cut off from the rest. Virtually every organization is affected by the international dimension. In Chapter 23 we will explore management in the international sector.

The task environment

Because the impact of the general environment is often rather vague, most organizations focus more precisely on what is called the task environment. Though it is complex, the task environment provides useful information more readily than the general environment does. The manager can identify environmental factors of specific interest to the organization rather than having to deal with the more abstract dimensions of the general environment.

Managers at Armstrong Rubber Company, for example, have little trouble identifying elements of that company's task environment. Most of the company's operating employees are represented by the United Rubber, Cork, Linoleum and Plastic Workers of America. Almost half of the tires that Armstrong manufactures go to one customer, Sears, Roebuck and Co. Primary competitors are Goodyear, Firestone, Goodrich, and other tire producers. Du Pont is a supplier of the primary raw material in Armstrong's new tire, the Tredloc. Emissions at Armstrong's plants are monitored by the Environmental Protection Agency. Finally, the company is the major stockholder of Copolymer Rubber & Chemical Corporation, a manufacturer of synthetic rubber.[15]

As mentioned earlier (and as suggested by this example), the task environment is composed of six dimensions: competitors, customers, suppliers, regulators, unions, and associates. Figure 3.3 shows the relationship of the task environment to the organization and to the general environment. Note that the dimensions of the general environment are broad and nonspecific, whereas the dimensions of the task environment are composed of specific organizations. Note also that the relationship between the organization and the task environment is much closer and more direct than that between the organization and the general environment.

Competitors

An organization's *competitors* are other organizations that compete with it for resources. The most obvious resources that competitors vie for are customer dollars. General Motors, Ford, Nissan, and Volvo are competitors; K mart and Sears are competitors; Texaco, Mobil, and Shell are competitors.

15. Gurney Breckenfeld, "The Niche Pickers at Armstrong Rubber," *Fortune*, September 6, 1982, pp. 100–105.

Figure 3.3
The task
environment

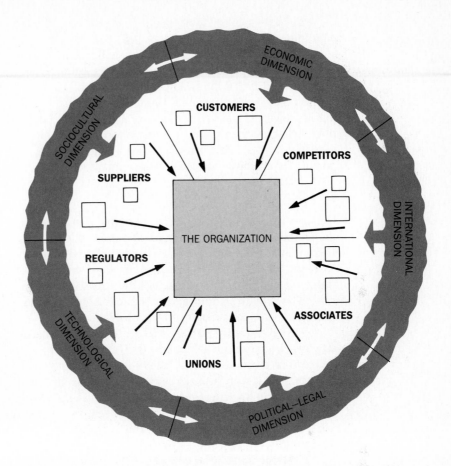

Competition can also be viewed from a different level of abstraction. In Chapter 1 we noted that General Motors competes not only with Ford and Nissan, but also with Schwinn, public transportation, and automobile repair outlets. Nor is competition limited to business firms. Universities compete with trade schools, the military, other universities, and the job market to attract good students. Art galleries compete with each other to attract the best exhibits.

From these latter examples, we see that organizations may compete for a variety of resources beyond customer dollars. Two entirely different types of organizations may compete to acquire a loan from a bank that has only limited funds to lend. In a large city, the police and fire departments may compete for the same tax dollars. Firms compete for quality labor, technological breakthroughs and patents, and scarce raw materials.

On occasion, the competitive environment creates some strange bedfellows. A group of Ford, Chrysler, and Chevrolet dealers with adjacent locations in Dallas once co-sponsored television commercials inviting customers to come out to the "Miracle Mile" for a full selection. Here was a Ford dealership working with what would usually be its competitors to compete with Ford dealers in other parts of the city. Similarly, at the corporate level, Ford, Chrysler, and

General Motors may lobby together to persuade the government to limit foreign imports.

Competitive relationships are usually complex. The manager should be alert to the competitive environment and careful not to oversimplify the information about it that flows into the organization. Information about competitors is often quite easily obtained. Sears can monitor J. C. Penney's prices by reading its newspaper advertisements or by sending someone to a store to inspect price tickets. Other kinds of information may be more difficult to obtain. Research activities, new product developments, and future advertising campaigns, for example, are often closely guarded secrets.

Customers

The marketing concept suggests that the primary goal of every organization should be customer satisfaction. Typically, the *customer* is the person who pays money to acquire an organization's product or service. In many cases, however, the chain of transaction is more complex. As consumers, for example, we do not buy a bottle of Coke from Coca-Cola. We buy it from Safeway, who bought it from an independent bottler, who bought the syrup and the right to use the name from Coca-Cola.

For several years, a regional office of Prudential had a "terrible communications problem" in its claims division. Work procedures had been established to receive and process claims from insurance policy holders. Over time, however, agents in the field began to act as go-betweens. Policy holders gave their claims to their agent, who filed the claims with the regional office. In effect, the claims division's customers were no longer the policy holders but were the agents instead. When this was finally recognized, a few simple changes in work procedures solved all the "communications" problems.

Customers need not be individuals. Schools, hospitals, government agencies, wholesalers, retailers, and manufacturers are just a few of the many kinds of organizations that may be major customers of other organizations. Managers should pay close attention to the customer dimension of the task environment. Common sources of information about customers include market research, surveys, consumer panels, and reports from sales representatives.

Suppliers

Suppliers provide resources for the organization. For example, suppliers for American Airlines include Boeing (aircraft), various food services (in-flight meals and refreshments), and local fuel companies (jet fuel). Suppliers for a manufacturer include the sources of raw materials as well as firms that sell machinery and other production devices.

Another kind of supplier provides the capital needed to operate the organization. Banks, stockholders, federal lending agencies, and other investors are all suppliers of capital for business firms. State governments, federal grant agencies, and successful alumni are suppliers of capital for state universities. Still other suppliers provide human resources for the organization. Examples include public and private employment agencies and college placement offices.

Some suppliers furnish the organization with the information it needs to carry out its mission. Many companies subscribe to periodicals such as the *Wall Street Journal, Fortune,* and *Business Week* to help their managers keep abreast of news. Market research firms are used by some companies. And some firms specialize in developing economic forecasts and in keeping managers informed about pending legislation.

Most organizations try to avoid depending exclusively on individual suppliers. When a firm buys all of a certain resource from one supplier, it may be crippled if the supplier goes out of business, is faced with a strike, or raises prices to a prohibitive level. Most organizations try to develop and maintain relationships with a variety of suppliers.

Another strategy some firms use is to gain control of a key supplier or suppliers. Although Du Pont evidently acquired Conoco for other reasons, it also obtained a reliable source of petroleum for its plastics and chemical products when it acquired the oil company. Sears manufactures many of the products it sells.

Dealing with suppliers is an important task of management. It is wise to maintain good relationships with suppliers and to avoid supplier dependence by establishing a network of suppliers for the various resources the organization needs to function.

Regulators

Regulators are units in the task environment that have the potential to actively control, regulate, or influence an organization's policies and practices. There are two important kinds of regulators: governmental agencies and interest groups.

Governmental agencies. Regulatory agencies are usually created by the government to protect the public from certain business practices or to protect organizations from one another. Powerful federal regulatory agencies include the Environmental Protection Agency (EPA), the Occupational Safety and Health Administration (OSHA), the Interstate Commerce Commission (ICC), the Securities and Exchange Commission (SEC), the Food and Drug Administration (FDA), the Federal Communications Commission (FCC), and the Equal Employment Opportunity Commission (EEOC). They are typically given official power to conduct investigations, set standards and rates, and levy fines or take other action against firms that violate the laws the agencies were created to enforce.

Many of these agencies play important roles in protecting the rights of individuals. The FDA, for example, helps ensure that the food we eat is free from contaminants, and the EPA tries to keep our environment clean. Most of the agencies have a significant degree of power to carry out their mandates. OSHA, for example, can force a business to stop operating until unsafe working conditions have been corrected.

The costs a firm incurs in complying with government regulations may be substantial, but these costs are usually passed on to the customer. Even so, many organizations complain that there is too much regulation at the present time. One recent study found that 48 major companies spent $2.6 billion in one year—over and above normal environmental protection, employee safety, and similar costs—due to stringent government regulations. On the basis of these findings, the extra costs of government regulations for all businesses have been estimated at more than $100 billion per year.[16] Obviously, the impact of regulatory agencies on organizations is considerable.

Although federal regulators get a lot of publicity, the effect of state and local agencies is also significant. California has more stringent automobile emission requirements than those established by the EPA. And public utility rates are usually set by local agencies.

A good deal of attention is focused on the regulation of business firms, but not-for-profit organizations must also deal with regulatory agencies. Most states, for example, have coordinating boards that regulate colleges and universities.

Interest groups. The other basic form of regulator is the interest group. Rather than being created by some branch of the government, an interest group is organized by its members to attempt to influence organizations. Prominent interest groups include the National Organization for Women (NOW), the Moral Majority, the Airline Passengers Association, the League of Women Voters, the Sierra Club, various consumer groups (such as Ralph Nader's Center for Study of Responsive Law and the Consumers Union), and industry self-regulation groups like the National Advertising Review Board and the Council of Better Business Bureaus.

Interest groups lack the official power of governmental agencies. They can, however, exert considerable influence by using the media to call attention to their positions. Ralph Nader's organization, for instance, had a significant effect on automobile safety at General Motors.

Unions

Labor unions are an important element of the task environment for many organizations. The National Labor Relations Act of 1935 requires organizations to recognize and bargain with a union if that union has been legally established by the organization's employees. Presently, around 23 percent of the American labor force is represented by unions. Some large firms such as Ford, Exxon, and General Motors may have to deal with a great many unions. Even when an organization's labor force is not unionized, management may still be concerned with this element of the task environment. During the 1970s, Farah Manufacturing Company, a Southwestern clothing company, waged a bitter legal fight to keep unions out of the company's plants in Texas and New Mexico.[17] K mart, J. P. Stevens, and Delta Air Lines have also actively sought to avoid unionization.

16. "Many Businesses Blame Governmental Policies for Productivity Lag," *Wall Street Journal*, October 28, 1980, pp. 1, 22.

17. See Rex Hardesty, "Farah: The Union Struggle in the 70s," *American Federationist*, June 1973, pp. 6–8.

Many people think primarily of blue-collar workers as union members, but many government employees, teachers, and other white-collar workers are also represented by unions. In recent years the activities of these nontraditional unions have attracted much attention. Recall the strikes by the major league baseball players and the air traffic controllers in 1981 and by the National Football League Players Association in 1982.

Associates

The associate dimension is seldom discussed as part of the task environment, but associates are destined to play an increasingly important role in the task environment of many organizations. We can define *associates* as two or more relatively autonomous organizations that are controlled by another organization, such as a holding company or parent firm. Examples of associates include the following:

1. Occidental Life, Budget Rent-A-Car, and Transamerica Financial Corporation (among others) are associates owned by Transamerica Corporation.
2. Miller Brewing Company and The Seven-Up Company are associates owned by Philip Morris, Inc. This "family" of associates is shown in Figure 3–4.
3. J. I. Case Company and Southwestern Life (among others) are associates owned by Tenneco Corporation.
4. Many local banks are now owned by large holding companies.

The success of associate relationships varies tremendously. When Philip Morris acquired Miller, its advertising expertise, capital, and creativity helped vault Miller to the number-two spot in its industry. On the other hand, United Artists was unhappy as an associate when it saw its hard-earned profits going to Transamerica. As a result, UA's management actively sought to sever ties with Transamerica.[18] Due to the current trend toward merger, diversification, and acquisition, many firms are likely to find themselves associates of other organizations in the future.

In summary, organizations must deal with all six primary dimensions of the task environment. For some organizations, of course, certain dimensions

Figure 3.4
The Philip Morris
group of associates

18. See "Transamerica's New Chief Wastes No Time on Plans to Revive Sluggish Conglomerate," *Wall Street Journal,* January 12, 1981, p. 23.

are more significant than others. Unions may be less important to non-unionized firms. For most large organizations, however, all six dimensions are extremely important.

Organization–environment relationships

Contemporary organization theory has focused a great deal of attention on how the environment of an organization affects that organization. We will describe the nature of those effects on the organization, and then we will discuss how the organization, in turn, influences the environment.

Environment ⟶ organization

An organization's general and task environments affect the organization in a variety of ways. The most common approach to analyzing these effects is based on the work of J. D. Thompson,[19] a noted organization theorist. Thompson suggests that elements in the task environment can be characterized along two dimensions: degree of change and degree of homogeneity. The degree of change in the task environment is the extent to which that environment is relatively stable or relatively dynamic. The degree of homogeneity is the extent to which it is relatively simple (few elements, little segmentation) or relatively complex (many elements, much segmentation).

Consider, for a moment, four different companies. Armstrong Rubber operates in a relatively simple environment, because relatively few other organizations and elements are a part of its task environment. Sears deals with many competitors, customers, and suppliers and therefore has a more complex task environment. The task environment of Texas Instruments changes rapidly, so it can be classified as dynamic. A small, locally owned retail establishment that has operated in one location for many years and has a loyal customer base is operating in a relatively stable environment.

We can use Figure 3.5 to analyze these companies in terms of degree of change and degree of homogeneity. When we do so, four situations emerge with different "levels of uncertainty." (As we shall see in Chapter 11, uncertainty plays a major role in shaping the organization.)

Stable-simple environments. When environmental conditions are relatively stable and simple, the organization experiences little uncertainty and is likely to adopt a rigid structure. The rationale for this bureaucratic structure is that, in the face of little uncertainty, rules, regulations, and standard operating procedures can usually keep things running smoothly. Firms in this situation include many franchised food operations (such as McDonald's and Kentucky

19. Thompson, *Organizations in Action.* For another interesting approach, see Paul R. Lawrence and Jay W. Lorsch, *Organization and Environment* (Homewood, Il.: Irwin, 1969).

Figure 3.5
The nature of the
external
environment

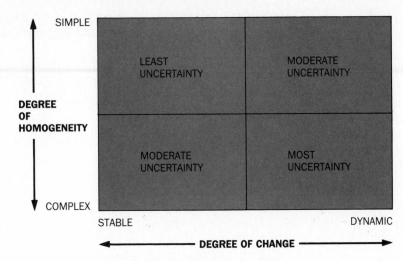

Source: Adapted from J. D. Thompson, *Organizations in Action* (New York: McGraw-Hill, 1967), p. 72. Used with permission of the publisher.

Fried Chicken) and most container manufacturers. McDonald's, for example, focuses on a certain segment of the consumer market, produces a limited product line, has a constant source of suppliers, and faces relatively consistent competition from Burger King and Wendy's. Furthermore, the fast-food industry has few unions and is influenced by few regulatory agencies.

Dynamic-simple environments. Organizations with dynamic but simple environments generally face a moderate degree of uncertainty. The usual method for dealing with this level of uncertainty is a modified version of the bureaucratic structure. Rules and regulations still predominate, but certain areas (such as marketing) are likely to have the power to monitor and deal with rapid changes in environmental conditions. Examples of organizations functioning in such environments include clothing manufacturers (targeting on a certain kind of clothing buyers but sensitive to fashion-induced changes) and record producers (catering to certain kinds of record buyers but alert to changing tastes in music). A clothing manufacturer like Levi Strauss, for example, faces few competitors (Wrangler and Lee), has few suppliers and few regulators, and uses limited distribution channels. However, this relatively simple task environment also changes quite rapidly as competitors adjust prices and styles, consumer tastes change, and new fabrics become available.

Stable-complex environments. The third combination of environmental factors is one of stability and complexity. Again, a moderate amount of uncertainty results, but a different form of organization is appropriate. Usually the firm is somewhat decentralized, and it groups its activities around different products or product lines in response to complex environmental elements.

General Motors, for example, is structured along these lines. Each division is designed to meet the needs of a particular segment of the environment. Chevrolet focuses on the lower end of the market, Cadillac concentrates on the upper end of the market, and Oldsmobile, Pontiac, and Buick position themselves in between. Overall, the organization must deal with a myriad of suppliers, regulators, consumer groups, and competitors. Yet change occurs quite slowly.

Dynamic-complex environments. The general and task environment dimensions may also interact in a very dynamic and complex way to yield a high degree of uncertainty. That is, the environment has a large number of elements and the nature of those elements is constantly changing. Here firms might find it advantageous to adopt a much less bureaucratic approach. The manager faces a larger number of environmental variables, and these forces are constantly changing. Hence more emphasis is placed on communication, decentralization, and managerial autonomy. Texas Instruments and other firms in the electronics field face these conditions because of the rapid rate of technological innovation and change in consumer markets that characterize their industry, their suppliers, and their competitors.

Organization $\longrightarrow$ environment

In this section we briefly outline a few strategies that firms have used to influence the external environment. In general, organizations find it much easier to influence specific units in the task environment than to influence the broader dimensions of the general environment (see Figure 3.6).

Influencing suppliers. Firms use a variety of techniques for influencing their suppliers. One important strategy is to use a number of different suppliers in order to limit the firm's dependence on any one. The organization may try to sign long-term contracts with fixed prices as a hedge against inflation. It may also attempt to become a supplier's largest customer in order to make the supplier more dependent on it. Or it may become its own supplier. Sears, for example, owns many of the firms that produce the products it sells. Some of these suppliers were purchased by Sears; others were formed for the specific purpose of supplying merchandise.

Influencing competitors. Influencing competitors is obviously more difficult. In a sense, though, almost any major activity a firm engages in affects its competitors. When General Motors begins to offer factory rebates, Ford and Chrysler may be forced to follow suit. When Prudential lowers its life insurance rates, New York Life and Mutual of Omaha are likely to do the same. However, some specific techniques for influencing competitors, such as price fixing and restraint of trade, are prohibited by law.

Influencing customers. Organizations may influence their customers in a variety of ways. Two common methods are changing the customer "mix"

Figure 3.6
The organization
influencing its
environments

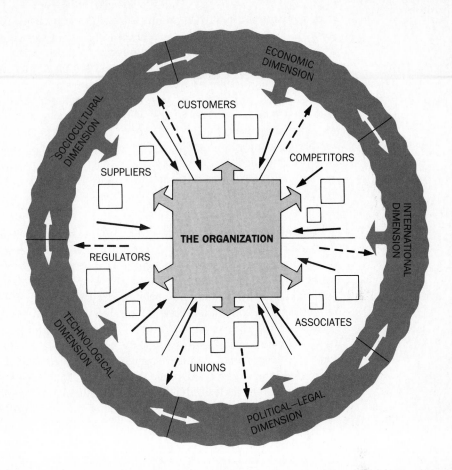

and changing the needs of present customers. The former strategy involves creating new uses for a product, finding entirely new customers, or taking customers away from competitors. For example, in recent years Arm & Hammer baking soda has been advertised as a deodorizer for refrigerators. Hence, people who normally might buy one box of soda for baking may now buy an additional box for their refrigerator. The other approach to influencing customers is to convince them that they need something they didn't need before. Automobile manufacturers use this strategy to convince people that they need a new car every two or three years. Apparently, people can also be convinced that they need Pet Rocks, Rubik's Cubes, and other novelties.

Influencing regulators. Organizations employ a number of strategies for influencing their regulators. Common approaches include lobbying and bargaining. Lobbying involves sending a company or industry representative to Washington in an effort to influence relevant agencies, groups, and committees. For example, the United States Chamber of Commerce lobby, the nation's largest business lobby, has an annual budget approaching $100 million.[20] The automobile companies have been successful on several occasions in bargaining with the Environmental Protection Agency to extend deadlines for compliance with pollution control and mileage standards. Some firms have also attempted to influence regulators via illegal offers of bribes.[21]

Influencing interest groups is more difficult, although some firms attempt to do so. When members of the Moral Majority were strongly criticizing the television networks, for example, ABC ran a movie that depicted in an unfavorable light an evangelist who was much like that group's leader. The purpose of the movie was to present the public with an alternative perspective on the actions of the Moral Majority and perhaps to reduce the group's influence and power.

Influencing unions. Most bargaining sessions between management and unions are attempts at mutual influence. Management tries to get the union to accept its contract proposals, for instance, and unions try to get management to sweeten its offer. When unions aren't represented in an organization, management usually attempts to keep them out. When Honda opened its first plant in the United States, it helped establish a plant union in an effort to head off the United Auto Workers. Many of the things an organization can do vis-à-vis unions are spelled out by laws such as the National Labor Relations Act. Occasionally, in the spirit of enlightened self-interest, unions have responded cooperatively to particular requests of an organization. During the crisis at Chrysler, for example, the UAW made significant wage concessions to help the firm survive.

Influencing associates. The extent to which a firm can influence an associate is a function of the two units' relative sizes and roles in the overall organization. A large and significant division or unit (such as Chevrolet at General Motors) may wield considerable influence over a smaller and less important division (such as GMC trucks).

We should also note that some firms try to influence their environments in less specific ways. Mobil has developed a number of ads touting the doctrine of free enterprise for business in general and the petroleum industry in particular. Some firms even "exchange" their environment for another. For example, Clorox Company currently derives only about 25 percent of its revenue from the product for which it is named.[22] By acquiring product lines and companies in other markets, the firm has literally exchanged one environment for several.

20. See Richard I. Kirkland, "Fat Days for the Chamber of Commerce," *Fortune*, September 21, 1981, pp. 144–158; and David W. Fischer, "Strategies Toward Political Pressure," *Academy of Management Review*, January 1983, pp. 71–78.

21. See W. Robertson, "The Directors Woke Up Too Late at Gulf," *Fortune*, June 1976, pp. 120–125.

22. "Pocket-Sized P&G," *Fortune*, July 27, 1981, p. 14.

Figure 3.7
The boundary
spanning process

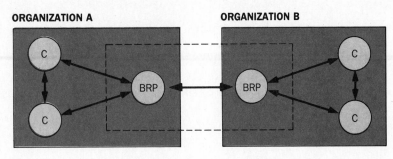

Key:

BRP = Boundary Role Person
  C = Constituent

Source: Adapted from J. S. Adams, "The Structure and Dynamics of Behavior in
Organization Boundary Roles," in M. Dunnette (ed.), *Handbook of Industrial and
Organizational Psychology* (New York: Wiley, 1983). Used with permission of the
publisher.

Boundary spanning processes

The boundaries, or points of contact, between organizations are especially sensitive areas. *Boundary roles* are positions that link two or more systems in
different organizations,[23] and *boundary spanners* are individuals who occupy
boundary roles in an organization. For example, salespersons link the company
with its customers, and purchasing agents link the company with its suppliers.
Some theorists also relate boundary spanning to the coordination of departments or units within an organization; we will explore this point further in
Chapter 9.

Figure 3.7 shows how the boundary spanning process works. The two
circles labeled BRP (boundary role person) represent boundary spanners of two
different organizations. The dotted region denotes their interaction. The four
circles marked C are the constituents of each boundary spanner.

The boundary spanner in organization A may be a purchasing agent
looking for a particular type of machine. His or her constituents are primarily
the people who will use the machine and those who will pay for it. The boundary spanner in organization B may be an industrial sales representative for a
firm that manufactures the kind of machine that firm A needs. His or her
constituents may be the people who will design the specific machine needed
by firm A and those who will build it. The two BRP's act as agents or representatives for their organizations in negotiating an agreement that meets the
needs of their constituents.

23. See J. Stacy Adams, "The Structure and Dynamics of Behavior in Organization Boundary
Roles," in Marvin Dunnette (ed.), *Handbook of Industrial and Organizational Psychology* (New
York: Wiley, 1983); and Robert Miles, *Macro Organizational Behavior* (Santa Monica, Calif.: Good-
year, 1980).

Boundary spanners perform six basic functions:

1. They represent the organization to the environment.
2. They monitor the environment for information that may be of value to the organization.
3. They try to protect the organization from threats from the environment.
4. They serve as gatekeepers and information processors.
5. They serve as negotiating agents with environmental units for the purposes of acquiring inputs and disposing of outputs.
6. They link organizations and coordinate activities among them.[24]

Given the importance and uncertainty of an organization's external environments, boundary spanning processes are essential. Managers should make sure that boundary roles are properly designed and that they are filled by people with the right combination of personality, experience, and skill.

Social responsibility

A large part of an organization's response to the environment (but at a more general level), is called social responsibility. *Social responsibility* has been defined as the organization's obligation to take actions that protect and improve the welfare of society as a whole, along with advancing its own interests.[25] Our discussion of social responsibility will focus on managerial ethics, organizational responsibility to society, and a means of evaluating an organization's level of social responsibility.

Managerial ethics

Socially responsible behavior by managers is usually a matter of ethics. Ethical behavior is behavior that is consistent with prevailing social and cultural norms and mores. It is important to note the distinction between ethical behavior and legal behavior. Legal behavior is that which is not prohibited by laws and regulations, whereas ethical behavior is more fluid and may go beyond mere legality. Other factors that help define ethical behavior include codes of ethics and social pressures.

Many examples of unethical behavior have been reported over the last several years. Common examples include embezzlement, political bribes and gifts, theft, the use of improper reporting procedures, and violations of privacy. For example, two top executives at Fruehauf Trailer Company were recently found guilty of conspiring to defraud the government of excise taxes,

24. See Miles, *Macro Organizational Behavior*, pp. 320–339.

25. See Keith Davis and Robert L. Blomstrom, *Business and Society: Environment and Responsibility*, 3rd ed. (New York: McGraw-Hill, 1975), p. 6.

and Southwestern Bell has been found guilty of illegally tapping an employee's telephone.[26]

Why do managers stoop to such practices? One reason is that they may be rewarded for high levels of performance, regardless of how this performance is achieved. If a political bribe will result in a favorable zoning change, a manager may feel compelled to proceed. Competition for scarce resources may also prompt unethical behavior. Two sales representatives competing for the same contract, for example, might consider adding "inducements" to get the contract. Even during their education, future managers are often exposed to ethical dilemmas. For example, controversy arose at the Harvard Business School when one student team that was competing in a simulation exercise obtained the computer code of another team and used that code to obtain secret information about its competitor.[27]

Organizational responsibility

The dominant view of business's responsibility to society has changed dramatically over the past several decades. As shown in Figure 3.8, three different attitudes toward organizational responsibility have evolved.[28]

Phase 1. Profit-maximizing management was the dominant philosophy of business responsibility for many decades up until the 1930s. This viewpoint rests on the assumption that pursuing the interests of the firm should take precedence over serving the interests of society. Managers have affirmed this opinion in expressions ranging from "What's good for General Motors is good for the country" all the way to Vanderbilt's exclamation, "The public? The public be damned!" During the Depression, however, such an adversarial posture began to seem inappropriate.

Figure 3.8
The changing role of
business in society

26. See Walter Kiechel, "The Crime at the Top in Fruehauf Corp.," *Fortune*, January 29, 1979, pp. 32–35; and A. F. Westin, "The Problem of Employee Privacy Still Troubles Management," *Fortune*, June 4, 1979, pp. 120–126.

27. See Thomas Moore, "Industrial Espionage at the Harvard B-School," *Fortune*, September 6, 1982, pp. 70–76.

28. See Robert Hay and Edmund Gray, "Social Responsibilities of Business Managers," *Academy of Management Journal*, March 1974, pp. 135–143.

Phase 2. Since the Depression, most major organizations have evolved as corporations with large numbers of stockholders. Managers have become trustees for thousands of owners. Over the years, trusteeship management has come to be viewed as the process of mediating the conflicting demands of stockholders, suppliers, customers, and the public. This view of organizational responsibility rests on the assumption that business and society are partners and that they must work together for their mutual survival.

Phase 3. Quality-of-life management began to emerge in the 1960s. This period of our history was characterized by a great deal of unrest, disillusionment, and distrust of business. Advocates of the quality-of-life viewpoint argue that business and society should not be partners. Instead, the needs of business should be subordinate to the needs of society. Stated differently, quality-of-life management reverses the profit-maximizing management assertion and suggests that "what's good for society is good for business."

At the present time, the corporate philosophies of most organizations are probably consistent with the tenets of trusteeship management. However, a reasonable number of organizations subscribe to each of the other two viewpoints. Whether trusteeship management continues to be dominant or a new model emerges remains to be seen.

Forces affecting responsibility

A variety of forces act to influence social responsibility on the part of organizations. Some of these forces tend to increase social responsibility; others tend to reduce it.[29]

Forces encouraging responsibility. Beyond individual beliefs, ethics, and value systems, other factors enhance social responsibility: (1) behaving responsibly improves the organization's image, (2) it is in the best interest of the organization to improve the communities where it does business, (3) social responsibility improves the business system, and (4) it may be illegal to do otherwise. A number of specific laws, such as the Water Quality Act of 1965 and the Highway Safety Act of 1973, force organizations to do certain things that are considered socially responsible. Recently, an attempt was made to pass the Corporate Democracy Act, which is intended to increase the accountability of corporate managers to all of their constituencies.[30]

Forces discouraging responsibility. There are also a number of forces that act to constrain social responsibility: (1) attempts to be socially responsible

29. See R. Joseph Mansen, Jr., "The Social Attitudes of Management," in Joseph W. McGuire (ed.), *Contemporary Management* (Englewood Cliffs, N.J.: Prentice-Hall, 1974), p. 616; and Rich Stranel, "A Systems Paradigm of Organizational Adaptations to the Social Environment," *Academy of Management Review*, January 1983, pp. 90–96.

30. See Gerald Keim, Barry Baysinger, and Roger Meiners, "The Corporate Democracy Act: Would the Majority Rule?" *Business Horizons*, March–April 1981, pp. 30–35.

may result in decreased profits for stockholders, (2) social actions are difficult to measure, (3) socially responsible activities may further increase the prices an organization must charge its customers, and (4) business may already have too much power and too little accountability. That is, increased social involvement would tend to further increase the business sector's power, but the public would still have no control over the thrust and outcomes of the social behavior that businesses engaged in.

Approaches to responsibility

Organizations can approach issues of social responsibility in a variety of ways. At one extreme is tokenism, a symbolic approach to a situation. Naming a black or a woman to a major committee as a symbolic gesture rather than because of the appointee's qualifications is an example of tokenism. Companies may be attracted to tokenism because it is simple and visible, but in the long run it is usually not very effective.

At the other extreme are companies and managers who are highly committed to social responsibility. Kenneth Dayton, chairman of the Dayton-Hudson department store chain, urges corporations to donate 5 percent of their pretax profits to charity. (Five percent is the maximum amount that is tax-deductible.) In 1981 Exxon gave away $45 million, and AT&T donated $47 million to various social causes.[31] McDonald's continues to develop its program of Ronald McDonald Houses to assist families of children with cancer.

Of course, more moderate approaches tend to be the norm. Most companies make at least some reasonable attempts to be socially responsible, without losing sight of the fact that their primary purpose is to generate profits for their stockholders. At present, about 1 out of every 10 companies gives 2 percent or more of its pretax profits to social causes. A recently formed Presidential Task Force has recommended that, by 1986, every U.S. company should be giving at this level. The task force also suggested that organizations encourage their employees to contribute their time to worthwhile volunteer causes.[32]

The social audit

An interesting approach to assessing an organization's social responsibility is the social audit. A *social audit* is an internal process designed to measure, monitor, and evaluate the social objectives and programs of an organization.[33] One common approach is to assess the costs and benefits of the social programs an organization undertakes. For example, Exxon might weigh the benefits of participating in a set of social programs against the total costs of

31. See Marvin N. Olasky, "Reagan's Second Thoughts on Corporate Giving," *Fortune*, September 20, 1982, pp. 130–136.

32. See Olasky, "Reagan's Second Thoughts on Corporate Giving."

33. See Archie Carroll and George Beiler, "Landmarks in the Evolution of the Social Audit," *Academy of Management Journal*, September 1975, pp. 589–599.

participating. Another approach is to tailor the audit to each social program. The advantage of this approach is that it allows the firm to evaluate and alter one or a few programs on their own merits without disrupting the overall framework of the firm's efforts to live up to its social responsibility.

At present, the use of social audits is not very widespread. No standard audit format or procedure exists, many managers are reluctant to subject themselves to such audits, and there are no objective evaluation standards. When a financial audit is performed, the auditors can conclude that the firm's records are in good order, because what constitutes "good order" is clearly defined by various financial groups and governmental agencies. Unfortunately, we do not know what good order is in the context of social responsibility.

The use of social audits will probably become more popular in the future. Managers are growing increasingly aware of their responsibilities in society. The social audit may prove to be a valuable tool in assessing the extent to which the organization is responding to the needs of its external environments.

Summary of key points

Environmental factors play a major role in determining an organization's success or failure. The environment is the set of forces and conditions that surround and permeate an organization.

Organizations have three different environments. The general environment is composed of those nonspecific dimensions of the organization's surroundings that might affect the activities of the organization. The task environment consists of specific dimensions of the organization's surroundings that are very likely to influence the organization. The internal environment of an organization is the perceptions that the members of an organization share regarding the organization's nature, style, and character.

The general environment consists of five dimensions: economic (the economic system that prevails in the country where the organization operates), technological (available means for transforming inputs into outputs), sociocultural (the customs, values, and mores of the society in which the firm operates), political–legal (the political system where the organization operates), and international (competition and trade in and from other countries).

The task environment consists of six dimensions: competitors (those organizations that compete for resources), customers (those people and/or organizations that purchase the organization's outputs), suppliers (those that supply resources to the organization), regulators (environmental units—such as governmental agencies and interest groups—that attempt to actively control, regulate, or influence an organization's policies and practices), unions (organized groups of employees), and associates (two or more relatively autonomous organizations that are controlled by another organization).

The degree of change and the degree of homogeneity in an organization's general and task environments result in varying degrees of uncertainty. Uncertainty, in turn, affects the organization in a variety of ways. Organizations attempt to influence the specific dimensions of their task environments, and they occasionally try to influence broader elements of their general environment as well.

Boundary spanners are people who link two or more organizations or units within organizations. Boundary spanners represent the organization to the environment, scan and monitor the environment, help protect the organization from the environment, function in gatekeeping and information processing, negotiate, and link and coordinate.

Social responsibility refers to the organization's obligation to take actions that protect and improve the welfare of society as a whole. Appropriate managerial behavior is primarily a matter of ethics; unethical behaviors include political bribes and gifts, the use of improper reporting procedures, and violations of privacy. Approaches to the organization's responsibilities to society include profit-maximizing management, trusteeship management and quality-of-life management. Approaches to social responsibility range from tokenism to very strong commitment, but most organizations adopt a middle-of-the-road approach. The social audit is a potentially valuable technique for measuring, monitoring, and evaluating the social objectives and programs of an organization.

QUESTIONS FOR DISCUSSION

1. In your opinion, is the general or the task environment more important? Why?
2. Can you cite examples of organizations that are *very* susceptible to environmental forces? What other organizations are more insulated from their environments?
3. Can you identify instances in which each of the dimensions of the general environment is more important than the others?
4. Other than those represented by the six dimensions of the task environment, can you suggest other specific environmental units that are of interest to organizations?
5. How can an organization accurately identify all of the elements of its task environment and be sure that it hasn't overlooked any?
6. Which "direction" of influence between the organization and its environments is likely to be the strongest? Can you suggest examples in which each direction is stronger than the other?
7. What kinds of businesses have the most potential to influence their environment? What kinds have the least?
8. Identify several examples of boundary spanning roles other than those mentioned in the chapter.
9. In what ways would the job of a boundary spanner be attractive? In what ways would it be unattractive?
10. Which philosophy of organizational responsibility is likely to be predominant in the future? Are there other philosophies you can suggest?
11. Beyond the factors discussed in this chapter, what other arguments can you develop for and against social responsibility in the business sector?

C A S E   3.1

At the beginning of this chapter, you read a scenario about a company president who stole over $84,000 from his company. You were asked what you, as a member of the board of directors of the company, would do about this situation. The company being described was Columbia Pictures, its president David Begelman. The case that follows describes what Columbia's board of directors did and then raises some issues for your consideration.

Unethical conduct at Columbia Pictures

David Begelman became the president of Columbia Pictures during 1973. In addition to a very handsome salary, estimated at around a quarter of a million dollars a year, he was also provided with a number of attractive perquisites, such as subsidized housing (a Beverly Hills home with a lease of approximately $5,000 a month) and household help. Begelman's primary duties were to oversee Columbia's studio in California; Alan Hirschfield was CEO and controlled the parent company's operations in New York. Together the two were credited with turning Columbia around. Before their arrival the company was on the verge of failure, and they engineered a dramatic recovery. A primary reason for this recovery was the development of the movie *Close Encounters of the Third Kind.* One of the most profitable movies in history, *Close Encounters* grossed well over $100 million.

On September 2, 1976, David Begelman ordered a check drawn in the amount of $10,000 and payable to the actor Cliff Robertson. Begelman forged Robertson's endorsement, had the check initialed by a bank officer who knew him, and then cashed it. The incident was discovered several months later when the accounting department at Columbia mailed a routine tax form to Robertson, who, of course, knew nothing about the money. Some months later Begelman called and told him that a young man had confessed to forging the check and had been fired; the two men agreed not to press charges. Robertson's accountant did, however, need a copy of the check for his records. When the copy was later shown to the bank officer, he remembered that Begelman himself had cashed it.

After the police contacted Hirschfield, Begelman indicated to him that this was the only time he had engaged in such activities. He told a member of the board of directors, Herbert Allen, the same thing. On September 30, 1977, Columbia suspended Begelman (with full pay) until an investigation of "certain unauthorized financial transactions" could be completed. Over the next several weeks, that investigation revealed that Begelman had forged a number of other checks, had padded his expense reports, and had overbilled the company for work done on the house. All told, the company president was found to have stolen $84,208.

The board of directors then convened to decide what to do. After much heated debate, all of the board members except two voted to reinstate Begelman as president. Their rationale was that a psychiatrist had testified that certain emotional problems that had driven Begelman to steal had been corrected and the $84,000 was a small price to pay for $100 million in profits. After first refusing, Begelman eventually accepted the offer of reinstatement.

It should also be noted that Columbia did not release any of this information. It was eventually published in the *Wall Street Journal* and the *Washington Post.* Two months after being reinstated, Begelman stepped down again to become an independent producer. Early in 1980, Metro-Goldwyn-Mayer hired David Begelman (at a salary of around half a million dollars a year) to head its film division. At MGM Begelman rapidly expanded film production. Many of his pictures went over budget and were box office flops. He eventually left this post in mid-1982 by mutual agreement with MGM.

CASE
QUESTIONS

1. Did the board of directors at Columbia act in a socially responsible manner? Which philosophy of management best describes the board's behavior?

2. Could unique characteristics of the film industry's environments in any way justify what happened? Do you think the issue would have been resolved in the same fashion if Begelman had worked for General Motors, American Airlines, or Westinghouse? Why or why not?

3. Why do you think MGM hired Begelman? How can it justify that action?

4. Why do you think Begelman, who had been so effective at Columbia, was so unsuccessful at MGM?

CASE
REFERENCES

"David Begelman Steps Down, Not Out." *Variety,* February 8, 1978, pp. 5–7.

Dorfman, Dan. "Inside the Scandal at Columbia Pictures," *New York,* January 16, 1978, pp. 8–10.

McClintock, David. *Indecent Exposure* (New York: Morrow, 1982).

Tobias, Andrew. *Getting by on $100,000 a Year and Other Sad Tales* (New York: Simon and Schuster, 1980).

"United Artists' David Begelman Vacates Two Posts," *Wall Street Journal,* July 13, 1982, p. 3.

C A S E   3.2

Dealing with changing environments

Bill Halten slumped down into his seat on the airplane by Nancy Baysinger. They were on their way to a corporate planning session in Chicago. Bill was exhausted. He had been up late the night before putting the finishing touches on his presentation.

Bill and Nancy work for Adam Business Services, a rapidly growing company that handles a variety of business products and services. Adam Business Services, or ABS, was founded 20 years ago by Carl Adam. In the beginning, ABS sold a basic line

of office products—paper, pens, typewriter ribbons, and so on—
and it provided typing services on a per-page basis for selected
customers.

About eight years ago, Bill Halten was hired to head the
company's sales and marketing department. Two years later,
Carl Adam sold ABS to Consolidated Industries, a rapidly growing conglomerate based in Chicago. Shortly thereafter Nancy Baysinger was hired, and the marketing effort was split between her
and Bill. Bill handles office products and Nancy manages office
services.

Consolidated began to pump a lot of money into ABS and
pushed the company to rapidly expand its line of products and
services as well as its market area. Bill's product group now
includes typewriters, personal computers, word processing equipment, office copiers, modular office furniture, and other new
components of automated office systems. Nancy's area of responsibility still includes in-house typing but has also expanded.
She markets a temporary-personnel service, a training service for
the equipment Bill handles, and a service for data entry and com-
putation for companies that don't have their own computers.

"You know," Bill groaned, "this business is a lot different
from what it used to be. Back when Carl Adam was in charge we
kept things simple. We just called on a small number of big customers, we bought all of our stuff from one wholesaler, and we
never had any problems with the government. We didn't even have
any unions then. Now things are a lot different. It seems like we're
competing with the whole world—IBM, Xerox, and Apple, not to
mention the other office products companies. And we try to sell to
everybody! At last count, we were buying from over a hundred different suppliers.

"The Federal Trade Commission has decided to investigate
our new advertising campaign on the east coast. Seems they think
our discounts are putting some of the smaller outfits out of business. And when Consolidated got us, we got their unions. Just last
week, we lost a big account because a secretary refused to take a
call after 5:00. And Consolidated has cut off our money. At first
they gave us everything we wanted, but now they're asking us to
support some of the new acquisitions. Yes, things are a lot
tougher now than they were before."

"I'm not sure what it was like before Consolidated, Bill, but it
seems to me that we've got it pretty good," responded Nancy.
"Personally, I like the excitement and the fast pace of this company. We're really going places. And besides, things just have to
get more hectic when you're growing. I'm sure Carl was a nice guy
to work for, but from what I've heard he sure kept a low profile. If
he hadn't sold the company, we'd probably still be just a small-
time operation. Now, though, we're a leader in the industry and I
think the best is still ahead."

CASE
QUESTIONS

1. Is Bill responding more to the general environment or to the task environment? Identify the primary dimensions that he is concerned with.
2. What has caused the increased complexity of the company's environment? Does this always occur?
3. What reasons might account for the different perspectives held by Bill and Nancy?
4. Are Bill and Nancy boundary spanners? Why or why not?

Planning and Decision Making In Organizations

4

ORGANIZATIONAL GOALS

1. Describe the place of goals and goal setting in the planning process.

2. Discuss five different ways of analyzing goals.

3. Explain the importance of a goal framework and how it can contribute to goal optimization.

4. Identify barriers that may interfere with the goal setting process.

5. Describe techniques for making goal setting more effective.

6. Describe how management by objectives (MBO) works and discuss its strengths and weaknesses.

OPENING INCIDENT

You have just been hired as the chief executive officer of the largest diversified company in the United States. Within the corporate framework there are 250 individual businesses. Although the company has always been profitable, the company's stock is not particularly attractive to investors. One reason for this lack of interest is that the company has not always maintained a clear vision of what it was and where it was going. You believe steps are necessary to sharpen the company's vision and focus. What would you do?

McDonald's tries to increase its sales volume by a specified amount. Safeway plans to open a certain number of stores next year. IBM expects to achieve a predicted rate of return for its investors. A major state university anticipates admitting a designated number of students each fall. And at the beginning of any given sports season, virtually all coaches say they expect a good season. The underlying theme in all these situations is that they involve goals and objectives. An anticipated or expected level of sales, number of stores opened, rate of return on investment, increase in enrollment, or seasonal record of wins and losses—all are organizational goals.

Establishing goals is one of the first phases of the planning process: we must know where we want to go before we can decide how to get there. An organization has to decide what it wants to "look like" at a particular time in the future before it can develop tactics and strategies to guide its on-going activities. In fact, this is our definition of a *goal:* it is an end state that the organization hopes to attain.

If Safeway establishes a goal of opening 60 new stores in 1990, this goal becomes the focal point for marketing, distribution, financial, and personnel planning between now and that time. After setting a goal of a 5 percent increase in enrollment for next year, university administrators know how to proceed with resource requests, faculty hiring, and class scheduling. The proper development of organizational goals is clearly an important function of management.

This chapter examines the analysis and development of goals. First we provide an overview of the planning process and indicate the place of goals in that process. We then discuss the nature of organizational goals. A goal framework for dealing with multiple and/or conflicting goals will help us resolve discrepancies in an organization's goal set. We also identify barriers and problems that may interfere with the goal-setting process, and we describe how these barriers can be overcome and the goal-setting process made more effective. Finally, we discuss one particularly useful strategy for setting goals and evaluating the results, management by objectives (MBO).

The planning process

To really understand the importance of organizational goals, we must approach them from the standpoint of the planning process. A number of different planning frameworks have been developed by theorists and researchers.[1] The planning framework we will use for our discussion of goals and their role in planning is shown in Figure 4.1. According to the model shown in Figure 4.1, planning begins with the five planning "premises" of purpose, mission, environment, values, and experience. An organization's purpose is the reason for its existence, and its mission is the way it tries to live up to that purpose. These concepts will be discussed in more detail later in this chapter.

The organization's environment was discussed in Chapter 3. Any or all of the dimensions of an organization's general environment (economic, technological, sociocultural, political, and international) and its task environment (competitors, customers, suppliers, regulators, unions, and associates) can come into play as the planning process is executed. Managerial values were also treated in Chapter 3. Values and ethics play a role in determining how much resource a manager is willing to devote to social responsibility, how a manager responds when a competitor is particularly vulnerable, and the like.

Finally, experience gained from previous planning cycles influences how subsequent planning activities are carried out. An organization that has made substantial in-roads in a new market may choose to increase its efforts in the

Figure 4.1
The planning framework

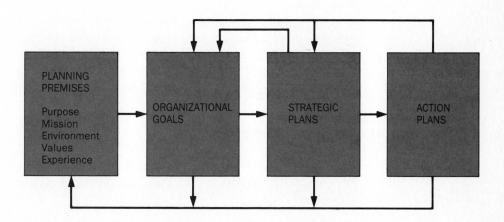

1. See Arthur A. Thompson, Jr., and A. J. Strickland III, *Strategy Formulation and Implementation* (Dallas: Business Publications, 1980) for one interesting framework.

future. On the other hand, if the attempt to enter the new market failed, the organization may decide to pull out—and also to investigate how the original plan to enter that market was developed.

Managers use these premises as a foundation in setting organizational goals. Goals can range from short-term to very long-term objectives and they may span different horizontal levels in the organization and different functional areas (such as marketing, production, and finance).

After the organization's goals are defined, managers develop strategic plans to attain those goals. The development of strategies and strategic plans is so important to the organization that it is often carried out by upper-level managers. Chapter 5 is devoted to strategic planning.

Strategic planning leads to action plans. Whereas strategies are typically long-range in nature, action plans often cover a shorter period of time. They are intended to help the manager carry out strategic plans in a step-by-step, systematic fashion. Common types of action plans include tactical plans, single-use plans, and standing plans. We will discuss action planning in Chapter 6.

Finally, as Figure 4.1 suggests, both strategic plans and action plans can affect organizational goals in a cyclical fashion. For example, as a result of carrying out an action plan and reviewing the results, it may become necessary to modify one or more goals, such as growth rate or market share. And, to complete the circle, organizational goals, strategic plans, and action plans all affect future planning premises. The experience they provide can definitely alter the purpose, mission, values, and environment of an organization.

A number of organizations follow this basic planning framework. Texas Instruments, for example, uses a system it calls OST (objectives, strategies, tactics). Top management at TI establishes a series of broad, general business objectives. Top managers and engineers then develop strategies to achieve those objectives. Middle and first-line managers carry out a variety of tactical plans derived from these strategies.[2]

Of course, the planning framework that has been described is not an inflexible model of how the planning process should be carried out. It is simply a general construct illustrating how the components of the process are logically related to one another. Having examined the overall planning process, we are ready to return to organizational goals and how they are developed.

The nature of organizational goals

All organizations have multiple goals, or a set of goals they work to achieve.[3] To speak of an organization's "goal," as though it had only one, is a great

---

2. See Bro Uttal, "Texas Instruments Regroups," *Fortune*, August 9, 1982, pp. 40–45.

3. See Herbert A. Simon, "On the Concept of Organizational Goal," *Administrative Science Quarterly*, March 1964, pp. 1–22. See Arthur G. Bedeian, *Organizations: Theory and Analysis* (Hinsdale, Ill.: Dryden, 1980), Chapter 4, pp. 77–104 for a recent review. See also George Steiner, *Top Management Planning* (New York: MacMillan, 1969).

oversimplification. Because organizations have many goals of different kinds, it is important that they be coordinated and that they all move the organization in the same direction. We will begin by analyzing five characteristics in which individual goals can differ. Then we will consider a matrix approach for analyzing an organization's entire goal set, with a view to optimizing goal achievement throughout the organization.

It is useful to differentiate among individual goals in terms of five variables. These are level of abstraction, focus or subject matter, degree of openness, organizational level, and time frame.

Level of abstraction

Assume for a moment that it would be possible to pick up a telephone and call a number of top managers to ask them what their organizations' goals are. You might get any or all of the following answers:

We want to make a positive contribution to society.
We want to increase sales by 3 percent next year.
We want to improve the quality of health care delivery.
We want to cut costs by 4½ percent.
We want to provide a reasonable return to our stockholders.
We want to become the sales leader in our industry by the year 2000.

All of these statements are goals that the organization is attempting to work toward, but the goals vary in specificity, time frame, and so on. They exhibit different levels of abstraction.[4]

As shown in Figure 4.2, goals at the highest level of abstraction express the organization's overall purpose, whereas organizational objectives at the lowest level of abstraction are relatively specific and concrete. At an intermediate level of abstraction is the organization's mission, the goal that best sets it apart from similar organizations.

The organization's purpose. The *purpose* of an organization can be viewed as its basic goal, defined by the societal context in which it operates. In the United States, the purpose of business firms such as Tenneco, U.S. Steel, and Eastman Kodak is to earn a profit for the firms' owners. The purpose of the University of Illinois, Houston Community College, and Vanderbilt University is to discover and transmit knowledge. The purpose of the city of New York and the state of Kansas is to provide their citizens with social services and protection. The primary purpose of hospitals is to supply health care.

Although it may seem obvious, a basic goal of all organizations is *survival*. To carry out its avowed purpose, a firm must survive long enough to do so. This is true of organizations in all parts of society, whether businesses, governmental units, or not-for-profit private organizations. Most organizations are ul-

4. See Heinz Weihrich and Jack Mendlesen, *Management: An MBO Approach* (Dubuque, Iowa: Wm. C. Brown, 1978) for a discussion of goal abstraction.

Figure 4.2
Levels of
abstraction and
organizational goals

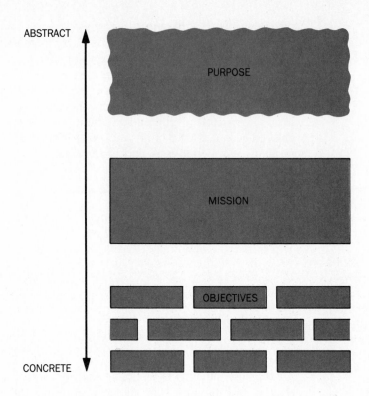

timately concerned with ensuring their own survival. W. T. Grant, Studebaker, and the Penn Central Railroad are organizations that failed to achieve this goal.

We should note, however, that long-term survival may *not* be the most appropriate goal for all situations. Some task forces have a limited mission; when that mission is accomplished, they cease to exist. A small town may establish a special committee to engage architects for a new school, arrange the details of financing, and supervise construction. Once the building is erected, the committee dissolves. A more unusual case is that of UV Industries. In early 1979, UV found itself in a position where surplus cash and tax laws made it most advantageous to liquidate itself and distribute the cash to its stockholders.[5]

What determines the general purpose of an organization? Certainly the aims of its founders and managers have much to do with an organization's purpose. But this purpose must also be deemed appropriate by society at large. Imagine the public's reaction if the University of Illinois or the city of New York announced that its goal was to make a 10 percent profit next year! Ultimately, an organization's purpose derives from the societal context in which the organization operates.

5. See Peter W. Bernstein, "A Company That's Worth More Dead Than Alive," *Fortune*, February 26, 1979, pp. 42–44.

The organization's mission. As noted in Figure 4.2, an organization's mission exhibits an intermediate level of abstraction. Although society frames an organization's general purpose, managers choose the path to take in order to best achieve that purpose; their choice is the organization's *mission.*

Monsanto and Apple Computer have decided to carry out their purpose (making a profit) by manufacturing chemicals and personal computers, respectively. Even within the same industry, different firms may adopt variations of the same mission. In retailing, K mart and Neiman-Marcus both attempt to make a profit by selling merchandise at a markup to consumers, but they carry vastly different kinds of merchandise and try to meet the needs of different kinds of customers. In similar fashion, educational institutions such as the University of Illinois and Houston Community College have the same purpose, but the former emphasizes the discovery of knowledge (research) whereas the latter focuses more on the transmission of knowledge (teaching).

The organization's objectives. At the lowest level of abstraction are the organization's objectives. *Objectives* are statements of how an organization intends to fulfill its mission. They are generally expressed in more specific terms and include a more definite time frame than the organization's mission. Nabisco, the nation's largest mass-producer of cookies, recently announced its entry into the salty snacks (chips, pretzels, cheese puffs) market long dominated by Frito-Lay. Its target objective is to become number two in the industry, behind Frito-Lay and ahead of Borden.[6] This decision doesn't reflect a change in mission (the new product line is still in the packaged-food industry), but it does represent a new and specific objective for fulfilling that mission.

Thus a business firm plans to fulfill its purpose (earning a profit) by adopting a mission (competing in a certain industry). In all likelihood, the firm will also develop specific goals for the level of sales it wants to achieve, the growth rate it hopes to maintain, and the image it wishes to cultivate. Each of these specific goals is an objective the firm hopes to meet. Organizations typically have a fairly large number of objectives.

Table 4.1 provides examples of the purpose, mission, and objectives of two business firms, a university, and a hospital. Note the diversity across the different kinds of organizations. Also note that, even though Boeing and American Motors have the same purpose, their mission and objectives are quite different.

Focus or subject matter

Some goals are financial, others social or environmental or political. Whatever the subject matter of the goal, we refer to it as the goal's *focus.* Writers on organizational strategy and goals have suggested several ways to classify the areas that organizations focus on.

Perhaps the best-known categorization is that of Peter Drucker.[7] He ob-

6. See Ann M. Morrison, "Cookies Are Frito-Lay's New Bag," *Fortune,* August 9, 1982, pp. 64–67.
7. See Peter F. Drucker, *The Practice of Management* (New York: Harper and Brothers, 1954).

Table 4.1 Examples of purposes, missions, and hypothetical objectives

Type of Goal	Boeing Co.	American Motors Corp.	University of Minnesota	Los Angeles County Hospital
Purpose	Earn profit for owners.	Earn profit for owners.	Develop and transmit knowledge.	Provide health care.
Mission	Manufacture aircraft for sale.	Manufacture road vehicles for sale.	Provide broad-based academic programs to serve needs of citizens of the state.	Offer a full range of medical services for the citizens of Los Angeles.
Objectives	Increase sales by 6% each of next 5 years.	Maintain leadership in sales of off-the-road vehicles.	Increase funded research by 10% next year.	Increase number of beds by 175 next year.
	Provide 12% ROI to stockholders each of next 3 years.	Increase worker productivity by 8% by 1990.	Decrease dependence on state funding.	Decrease by 10% time in emergency room before contact with physician.
	Decrease employee turnover by 3% each of next 4 years.	Establish long-term relationship with a foreign manufacturer.	Increase enrollment by 2% each of next 4 years.	Increase patient costs for hospital visit by no more than 5% next year.

serves that well-managed businesses have goals in the areas of market standing, innovation, productivity, physical and financial resources, profitability, manager performance and development, worker performance and attitude, and public responsibility. Table 4.2 enlarges on each of these areas.

Drucker's list is intended for business organizations. A different viewpoint is needed for hospitals, universities, governmental agencies, and other not-for-profit organizations. Warren Bennis has suggested that *all* organizations should attempt to achieve goals of six basic kinds.[8]

1. Identification (of the organization's purpose and mission)
2. Integration (of individual and organizational goals)
3. Social influence (equitable distribution of power)
4. Collaboration (the control of conflict)
5. Adaptation (to environmental change)
6. Revitalization (to combat decline and decay)

If we synthesize the goal categories suggested by Drucker, Bennis, and others,[9] we see that organizational goals focus on four major areas: financial and other monetary measures, environmental relationships, participants in the organization, and survival.

8. See Warren G. Bennis, *Organizational Development* (Reading, Mass.: Addison-Wesley, 1969).
9. See also Richard M. Steers, *Organizational Effectiveness: A Behavioral View* (Santa Monica, Calif.: Goodyear, 1977) for a discussion of other perspectives on goals.

Table 4.2 Drucker's goals for well-managed businesses

1. **Market standing.** An indication of the percentage market share desired by the firm and/or the specification of a competitive niche.
2. **Innovation.** Recognition of the need to develop new services or products.
3. **Productivity.** An efficiency measure that relates resources used to output generated.
4. **Physical and financial resources.** The acquisition and efficient use of physical and financial resources.
5. **Profitability.** An indication of the firm's profitability as measured by one or more financial indexes, such as return on investment.
6. **Manager performance and development.** Effective conduct of the managerial roles and development of potential in the individual.
7. **Worker performance and attitude.** Effective conduct of the operational roles and maintenance of positive attitudes on the part of employees.
8. **Public responsibility.** A consideration for the firm's impact on society.

Source: Data from pp. 65–83 from *The Practice of Management* by Peter F. Drucker (New York: Harper & Brothers, 1954). Copyright 1954 by Peter F. Drucker.

Financial goals involve costs and other monetary measures. For a business like Dow Chemical or RCA, financial goals may include target levels of profit, a certain return on investment, productivity levels, sales, and so on. Financial goals for hospitals may relate more to cost control and effective use of space.

Environmental goals describe how the organization wants to relate to its external environments. Examples include adaptability, growth, social responsibility, market share, and so on. Environmental goals may be stated less specifically than financial goals.

Participant goals involve the people in the organization. They include objective variables such as turnover and absenteeism and such nonquantifiable factors as worker satisfaction, personal development, and quality of life at work.

Survival, as discussed earlier, is also a basic goal.

Degree of openness

A distinction can also be made between what Charles Perrow calls official goals and operative goals.[10] The *official goals* of an organization are those that derive from the purpose and mission of the organization and that the organization espouses formally and publicly in annual reports and company publications. They include such broad considerations as turning a reasonable profit for the owners and making a positive contribution to society. Official goals are the goals that society wants the organization to seek (or at least is willing to allow it to seek).

Operative goals, on the other hand, represent the unpublicized, private

10. See Charles Perrow, "The Analysis of Goals in Complex Organizations," *American Sociological Review*, December 1961, pp. 846–847.

goals of an organization. These goals may be widely shared among all managers in a firm, or they may be held by only a few individuals. Among the operative goals of a business firm might be to delay the purchase of antipollution equipment as long as possible, to force a competitor out of the market, or to increase the profit margin by 4 percent. Similarly, a public library might have an operative goal of an 8 percent budget increase because it recognizes that its formal request of a 15 percent increase is not likely to be granted by the city.

Organizational level

Another way to differentiate goals is by their level in the organization. Most of our examples so far have been drawn from the organizational level—they have been goals that the overall organization hopes to achieve. At least four other organizational levels, however, have their own sets of goals.

First, the various departments, divisions, and other primary subunits have goals associated with the functions of those subunits. Thus a marketing department has sales and market-share goals, and a production department has efficiency, cost, and quality goals. Second, work groups within departments have goals. The goal of one sales unit may be a 6 percent increase in sales, while another unit has an 8 percent goal. Third, individuals typically set goals for themselves. Beyond work-related goals such as increasing sales, individual goals may also include taking career steps. Finally, if an organization is an associate (see Chapter 3), it may have goals suggested and/or imposed by its parent company.

Time frame for goals

The goal set is further complicated by the fact that goals extend over different time periods. Some goals, such as sales per year and annual return on investment, have by definition a short time horizon. Employee turnover and various production costs are also typically short-run goals. As shown in Figure 4.3, short-run goals tend to be quite specific. For example, a short-run goal such as achieving an annual sales volume of $1,000,000 next year indicates a given dollar amount. In general, the lower the organizational level, the more specific and short-run are the goals.

Slightly less specific are intermediate goals. These are goals that the company plans to achieve in longer than one year but (usually) in less than five years. If Montgomery Ward wanted to open 50 new stores, it is unlikely that it could find the right locations, arrange the necessary financing, and get them all built in one year. Hence they might anticipate opening 10–15 stores next year, 15–20 the following year, and the remainder in the third year. By our definition, the goal of opening 50 stores has an intermediate time frame. (Note that these yearly subgoals are slightly less specific in that they indicate a range.)

Finally, long-run goals are goals that will be attained some time after five years have elapsed. As shown in Figure 4.3, these goals have a still lower level of specificity. Goals such as discovering new oil reserves, increasing market

Figure 4.3
The time frame for
goals

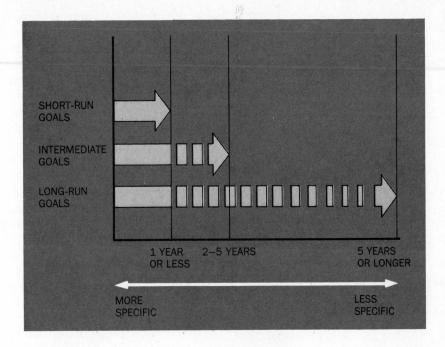

share, or developing new markets are likely to be long-run goals. Some long-run goals may be stated in fairly specific terms, but they are still much more susceptible to change than shorter-run goals. For example, a firm might set a long-run market-share goal of 26 percent by the year 2000. Due to changing conditions, however, the same goal might be revised down to 25.5 percent next year and up to 27 percent the following year. This process will be more fully discussed in Chapter 6.

One final note about time frames: organizations vary in what they regard as short-run and long-run goals. A mom-and-pop grocery store may view any goals over two years distant as very long-run; a coal company may more readily project twenty years into the future.

Managing multiple goals

The goal framework

Having discovered that goals differ in level of abstraction, subject matter, degree of openness, organizational level, and time frame, we can appreciate that managers face a complex maze of goals. Making sense of them is essential.

Establishing a goal framework is a good way to identify and reconcile various discrepancies that may exist in an organization's goal set. These discrepancies may arise between goals and also across time. For example, one way for a firm to maximize profits in the short run is to spend little on research and development; yet when R&D is neglected, long-term profits may plummet. Similarly, a firm can reduce costs by using inexpensive waste-disposal processes or pumping waste into rivers. Besides probably being illegal, such actions would also conflict with the frequently espoused goal of making a positive contribution to society.

One kind of goal framework is the matrix shown in Figure 4.4. If it is arranged so that organizational levels (imposed, organizational, subunit, work group, and individual), for example, intersect with focuses (financial, environmental and participant, and survival), then discrepancies and gaps in the organization's goal set will reveal themselves. Or the matrix may be set up so that time frames intersect with focuses, or degrees of openness with levels of abstraction. The important point is that such a matrix highlights sixteen or twenty subcategories of goals, and interesting relationships may emerge.

Figure 4.4
One type of goal framework

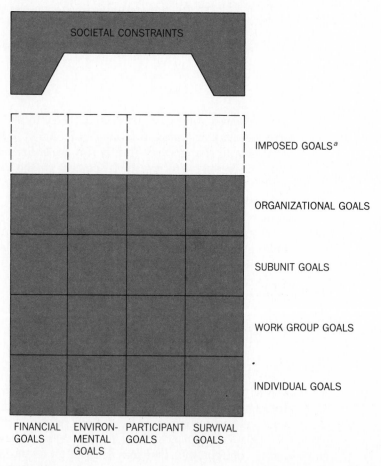

aRelevant for Associates.

For example, top management may advocate social responsibility, whereas a subunit may have an operative goal of pursuing profit regardless of the effect on the physical environment. Or a work group may be making long-range plans, not knowing that the division manager plans to phase the group out within a year and distribute its members among other departments.

Goal optimization

Seldom can managers maximize, or completely achieve, any goal or set of goals. Rather, they must optimize their relevant goal set if they are to be successful.

Consider a few of the goals of production or plant managers for a manufacturing firm such as Johnson & Johnson or American Cyanamid: minimize manufacturing costs, reduce employee turnover, and eliminate waste or scrappage. One technique for minimizing costs and scrappage calls for close supervision and tight controls. But workers may dislike this system and turnover may increase. The successful manager may find it more effective to tolerate slightly higher costs and scrappage levels in order to keep turnover at a low level. Such an approach may well result in the lowest *overall* cost. This process of balancing goals is *optimization,* an important part of the planning process in organizations.

Establishing business goals

Given the diversity of goals a business can establish, the process of goal development is usually quite complex. To integrate organizational goals with the strategic planning process, it has recently been suggested that goals should focus on five primary policy issues: the business posture, the business mix, market share and growth rate, resource allocation and risk analysis, and social issues.[11]

The business posture. The *business posture* of a firm is the stance it adopts in its primary business and operations. Various postures a business might assume include growth, stability, and survival. Growth postures suggest aggressive actions and the development of momentum. A posture of stability is often appropriate when sales or profits are no longer increasing or when the organization is contemplating changes in mission and strategy. Survival becomes paramount when the industry is declining or when the organization has made major errors.

The business mix. The *business mix* refers to the combination of products and services an organization intends to market. Some companies provide a variety of products and services within a single organizational framework. General Electric Company consists of 250 individual businesses within the

11. This section draws from Y. N. Chang and Filemon Campo-Flores, *Business Policy and Strategy* (Santa Monica, Calif.: Goodyear, 1980), pp. 111–117.

larger corporate organization. In other situations, different products and services are associated with distinct companies. Transamerica Corporation is a holding company with subsidiaries operating in a variety of businesses. Although Transamerica retains control, each subsidiary has its own public identity. We will learn much more about the concept of the business mix in Chapter 5.

Market share and growth rate. Companies usually develop goals relating to market share and growth rate. *Market share* is generally expressed as the percentage of the total market for a particular good or service that is controlled by an organization. If the total market for personal computers is 250,000 per year and IBM sells 100,000 personal computers per year, IBM's market share is 40 percent. The value of increasing one's market share must continually be weighed against the costs of increasing it.

Growth rate must also be approached from a realistic standpoint. In general, the larger an organization becomes, the more difficult is further growth. It would be difficult or impossible for General Motors or Exxon to increase its sales by 25 percent next year, but a local GM dealer or a small independent driller might well be able to attain such a growth rate.

Resource allocation and risk analysis. The organization must also consider resource allocation and risk analysis as it develops its goals. By *resource allocation* we mean the extent to which the organization intends to allocate its resources across possible demands for those resources. For example, a goal of rapid growth entails plowing profits back into the business and merely maintaining dividend payments. A goal of a high return to investors, however, dictates high dividends and (usually) a slower growth rate.

Risk analysis leads to an understanding of the risks associated with various courses of action. It is generally more risky to enter new markets rapidly or to borrow heavily than it is to expand slowly or to not borrow. Of course, a riskier course of action may also have a higher potential payoff.

Social issues. Finally, organizational goals must often encompass social issues. Social responsibility is a major concern for many companies, which have begun to incorporate social issues and concerns into their goal development process. Such goals may be general statements of organizational social concern or specific statements addressing particular environmental, consumer, or human issues.

An illustration. An example should provide additional insight into business goals. Table 4.3 summarizes the major goals of Hewlett-Packard Company, the electronics firm. Goal 1 (profit) has business posture, growth, and risk overtones. Goal 2 (customers) includes implications for posture and resource allocation. Goal 3 (field of interest) reflects considerations of posture, business mix, market share, growth, and resource allocation. Goal 4 (growth) is also related to mix, growth, and risk analysis. Goals 5 through 7 (people, management, and citizenship) all have overtones of social issues, and Goal 6 also relates to risk analysis.

Table 4.3 Hewlett-Packard's business goals

1. **Profit.** To achieve sufficient profit to finance our company growth and to provide the resources we need to achieve our other corporate objectives.
2. **Customers.** To provide products and services of the greatest possible value to our customers, thereby gaining and holding their respect and loyalty.
3. **Field of interest.** To enter new fields only when the ideas we have, together with our technical, manufacturing, and marketing skills, assure that we can make a needed and profitable contribution to the field.
4. **Growth.** To let our growth be limited only by our profits and our ability to develop and produce technical products that satisfy real customer needs.
5. **People.** To help our own people share in the company's success, which they make possible: to provide job security based on their performance, to recognize their individual achievements, and to help them gain a sense of satisfaction and accomplishment from their work.
6. **Management.** To foster initiative and creativity by allowing the individual great freedom of action in attaining well-defined objectives.
7. **Citizenship.** To honor our obligations to society by being an economic, intellectual, and social asset to each nation and each community in which we operate.

Source: © 1979 by the Regents of the University of California. Reprinted from *California Management Review*, volume XXII, no. 2, pp. 71–79 by permission of the Regents.

Barriers to the goal-setting process

A number of barriers can interfere with the goal-setting process.[12] Four of the more common barriers are inappropriate goals, unattainable goals, an over-emphasis on quantitative or qualitative goals, and improper reward systems. These barriers are depicted in Figure 4.5. The following sections describe each barrier in more detail.

Inappropriate goals

Inappropriate goals come in any number of forms. Paying a large dividend to stockholders may be inappropriate if it comes at the expense of necessary research and development. Driving a competitor out of business, paying off local officials to obtain a favorable zoning decision, and evading antipollution regulations are illegal as well as inappropriate.

Inappropriate goals may also arise from what is called a *means–end inversion.* In this situation, the means selected to obtain an end (or goal) become the end itself. For example, a police department may adopt a goal of reducing traffic accidents. As a means of achieving this goal, officers may attempt to issue ten traffic citations per day. Over time, the goal of reducing accidents may be replaced by the goal of issuing ten citations per day.

Let us take a business example of means–end inversion involving profits

12. See James L. Gibson, John M. Ivancevich, and James H. Donnelly, Jr., *Organizations*, 4th ed. (Dallas: BPI, 1982), pp. 114–119. See also Edwin A. Locke, "The Ubiquity of the Technique of Goal Setting in Theories of and Approaches to Employee Motivation," *Academy of Management Review*, July 1978, pp. 594–602.

Figure 4.5
Barriers to setting
good goals

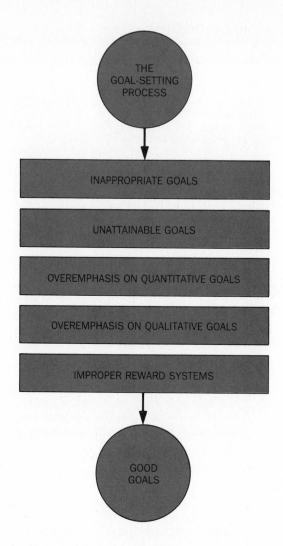

and market share. As a means of achieving a high level of profits, a company
might attempt to increase its market share. An increase in market share might
necessitate boosting advertising and cutting prices. But these activities also decrease profits. Not only does increasing the company's market share become a
goal in its own right, but it actually detracts from the original goal of increasing
profits.

Other inappropriate goals are those that are inconsistent with the organization's purpose and/or mission. Imagine a business violating its basic purpose
by giving all its profits to charity. Imagine a church attempting to earn a profit!
Violations of organizational mission are less obvious than violations of purpose; they arise when a firm develops a goal that is too far removed from what
it does best. When General Electric and RCA tried to enter the computer market in the late 1960s, they ultimately found this goal inappropriate to their

corporate mission. GE has been most successful in marketing products to ultimate customers, but selling computers meant dealing with corporate customers
instead. Unable to adapt, GE was forced to drop out of the computer market
and sell its operation to Honeywell.[13]

Unattainable goals

Another obstacle to the goal setting process is unattainable objectives—objectives so extreme that accomplishing them is virtually impossible. By the same
token, one does not want to develop objectives that are so easily attainable that
employees see them as a joke or an insult. Objectives must be challenging but
within reach.[14]

Setting an unattainable objective is destructive for one simple reason: no
matter how well an individual, unit, or organization performs, if objectives are
not met, many people assume that someone has failed. Consider a football
team that has not won a game in four years and has had a dismal recruiting
year. When a new coach predicts an undefeated season and a national championship for the team, he sets up an unattainable goal. Even if the team fin-
ishes with a 7–4 record and goes to a minor Bowl, some people will point out
that the coach failed to meet his goal.

What are some unattainable objectives for business organizations? For
most firms, to double sales in 2 years, to increase productivity by 46 percent
next year, or to develop 96 new products over the next 4 years would be unrealistic goals. The long-range interests of the organization would be better
served by setting more reasonable objectives.

Some firms, of course, do manage to post impressive accomplishments
or even to achieve a major turnaround. This is usually the result of a "crash
program"—a combination of good strategic planning and the investment of
unusually large amounts of the organization's monetary, physical, human, and
information resources. Such a program can rarely be sustained over the long
term. Sometimes, too, a firm enjoys a success that is quite unexpected. Ideal
Toy Corporation lost $15.5 million in 1980 and then made more than a
$9 million profit in 1981 because of its sales of Rubik's Cube. The rights to the
cube had been acquired on short notice after many larger firms had turned
them down.[15]

The point is that, although major successes in short time periods *can* occur, most long-term successes are the result of a steady application of the organization's resources, via good strategic planning, to attainable goals.

Overemphasis on quantitative or qualitative goals

Another barrier to goal setting is placing too much emphasis on either quantitative *or* qualitative goals. In some settings quantitative goals are necessarily

---

13. See Ann M. Morrison, "Trying to Bring GE to Life," *Fortune*, January 25, 1982, pp. 50–57.

14. See Locke, "The Ubiquity of the Technique of Goal Setting."

15. "Cubist Profits," *Fortune*, January 11, 1982, pp. 7–8.

emphasized. Making a certain profit margin, increasing productivity to a designated level, publishing a certain number of articles, and winning a specific number of games are all worthwhile objectives. Because they are quantitative, they are convenient benchmarks against which to measure actual performance. But because of this convenience, managers tend to overemphasize quantitative objectives as an indicator of performance. For example, a sales representative may have two basic objectives for this year: increase sales by 10 percent and improve customer relations. At the end of the year, the representative's sales manager is likely to place more weight on the sales increase, simply because it can be more objectively assessed than on improvement in customer relations. This may result in short-sighted and unfair slighting of the less tangible aspects of the employee's performance.

Equally significant problems may arise if only qualitative goals are developed. If a manager's objectives for the year are to revitalize her or his unit, develop the unit's human resources, and make a greater social contribution, assessing her or his performance at the end of the year will be quite difficult. After all, how do we decide whether "a greater social contribution" has been made?

Some goals, especially those relating to financial considerations, are by nature quantifiable, objective, and verifiable. Other goals, such as employee satisfaction and development and many aspects of environmental relations, are difficult if not impossible to quantify. Both kinds of goals should be considered in developing goals and in evaluating the results.

Improper reward systems

In some settings, an improper reward system acts as a barrier to the goal-setting process. For a number of reasons, people may be rewarded for poor goal setting, and they may go unrewarded or even be punished for proper goal setting. A manager might set the objective of simply decreasing turnover next year. If turnover is decreased by even a fraction, this manager may be able to claim success and be rewarded for the accomplishment. In an identical situation, a manager who attempts to decrease turnover by 5 percent but is able to achieve a decrease of only 3 percent may receive a smaller reward because of her or his failure to reach the "letter" of the established goal.

Moreover, in some situations people may be rewarded for achieving goals that are counterproductive to the organization's intent. United Fund solicitors, for example, may be rewarded (in the form of compliments and congratulations) for dollars pledged rather than actual dollars collected. Such solicitors have an incentive to accept pledges from people who are not likely to pay, and these unfulfilled pledges distort the United Fund's expectations of donations that are forthcoming.

We have identified four important barriers to effective goal setting in organizations: inappropriate goals, unattainable goals, an overemphasis on quantitative or qualitative goals, and improper reward systems. Other factors that may disrupt the goal setting process include poorly stated goals and contradictory goals. Let us now consider some techniques for overcoming many of these barriers.

Making goal setting effective

Techniques, suggestions, and guidelines exist for making goal setting and planning much more effective. These guidelines are listed in Table 4.4 and summarized in the following paragraphs.

Understanding the purposes of goals

One of the best ways to facilitate the goal setting process is to make sure that managers understand the two main purposes of goals.[16] Goals provide a target to shoot for and establish a framework around which other planning activities develop. As in target shooting, managers do not have to hit the bull's eye every time in order to win. As a framework, goals define where the organization, unit, or individual is expected to be at various times in the future, and they suggest ways of getting there.

An example from the photography industry will serve to illustrate the nature of goals as targets. In mid-1982, Canon announced a plan to introduce a 35-mm pocket snapshot camera in the United States. A company executive noted that Canon hoped eventually to capture 15 to 20 percent of the snapshooter market. This range then becomes a target. The company would no doubt like to have 20 percent of the market, but it has probably already determined that a 15 percent share would be satisfactory.[17]

Managers should be encouraged to develop objectives that are appropriate to the organization's purpose and mission. They should know that placing too much emphasis on either quantitative or qualitative objectives may be a

Table 4.4 Making goal setting more effective

1. Managers should understand the purposes of goals.
2. Objectives should be properly stated.
   a. They should be specific.
   b. They should be concise.
   c. They should be time-related.
3. Goals should be horizontally and vertically consistent.
4. Managers must accept and be committed to the goals.
5. The goal-setting process should be integrated with the reward system, but it should also have a diagnostic component.

16. See Steers, *Organizational Effectiveness*, Chapter 2.

17. See Thomas Moore, "Canon Takes Aim at the Snapshooter," *Fortune*, July 28, 1982, pp. 38–39.

problem. And they should understand that absolute goal attainment is not always necessary for success in the organization.

Stating objectives properly

Making sure that objectives are properly stated is another way to improve the goal-setting process. As much as possible, objectives should be specific, concise, and time-related.[18]

Specificity. Objectives should identify the specific outcome being sought. The goal of increasing productivity is not a specific objective; a goal of increasing productivity by 3 percent is more specific. Adding a target date would make the objective more specific still. Quantitative objectives are likely to be more specific than qualitative ones. But even when a manager establishes a qualitative goal such as improving employee morale, he or she can still identify measurable indicators of morale. For example, the manager might attempt to reduce the number of employee grievances by 4 percent.

This specificity should not be carried to an extreme, of course. If Canon stated that, on March 12, 1986, it wanted to control 17.64 percent of the snapshooter market, it would be carrying specificity too far.

Conciseness. Athough an objective may include all relevant variables, it should not be too wordy. Consider the objective of "increasing and expanding our market penetration and share during the period from January 1, 1985 to December 31, 1985 by a percentage ranging from 10 percent to 12 percent through additional promotional activities such as sales contests, selected price reductions, and an improved quantity-discount program." This is too wordy, whereas a goal of "increasing our market share by 10 percent to 12 percent in 1985" is clear and to the point. The methods for attaining the goal (the additional promotional activities) will be a part of the planning process rather than part of the goal-setting process. We will discuss the planning process in Chapter 5.

The time factor. Finally, a good objective should specify relevant time frames. For short-, intermediate-, and long-run goals, the time involved should be pinpointed in the goal itself. The objective we just developed for market share tells the manager that, on December 31, 1985, the firm's market share should be 10 percent to 12 percent larger than it was at the beginning of the year.

Goal consistency

A third way to improve the goal-setting process is to make sure that goals are consistent both horizontally and vertically. As we noted before, organizations

18. See Locke, "The Ubiquity of the Technique of Goal Setting."

have a myriad of goals, and it is important that they not conflict with each other.[19]

By horizontal consistency, we mean that goals for different subunits and for their managers should be consistent with each other. For example, if marketing acts to increase its product line, production costs will probably rise. So under these circumstances the production department should probably *not* adopt a goal of reducing costs.

Vertical consistency suggests that goals of individual managers should agree with work-group goals, work-group goals should be consistent with subunit goals, and subunit goals should be consistent with organizational goals. Again using marketing as an example, suppose the sales division of a firm has a goal of an 8 percent increase in sales. For this goal to be accomplished, the sales goals of various districts must add up to yield at least an 8 percent increase. One method for facilitating vertical goal consistency, called management by objectives, is discussed later in this chapter.

Goal acceptance and commitment

A high level of acceptance and commitment on the part of individual managers is essential to meeting the organization's goal. People are not likely to work whole-heartedly toward attaining any goal that they do not accept or are not committed to.[20]

To encourage goal acceptance by those who work for them, managers should demonstrate their own acceptance of the goals. That is, they should indicate that the goals are appropriate and attainable and in the best interests of all concerned. They should also allow broad-based participation in the goal setting process when appropriate, and they should ensure proper communication of the goals, the means by which they were developed, and the probable consequences of successful goal attainment. Commitment can be developed by the same methods. People are likely to be more committed to goals that they helped develop and understand clearly. And commitment is likely to persist over time if people are rewarded for successful goal attainment.

Effective reward systems

The effectiveness of goal setting is enhanced if the goal setting is integrated with the organization's reward system.[21] Individuals should be rewarded first for effective goal setting and then for successful goal attainment. However, they should be assured that failure to attain a goal will not necessarily have punitive consequences. After all, failure sometimes results from factors outside

19. See Steiner, *Top Management Planning* for a classic treatment of goal consistency. A more recent perspective on goal consistency is presented by William Ouchi, "Markets, Bureaucracies, and Clans," *Administrative Science Quarterly*, March 1980, pp. 129–141.

20. See Gary P. Latham and Gary A. Yukl, "A Review of Research on the Application of Goal Setting in Organizations," *Academy of Management Journal*, December 1975, pp. 824–845.

21. See Locke, "The Ubiquity of the Technique of Goal Setting."

the manager's control. Changing economic conditions, changing governmental regulations, and activities in the marketplace may all make goal attainment unlikely. To the extent that the manager could not have predicted these events in advance, he or she should not be held responsible for the results. Accordingly, the goal setting process should have a "diagnostic" as well as an evaluative component.

An example will serve to illustrate both the diagnostic and the evaluative components of goal setting and rewards. Consider the case of a sales manager reviewing performance with three sales representatives. One representative may have not established appropriate objectives to begin with. His or her evaluation should perhaps focus on how the representative can do a better job of setting objectives in the future. The second sales representative may have set appropriate goals but not met them due to unexpected circumstances. For this person, the evaluation can focus on diagnosing whether those unexpected circumstances could have been foreseen, how they can be avoided in the future, and so forth. The third sales representative, who set proper goals and then met them, should be rewarded.

Management by objectives

Management by objectives, or MBO, is a particularly useful and popular technique for systematizing the goal setting process. In this section, we will discuss the nature and purpose of MBO, the steps in the MBO process, and the effectiveness of MBO as a management technique.

The nature and purpose of MBO

Although it is hard to pinpoint the actual origins of MBO, most people credit Peter Drucker with developing it.[22] In *management by objectives,* a manager and a subordinate collaborate in setting goals for the subordinate, with the understanding that the extent to which these goals are attained will be a major factor in evaluating and rewarding the subordinate's performance.

MBO, then, is concerned with goal setting for individual managers and their units or work groups, as opposed to the overall organization. As we shall see, however, goal setting in an MBO system should start at the top of the organization. And the goals of top management should reflect the organization's goals.

The purpose of MBO is to give subordinates a voice in the goal setting process and to clarify for them exactly what they are expected to accomplish in a given time. We will describe MBO in its "pure" form, although each organization that adopts MBO is likely to make at least minor adjustments because of its own unique situation.[23] Indeed, many firms have come up with their

22. See Drucker, *The Practice of Management.*

23. See John Ivancevich, J. Timothy McMahon, J. William Streidl, and Andrew D. Szilagyi, "Goal Setting: The Tenneco Approach to Personnel Development and Management Effectiveness," *Organizational Dynamics,* Winter 1978, pp. 48–80 for a discussion of one variation of MBO.

Figure 4.6
The MBO process

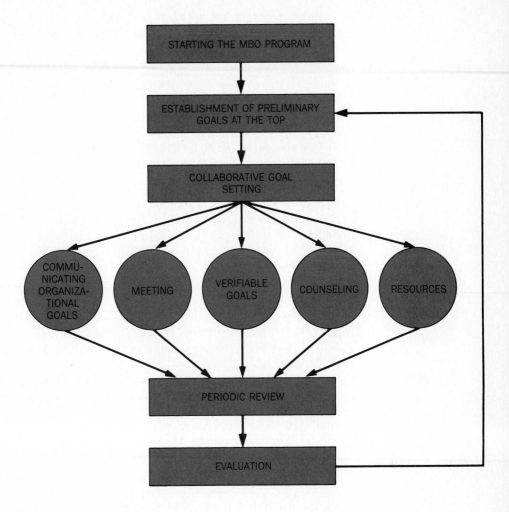

own names for MBO. Some of the more popular include "management for (or by) results," "management by goals," and "objectives management." The actual mechanics of the MBO process, summarized in the next section, are shown in Figure 4.6.[24]

The MBO process

Starting an MBO program. For an MBO program to be successful, it must start at the top of the organization. That is, top managers must communicate why they have adopted MBO, what they think it will do, and the fact that they have accepted and are committed to MBO. Employees must also be educated about what MBO is and what their role in it will be.

24. For discussions of the MBO process, see Stephen J. Carroll and Henry L. Tosi, *Management by Objectives* (New York: MacMillan, 1973); and A. P. Raia, *Managing by Objectives* (Glenview, Il.: Scott, Foresman, 1974).

Establishment of preliminary goals. Having adopted the MBO philosophy, it is necessary to develop preliminary organizational goals and objectives (if this has not already been done). These goals are usually set by top management and reflect the organization's basic mission and strategy. Some of these goals will coincide with the organization's budgeting cycle; others will involve a longer time. The idea is that goals set at the top will cascade down the organization in a systematic way.

Collaborative goal setting. Although establishing the organization's preliminary goals is extremely important, collaborative goal setting is the essence of MBO. This collaboration involves a series of distinct steps:

1. Superiors tell their subordinates what organizational and unit goals have been established. Subordinates are asked to think about how they can help achieve these goals and objectives.
2. Superiors meet with their subordinates on a one-to-one basis. The purpose of these meetings is to arrive at a set of objectives for each subordinate that both the subordinate and the superior have helped develop and to which both are committed.
3. Each objective should be as verifiable (quantitative) as possible and should specify a time frame for its accomplishment. In general, objectives should meet the three criteria of specificity, conciseness, and time-relatedness. And they should be written down.
4. Superiors must play the role of counselors in the goal setting meeting. They must, for example, ensure that the subordinates' goals are attainable and that they will facilitate both the unit's and the organization's goals.
5. Finally, the meeting should spell out the resources that the subordinate will need to work effectively toward goal attainment. For example, if a sales manager's goals for increasing sales are predicated on the assumption that his or her district will receive 4 new sales representatives and a 15 percent travel budget increase, these assumptions need to be agreed on. Similarly, if a production manager needs another quality control inspector in order to achieve a certain quality goal, some indication of whether this new inspector's position will be approved is required before the goal is accepted.

Periodic reviews. During the course of the time specified for goal attainment, it is usually advisable to conduct periodic reviews. That is, if the objectives are established for a one-year period, it may be a good idea for subordinate and supervisor to meet quarterly to discuss progress to date. Additions to, deletions from, and notes regarding the goals of a particular employee may be appropriate, especially if organizational goals have changed or if necessary resources are unavailable.

Evaluation. At the end of the MBO cycle, the manager meets with each subordinate again to review the degree of goal attainment. They discuss which goals the employee was able to meet and which were not met. The reasons for both success and failure are explored. (This is the diagnostic phase.) Finally, the employee is rewarded (praise, a pay increase, or promotion) on the basis of his or her goal attainment. In an on-going MBO program, this evaluation meeting may also serve as the collaborative goal setting meeting for the next time period.

The effectiveness of MBO

A fairly large number of organizations use some form of MBO. Alcoa, Tenneco, RCA, Du Pont, General Motors, General Foods, and Black & Decker have all adopted the technique.[25] In fact, approximately 40 percent of *Fortune's* list of the 500 largest industrial firms in the United States use some form of MBO. As might be expected, both strengths and weaknesses have been identified in MBO.

Strengths. A primary benefit of MBO is improved employee motivation. By clarifying exactly what is expected, by allowing the employee a voice in determining expectations, and by basing rewards on the achievement of these expectations, organizations create a powerful motivational system for their employees.

Communication is also enhanced through the process of goal discussion and collaboration. And performance appraisals may be done more objectively with less reliance on arbitrary or subjective assessment. MBO also focuses attention on appropriate goals, helps identify superior managerial talent for future promotion, and provides a systematic management philosophy that can have a positive effect on the overall organization.

Finally, MBO has implications for control, the process of monitoring progress toward goal attainment. The periodic development and subsequent evaluation of individual goals helps keep the organization on course toward its long-run goals.

Criticisms. MBO has been criticized for certain shortcomings. Perhaps the major problem that can derail an MBO program is lack of top management support. Some organizations have decided to use MBO, but then its implementation has been delegated to lower management. This limits the program's effectiveness, because the goals cascading down the organization may not actually be the goals of top management and because others in the organization are not motivated to accept and become committed to MBO.

Another problem with MBO is that some firms overemphasize quantitative goals and burden their systems with too much paperwork and recordkeeping. Some managers will not or cannot sit down and work out goals with their subordinates. Rather, they "suggest" or even "assign" goals to people. The result is resentment and a lack of commitment to the MBO program.

---

25. See Ivancevich et al., "Goal Setting"; and Carroll and Tosi, *Management by Objectives* for descriptions of MBO at Tenneco and Black & Decker, respectively.

In summary, management by objectives is a useful technique for structuring goals in a wide variety of organizational settings. It can serve to clarify expectations, enhance motivation, and facilitate more equitable performance appraisals. However, to succeed with MBO, managers must work to overcome the problems identified above.[26]

Summary of key points

A goal is an end state that the organization hopes to attain. Formulating organizational goals is an important part of the planning process. In particular, goals are derived from the five basic premises of purpose, mission, environment, values, and experience. The resulting goals help determine strategic plans and action plans.

Organizational goals can be differentiated along five major dimensions. In terms of *abstraction*, important kinds of goals are purpose (the organization's basic goals as derived from society), mission (the path taken by decision makers in fulfilling the organization's purpose), and objectives (statements of how an organization hopes to fulfill its mission). The *focus* of goals may be on financial, environmental, or participant issues, or it may relate to survival. The degree of *openness* of goals indicates the extent to which they may be official or operative. By organizational *level*, we mean that goals are established not only for the entire organization, but also for subunits, work groups, and individuals. Finally, goals have different *time frames*. In particular, they may be short-run, intermediate, or long-run.

Constructing the goal framework for organizations involves analyzing the goal set in matrix form along any two or more dimensions. For example, analyzing the goal set in terms of level and focus will help identify discrepancies and gaps. A major job of management is to achieve goal optimization.

In terms of establishing business goals, a strategic stance suggests five basic policy issues to be addressed by the organization's goals. These issues are the business posture, the business mix, market share and growth rate, resource allocation and risk analysis, and social issues.

Primary barriers to the goal setting process include inappropriate goals, unattainable goals, an overemphasis on quantitative or qualitative goals, and an improper reward system. Methods for overcoming these obstacles and otherwise making the goal setting process more effective include understanding the purpose of goals, stating objectives properly, ensuring goal consistency, facilitating acceptance of and commitment to organizational goals, and establishing a reward system that reinforces effective goal setting and goal attainment.

One particularly useful technique for systematizing the goal setting process is management by objectives, or MBO. MBO is a process of collaborative goal setting. Superiors and subordinates jointly establish and record goals for the subordinate that are consistent with the goals of the superior. At the end

26. See Jack N. Kondrasuk, "Studies in MBO Effectiveness," *Academy of Management Review,* July 1981, pp. 419–430 for a recent review.

of a designated period of time, the subordinate's performance is evaluated, and the degree of goal attainment becomes the basis for rewards.

QUESTIONS FOR DISCUSSION

1. Some people consider goal setting a part of the planning process, but others argue that the two are distinct activities. Discuss the merits of each viewpoint.
2. An organization's purpose is derived from the societal context in which it operates. Think about some societies that are very different from our own. What might the purposes of organizations in these societies be?
3. Is it possible for an organization to have more than one purpose? More than one mission?
4. Why is it useful to think about the organization's goal set in terms of focus, level, time span, abstraction, and openness?
5. Do small groups or individuals have official and operative goals similar to the official and operative goals of corporations?
6. Explain why the concept of optimization is so important when considering goals.
7. Try to identify some of the financial, environment, participant, and survival goals of your school or university.
8. Which goals do you think are most frequently neglected by managers—short-run, intermediate, or long-run? How might this relate to the reward system used in the company?
9. Select an organization with which you are familiar. Can you suggest some of its goals along the lines of the business goals identified in this chapter?
10. Can you identify any other barriers to effective goal setting?
11. The old adage "People support what they help create" is another way of saying that goal acceptance and commitment are important in attaining goals. List some ways to get employees involved in the goal-setting process.
12. If you were a management consultant, what arguments would you advance to convince top management that it should adopt management by objectives?
13. Could you use MBO in your class? Discuss the pros and cons of this system for use in a classroom setting.

C A S E 4.1

At the beginning of this chapter, you read a scenario about the new chief executive officer of a large, diversified corporation consisting of 250 individual businesses. Though remaining profitable, the company has occasionally lacked vision and focus. The company being described was General Electric; the new CEO John F.

General Electric clarifies its corporate goals

Welch. The case that follows explains what GE and Welch have done and then raises some other issues for your consideration.

General Electric Company is the largest diversified company in the United States, and it has historically been one of the best managed. All told, GE consists of 250 individual businesses that produce products ranging from light bulbs to appliances. The company has also been consistently profitable; in one recent year, 44 percent of its after-tax profits were paid out in dividends. Yet investors have not been particularly enamored of GE stock. The company is so large, and its sales so stable, that many people have assumed that GE stock will not provide a reasonable return on investment.

Part of the problem with GE's image is that the company has not always had a clear vision of what it was and where it was going. The company seemed to lack focus and tried to do too many things at once. One former chief executive, for example, plunged GE into three risky ventures simultaneously: nuclear energy, computers, and commercial jet engines. His successor sold the disastrous computer operation to Honeywell in 1970. As recently as 1981, however, GE's nuclear operation was still not on track: managers were caught developing plans on the assumption that three new reactors would be built in this country each year, even though most planned facilities have been abandoned.

In April 1981, John F. Welch quickly decided that one of his top priorities was to make the company more attractive to investors by sharpening its focus and increasing its domination of product markets. He established an ambitious goal for each of GE's 250 businesses: to be number one or number two in its industry or to achieve a marketing advantage through technological innovation within three to five years. The rationale for this goal was that it is most feasible in a time of slow economic growth. That is, as sales volumes decrease and productivity becomes even more of a concern, strong companies have an even greater competitive advantage over weaker companies than during good times. Hence dominant market positions become especially important.

Welch has structured the company, then, such that each business manager has the same clear-cut set of goals. Units that have no real chance of achieving this goal are likely candidates for being phased out. GE's reward structure will also probably be changed so that managers who achieve the goal will receive substantial rewards for their efforts.

For the future, GE has carved out a number of areas in which it wants to make major in-roads. One area targeted for fast growth is plastics. Another is equipment for sophisticated medical diagnostic purposes. Perhaps the area that has generated the most enthusiasm for GE managers, however, is manufacturing automation. Robots are already being produced under license from foreign manufacturers, and the company will soon begin making its own. At present, GE's emphasis on technological innovation is internally oriented. With the passage of time, however, it will begin to have an impact externally as well.

Of course, there are some uncertainties about GE's chosen course of action and Welch's goals for GE's various businesses. Some analysts, for example, question GE's commitment to automation, given the number of setbacks it is likely to encounter. Disposing of businesses that cannot achieve Welch's goals may be a problem in some cases. Finally, convincing investors that GE stock is as solid as ever and *also* a good bet for growth will be a difficult selling job.

CASE QUESTIONS

1. What do you think of GE's goals for its businesses? What kinds of problems might arise from efforts to meet these goals?
2. Characterize these goals in terms of abstraction, focus, openness, level, and time frame.
3. What barriers to these goals might arise? What steps, if any, has GE taken to overcome these barriers?
4. Is GE's venture into automation consistent or inconsistent with the company's efforts to sharpen its vision and focus?

CASE REFERENCES

"The $5-Billion Man—Pushing the New Strategy at GE," *Fortune*, April 18, 1983, p. 6.

"GE Promotes Factory Automation, But Some Doubt Big Market Exists." *Wall Street Journal*, October 21, 1982, p. 33.

"GE's Wizards Turning from the Bottom Line to Share of the Market." *Wall Street Journal*, July 12, 1982, pp. 1, 14.

Morrison, Ann. "Trying to Bring GE to Life." *Fortune*, January 25, 1982, pp. 50–57.

C A S E 4.2

Dan Thomas shook his head. He had just come from an executive committee meeting and was quite frustrated. Dan is the vice president for production at May Furniture. May manufactures and markets a full line of medium-priced furniture. The company currently does quite well with living room and bedroom furniture but has been struggling with its line of dining tables and children's furniture.

The company's executive committee comprises Dan; the vice presidents for marketing, finance, and personnel and human resources; the controller; the legal advisor; the assistant to the president; and the president himself, Luke May. May's father founded the company about 50 years ago. In addition to being president, May is also the majority stockholder.

The executive committee meets monthly to discuss matters of strategy and policy. At this morning's meeting, Luke May delivered a stern message about the company's recent sluggish per-

Setting and meeting organizational goals

formance and his intent to turn things around. In particular, he outlined a series of 5-year goals for the company.

1. Increase sales of bedroom and living room furniture by 20 percent.
2. Increase sales of dining tables and children's furniture by 100 percent.
3. Cut overall operating cost by 10 percent.
4. Cut employee turnover by 3 percent.
5. Introduce a new line of metal patio furniture with projected annual sales of $5 million in 5 years.

These goals, May explained, are intended to increase income and lower expenses, thereby improving the company's profit picture.

Dan had not said anything at the meeting. As a rule he preferred to sit back and listen, reflect, frame his thoughts slowly and carefully, and then deal with situations on a person-to-person basis. He already recognized that a confrontation with Luke May was coming.

"The man just has no conception of what these goals mean," thought Dan. "They all sound good, but they just don't fit together right." As he thought, he jotted down notes he would use when he talked to May.

Goal 1. Too easy; our best line; we can do better than 20 percent without trying.
Goal 2. Too hard; we're not competitive in these markets; there's no way we can double sales in just 5 years.
Goal 3. Sounds good, but doesn't fit with goal 2. To increase sales at all, we'll have to improve product design and quality, expand product lines, and advertise more. This will increase costs, not cut them.
Goal 4. Again, sounds good but contradicts all previous goals. As we try to increase sales and cut costs, we'll be putting more pressure on everyone. That will drive some people away and increase turnover.
Goal 5. This makes the least sense of all. All our other products are made of wood. To make metal furniture, we'll need new machinery, operators, etc.; no market research done; we don't know if we'll sell $5 or $50 million.

After reading over his notes, Dan realized that he had a firm foundation for questioning the goals imposed by May. Something else was nagging at him, however. He had suspected for some time now that Luke May had lost interest in the company. He was in his mid-50s and would be retiring soon. He had never married and had groomed no one in the immediate family to take over the business. What would happen when May retired?

Dan suspected that May wanted to sell the company, perhaps to some big furniture company or a conglomerate. By jacking up sales and profits and by expanding into new markets, May could make the company much more attractive and make a killing if he decided to sell. "If that's what's on his mind," Dan thought, "it doesn't matter what I say. He doesn't care about what the company will look like after he leaves. He's willing to sacrifice the future for the short term."

CASE
QUESTIONS

1. Characterize May Furniture's goals in terms of their abstraction, focus, openness, level, and time frame.
2. How could the concept of optimization be used to help May formulate more appropriate goals?
3. Why is Dan unwilling to accept the proposed set of goals? What, if anything, could have been done differently to make them more appealing to Dan?

5

STRATEGIC PLANNING: THE PLANNING PROCESS

CHAPTER OBJECTIVES

1. Describe strategic planning.

2. Outline the focus of strategic planning in terms of its components and levels.

3. Discuss the general processes involved in developing and implementing the organization's strategy.

4. List the five functional strategies and explain why they are important in implementing the mission and primary goals of the organization.

5. Explain how the levels and processes of strategy can be integrated.

6. Discuss the entrepreneurial, engineering, and administrative problems of management and the four different approaches that organizations take to solve these problems.

7. List the characteristics of strategic business units, and describe how SBUs are classified in terms of the business portfolio matrix.

8. Describe, and discuss the merits of, several other contemporary approaches to strategic planning.

CHAPTER OUTLINE

The nature of strategic planning

The focus of strategic planning
The components of strategy
The levels of strategy

The strategic process
Scanning the environment
Environmental analysis
Establishing the mission and primary goals
Developing policies
Developing functional strategies
Integrating levels and processes of strategy

The adaptation model of strategy
The problems of management
The strategic typology

The business portfolio matrix approach to strategy
Strategic business units
The portfolio matrix
Selection of alternatives

Other contemporary frameworks for strategy
The technology life-cycle approach to strategy
The generic strategies approach
Global strategies
Anti-strategy

Strategic planning: A synthesis of contemporary viewpoints

Summary of key points

OPENING INCIDENT

You are a top manager at one of the leading firms in your industry. Recent environmental changes, however, threaten the very existence of that industry. The medical profession has demonstrated that the use of your primary product is a health hazard, and Congress has ruled that you will no longer be allowed to advertise on television. What would you do?

In August 1981, Pan American World Airways was projecting a year-end deficit of $400 million. When Pan Am's bankers heard this disturbing news, they cut the company's line of credit by more than 50 percent. To meet its financial obligations, Pan Am was forced to complete a hasty agreement to sell its profitable Intercontinental Hotels subsidiary to a British conglomerate.[1] This action represented a plan, of sorts, to enable the airline to meet one of its basic goals: survival.

In the early 1980s another major company was undergoing dramatic changes of a very different nature. Over the course of its existence, International Telephone and Telegraph had evolved into the largest conglomerate in the world. But ITT's financial performance was not what it should be. To improve the firm's financial posture and create a leaner, less complex organization, a new management team at ITT has embarked on a long-term program of divestiture.[2] This program of selling or otherwise disposing of parts of the company is also a plan, but a plan quite different from the one followed by Pan Am. ITT is engaging in a long-term strategy, whereas Pan Am has adopted a stop-gap measure to pay its bills.

Strategy and strategic planning are the subject of this chapter. Strategic planning follows the development of organizational goals, which we discussed in Chapter 4. It outlines the methods the organization has chosen to identify and fulfill its mission(s). *Strategy* is the pattern of the organization's goals and the major policies and plans it has for achieving these goals, stated in a way that defines what business the company is in or wants to be in and the kind

---

1. "Check Out: Pan Am Sells Its Hotels," *Fortune*, September 21, 1981, p. 13.
2. Geoffrey Colvin. "The De-Geneening of ITT," *Fortune*, January 11, 1982, pp. 34–39.

of company it is or wants to be.[3] *Strategic planning*, then, is the process of developing strategy.

First we discuss the nature of strategic planning. Next we summarize the focus of strategic planning. The processes involved in strategic planning are described in the third section. The remaining sections outline important contemporary models and frameworks of strategic planning.

The nature of strategic planning

Why would an organization buy a company that had lost almost $2 million the previous year and operated in an industry where only 8 of 26 companies made a profit in 1980? Because it meshed with the organization's strategy. The organization in question, the Chicago-based Tribune Company, paid $20.5 million for the Chicago Cubs baseball team. Another Tribune subsidiary, WGN-TV, expects to earn over $6 million in commercials from televising Cubs games. By pumping more money into the team, Tribune Company hopes to make the Cubs more competitive on the field. If this is achieved, ticket sales will increase and television revenues will go even higher. The man hired to manage the Cubs, Dallas Green, immediately embarked on a number of efforts intended to increase season-ticket sales and revive the team's farm system.[4]

This example illustrates most of the major elements of strategic planning:

1. It focuses on matching the resources and skills of the organization with the opportunities and risks present in the external environment.
2. It is performed by top-level managers.
3. It has a long-run time frame.
4. It is expressed in relatively general, nonspecific terms.

The Tribune Company reacted to environmental circumstances (including the fact that a new pay-TV service in Chicago was broadcasting games of the city's other baseball team, the White Sox); the decision was made by Tribune's top management; the company has taken a long-range perspective; and the notion of diversifying into other entertainment areas was considered in developing this particular strategy.

Contrast this with the other basic approach to planning, tactical planning. *Tactical planning* is characterized by specific tactics for achieving short-run objectives, the involvement of middle-level managers, and a higher level of detail and specificity. In an example of tactical planning, Dallas Green, a middle manager, is focusing on specific attendance increases for future seasons and has mapped advertising campaigns to achieve these increases.

---

3. See Kenneth Andrews, *The Concept of Corporate Strategy* (Homewood, Il.: Dow Jones–Irwin, 1971).

4. See Thomas Moore, "Why Tribune Company Is Feeding the Chicago Cubs," *Fortune*, June 28, 1982, pp. 44–50.

Figure 5.1
The relationship
between strategic
planning and
tactical planning

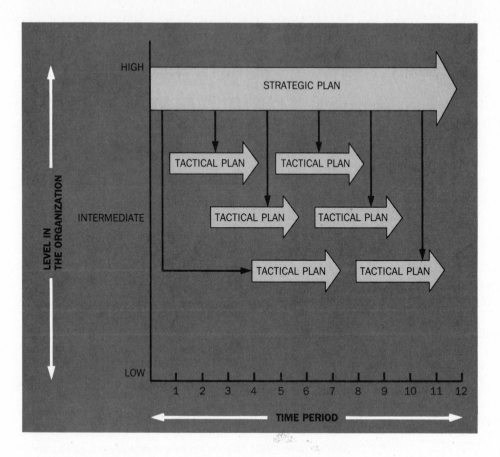

Figure 5.1 illustrates the general relationship between strategic and tactical planning. Note in particular the time period and level of responsibility for each. Tactical planning will be discussed in Chapter 6.

The focus of strategic planning

To develop an understanding of strategic planning, it is useful to understand the focus of strategy. The focus of strategy, in turn, is determined by its components and its level.[5]

The components of strategy

A well-conceived strategy includes four basic components: scope, resource deployment, competitive advantages, and synergy.

5. This section is based on Charles W. Hofer and Dan Schendel, *Strategy Formulation: Analytical Concepts* (St. Paul, Minn.: West, 1978), pp. 25–29.

Scope. The scope component of a strategy specifies the present and planned interactions between the organization and its environment. Sometimes referred to as the "statement of the organization's domain," the *scope* component specifies what markets the organization expects to compete in. For example, Texas Instruments focuses on the electronics industry and its dimensions (such as semiconductors, consumer electronics, and so forth) but does not produce automobiles or candy.

Resource deployment. The strategy should include an outline of the organization's projected *resource deployment*—how it will distribute its resources across various areas. In the case at the end of Chapter 4, for example, we saw that General Electric wants each of its businesses to be number one or two in its industry. If a business can't achieve this, it will probably be phased out.[6] By this means, resources will be slanted toward successful businesses and away from less successful ones.

Competitive advantages. The strategy should specify the *competitive advantages* that result from the organization's scope and pattern of resource deployment. For example, Walt Disney Productions has defined its scope as the entertainment industry and allocated resources across its theme parks and film divisions. The latest Disney ventures, Epcot Center in Florida and a Disneyland-type park in Japan, represent approaches to capitalizing on the competitive advantages it has built up over the years.[7]

Synergy. Strategy should also take into account the synergy expected to result from decisions about scope, resource deployment, and competitive advantages. For example, Disney hopes that the expected success of Epcot Center will have a positive impact on its film division, which has not been particularly effective in recent years.

The levels of strategy

Just like organizational goals, strategies vary by level. In particular, organizations can develop corporate strategy, business strategy, and functional strategy.[8]

Corporate strategy. *Corporate strategy* is the course charted for the total organization. It attempts to specify what set of businesses the organization intends to be in. Hence corporate strategy is primarily concerned with the scope and resource deployment components of strategy.

To illustrate corporate strategy, consider the case of RCA. At the corporate level, RCA is composed of the NBC television network, Hertz, C.I.T. Financial Corporation, RCA Consumer Electronics, RCA Records, Banquet

6. See Ann Morrison, "Trying to Bring GE to Life," *Fortune*, January 25, 1982, pp. 50–57.

7. See "Disney's Epcot Center, Big $1 Billion Gamble, Opens in Florida," *Wall Street Journal*, September 16, 1982, pp. 1, 19.

8. See Hofer and Schendel, *Strategy Formulation*.

Foods, and other divisions. Corporate strategy, then, has been aimed at determining what businesses to buy, what businesses to sell, and so on. (For example, the company is currently attempting to sell Hertz.[9])

Business strategy. While corporate strategy focuses on what businesses the company should be in, setting *business strategy* involves determining how best to compete in a particular market or industry. Whereas RCA has a corporate strategy, NBC, C.I.T. Financial Corporation, RCA Consumer Electronics, and the other divisions each have their own business strategy. RCA Consumer Electronics, for example, has recently been concentrating its efforts on its new videodisc player. The company believes that the price and simplicity of the videodisc players and discs will eventually make this a profitable enterprise for the company.[10] Business strategy, then, is focused less on scope and resource deployment than on competitive advantage and synergy.

Functional strategy. A *functional strategy* is a strategy developed for a major functional area such as marketing or finance. For its videodisc player, RCA Consumer Electronics has developed a marketing strategy based on the concepts of price and ease of operation. Extensive television advertising campaigns were mounted and rebate programs developed to get these messages across.[11] We will discuss functional strategies in more detail later in this chapter.

The strategic process

The several processes involved in developing strategy do not necessarily occur in a logical sequence. Rather, they are undertaken simultaneously by various managers and then integrated into the strategic plans for the organization as a whole.

Scanning the environment

An organization's environment plays a major role in shaping strategy. The top managers of an organization must know what is going on in business, government, and society at large if they are to chart a meaningful course for the organization. In Chapter 3 we discussed general and task environments, boundary spanning processes, and social responsibility from a somewhat different angle. Our concern at this point is more specific: we are interested in scanning the environment for information, in how such information is gleaned,

---

9. See A. F. Ehrbar, "Splitting Up RCA," *Fortune*, March 22, 1982, pp. 62–76.

10. See Edward Meadows, "The Slippery Market for Videodiscs," *Fortune*, November 2, 1981, pp. 82–88.

11. See Meadows, "The Slippery Market for Videodiscs."

and in how it is used. As we shall see, information is a major factor in strategic planning.

Kinds of information. Information about the environment can be roughly divided into six different categories.[12]

1. **Market information.** Data about market potential, competition, pricing, customers, and the like are of particular value to business organizations in highly competitive situations.
2. **Technical information.** Manufacturers, especially, need information on technological innovations, licensing and patent information, and so forth.
3. **Broad issues.** All organizations need information on governmental regulation, social needs and/or changes, and the economic outlook.
4. **Acquisition leads.** Information on possible purchase and/or merger opportunities is particularly useful to organizations that are open to a strategy of acquisition and expansion.
5. **Miscellaneous information.** Information on resource availability, supplier behavior, and so on is important to a variety of organizations.
6. **International information.** This is of interest to most organizations, especially those competing in foreign markets.

As environmental elements become more complex and uncertain, other kinds of information may also become important.

Sources of information. Managers get information from four kinds of sources: outside personal, outside impersonal, inside impersonal, and inside personal.[13] These four kinds of sources are shown in Figure 5.2. Outside personal sources are those that are located outside the organization but are available through some personal relationship with a customer, banker, or someone else. These particular sources of information are not widely available to everyone. Outside impersonal sources include newspapers and trade publications. Impersonal sources may also be found within the organization; these inside impersonal sources include scheduled meetings and routine reports. Finally, inside personal sources are individuals at all levels within the organization. Research suggests that personal sources are much more widely available and more widely used than impersonal sources.[14]

Uses of information. Of course, the real value of environmental scanning lies in the ways in which different kinds of information are actually used by managers. One important use is to make forecasts, or predictions, about what certain elements of the future will look like. A statement that unemployment will be 10 percent in 1990 is a forecast. Several popular forecasting techniques will be discussed in Chapter 8.

12. See F. J. Aguilar, *Scanning the Business Environment* (New York: Macmillan, 1973).
13. Aguilar, *Scanning the Business Environment*.
14. Aguilar, *Scanning the Business Environment*.

Figure 5.2
Managers' sources
of information

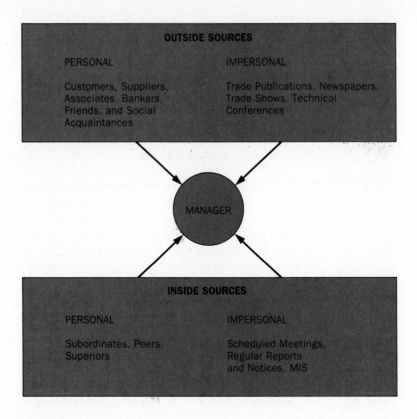

Another important use of information is to help managers make decisions. Managers would have a difficult time setting appropriate prices if they had no idea what the demand was for certain products or services, what competitive prices were, and so forth. Decision making will be explored in more depth in Chapter 7.

Finally, information plays a vital role in the strategic planning process. Unlike forecasting, strategic planning focuses on what managers *want* some element of the future to look like. Information, then, will be an important element in our remaining discussion of strategic planning.

Environmental analysis

The primary purpose of environmental analysis is to identify opportunities for the organization. It also identifies threats, roadblocks, and other undesirable possibilities. The following examples illustrate the role of information.

1. Information about a competitor entering or leaving a particular market segment might suggest that the company avoid it, enter it, and/or continue scanning.

2. Information about technological innovations might suggest that the company build a new plant, scrap an existing plant, and/or continue scanning.

3. Information about impending government regulation or deregulation might suggest that the company take any number of actions.

Environmental analysis, then, is the manager's assessment of the information gleaned from environmental scanning.

Establishing the mission and primary goals

Every organization must first define its mission before it can develop effective strategies. Companies like Procter & Gamble and Texas Instruments, for example, must decide what business the company is in and what it hopes to accomplish. Universities must decide whether to stress research or teaching; hospitals must decide whether to emphasize general patient care or treatment of specific diseases such as cancer. Environmental scanning and analysis may play a part in defining an organization's basic mission as well as in developing strategies for carrying out that mission.

Developing policies

Once an organization has defined its mission and analyzed pertinent factors in the environment, it must develop guiding policies that will move the organization toward its goals. A firm may formulate, as a major goal, growth through acquisition of other companies. Environmental analysis may reveal that the firm has a good credit line and is seen as a good "parent" company. Management might then develop policies that describe what criteria a prospective acquisition must meet before the purchase is made. For example, the firm might set a policy of acquiring firms that have realistic targets of 15 percent annual growth in sales and 20 percent growth in profits. Policies, then, are general guidelines for decision making as the firm attempts to fulfill its mission.

Developing functional strategies

Another major component in strategic planning is the creation of functional strategies. Many organizations develop six such strategies: marketing, financial, production, research and development, personnel, and organization design. Issues that strategies typically address in each of these six functional areas are summarized in Table 5.1.

Marketing strategy. For many organizations, the marketing strategy is the most important functional strategy, and it usually reflects the company's overall strategy. The Southland Corporation, for example, recognized the value of locating its 7-Eleven convenience stores on corner sites, pushing into gasoline retailing when the major oil companies were cutting back, and being

Table 5.1 Functional strategies

Functional area	Major concerns
Marketing	Product mix Market position Distribution channels Sales promotions Pricing issues Public policy
Finance	Debt policies Dividend policies Assets management Capitalization structure
Production	Productivity improvement Production planning Plant location Government regulation
Research and development	Product development Technological forecasting Patents and licenses
Personnel	Personnel policies Labor relations Executive development Governmental regulation
Organization design	Degree of decentralization Methods of coordination Bases of departmentalization

among the first to introduce video games and fast foods in its stores. Each of these actions was designed to satisfy specific consumer needs and was taken a step before the competitors. Promoting itself as a one-stop convenience outlet, the company increased its sales by 22 percent and its earnings by 20.4 percent each year from 1977 through 1982.[15]

The marketing strategy deals with a number of major issues confronting the organization. One of these is the product mix. For General Motors's Chevrolet Division, the product mix would include the various lines, such as

15. See Shawn Tully, "Look Who's a Champ of Gasoline Marketing," *Fortune*, November 1, 1982, pp. 149–154.

Camero, Citation, and Chevette, and different versions of each model. Other major issues in marketing strategy include desired market position (K mart and Sears compete for first place in retailing), distribution channels (a major reason for the initial success of Timex was its decision to sell watches in drug-stores), sales promotion (such as advertising budget and the size of the sales force), pricing policies (such as setting an initially high price to skim off the "cream," followed by planned price cuts), and public policy (dealing with legal, cultural, and/or regulatory constraints).

Financial strategy. Developing the right financial strategy is essential to an organization. An important part of this strategy is deciding on the most appropriate capital structure. That is, what combination of common stock, pre-ferred stock, and long-term debt (such as bonds) will provide the firm with the capital it needs at the lowest possible costs? Another element in financial strat-egy is debt policy: how much borrowing will be allowed and in what forms? Assets management focuses on the handling of current and long-term assets. For example, how should the firm invest a cash surplus to optimize both re-turn and availability? Finally, dividend policy determines what proportion of earnings is distributed to stockholders and what proportion is retained for growth and development. Disney has adopted a financial strategy of low debt. As a result, even though Epcot Center cost nearly $1 billion, it was financed almost entirely by operating funds. RCA, on the other hand, is almost $2.9 billion in debt.[16]

Production strategy. In some ways, an organization's production strat-egy stems from its marketing strategy. For example, if the marketing strategy calls for promoting high-quality, high-priced products, production naturally fo-cuses on quality, with cost only a secondary consideration. Several major is-sues still remain, however. For example, methods for improving productivity need to be developed. In our current productivity crisis, this aspect of produc-tion strategy is becoming increasingly important. Production planning (when to produce, how much to produce, and how to produce) is especially impor-tant for manufacturers. Production strategy also involves decisions about where to locate plants. Finally, production strategy must take into account the regulations of governmental bodies such as the Environmental Protection Agency (EPA) and the Occupational Safety and Health Administration (OSHA).

An area of great significance for the production strategies of many com-panies is robotics. Some companies (such as General Electric, Nissan, and Toyota) are investing large sums of money in automated technology, while other manufacturers (such as Du Pont and Exxon) are proceeding more slowly. It remains to be seen whether the aggressive or the conservative approach is best.

16. See "Disney's Epcot Center, Big $1 Billion Gamble, Opens in Florida"; and Ehrbar, "Split-ting Up RCA."

Research and development strategy. Most large organizations, and many smaller ones as well, find it important to have a research and development strategy. A primary area of concern here is making decisions about product development. Should the firm concentrate on new products or on the modification of existing products? What use should be made of technological forecasting—predictions of technical trends, new discoveries and breakthroughs, and so on? R&D strategies might also include a policy on patents and licenses. If a firm develops a new product or procedure and patents it, other firms cannot use it. However, it may be profitable to license the use of the patent—that is, to sacrifice some degree of competitive advantage in return for fees gained by allowing other firms to use the product or procedure also.

An organization that has used a strong R&D strategy for its own benefit is Bridgestone Tire Company. By investing heavily in R&D, Bridgestone has increased worker productivity by 10 percent a year since the mid-1970s and has vaulted from the number-eight tire manufacturer in the world to the number-four spot.[17]

Personnel strategy. Many organizations find it necessary to develop a personnel strategy. Personnel policies are required on such matters as compensation, selection, and performance appraisal. Another aspect of personnel strategy is labor relations, especially negotiations with organized labor. Government regulations, such as the Civil Rights Act of 1964, also need to be taken into account. And executive development often warrants strategic attention. For example, if an organization anticipates opening eight new plants in six years, it must start now to locate and develop potential managers for those plants.

We mentioned in Chapter 1 that some companies (such as Procter & Gamble, General Foods, and General Mills) have developed training programs that are so good they are thought of by some recruiters as second M.B.A.'s.[18] As a result, each firm has a strong human resource base. This approach represents one form of personnel strategy.

Organization design strategy. Organization design strategy is concerned with how the organization structures itself—how positions, departments, and divisions are arranged. The appropriate design makes it more likely that the firm will successfully carry out its strategic plans. Organization design is beyond the scope of our discussion at this point, but it is explored in depth in Chapters 9–12.

Integrating levels and processes of strategy

We are now in a position to describe, in general terms, how the various levels and dimensions of strategy are integrated in organizations. Figure 5.3 presents our view of how these processes are interrelated.

17. See Bernard Krisher, "A Different Kind of Tiremaker Rolls into Nashville," *Fortune,* March 22, 1982, pp. 136–146.

18. See Ann Morrison, "The General Mills Brand of Managers," *Fortune,* January 12, 1981, pp. 98–107.

Figure 5.3
Integrating strategy
levels and
processes

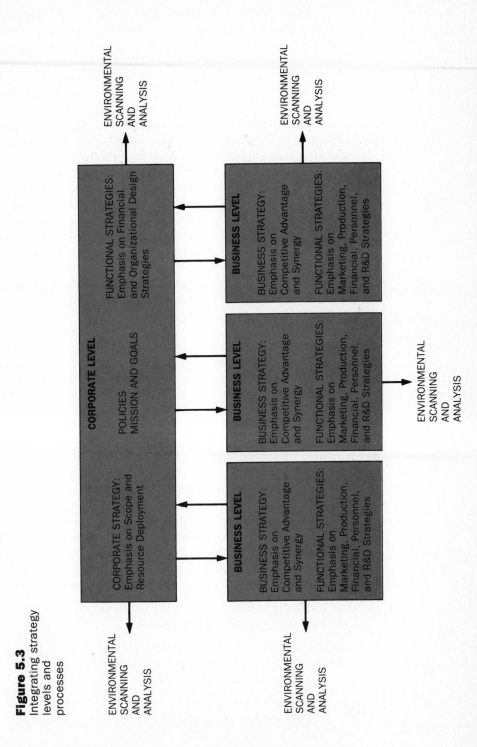

This framework suggests that, at the corporate level, several aspects of strategy are relevant. Managers at this level scan and analyze the environment, develop corporate strategy (emphasizing scope and resource deployment), determine the organization's missions and goals, establish policies, and develop functional strategies. The functional strategies that are most relevant at the corporate level concern the financial structure and base of the organization and the organization's overall design and arrangement.[19]

At the business level, managers also scan and analyze the environment. Business level strategy, as noted earlier, tends to focus more on competitive advantage and synergy. Functional strategies that are particularly important for most businesses include marketing, production, finance, personnel, and R&D.[20]

Finally, we should note the interaction between corporate-level and business-level strategies. If a firm competes in a number of different industries, its strategic planning will probably be done in a "top-down" fashion. That is, corporate-level strategy is developed first and business-level strategies follow. On the other hand, if the organization has few products or product lines and competes in few markets, a "bottom-up" process is more often used. The corporate-level strategy is developed from the business-level strategy.[21] This process of integrating corporate-level and business-level strategies will be explained in more detail in Chapter 6.

This framework is offered to provide a general picture of how the various processes and elements of strategy are interrelated. Due to the importance of strategy for organizational success, a number of more complete models, theories, and frameworks for strategy have been developed by researchers and managers. In the following sections, we explore some of the more important and potentially useful frameworks for strategy and strategic planning.

The adaptation model of strategy

The adaptation model of organizational strategy was developed in 1978 by Raymond E. Miles and Charles C. Snow.[22] The adaptation model argues that the basic task of strategic management is to maintain an effective alignment with the organization's environment while also managing internal interdependencies. That is, the firm should attempt to match its mission and goals with opportunities and threats in the environment. This process of environmental alignment is carried out by dealing with three basic problems of management.

The problems of management

The three basic management problems that determine the adaptation process are the entrepreneurial problem, the engineering problem, and the administra-

19. See Hofer and Schendel, *Strategy Formulation.*

20. See Hofer and Schendel, *Strategy Formulation.*

21. See Hofer and Schendel, *Strategy Formulation.*

22. Raymond E. Miles and Charles C. Snow, *Organizational Strategy, Structure, and Process* (New York: McGraw-Hill, 1978).

tive problem. In on-going organizations, these problems must be addressed simultaneously, but it is only logical to take them up in the order we have suggested.

The entrepreneurial problem. The entrepreneurial problem consists of defining the organization's mission. In a new organization, this means determining what specific goods or services the organization will provide and what target market or market segment it will attempt to penetrate. In the on-going firm, the entrepreneurial problem is whether to add to and/or modify the existing mix of goals, services, markets, and segments. Hence the process is the same as the scope component of the corporate strategy, in which the firm determines what businesses it wants to compete in. R. J. Reynolds's acquisition of Del Monte represents one firm's attempt to deal with the on-going entrepreneurial problem. The management of R. J. Reynolds recognized the threats being posed to the tobacco market by governmental regulation, public opinion, and so forth. Company officials decided that the organization must expand into new businesses to counter these threats. Entry into the food industry represents one solution to R. J. Reynolds's entrepreneurial problem.[23]

The engineering problem. The engineering problem is to establish a system for producing, controlling, and distributing the goods or services identified in the solution to the entrepreneurial problem. A decision to begin production with an assembly-line technology and a later decision to convert to an automated system using robots are both solutions to a manufacturer's engineering problem. In a service firm like a dry-cleaning establishment, deciding whether to have a store employee do minor mending or to send it out to a tailor is also part of the engineering problem. In a university, decisions regarding the numbers of classes, the size and location of classes, and the prerequisites to various classes are all associated with the engineering problem, which is actually similar to a functional production strategy.

The administrative problem. The administrative problem revolves around developing and refining an appropriate organizational design for achieving the solutions to the entrepreneurial and engineering problems. Decisions about decentralization and spans of control are related to the administrative problem. (The concepts of organization structure and design are discussed more fully in Chapters 9–12.) Clearly, this problem is similar to the functional strategy of organization design.

The administrative problem has both a lag aspect and a lead aspect. That is, the organization's structure must be consistent with present solutions to the company's current entrepreneurial and engineering problems (the *lag* characteristic). But it must also facilitate the recognition and solution of future entrepreneurial and engineering problems (the *lead* characteristic). In other words, an organization's structure should fit both present and future.

---

23. See Gwen Kinkead, "A Low-Nicotine Tour Through R. J. Reynolds," *Fortune*, January 11, 1982, pp. 76–80.

Figure 5.4
The adaptation
process

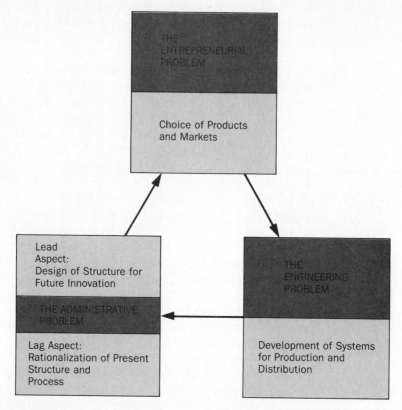

Source: Adapted from Raymond E. Miles and Charles C. Snow, *Organizational
Strategy, Structure, and Process* (New York: McGraw-Hill, 1978), p. 24. Used
with permission of the publisher.

The relationships among the entrepreneurial, engineering, and administrative problem-solving processes are shown in Figure 5.4.

The strategic typology

Different organizations approach their entrepreneurial, engineering, and administrative problems in different ways. Miles and Snow have identified four basic approaches, or strategies, that organizations are likely to adopt.[24] In this classification scheme or typology, the organizations themselves are called defenders, prospectors, analyzers, and reactors.

24. Miles and Snow, *Organizational Strategy, Structure, and Process.* See also Donald C. Hambrick, "Some Tests of the Effectiveness and Functional Attributes of Miles's and Snow's Strategic Types," *Academy of Management Journal,* March 1983, pp. 5–26.

Defenders. *Defenders* are organizations that attempt to create or maintain an environment for which a stable form of organization is optimal. That is, the overriding concern of management is stability. Defenders solve their entrepreneurial problem by attempting to carve out a relatively narrow niche in the market for themselves and to direct a limited set of products or services at that niche. Although defenders may employ competitive pricing and/or high-quality production standards to guard their positions, they are likely to ignore trends and developments outside their chosen domains. Defenders solve the engineering problem by concentrating on the most efficient production and distribution techniques, with little regard for long-term effectiveness. They solve the administrative problem by maintaining a rigid, bureaucratic form of organization to facilitate control and efficiency. Organizations that might be classified as defenders include McDonald's, a book publisher, a small hospital, and most federal employers. Each of these organizations has chosen a certain position in the environment, and its major goal is to maintain that position.

Prospectors. The prospector is almost the exact opposite of the defender. The *prospector* attempts to create and maintain a dynamic environment for itself. Specifically, prospectors develop a knack for discovering and then exploiting new product and market opportunities. Their entrepreneurial problem is how best to locate and then systematically develop these opportunities. Because prospectors focus on new products and markets, their engineering problem is how to avoid a long-term commitment to any single type of technology. Prospectors typically deal with this problem by using several technologies, each with little routine and mechanization. This allows the organization to shift from one product or market to another without having to totally scrap existing technology and invest in entirely new plants and equipment. The administrative problem for the prospector is how to facilitate rather than control operations within the organization. Examples of prospectors might include Westinghouse, Bendix, and Litton Industries.

Analyzers. The third kind of organization described by Miles and Snow is the analyzer. The *analyzer* is a mid-range organization in terms of its adjustment strategy. That is, it attempts to integrate the strategies of both defenders and prospectors in one organization. Its entrepreneurial problem is to identify and take advantage of new products and markets while maintaining a nucleus of traditional products and customers. The engineering problem for the analyzer is to achieve a balance between the conflicting demands for flexibility and stability in the organization's technology. Its administrative problem is to structure the organization in such a way as to support the forces for stability associated with the on-going nucleus of products and technologies *and* to accommodate the forces for dynamism stimulated by the desire for new products and new technologies. The organization must have some units and groups maintaining the traditional products and other units exploring and developing new products and markets.

A prime example of an analyzer is Procter & Gamble. This firm has a core of traditional products, such as Crest toothpaste and Head and Shoulders shampoo, but it also maintains a fairly aggressive expansion policy, as shown by its recent forays into soft drinks and coffee.

Reactors. Essentially, *reactors* are strategic failures. Their inappropriate responses to the environment result in poor performance, which causes them to become less aggressive in the future. Several factors might cause organizations to become reactors.

1. Top management may not have clearly articulated the organization's strategy.
2. Management may not fully shape the organization's structure and processes to fit a chosen strategy.
3. Management may have a tendency to maintain the organization's current strategy–structure relationship despite overwhelming changes in environmental conditions.[25]

An excellent illustration of an organization employing the reactor mode of operation was W. T. Grant, one of the United States's largest retailers before its bankruptcy in 1976. In response to the success of K mart in the discounting area, Grant adopted the ill-conceived strategy of expanding rapidly without the necessary resources. Further, the company had inadequate training programs for its managers and too few controls over day-to-day operations. The company simply tried to do too many things too fast, and then it refused to step back and retrench.

In summary, the adaptation model of strategy offers insight into three basic problems: entrepreneurial, engineering, and administrative. Classifying organizations as defenders, prospectors, analyzers, or reactors also provides an important perspective on the strategic planning process. But which strategic posture is best suited to which environmental conditions? Figure 5.5 suggests some relationships among form of organization, degree of environmental stability, and degree of "organization–environment congruence."

This arrangement suggests that the appropriateness of defender, analyzer, or prospector strategies varies according to the stability of the organization's environment. When there is a high degree of environmental stability, a defender strategy may be appropriate. Hence a defender operating in a stable environment has a high degree of organization–environment congruence. Prospectors and analyzers in that same environment have a lower degree of congruence.

For low levels of stability (a dynamic, changing environment), the prospector strategy may be more effective. Analyzers and defenders in this situation will have a lower degree of organization–environment congruence and may therefore be less effective. Finally, the analyzer strategy may exhibit a

25. Miles and Snow, *Organizational Strategy, Structure, and Process.*

Figure 5.5
The strategic
taxonomy of the
adaptation model

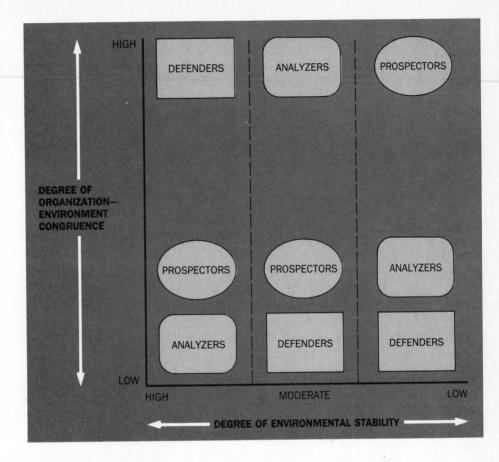

higher level of organization–environment congruence under conditions of moderate stability.

The primary contributions of the adaptation model are that it underscores the importance of organization–environment congruence, it helps organizations better understand their strategic positions relative to those of other organizations, and it focuses attention on some of the primary problems of management.

The business portfolio matrix approach to strategy

This approach to strategy began at General Electric and was eventually developed into a complete framework by the Boston Consulting Group. Essentially, the business portfolio matrix approach to strategy consists of three phases: identification of strategic business units, classification of these units into a matrix, and selection of alternatives for dealing with the units.

Strategic business units

The concept of *strategic business units* (SBUs) was the contribution of General Electric. In 1971 managers at GE realized that they needed a more logical framework for viewing their organization. They decided to view the firm as a portfolio of businesses. For example, one SBU was defined as all food preparation appliances (toaster ovens, ranges, and so on). A total of 43 SBUs were identified within the company. In short order, several other firms, including Union Carbide and General Foods, began to view themselves in terms of SBUs.

Generally, SBUs have the following characteristics:

1. Each one has its own mission.
2. Each is a single unit or set of related units.
3. Each has its own competitors.
4. Each can have its own unique strategy apart from that of other units in the organization.

Hence General Electric has an overall corporate strategy, but each SBU within the company can adopt its own business strategy.

An organization can define SBUs at a number of different levels. Philip Morris, for example, might classify Seven-Up, Miller Brewing, and Philip Morris USA as SBUs. Each has a different kind of product. For its part, General Motors could view each of its automobile divisions—Chevrolet, Pontiac, and

Figure 5.6
Some of Sears, Roebuck and Company's SBUs

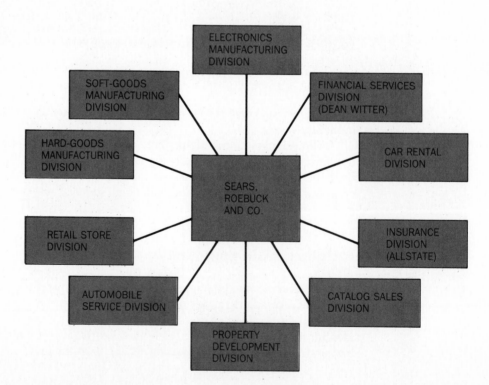

Figure 5.7
The business
portfolio matrix

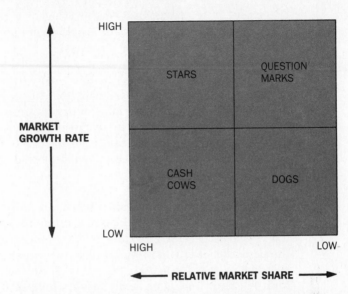

Source: "The Product Portfolio," 1970 The Boston Consulting Group, Inc. All
rights reserved. Published by permission.

so on—as a separate SBU. An SBU diagram for Sears, Roebuck is given in
Figure 5.6.

When all SBUs have been appropriately identified, the next step in using
the business portfolio matrix approach to strategy is to classify the various
SBUs into categories described by the matrix. The development and refinement
of the matrix itself was primarily the work of the Boston Consulting Group.[26]

The portfolio matrix

Essentially, the *portfolio matrix* categorizes SBUs in terms of their rate of market growth and their relative share of that market. The object is to assist managers in allocating resources to each SBU. (Hence the resource deployment
component of corporate strategy becomes relevant here.) When market share
and growth rate are classified as high or low, the 2 × 2 matrix shown in
Figure 5.7 emerges. In the following paragraphs, we will discuss each of the
four kinds of SBUs identified in the portfolio matrix.

Stars. In the upper-left cell of the matrix are the SBUs called stars. *Stars*
have a relatively large share of a high-growth market. Typically, stars require
a large amount of short-run cash to support their rapid growth, and managers
try to invest in the future by maximizing long-term potential. A good example
of a star in the early 1980s was the Atari home video games. In 1980 Atari had

26. Allan Gerald, "A Note on the Boston Consulting Group Concept of Competitive Analysis
and Corporate Strategy," *Intercollegiate Case Clearing House*, ICCH 9–175–175 (June 1976).

80 percent of a market that was growing at a rate of over 100 percent per year.[27] Other recent stars include Apple computers, cable TV franchises in urban areas, and Steven Speilberg movies.

Cash cows. As markets mature, many stars become cash cows for the organization. A *cash cow* is an SBU that has a large share of a low-growth market. A cash cow requires little money for growth and expansion, so it generates surplus revenue that the company can use in other areas (to promote stars, for example). Current cash cows include Heineken beer (60 percent of a stagnant Dutch beer market) and Wonder bread (the largest share of a declining white bread market).

Question marks. *Question marks* are SBUs with a relatively low share of a high-growth market. Managers must decide whether to commit the financial resources necessary to transform the SBU into a star or to de-emphasize the particular SBU within the overall portfolio strategy. Because SBUs seldom stay in the question mark category very long, current examples are hard to find. A classic case is General Electric's decision to drop its computer operations. Another recent example occurred in the contact lens industry. In 1981 the market for contacts was growing at a rate of 20 percent per year. For the industry giant, Bausch & Lomb, its contact lens line was clearly a star. For its competitors, including divisions of Revlon and Johnson & Johnson, these SBUs were question marks.

Dogs. If question marks are relatively difficult to track over time, *dogs* are even harder to identify; an SBU with a small share of a low-growth market is not likely to be around very long. Dogs are often unable to support themselves and are frequently a cash drain on other SBUs within the organization. A small slide rule division, a Latin department in a technical school, and a unit producing console black-and-white televisions could all be categorized as dogs. Several examples of stars, cash cows, question marks, and dogs are listed in Table 5.2.

Selection of alternatives

After SBUs have been identified and classified within the business portfolio matrix, the final stage of this strategic approach is to establish methods for managing each SBU. That is, a business strategy is developed for each SBU; the corporate strategy is also involved, because issues of resource deployment are important. A variety of alternative strategies can be adopted.

Growth. A growth strategy is generally appropriate for stars and for question marks that have a reasonable chance of becoming stars in the future. The organization adopts a conscious commitment to pump resources into the

27. Peter W. Bernstein, "Atari and the Video-Game Explosion," *Fortune*, July 27, 1981, pp. 40–46.

Table 5.2 Examples from the business portfolio matrix

Category	Examples
Stars	Home video games
	High-mileage, low-cost cars
	"Star Wars" movie series
Cash cows	Crest toothpaste
	Right Guard aerosol deodorant
	Levi's jeans
Question marks	Automated manufacturing systems
	Videodisc players
	Amtrak
Dogs	Buggy whips
	Slide rules
	White dress socks
	Edsels

SBU in order to increase both the size of the market and its own share of that market. The organization may even sacrifice short-run profits in order to attain a favorable long-run position. RCA, for example, sank $200 million into its videodisc player in an attempt to create a star. Other growth techniques include diversification (adding products and/or services to existing lines), merger, joint venture (such as American Motors Corporation's link up with Renault), and vertical integration (as when a company supplies its own raw materials or sells directly to the ultimate consumer).

Stable growth or hold. For other SBUs a more appropriate technique is to maintain a modest level of growth or simply to maintain the status quo. This approach is most useful for cash cows. For these SBUs, market growth has leveled off and the organization can reap the benefits of past investments. For a product like Crest toothpaste, for example, Procter & Gamble is not likely to anticipate any extended period of rapid growth. Instead, the company will invest in advertising and promotion only to the extent necessary to maintain a modest growth rate and a stable market share.

Retrenchment or turnaround. Retrenchment or turnaround techniques may be called for when a question mark fails to move into the star category, or when a cash cow begins to lose ground. The organization may try to stimulate the market, to find new uses for its product (for example, promoting Arm & Hammer baking soda as a deodorizer), or to change its image in the eyes of its customers.

Divestiture. The appropriate strategy for some SBUs (especially those in the dog category) is divestiture. The organization may sell the SBU or simply close down that particular product or service line. RCA has attempted to sell major SBUs such as Hertz in an effort to raise cash; K mart closed its Kresge stores (to concentrate on discounting) and Woolworth closed its Woolco stores (to get out of discounting) in an attempt to rid themselves of SBUs that had become dogs.

The business portfolio matrix approach to strategy has been popular for several years. Though criticisms have been leveled at it (for example, some managers use the matrix too mechanically, and some dogs that are divested may still have potential), recent scientific studies have generally supported the validity of this approach.[28] Hence the business portfolio matrix approach to strategy is likely to remain popular for some time.

Other contemporary frameworks for strategy

The adaptation and business portfolio matrix approaches to strategy have been widely discussed in management literature and widely used by practicing managers. In this section, we will briefly summarize other contemporary perspectives on strategy and strategic planning that may become just as popular in the future.

The technology life-cycle approach to strategy

One new approach to strategic planning is the technology life-cycle approach.[29] The basic assumptions of this approach are that each technology has a limited life expectancy and that effective strategic planning should anticipate new technologies to replace the old. Two examples should serve to illustrate how technological progress can affect organizational performance.

In the late 1970s, Gulf Oil established a five-year strategy for attaining the number-two position in the market for low-density polyethylene film (used for garbage bags, sandwich bags, and so on). One assumption underlying this strategy was that no technological innovations for producing the film would emerge during the five-year period, so few resources were committed to research and development. Midway through the plan, however, Union Carbide

28. See Donald C. Hambrick, Ian C. MacMillan, and Diana L. Day, "Strategic Attributes and Performance in the BCG Matrix—A PIMS-Based Analysis of Industrial Product Businesses," *Academy of Management Journal*, September 1982, pp. 510–531; and Ian C. MacMillan, Donald C. Hambrick, and Diana L. Day, "The Product Portfolio and Profitability—A PIMS-Based Analysis of Industrial Product Businesses," *Academy of Management Journal*, December 1982, pp. 733–755.

29. Walter Kiechel III, "The Decline of the Experience Curve," *Fortune*, October 5, 1981, pp. 139–146.

announced a breakthrough that would reduce production costs by 20 percent. This event, coupled with an error in Gulf's assessment of market growth, jeopardized the company's strategy.[30] Had Gulf's managers used the technology life-cycle perspective, they might not only have considered that a potential breakthrough *might* occur, but they might even have *assumed* that it would.

Sometimes a technological breakthrough may create an entirely new product. Such was the case when electronic cash registers replaced the older mechanical machines, and because National Cash Register didn't anticipate this innovation, it lost its position in the market to Burroughs, which had properly planned for the change. At present, the technology life-cycle approach has been developed only very generally, and no guiding framework exists. Due to the current emphasis on technological innovation and enhancement of productivity, however, it seems likely that this approach to strategy will become increasingly useful.

The generic strategies approach

Another approach to strategic planning that is likely to become important is the generic strategies approach. Developed by Michael Porter, this perspective holds that there are three generic strategies that firms can adopt.[31] The label *generic* is used because a strategy may be appropriate to a wide variety of organizations across diverse industries. Porter suggests that organizations should develop a feeling for their industry and then define a competitive niche by adopting one of the three generic strategies.

Differentiation. The differentiation strategy involves developing an image of the organization's product or service in such a way that customers perceive it as being different from all others. The product or service could be differentiated in terms of quality, design, future service, or any of a number of other attributes. The rationale for such differentiation is that the organization can charge higher prices (and therefore make more profit per unit) for a unique product. Examples of products or services that have been successfully differentiated include:

1. Seiko watches, Volvo automobiles, and the Stanford M.B.A. (high quality)
2. Calvin Klein jeans and limited-edition plates, coins, and other commemoratives (unique design)
3. Caterpillar tractors and Curtis Mathes televisions (good long-run service)

Overall cost leadership. Organizations that adopt this strategy attempt to maximize sales by minimizing cost per unit and hence prices. That is, the

---

30. "The New Planning," *Business Week,* December 18, 1978, pp. 62–68.
31. Michael Porter, *Competitive Strategy* (New York: Free Press, 1980).

organization tries to increase its sales volume by charging low prices, or exercising "cost leadership." Examples of products reflecting this view include Bic pens, Black & Decker power tools, and J. C. Penney's line of Fox clothing. Discount retailers such as K mart also use this strategy.

Focus. In this strategy, products or services are targeted at certain geographic locations, certain customer groups, and so on. Products or services that have successfully focused on specific segments of the total market include cosmetics for blacks, Izod clothing, and regional foods such as chili in the Southwest and clam chowder in the Northeast.

Global strategies

Working with three colleagues, Michael Porter has also developed a framework for strategic planning at the international level.[32] Porter argues that many firms competing in international markets view themselves as multinationals; that is, they view each market or country separately. A more effective approach is to view the organization from an integrated global perspective, realizing that all countries and markets are interrelated. Just as domestic firms, for example, locate plants in areas offering inexpensive labor and low taxes and then ship the finished goods to major urban markets, the global firm may locate its plants in underdeveloped countries (where inflation is low and labor cheap) and then ship goods to more attractive markets in other countries.

Another point Porter and his associates make is that an individual company may have little control over whether it develops a global strategy. They argue that entire industries, not individual companies, become global. Hence any given organization may have to adopt a global strategy to keep pace with the competition.

Anti-strategy

A final contemporary approach to strategy might be labeled *anti-strategy*.[33] This is not really a strategic framework at all but an argument against the current uses of strategy.

This view points to the lack of strategic planning by successful Japanese firms as evidence that American firms may rely too heavily on the various strategic models we have summarized. The idea is that the success of Japanese business is partially attributable to the willingness of upper management to guide and channel input from the lower ranks of the organization and to determine how to do things best on a trial-and-error basis. American firms, ac-

32. Thomas M. Hout, Michael E. Porter, Eileen Rudden, and Eric Vogt, "Global Industries: New Rules for the Competitive Game," Boston: Graduate School of Business Administration, Harvard University, Working Paper, HBS 80–53.

33. Richard T. Pascale, "Our Curious Addiction to Corporate Grand Strategy, *Fortune*, January 25, 1982, pp. 115–116.

cording to this view, rely too much on a grand strategy developed at the top and then imposed as a narrow corridor through which the organization is made to move. It is unlikely that the concept of anti-strategy will ever be widely accepted by American managers. It does, however, warn of the pitfalls in taking a mechanistic view of strategic planning.

Strategic planning: A synthesis of contemporary viewpoints

Why are there so many models and frameworks? The reason is that there are no "guaranteed" strategies for success in any field of endeavor. If there were, all organizations would use them. Successful organizations may attribute part of their good fortune to a well-conceived strategy, but common sense, hard work, and pure luck also contribute to the performance of most organizations. It is fair to say that systematic strategic planning usually improves an organization's chances for success. Moreover, the manager gains breadth and insight from considering the various strategies.

Examining the adaptation model, most managers can easily relate to the three basic problems of management (entrepreneurial, engineering, and administrative). And considering how best to avoid the pitfalls of the reactor "strategy" is most instructive. The business portfolio matrix approach calls attention to the very useful concept of strategic business units (SBUs), the role that different SBUs play in the overall organization, and the variety of alternatives available for dealing with each SBU. The technology life-cycle view focuses managerial attention on the dangers of ignoring technological innovation. The generic strategies approach, including differentiation, focus, and overall cost leadership, is useful in many situations. The global strategy perspective suggests that an organization must monitor the involvement of its industry in international markets and then adopt a global perspective when and if that becomes appropriate in order to compete effectively. And even while warning against a mechanistic approach to strategic planning, the anti-strategy view concedes that no strategic planning at all may be hazardous to organizational health.

Further, we should note that the various frameworks and models seldom offer contradictory guidelines. In fact, they generally complement one another. For example, the composition of the SBU portfolio is closely related to both the entrepreneurial and the administrative problems. The technology life-cycle concept could be useful in handling the engineering problem. Managers can use generic strategies to help identify various SBUs within a portfolio and to further their understanding of defenders, prospectors, and analyzers. And the concepts of corporate, business, and functional strategies mesh very well with many of the other perspectives.

In the final analysis, managers should try to strike an optimal balance in their use of strategic frameworks and models. On the one hand, they should be familiar with the strategic planning models in order to use them to the degree they feel is appropriate. This familiarity also allows the manager to use only a part of a particular framework, or to modify a framework to fit his or her unique situation. On the other hand, managers should not rely so heavily on any framework that they fail to take full advantage of their own insight and experience.

Summary of key points

Strategy is the pattern of goals and the major policies and plans for achieving those goals, stated in a way that defines what business the company is in or wants to be in and the kind of company it is or wants to be. Strategic planning, then, is the process of developing strategy.

Strategic planning focuses on matching the resources of the organization with the opportunities and risks in the external environment. It is performed by top-level managers, has a long-run time frame, and is expressed in relatively general, nonspecific terms. (Herein it contrasts with tactical planning, which is more specific and involves middle-level managers, a shorter time frame, and more specific detail.)

Strategy can be characterized along two dimensions: its components and its level. The four basic components of strategy are scope, resource deployment, competitive advantages, and synergy. Scope specifies what markets the organization expects to compete in, whereas resource deployment involves allocating resources across different areas. Analysis of the company's competitive advantages identifies areas in which it should be particularly strong, and synergy accounts for interactions between areas of the organization. Strategy can also be viewed from three levels: corporate, business, and functional. Corporate strategy specifies what set of businesses the organization intends to be in. Business strategy, in turn, involves the strategy for each business within the organization. Functional strategies focus on marketing, finance, production, research and development, personnel, and organization design.

For most organizations, the strategic process involves a variety of activities. Common activities include scanning the environment, analyzing the environment, establishing the company's mission and primary goals, developing policies, and developing functional strategies.

The adaptation model of strategy identifies three basic problems that management encounters in attempting to achieve an effective environmental alignment: entrepreneurial, engineering, and administrative problems. Depending on how an organization deals with these problems, it may act as a defender, prospector, analyzer, or reactor.

The business portfolio matrix approach to strategy suggests the identification of strategic business units (SBUs); the classification of each SBU as a star, cash cow, question mark, or dog within the portfolio matrix; and the selection of strategies for each SBU as a function of its location within the matrix.

Other contemporary frameworks for strategic planning include the technology life-cycle approach, the generic strategies approach, global strategies, and anti-strategy. There is no one best model of strategic planning. Each model of strategy has something useful to offer successful managers, and they should be viewed as complementary frameworks for the strategic planning process.

QUESTIONS FOR DISCUSSION

1. Why is the concept of strategy so important to contemporary organizations?
2. Is it possible for a single-product firm to differentiate its corporate and business strategies?
3. What factors might have been included in an environmental analysis of the United States automobile industry in the early 1980s?
4. Why are environmental scanning and analysis so important to strategic planning?
5. Discuss the six functional strategies and explain how they are related to one another. Can they be ranked in order of their importance to certain kinds of firms? How well could a firm survive if it neglected to develop one or more of these strategies?
6. Some people argue that goal setting and strategy are different processes, whereas others view them as part of the same process. Discuss the merits of each viewpoint.
7. Miles and Snow describe four approaches for *organizations* to take in response to their entrepreneurial, engineering, and administrative problems. Can you think of examples wherein *individuals* might act as defenders, prospectors, analyzers, and reactors?
8. Identify examples of defenders, prospectors, analyzers, and reactors other than those discussed in the text.
9. If you were a manager with an SBU classified as a question mark, how might you turn it into a star?
10. Can you think of any reasons why you might want to keep a dog in your corporate portfolio of SBU's? (Hint: consider market niches and competition.)
11. Identify examples of stars, question marks, cash cows, and dogs other than those discussed in the text.
12. Use both the adaptation model and the portfolio matrix model to characterize your business or university.
13. Which of the four recent frameworks do you think has the greatest potential for the future?
14. Identify major consistencies and contradictions among the four recent frameworks, the adaptation model, and the business portfolio matrix.
15. Compare and contrast the adaptation model and the portfolio matrix approach.
16. Consider a corporation that is still operated and controlled by its original founder. How might this affect the choice of strategic alternatives (growth, stable growth, retrenchment or liquidation)? Are there circumstances in which the entrepreneur might not be willing to choose the

alternative that seems best, given the market growth and position of the firm?

C A S E   5.1

At the beginning of this chapter, you read about a successful firm whose entire industry was threatened. The medical profession had determined that the company's primary product was a health hazard, and television advertising for the product was barred. The industry in question was the tobacco industry, the company Philip Morris. The case that follows describes what Philip Morris did and then raises some issues for your consideration.

Philip Morris changes strategy

When the surgeon general's report linking cigarette smoking and cancer was released in the 1950s, tobacco companies quickly realized that, if *they* were to remain healthy, new strategies would be needed. The environmental threat posed by consumer warnings on packaging and bans on television advertising was simply too great to ignore. Hence most of the leading tobacco manufacturers began to look for ways to diversify into new markets.

Philip Morris, Inc. was among the largest and most profitable tobacco companies. Its leading product, Marlboro, is the best-selling cigarette in the world. The company's financial prowess, then, enabled it to acquire other firms.

In 1959 Philip Morris purchased the Miller Brewing Company for $130 million. Its experience with Miller is one of marketing's greatest success stories. Prior to the acquisition, the beer industry was somewhat conservative and old-fashioned in its approach to marketing. Philip Morris, however, brought with it a different perspective (one that had vaulted Marlboro to industry leadership), and a huge marketing budget. First Miller's leading product, Miller High Life beer, needed to be repositioned. The same number of beer drinkers bought Miller as bought Schlitz and Budweiser, but Miller was bought by light drinkers (the typical Miller drinker consumed one or two beers at a time). A new advertising campaign, built around the slogan "If you've got the time, we've got the beer" made Miller more appealing to the heavy beer drinkers. Miller quickly became the number-two seller in the industry, behind Budweiser. In subsequent actions, Miller introduced the very successful Lite ("Lite Beer from Miller—everything you always wanted in a beer, and less") to appeal to calorie-conscious drinkers who wanted a less-filling beer and Lowenbrau ("Tonight let it be Lowenbrau"), aimed at the more sophisticated and status-conscious drinkers. Yet, despite the enormous success of this marketing strategy, Miller has not been particularly profitable for Philip Morris. In 1980 Miller accounted for 30 percent of Philip Morris's sales but only 11 percent of its profits.

In 1978 Philip Morris acquired The Seven-Up Company for $515 million. The new owner moved more slowly in attempting to stimulate this company, however. By 1980 Seven-Up had dropped from third to fourth in the soft-drink market and lost $7 million, but in 1982 it appeared that Seven-Up was ready to make a big push. First the company began a series of advertising campaigns calling attention to the fact that Seven-Up contains no caffeine. Next it introduced a new cola, Like, also touted as being nearly caffeine-free. Early indications suggested that consumers were responding favorably to both Seven-Up and Like. Whether this strategy will be successful or not, of course, remains to be seen.

Philip Morris's most recent acquisition, Rothmans International, brings the company full circle to its roots in the tobacco industry. Rothmans is the fourth-largest cigarette company in the world (Philip Morris is number two). Currently headquartered in Great Britain, Rothmans markets a line of cigarettes called Rothmans, Peter Stuyvestant, Cartier, and Dunhill around the world. Rothmans's international networks could give Philip Morris a truly global presence. It should be able to control the existing markets and product lines, while using them to increase the international market for its existing products, such as Marlboro and Merit.

CASE
QUESTIONS

1. Cite examples of corporate, business, and functional strategies in this case.
2. Classify each of the products or product lines mentioned in this case according to the business portfolio matrix.
3. Given that environmental threats initially prompted Philip Morris's diversification, what reasons can you suggest for the move back into the tobacco industry?
4. If Philip Morris is successful with Rothmans, what might be next on its agenda?

CASE
REFERENCES

Bernstein, Peter W. "Seven-Up's Sudden Taste for Cola." *Fortune,* May 17, 1982, pp. 101–103.

Clark, John. *Business Today—Successes and Failures* (New York: Random House, 1979).

Kinkead, Gwen. "Philip Morris Undiversifies." *Fortune,* June 29, 1981, pp. 62–65.

"Miller Brewing Company's High Life Shipments Go Flat Despite Rise in Overall Volume." *Wall Street Journal,* January 22, 1981, p. 38.

C A S E   5.2

Ron Garvey, Chairman of Spearman Consolidated, was preparing his notes for the company's annual planning conference. Spearman Consolidated is a rapidly growing conglomerate. Formed over 30 years ago by venture capitalist Henry Spearman, the company now consists of 10 businesses. Each business was acquired be-

Taking the business portfolio matrix approach to strategy

cause it showed potential for increasing the company's profits. When businesses fail to attain target profits, they are usually sold in short order. The purpose of Spearman's planning conference is to evaluate present holdings and to map out strategies for future acquisitions. Garvey expects the next year to be quite hectic for Spearman and wants to make sure the participants in the planning conference understand the company's position.

Among Spearman's 10 businesses, Amalgamated Electronics has really had a banner year. The Amalgamated home computer has increased its market share to 10 percent, and all signs indicate continued rapid growth. American Video has also had a super year. This company produces arcade video games and licenses its most popular games to Atari and Mattel. During the last year, five of the most popular new video games were developed by American; one of them, Space Creatures, has already drawn a record licensing fee and the other four are expected to do quite well. Record sales increases were also posted by Peterson Air Freight. It actually tripled its sales and increased its market share by 15 percent.

Cook Advertising, however, was a different story. The advertising industry is growing, but Cook just can't seem to make a dent. Spearman poured a lot of money into Cook's operating budget, but Garvey doesn't know whether the investment will pay off. The same can be said of Woodman Luggage. Spearman spent over half a million dollars promoting Woodman, but sales increases were disappointing.

The money Spearman spent on Cook Advertising and Woodman Luggage came primarily from surpluses generated by three other businesses. Fisher Apparel, Shaw Sporting Goods, and Abelson's Department Stores have been a part of Spearman Consolidated for many years. Each produces a healthy profit each year, although their growth rates have leveled off considerably. Spearman typically uses the profits from these companies to stimulate growth in other businesses.

Two companies that are *not* likely to receive any more of these surplus profits, Garvey notes, are Lucas Amusements and General Office Equipment. Lucas Amusements is basically a traveling amusement park playing engagements at county fairs and shopping malls. Last year Lucas lost almost $1 million, and engagements are dropping by about 6 percent per year. General Office Equipment is in even worse shape. Its line of manual office typewriters and adding machines has posted sales declines of 15 percent each year for the last 5 years.

Garvey expects a major overhaul at Spearman this year. Marginal businesses must be dropped and appropriate new acquisitions investigated.

CASE
QUESTIONS

1. Characterize Spearman Consolidated in terms of the business portfolio matrix.
2. Is Spearman a defender, a prospector, an analyzer, or a reactor?
3. What businesses should be disposed of? What industries might Consolidated explore for acquisition?

6

DEVELOPING AND IMPLEMENTING PLANS

1. Discuss planning as an organizational subsystem that interacts with its environment.

2. List factors to consider in organizing the planning staff, and describe the responsibilities of the planning staff.

3. Describe three types of action plans, the different situations in which they might be used, and how they are important in the day-to-day activities of the organization.

4. Explain the characteristics of short-range, intermediate, and long-range planning.

5. Discuss ways in which the organization structure and the planning process interact.

6. Explain the concept of contingency planning and identify the points at which it comes into play during the planning process.

7. Discuss barriers to the planning process and techniques for overcoming them.

CHAPTER OUTLINE

165

OPENING INCIDENT

You are a manager at one of the oldest companies in the United States. The foundation of your company's operations has always been glass manufacturing and processing. Over the last several years, however, the market for your primary products, glass for light bulbs and television picture tubes, has essentially disappeared. You realize that your company needs a new direction if it is to survive, yet you are reluctant to move too far away from glass manufacturing and processing. What would you do?

I n 1970 Karl Bays was appointed president of American Hospital Supply Corporation, a struggling company going nowhere. Bays recognized that the health care environment was rapidly changing. Stemming primarily from political activity (for example, federal subsidies for hospital construction and Medicare), changing sociocultural attitudes (such as the emerging belief that high-quality health care is a right rather than a privilege), and technological innovation (for example, rapid breakthroughs in health care techniques), it became apparent that the health care industry was on the verge of a revolution. Bays reasoned that, if hospital suppliers were to survive, they would have to change too.

American Hospital Supply established goals (the first phase of planning, discussed in Chapter 4) of surviving the shift and becoming number one in the new environment, and it developed a strategy (the next phase of planning, discussed in Chapter 5) for achieving those goals. But Bays had to do more than just sit back and wait for things to fall into place. What he did was to computerize the company's inventory control and record-keeping activities, move into manufacturing, and overhaul AHS's distribution system.[1] These three activities represent plans developed to carry out AHS's strategy, the kind of planning this chapter is concerned with.

A *plan* is a framework for goal accomplishment. It usually outlines how the organization intends to move toward its goals in a logical and systematic fashion. *Planning,* then, is the process of developing organizational plans. Strategic planning, as discussed in Chapter 5, focuses on general, long-run issues. This chapter deals with more operational, day-to-day planning. First we will discuss the role of planning as an organizational subsystem. Next we will explore the relationship of the planning staff and planning activities to the

1. See Anne B. Pillsbury, "The Hard-Selling Supplier to the Sick," *Fortune,* July 26, 1982, pp. 56–61.

overall organization. Three kinds of action plans are described next. Then, after dealing with the time frame for planning activities, we discuss relationships between organization structure and the planning process. Contingency plans are the topic of the next section. Finally, we deal with barriers to the planning process and ways to overcome them.

Planning as an organizational subsystem

A useful way to understand how planning is done in organizations is to adopt a systems theory perspective. Systems theory was briefly introduced in Chapter 1 and discussed more fully in Chapter 2. For planning, the concepts of subsystems and open systems are especially relevant. Remember that subsystems are really systems within larger systems and that an open system is one that interacts with its environment.

Figure 6.1 illustrates how the planning process encourages an open-systems view of organizations. As we saw in Chapter 5, information is a primary input to the planning process. Much of it comes into the organization from outside sources that fuel the planning process. Input to the planning process also comes from managers at all levels of the organization. Figure 6.1 reflects the hope that the planning process will help the organization move to a more favorable position within its environment—or even move to an entirely different environment.

Nike provides a good illustration of how a company can adjust to chang-

Figure 6.1
Planning as a component of an open system

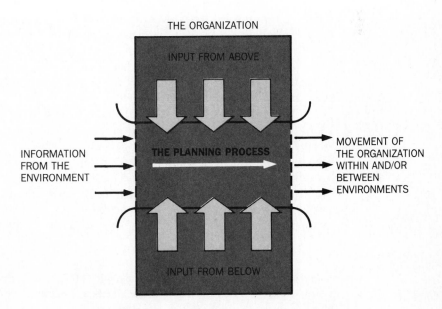

ing environmental conditions through on-going planning activities. During the late 1970s, the company emphasized athletic shoes during the jogging boom. As the demand for running shoes leveled off in the early 1980s, Nike was prepared to diversify into casual and children's shoes and athletic clothing as well as to increase its international thrust.[2] Such timely shifts are possible only when a company stays in close contact with important dimensions of its environment and plans ahead to adapt to changes.

As a subsystem of the organization, planning plays an even more important role in determining the organization's success. Planning is one of several subsystems exhibiting various degrees of interrelatedness and interdependence. In Chapter 5 we noted that, as a part of overall strategic planning, organizations develop strategies for the marketing, finance, research and development, production, organization design, and personnel functions. The strategies of all the organization's functions are highly interrelated.

The research and development unit of an electronics firm, for example, may discover a new technique for consolidating the controls and electricity-usage monitors for all of a home's appliances into one central control panel. The marketing department takes this information, conducts market surveys and feasibility studies to ascertain the product's potential, and then decides whether to proceed. Production must then deal with issues such as whether to build a new plant to produce the control panel (and, if so, where to build the plant, how it will be arranged, and so on) or to use an existing facility. Personnel, in the meantime, is concerned with developing the management team for the new operation and training the sales force to market the product effectively. And finance is involved throughout the process, assisting with the initial feasibility study, determining how best to pay for the new facility, and so on.

Clearly, each of the organization's subsystems uses information from the others as input to its own planning activities. Production must know what the expected selling prices will be (from marketing) and what profit margin is needed (from finance) in order to estimate target cost figures; personnel must know projected sales levels (from marketing) and production volume (from production) to estimate the number of employees needed to successfully develop and introduce the new product.

Planning, then, goes on throughout an organization. It facilitates the organization's interaction with its environment and helps it take an open-systems stance. Managers who fail to plan effectively and who do not adequately monitor environmental shifts are asking for trouble. As a subsystem of the organization, planning cuts across departmental boundaries to integrate and coordinate functional units. To develop plans properly, managers must frame them in terms of functional areas, and the nature of each area's plans makes this framing process easier.[3]

2. See Myron Magnet, "Nike Starts the Second Mile," *Fortune*, November 1, 1982, pp. 158–166.

3. See Charles W. Hofer and Dan Schendel, *Strategy Formulation: Analytical Concepts* (St. Paul, Minn.: West, 1978).

Planning's place in the organization

We are now ready to investigate precisely who does the planning in organizations, or the *place* of planning in the organization. Obviously, all managers engage in planning to some degree. Marketing sales managers develop plans for target markets, market penetration, and sales increases. Production managers plan cost-cutting programs and better inventory control methods. As a general rule, the larger an organization becomes, the more the primary planning activities become associated with groups of managers as opposed to individual managers. This section explores three perspectives on the place of planning in the organization structure.

The planning staff

Many larger organizations develop a professional *planning staff.*[4] Cities Service, Tenneco, General Motors, General Electric, Ford, and Boeing all have such a staff.[5] Organizations set up a planning staff for one or more of the following reasons:

1. **Planning takes time.** A planning staff can reduce the workload of individual managers.
2. **Planning takes coordination.** A planning staff can help integrate and coordinate the planning activities of individual managers.
3. **Planning takes expertise.** A planning staff can bring to a particular problem more tools and techniques than any single individual.
4. **Planning takes objectivity.** A planning staff can take a broader view than individual managers and go beyond pet projects and particular departments.

Organizing the planning staff. There are many possible approaches to organizing the planning staff; two extreme approaches are illustrated in Figure 6.2. The pure staff arrangement places the planning staff in an advisory role. The planning staff is completely removed from formal lines of authority. Under the matrix staff arrangement, the planning staff operates at the same level as other units, with the same degree of authority. Representatives from each unit are formed into teams to work on various projects; two such teams are indicated by the shaded areas in Figure 6.2. (More information about the matrix form of organization structure is found in Chapter 11.)

Of course, top management must decide how the planning staff is to be organized. Factors that influence this decision include:

1. **Degree of centralization.** In highly centralized organizations, top managers are likely to keep the planning staff under their own control (perhaps with a pure staff arrangement). In decentralized organizations the plan-

4. See George A. Steiner, *Top Management Planning* (New York: Macmillan, 1969).
5. See Peter Nulty, "Treasure Hunt at Cities Service," *Fortune*, June 28, 1982, pp. 53–55; and Ann M. Morrison, "Trying to Bring GE to Life," *Fortune*, January 25, 1982, pp. 50–57.

Figure 6.2
Approaches to
organizing the
planning staff

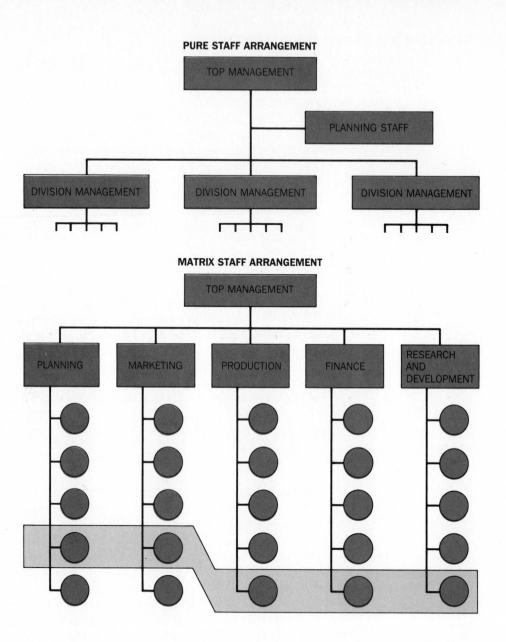

ning staff may be given more power. Some decentralized firms even have several planning staffs. General Motors has a planning group for each automobile division, as well as a corporate planning staff.

2. **Nature of the environment.** The more dynamic and complex an organization's environment, the more likely the planning staff is to enjoy more resources, responsibility, and power. Texas Instruments has recently recognized that its mechanistic, centralized planning system has occasionally

caused the company to react too slowly to environmental shifts. As a result, the company is moving to give corporate planners more authority.[6]

3. **The personality of top managers.** Some managers simply prefer to retain more control than others over planning activities, so a planning staff reporting to this kind of manager is likely to have little power or responsibility. General Electric's new CEO has frozen the budget of the company's planning staff in an effort to reduce the numbers and power of the corporate planners.[7]

Responsibilities of the planning staff. A planning staff generally has three basic areas of responsibility. First, it assists top management in developing goals, policies, and strategies for the organization. The planning staff facilitates this process by scanning and monitoring the environment of the organization.

A second major responsibility of the planning staff is to coordinate the planning of different levels and units within the organization. For example, when a firm is about to introduce a new product, the planning staff may ensure that the sales and promotional efforts of the marketing division, the production and inventory levels of the manufacturing division, and the cash available to finance all of these activities mesh. Each division's needs and output must be consistent with those of the other divisions, and all must be geared to the company's overall objective.

Finally, the planning staff acts as an organizational resource for managers who lack expertise in strategic planning. Managers who are new to their position and managers of relatively new units in the organization may fall in this category.

Planning within diversified organizations

Whether or not organizations have formal planning staffs, group-level planning is essential. Richard Vancil and Peter Lorange suggest that strategic planning is developed in large, diversified organizations via a three-level, three-cycle process.[8]

Three levels of strategy. According to Vancil and Lorange, strategy is developed as a result of the efforts of three levels of management: top-level managers, divisional managers, and functional managers (marketing managers, production managers, and so on) within each division. If the organization has a planning staff, its contributions are made at the top level. What emerges from this top level is an overall strategy and goal set. This overall strategy is the same as the *corporate strategy* discussed in Chapter 5.[9] Implicit within this strategy and goal set is an allocation of resources across *divisions*.

6. See Bro Uttal, "Texas Instruments Regroups," *Fortune,* August 9, 1982, pp. 40–45.

7. See Morrison, "Trying to Bring GE to Life."

8. See Richard F. Vancil and Peter Lorange, "Strategic Planning in Diversified Companies," *Harvard Business Review,* January–February 1975, pp. 81–90.

9. See Hofer and Schendel, *Strategy Formulation.*

Divisional managers then formulate a strategy and goal set for their own divisions. Divisions are typically subdivided into departments, and a major activity at this point is the allocation of resources across *departments*. This idea is analogous to the *business strategy* introduced previously.[10] For example, Philip Morris USA, Miller Brewing, and Seven-Up all develop their own strategies.

Finally, the functional or department managers develop tactical plans to help the division accomplish its goals.

Three cycles of strategy. Strategy is rarely developed in a rigid, mechanical fashion. Although the variations are endless, Vancil and Lorange identified a three-cycle process that most organizations tend to follow. In each cycle, top management consults lower levels of management and then takes some kind of action, as shown in Figure 6.3.

In the first cycle, top management develops a preliminary strategy and goal set for the entire organization. It then calls on division heads to develop strategy and objectives for their units and to propose resource allocations. (In this context, *resource* means primarily money, though space, equipment, and personnel may also be involved.) Cycle 1 ends when top management approves the divisional goals and strategies.

In the second cycle, top management asks the divisions to consult with their department heads to develop specific programs and alternatives. After receiving these recommendations, top management makes tentative resource allocations.

In Cycle 3, top management calls for division budgets. Division heads in turn call for department budgets. These are submitted for approval and then passed up the line to top management, which approves the budgets for the coming year. A one-year budgetary cycle is thought to provide enough time to work toward accomplishing goals but to be brief enough to allow a reasonable degree of financial control.

The individual planner

Even when organizations have large, sophisticated planning staffs and well-developed planning cycles, individual managers are the key to successful planning. They must be willing and able to make appropriate contributions to any overall planning framework. But they must also be willing to take the initiative in planning for their units of responsibility and their own individual activities. For example, when Howard Morgens joined Procter & Gamble several decades ago, he alone recognized the future importance of television advertising. He took the company to the forefront of that advertising medium. Even today, Procter & Gamble is recognized as one of the strongest sales and marketing companies in the world.[11] Individual managers (occasionally acting alone but

10. See Hofer and Schendel, *Strategy Formulation*.

11. See Arthur M. Louis, "The Hall of Fame for U.S. Business Leadership," *Fortune*, March 22, 1982, pp. 101–107.

Figure 6.3
Developing strategy
in a diversified
organization

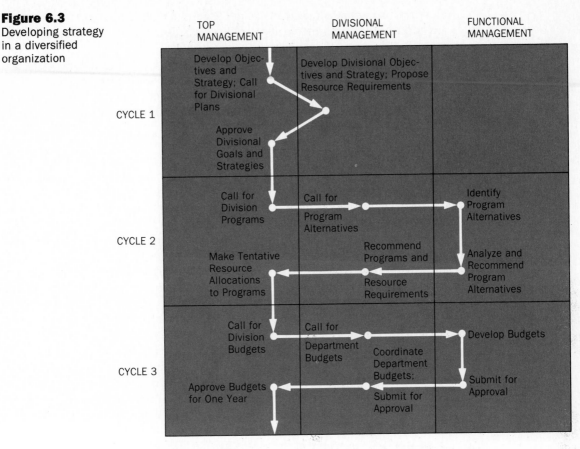

more often working within the context of a larger group) are the core of the
planning process in organizations.

The use of action plans

Whereas strategic planning establishes the broad, general framework for an
organization, *action plans* focus on day-to-day activities. We will discuss three
kinds of action plans: tactical plans, single-use plans, and standing plans.

Tactical plans

Most people have heard of "winning the battle but losing the war." *Tactical
plans* are to battles what strategy is to a war: an organized sequence of steps

designed to execute strategic plans and achieve strategic goals. Strategy focuses on resources, environment, and mission, whereas tactics deal primarily with people and action.

At the beginning of this chapter, we read a scenario about American Hospital Supply. AHS developed a strategy of making itself more congruent with the changing health care environment. One means (tactic) chosen to execute this strategy was to computerize the company's inventory control system.[12] Tactics, then, are the building blocks of strategy.

How to engage in tactical planning. Effective tactical planning depends on many factors that vary from one situation to another, but there are some general guidelines.

First, the planner must recognize that tactics include a number of subobjectives leading to a broader strategic objective. In early 1982 Dayton-Hudson announced strategic plans to invest $2.7 billion in 750 new retail stores (primarily Target, B. Dalton, and Mervyn's) over a 5-year period.[13] Tactical planning within the organization focused on how best to allocate the funds and number of openings each year. Each year's target was a subobjective within the overall strategy.

Second, although strategies are stated in general terms, tactics must deal more with specific resource and time constraints. Consider the Dayton-Hudson example again. Managers engaged in tactical planning must deal with the very concrete problems of how to locate a certain number of sites within a short time and how best to finance each year's construction costs.

Finally, tactical planning requires the use of human resources. Managers involved in tactical planning spend a great deal of time working with other people. An executive at Dayton-Hudson who is involved in the expansion program works with people in the marketing department (locating sites), the legal staff (analyzing leases with shopping malls), the personnel department (identifying and training new store managers), and so forth.

Executing tactical plans. The ultimate success of any tactical plan depends on the way it is carried out. If a strategy calls for a 10-year sales increase of 40 percent and an initial tactical plan of a 7 percent increase in the first year, then the marketing department must devote extra effort, time, and energy to achieving this increase. Similarly, a tactical subobjective of cutting production costs by 1.5% in 6 months suggests that employees and first-line supervisors must work harder and "smarter" to attain the desired cost savings.

Tactical planning is carried out at all levels of management. Plant managers, for example, must develop tactical plans consistent with those of the manufacturing managers above them, and first-line supervisors must have tactical plans that correspond to those of the plant managers. Under ideal circumstances, tactical plans should cascade down the organization in much the same way as objectives do under management by objectives. At Dayton-Hudson, this cascading effect might involve top management identifying the need for

12. See Pillsbury, "The Hard-Selling Supplier to the Sick."
13. "Dayton-Hudson Presses on with a Huge Expansion," *Fortune*, January 11, 1982, p. 7.

750 new store managers, divisional managers allocating them across various kinds of stores, and then successful managers of existing stores recruiting and training a specified number of potential new managers.

Single-use plans

Programs and projects usually require *single-use plans*, which are plans developed to carry out a course of action that is not likely to be repeated in the future.

Programs. A *program* is a single-use plan for a large set of activities. It could consist of appropriate techniques for introducing a new product line, opening a new facility, or changing an organization's mission. Guidelines for effective program development include the following:[14]

1. Divide the total set of activities into meaningful steps.
2. Study the relationships among steps, taking special note of any required sequence of steps.
3. Assign responsibility for each step to appropriate managers and/or units.
4. Determine and allocate the resources needed for each step.
5. Estimate the starting and completion dates for each step.
6. Assign target dates for completion of each step.

An example of a major corporate program is Mobil's entry into the disposable-plate market with its line of Hefty plates. The program involved the steps of marketing research, production planning and control, distribution, product pricing and packaging, and ultimate entry into the market. Top management followed more or less the guidelines listed above, making assignments to appropriate divisions within the firm and allocating them the necessary resources. Each unit developed tentative time frames for the completion of its part of the program; these tentative time frames were eventually coordinated into a formal program. Hefty plates first went on sale in 1978; by 1981 they had become the third-best-selling line in the market.[15]

Projects. A *project* is very similar to a program but is generally of less scope and complexity. A project may be a part of a broader program or it may be a self-contained single-use plan. Hence part of Mobil's program to enter the disposable-plate market might have been the project of building a new plant. Other examples of projects include developing a new product within an existing product line and setting up a new benefit option within the current salary package.

Most programs and projects are developed in conjunction with a *budget:* a statement of the resources allocated for a particular set of activities (such as a program or a project) and a further statement of how the resources are to be

14. See William H. Newman and J. P. Logan, *Strategy, Policy, and Central Management*, 8th ed. (Cincinnati, Ohio: Southwestern, 1981).
15. See Jeremy Main, "Plate Wars," *Fortune*, February 22, 1982, pp. 76–80.

divided among the activities. A program for developing a new product might be accompanied by a $3 million budget; $1 million of this could be designated for research and development and marketing research, $1.5 million for modifications to an existing production facility and initial production costs, and the remainder for promotion and advertising. Budgets are not only a plan for spending but also a control device to ensure that funds are spent in the proper manner. We will return to budgets in Part Five.

Standing plans

Whereas single-use plans (programs and projects) are for nonrecurring situations, *standing plans* are used for activities that recur regularly over a period of time. We will discuss three kinds of standing plans: policies, standard operating procedures, and rules and regulations.

Policies. As a general guide for action, a *policy* is the most general form of standing plan. A university, for example, might establish the policy that people applying for admission need a certain minimum score on their entrance exams and a certain minimum standing in their high school classes. When applicants fail to reach these minimums, admissions officers routinely deny admission. A policy may also describe how exceptions are to be handled. The university's policy statement might create an Admissions Appeals Committee to evaluate applicants who do not meet minimum requirements but who may warrant special consideration.

Standard operating procedures. Another type of standing plan is the *standard operating procedure,* or SOP. An SOP is more specific than a policy in that it outlines the steps to be followed in particular circumstances. The admissions clerk at the university, for example, might be told that, when an application is received, he or she should (1) set up a file for the applicant; (2) add test score records, transcripts, and letters of reference to the file as they are received; and (3) give the file to the appropriate admissions director when it is complete. SOPs describe in detail how a recurring task or activity is to be handled.

Rules and regulations. The narrowest of the standing plans, *rules and regulations,* describe exactly how specific activities are to be carried out. Rather than guiding decision making, rules and regulations substitute for decision making in various situations. The university admissions office might have a rule that, if an applicant's file is not complete two months prior to the beginning of a semester, the student will not be admitted until the next semester. Of course, a manager at a high enough level can suspend or bend the rules. If the high school transcript of the daughter of a prominent alumnus arrives a few days late, the director of admissions would probably waive the two-month rule. Rules and regulations can be a problem if they become excessive and/or if they are enforced too rigidly.

SOPs and rules and regulations are similar in many ways. They are both

Table 6.1 Action plans in organizations

Type of action plan	Primary purpose	Forms
Tactical plans	To systematically implement the organization's strategic plans	Various
Single-use plans	To carry out a course of action that is not likely to be repeated in the future	1. Programs 2. Projects
Standing plans	To carry out a course of action that is likely to be repeated regularly over a period of time	1. Policies 2. Standard operating procedures 3. Rules and regulations

relatively narrow in scope and each can serve as a substitute for decision making. However, an SOP typically describes a sequence of activities, whereas rules and regulations focus on one activity. Recall our examples: the admissions desk SOP consisted of three activities, whereas the two-month rule related to one activity only. In an industrial setting, the SOP for orienting a new employee could involve enrolling the person in various benefit options, introducing him or her to coworkers and supervisors, and providing a tour of the facilities. A pertinent rule for the new employee might involve when to come to work each day.

Summary of action plans

We have identified three categories of action plans: tactical plans, single-use plans, and standing plans. Table 6.1 summarizes these categories, their purposes, and the forms they take. Action plans are necessary in order to implement strategy, and they help managers focus quite specifically on day-to-day activities and events.

The time frame for planning

The timing issue is intimately related to strategy and action plans. Chapter 4 described long-run, intermediate, and short-run goals. By the same token, many organizations develop long-range, intermediate, and short-range plans.

Long-range planning

Long-range planning, which is similar to strategic planning but somewhat more specific, covers many years, perhaps even decades. (General Motors and Exxon routinely develop plans for 10–20-year intervals.) We must make a careful distinction between long-range planning and strategic planning. A strategic plan is a general description of how the organization hopes to fulfill its mission. A long-range plan is a component of a strategic plan, and it is usually associated with a functional strategy.

Assume for a moment that an organization has developed a strategy calling for a major expansion over a 10-year period. The personnel functional strategy, then, must deal with an increased need for human resources. The personnel manager will probably develop a long-range plan describing how many potential managers must be identified each year, whether they should come from inside or outside of the organization, and how they are to be "groomed" for the job. Put another way, the long-range plan is a central component of a functional strategy. Nevertheless, some functional strategies have multiple long-range plans, and some long-range plans may be developed apart from functional strategies.

The time span for long-range planning varies from one organization to another. To simplify our classification, we will regard any plan that extends beyond 5 years as long-range. Managers of organizations in complex, volatile environments face a special dilemma. These organizations probably need a longer time horizon than organizations in less dynamic environments. Yet this very complexity makes long-range planning more difficult.

Areas of long-range planning may include major expansion, development of top managers, large issues of new stocks and bonds, new product/service development, and new plant construction. In recent years, Union Carbide moved its corporate headquarters from Manhattan to up-state New York, Sears entered the financial services industry, Disney opened Epcot Center, and Hilton issued $75 million in 10-year bonds. Each of these activities no doubt resulted from long-range planning undertaken in the past and is expected to play a major role in corporate operations for a long time to come.

Like strategic plans, long-range plans are usually developed on a tentative basis and are subject to change with the passage of time. Disney, for example, expects Epcot to play a major role in its activities for decades. In ten years, however, Epcot's role may be more or less significant than is presently projected.[16]

Intermediate planning

Intermediate plans are somewhat less tentative and less subject to change, and they usually range from 1 to 5 years. Whereas long-range plans serve more as general guidelines derived from an organization's strategy, intermediate plans are more relevant on a day-to-day basis for middle and first-line managers. A

16. See Irwin Ross, "Disney Gambles on Tomorrow," *Fortune*, October 4, 1982, pp. 62–68.

long-range plan may call for achieving sales leadership in a particular industry in 8 years, whereas the supporting intermediate plan is likely to call for a 3 percent sales increase in each of the next 4 years. Thus tactical plans tend to have an intermediate time horizon.

Long-range planning is plagued by the uncertainties associated with long time horizons, so, for many organizations, intermediate planning has become the central focus of planning activities. For example, International Harvester recently developed major planning efforts in the areas of finance, product mix, and personnel. During the early 1980s, as IH was on the brink of bankruptcy, the company established procedures for cutting its work force, jettisoning unprofitable products, and restructuring its debt. In each case the planning horizon was less than 5 years.[17]

Most intermediate plans are components of long-range and/or strategic plans. For example, if a long-range plan calls for an 18 percent increase in labor force, an intermediate plan for contributing to that growth may be appropriate. In other instances, intermediate plans may be developed apart from long-range and strategic plans. In the International Harvester situation, the company was more concerned with surviving the next few years than with taking a long-run perspective.

Short-range planning

Finally, managers develop sets of plans dealing with a time frame of 1 year or less. These short-range plans have more impact on the manager's day-to-day activities than long-range or intermediate plans. For example, in the burgeoning and dynamic video game market of the early 1980s, manufacturers had to take a short-range perspective. Managers didn't know what technological breakthroughs or market shifts might occur in 4 months, much less 4 years.[18] But it would have been foolish not to take advantage of overwhelming demand merely for the lack of a long-range plan.

Short-range plans generally fall into one of two categories: operational plans and reaction plans.

Operational plans. Operational plans are those that have been systematically developed and derived from a broader framework of plans. That is, *operational plans* serve to operationalize strategic, long-range, or intermediate plans. If a long-range plan calls for an 18 percent increase in an organization's labor force and an intermediate plan calls for 8 percent of that increase to be attained in the next 4 years, a short-range operational plan may be to increase the labor force by 1.5 percent *this* year.

Reaction plans. *Reaction plans* are plans designed to allow the company to react to an unforeseen circumstance. This circumstance may or may

17. See ''How International Harvester Hopes to Return to the Black,'' *Fortune*, January 25, 1982, pp. 7–8.
18. See Peter Nulty, ''Why the Craze Won't Quite,'' *Fortune*, November 15, 1982, pp. 114–124.

not be a desirable situation for the organization, and the reaction may or may not be fully appropriate. When Chrysler contemplated selling its profitable military division in early 1982, this was a short-range plan to acquire cash to meet financial obligations. Chrysler wanted to keep the division (it was one of the company's few profitable operations in recent years), but a severe cash shortage necessitated extreme measures to raise money. In the same year Ethyl Corporation developed a short-range plan to purchase First Colony Life, a fast-growing insurance company. This plan was a reaction to a good investment

Figure 6.4
Integrating planning time frames

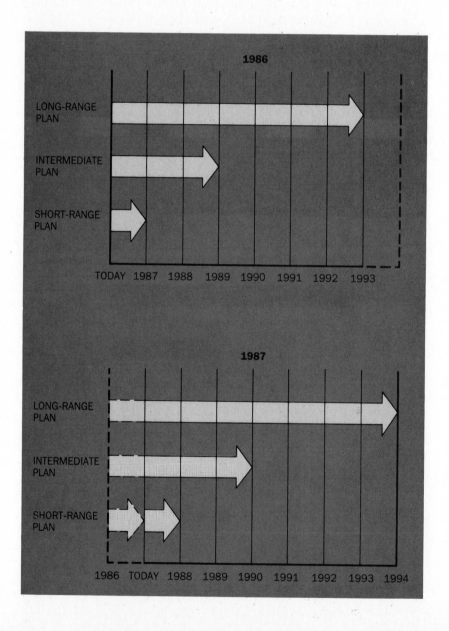

situation for Ethyl. That is, because First Colony had sky-rocketing sales and because Ethyl was looking for a good investment, the match was ideal.[19]

In general, managers need to avoid concentrating too much on short-range planning. Short-range plans tend to focus on immediate quantitative outcomes, and the manager who becomes preoccupied with them may neglect crucial intermediate and long-range planning activities.

Integrating time frames

A potential problem that managers face when planning across different time horizons is balancing and integrating plans. Short-range plans calling for personnel cuts may be inconsistent with a long-range plan for increasing productivity. But a series of short-range and intermediate plans for increasing sales probably are congruent with a long-range plan for increasing sales. Here the short- and long-range plans support each other. The challenge is to achieve and maintain consistency and congruency across planning time horizons. (The discussion on goal-set analysis in Chapter 4 may be useful in this regard.)

Figure 6.4 also shows how plans might be formally integrated. Beginning in 1986, a hypothetical organization has a long-range plan extending over several years, an intermediate plan extending over 3 years, and a 1-year short-range plan. A year later, in 1987, the short-range plan has, of course, been completed (not necessarily with 100 percent success). Hence the organization develops a new short-range plan for the coming year. Using additional information now available, the organization can also revise and extend its intermediate and long-range plans from their original 3- and 7-year lengths.

Adapting organization structure to the planning process

For plans to be implemented effectively, it is important that the organization structure be appropriately matched with the planning process. Organization structure is not fully discussed until Part Five, so our description of structural components will necessarily be somewhat general.

Organizational components and planning

In most larger organizations, five basic parts of the organization structure are involved in the planning process.[20] These components are shown in Figure 6.5.

Board of directors. At the top of a corporation is the board of directors, a group of people elected by the company's stockholders. Among other responsibilities, the board of directors has the duty to establish the corporate

19. See "Defense Jewel" and "Joining Agility and Innovation," *Fortune*, February 22, 1982, pp. 7–8.

20. See Y. N. Chang and Filemon Campo-Flores, *Business Policy and Strategy* (Santa Monica, Calif.: Goodyear, 1980).

Figure 6.5
The planning
process for a typical
corporation

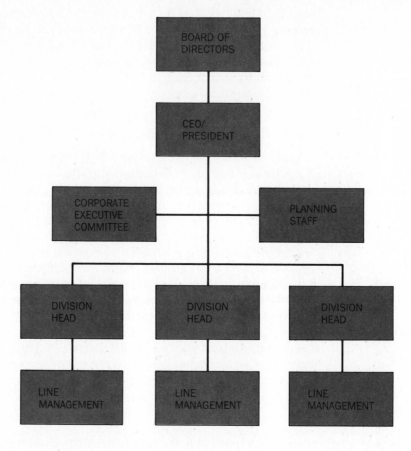

mission and strategy. In some companies the board takes an active role in the planning process. At CBS, for example, board chairman William S. Paley has traditionally played a major role in charting the company's direction and mission. In other companies the board selects a competent chief executive and delegates planning to that individual. Jim Treybig, of Tandem Computers, delegates much of the company's planning activities to a senior vice president.[21]

The chief executive officer. The chief executive officer (CEO) is usually the president or the chairman of the board of directors. In any case the CEO is probably the single most important individual in any organization's planning process. Even when the board takes the lead in developing strategy, the CEO plays a major role in the complete planning process and is responsible for implementing the strategy. When the board delegates the entire planning process, the CEO obviously must spearhead the development of an appropri-

21. See Stratford P. Sherman, "CBS Places Its Bets on the Future," *Fortune*, August 9, 1982, pp. 70–76; and Myron Magnet, "Managing by Mystique at Tandem Computers," *Fortune*, June 28, 1982, pp. 84–91.

ate mission and strategy. The board and CEO, then, assume directive roles in planning. The other three organizational components involved in the planning process have more of an advisory or consulting role.

The planning staff. The planning staff may have varying degrees of power. At one extreme, it may simply respond to the CEO's assignments and directives. This is how the staff at General Electric now functions.[22] In other cases, the planning staff may take the initiative in determining what needs to be done and how best to do it.

The executive committee. Another group that plays a major role in the planning process of many organizations is some form of executive committee. The executive committee is usually composed of the top executives in the organization. In the hypothetical organization shown in Figure 6.5, the executive committee could perhaps consist of the three division heads and be chaired by the CEO. Committee members usually meet on a regular basis to provide input to the CEO on the proposals that affect their own units and to review the various strategic plans that develop from this input. The number of individuals on an executive committee varies considerably from one organization to another; a very large organization might have several dozen. Members of the executive committee are frequently assigned to various staff committees, subcommittees, and task forces to concentrate on specific projects or problems that might confront the entire organization at some time in the future.

Line management. The final structural component of most organizations' planning activities is line management. Line managers are those individuals with formal authority and responsibility for the management of the organization (more information about line management will be presented in Chapter 10). Line managers play an important role in an organization's planning process for two reasons. First, they are a valuable source of inside information for other managers as plans are formulated and implemented. Second, it is usually the line managers at the middle and lower levels of the organization who must execute the plans developed by top management. Line management identifies, analyzes, and recommends program alternatives, develops budgets and submits them for approval, and finally sets the plans in motion.

Other organization processes and planning

Another element of organizational structure that affects planning is decentralization. Decentralization is the extent to which decision-making power and autonomy are passed down to lower levels in the organization (decentralization will be explored in depth in Chapter 9). When organizations are decentralized, more planning responsibility is given to managers at lower levels in the organization; when organizations are centralized, managers at the top retain more control over planning.

22. See Morrison, "Trying to Bring GE to Life."

Recently General Electric has moved toward decentralizing its planning process. As described earlier in this chapter, GE decided to de-emphasize the centralized planning being done by the firm's planning staff. This was accomplished by freezing the unit's budget. Much more planning power was then given to the line managers in charge of GE's 250 individual businesses by encouraging and rewarding initiative and innovation.[23]

Another organizational element that is closely related to the planning process is management by objectives.[24] As discussed in Chapter 4, MBO is a technique for creating an integrated and coordinated set of individual and organizational goals through the process of collaborative goal setting. From another perspective, MBO can also be viewed as a mechanism for developing plans. As we saw, top management has the responsibility for preliminary goal setting and strategic planning for the organization. And when top managers and their subordinates meet to work out goals for each subordinate, they are taking the first step in translating strategy into tactical and action plans. As each successive manager meets in turn with his or her subordinates to set goals, strategic plans are integrated into a day-to-day scheme outlining the contribution of each individual employee's time and talents.

Contingency planning

Another important element of an effective planning system is contingency plans. *Contingency planning* is the development of alternative courses of action to be taken if an intended plan is unexpectedly disrupted or rendered inappropriate. For example, suppose a rapidly expanding franchise food company has made plans to build 100 new units during each of the next 4 years. Its top managers realize, however, that a shift in the economy might call for a different rate of expansion. Therefore, the firm develops two contingency plans: (1) if the economy begins to expand beyond some specific level (contingency event), then (contingency plan) the rate of the company's growth will increase from 100 to 150 new stores per year, or (2) if inflation increases substantially, the expansion rate will drop from 100 to 75 new stores per year. The organization has now specified two crucial contingencies (expansion or inflation in the economy beyond the expected range) and two alternative plans (increased or decreased growth).

The mechanics of contingency planning are shown in Figure 6.6. In relation to an organization's on-going planning process, contingency planning comes into play at and between what we will call four action points. At action point 1, the basic plans of the organization are developed. These plans include strategic plans and tactical, single-use, and standing plans. As a part of this development process, managers usually consider various contingency events. Certain management groups even assign someone the role of devil's advocate

---

23. See Morrison, "Trying to Bring GE to Life."

24. See Stephen J. Carroll and Henry L. Tosi, *Management by Objectives* (New York: Macmillan, 1973) for a discussion of MBO as a planning method.

Figure 6.6
Contingency
planning

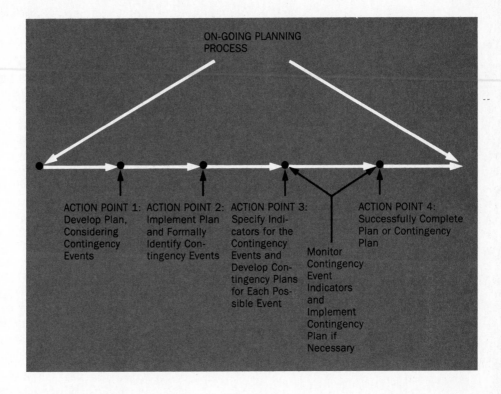

to ask "But what if . . ." about each course of action. Moreover, most managers consider probabilities from the beginning and base their plans on the extent to which various assumptions are likely to be realized. If our plan is based on a market increase of 10 percent, and if this 10 percent increase has a 98 percent chance of happening, we are probably on sound footing. If our 10 percent increase has only a 15 percent chance of coming true, however, we should not depend too heavily on its happening. Various other contingencies (such as a market increase greater than or less than 10 percent) should also be considered.

At action point 2, the plan that has been chosen is put into effect. The most important contingency events are also identified in a more formal manner. Because there could theoretically be an almost infinite array of contingency events, it is important to pinpoint those that have the greatest probability of happening. Only those events that are likely to occur and whose effects would have a substantial impact on the organization are used in the contingency planning process.

Next, at action point 3, the company specifies certain indicators or signs that might suggest that a contingency event is about to take place. For example, a company might decide that an annual inflation rate of more than 15 percent should be considered a contingency event. In that case, a good early indicator might be a *monthly* inflation rate of 1.5 percent or greater for 3 consecutive months. As indicators of contingency events are being defined, the contingency plans themselves should also be developed. Possible contingency plans for various situations include delaying plant construction, developing a new manufacturing process, and cutting prices.

After this stage, the managers of the organization monitor the indicators identified at action point 3. If the situation dictates, a contingency plan may be implemented. Otherwise the primary plan of action continues in force. Finally, action point 4 marks the successful completion of the plan or contingency plan.

Contingency planning is becoming more important to most organizations, especially those operating in particularly complex and/or dynamic environments. It is appropriate for all types of plans, whether strategic or tactical, whether long-range, intermediate, or short-range.

Barriers to the planning process

Very few plans unfold as smoothly or systematically as we might like. A number of barriers to the goal-setting process were discussed in Chapter 4, and, because goal setting is a part of the planning process, these barriers also apply to planning. The following section identifies other barriers that relate less to goal setting and more to planning at a general level. And it suggests methods for overcoming such obstacles. Table 6.2 summarizes these issues.[25]

The major barriers

Dynamic and complex environments. Often, a major barrier to effective planning is the nature of an organization's environment. When an electronics firm develops a long-range plan, it tries to take into account how much technological innovation is likely to occur during that interval. But forecasting such uncontrollable external events is very difficult. During the early boom years of personal computers, data were stored primarily on floppy disks. Due to limited storage capacity, however, a new form of micro disk drive was developed. Whereas the typical floppy disk can hold 250 typed pages of information, the new disk drive can store 1,250 pages. In the years to come, even more breakthroughs are likely.[26] Anticipating these rapid and significant changes certainly complicates the planning process. Changes in any of the elements of an organization's task or general environments, then, can radically alter its plans and obstruct the planning process.

Reluctance to establish goals. Another barrier to effective planning is the reluctance of some managers to establish goals for themselves and their

25. See George A. Steiner, *Strategic Planning: What Every Manager Must Know* (New York: Free Press, 1979) for a general discussion of problems in the planning process.

26. See Peter Nulty, "Big Memories for Little Computers," *Fortune*, February 8, 1982, pp. 50–56.

Table 6.2 Barriers to planning and methods for dealing with them

Barriers to planning	Methods for overcoming the barriers
1. Environment	1. Start at top
2. Reluctance to establish goals	2. Recognizing the limits
	3. Communication
3. Resistance to change	4. Participation
4. Constraints	5. Integrating time frames
5. Time and expense	6. Contingency planning

units of responsibility. The reason for this reluctance may be lack of confidence or fear of failure. If a manager sets a goal that is specific, concise, and time-related, then whether he or she attains it will be obvious. Managers who consciously or unconsciously try to avoid this degree of accountability are likely to hinder the organization's planning efforts. Other factors contributing to a manager's reluctance to establish goals may include a lack of ability, a lack of information, or a poor reward system.

Resistance to change. A third major barrier to the planning process is resistance to change. Almost by definition, planning involves changing one or more aspects of the organization's current situation. Managers resist change for any number of reasons, including fear of the unknown, a preference for familiar goals and plans, and economic insecurity. We will give more attention to resistance to change in our discussion of organizational change in Chapter 12.

Constraints. Constraints that limit what an organization can do are another major obstacle in the planning process. For example, an organization may have such a heavy investment in plant and equipment that it *cannot* acquire new equipment. Labor contracts can also be major constraints. In the early 1980s, Ford, General Motors, and Chrysler each went through complex negotiations with the United Auto Workers union to change labor contracts so that the firms could develop new plans for dealing with sagging domestic sales.[27] Other possible constraints include governmental regulations, a shortage of managerial talent, and a scarcity of raw materials.

Time and expense. Some managers fail to plan effectively because good planning is time-consuming and expensive. It is easy to say "I'm too busy to plan today; I'll do it tomorrow" or to put off good planning for lack of funds.

27. See Irwin Ross, "The New UAW Contract: A Fortune Proposal," *Fortune,* February 8, 1982, pp. 40-45.

A planning system may require, for example, technical expertise and/or a data base that is not available within the organization. It then becomes necessary to purchase the needed expertise and information.

Overcoming the barriers

Fortunately, there are techniques and guidelines that managers can use to overcome some of these planning barriers.

Start at the top. Effective planning must start at the top of the organization. Top management must take the lead in establishing the importance of planning and in determining the mission and strategy the organization is to follow.

Recognizing the limits to planning. Though it may sound paradoxical, another guideline for effective planning is to recognize that it has its limits. Planning is not a panacea that will solve all of an organization's problems, nor is it an iron-clad set of procedures to be followed at any cost. Managers should recognize that good planning does not necessarily ensure success and that adjustments and exceptions are to be expected as the plan unfolds.

Communication. Not only must planning be initiated at the top, but it must also be communicated to others in the organization. Everyone involved in the planning process should know what the overriding organizational strategy is, what the various functional strategies are, and how they are all to be integrated and coordinated.

Participation. We noted at several points in this chapter the role that line and/or functional managers play in the planning process. These individuals almost always have valuable information to contribute, and it is usually up to them to execute the plans, so their involvement and participation are obviously critical. Moreover, all managers are more committed to plans that they have helped to shape. Even when an organization is somewhat centralized and/or uses a planning staff, managers from a variety of levels in the organization should be involved in the planning process.

Integrating time frames. Planning should be a dynamic process in which long-range and intermediate plans are frequently revised and updated in response to new information and the completion of short-range plans.

Contingency planning. Contingency planning is especially useful when environmental turbulence is likely. Proper contingency planning enables the organization to avoid "crisis" management. When a contingency event occurs, the prepared organization will be able to make a smooth transition to the appropriate contingency plan rather than having to react hastily by throwing a new plan together on short notice.

In this section, we have discussed five barriers to effective planning and six methods for at least partially overcoming them. One generalization we can draw from this discussion is that planning is most effective when managers at all levels of the organization recognize the purposes, values, and limitations of planning and when they understand the importance of treating planning as a major managerial function.

Summary of key points

The planning process encourages and is consistent with an open-systems view of organizations. Planning can also be viewed as an organizational subsystem.

Many large organizations use a planning staff to facilitate the planning process. This staff may be located in various places within the organization, and it may have functional authority or be simply advisory. One useful concept of how planning operates in large, diversified organizations identifies three levels of strategy (top-level managers, divisional managers, and functional managers) and three cycles of strategy. Even when organizations have a large planning staff, managers should never neglect planning as individuals for their own units.

Three kinds of action plans are tactical plans, single-use plans, and standing plans. Tactics are an organized sequence of plans designed to execute strategic decisions and achieve strategic goals. Single-use plans are plans designed to carry out a course of action that is not likely to be repeated in the future. Programs and projects are examples of single-use plans. Standing plans, at the other extreme, are plans designed to carry out a course of action that is likely to be repeated several times. Policies, standard operating procedures, and rules and regulations are all standing plans.

Organizations plan over three time horizons: long-range (greater than 5 years), intermediate (between 1 and 5 years), and short-range (1 year or less). Short-range plans also include operational and reaction plans. It is crucial that plans spanning different time horizons be properly integrated.

Five organizational components involved in planning are the board of directors, chief executive officer, planning staff, executive committee, and line management. Decentralization and management by objectives may be closely related to the planning process.

Contingency planning is the development of alternative courses of action to be taken if an intended plan is unexpectedly disrupted. Contingency planning is becoming an increasingly important part of the planning process in many organizations.

Barriers to the planning process include dynamic and complex environments, a reluctance to establish goals, resistance to change, various constraints, and the time and expense involved. Methods for overcoming these barriers include starting at the top, recognizing the limits of planning, careful communication, a broad base of participation, effective integration of time frames, and contingency planning.

QUESTIONS FOR DISCUSSION

1. Think about large not-for-profit organizations such as Boy Scouts of America, or the United Way. Do these organizations need planning staffs? Could the absence of a planning staff affect the success of these organizations in the same way in which it would affect the success of a manufacturing company?

2. Are the processes of planning within diversified organizations applicable to nondiversified firms? Why or why not?

3. In your opinion, which kind of action plan (tactical, single-use, or standing) should a new company develop first, and why? Could they all be developed simultaneously?

4. How closely linked should strategic and action plans be to one another? Can they be too closely linked?

5. What effects did the poor economic forecasts and threats of recession have on short-, intermediate and long-range planning in the early 1980s? Discuss the ideas of uncertainty versus certainty, and good versus bad outlooks for the future.

6. Identify several policies, standard operating procedures, and rules and regulations at your university or business. Are they related to the organization's strategy or other action plans? How could they be made more consistent with each other?

7. Think about your personal plans for the future. Do you tend to think one year, five years, or ten years in advance?

8. What are the advantages and disadvantages of the various time horizons for planning?

9. You are the CEO of a large conglomerate. Many of your SBUs operate in environments that are both risky and rapidly changing. Which organizational component would you rely on most for planning—the board of directors, the executive committee, or line management?

10. Do *you* ever engage in contingency planning? In what context?

11. Is it possible to develop too many contingency plans? What are the advantages and disadvantages of contingency planning?

12. Can you identify any other barriers to effective planning? Are there other ways to overcome the barriers mentioned in the chapter?

C A S E 6.1

At the beginning of this chapter, you read a scenario about an old company whose primary markets are disappearing. The company wants to maintain its base in glass manufacturing and processing, but it also recognizes the need to move in new directions. The company being described was Corning Glass Works. The case that follows explains what Corning is doing and then raises some other issues for your consideration.

Organizational plans at Corning Glass Works

Corning Glass Works, founded over 130 years ago, is one of this country's oldest companies. Corning glass blowers created Thomas Edison's first light bulb in 1880. The company is still operated by descendants of the original founder and has always had glass manufacturing and processing as its base.

This strategy, however, has recently caused problems for Corning. One of its mainstays, lamp glass for bulbs, has declined from yielding a third of the company's revenues 35 years ago to supplying only an insignificant portion of revenues today. The division that produces glass for television picture tubes has also fallen on hard times. Competition from other countries has made this business unprofitable for the company.

In response to these problems, top management at Corning has formulated a new strategy for the company that consists of three major components. First, the company will decrease its involvement in low-growth industries like light bulbs and television picture tubes. Second, Corning will attempt to reduce its dependence on cyclical businesses (businesses characterized by extreme fluctuations in demand). Finally, the company intends to expand aggressively into businesses with high-growth potential.

One such area is the optical waveguide business. An optical waveguide is a small glass fiber strand capable of transmitting sound coded into light signals. The primary market for optical waveguides is for telephone systems, but they also have potential uses in cable TV, computer networks, and medical equipment. Corning expects to eventually achieve sales of $400 million a year in this market.

Another area in which the company anticipates a boom is biotechnology aimed at controlling enzymes during manufacturing processes. In industries such as brewing and leather finishing, enzymes are needed but must also be controlled so as not to contaminate finished products. A recently formulated joint venture with Kroger supermarkets is intended to develop that technology more fully in the food business.

A third new major thrust that Corning is undertaking is in its medical division. The company has long dominated the market for glass beakers and test tubes. Recently however, the focus has shifted to electronic diagnostic equipment. The company hopes to attain one of the top two positions in this industry.

Corning also has a number of less ambitious but equally important programs underway. On one front, the company is now marketing a more sophisticated line of glass cooking ware to gourmet shops (existing lines of Pyrex and Corning Ware are sold primarily through discount and/or department stores). A line of sunglasses was introduced in 1983 (Corning manufactures the glass lens that changes tint in response to sunlight). Another new division, Corning Engineering, is attempting to market technology to underdeveloped countries. Finally, Corning has embarked on an ambitious program to increase productivity. Through such techniques as reducing personnel and increasing efficiency, the company hopes to become more profitable.

Corning does face problems with these new ventures, however. For example, if Corning is to realize anticipated profits with its optical waveguides and enzyme control methods, markets are going to have to expand rapidly. Another criticism of Corning is that its top management has often been more interested in maintaining a certain image than in earning profits.

CASE
QUESTIONS

1. Can you identify examples of strategic plans and tactical plans in this case?
2. Outline a series of action plans that Corning might pursue.
3. Are there areas wherein contingency plans might be especially useful? If so, where?
4. Identify some potential planning barriers that Corning may encounter, and suggest ways of dealing with them.
5. Identify long-range, intermediate, and short-range plans in this case.

CASE
REFERENCES

"Corning to Enter Sunglass Business Starting Next Year." *Wall Street Journal,* March 9, 1982, p. 32.

"Corning Glass Plans Purchase of Gilford Instruments." *Wall Street Journal,* June 2, 1980, p. 12.

"It Takes a Lot of Practice (Corning Glass Works)." *Forbes,* September 13, 1982, p. 82.

Magnet, Myron. "Corning Glass Shapes Up." *Fortune,* December 13, 1982, pp. 90–109.

C A S E 6.2

David Green was pleased. He was on an airplane returning from a five-day management development seminar held at the state university. The seminar was entitled "Effective Managerial Planning." Green felt that the seminar was going to be of great benefit to his company.

David Green had inherited his company, Oilfield Supply, Inc., from his father almost eight years ago. Green's father founded the company in the 1930s as a supplier of oilfield equipment and related materials. The elder Green was not particularly ambitious; he wanted merely to earn a profit sufficient to support his family. David, however, had a different view—he wanted to turn Oilfield Supply into a big company.

After assuming ownership, Green spent two years learning the ropes and trying to decide what approach he should take to spark growth. A consultant recommended that the company adopt a formal strategic planning system. Because David knew nothing about strategic planning, the consultant developed a suggested strategy and presented it to the company's executive committee.

Following through on strategic planning

Though none of the committee members were critical of the plan, they were also not particularly enthusiastic about it. Nonetheless, Green adopted it for the company and committed Oilfield Supply to follow the strategy suggested by the consultant. Basically, the strategy consisted of three components: (1) Oilfield Supply would stop manufacturing its products and instead buy them from other manufacturers. (2) Using the money obtained from selling existing manufacturing facilities, OS would develop a new distribution system to cut delivery times in half. (3) The company would develop a new division to service off-shore drilling platforms.

For some reason, the results had not been what Green anticipated. Most of the strategic plan simply never seemed to get off the ground. True, the company had increased its sales substantially, but this was primarily attributable to the oil boom of the late 1970s. Oilfield Supply was still producing some of its products, although a couple of plants had been sold. The new distribution system had cut delivery times by 10 percent but was still a long way from its original target. And the new division was not yet turning a profit.

Green now feels that he has the solution, though: action planning. An elaborate strategy had been laid out for his firm, but it was never translated into operational terms. In particular, Green felt, OS needed a program to get completely out of manufacturing, a tactical plan to revamp its distribution system, and another tactical plan to turn its new division around. Green also recognized that the company needed more standing plans and that some consideration should be given to long-range planning.

CASE
QUESTIONS

1. Do you agree or disagree with Green's assessment of his current situation?
2. Are there any potential pitfalls you see ahead?
3. Besides a lack of action plans, what else could account for the company's mediocre performance?

7

MANAGERIAL DECISION MAKING

CHAPTER OBJECTIVES

1. Define *decision making*, explain how it differs from problem solving, and discuss the three states under which decisions can be made.

2. Identify the major assumptions of classical decision theory, and compare them to the assumptions of behavioral decision theory.

3. List the six steps in the decision making process and briefly describe each.

4. Summarize the advantages and disadvantages of group decision making, and discuss two common techniques for group decision making.

5. Discuss the nature of creativity and explain how it can be managed and maintained in organizations.

OPENING INCIDENT

You are the chief executive of one of the country's largest retailers. Almost 20 years ago, your company ventured half-heartedly into a new area of retailing. Today that division employs almost 25,000 people, has 336 outlets, and produces $2 billion in annual sales. Yet losses from the division run into the millions each year, and recent attempts to turn things around have not been successful. What would you do?

After decades of avoiding big retailing chains and focusing more on department and specialty stores, Levi Strauss recently began selling to Sears and J. C. Penney. The city of San Francisco decided that, rather than abandon its famed cable car system, it would spend $60 million and two years to renovate the system's trackage and machinery. Finally, CBS, HBO, and Columbia Pictures recently entered into a joint venture to form a new motion picture studio. Each company stands to gain: CBS gets a foothold in cable, HBO gets a new source of movies, and Columbia gets capital to finance more movies.[1]

What do these activities have in common? Each represents a major organizational decision. Levi Strauss decided to expand its marketing strategy. San Francisco decided to renovate its transportation system rather than replace it with a more contemporary system. CBS, HBO, and Columbia Pictures decided to pool their financial resources in such a way as to benefit each company.

The last three chapters have dealt with issues of organizational goals and objectives, strategy and strategic planning, and the development and implementation of plans. Implicit in these activities is the idea of decision making. Selecting a 10 percent sales increase instead of a 9 percent or 11 percent increase is a decision. To adopt one particular strategy over another (to take, for example, a prospector stance rather than an analyzer stance) is to make a decision. Choosing among various action plans, time frames, structural methods for dealing with planning, contingency plans, and methods for overcoming barriers to effective planning are all managerial decisions.

This chapter explores the decision making process itself. First we discuss the nature of decision making. We then describe two dominant models of decision making: classical and behavioral. Steps in the decision making process are summarized next. And, after a discussion of group decision making, we conclude by examining the role of creativity in decision making.

1. See "Visibility," *Fortune*, February 8, 1982, p. 14; "Will San Francisco Dissolve into the Fog Without Cable Cars?" *Wall Street Journal*, July 16, 1982, pp. 1, 6; and "Three's Company," *Fortune*, December 27, 1982, pp. 7–8.

The nature of decision making

Decisions are an integral part of all managerial activities, including organizing, leading, and controlling. However, decision making is usually most closely associated with the planning function, because it is an important tool for most planning activities.

Decision making defined

Decision making can be defined as the process of choosing one alternative from among a set of rational alternatives. (Of course, what is rational for one person may not be rational for another; this point will be pursued later in the chapter.) To fully appreciate our definition, we must first distinguish between decision making and problem solving and then describe what we mean by effective decision making.

In solving a mathematical problem (such as 6 × 8), a student theoretically can choose from among an infinite number of answers, but after considering a few of these answers, the student will probably recognize that only *one* is correct. Similarly, if a manager encounters a situation for which only one course of action is available, that course of action is the only solution to the problem. If two or more reasonable alternatives are available, however, the manager must make a decision. The primary distinction between problem solving and decision making is that the former involves determining the one correct solution, whereas the latter involves selecting one solution from among several alternatives, each of which could be correct under different circumstances.

Effective decision making requires an understanding of the situation. Most people would consider an effective decision to be one that *optimizes* some factor such as profits, sales, employee welfare, or market share. In some situations, though, an effective decision may be one that *minimizes* loss, expenses, or employee turnover. It may even mean selecting the best method for going out of business or terminating a contract.

The factors underlying a decision also influence its effectiveness. In early 1982, Brunswick Corporation of Skokie, Illinois, sold its most profitable division (Sherwood Medical Company) to American Home Products. Its objective was simply to make itself less attractive to Whittaker Corporation, which was considering buying the entire organization primarily to acquire Sherwood Medical Company. As a result, Whittaker did decide not to acquire Brunswick.[2] Given Brunswick's apparent goal of maintaining its autonomy, the decision to sell a profitable division was probably effective. Similarly, the effectiveness of any decision must be assessed in terms of the decision maker's underlying goal.

The decision making context

Decision theorists often debate whether decision making is better considered an individual phenomenon or an organizational phenomenon. That is, do

2. See "Selling the Jewel," *Fortune*, March 8, 1982, p. 8.

Figure 7.1
The decision making
context

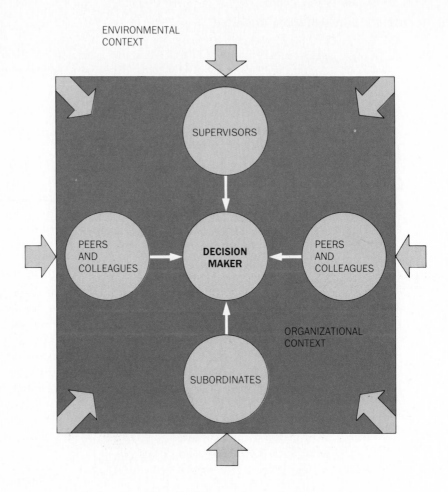

managers or organizations make decisions? In this text, managerial decision making is treated as essentially an individual process, but a process that occurs in an organizational context.[3] Figure 7.1 illustrates this point. At the center of the process is the individual decision making manager, but any given decision is likely to be influenced by a number of other people, departments, and/or organizations. Important influences shown in Figure 7.1 include supervisors, peers and colleagues, subordinates, other organizational components (such as other departments and their managers), and the environment (including elements of the task environment, such as competitors and suppliers, as well as general environmental factors such as technology and the economy).

3. See David W. Miller and Martin K. Starr, *The Structure of Human Decisions* (Englewood Cliffs, N.J.: Prentice-Hall, 1976); and Irving Janis and Leon Mann, *Decision Making* (New York: Free Press, 1977) for analyses of individual decision making. Alvar Elbing, *Behavioral Decisions in Organizations*, 2nd ed. (Glenview, Il.: Scott, Foresman, 1978) provides a thorough analysis of the organizational context of decision making.

Decision making conditions

Even though decision making is basically an individual process, the surrounding conditions can vary dramatically. In organizations, managers make decisions under conditions of certainty, risk, or uncertainty.[4] These conditions are represented in Figure 7.2.

Decision making under certainty. When managers know with certainty what their alternatives are and what conditions are associated with each alternative, a state of *certainty* exists. Suppose a manager is faced with the task of investing the organization's surplus cash. A bank might pay 7 percent interest on the money and allow withdrawals on 24-hour notice. Another institution might pay 9 percent but require a 30-day notice. A third institution might

Figure 7.2
Decision making
conditions

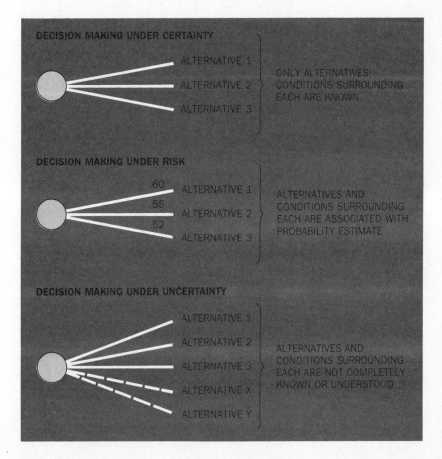

4. See Kenneth MacCrimmon and Ronald Taylor, "Decision Making and Problem Solving," in Marvin Dunnett (ed.), *Handbook of Industrial and Organizational Psychology* (Chicago: Rand McNally, 1976), pp. 1397–1454.

pay 12 percent but also impose an 8 percent penalty for withdrawal before the end of 6 months. The manager, then, knows the alternatives (7, 9, or 12 percent interest) and the conditions associated with each (penalty and/or required notice for withdrawal). A condition of certainty exists: the investment can be made with the full knowledge of what the payoff (and possible costs) will be.

In organizational settings, few decisions are made under conditions of certainty. The complexity and turbulence of contemporary society make such situations rare. Even the investment decision we just considered is not completely realistic, because the manager may not have been aware of all the possible alternatives. In some cases, the awarding of a contract on the basis of bids approaches a state of certainty, but contractors typically write cost-increase and/or inflation clauses into contracts so that, even here, the manager may not be 100 percent certain of the conditions surrounding each alternative.

Decision making under risk. A more common decision making situation is a state of risk. Under a state of *risk,* the availability of each alternative, the likelihood of its occurrence, and its potential payoffs and costs are all associated with a probability estimate.

Suppose a swimming pool dealer decides to acquire another business to bolster sales during slack seasons. Two candidates look attractive and the dealer must decide between them. Acquisition candidate number one has a stable product line with a stable growth rate. Candidate number two is much more aggressive but has had an erratic rate of growth. The manager can choose the first alternative, which will provide a safe, constant, but average return, or the second alternative, which has the potential to provide a spectacular return but might also turn out to be a financial loser. After careful study of the second alternative, the manager might decide with some confidence that it has a 10 percent chance of going broke, a 50 percent chance of doing just as well as the first candidate, and a 40 percent chance of doing much better. In investing the firm's money, then, the manager must decide how much risk he or she is willing to assume.

Obviously, the key element in decision making under a state of risk is accurately determining the probabilities associated with each alternative. In our example, if the second candidate had a 60 percent chance of going broke, a 20 percent chance of matching the first candidate's performance, and a 20 percent chance of excelling, a completely different situation would exist.

Hiram Walker Resources, a Canadian beverage producer, reported a decrease in the value of its assets of approximately $145 million after taxes in 1982. This loss stemmed from the purchase in 1981 of $630 million worth of U.S. gas and oil properties. The problem was that management at Hiram Walker assigned the wrong probabilities to future oil price changes and to the amount of gas and oil reserves actually on the properties. When prices declined and the reserves turned out to be smaller than predicted, the book value of the acquisitions plummeted.[5]

5. See Alexander Stuart, "Hiram Walker's Unhappy Morning After," *Fortune,* March 8, 1982, pp. 65–72.

Decision making under uncertainty. Most of the significant decision making in contemporary organizations is done under a state of *uncertainty,* wherein the decision maker does not know what all the alternatives are, what the probability is that each will occur, or what consequences each is likely to have. This uncertainty stems from the complexity and dynamism of contemporary organizations and their environments.

Consider a problem of technological innovation. A manufacturing manager faces the task of expanding production facilities to keep pace with the market. The obvious solution is to build a new plant. There is some chance, however, that a technological breakthrough may occur within two years and make existing production processes obsolete. The probability that the breakthrough will occur, if it does, and the probabilities associated with different times when it might occur are not known, resulting in a condition of uncertainty.

This decision situation is shown in a tree diagram in Figure 7.3, where it

Figure 7.3
Deciding under conditions of uncertainty

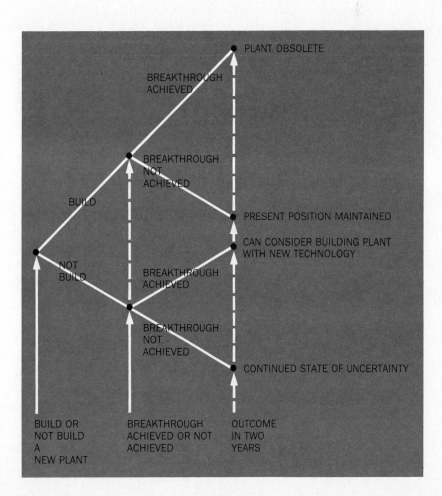

is apparent that four outcomes are possible. If the manager builds today and the breakthrough occurs in two years, the plant becomes obsolete (hence the decision was "wrong"). If the manager builds and the breakthrough does not occur, the manager can maintain market position (the decision was "right"). If the manager does not build today and the breakthrough occurs in two years, the manager can then build with the new technology (again, the "right" decision). Finally, the manager could elect not to build today and the breakthrough also may not occur. In two years, then, the same situation of uncertainty may exist (the decision might be "wrong" or "right," depending on the information available in two years). In situations like this, the manager must rely heavily on intuition and past experience. (More information about decision trees appears in the next chapter.)

A real decision made under uncertainty involved the short-lived World Football League in the early 1970s. Investors entered into the new sports league just as the nation's economy was taking a downturn and the interest in professional football was approaching the peak of its rapid growth cycle. Even though the league got off to a fairly smooth start, poor attendance and high player salaries caused it to fold in less than two years.[6]

On a more positive note, all successful organizations have made many effective decisions under uncertainty. For example, Financial Corporation of America has boosted its growth rate and profits dramatically by venturing into new and uncertain areas of investment and lending. The company increased its assets by 65 percent in 1982, while other savings and loan institutions lost an average of 73 cents on each $100 of assets.[7]

The key to effective decision making under uncertainty is to acquire as much relevant information as possible and to approach the situation from a logical and rational perspective. Intuition, judgment, and experience always play major roles in the decision making process under conditions of uncertainty.

Models of the decision making process

Over the years, the process of managerial decision making has been described from a variety of perspectives. The two most common approaches are called classical decision theory and behavioral decision theory.

Classical decision theory

Earlier in this chapter we noted that rationality is defined from the point of view of the individual. Classical decision theory, however, which was the dominant view of decision making during the first part of this century, assumed that rationality could always be defined from an economic perspective.

6. See John Clark, *Business Today—Successes and Failures* (New York: Random House, 1979).

7. See Gary Hector, "An S&L's Breathtaking Stunt," *Fortune*, July 12, 1982, pp. 69–80. See also Gary Hector, "A Daredevil S&L Shoots for Top Spot," *Fortune*, April 18, 1983, p. 111.

That is, managers were believed always to make decisions that were in the economic best interests of the organization. This view would assume that, if a manager determined that his or her own position in the firm was superfluous, he or she would recommend that it be eliminated. Classical decision theory also made certain other assumptions about the decision making process:

1. Decision makers have complete information regarding the decision situation.
2. Decision makers have complete information regarding all possible alternatives.
3. Decision makers have a rational system for ordering preferences in a hierarchy of importance.
4. The decision makers' goal is always to make the final choice in a fashion that will maximize the economic payoff to the organization.

Hence classical decision theory assumed that decision conditions could be altered so as to achieve some level of certainty. Armed with complete knowledge, managers could then select the alternative that best met the needs of the organization.

Managerial thinking during the heyday of classical decision theory was heavily influenced by economic concepts, including the concept that human behavior is unerringly rational. Many managers even today assume that they and others will be rational decision makers. But it has been shown that in many cases our personal preferences, attitudes, emotions, and motives influence our decision making behavior. A model of decision making that better reflects these subjective considerations is behavioral decision theory.

Behavioral decision theory

One of the first writers to recognize that rationality and economic criteria do not accurately describe decision making processes was Herbert A. Simon.[8] (Simon was subsequently awarded the Nobel Prize in economics for his contributions.) In contrast to classical ideas, behavioral decision theory makes the following assumptions about the decision making process:

1. Decision makers have *incomplete* information regarding the decision situation.
2. Decision makers have *incomplete* information regarding all possible alternatives.
3. Decision makers are *unable* and/or *unwilling* to fully anticipate the consequences of each available alternative.

One important concept that Simon derived from these ideas is the notion of **bounded rationality.** He specifically notes that decision makers are limited by their values and unconscious reflexes, skills, and habits. They are also lim-

---

8. See Herbert A. Simon, *Administrative Behavior.* (New York: Free Press, 1945). Simon's ideas have been recently refined and updated in Herbert A. Simon, *Administrative Behavior*, 3rd ed. (New York: Free Press, 1976).

ited by less-than-complete information and knowledge. Further, he argues that "the individual can be rational in terms of the organization's goals only to the extent that he is *able* to pursue a particular course of action, he has a correct conception of the *goal* of the action, and he is correctly *informed* about the conditions surrounding his choice. Within the boundaries laid down by these factors his choices are rational-goal-oriented."[9] Essentially, Simon suggests that people may try to be rational decision makers but that their rationality has limits.

Consider the case of a manager attempting to decide where to locate a new manufacturing facility. To be rational, he or she must have the power and ability to make the correct decision, must clearly understand what the new facility is to do, and must have complete information about all alternatives. It is very unlikely that all of these conditions will be met, so the decision maker's rationality is bounded by situational factors.

Another important concept developed by Simon is *satisficing*, which suggests that, rather than conducting an exhaustive search for the best possible alternative, decision makers tend to search only until they identify an alternative that meets some minimum standard of sufficiency. In the case of the manager who must choose a site for a new plant, some of the minimum requirements for the site may be that it must be within 500 yards of a railroad spur and within 2 miles of a major highway, be located in a community of at least 40,000 people, and cost less than $1,000,000. After a period of searching, the manager may locate a site 490 yards from a railroad spur, 1.8 miles from a highway, in a community of 41,000 people, and with a price tag of $950,000. The satisficing concept suggests that she or he will select this site even though further searching might reveal a better one.

People tend to satisfice for a variety of reasons. Managers may simply be unwilling to ignore their own motives and therefore not be able to continue searching after a minimally acceptable alternative is identified. The decision maker may be unable to weigh and evaluate large numbers of alternatives and criteria. Subjective and personal considerations often intervene in decision situations. For example, the final criterion used to select a plant site might be its proximity to the manager's home town. For all these reasons, the satisficing process plays a major role in decision making.

In the remainder of this chapter, we will attempt to describe decision making from two perspectives: (1) how it should be done from a rational and objective perspective and (2) how behavioral considerations such as bounded rationality and satisficing influence the overall process.

Steps in decision making

Most decision making consists of several separate steps, which are summarized in Table 7.1. As we have demonstrated, however, actual decision making may not always be as rational as Table 7.1 implies. As we consider the steps in-

9. See Simon, *Administrative Behavior*, 3rd ed., p. 241.

Table 7.1 Steps in the decision making process

Step	Detail	Example
1. Recognizing and defining the situation	Some stimulus or spark indicates that a decision must be made. The stimulus or spark may be positive or negative.	A plant manager sees that employee turnover has increased by 5 percent.
2. Developing alternatives	Both obvious and creative alternatives are desired. In general, the more significant the decision, the more alternatives should be generated.	The plant manager can increase wages, increase benefits, or change hiring standards.
3. Evaluating alternatives	Each alternative is evaluated to determine its feasibility, its satisfactoriness, and its consequences.	Increasing benefits may not be feasible. Increasing wages and changing hiring standards may satisfy all conditions.
4. Selecting the best alternative	Consider all situational factors, and choose the alternative that best fits the manager's situation.	Changing hiring standards will take an extended period of time to cut turnover, so increase wages.
5. Implementing the chosen alternative	The chosen alternative is implemented into the organizational system.	The plant manager may need permission of corporate headquarters. The personnel department establishes a new wage structure.
6. Follow-up and evaluation	At some time in the future, the manager should ascertain the extent to which the alternative chosen in step 4 and implemented in step 5 has worked.	The plant manager notes that, six months later, turnover has dropped to its previous level.

volved in the decision making process, we should interpret the table as normative ("how it should be done"). And at appropriate places, we will note how behavioral decision theory can contribute to our understanding of decision making.

Recognizing and defining the situation

The first step in making a decision is recognizing that a decision is necessary—there must be some stimulus or spark to initiate the process. For many small-scale decisions, the stimulus may occur without any prior warning. When a piece of equipment breaks, the manager must decide whether to repair or replace it. The stimulus for a decision may be positive as well as negative. A manager who must decide how to invest surplus funds, for example, clearly faces a decision situation. Hence a "problem" can be either a good thing or a bad thing. In this sense, a decision about which of two attractive job offers to accept is a problem.

An effective manager is able to anticipate major decision situations so as to not be caught unprepared. A series of cues should serve to indicate that a decision situation is imminent. In 1980 International Harvester lost $397 million; in 1981 the loss was $393 million. Factors contributing to these massive losses included a six-month strike by the United Auto Workers and a shrinking market.[10] Management might have anticipated such a disastrous situation by being more sensitive to labor relations and by better interpreting various financial reports and sales projections. The situation clearly called for a number of major decisions in order to put the company in the black again.

In addition to recognizing the need for a decision or set of decisions, the manager must also define the situation, which is partly a matter of determining how the problem that is being addressed came about. This is an important step, because the situation definition plays a major role in subsequent steps. Suppose, for example, that a manufacturer of venetian blinds has had decreasing sales for the last two years. One manager might define this as a situation in which the product's appeal to the public has run its course and begin to search for a replacement product. Another manager might define the situation as a case of slippage in advertising and promotion and look for ways to improve them. The problem—declining sales—is the same in both cases, but the two different definitions of the situation call for two very different solutions.

Also clearly apparent in this situation is the behavioral impact on problem definition. That is, individual predispositions and values usually affect how people define problems. If the venetian blind manager doesn't like the product and feels that demand for it has run its course, declining sales can be used as evidence to support its elimination. Another manager, who helped develop this particular product line and started with the company by selling venetian blinds, may be more inclined to increase advertising and promotion.

Developing alternatives

Once the decision situation has been recognized and appropriately defined, the second step in the process is to develop alternative courses of action to deal with the situation. It is generally useful to design the process in such a way that both obvious, standard solutions *and* creative, innovative solutions or alternatives are generated.

A useful technique for stimulating creativity is brainstorming. In a brainstorming session, individuals in a group suggest as many alternatives as they can think of, no matter how novel or unusual. One of the rules of brainstorming is that criticism and evaluation must be withheld, so people feel free to offer suggestions that might otherwise seem unacceptable. Ideas generated in such an atmosphere often turn out to be of surprising value. (We will discuss creativity and brainstorming in more detail later in this chapter.)

In general, the more important the decision, the more attention is directed to developing alternatives. If the decision involves where to build a multimillion-dollar office building, a great deal of time and expertise will be

10. See "How International Harvester Hopes to Return to the Black," *Fortune,* January 25, 1982, p. 7.

devoted to identifying the best locations. After Union Carbide decided in 1976 to move its corporate headquarters from New York City, the company spent two years searching for the best location before selecting Danbury, Connecticut.[11] If the problem is to choose a color for the company softball team uniforms, less time and expertise will be brought to bear.

In the financial dilemma faced by International Harvester, management identified several alternatives for dealing with the situation. These included reducing fixed costs, disposing of subsidiaries, reducing the size of the work force, and seeking wage concessions from the UAW.[12]

Differences between the classical and the behavioral views of decision making become apparent here. The former assumes that all alternatives will be identified, whereas the latter suggests that only some alternatives will be considered. This second situation clearly occurs most frequently.

Although managers should encourage creative solutions, they should also recognize that various constraints often limit their alternatives. Common constraints include legal restrictions, moral and ethical norms, authority constraints, or constraints imposed by the power and authority of the manager, available technology, economic considerations, and unofficial social norms.[13]

Evaluating alternatives

The third step in the decision making process is evaluating each of the alternatives generated in the previous step. Usually, each alternative should be assessed to determine its feasibility, its satisfactoriness, and its consequences. The process of applying these criteria is shown in Figure 7.4.

The first question to ask is whether a proposed alternative exhibits feasibility. Is it within the realm of probability and practicality? For a small, struggling firm, an alternative requiring a huge financial outlay would probably be out of the question. Even larger firms have financial limits that would rule out various alternatives. Other alternatives may not be feasible because of legal barriers such as legislation and zoning ordinances. And limited human, material, and information resources may make other alternatives impracticable.

When an alternative has passed the test of feasibility, it must next be examined to see how satisfactory it would be. Satisfactoriness refers to the extent to which the alternative will satisfy the conditions of the decision situation. For example, a manager may be searching for ways to expand production capability by 50 percent. One alternative is to purchase an existing plant from another company. Upon examination, however, the manager may discover that the plant would increase production capability by only 35 percent, which is unsatisfactory. Depending on the circumstances, the manager may decide to buy the plant anyway and search for other ways to achieve the remaining

11. See Walter McQuade, "Union Carbide Takes to the Woods," *Fortune*, December 13, 1982, pp. 164–174.

12. See "How International Harvester Hopes to Return to the Black."

13. See Fremont Shull, Andre Delbecq, and L. L. Cummings, *Organizational Decision Making* (New York: McGraw-Hill, 1970).

Figure 7.4
Evaluating alternatives in the decision making process

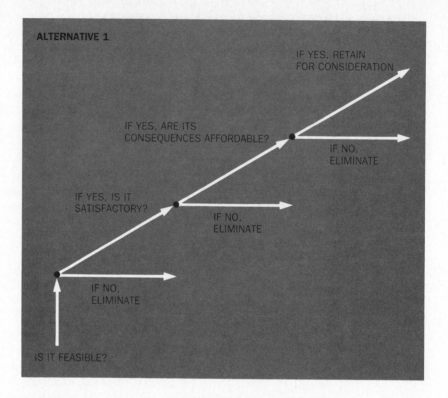

15 percent expansion. Or she or he may simply drop the proposed purchase of that plant from consideration.

Finally, when an alternative has proved both feasible and satisfactory, its probable consequences must still be assessed. To what extent will adopting a particular alternative influence various parts of the organization? What costs (both financial and nonfinancial) will be associated with such influences? For example, a plan to boost sales by cutting prices may also disrupt cash flows, require a new advertising program, and alter the behavior of sales representatives because of a different commission structure. (This bears out what we learned from systems theory in Chapter 2—that changes in one subsystem are likely to affect other subsystems as well.) The manager, then, must put "price-tags" on the consequences of each alternative. Even an alternative that is both feasible and satisfactory must be eliminated if its consequences are too expensive for the total system.

Selecting the best alternative

Even though many alternatives will fail to pass the triple test of feasibility, satisfactoriness, and affordable consequences, it is likely that two or more alternatives will remain. Choosing the best of these is the real crux of the decision making process. Several points should be considered when selecting an alternative.

One approach is to choose the alternative with the highest combined level of feasibility, satisfactoriness, and affordable consequences. Though most situations do not lend themselves to objective, mathematical analysis, the manager can usually develop subjective estimates and weights for making the decision.

Closely related is the issue of optimization versus maximization (introduced in Chapter 4). Because any decision situation is likely to affect several individuals and/or subunits in an organization, any feasible alternative will probably not maximize, or completely achieve, all of the relevant goals. Suppose a team manager needs to select a starting centerfielder for a baseball team. Player A might hit .350 but not be able to catch a fly ball, player B might hit only .175 but be perfect in the field, and player C might hit .290 and be a solid but not perfect fielder. Most managers would select player C because of the optimal balance of hitting and fielding.

Managers charged with selecting the best should always remember to consider the idea of multiple acceptable alternatives. It may not be necessary to select just one alternative and reject all the others. In our baseball example, the team manager might decide that player C will start each game, player A will be retained as a pinch-hitter, and player B will be retained as a defensive substitute. In many hiring decisions, the candidates remaining after step 3 (evaluation) are ranked. If person number 1 rejects the offer, it is automatically extended to person number 2, and so on. In our earlier example of a need to increase production capability by 50 percent, an optimal solution might be to increase capability by 35 percent by purchasing the additional plant and then pick up the other 15 percent by expanding an existing plant.

Implementation

After one or more alternatives have been selected, the manager must put the alternative(s) into effect. In some decision situations, implementation may be fairly easy; in other situations it may be quite difficult. Take the case of an acquisition. The manager must decide how to integrate all the activities of the new business, ranging from purchasing to personnel practices to distribution, into an on-going organizational framework.

The key to effective implementation is action planning. Tactical plans, operational plans and programs, and standing plans are all appropriate techniques for solving organizational problems arising from decision situations. A program, for example, might be developed for the express purpose of implementing a course of action that has been selected for resolving an organizational problem. A manufacturer may have determined that a decline in overall profitability has been caused by technological obsolescence in one of its plants. The solution may be to close the plant. Lower-level managers, in turn, might develop a program for funneling customer orders from that plant to other facilities, for relocating personnel, for disposing of the equipment, and so on.

Another issue to consider when implementing decisions is people's resistance to change. The reasons for such resistance include insecurity, inconvenience, and fear of the unknown. Hence managers should anticipate potential resistance at various stages of the implementation process. More information on resistance to change appears in Chapter 12.

In a related vein, managers should recognize that, even when all alternatives have been evaluated as precisely as possible and the consequences of each alternative weighed, it is likely that unanticipated consequences will also arise. Unexpected cost increases, a less-than-perfect "fit" with existing organizational subsystems, unpredicted effects on cash-flow operating expenses, and any number of other situations could develop after the implementation process has begun.

Follow-up and evaluation

As the final step in the decision making process, managers should be sure to evaluate the effectiveness of their decision. That is, they should make sure that the alternative chosen in step 4 and implemented in step 5 accomplished the desired result. If the initial situation was an increase in absenteeism and turnover, the alternative chosen to deal with this situation may have been an incentive system to reward attendance. If attendance does in fact improve to the desired level, the manager can assume that the optimal alternative was chosen and the situation has been corrected. On the other hand, if attendance does not improve, the manager should recognize that the chosen alternative is not working and that other action may be necessary.

When an implemented alternative appears not to be working, the manager can respond in any of several ways. One of the alternatives that was identified previously (the second or third choice) could be adopted. Or the manager might recognize that the situation was not correctly defined to start with and begin the decision making process all over again. Finally, the manager might decide that the alternative originally chosen *is* in fact appropriate, but that it simply has not yet had time to work or should be implemented in a different way.

An effective process for evaluating alternatives is shown in Figure 7.5.

Figure 7.5
Evaluating the effectiveness of decisions

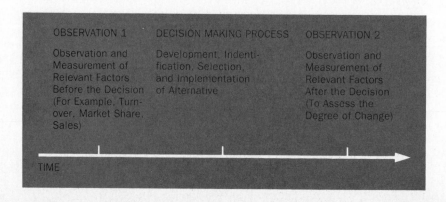

OBSERVATION 1

Observation and Measurement of Relevant Factors Before the Decision (For Example, Turnover, Market Share, Sales)

DECISION MAKING PROCESS

Development, Indentification, Selection, and Implementation of Alternative

OBSERVATION 2

Observation and Measurement of Relevant Factors After the Decision (To Assess the Degree of Change)

TIME

"That makes four 'Yes'es and one 'No, no, a thousand times no.'"

Drawing by Vietor © 1982 The New Yorker Magazine, Inc.

Prior to the actual decision, existing conditions relevant to the decision itself are observed, assessed, and/or measured. This step can be viewed as being complementary to step 1 in the decision making process (see Table 7.1). In many cases, for example, managers may have to observe closely or measure a situation in order to be certain that a problem exists. The middle box in Figure 7.5 represents steps 2 through 5 of the decision making process. Finally, a post-decision observation should be made to determine how successful the decision was in solving the original problem.

Group decision making

In more and more organizations today, important decisions are made by groups rather than individuals. Examples range from executive committees to design teams to marketing planning groups. Both business and nonbusiness organizations rely on group decision making, and very often decisions are reached through some kind of consensus process rather than by taking a vote. This section explores the advantages and disadvantages of group decision making and then discusses two popular techniques for managing the process.

Advantages of group decision making

The advantages and disadvantages of group decision making are summarized in Table 7.2.[14] One advantage of group decision making over individual decision making is that there is simply more information available in a group set-

14. See Norman P. R. Maier, "Assets and Liabilities in Group Problem Solving: The Need for an Integrative Function," in J. Richard Hackman, Edward E. Lawler, III, and Lyman W. Porter (eds.), *Perspectives on Behavior in Organizations*, 2nd ed. (New York: McGraw-Hill, 1983), pp. 385–392.

Table 7.2 Advantages and disadvantages of group decision making

Advantages	Disadvantages
1. More information and knowledge are available.	1. The process takes longer, so it is costlier.
2. More alternatives are likely to be generated.	2. Compromise decisions resulting from indecisiveness may emerge.
3. More acceptance of the final decision is likely.	3. One person may dominate the group.
4. Enhanced communication of the decision may result.	4. Groupthink may occur.
5. More accurate decisions generally emerge.	

ting. As suggested by the old axiom "two heads are better than one," when a group is assembled, a variety of education, experience, and perspective is represented. If one manager is very familiar with television and radio advertising and another is an expert on in-store promotion, their pooled expertise in devising an overall advertising campaign is substantially greater than that possessed by either working alone. Partly as a result of this increased information, groups typically can identify and evaluate more alternatives than one individual could. Furthermore, people who are involved in making a decision are more likely to be genuinely committed to the final alternative selected than if someone else had made the decision and imposed it on them. The people involved in a group decision understand the logic and rationale behind it and are better equipped to communicate the decision to their work groups or departments. Finally, research evidence suggests that groups actually may make better decisions than individuals.[15]

Disadvantages of group decision making

Perhaps the biggest drawback of group decision making, compared with individual decision making, is the additional time and (hence) the greater expense entailed. The increased time stems from interaction and discussion among group members. If a manager's time is worth, say, $50 an hour, and if the manager spends 2 hours making a decision, the cost of the decision activity to the organization is $100. For the same decision, a group of 5 managers might require 3 hours of time. At the same $50-an-hour rate, the organization is paying $750 for the decision. If the group decision is somehow better, the additional expense may be justified, but group decision making *is* more costly and should be used only when the results are likely to justify the expense.

15. See James H. Davis, *Group Performance* (Reading, Mass.: Addison-Wesley, 1969); and Linda N. Jewell and H. Joseph Reitz, *Group Effectiveness in Organizations* (Glenview, Il.: Scott, Foresman, 1981).

Group decisions may also represent undesirable compromises. For example, hiring a compromise top manager may be a bad decision in the long run because he or she may not be able to respond adequately to *any* of the various special subunits in the organization.

Sometimes one individual dominates the group process to the point where others cannot make a full contribution. This dominance may stem from a desire for power or a naturally dominant personality. The problem is that what appears to emerge as a group decision may actually be the decision of one person.

Finally, a group may succumb to a phenomenon known as groupthink. *Groupthink* occurs when the group's desire for consensus and cohesiveness overwhelms its desire to reach the best possible decisions.[16] Under the insidious influence of groupthink, the group may arrive at decisions that are not in the best interest of either the group or the organization, but rather avoid conflict among group members. One of the clearest examples of groupthink that has been documented arose among President John F. Kennedy and his advisers as they came to their decision to support the Bay of Pigs invasion of Cuba in the early 1960s. The Bay of Pigs invasion, intended to undermine Fidel Castro's government, turned out to be one of this country's greatest military fiascos. Yet Kennedy and all of his key advisers had given the invasion their whole-hearted support because they felt that the United States' involvement would be kept secret, that the Cuban military was not effective, that the invasion would spark the Cuban underground into action, and that retreat would be possible if the invasion failed. When all of these assumptions proved wrong, the tragedy that ensued was inevitable.

Fortunately, there are a few things a group can do to avoid groupthink. Each member of the group should critically evaluate all alternatives. The leader should not make her or his own position known too early so that divergent viewpoints can be presented. At least one member of the group should be assigned the role of devil's advocate. And, after reading a preliminary decision, the group should hold a follow-up meeting wherein divergent viewpoints can be raised again, if any group member wishes to do so.[17]

Techniques for group decision making

A number of techniques have been developed to manage or structure the group decision making process. Two of the more popular techniques are the Delphi technique and the nominal group technique. These are summarized in Table 7.3.

The Delphi technique. The *Delphi technique* is a method for developing a consensus of expert opinion. Developed by the Rand Corporation, the Delphi technique solicits input from a panel of experts who contribute individually. Their opinions are combined and, in effect, averaged. Assume that the prob-

16. See Irving L. Janis, *Groupthink*, 2nd ed. (Boston: Houghton Mifflin, 1982).
17. See Janis, *Groupthink.*

Table 7.3 Techniques for group decision making

1. **The Delphi technique.** The systematic refinement of expert opinion. Not feasible for routine decisions. More appropriate for broad, long-range issues such as future technological breakthroughs, economic conditions, and so forth.
2. **The nominal group technique.** Used to generate creative and innovative alternatives. More feasible for routine decisions. Involves generating, discussing, and voting on a variety of alternatives.

lem is to establish an expected date for a major technological breakthrough in converting coal into usable energy. The first step in using the Delphi technique is to obtain the cooperation of a panel of experts. For this situation, experts might include various research scientists, university researchers, and executives in a relevant energy industry. At first, the experts are asked to anonymously predict a time frame for the expected breakthrough. The persons conducting the Delphi collect the responses, average them, and ask the experts for another prediction. In this round, the experts who provided unusual or extreme predictions are asked to justify them. These explanations may then be relayed to the other experts. When the predictions stabilize, the average prediction is taken to represent the decision of the "group" of experts.

The time, expense, and logistics of the Delphi technique rule out its use for routine, everyday decisions, but it has been successfully used for forecasting technological breakthroughs, market potential for new products, research and development patterns, and future economic conditions.[18]

Nominal group technique. Another valuable method for managing group decision making is the *nominal group technique,* or NGT. Unlike the Delphi method, wherein group members do not see one another, group members in an NGT session are in the same room. As implied by the term *nominal,* however, the members represent a group in name only; they do not interact in a fashion typical of most groups.

Nominal groups are used most often to generate creative and innovative alternatives or ideas. To begin, the manager assembles a group of knowledgeable people and outlines the problem to them. The group members are then asked to individually write down as many alternatives as they can think of. The members then take turns stating their ideas, which are recorded on a flip chart or blackboard at the front of the room. Discussion is limited to simple clarification. After all alternatives have been listed, more open discussion takes place. Group members then vote, usually by rank-ordering the various alter-

18. See Andre L. Delbecq, Andrew H. Van de Ven, and David H. Gustafson, *Group Techniques for Program Planning* (Glenview, Il.: Scott, Foresman, 1975); and Jewell and Reitz, *Group Effectiveness in Organizations.*

natives. The highest-ranking alternative represents the decision of the group. Of course, the manager in charge may retain the authority to accept or reject the group decision.

Obviously the NGT is similar to brainstorming. The primary advantage of the NGT is that it identifies a large number of alternatives while minimizing individual inhibitions about expressing unusual or novel ideas. On the negative side, if the manager ultimately rejects the group decision, enthusiasm for participating in the future is likely to be dampened. On balance, the NGT appears to be a valuable tool for group decision making.[19]

Creativity in decision making

Creativity and its role in decision making are nebulous concepts. *Creativity* can be defined as the process of developing original, imaginative, and innovative perspectives on situations. Of course, it is not something that a manager can turn on or off like an electric calculator or apply mechanically like a mathematical model. Still it is important to understand what creativity is and how to nurture and harness it for purposes of decision making.

The nature of creativity

Given the abstract nature of creativity, it is not surprising that we know little about it and how it works. Nonetheless, research has provided some insights about creativity and how it affects us as individuals.

The process of creativity. Most creative accomplishments involve four general phases or stages: preparation, incubation, insight, and verification.[20] (See Figure 7.6.)

Figure 7.6
The creativity process

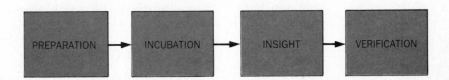

PREPARATION → INCUBATION → INSIGHT → VERIFICATION

19. See Delbecq et al., *Group Techniques for Program Planning;* Jewell and Reitz, *Group Effectiveness in Organizations;* and Richard Woodman, "Use of the Nominal Group Technique for Idea Generation and Decision Making," *The Texas Business Executive,* Spring 1981, pp. 50–53.

20. See Thomas V. Busse and Richard S. Mansfield, "Theories of the Creative Process: A Review and a Perspective," *Journal of Creative Behavior,* Vol. 4, No. 2, 1980, pp. 91–103, 132, for other perspectives on the process of creativity.

Education and formal training are often a part of the preparation phase of creativity. (It is unlikely that an uneducated person could achieve great breakthroughs in theoretical physics.) Preparation can also involve a much shorter and narrower perspective, however. An artist creating a new advertising campaign may prepare by researching the product and the promotional campaigns used for competing products. This preparation may take only a few days or weeks.

Incubation usually involves a period of relaxation after a sustained period of preparation. The phrase "let's sleep on it" refers to the need for incubation. The human mind gathers and sorts data, but then it needs time to let things jell and fall into place. Incubation may occur when one is sleeping, visiting with friends, driving, chopping wood, painting, or doing whatever the individual finds relaxing. The point is simply that, after preparing for a situation, creative people usually spend some time directing their energies toward other pursuits before confronting that situation again.

During the insight phase, the individual becomes aware of a new idea or solution. Insight may occur rapidly or develop gradually. It may be triggered by a new fact, or it may represent a systematic synthesis of all the information gathered during the preparation phase.

Finally, the individual must verify the appropriateness of the solution or the idea. If a new product would cost more to build than consumers would be willing to pay, it would obviously not be a good idea to build the product. The verification process usually includes confirming the newness of the idea and then communicating it to appropriate audiences.

Characteristics of creative people. Just as everyone wants to be considered intelligent and hard-working, people like to feel that they are creative. Unfortunately, however, not everyone is. Researchers have investigated relationships between creativity and a variety of individual characteristics with varying degrees of success. There appears to be little overlap between intelligence and creativity, for example,[21] and there appears to be no difference in creativity between males and females. Other characteristics have been shown to be more consistently related to creativity. The typical period of greatest creativity for most people seems to be between the ages of 30 and 40. Creative people also tend to be less susceptible to social influence than less creative people.

Managing creativity in organizations

For the concept of creativity to be of value to the manager, it must be useful in decision making and other organizational activities. Creative processes must be harnessed and focused on organizational problems. Two widely used techniques for channeling creativity are brainstorming and synectics.

---

21. See Anne Anastasi and C. E. Schaefer, "Note on the Concepts of Creativity and Intelligence," *Journal of Creative Behavior*, Vol. 5, No. 2, 1971, pp. 113–116.

Brainstorming. Brainstorming, as introduced earlier in this chapter, is a technique for stimulating novel and imaginative ideas and alternatives. The basic ground rules for a brainstorming session are as follows:[22]

1. Participants are encouraged to suggest wild and extreme ideas.
2. Participants are encouraged to build on suggestions made by others.
3. Participants are forbidden to criticize the ideas of others.

The purpose of brainstorming is to foster free thinking while sparing participants the inhibiting threat of ridicule. Brainstorming is used in advertising, new product development, and other complex decision situations. Though brainstorming is most often performed by groups, some research suggests that individual brainstorming may be even more effective.[23]

Synectics. A second method for sparking creativity is synectics.[24] Whereas brainstorming focuses on generating a large number of alternatives, synectics attempts to identify one radically different new idea or solution. In order to discourage obvious or easy solutions, the group leader does not explain the exact nature of the situation at first. Instead, she or he leads the discussion toward the general area of the situation of interest. For example, an assignment for a group of restaurant chain managers might be to identify a new concept in family dining. The leader could begin by having the group discuss family leisure activities. Areas the group might explore could include movies, electronic game parlors, and recreational activities. The leader could then direct the discussion toward leisure activities having more to do with eating out. Focusing originally on leisure as opposed to dining should put group members in a frame of mind to develop new and unusual ideas. One solution that might emerge is a restaurant–electronic game complex where families could play the games and also purchase pizza and hamburgers. And, in fact, this is almost exactly the thought process Nolan Bushnell used when he developed Pizza Time Theatre and its mascot, Chuck E. Cheese.[25]

Maintaining creativity in organizations

Whereas brainstorming and synectics are useful for harnessing creativity, organizations may be even better served by trying to foster conditions that will stimulate and maintain creativity over time. A variety of activities can help maintain creativity in organizations.[26] People who come up with creative ideas

22. See Jewell and Reitz, *Group Effectiveness in Organizations*, p. 96.

23. See Donald W. Taylor, Paul C. Berry, and Clifford H. Block, "Does Group Participation When Using Brainstorming Techniques Facilitate or Inhibit Creative Thinking?" *Administrative Science Quarterly*, June 1958, pp. 23–47.

24. See William J. Gordon, *Synectics* (New York: Collier Books, 1968).

25. See Gwen Kinkead, "High Profits from a Weird Pizza Combination," *Fortune*, July 26, 1982, pp. 62–66.

26. See H. Joseph Reitz, *Behavior in Organizations*, rev. ed. (Homewood, Il.: Irwin, 1981), pp. 186–189.

should be rewarded, and, though creativity can't be turned on and off, goals and deadlines often spark creative behavior. Putting things off can cause problems, and the pressure of a deadline can be the catalyst that people need to achieve creative insights. Extended effort over a period of time can also result in creative outcomes. Finally, organizations must make sure that they do not unduly constrain and limit individual freedom and autonomy. Virtually any decision situation requires some set of parameters and guidelines, but people must be given the time and resources for preparation and incubation if creative insights are to emerge.

Summary of key points

Decisions are an integral part of all managerial activities (planning, organizing, leading, and controlling), but they are perhaps most central to the planning process.

Decision making can be defined as choosing one alternative from among a set of rational alternatives. Problem solving and decision making are distinguishable in that the former results in one "correct" answer, whereas the latter requires the individual to choose from among more than one potentially "correct" answer. Decision making processes are considered an individual phenomenon, albeit a phenomenon that occurs in an organizational context consisting of superiors, subordinates, peers, and colleagues, as well as various groups, units, departments, and environmental factors.

Decisions may be made under states of certainty, risk, or uncertainty. Classical decision theory assumes that managers have complete information, that they will behave rationally, and that economic criteria will always guide their decision processes. The more realistic behavioral decision theory recognizes that managers will have incomplete information, that they will not always behave rationally, and that they will take into account factors other than economic criteria. Behavioral decision theory also includes the concepts of bounded rationality and satisficing.

The primary steps in an ideal decision making process are (1) recognizing and defining the situation, (2) developing alternatives that might be appropriate, (3) evaluating each alternative in terms of its feasibility, satisfactoriness, and potential consequences, (4) selecting the best alternative, (5) implementing the chosen alternative, and (6) following up and evaluating the effectiveness of the alternative after it is implemented.

Group decision making has a number of advantages and disadvantages compared to individual decision making. The Delphi technique and the nominal group technique are methods for increasing the advantages and limiting the disadvantages of group decision making.

Creativity is an important element in decision making. The creative process typically involves preparation, incubation, insight, and verification. Some people are more creative than others, although little is known about what causes these differences. Two techniques that are sometimes used to manage creativity are brainstorming and synectics. Creativity can be maintained by reinforcing creative behavior, establishing goals and deadlines, encouraging extended effort, and recognizing the value of affording employees freedom and autonomy.

QUESTIONS FOR DISCUSSION

1. Try to think of five examples of decision making under certainty. Why is this difficult to do? How do the different states affect the decision making process?
2. Think of decisions you have made under conditions of risk and uncertainty. Which type is easier to make? Why?
3. Which of the assumptions of the classical decision making theories do you think is the most unrealistic? Why?
4. Can you think of examples of satisficing that you have either engaged in yourself or observed in others?
5. Which of the six steps in the decision making process seem to be ignored most frequently by practicing managers? Discuss the argument that the only step which really should be taken formally is the selection step.
6. Think about decisions you have had to make in your life, such as selecting a college or university and choosing a major. Did you follow a rational or a behavioral decision model? Did you consciously take all six steps described in the text?
7. Can you think of other advantages or disadvantages of group decision making? Give examples of the advantages and disadvantages of group decision making drawn from groups you have been a part of.
8. In addition to "withholding criticism," what other "rules" would be helpful during a brainstorming session?
9. Can creativity be learned? Why or why not?
10. Think of some creative new products that have been particularly successful and some that have been unsuccessful. Why did they succeed or fail? Can an unsuccessful idea really be creative?

C A S E 7.1

At the beginning of this chapter, you read an incident about a large retailer who, twenty years earlier, had moved half-heartedly into a new area of retailing. The new division had grown to become a major part of the company but was still losing money. The retailer in question was F. W. Woolworth Company, the division Woolco discount stores. The case that follows describes what Woolworth did and then raises some issues for your consideration.

Evaluating Woolworth's decisions

In 1962 an event occurred that would forever change the face of nonfood retailing in the United States. The Kresge company opened the first K mart store and plunged full-speed-ahead into large-scale discount retailing. Kresge would become the second largest nonfood retailer (behind Sears); it eventually changed its corporate name to K mart to reflect its commitment to this form of retailing.

Before 1962 Kresge had battled for the consumer's dollar against such other variety stores as Woolworth, W. T. Grant, and Ben Franklin. In the same year that the first K mart opened, Woolworth also opened its own large discount store, Woolco. Whereas Kresge was soon opening as many as 200 K mart stores per year, Woolworth expanded much more slowly. By 1977 there were 381 Woolco stores open, compared with 1,367 K marts.

Woolworth originally established separate operating divisions for its existing Woolworth stores and its new Woolco stores, but in 1971, management was forced to change this method of organization because of in-fighting and conflict between the two divisions.

Even though K mart had recently begun to diversify, discounting has been and will continue to be the core of its operations. At Woolworth, however, management made a conscious decision to remain broad-based and to avoid dependence on one division. In 1963 the company purchased Kinney Shoe, and in 1969 acquired the Richman Brothers clothing chain. Kinney later branched out into athletic shoes with a chain of Foot Locker stores.

By 1982 there were 336 Woolco stores in operation, employing almost 25,000 people. The Woolco stores accounted for around $2 billion in annual sales, but they were marginally profitable at best. In the final half of 1982, Woolco stores lost $21 million for Woolworth.

Woolworth management made repeated attempts in the late 1970s and early 1980s to turn Woolco around, including hiring a new top manager away from Target. It was all to no avail. In late 1982 Edward Gibbons, CEO of Woolworth, announced that in early 1983 the company would close all 336 Woolco stores. Further, the company would divest itself of its 52.6 percent ownership of 1,000 Woolworth stores in Great Britain. In one of the largest retailing liquidations in history, Woolworth reduced its size by almost 30 percent.

Woolworth's plan is to concentrate on its remaining divisions and expand cautiously into other areas. Both Kinney and Richman are doing well. The company's Foot Locker chain has been especially successful. One new venture is J. Brannam, a shortened version of "just brand names." J. Brannam will sell brand-name merchandise aimed at upper-middle-class consumers—but at discount prices.

In addition, the company plans to retain its chain of Woolworth variety stores. As the largest such chain in the country, Woolworth stores may be able to generate reasonable profits by handling merchandise with broad appeal at cut-rate prices. Tough times remain, however, if the company is to reclaim its former status in the eyes of the American shopper.

CASE QUESTIONS

1. Identify the major decisions made by Kresge and Woolworth in this case and compare their relative effectiveness. Characterize each decision in terms of the conditions surrounding it at the time.

2. Besides closing the Woolco stores, what other alternatives did Woolworth have?

3. Brainstorm some other areas of retailing that Woolworth might pursue.

CASE REFERENCES

Clark, John. *Business Today—Successes and Failures.* New York: Random House, 1979.

Tracy, Eleanor J. "Ed Gibbons' Legacy to Woolworth." *Fortune,* November 29, 1982, pp. 128–129.

"Woolworth Calls It Quits for Woolco." *Newsweek,* October 4, 1982, p. 70.

"Woolworth's President, Anderson, Quits Amid Reputed Strife Over New Chairman." *Wall Street Journal,* January 13, 1983, pp. 1, 6.

C A S E 7.2

What goes into making a decision?

". . . The site selection committee, therefore, recommends that the new manufacturing facility for Hall Industries be constructed in either Chicago, Kansas City, or St. Louis on one of the plots currently held at option." Carl Peterson re-read the last sentence of the recommendation one more time and then put the report in a desk drawer. "Yes," he thought, "this is going to be quite a decision."

Hall Industries is a rapidly growing manufacturing and distributing company with nationwide operations. About a year ago, it became apparent that a new plant was needed. Existing facilities were concentrated in California, New Jersey, and Florida, so it seemed logical to build the new plant in the Midwest. The company president appointed a committee to study possible building sites, to purchase options to buy on any sites that seemed especially attractive, and to submit that list of sites to the president for further consideration. After spending nine months studying various possible locations for the new plant, the committee recommended four sites: two in Chicago and one each in Kansas City and St. Louis. Each site met the company's requirements in terms of utility and tax rates, price, labor market, and access to transportation.

The newly appointed manager of that plant, Carl Peterson, was to make the final decision himself. Carl had joined Hall Industries six years ago, after working for eight years in the automobile industry and then returning to school for his M.B.A. Carl had risen rapidly through the ranks at Hall Industries, and he has spent the last year as assistant plant manager at the San Diego facility. After being notified of his appointment, Carl was elated. He immediately set to work studying the four possible locations recommended by the site selection committee.

One of the Chicago sites was clearly a little better than the others on most dimensions; it was also a little more expensive. After Carl spent weeks and weeks going over the numbers, that site seemed to emerge as the best choice. Yet Carl resisted making a final choice because of other factors that kept creeping into the back of his mind.

First there were his parents. His mother and father lived in a small central-Missouri town that was within a two-hour drive of either Kansas City or St. Louis but was several hours from Chicago. Carl was very close to his parents and visited them several times a year. And then there was his wife. Helen had a promising career as a banking officer, and her future was also at stake in the move. She felt she could find a new position in any of the cities under consideration but had argued that St. Louis was the least desirable. She enjoyed the city itself, but she felt that the business climate there was less conducive to her career.

There were also the issues of housing and transportation. Like their parents before them, both Carl and his wife wanted a large house and a few acres of land. The site in Kansas City would allow them to have their house in the country, and would only necessitate a fifteen-minute drive into the city. The Chicago site, however, would require a commute of over an hour each way. Further, for Carl, the commute would involve at least thirty minutes in a car to the train station and another thirty minutes on the train. While the company will cover all relocation costs for Carl and his wife, it will not provide any extra allowance for daily transportation expenses.

Carl argued to himself that, even though one of the Chicago sites was slightly better than the others, they were all perfectly suitable for the company. And after all, he and his family had to live there. Why shouldn't he consider not only the company's needs, but his own needs as well? As Carl continued to daydream, he wondered what kind of season the Kansas City Royals were going to have next year.

CASE
QUESTIONS

1. Analyze this situation in terms of classical and behavioral decision making.

2. Is Carl following the six steps in the decision making process?

3. Do you agree or disagree with Carl that he should consider personal factors as well as the company's interests in making his decision?

8

QUANTITATIVE TECHNIQUES FOR PLANNING AND DECISION MAKING

CHAPTER OBJECTIVES

1. Define forecasting and show how it is an important part of the planning process; discuss the various approaches to forecasting and explain how each could be important to many kinds of organizations; and describe several forecasting techniques.

2. Describe the basic concepts of linear programming, break-even analysis, simulations, and PERT, and cite cases in which these analytical methods are appropriate.

3. Explain how decision making techniques such as the pay-off matrix and decision trees are used, and list other quantitative techniques that are available to assist managers in making decisions.

4. Discuss the advantages and disadvantages of using quantitative techniques for planning and decision making.

Forecasting
Sales forecasting
Technological forecasting
Other types of forecasting
Forecasting techniques

Other planning techniques
Linear programming
Break-even analysis
Organizational simulation
PERT

Quantitative approaches to decision making
The pay-off matrix
Decision trees
Other quantitative techniques for decision making
The role of the computer in decision making

The pros and cons of quantitative techniques
Problems and disadvantages
Strengths and advantages

Summary of key points

OPENING INCIDENT

The year is 1978. You are a manager at a major aircraft manufacturer. Your company is the thirty-first largest business in the United States, the world's largest manufacturer of jet transports, and the country's largest exporter. A recent forecast predicts that the market for new aircraft may exceed $82 billion over the next 10 years. You also know that the price of jet fuel has gone through the roof. Your company has large financial reserves to draw on. What would you do?

The General Motors assembly plant in Oklahoma City has the capability to manufacture two different kinds of cars simultaneously on the same assembly line. Management can vary the mix according to market conditions, inventory levels, and so on. Plant managers at the Ford plant in Wayne, Michigan, set production schedules four weeks in advance. Orders for engines are then phoned out every night. The engine plant, twenty miles away, ships the engines needed for the next day in the right order so that they can be taken directly to the assembly line. This procedure greatly reduces the inventory needs of the Wayne plant, thereby reducing costs.[1]

What do these examples have in common? Aside from the fact that they are both drawn from the automobile industry, each underscores the increasing importance of quantitative techniques and procedures to managers. Imagine maintaining inventories of thousands of parts for two different kinds of cars at the same facility and then coordinating their delivery to one assembly line where both cars are being produced! Planning a production run weeks in advance while maintaining a daily ordering system is equally complex. It is extremely unlikely that either of these systems could function without the aid of quantitative techniques and computers to execute them.

The previous four chapters dealt with the important managerial activities of planning and decision making. Our approach so far has been fairly general and descriptive; now we will look at the details. An analogy from the construction industry will make this new approach clearer. Our discussions of planning and decision making were like a description of the basic processes for constructing an office building or a house: structural configurations, alternative materials, stress and load requirements, and so forth. To carry out those activities, however, the builder needs to know how to use tools (such as hammers and saws) and equipment (such as riveting machines and drill presses).

---

1. See Charles G. Burck, "Can Detroit Catch Up?" *Fortune*, February 8, 1982, pp. 34–39. See also Gene Bylinsky, "The Race to the Automatic Factory," *Fortune*, February 21, 1983, pp. 52–64.

We are ready to discuss the "tools and equipment" required for effective planning and decision making. We will discuss forecasting techniques often used in planning and then turn to other planning aids. Techniques for decision making are discussed in the next section. The chapter concludes by considering the strengths and weaknesses of quantitative approaches to planning and decision making.

Forecasting

To plan, one must make assumptions about future events, but planners cannot simply look into a crystal ball. In most cases, they must perform some type of forecasting to identify probable future circumstances, and they must often forecast across several time horizons. *Forecasting,* then, is the process of developing assumptions or premises about the future that managers can use in planning or decision making.[2] We will deal most extensively with sales forecasting and technological forecasting. Then, after a brief look at other areas of forecasting, we will summarize several forecasting techniques.

Sales forecasting

Chapter 5 described how, in the late 1970s, Gulf Oil embarked on a strategy designed to attain the number-two position in the market for low-density polyethylene film. One error the company made pertained to technology, another to projected demand. In particular, Gulf forecasted a 10 percent annual growth rate in demand. Management decided that building a new manufacturing plant would help Gulf increase its share of this projected growth. When growth turned out to be only 8 percent per year, building the new plant was postponed.[3] Obviously, accurate sales forecasting is important. Gulf was willing to spend millions of dollars as a result of a sales forecast and was then forced to postpone the whole project when the forecast turned out to be wrong.

As the term implies, *sales forecasting* is concerned with predicting future sales. Because monetary resources flowing into an organization are necessary to finance both current and future operations, sales forecasts are of vital importance. Consider the following questions that might be answered by forecasting.

1. How much of a given product should we produce next week, next month, or next year?
2. How much money will we have available to spend on research and development and on new-product test-marketing?
3. When and to what degree will we need to expand our existing production facilities?
4. How should we respond to union demands for a 15 percent pay increase?

2. See George A. Steiner, *Top Management Planning* (New York: Macmillan, 1969).
3. See "The New Planning," *Business Week,* December 18, 1978, pp. 62–68.

None of these questions can be adequately answered without some notion of what future revenues are likely to be, so sales forecasting is generally one of the first steps in planning.

Unfortunately, the term *sales forecasting* suggests that this form of forecasting is appropriate only for organizations that have something to sell. But other kinds of organizations also depend on financial resources, and they also must forecast. The University of Nebraska must forecast future state aid in order to plan course offerings, staff size, and so on. Hospitals must forecast their future income from patient fees, insurance payments, and other sources in order to assess their ability to expand. Although we will continue to use the conventional term, keep in mind that what is really at issue is *revenue* forecasting.

Once projected, the sales (or revenue) forecast becomes a guiding framework for a variety of other activities. Raw material expenditures, advertising budgets, sales commission structures, and similar operating costs are all based on projected sales figures.

Chapter 6 explained how firms integrate short-range, intermediate, and long-range planning horizons via systematic updating and refining. In like fashion, organizations often forecast sales across several time horizons. The longer-run forecasts may then be updated and refined as various shorter-run cycles are completed. Gulf's original long-range forecast has been shown to be incorrect, so the company has no doubt revised its predictions accordingly.

For obvious reasons, a forecast should be as accurate as possible, and the accuracy of sales forecasting tends to increase as organizations learn from their previous forecasting experience. But the more uncertain and complex future conditions are likely to be, the more difficult it is to develop accurate forecasts. For this reason, forecasts are more useful to managers if they are expressed as a range rather than as an absolute index or number. If projected sales increases are expected to be in the range of 10–12 percent, a manager can consider all the implications for the entire range. A 10 percent increase can dictate one set of activities; a 12 percent increase can call for a different set of activities.

Technological forecasting

Technological forecasting focuses on predicting what future technologies are likely to emerge and when they are likely to be economically feasible. (We first considered this area of forecasting in Chapter 5 in our discussion of the technology life-cycle perspective on strategy.)

In an era when technological breakthrough and innovation have become the rule rather than the exception, it is extremely important that managers be able to anticipate new developments in advance. If a manager invests heavily in existing technology (such as production processes, equipment, and computer systems) and this technology becomes obsolete in the near future, the company has wasted its resources. This was the mistake Gulf made when it failed to anticipate technological breakthroughs in devising its strategy to become the number-two company in the low-density polyethylene film market. When Union Carbide developed a new process that cut production costs by 20 percent, Gulf was placed at a competitive disadvantage.

The most striking technological innovations in recent years have been in electronics, especially semiconductors. Home computers, electronic games, and sophisticated communications equipment are all evidence of the electronics explosion. Other areas of rapid innovation include lasers, synthetic fabrics and materials, construction equipment and methods, health care, and robotics.

The Delphi technique and brainstorming, both discussed in Chapter 7, are the methods most organizations use in technological forecasting. Given the increasing importance of technology and the rapid pace of technological innovation, it follows that managers will grow increasingly concerned with technological forecasting in the years to come.[4]

Other types of forecasting

Other types of forecasting are also important to many organizations. Resource forecasting, for example, projects future needs for resources such as personnel and raw materials. Here the emphasis is on the organization's inputs from the environment rather than its outputs. General economic conditions are the subject of other forecasts. Some organizations undertake population and/or market size forecasting. And government fiscal policy and various governmental regulations affect most firms. It is no exaggeration to say that virtually any component in an organization's general and task environments is an appropriate area for forecasting.

Forecasting techniques

To carry out the various kinds of forecasting we have identified, several techniques are available to managers. We will consider time-series analysis, causal modeling, several qualitative techniques, and a few special techniques.

Time-series analysis. The underlying assumption of time-series analysis is that the past is a good predictor of the future. This technique is most useful when the manager has quite a lot of historical data available and when stable trends and patterns are apparent.

In a *time-series analysis,* the variable under consideration (such as sales or enrollment) is plotted across time and a "best-fit" line is calculated. Figure 8.1 shows how a time-series analysis might look. The X's represent the number of units sold for each year from 1976 through 1984. The "best-fit" line has also been drawn in. If a manager wants to know what sales to expect in 1985, he or she simply extends the pattern. The projected sales level in this example is around 8,200 units.

It is important to add that real time-series analysis involves much more than simply plotting sales data and then using a ruler and a pencil to extend the line. Sophisticated mathematical procedures, among other things, are nec-

4. See Wickham Skinner, "The Impact of Changing Technology on the Working Environment," in Clark Kerr and Jerome Rosow (eds.), *Work in America—The Decade Ahead* (New York: Van Nostrand, 1979), pp. 204–230 for a discussion of the impact of technology. See R. Balachandra, "Technological Forecasting: Who Does It and How Useful Is It?" *Technological Forecasting and Social Change,* January 1980, pp. 75–85.

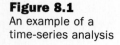

Figure 8.1
An example of a
time-series analysis

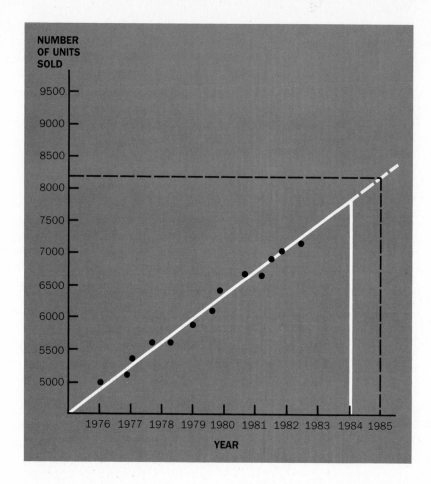

essary to account for seasonal and cyclical fluctuations and to identify the true "best-fit" line. In real situations, data seldom follow the neat pattern found in Figure 8.1. Indeed, the data points may be so widely dispersed that they mask meaningful trends from all but painstaking inspection.[5]

Causal modeling. Another useful forecasting technique is causal modeling. Actually, the term *causal modeling* represents a group of several different techniques.[6] Table 8.1 summarizes three of the more useful approaches.

Regression models are statistical equations created to predict a variable (such as sales volume) that depends on a number of other variables (such as price and advertising). The variable being predicted is called the dependent

5. See Everette S. Gardner and David G. Damenbring, "Forecasting with Exponential Smoothing: Some Guidelines for Model Selection," *Decision Sciences*, April 1980, pp. 370–383 for a recent technical review of time-series analysis.

6. See John C. Chambers, S. K. Mullick, and D. Smith, "How to Choose the Right Forecasting Technique," *Harvard Business Review*, July–August 1971, pp. 45–74.

Table 8.1 Examples of causal modeling forecasting techniques

Regression models	Used to predict one variable (called dependent variable) on the basis of known or assumed other variables (called independent variables). For example, we might predict that a certain level of product sales will be caused by certain price, advertising, and economic levels.
Econometric models	Make use of several multiple-regression equations to consider the impact of major economic shifts.
Economic indicators	Various population statistics, indexes, or parameters that predict organizationally relevant variables such as discretionary income. Examples include cost-of-living index, change in GNP, and level of unemployment.

variable; the variables used to make the prediction are called independent variables. The following is a typical regression equation:

$$y = ax_1 + bx_2 + cx_3 + d$$

where: y = the dependent variable (sales, in this case)

x_1, x_2, and x_3 = independent variables (advertising, price, and commissions)

a, b, and c = weights for the independent variables calculated during development of the regression model

d = a constant

To use the model, a manager could plug in various alternatives for advertising, price, and commissions and then compute y. The value of y represents the forecast.[7]

Econometric models employ regression techniques at a much more complex level. Econometric models attempt to predict major economic shifts and the potential impact of those shifts on the organization. They might be used to predict various age and economic groups that will characterize different regions of the United States in the year 2000 and to further predict the kinds of products and services these groups may want. A complete econometric model may consist of hundreds or even thousands of equations. Large computers are necessary to apply them. Many smaller firms (and most larger ones) do not have the resources to develop econometric models. Instead, they may use existing models at universities and research centers.[8]

Economic indicators, another type of causal model, are population statis-

7. See Fred N. Kerlinger and Elazar J. Pedhazur, *Multiple Regression in Behavioral Research* (New York: Holt, 1973).

8. See James L. Murphy, *Introductory Econometrics* (Homewood, Il.: Irwin, 1973).

tics or indexes that reflect the economic well-being of that population. Examples of widely used economic indicators include the current rates of inflation and unemployment. In using such indicators, the manager draws on past experiences that have revealed a relationship between a particular indicator and one or more facets of the company's operations. If managers in the sailboat manufacturing division of AMF, a large sporting-goods company, have noticed that decreases in unemployment among professionals have always been followed by an increased demand for sailboats, they will know what to expect if they hear reports of further declines in unemployment.[9]

Qualitative techniques. Table 8.2 summarizes several qualitative techniques that can be used for forecasting. The Delphi technique was described in Chapter 7 as a mechanism for managing group decision making activities, but the procedure can also be used to develop forecasts. A variation on it—the panel or jury-of-expert-opinion approach, involves carrying out a Delphi process with members of top management. And the Delphi technique may be particularly useful in the area of technological forecasting.

The sales-force-composition method of sales forecasting is a pooling of the predictions and opinions of experienced sales personnel. Because of their experience, such persons are often able to forecast quite accurately what various customers will do. Of course, managerial expertise is also needed to combine, interpret, and act on the predictions from sales personnel.

Finally, the customer evaluation technique goes beyond an organization's sales force and collects data from customers of the organization. The customers provide estimates of their own future needs for the goods and services the organization supplies. Again, managers must combine, interpret, and act on this information. There are two major limitations to this approach. Customers may be less interested in taking time to develop accurate predictions than are members of the organization itself, and the method makes no provision for dealing with new customers the organization may acquire.

Special techniques. Special circumstances sometimes require special techniques. The two we will summarize here are most useful for technological forecasting.

Morphological analysis involves identifying relevant dimensions of a subject, specifying all the variations and combinations of those dimensions, and then finding practical applications for them. This technique is especially helpful in finding new uses for various products. For example, suppose a manufacturer's primary product is used in four other products made by other companies. A morphological analysis might reveal what effects technological change might have on the future demand by each of the other companies and also other potential future uses for the product.

Substitution effect models predict how, when, and under what circumstances a new product or technology will replace an existing one. The decision to substitute is usually made when economic factors (such as production costs)

9. See United States Department of Commerce, *Survey of Current Business,* various issues, for a discussion of current economic indicators and their meaning for business.

Table 8.2 Examples of qualitative forecasting techniques

Delphi	The systematic refinement of expert opinion.
Sales-force-composite	A combination of predictions or opinions drawn from experienced sales personnel and used to forecast sales for a designated time period.
Customer expectation model	A combination of predictions from long-standing customers, of their future product or service needs.

would be improved by the new technology. In other words, a company should adopt the new technology when it is likely to pay off.

In most instances, morphological analysis and substitution effect models are used along with other forecasting methods such as the Delphi technique.

Selection of a technique. Selecting an appropriate forecasting technique can be as important as applying it correctly. Some techniques are appropriate only for specific circumstances. The sales-force-composition technique is good only for sales forecasting, and morphological analysis is intended for technological forecasting. Other techniques, like the Delphi method, are useful in a variety of situations. Some techniques, like the econometric models, require the use of computers, whereas others, like customer evaluation models, can be carried out with little mathematical expertise. For the most part, selection of a particular technique depends on the nature of the problem, the experience and preferences of the manager, and available resources. For more information about selecting the right technique, consult any of several recent articles and books dealing with this topic.[10]

Other planning techniques

Besides the forecasting techniques, other quantitative techniques are available for other planning purposes. Four of the most popular are linear programming, break-even analysis, simulation, and PERT.

Linear programming

Linear programming is one of the most widely used quantitative tools for planning.[11] *Linear programming,* or LP, is a procedure for calculating the optimal combination of resources and activities.[12] It is appropriate when there is some

10. See in particular Chambers et al., "How to Choose the Right Forecasting Technique"; and J. Scott Armstrong, *Long-Range Forecasting: From Crystal Ball to Computers* (New York: Wiley, 1978).

11. Thad B. Green, W. B. Newsome, and S. R. Jones, "A Survey of the Applications of Quantitative Techniques to Production/Operations Management in Large Corporations," *Academy of Management Journal,* December 1977, pp. 669–676.

12. See Robert E. Markland, *Topics in Management Science,* 2nd ed. (New York: Wiley, 1983).

Table 8.3 Production data for tuners and receivers

| Department | Number of hours required per unit | | Production capacity per day (in hours) |
	Tuners (T)	Receivers (R)	
Production (PR)	10	6	150
Inspection and testing (IT)	4	4	80
Profit margin	$30	$20	

objective to be met (such as a sales quota or a certain production level) within a set of constraints (such as a limited advertising budget or limited production capabilities). In LP, the objective function must be expressed as a linear function and constraints affecting that objective must be expressed as a system of linear equalities or inequalities.

Assume that a small electronics corporation produces two basic products, a high-quality cable television tuner and a high-quality receiver for picking up television audio and playing it through a stereo amplifier. Both products go through the same two departments: production, and inspection and testing. Each product has a known profit margin and a high level of demand. The production manager's job, then, is to produce the optimal combination of tuners (T) and receivers (R) so as to maximize profits and use the time in production (PR) and in inspection and testing (IT) most efficiently. Table 8.3 gives the information we need to use linear programming to solve this problem.

The *objective function* is that which we want to achieve. In technical terms, it is a mathematical representation of the desirability of the consequences of a particular decision.[13] In our example, the objective function can be represented as follows:

$$\text{Profit}_{\text{maximize}} = \$30 X_T + \$20 X_R$$

where: X_T is the number of tuners to be produced, and
X_R is the number of
receivers to be produced

The $30 and $20, of course, are the respective profit margins of the tuner and receiver, as noted in Table 8.3. The objective, then, is to maximize profits.

However, this objective must be accomplished within a set of constraints. In our example, these constraints are the time required to produce each product in each department and the total amount of time available. These data are also found in Table 8.3. Relevant constraint equations are

$$10T + 6R \leq 150$$

$$4T + 4R \leq 80$$

13. See Markland, *Topics in Management Science.*

and, of course

$$T \geqslant 0$$

$$R \geqslant 0$$

One approach to solving the problem is the graphical method. To graph the various combinations, we first assume that production of each product is maximized when production of the other is at zero. The resultant solutions are then plotted on a coordinate axis. In the PR department, if product $T = 0$, then

$$10T + 6R \leq 150$$

$$10(0) + 6R \leq 150$$

$$R \leq 25$$

In the same department, if product $R = 0$, then

$$10T + 6R \leq 150$$

$$10T + 6(0) \leq 150$$

$$T \leq 15$$

Similarly, in the IT department, if no tuners are produced,

$$4T + 4R \leq 80$$

$$4(0) + 4R \leq 80$$

$$R \leq 20$$

and, if no receivers are produced,

$$4T + 4R \leq 80$$

$$4T + 4(0) \leq 80$$

$$T \leq 20$$

Figure 8.2 shows how the resulting graph would look. The shaded region represents the *feasibility space,* or production combinations that do not exceed the capacity of either department. The optimal number of products will be defined at one of the four corners of the shaded area in Figure 8.2. That is, the firm should produce 20 receivers only (point C), 15 tuners only (point B), 13 receivers and 7 tuners (point E), or no products at all. Given the assumption that production of both tuners and receivers is to be greater than 0, it follows that point E is the optimal solution. (Note that point E is the intersection of the two constraints.) That combination requires 148 hours in PR and 80 hours in IT and yields $470 in profit. (Note also that, if only receivers were produced, the profit would be $400 and that producing only tuners would mean $450 in profit.)

Only two alternatives can be handled by the graphical method, and our example was extremely simple. When there are other alternatives, an algebraic

Figure 8.2
The graphical
solution of a linear
programming
problem

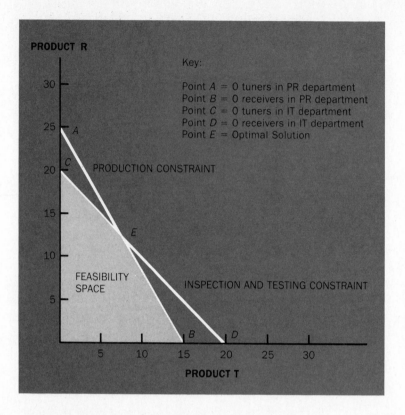

method must be employed. Real-world problems may require several hundred equations and variables. High-speed computers are needed to solve these kinds of problems.

One particularly sophisticated linear programming technique is the simplex method. We noted earlier that the optimal graphical solution would appear at an intersection of constraint equations and/or axes. Such an intersection is called a vertex. A simplex algorithm identifies all of the vertices in a complex feasibility space and then tests each one until the optimal solution is identified.

Linear programming is a powerful technique. It can play a key role in planning and decision making, and it can provide the manager with valuable insights into problems at hand. LP can be used to schedule production, select an optimal portfolio of investments, allocate sales representatives to territories, or produce an item at some minimum cost.[14]

Break-even analysis

Linear programming is called a normative procedure because it prescribes the optimal solution to a problem. Break-even analysis, on the other hand, is a

14. See Markland, *Topics in Management Science.*

descriptive procedure because it simply describes relationships among variables. Then it is up to the manager to make the decisions.

Break-even analysis is basically a technique for financial planning. We can define *break-even analysis* as a procedure for identifying that point at which revenues and costs are equal and the project is yielding neither profit or loss. It might be used, then, to analyze the effects on profits of different price/output combinations or various levels of output.[15]

Figure 8.3 represents the key cost variables in break-even analysis. Most situations include three cost considerations: fixed costs, variable costs, and total costs. Fixed costs are costs incurred regardless of what is being produced. They include rent or mortgage payments on the building, managerial salaries, and depreciation of plant and equipment. Variable costs are those that vary with the number of units produced, such as the cost of raw materials and direct labor used to make each unit. Total costs are simply fixed costs plus variable costs.

Other important factors in break-even analysis are revenue and profit. Revenue, the total dollar amount of sales, is computed by multiplying the number of units sold by the sales price of each. Profit is then determined by subtracting total costs from total revenues. When revenues and profits are considered in conjunction with total costs, the break-even graph shown in Figure

Figure 8.3
An example of cost factors for break-even analysis

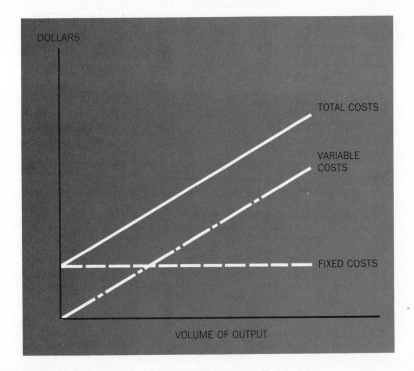

15. See Roger C. Pfaffenberger and James H. Patterson, *Statistical Methods,* 2nd ed. (Homewood, Ill: Irwin, 1981).

Figure 8.4
Break-even analysis

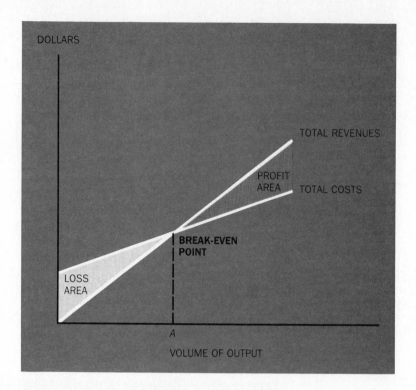

8.4 emerges. The point at which the lines representing total costs and total revenues cross is the break-even point. Note that, because of the fixed costs, the line for total costs never begins at zero. In Figure 8.4, if this company sells more units than are represented by point *A*, it will realize a profit; selling below that level will result in a loss.

Mathematically, the break-even point (expressed as units of production or volume) is shown by the formula

$$BEP = \frac{TFC}{P - VC}$$

where: BEP = break-even point

TFC = total fixed costs

P = price per unit

VC = variable cost per unit

Assume you are considering the production of a new garden hoe with a curved handle. You have determined that an acceptable selling price will be $20. You have also determined that the variable costs per hoe will be $15, and you have total fixed costs of $400,000 per year. The question is how many hoes you must sell each year to break even. Using the break-even model, you find that

$$\text{BEP} = \frac{\text{TFC}}{\text{P} - \text{VC}}$$

$$= \frac{400,000}{20 - 15}$$

$$= 80,000 \text{ units}$$

You must sell 80,000 hoes to break even. Further analysis would also show that, if you raised your price to $25 per hoe, you would need to sell 40,000 to break even, and so on.

Break-even analysis is an extremely popular planning technique, but it has two major weaknesses. It considers revenues only up to the break-even point, and it makes no allowance for the time value of money. That is, because the funds used to cover fixed and variable costs could be used for other purposes (such as investment), the organization is losing interest income by tying up money prior to reaching the break-even point—an aspect of the situation that the break-even model does not account for. Most situations require that, after the preliminary break-even analysis has been completed, more sophisticated techniques (such as rate-of-return analysis or discounted-present-value analysis) be called into play. These techniques can help the manager decide whether to proceed or to divert resources into other areas.

Organizational simulation

Another useful planning device is simulation. The word *simulate* means "to copy" or "to represent." An *organizational simulation,* then, is a model of a real-world situation that can be manipulated to discover how it "behaves." Like break-even analysis, simulation is a descriptive rather than a prescriptive technique.

An appropriate situation for simulation would be the planning of a major new airport in a metropolitan area. Issues to be addressed would include: the number of runways, the direction of those runways, the number of terminals and gates, the allocation of various carriers among the terminals and gates, and the technology and personnel needed to achieve a target frequency of take-offs and landings. (Of course, a real example would be even more complex than this.)

The simulation model would interrelate these and other important factors. The planner could then plug in several different values for each factor and observe the probable results. For example, the manager could ascertain the effects on take-offs and landings of having three runways instead of four or explore the results of spreading United Air Lines, American Airlines, and Eastern Air Lines across different terminals rather than grouping them in one.

Simulation problems are in some ways similar to those addressed by linear programming, but simulation is more useful in very complex situations characterized by diverse constraints and opportunities. The development of sophisticated simulation models may require the expertise of outside specialists or consultants, and the complexity of simulation almost always necessitates the use of a computer. For these reasons, simulation is more likely to be used as a technique for planning in larger organizations that have the required resources.[16]

PERT

PERT, an acronym for Program Evaluation and Review Technique, is not only an important quantitative technique for planning, but a valuable control device as well. In the late 1950s, the U.S. Navy was faced with the enormous task of coordinating the activities of 3,000 contractors during the development of the Polaris nuclear submarine. Working with Lockheed Aircraft and a large consulting firm, the Navy developed PERT. It credits the technique with saving two years that would otherwise have been required to complete the overall project.

From the standpoint of planning, *PERT* allows a manager to plan a project far in advance and to estimate the time needed for completion. Thus it can pinpoint bottlenecks and identify areas that may need modification. PERT also facilitates the control function by allowing comparison of actual progress to planned progress.[17]

Basically, PERT involves the creation of a network of all activities neces-

Table 8.4 Introducing a new product: activities and events

Activities	Events
	1. Origin of project.
a. Produce limited quantity for test marketing.	2. Completion of production for test marketing.
b. Design preliminary package.	3. Completion of design for preliminary package.
c. Locate test market.	4. Test market located.
d. Obtain local merchant cooperation.	5. Local merchant cooperation obtained.
e. Ship product to selected retail outlets.	6. Product for test marketing shipped to retail outlets.
f. Monitor sales and customer reactions.	7. Sales and customer reactions monitored.
g. Survey customers in test-market area.	8. Customers in test-market area surveyed.
h. Make needed product changes.	9. Product changes made.
i. Make needed package changes.	10. Package changes made.
j. Begin national advertising.	11. National advertising carried out.
k. Begin national distribution.	12. National distribution completed.

16. See Robert H. Bonczek, Clyde W. Holsapple, and Andrew B. Whinston, "The Evolving Role of Models in Decision Support Systems," *Decision Sciences,* April 1980, pp. 337–356.

17. See Harold Fearon, William Ruch, Patrick Decker, Ross Reck, Vincent Renter, and C. David Wieters, *Fundamentals of Production/Operations Management* (St. Paul, Minn.: West, 1979).

Figure 8.5
A PERT network for introducing a new product

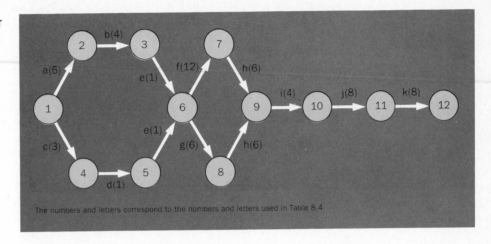

The numbers and letters correspond to the numbers and letters used in Table 8.4.

sary to complete a particular project. The steps involved in using PERT are as follows:

1. Identify the activities to be performed and the events that will mark their completion.
2. Develop a network of the relationships among activities and events.
3. Analyze the time necessary to get from each event to the next and the total time required to complete the project.
4. Refine the network.
5. Use the network to control the project.

Let us consider how a marketing manager might use PERT to plan the test marketing and nationwide introduction of a new product. Table 8.4 identifies the basic steps involved in carrying out this project. These activities are now grouped into a network, as shown in Figure 8.5, where each completed event is represented by a number in a circle. The activities are indicated by letters on the lines connecting the events. Note that some activities are performed independently of one another (for example, production and the location of a test-market site can be carried on simultaneously), whereas others must be performed in sequence (surveying customers in the test-market area should be done before making changes in the product).

The time to get from each activity to the next must then be determined. The time between activities is usually calculated by averaging the manager's estimates of the most optimistic time, the most likely time weighted by 4, and the most pessimistic time. That is,

$$\text{Expected time} = \frac{a + 4b + c}{6}$$

where: a = optimistic time

b = most likely time

c = pessimistic time

The expected number of weeks for each activity in our example is shown in parentheses in Figure 8.5. (Another technique called the critical path method, or CPM, is useful when the times between events are known in advance; other minor differences between PERT and CPM are beyond the scope of this discussion.)

The manager then analyzes the network to locate the longest sequence through it. This sequence, known as the critical path, represents the shortest time in which we can expect to complete the project. Analysis of Figure 8.5 indicates that, of the four sequences that must unfold, the path of 1–2–3–6–7–9–10–11–12 is the critical path in this case, with an expected duration of 49 weeks.

After this preliminary analysis, the manager might be able to refine the network by somehow shortening the critical path. For example, early work on the preliminary package might begin before the test products are finished. Or the manager might decide that 10 weeks (rather than 12) are sufficient to monitor sales and customer reactions. Each of these actions results in a shorter critical path and therefore a shorter time until project completion. In many construction projects using PERT, employees can be shifted from activities that are not critical at the time to activities that are critical at that point in the path. Thus PERT reveals ways to reduce the total time needed to complete the project.

Finally, the PERT network can be used as a control technique to keep the project on schedule (the use of PERT in organizational control will be discussed in Chapter 18). As in linear programming and simulation, computers are often used to handle large-scale and complex PERT networks. Our example was extremely simple in order to illustrate how the technique works. For real projects, sophisticated versions of PERT (and CPM) that incorporate probabilistic methods and cost considerations are usually far more appropriate.[18]

Quantitative approaches to decision making

The previous section discussed four useful quantitative techniques for planning. This section describes quantitative techniques that are more directly relevant to decision making. To illustrate the differences, consider the previous example of PERT's use for planning the test-marketing and introduction of a new product. Although this overall process is clearly a planning activity, each set of activities and events represents a decision. Designing the preliminary package, selecting test-market sites, and evaluating survey results all involve decisions. The techniques discussed in this section are more relevant to these smaller-scale issues. They typically involve a shorter time and have a somewhat narrower focus.

---

18. See Everett E. Adam, Jr. and Ronald J. Ebert, *Production and Operations Management*, 2nd ed. (Englewood Cliffs, N.J.: Prentice-Hall, 1982).

The pay-off matrix

One useful quantitative technique for decision making is the *pay-off matrix,* which specifies the value of various alternatives as a function of different possible outcomes associated with each. To use a pay-off matrix requires that there be several alternatives available, that several different events could occur, and that the consequences depend on which alternative is selected and on which event or set of events occurs. An important concept in understanding the pay-off matrix, then, is probability.

A probability is the likelihood, expressed as a percentage, that a particular event will or will not occur. If we believe that a particular event will occur 75 times out of 100, we can say that the probability of its occurring is 75 percent, or .75. Probabilities range in value from 0 (no chance of occurrence) to 1.00 (certain occurrence). The latter might also be referred to as 100 percent. In the business world, there are few probabilities of either 0 or 1.00.

Furthermore, the certainty of a particular probability may vary. The probability of tossing a fair coin and getting a "head" is always 50 percent. On the other hand, when a weather forecaster tells us that there is a 40 percent chance of rain tomorrow, we all know from experience that the real likelihood of rain varies significantly. Most probabilities that managers use also vary: they are often based on subjective judgment, intuition, and historical data.

The most useful probabilities for a pay-off matrix are those that pertain to *expected value.* The expected value of an alternative is the sum of all possible values multiplied by their respective probabilities. Suppose, for example, that an investor is considering investing in a new company. If he believes there is a .40 probability of making $100,000, a .30 probability of making $30,000, and a .30 probability of losing $20,000, the expected value (EV) of this alternative is

$$EV = .40(100,000) + .30(30,000) + .30(-20,000)$$

$$= 40,000 + 9,000 - 6,000 = \$43,000$$

The investor can then weigh the expected value of the investment against the expected values of various alternatives. The highest EV signals the investment that should be selected. Let us use the same investor to illustrate how a pay-off matrix works. Suppose that he has $20,000 to invest. For some reason, he has decided not to invest in the new company but has located three alternatives. Because the expected value of each alternative depends on short-run changes in the economy, he decides to develop a pay-off matrix. Figure 8.6 shows what the pay-off matrix might look like.

The expected value of alternative 1 is:

$$EV = .30(-10,000) + .70(50,000)$$

$$= -3,000 + 35,000 = \$32,000$$

The expected value of alternative 2 is:

$$EV = .30(90,000) + .70(-15,000)$$

$$= 27,000 + (-10,500) = \$16,500$$

Figure 8.6
An example of a
pay-off matrix

		HIGH INFLATION (Probability of .30)	LOW INFLATION (Probability of .70)
INVESTMENT ALTERNATIVE 1	LEISURE PRODUCTS CO.	-$10,000	+$50,000
INVESTMENT ALTERNATIVE 2	ENERGY ENHANCEMENT CO.	+$90,000	-$15,000
INVESTMENT ALTERNATIVE 3	FOOD PRODUCING CO.	+$30,000	+$25,000

And the expected value of alternative 3 is:

$$EV = .30(30,000) + .70(25,000)$$

$$= 9,000 + 17,500 = \$26,500$$

Alternative 1, then, has the highest expected value. Other uses for pay-off matrices include determining order quantities, deciding whether to repair or replace broken machinery, and deciding which of several new products to introduce. Of course, the real key to effective use of the pay-off matrix approach is making accurate estimates of the relevant probabilities.[19]

Decision trees

Decision trees are like pay-off matrices in that they are intended to enhance a manager's ability to evaluate alternatives and make use of expected values. However, they are most appropriate when the decisions and alternatives follow a sequential pattern.[20]

Figure 8.7 illustrates a hypothetical decision tree. The firm represented in the figure is trying to determine whether it should begin exporting to France or to China. (It is restricted to only one of these alternatives by limited capacity.) Whichever alternative is selected, demand for the product in that particular country may turn out to be high or low. In France, there is a .80 chance of high demand and a .20 chance of low demand. The anticipated payoffs in these situations are predicted to be $20 million and $3 million, respectively. In China, the probabilities of high versus low demand are .60 and .40, respectively, and the associated payoffs are presumed to be $25 million and $6 million. As shown in the figure, the expected value of shipping to France is

19. For a recent technical discussion of pay-off matrices, see Pfaffenberger and Patterson, *Statistical Methods*.

20. See N. Paul Loomba, *Management: A Quantitative Perspective* (New York: Macmillan, 1978).

Figure 8.7
A hypothetical
example of a
decision tree

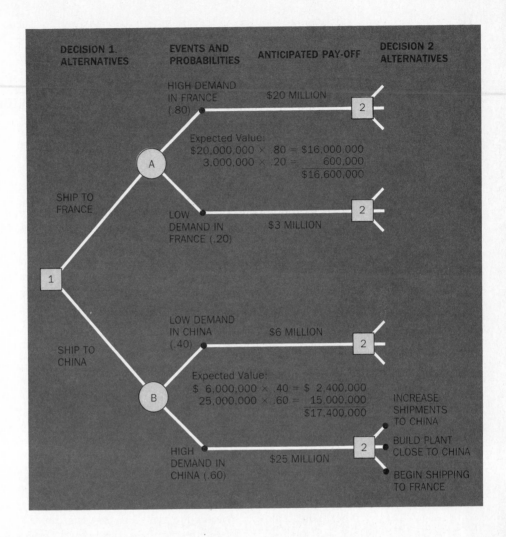

$16,600,000, whereas the expected value of shipping to China is $17,400,000.

The astute reader will note that this part of the decision could also have been set up as a pay-off matrix. However, the real value of decision trees is that we can extend the model to include additional decisions. Assume, for example, that the company begins shipping to China. If high demand does in fact materialize, the company will reach another decision situation. It might ask, "Should we (1) use surplus revenues to increase shipments to China, (2) use surplus revenues to build a plant close to China in order to cut shipping costs, or (3) use surplus revenues to begin shipping to France?" Various outcomes are possible for each decision, and each outcome will also have both a probability and an anticipated pay-off. It is possible to compute expected values back through several tiers of decisions all the way to the initial one. Just as with pay-off matrices, determining probabilities accurately is the crucial element in the process. Properly used, a decision tree provides managers with a road map through complex decision situations.[21]

Other quantitative techniques for decision making

In addition to pay-off matrices and decision trees, a number of other quantitative methods are also available to facilitate decision making.

Inventory models. *Inventory models* are guidelines that help the manager decide how much inventory to maintain. By inventory we mean both raw materials (inputs) and finished goods (outputs). In the case of finished goods, both extremes are bad: excess inventory ties up capital, whereas a small inventory may result in shortages and customer dissatisfaction. For raw materials, too much inventory again ties up capital. But if a company runs out of resources, work stoppages occur. Finally, because the process of placing an order for raw materials and supplies has associated costs (such as clerical time, shipping expenses, and higher unit costs for small quantities), it is important to minimize the frequency of ordering. Inventory models help the manager make decisions in such a way as to optimize the size of inventory.[22] (Because inventory models are most often used as a method of control, we will discuss them in more detail in Chapter 18.)

Queuing models. *Queuing models* are intended to help managers deal with waiting-line situations. We are all familiar with such situations: shoppers waiting to pay for groceries at Safeway, drivers waiting to buy gas at a Gulf station, travelers calling American Airlines for reservations, and customers waiting for a teller at Citibank.

Take the Safeway example. If a store manager has only one check-out stand in operation, the store's cost for check-out personnel is very low. On the other hand, many customers are upset by the long line that frequently develops. To solve the problem, the store manager could decide to keep 20 check-out stands open at all times. Customers would like the short waiting period, but personnel costs would be very high. A queuing model would be appropriate in this case to help the manager determine the optimal number of check-out stands: the number that would balance personnel costs and customer waiting time.[23]

21. See Adam and Ebert, *Production and Operations Management* for a recent review of decision trees and their applicability to management.

22. See Adam and Ebert, *Production and Operations Management;* Markland, *Topics in Management Science;* and Jose Tanchoco, Robert Davis, and Richard Wysk, "Economic Order Quantities Based on Unit-Load and Material-Handling Considerations," *Decision Sciences,* July 1980, pp. 514–521.

23. See Markland, *Topics in Management Science;* and E. H. Warren, Jr., "Estimating Waiting Time in a Queuing System," *Decision Sciences,* January 1981, pp. 112–117.

Distribution models. A decision facing many marketing managers relates to the distribution of the organization's products. Specifically, the manager must decide where the products should go and how to transport them. Railroads, trucking, air freight—each has associated shipping costs. The problem is to identify the combination of routes that optimizes distribution effectiveness and distribution costs. Linear programming is usually the basis for *distribution models,* although they may also be developed as simulations.[24]

Game theory. *Game theory* was originally developed to predict the effect of one's decision on one's competitors. Models developed from game theory are intended to predict how a competitor will react to various activities that an organization might undertake, such as price changes, promotional changes, and new products. If Coca-Cola were considering raising by 10 percent the price it charges bottlers for syrup, it might use a game theory model to predict whether Pepsi-Cola and Dr Pepper would follow suit. If the model revealed that they would, Coca-Cola would probably proceed. Otherwise it would probably maintain the existing price. Unfortunately, game theory has not yet proved as useful as it was originally expected to be. The complexities of the real world combined with the limitations of the technique itself restrict its applicability. Game theory does provide a useful conceptual framework for analyzing competitive behavior, however, and its usefulness may be improved in the future.[25]

The role of the computer in decision making

As indicated throughout this chapter, many of the quantitative techniques for planning and decision making are most effective when used with a computer. In fact, complex linear programming (especially the simplex method), simulation, econometric modeling, and PERT problems are nearly impossible without one.

Due to the high cost of computer technology in the early years, many of these techniques were unavailable to most small and many medium-sized organizations. Recent years, however, have seen a veritable computer explosion. By 1990, it has been predicted, 60 percent of all jobs in the United States will rely to some extent on information-processing computer activities.[26] Many elementary school children now use computers to learn basic skills. Perhaps the most significant factor in this explosion has been the development of minicomputers and microcomputers, which have tremendous capabilities but are relatively inexpensive.

24. See Adam and Ebert, *Production and Operations Management.*

25. See Shiv K. Gupta and John M. Gozzolino, *Fundamentals of Operations Research for Management* (San Francisco: Holden-Day, 1974).

26. See Joseph L. Sardinas, Jr., *Computing Today: An Introduction to Business Data Processing* (Englewood Cliffs, N.J.: Prentice-Hall, 1981).

With the aid of the newest generation of computers, combined with the increased familiarity of most persons with computer technology, sophisticated planning and decision making tools and techniques should soon be within the grasp of all managers. A paradoxical consequence of enhanced computer technology is that, while it makes it easier to deal with environmental complexity and uncertainty, it increases the need to keep abreast of current computer developments.

The pros and cons of quantitative techniques

The pros and cons of quantitative aids and techniques for planning and decision making are summarized in Table 8.5. In this section we will discuss both sides of the issue.

Problems and disadvantages

One weakness of quantitative aids is that they may not always adequately reflect reality. Many models are based on assumptions that may not always be valid. Even with the most sophisticated and powerful technique, simplifying assumptions may be needed. For example, for most techniques the manager must identify and characterize all variables to be considered. When the solution is subsequently implemented, a variable that has gone unaccounted for may influence it in some way.

Many problems are not amenable to quantitative analysis because important aspects are intangible and/or nonquantifiable. Employee morale or satisfaction is often a major factor in managerial decisions. Even though

Table 8.5 Pros and cons of quantitative aids for planning and decision making

Problems and disadvantages	Strengths and advantages
1. Models may not reflect reality.	1. Models are powerful tools for certain kinds of situations.
2. Problems may involve intangible or nonquantifiable factors.	2. Models help simplify and organize complex problems.
3. The use of quantitative aids may be costly.	3. Properly designed models and formulas enhance rationality.
4. Resistance to change may be encountered.	4. The computer explosion facilitates its use in many settings.
5. Problems may arise with the management—management scientist interface.	

questionnaires exist that purport to measure satisfaction, the numbers obtained from such surveys are estimates at best. Other intangible factors include the image of the organization, emotional issues, and many facets of social responsibility. One recent survey has shown that some companies, such as IBM and Hewlett-Packard, have a much better reputation than other companies, such as RCA and International Harvester.[27] In decisions involving such activities as advertising, borrowing, and recruiting, the company's reputation may be an important consideration. Quantitative techniques have a difficult time accounting for these factors.

Third, the use of quantitative aids may still be quite costly. Few companies can afford to develop their own econometric models. Even though the computer explosion will increase the availability of quantitative aids, there is still some expense involved, and it will take time for many of these techniques to become widely used.

Resistance to change also limits the use of quantitative aids in some settings. If a manager for a retail chain has always based decisions for new locations on personal visits, observations, and intuition, she or he may be less than eager to begin using a computer-based model for evaluating and selecting sites.

Finally, problems may arise in the manager–management scientist interface. Experts trained in the use of highly sophisticated quantitative aids and techniques may not understand or appreciate other aspects of management. They may use too much technical jargon and may even attempt to oversell the quantitative techniques without conceding their limitations or assessing the overall situation. On the other hand, some managers may not fully appreciate the value and potential power of quantitative techniques. They may have trouble looking beyond the costs involved. Of course, as the jobs of manager and management scientist become increasingly similar, these difficulties should subside.

Strengths and advantages

On a more optimistic note, quantitative aids offer many advantages. For situations that are amenable to quantification, they can bring sophisticated mathematical processes to bear.

In a related vein, quantitative aids can help a manager simplify and organize complex problems. Both PERT and decision trees force a manager to develop a schematic diagram of a sequence of activities and/or decisions. By using them, the manager can better understand and appreciate the consequences of one activity or decision on other activities or decisions that will arise later.

Properly designed models and formulas also help decision makers "see reason." For example, a film investor might at first ridicule science fiction and

27. See Claire Makin, "Ranking Corporate Reputations," *Fortune*, January 10, 1983, pp. 34–44.

fantasy films as childish. However, when exposed to a pay-off matrix comparing the likelihood of financial success for a new film based on a serious literary work with that for a new George Lucas series, the investor may decide that childish fantasies are a good investment. Quantitative approaches force the manager to look beyond her or his prejudices and predispositions.

Finally, the computer explosion is rapidly making quantitative techniques available in a wider range of settings than ever. It will still take some time, but many managers stand to benefit from current technological innovations.

The crucial point to remember is that quantitative aids are a means to an end and not an end in themselves. Just as a carpenter uses a handsaw in some situations and an electric saw in others, a manager must recognize that a quantitative model may be useful in some situations but not in others that may call for a more intuitive approach. Knowing the difference is one mark of a good manager.

Summary of key points

Forecasting is the process of developing assumptions or premises about the future that managers can use in planning or decision making. Various approaches to forecasting include sales or revenue forecasting, technological forecasting, resource forecasting, general economic forecasting, population and/or market size forecasting, and governmental activity forecasting.

Techniques available for forecasting include time-series analysis, causal modeling, qualitative procedures (such as the Delphi technique and panel-of-expert-opinion, sales-force-composition, and customer evaluation models), and various specialized techniques (such as morphological analysis and substitution effect models).

Other popular planning aids and techniques include linear programming, break-even analysis, simulation, and PERT. Linear programming is appropriate when the objective and constraints of a problem can be expressed as linear functions and the intent is to allocate resources in an optimal fashion. Break-even analysis focuses on identifying the point at which revenues and costs are equal. A simulation is a model of a real-world situation that the manager can use to determine the probable effects of various actions. PERT involves the creation of a network that specifies all activities required to complete a project and the relationships among those activities.

Useful techniques that are more directly relevant to decision making include the pay-off matrix and decision trees. A pay-off matrix specifies the expected value of various alternatives as a function of different potential outcomes associated with each. A decision tree extends the pay-off matrix concept by considering a series of sequential alternatives and potential outcomes. Other decision making aids include inventory models, queuing models, distribution models, and game theory.

Computers will surely play an increasingly important role in making quantitative techniques for planning and decision making available in a wider variety of settings. There are a number of pros and cons associated with the use of quantitative techniques for planning and decision making. The major point to consider when evaluating the pros and cons of quantitative techniques is that they are tools and aids for facilitating effective planning and decision making, not an objective in and of themselves.

QUESTIONS FOR DISCUSSION

1. The text noted that universities have to do sales or revenue forecasting to determine future income from state financial aid. Discuss other kinds of forecasting that are important to a university. What information does the university administration need to develop these forecasts?

2. Which kind of forecasting is probably easiest? Which kind is probably most difficult? Why?

3. Some people argue that managers don't really have to know how to use the techniques discussed in this chapter—that a manager can always call on technicians to work things out. Do you agree or disagree?

4. Can break-even analysis be used when the variables are nonquantifiable? That is, is break-even analysis possible when one can't attach dollar values to costs and revenues?

5. Many colleges of business require a capstone course during the senior year that uses a simulation. Find out whether your college or school uses such a simulation and, if it does, how realistic the simulation is.

6. Try to develop a PERT network to plan a research project or other class project you are working on. What problems do you encounter? Could you also do this for something designed to take a longer period of time, such as your search for a job?

7. A discussion question in Chapter 7 asked you to recall a major decision you had made in your life and to think about whether you used a rational or a behavioral decision model. Using that same major decision, try to put the alternatives into a decision tree format. Would doing so have helped you make your decision? Would it have led you to a different decision?

8. Can you think of any additional pros or cons of using quantitative techniques? Give examples.

9. You are the CEO of a large corporation. You have a qualified staff of analysts, several computer programmers, and extra cash to spend on making effective decisions. Can you think of times when you might *not* want to do a full analysis and make the most careful decision possible?

10. What should you do when your intuition tells you one thing but the quantitative analysis of a situation tells you another? How will your actions differ depending on your position in the organization?

C A S E   8.1

At the beginning of this chapter, you read a scenario about a major jet aircraft manufacturer. In 1978 the company forecast a booming market for aircraft over the next ten years. The organization had large financial resources, so it appeared to be in a good position to take advantage of this growth. The company being described was Boeing. The case that follows recounts what Boeing chose to do, explains what the results were, and then raises some other issues for your consideration.

Boeing suffers due to inaccurate forecasting

For years, Boeing Company dominated both the domestic and the international market for jet transport planes. The 727 is the mainstay of most of the major United States airlines, while the 747 dominates the international routes. Sales to foreign carriers account for over 60 percent of Boeing's revenues. Historically, Boeing has always maintained a high level of financial strength.

In 1978 the company forecast that the market for new aircraft would exceed $82 billion through 1988. Further, Boeing felt that soaring jet fuel prices would cause many airlines to seek fuel-efficient planes. (The price of jet fuel had increased from 11 cents a gallon 5 years before to around $1.10 a gallon.) Given these conditions and Boeing's strong financial foundation, the company decided to commit over $3 billion to developing a new generation of aircraft that was both fuel-efficient and technologically advanced.

The Boeing 767 was projected as a large, wide-body plane with a seating capacity of from 211 to 289 passengers. The 757 is a smaller, single-aisle aircraft. The 757 was seen as a replacement for the 727. Both plans are designed with state-of-the-art technology.

During the four years needed to develop the 757 and the 767, however, three changes in Boeing's environments threw the company's plans off track. First, the airline industry fell on extremely hard times. Deregulation, fare wars, and excess capacity forced Braniff into backruptcy and left other carriers in weakened financial positions. In the early 1980s, many airlines were concerned more with just surviving than with building a new fleet.

Second, Airbus Industrie, a European consortium of aerospace companies, began making major in-roads in the international market. Many international carriers such as Lufthansa and KLM began placing more orders with Airbus than with Boeing. Two new Airbus planes, the A300 and the A310, will compete directly with the 757 and the 767.

Finally, increasing jet fuel prices turned out not to be so significant as originally projected. Prices have dropped and stabilized at around 95 cents a gallon. At the same time, soaring interest rates have made it more expensive to buy new aircraft. Hence the relative advantages of the 757 and the 767 are not as great as expected, while the costs make purchasing the planes more difficult.

As a result of these factors, sales of all of Boeing's planes—especially the 757 and the 767—are much lower than projected. Eastern purchased 27 of the 757s and took an option on 24 more. Delta has ordered 60 767s, and United has several 767s scheduled for delivery. But several other orders have been either delayed or canceled outright. In 1981 Air Florida canceled an order worth $105 million. Boeing has also been left holding three 747s that were built for Braniff but never delivered.

Although the short-term picture for Boeing may be bleak, the company is still strong financially. Boeing has hundreds of millions of dollars in reserves and, as a cushion, arranged a $3 billion line of credit in 1979. Further, the company has patience. The 727, the most successful plane in the history of aviation, took two years to become widely accepted. Top management expresses a similar commitment to both the 757 and the 767.

CASE
QUESTIONS

1. Are there any reasons to believe that Boeing could have done a better job in developing its 1978 forecast?
2. What actions should Boeing take now to get back on track?
3. What might Boeing's current forecasts look like?
4. What quantitative tools might Boeing use in its planning and decision making? In what areas might they be used?

CASE
REFERENCES

"Boeing's Tall Order (60 767 Jets)." *New York Times,* November 16, 1980, Section 3.

"The Crosscurrents Buffeting Airbus Industrie," *Business Week,* March 21, 1983, pp. 101–102.

Kraar, Louis. "Boeing Takes a Bold Plunge to Keep Flying High." *Fortune,* September 25, 1978, pp. 42–50.

"Slump Clouds the Take-Off of 767." *Wall Street Journal,* June 16, 1982, p. 29.

Stuart, Alexander. "Boeing's New Beauties Are a Tough Sell." *Fortune,* October 18, 1982, pp. 114–120.

C A S E   8.2

Jack Harrison and Brent Anderson recently formed a contract construction company. Both Harrison and Anderson have several years of experience in the construction industry. Harrison has worked

**Using decision
making techniques**

primarily in the construction of new homes; Anderson has devoted most of his time to large-scale construction. Their new company, H&A Construction, will concentrate primarily on building homes and small buildings.

H&A has recently won its first bid and has contracted to build a small convenience store in the local community. Basically, it has 120 days to build a 1,000-square-foot structure from prefabricated steel framing material, concrete blocks, wood, and brick. The convenience store company will then erect a facade and decorate the interior of the store.

Harrison and Anderson are having their first strategy meeting about how to tackle the job. Jack Harrison begins the meeting by describing how he plans to proceed. "I've got it all worked out," he says, "The PERT diagram I put together lays everything out for us. The first things we have to do are to order the steel, concrete blocks, wood, and bricks. I've already checked—we can get everything we need locally. We can lay the plumbing and get Bush Concrete to pour the foundation for us. By that time, the steel will be here and we'll erect the frame.

"Williams Electric would be a good outfit to do the wiring for us. All that will be left then will be to put up the walls and then lay in the roof. According to the PERT diagram, the critical path is 110 days. Even if we lose a few days to rain, it looks like we should still finish with time to spare."

"Now Jack," Brent responded, "You know I didn't go to college and all this PERT and critical path stuff is Greek to me. Everything you've said sounds fine, but I don't think we really need this fancy chart and all. It seems to me that we should just do the things we need to do and not spend our time worrying about any critical path."

Harrison was uncomfortable with his new partner's response. He tried to convince Anderson about the value of PERT and how useful it was for both planning and control. He tried to explain how they might be able to use linear programming, pay-off matrices, decision trees, and other quantitative techniques at some point in the future. But the harder he tried to convince Anderson of the potential value of this technique, the more his partner resisted. Finally, Anderson muttered something about wishing they could just build things and not worry about "fancy statistics." Then he walked out of the room.

As Harrison sat and reflected, he just couldn't understand his partner's attitude. He had studied these procedures in school and knew that they were valid. His previous boss had also used them. How could he convince Anderson that this was the way to do things?

CASE
QUESTIONS

1. Discuss Harrison and Anderson's different viewpoints. Is one more valid than the other? Why or why not?

2. What mistakes does each man appear to be making?

3. Does PERT seem useful for the job at hand? Do you think H&A Construction will ever be able to use the other techniques that Harrison mentioned?

The Organizing Process

PART CONTENTS

9

BUILDING BLOCKS OF ORGANIZATIONS

CHAPTER OBJECTIVES

1. Explain the concept of work specialization and the rationale behind its use in organizations.

2. List the common bases of departmentalization and discuss advantages and disadvantages of each.

3. Discuss delegation and decentralization as means of establishing patterns of authority on an individual level and on an organizational level.

4. Describe the span of management, and discuss situational factors in determining the appropriate span of management.

5. Explain the need for coordination of organizational activities, and discuss several coordination techniques.

O P E N I N G I N C I D E N T

You are a manager at a large apparel company. One of your products has sold over a billion units in its more than 120 years of existence. Your trademark is one of the most widely recognized in the world. Annual sales for the firm are approaching $3 billion. At present, your company is rapidly expanding its product mix and area of operations. Relatively new product lines have been purchased or developed in women's wear, infant clothing, athletic clothing, and hats. The current product mix consists of over 2,000 different styles, colors, and fabrics. The company's network of operations has spread worldwide. How should your company be structured?

After graduating with business degrees in management from a major state university, James Henderson and Rebecca Moore accepted positions as plant management trainees. Jim entered the management training program of a large cosmetics company, while Becky went to work for a smaller firm in the same industry. A couple of years later, they met again at a trade show. They went out to dinner one evening and began to discuss their respective careers. After a few drinks, Jim began to describe some of the things about his job that he didn't particularly like.

"And another thing," he continued, "is that I have such a narrow job. I mean, I'm only involved in a very small part of our total system. I'm not sure where the products come from before they get to our department, and after we finish with them I don't see them again until they're on the shelf at Kroger. And my boss refuses to let me make any decisions without checking with him first. I know I could do the job, but he just won't give me a chance. I sure didn't expect it to turn out like this back when we were in school."

"It doesn't sound like you're very happy with your work, Jim," said Becky. "I'm not sure I'd be happy with that job, either. As part of my training, my company transferred me across several departments, so I have a fairly good feel for our overall operation. I've been in on some pretty big decisions, too. Just a few weeks ago, my boss let me buy a new piece of machinery for the plant. I talked to the manufacturers' representatives, developed the cost estimates, and authorized the final purchase. I guess I've just been lucky."

Luck or not, Jim and Becky obviously have quite different perceptions of their work environments. As we shall see, much of this difference stems from different forms of organization structure. Jim's organization is evidently more specialized and centralized than Becky's. Of course, the mere fact that Jim seems to dislike his organization and Becky likes hers does not mean that everyone would react the same way.

As we noted in Chapter 1, after management has developed a set of workable plans, it must organize the human and other resources necessary to carry out these plans. Managerial processes are not discrete activities performed in a rigid sequence, but the organizing function logically follows the planning function. This chapter, the first of a four-chapter section on the organizing process, describes the "building blocks" of organizations: work specialization, departmentalization, delegation, decentralization, the span of management, and coordination of organizational activities. Subsequent chapters focus on getting work done in organizations, organization design, and organizational change and development.

Before beginning, however, we should take a moment to discuss what organization structure is and to differentiate it from organization design. The structure of a system such as an organization consists of its major components and dimensions. The design of a system reflects how the system defines and interrelates these components and dimensions. For example, a Ford automobile and a Chevrolet automobile have the same basic structure (engine, passenger compartment, trunk, fenders, and so on), but they also have unique designs (body style, engine size, and trunk capacity). When we discuss *organization structure,* we are concerned with the common elements that characterize all organizations, whereas *organization design* deals with unique definitions and interrelationships among these elements.

Work specialization

The most basic element of organization structure is *work specialization,* or the degree to which the overall task of the organization is broken down and divided into smaller, component parts. The concept of division of labor, which means basically the same thing as work specialization, is generally attributed to Adam Smith.[1] Smith described how specialization was used in a pin factory to improve productivity. One man drew the wire, another straightened it, a third cut it, a fourth ground the point, and so on. In this fashion, Smith claimed, 10 men were able to produce 48,000 pins in a day, whereas each man would have been able to produce only 20 pins per day working alone!

In the twentieth century, the best example of the impact of work specialization is the automobile assembly line, as pioneered by Henry Ford. Mass production stemming from work specialization techniques has had a profound impact in the United States[2] as well as the rest of the world.[3] High levels of low-cost production transformed our society during the first several decades of this century into one of the strongest economies in the history of the world.

The rationale for specialization

A good way to approach the rationale for specialization is to trace through a hypothetical example of the evolutionary nature of work specialization (see Fig-

1. Adam Smith, *Wealth of Nations* (New York: Modern Library, 1937; originally published in 1776).

2. See Max Lerner, *America as a Civilization* (New York: Simon and Schuster, 1957).

3. See Richard J. Barnet and Ronald E. Muller, *Global Reach* (New York: Simon and Schuster, 1974).

Figure 9.1
The evolution of
work specialization

PHASE 1: THE INDIVIDUAL ENTREPRENEUR

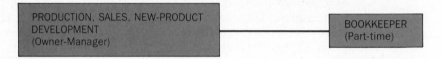

PRODUCTION, SALES, RECORD KEEPING,
NEW-PRODUCT DEVELOPMENT
(Owner-Manager)

PHASE 2: THE SMALL BUSINESS

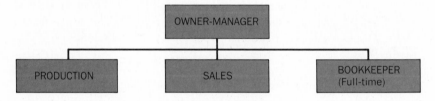

PRODUCTION, SALES, NEW-PRODUCT
DEVELOPMENT
(Owner-Manager)

BOOKKEEPER
(Part-time)

PHASE 3: THE GROWING BUSINESS

OWNER-MANAGER

PRODUCTION   SALES   BOOKKEEPER
(Full-time)

PHASE 4: THE LARGE BUSINESS

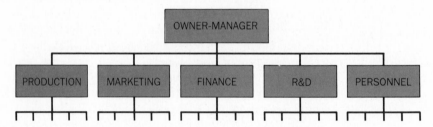

OWNER-MANAGER

PRODUCTION   MARKETING   FINANCE   R&D   PERSONNEL

ure 9.1). Assume that a part-time inventor discovers how to make an internal combustion engine that uses salt water for fuel. The inventor begins to produce the engines himself in his garage. As an individual entrepreneur, he makes the engines, sells them, keeps financial records, and also tries to develop other new products. Sooner or later, however, the operation will probably get too big for our inventor to handle all of these activities himself.

At this point, his operation becomes a small business, phase 2 in our diagram. He might begin to specialize by hiring a part-time bookkeeper to help with financial record keeping, an activity that was previously a part of his task. He has "broken off" a piece of it and given it to someone else. That is, in phase 2 he has begun to specialize.

With the passage of time, the business is likely to continue to grow. During this third phase, the owner may decide to employ a sales representative to market the product. Financial demands may call for a fulltime bookkeeper or even an accountant. He may also hire a fulltime production employee so that he can devote all his time to managing the overall enterprise and continuing his new-product development work.

Ultimately, the business may reach large-scale proportions. In the large business, highly skilled professionals may serve as vice presidents in each of the areas initially handled by individuals. Each vice president in turn, may coordinate division managers, product managers, and operating managers.

Thus the growth of the firm is marked by two parallel processes: (1) an increasingly large total task for the organization, and (2) pressure to "break off" various components of this total task. In addition to this evolutionary pressure to specialize, there are several more immediate justifications for specializing. Many of these ideas can be traced back to the writings of Adam Smith.[4]

Individual dexterity. If a worker has to learn only a small, simple task, he or she will probably become very proficient at that task. It is reasonable to expect individual skill and expertise to increase as work specialization increases.

Decreased transfer time. If an employee is performing several different tasks, it stands to reason that some time will be lost as the worker stops doing the first task and starts doing the next. Specialization is one way to eliminate this nonproductive transfer time.

Specialized equipment. The more narrowly defined a particular task is, the easier it may be to develop specialized machinery and equipment to assist with that task. Again, specialization is seen as a vehicle for increasing worker output.

Decreased training costs. Work specialization reduces training costs. The more specialized a job is, the easier it is to train someone to do it. When an employee who performs a highly specialized task is absent or resigns, the manager should be able to train someone new at relatively low cost.

Effects of specialization

Specialization of work has traditionally been assumed to boost efficiency and overall performance. And, although specialization is generally thought of in terms of operating jobs, many organizations have extended the basic elements of specialization to managerial and professional levels as well. A recent management overhaul at Porsche, the German sportscar manufacturer, resulted in increased specialization in both the engineering and development and the personnel units.[5]

4. Smith, *Wealth of Nations.*
5. See David B. Tinnin, "The American at the Wheel of Porsche," *Fortune,* April 5, 1982, pp. 78–87.

At the same time, however, specialization can have negative consequences. The foremost criticism is that workers who perform highly specialized jobs are likely to become bored and dissatisfied. That is, the job may be so specialized that it offers no challenge or stimulation. Boredom and monotony set in, absenteeism rises, and the quality of the work may suffer.

Furthermore, the anticipated benefits of specialization simply do not occur in some work settings. A study conducted at Maytag by M. D. Kilbridge revealed that, in the case under scrutiny, the time spent moving work-in-process from one worker to another was greater than the time needed for one individual to change from job to job.[6]

Some degree of work specialization characterizes most organizations. Although specialization often leads to gains in productivity, it should not be carried to extremes because of the negative consequences that could result. Managers should be sensitive to situations in which specialization should be avoided. The next chapter addresses the topic of job design, which involves determining the optimal level of work specialization to balance productivity gains against satisfaction losses.

Grouping jobs: Departmentalization

Another basic building block of organizations is departmentalization, the grouping of jobs according to some logical arrangement. In Figure 9.1 we considered a growing business. When that organization reached a certain size, it became impossible for the owner–manager to continue personal supervision of all the employees, so new managerial positions were created to supervise the work of others. The assignment of employees to particular managers was not done randomly; rather, jobs were grouped according to some plan. The logic embodied in such a plan is the basis for all *departmentalization:* the process of grouping jobs into manageable units. The following sections describe some of the more common kinds of departmentalization.

Functional departmentalization

An organization that exhibits functional departmentalization has chosen to group together those jobs wherein employees perform the same or similar activities. (The word *function* here is used differently from its use in referring to the basic managerial functions of planning and decision making, organizing, leading, and controlling. In this context, we are referring to generic activities carried out by organizations as opposed to specific dimensions of a manager's job.) An example of a firm that is departmentalized by function appears in Figure 9.2. This company, Johnson Products, manufactures and markets a line of cosmetics, toiletries, and fragrances for black women. One set of activities for this kind of organization involves the actual manufacturing of the products.

6. M. D. Kilbridge, "Reduced Costs Through Job Enlargement: A Case," *The Journal of Business,* 1960, Vol. 33, pp. 357–362.

Figure 9.2
Departmentalization
by function (Johnson
Products Company)

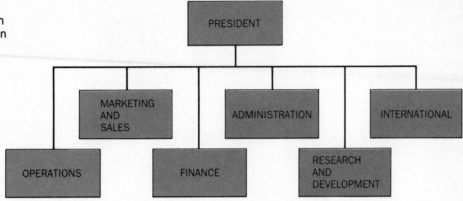

These activities have been grouped together and called operations, or production. The activities associated with advertising, promotion, and selling are grouped together as marketing and sales. Finance involves the management of the firm's financial resources, and administration carries out general management tasks. New-product development fits into the research and development department. Finally, activities concerned with business opportunities in other countries are grouped together in the international division.[7] (At higher levels of an organization, departments are usually called divisions, and it is also common to have departments within departments. These points will be explored later.)

Functional departmentalization is most common in smaller organizations, because it is very compatible with a relatively high level of work specialization. Referring again to our hypothetical firm in Figure 9.1, we can see that a functional form of organization emerged in response to increased levels of specialization.

The primary advantages of functional departmentalization are that: (1) each department can be staffed by experts in that functional area, (2) supervision is facilitated because an individual manager needs to be familiar with only a relatively narrow set of skills, and (3) coordination pressures on activities in each department are relatively easy to handle. On the other hand, as an organization begins to grow in size, several disadvantages of function departmentalization may emerge: (1) decision making tends to become slower and more bureaucratic, (2) employees may begin to concentrate too narrowly on their own units and lose sight of the total organizational system, and (3) accountability and performance become increasingly difficult to monitor (for example, it may not be possible to determine whether a new product's failure is due to production deficiencies or to a poor marketing campaign).

In summary, functional departmentalization is common and generally logical for smaller organizations. As the organization grows, however, the

7. See John Clark, *Business Today—Success and Failures* (New York: Random House, 1979) for a discussion of Johnson Products Company.

Figure 9.3
Departmentalization
by product
(Simplified view of
General Motors)

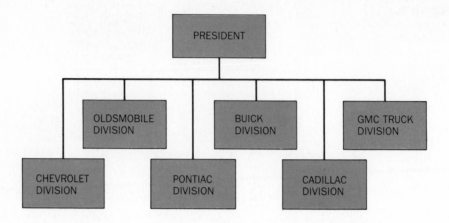

problems that functional departmentalization can engender begin to offset the advantages it confers. An alternative type of departmentalization, which is common in larger organizations and especially in those with a great many products or product lines, is product departmentalization.

Product departmentalization

Product departmentalization is the grouping and arranging of activities around products or product groups. The rationale for such an approach is that, when the number of products or product groups begins to get larger, the products are also likely to become more diverse. One firm, for example, may be manufacturing products ranging from jet engines to consumer appliances. The marketing, financial, production, personnel, and research and development activities associated with jet engines are likely to be much different from those associated with consumer appliances. Thus it is both more logical and more feasible to group the specialized activities for each product line than to insist, say, that one functional department market both jet engines and refrigerators.

Figure 9.3 shows a highly simplified version of the automotive activities of General Motors. The primary units focus on the Chevrolet, Oldsmobile, Pontiac, Buick, Cadillac, and GMC Truck product groups. Marketing, production, research and development, and many other functional activities are performed within each product group. (In recent years GM has begun to perform many of these activities across units as well.[8] More information about GM and its changes in structure will be presented in Chapter 11.)

The strategic business unit (SBU) approach to strategy described in Chapter 5 revolves around a product view of departmentalization. That is, each SBU can be viewed as a department responsible for one product or product group.

8. Charles G. Burck, "How GM Turned Itself Around," *Fortune*, January 16, 1978, pp. 86–100.

Figure 9.4
Departmentalization
by location
(Distribution
Division of Harris
County News)

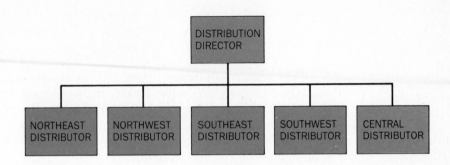

In 1978 Oki Electric Industry Company in Japan adopted an SBU structure. The company president created fifteen departments, or SBUs, centering on such high-profit products as computer terminal peripherals and integrated circuits. By 1981 the company's sales had increased by 12 percent to $880 million and its profits had increased by 28 percent to $19 million.[9]

The major advantages of product departmentalization are that: (1) activities associated with one product or product group can be easily integrated and coordinated, (2) the speed and effectiveness of decision making are enhanced, and (3) performance of individual products or product groups can be assessed more easily and objectively, thereby improving the accountability of departments for the results of their activities. Two major disadvantages of product departmentalization are that: (1) managers in each department tend to focus on their own product or product group to the exclusion of the rest of the organization and (2) administrative costs rise, because each department must have its own functional specialists such as marketing researchers and financial analysts.

Location departmentalization

Location departmentalization is used somewhat less frequently than function and product departmentalization. The geographic location isolated by this form of departmentalization may range in size from a hemisphere to only a few blocks of a large city.

Harris County News is a magazine distributor that is departmentalized by location (Harris County is the county in Texas where the city of Houston is located). The primary function of the company's distribution division is to pull old magazines off the racks and replace them with new issues in grocery stores, drugstores, bookstores, and so on. As shown in Figure 9.4, the company serves five basic geographic areas. Each department has its own shipping and receiving facility, fleet of delivery vans, and sales force. The manager of each department reports to a corporate executive (we have called this officer

9. "A U.S. Concept Revives Oki," *Business Week*, March 1, 1982, pp. 112–113.

the distribution director). Other organizations with location departmentalization include manufacturing, wholesaling, and transportation companies, police departments (precincts represent geographic areas of a city), and the Federal Reserve Bank.

The primary advantage of this form of departmentalization is that it enables the organization to respond easily to unique customer and environmental characteristics in the various regions. On the other hand, a larger administrative staff may be required (Harris County News has a personnel manager for each area), and the organization may have to invest in control systems to keep track of units in scattered locations.

Customer departmentalization

Under customer departmentalization, the organization structures its activities so as to respond to and interact with specific customers or customer groups. The lending activities in most banks, for example, are usually tailored to meet the needs of different kinds of customers. Figure 9.5 presents a partial view of the lending departments for a moderate-sized Midwestern bank. If an individual wants a personal loan to buy a new car, to purchase a television set, or to pay for a vacation, he or she is referred to the consumer loan department. Businesses borrow from the commercial loan department. A farmer who needs to buy a new tractor deals with the agricultural loan department. Larger banks may also have other lending departments for small businesses, large businesses, credit card operations such as Visa and Mastercard, and so on.

The basic advantage of customer departmentalization is that it allows the organization to use skilled specialists to deal with unique customers or customer groups. It takes a certain set of skills to evaluate a balance sheet and lend a business $50,000 for operating capital and a different set of skills to evaluate an individual's credit worthiness and lend $10,000 for a new car. However, customer departmentalization also requires a fairly large administrative staff to integrate the activities of the various departments. In banks, for example, coordination is necessary to make sure the organization doesn't overcommit itself in any one area, to handle collections on delinquent accounts from a diverse set of customers, and so forth.

Figure 9.5
Departmentalization by customer (Typical lending departments for a midwestern bank)

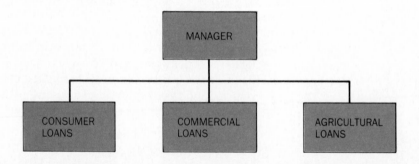

Miscellaneous forms of departmentalization

Departmentalization by function, product, location, or customer is adopted most frequently in grouping jobs in organizations, but two other approaches are occasionally used.

Departmentalization by time. Some organizations find it useful to group activities by time. The machine shop of Baker International in Houston, for example, operates on three shifts, each with a superintendent who reports to the plant manager and each with its own functional departments. Time (8:00 A.M.–4:00 P.M., 4:00 P.M.–12:00 midnight, and 12:00 midnight–8:00 A.M.) is thus the framework for many organizational activities. Other organizations that use time as a basis for grouping jobs include some hospitals and many airlines.

Departmentalization by sequence. In other situations departmentalization by sequence is appropriate. By sequence we mean some differentiating factor such as a number or letter. Many college students must register in sequence: last names starting with A through E in line 1, F through L in line 2, and so on, or student numbers less than 200000 at 8:00 A.M. and those between 200001 and 400000 at 10:00 A.M. Other areas that may be organized in sequence include credit departments (specific employees run credit checks according to customer name), insurance claims divisions (by policy number), and prisons (inmates eat according to serial number or cell block).

Final considerations

Two final points about departmentalization remain to be made. First, departments are often called something entirely different; divisions, units, sections, and bureaus are all common synonyms. The higher we look in an organization, the more likely we are to find departments referred to as divisions. Government departments are often known as bureaus. The underlying logic behind all the labels is the same, however: they represent groups of jobs that have been yoked together according to some unifying principle.

Second, almost any organization is likely to employ multiple bases of departmentalization, depending on level. At the top level, departmentalization might be by product. Each product division may be further divided into functional departments such as finance, marketing, and production. The marketing department of a division may have special units for different customer groups, and each customer department may have regional sales territories based on location. Finally, a plant in one of the product departments might operate three shifts and be departmentalized by time. Other possibilities for combining many forms of departmentalization in one organization will be presented in Chapter 11. At that time we will discuss matrix organization, which combines functional and product departmentalization at the same level.

Establishing patterns of authority: Delegation and decentralization

A third basic building block of organizations is the way in which authority is distributed. After considering the nature of authority in organizations, we will discuss how authority is distributed at both the individual level (referred to as delegation) and the organizational level (called decentralization).

The nature of authority

Authority is power that has been legitimized by the organization.[10] If a stranger walks up to you and tells you to run an errand for her, there is no compelling reason for you to do so (unless, of course, she's holding a gun). On the other hand, if you work for a manager who asks you to do something, a refusal can result in a reprimand, a delayed promotion, or even dismissal from your job. The difference is that the stranger has no authority over you, whereas your boss does.

Just as work specialization and departmentalization are natural outgrowths of increasing organizational size and complexity, so too is the establishment of patterns of authority. When our beleaguered inventor hired a professional sales representative (see Figure 9.1) he gave the salesperson not only a part of his own task, but authority over that task as well. The salesperson will serve as a representative of the company and must be able to commit the company to the sale of the product, grant discounts, and so forth. If every decision to be made requires the approval of the owner–manager, he is no better off than he was before he hired the sales representative. The power given to the salesperson to make certain kinds of decisions represents the establishment of a pattern of authority: there are some decisions that the salesperson can make alone, some that are to be made in consultation with others, and some on which the sales representative must defer to the boss. Our concern, then, is with such patterns of authority distribution. (We will further explore authority and power in Chapter 14.)

The delegation process

Delegation involves the establishment of a pattern of authority between a superior and one or more subordinates. Specifically, *delegation* is the process by which the manager assigns a portion of his or her total work load to others. The following sections give a number of reasons why delegation is useful, describe the delegation process, and explore problems that may impede effective delegation.

Reasons for delegation. The primary reason for delegation is to enable the manager to get more work done. Subordinates help ease the manager's

10. See John R. P. French and Bertran Raven, "The Bases of Social Power," in *Group Dynamics,* ed. Dorwin Cartwright and Alvin F. Zander, 2nd ed. (Evanston, Ill.: Row, Peterson, 1960), pp. 607–623.

burden by doing major portions of the organization's work. In some instances, too, a subordinate may have more expertise in addressing a particular problem than the manager does. The subordinate may have had special training in developing computer information systems or may be more familiar with a particular product line or geographic area. Delegation also helps develop the subordinate for future promotions. By participating in decision making and problem solving, subordinates learn more about overall operations and improve their managerial skills.

Parts of the delegation process. In theory, delegation from a manager to a subordinate consists of three basic parts (see Figure 9.6). First the manager assigns *responsibility*, or gives the person a job to do. The assignment of responsibility might range from telling a subordinate to prepare a report to placing the person in charge of a six-month task force. Along with the assignment, the individual is also given the *authority* to do the job. The manager may give the subordinate the power to requisition needed information from confidential files or to direct a group of other workers. Finally, the manager requires *accountability* from the subordinate. That is, the subordinate has an obligation to carry out the task assigned by the manager.

These three parts do not, of course, follow in rigid 1–2–3 order. Indeed, when a manager and a subordinate have developed a good working relationship, the major parts of the process may be implied rather than stated. The manager may simply mention that a particular job must be done. A perceptive subordinate may realize that the manager is actually assigning the job to her. From past experience with the boss, she may also know, without being told,

Figure 9.6
Parts of the
delegation process

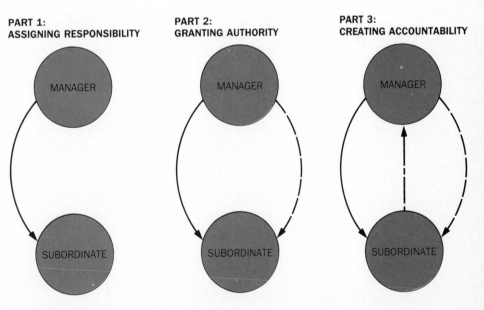

PART 1:
ASSIGNING RESPONSIBILITY

PART 2:
GRANTING AUTHORITY

PART 3:
CREATING ACCOUNTABILITY

that she has the necessary authority to do the job and that she is accountable to the boss for finishing the job as "agreed."[11]

Problems in delegation. Unfortunately, problems often arise in the delegation process. For a variety of reasons, a manager may be reluctant to delegate:

1. The manager may be so disorganized that he or she is unable to plan work in advance and, as a result, be unable to delegate appropriately.
2. The manager may worry that the subordinate will do too well and pose a threat to her or his own advancement.
3. The manager may not trust the subordinate to do the job well.

Similarly, some subordinates are reluctant to accept delegation:

1. They are afraid that failure will result in a reprimand or disciplinary action.
2. They may perceive that there are no rewards for accepting additional responsibility.
3. They may simply prefer to avoid risk and, therefore, want their boss to make all the decisions.

There are no "quick fixes" for these problems. Basically, it becomes an issue of communication. Subordinates must understand their own responsibility, authority, and accountability, and the manager must come to recognize the value of effective delegation. With the passage of time, subordinates should develop to the point where they can make substantial contributions to the organization. At the same time, the manager should recognize that a subordinate's satisfactory performance is not a threat to his or her own career, but an accomplishment on the part of both the subordinate who did the job *and* the manager who trained the subordinate and was astute enough to entrust the subordinate with the project. Responsibility for the outcome, however, continues to reside with the manager, who is accountable to a higher-level manager.

Decentralization

Just as authority can be delegated from one individual to another, organizations also develop patterns of authority across a wide variety of positions and departments. *Decentralization* is the extent to which power and authority are systematically delegated throughout the organization to middle and lower-level managers. General Electric, for example, has historically allowed middle and lower-level managers to make major decisions regarding their areas of responsibility.

It is important to recognize that decentralization is actually one end of a continuum anchored at the other end by *centralization,* the extent to which power and authority are systematically retained by higher-level managers. Hence a decentralized organization is one in which decision making power and

11. See Dale McConkey, *No Nonsense Delegation* (New York: AMACOM, 1974).

authority are delegated as far down the chain of command as possible. Conversely, in a centralized organization, decision making power and authority are retained at the higher levels of management. No organization is ever completely decentralized or completely centralized. These concepts are a matter of degree: some firms position themselves toward one end of the continuum, while some lean the other way.

What factors determine an organization's position on the decentralization–centralization continuum? The more common determinants include the following:[12]

1. **The external environments.** Usually, the greater the complexity and uncertainty of the environment, the greater the tendency to decentralize.
2. **History of the organization.** Firms have a tendency to do what they have done in the past, so there is likely to be some relationship between what an organization did in its earlier history and what it chooses to do today in terms of centralization or decentralization.
3. **Nature of the decision.** The costlier and riskier the decision, the more pressure there is to centralize.
4. **Abilities of lower-level managers.** If lower-level managers don't have the ability to make high-quality decisions, there is likely to be a high level of centralization. If lower-level managers are very well qualified, top management can take advantage of their talents by decentralizing; in fact, if top management fails to do so, talented lower-level managers may leave the organization.

There is no set of clear-cut guidelines for a manager to use in determining whether to centralize or decentralize. Many successful organizations (such as Sears, General Electric, and General Motors) routinely practice decentralization. Equally successful firms such as McDonald's and K mart have tended to remain centralized. Even within the same industry, different formulas for success have been applied. Du Pont and Dow are the two largest chemical companies in the United States, and each is among the twenty-five largest industrial firms in the country. Over the years, Du Pont has consistently remained decentralized in its operations, whereas Dow has been much more centralized. Both have been extremely successful.[13] Apparently the appropriate degree of decentralization is that which fits the circumstances.

The span of management

The fourth primary building block of an organization is the *span of management* (also called the span of control): the number of subordinates who report to a particular manager. One of the earliest examples of attention to the span of management is found in the Old Testament. Moses is advised by his

12. See Ernest Dale, *Organization* (New York: American Management Associations, 1967).

13. See Lee Smith, "Dow vs. Du Pont: Rival Formulas for Leadership," *Fortune*, September 10, 1979, pp. 74–84.

father, Jethro, to designate "rulers of thousands, and rulers of hundreds, rulers of fifties, and rulers of tens" (Exodus 18:13–26).

Narrow versus wide spans

The optimal span of management has been a primary concern of managers and researchers for many years. Should it be relatively narrow (with few subordinates per manager) or relatively wide (many subordinates)? What is the optimal number of subordinates that a manager can deal with?

One early writer, A. V. Graicunas, attempted to quantify problems connected with the span of management.[14] Graicunas noted that a manager must deal with three kinds of interactions with and among subordinates: direct (the manager's one-to-one relationship with each subordinate), cross (among the subordinates themselves), and group (between groups of subordinates). The number of possible interactions among group members can be determined by the following formula:

$$I = N\left(\frac{2^N}{2} + N - 1\right)$$

where I = total number of interactions with and among subordinates

N = number of subordinates

If a manager has 2 subordinates, 6 potential interactions exist. If the number of subordinates increases to 3, the possible interactions total 18; with 5 subordinates there are 100 possible interactions. Although Graicunas's formula offers no prescription for what N should be, it does demonstrate how complex a manager's work group can become when more subordinates are added. The key point is that, as the span of management increases, each additional subordinate adds more complexity to the overall group than the previous one did. Going from 9 to 10 subordinates is much different from going from 3 to 4.

Another early writer, Ralph C. Davis,[15] described two kinds of spans: an operative span for lower-level managers and an executive span for middle and top managers. He argues that operative spans can approach 30 subordinates, whereas executive spans should be limited to 3 to 9 (depending on the nature of the managers' jobs, growth rate of the company, and similar factors). Lyndall F. Urwick suggested that an executive span should never exceed 6 subordinates,[16] and General Ian Hamilton reached the same conclusion.[17] Today we recognize that the span of management is a crucial factor in structuring organizations but that there are no universal cut-and-dried prescriptions for an ideal

14. See A. V. Graicunas, "Relationships in Organizations," *Bulletin of the International Management Institute,* March 7, 1933, pp. 39–42.

15. See Ralph C. Davis, *Fundamentals of Top Management* (New York: Harper & Row, 1951).

16. See Lyndall F. Urwick, *Scientific Principles and Organization* (New York: American Management Associations, 1938), p. 8.

17. See Ian Hamilton, *The Soul and Body of an Army* (London: Edward Arnold, 1921), pp. 229–230.

© 1984 by Sidney Harris

or optimal span.[18] Later we will summarize some important variables that influence the appropriate span of management in a particular situation. First, however, we will describe how the span of management affects the overall structure of an organization.

Tall versus flat organizations

Imagine a hypothetical organization consisting of 36 operating employees and a maximum span of 6. As shown in Figure 9.7, the organization may have 6 lower-level managers, 2 middle managers coordinating the lower-level managers, and a single top manager. With a wider span of control, however, the

18. See David D. Van Fleet and Arthur G. Bedeian, "A History of the Span of Management," *Academy of Management Review*, 1977, pp. 356–372.

Figure 9.7
Tall versus flat
organizations

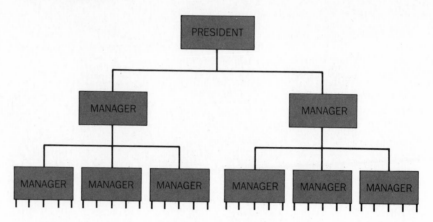

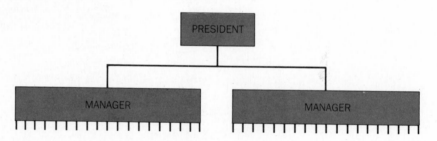

other organization in Figure 9.7 becomes feasible. Here the span is 18, with 2 managers supervising the same 36 employees and reporting to the president. The wider span eliminates one level of managerial positions and brings about a relatively "flat" organization structure.

In an early study at Sears, Roebuck and Company, James Worthy found that a relatively flat structure led to higher levels of employee morale and productivity.[19] It has also been argued that a tall structure is more expensive (due to the larger number of managers involved) and that it fosters more communication problems (due to the increased number of people whom vertical information must pass through).[20] On the other hand, a wide span of management in a flat organization may result in a manager having more administrative responsibility (because there are fewer managers) and more supervisory responsibility (because there are more subordinates reporting to each manager). If

19. See James C. Worthy, "Factors Influencing Employee Morale," *Harvard Business Review*, January 1950, pp. 61–73.

20. See Rocco Carzo, Jr., and John N. Yanouzas, "Effects of Flat and Tall Organization Structures," *Administrative Science Quarterly*, June 1969, pp. 178–191.

Table 9.1 Factors influencing the span of management

1. Competence of supervisor and subordinates
2. Physical dispersion of subordinates
3. Extent of nonsupervisory work in manager's job
4. Degree of required interaction
5. Extent of standardized procedures
6. Similarity of tasks being supervised
7. Frequency of new problems
8. Preferences of supervisors and subordinates

these additional responsibilities become excessive, the flat organization may suffer.

Avon, one of the largest cosmetics firms in the world (1981 sales of over $2.5 billion), recently modified its "height." Much of the company's early success in door-to-door selling was based on a program designed to boost the morale of the sales representatives through frequent sales meetings and a great deal of interaction with management. During a period of cost-cutting in the early 1970s, the frequency of the sales meetings dropped and managers paid less attention to the sales force. After losing considerable ground in the market place to competitors such as Revlon, Avon undertook several strategic actions to get back on the right track. One of the major changes it made was to eliminate two layers of management, creating a flatter organization. As a result, communication and employee morale improved.[21]

Determining the appropriate span

Of course the big question still remains. What is the appropriate span of management for a particular situation? The answer is that it depends on several factors. Some of these factors are listed in Table 9.1 and described in the following paragraphs.[22]

Competence. If a manager is competent and well-trained, he or she can supervise more subordinates. Similarly, if the subordinates are also competent and well-trained, they usually require less supervision. The more competent the manager and the subordinates, the wider the span of management can be.

Physical dispersion. The more widely the subordinates are scattered, the narrower the span can be. If an organization uses location departmentalization, sales managers may be scattered across a large part of the country. A regional sales manager could spend all of her or his time traveling if the span

21. See Linda S. Hayes, "The Changes in Avon's Makeup Aren't Just Cosmetic," *Fortune*, August 13, 1979, pp. 140–158.

22. See Harold Steiglitz, *Organizational Planning* (New York: National Industrial Conference Board, 1966), p. 15.

were wide. A narrower span solves this problem. On the other hand, if all the subordinates are in one location, the span can be somewhat wider.

Nonsupervisory work. Some managers, especially at the lower levels of an organization, spend most or all of their time supervising subordinates. Other managers spend a considerable amount of time doing paperwork, planning, and engaging in other managerial activities. The more such nonsupervisory duties a manager has, the narrower her or his span can be.

Required interaction. Some job situations require a great deal of interaction between supervisor and subordinates; other jobs require less. In general, the more interaction that is required, the narrower the span of management can be.

Standardized procedures. If there is a fairly comprehensive set of standard procedures, a relatively wide span is possible. Most difficulties can be handled by following a standard procedure. If only a few standard procedures exist, however, the supervisor usually has to play a larger role in overseeing day-to-day activities and may find a narrower span more appropriate.

Similarity of tasks. If most of the jobs being supervised are similar, a supervisor can handle a wider span. When each employee is performing a different task, more of the supervisor's time is spent on individual supervision.

Frequency of new problems. If new problems that require supervisory assistance arise frequently, a narrower span may be called for. If new problems are relatively rare, a wider span can be established.

Preferences. The preferences of both supervisor and subordinates may affect the optimal span. If the supervisor prefers to monitor her or his subordinates closely and/or the subordinates themselves prefer close supervision, a narrower span may be appropriate. Some managers prefer to spend less time actively supervising their employees, and many employees prefer to be more self-directed in their jobs. A wider span may be possible in these situations.

In some organizational settings, other factors may influence the optimal span of management, and the relative importance of each factor varies in different settings. It is also unlikely that all eight factors will suggest the same span; some may suggest a wider span, while others may indicate a need for a narrow span. The manager must assess the relative weight of each factor or set of factors when deciding what the optimal span of management is for his or her unique situation.

Coordination of organizational activities

The final major building block of organization structure is the coordination of organizational activities. *Coordination* is the achievement of compatible activities among parts of the organization. As shown in Figure 9.8, the activities of

Figure 9.8
The need for
internal
coordination

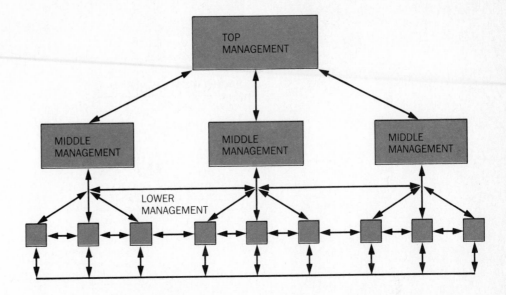

all individual employees and work units must be coordinated to ensure movement toward goal attainment. Even if we assume that interaction takes place between only 2 units at a time, the organization shown in Figure 9.8 will have to coordinate 51 activities!

Reasons for coordination

The primary reason for coordination is group (or department) interdependence. The greater the interdependence, the more coordination the company needs. James Thompson, a noted organizational scholar, has identified three major forms of interdependence: pooled, sequential, and reciprocal. These forms are shown in Figure 9.9.

Pooled interdependence. In groups that exhibit pooled interdependence, the various units operate with little interaction; the output of the units is simply pooled at the organizational level. The commercial, consumer, and agricultural loan departments of a moderate-sized bank, like the one used in our earlier example for customer departmentalization, are likely to operate in a pooled fashion. Each has its own budget, its own staff, and its own loan criteria. The profits (or losses) are "added together" at the organizational level. The units are interdependent to the extent that the final success or failure of one unit affects the others, but they do not generally interact on a day-to-day basis.

Sequential interdependence. In sequential interdependence, the output of one unit becomes the input for another in a sequential fashion. At General Motors, one plant may assemble engines and then ship them to a final assembly site at another plant where the cars are completed. The plants are

Figure 9.9
Three forms of
interdependence

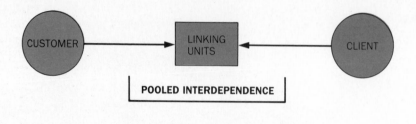

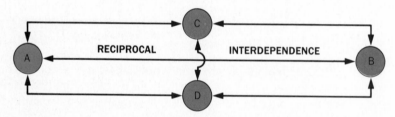

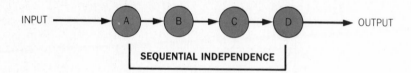

Source: *Organizations in Action* by J. Thompson. Copyright © 1967, McGraw-Hill Book Company. Used with permission.

interdependent in that the final assembly plant must have the engines from engine assembly before it can operate.

Reciprocal interdependence. When activities flow both ways between units, reciprocal interdependence comes into play. In a hospital, each ward or unit (such as intensive care, pediatrics, and so on) provides inputs to surgery. After surgery, patients are sent back to their respective wards. There is a two-way flow between units. Obviously, coordination requirements will be the greatest for this complex form of interdependence.

Coordination techniques

Some of the more useful devices for maintaining coordination among inter-dependent units are the managerial hierarchy, rules and procedures, liaison roles, task forces, and integrating departments.[23]

The managerial hierarchy. When hierarchy is used to achieve coordi-nation, one manager is placed in charge of the interdependent departments or

23. See Jay R. Galbraith, *Organizational Design* (Reading, Mass.: Addison Wesley, 1977).

units. In K mart distribution centers, major activities include receiving and unloading bulk shipments from railroad cars and loading other shipments onto trucks for distribution to retail outlets. The two groups (receiving and shipping) are interdependent in that they share the loading docks and such equipment as forklifts. In order to ensure coordination and to minimize conflict, one manager is in charge of the whole operation. Unfortunately, bestowing such managerial attention may not be the most efficient use of executive time or talent in many situations.

Rules and procedures. Routine coordination activities can often be handled via rules and standard procedures. In the K mart distribution center, an outgoing truck shipment has priority over an incoming rail shipment. When trucks are to be loaded, the shipping unit is given access to all of the center's auxiliary forklifts. This priority is embodied in a rule. As useful as rules and procedures often are in routine situations, they are not so effective when coordination problems are complex or unusual.

Liaison roles. The role of boundary spanners in organizations was introduced in Chapter 2, where we focused our attention on boundary spanners operating between the total organization and elements of the environment but also noted that there could be internal boundary spanners as well. Such an internal boundary spanner is often called a liaison.

The individual in a liaison role coordinates two or more interdependent units by acting as a common point of contact. This individual usually doesn't have any formal authority over the groups but simply facilitates the flow of information. Two engineering groups working on component systems for a large project might interact through a liaison. The liaison maintains familiarity with each group as well as with the overall project. She or he can answer questions and otherwise serve to integrate the activities of all the groups.[24]

Task forces. A task force may be created when the need for coordination is especially acute. When interdependence is very complex and several units are involved, one liaison person may not be sufficient. A task force might be assembled by drawing one representative from each group. The coordination function is thus spread across several individuals, each of whom has special information about one of the groups involved. When the project is completed, task force members return to their original positions.[25]

A college overhauling its degree requirements might establish a task force made up of representatives from each department affected by the change. Teams and committees may perform like functions, but their activities are somewhat different; we will discuss teams in Chapter 11 and committees in Chapter 10.

24. For a recent discussion, see Elizabeth V. Reynolds and J. David Johnson, "Liaison Emergence: Relating Theoretical Perspectives." *The Academy of Management Review*, October 1982, pp. 551–559.

25. See Galbraith, *Organizational Design*.

Integrating departments. Integrating departments are somewhat similar to task forces, but they are established on a more permanent basis. An integrating department generally has some permanent members, while others are assigned temporarily from units that are particularly in need of coordination. One study found that successful firms in the plastics industry, which is characterized by complex and dynamic environments, used integrating departments to maintain internal integration and coordination.[26] An integrating department usually has more authority than a task force and may be given some budgetary control by the organization.

Selecting a technique

In general, the greater the degree of interdependence, the more attention the company must devote to coordination. When interdependence is of a pooled or simple sequential nature, the managerial hierarchy and/or rules and procedures are often sufficient. When more complex forms of sequential or simpler forms of reciprocal interdependence exist, liaisons or task forces may be more useful. When reciprocal interdependence is complex, task forces or integrating departments are needed. Of course, the manager must also rely on her or his own experience and insights when establishing a coordination framework for the organization.

Summary of key points

Work specialization, the first building block of an organization, breaks down the total organizational task into smaller component parts. Specialization is generally assumed to enhance individual dexterity, reduce transfer time, facilitate the development of specialized equipment, and lower training costs. On the other hand, highly specialized tasks are likely to increase worker boredom, dissatisfaction, absenteeism, and turnover.

Another major building block of organizations is departmentalization, the grouping of jobs according to some logical arrangement. Departmentalization may be based on function, product, location, customer, or other categories. Most organizations employ multiple bases of departmentalization.

Establishing patterns of authority is also a major part of structuring an organization. Authority represents power that has been legitimized by the organization. The process of establishing a pattern of authority between a manager and a subordinate is termed delegation, which consists of three basic components: assigning responsibility, granting authority, and creating accountability. At the overall organizational level, the establishment of patterns of authority is called decentralization. Factors influencing the degree of decentralization that is likely to prevail in an organization include the external environ-

26. See Paul R. Lawrence and Jay W. Lorsch, "Differentiation and Integration in Complex Organizations," *Administrative Science Quarterly*, March 1967, pp. 1–47.

ments, the history of the organization, the nature of relevant decisions, and the abilities of lower-level managers.

The fourth major organizational building block is the span of management, or the number of subordinates who report directly to a manager. Early management theorists attempted to identify the optimal span of management, but today we recognize that the appropriate span for any given situation depends on a variety of factors. Organizations that have narrow spans of management tend to be "taller" (that is, they have more levels of management), whereas wider spans lead to relatively "flat" organizations (with fewer levels of management).

A final building block identified in this chapter is the coordination of organizational activities, which is needed because many organizational units are interdependent. Interdependence may be pooled, sequential, or reciprocal. Popular coordination techniques include the managerial hierarchy, rules and procedures, liaison roles, task forces, and integrating departments.

QUESTIONS FOR DISCUSSION

1. Work specialization is readily applied in organizations that manufacture a product. Think about other organizations that provide services, such as management consulting firms, hospitals, restaurants, and universities. Should these service organizations use work specialization? Why or why not?

2. In general, do you think specialization will increase or decrease in the future? Why?

3. If you were the CEO of a large conglomerate, what kind of departmentalization would you use? If you were a small entrepreneur, *how* and *when* should you change from functional to product departmentalization?

4. Think of an organization you are familiar with that is departmentalized by function, product, location, or customer. Describe why you think the organization is departmentalized that way, and speculate about what it might look like if a different base were adopted.

5. Look at Figure 9.1 again and suppose that the inventor has hired an accountant and a sales representative. Why might it be difficult for the entrepreneur to delegate authority? What arguments would you use to convince the inventor that these patterns of authority are important to the success of the organization?

6. Assume that an organization with a long history of centralization was purchased by another organization that practiced decentralization. What kinds of problems would probably result?

7. Consider the home computer industry in the early 1980s. The environment of the business was rapidly changing, with high technology, decreasing costs, larger marketing areas, and cutthroat competition. How might these environmental factors influence the appropriate span of management?

8. What is the span of management of the president of your university or organization? Do you think it is appropriate? What kinds of factors probably influenced it?

9. Using football, chess, and debating teams as examples, describe the type of interdependencies that exist between members, and, in each case, suggest which coordination techniques might be most effective. (*Hint:* Are defensive linemen coached separately? Is this an example of putting one manager in charge of an interdependent department?)

10. Why does increased interdependence require additional coordination? What would probably happen if two reciprocally interdependent units decided not to worry about coordination?

C A S E 9.1

Departmentalization at Levi Strauss

At the beginning of this chapter you read a scenario about a rapidly expanding, worldwide apparel company. Having diversified into women's wear, infant clothing, athletic clothing, and hats, the company has a product line consisting of over 2,000 different styles, colors, and fabrics. You were asked how the company should be structured. The company being described was Levi Strauss. The case that follows details how Levi's has been structured and then raises some other issues for your consideration.

Levi Strauss & Company was founded over 100 years ago by an impoverished Bavarian immigrant. Young Levi realized that prospectors needed sturdy, long-lasting pants. Moving from canvas to denim and developing a riveting technique for reinforcing points of strain, Levi's has gone on to sell more than one billion pairs of pants since those early years. The unique pocket stitching and the identifying tab Levi's uses on its jeans have become two of the most widely recognized trademarks in the world.

During the 1950s, Levi Strauss & Company began to expand in a number of different areas. White Levi's were introduced, the company began exporting jeans worldwide, and it developed the technology that led to permanent press fabric treatment. In 1971 Levi's issued its first public stock offering; the object was to finance growth and expansion into different areas.

In 1977 top management increased Levi's pace of expansion by acquiring Koracorp Industries, a leading manufacturer of women's wear, hats, infant clothing, and up-scale men's suits. Recent ventures have also included a line of athletic clothing (Levi's Activewear) and western hats (Resistol). Levi's has also begun to sell to major department store chains such as J. C. Penney and Sears.

At present, Levi's is the world's largest apparel manufacturer, with annual sales of almost $3 billion. The company's current product lines are composed of over 2,000 items of varying style, color, and fabric. To cope with this diverse and large-scale network of operations, Levi's has developed a unique form of organization structure employing a variety of bases of departmentalization.

At the corporate level, Levi Strauss & Company is divided into three strategic business units (SBUs): Levi Strauss USA, Levi Strauss International, and the New Business Group. As the term suggests, Levi Strauss USA handles the company's domestic operations. Three operating divisions are organized along product lines. Each division handles its own manufacturing, merchandising, distribution, and financial activities and is accountable for its own performance. A variety of staff units provide support services for each of the product divisions and coordinate activities across product lines. Decision making is highly decentralized to managers directly involved in the activities affected.

Levi Strauss International is responsible for all activities outside of the United States. This unit is organized by location, with Continental Europe, Northern Europe, Canada, Latin America, and the Asia/Pacific region each comprising a division. Each of these regional divisions, in turn, is organized in a fashion similar to Levi Strauss USA.

The New Business Group has a dual focus. It contains Levi's export—import operation, EXIMCO. And it also serves as a temporary home for new acquisitions until they can be integrated into an established division or group. The divisions in this unit report directly to the president.

In the years ahead, Levi Strauss & Company faces a number of problems and challenges. The company faces increased domestic competition from other brands such as Wrangler and Lee, as well as from designer jeans. Over the long run, competition from abroad should also increase. Low wages paid to apparel workers in other countries (20–25 cents per hour in some Asian countries) offer a distinct price advantage to foreign manufacturers. The traditional jeans market, long Levi's cornerstone, has begun to decline in recent years. Finally, the federal government will play an increasingly important role in Levi's future as international markets and trade relations become ever more complex. (This case was developed from a class report prepared by Tony Cataliotti, Jaime Pabon, and Andy Pearl.)

CASE
QUESTIONS

1. Can you diagram Levi's organization structure?
2. What advantages and disadvantages do you see in the organization structure adopted by Levi Strauss & Company?
3. What kinds of structural modifications might help Levi's perform effectively in the future?

CASE
REFERENCES

"Adding Koracorp to Levi's Wardrobe." *Business Week,* June 4, 1979, pp. 69–70.

"Levi Goes to Market." *Forbes,* June 11, 1979, pp. 106–107.

"Levi's Problems Finding a Fit." *New York Times,* November 8, 1980, pp. 20, 32.

Quirt, John. "Levi Strauss Is Stretching Its Wardrobe." *Fortune,* November 19, 1979, pp. 86–89.

C A S E 9.2

One morning while car-pooling to work, Sara Garcia and Roger Majors were discussing their subordinates. Sara seemed particularly bothered by two of the people she supervised. "The problem," she complained, "is that they just don't seem to want to take any initiative. When they were hired, I remember very carefully explaining to them that for the first few months they would need to check with me before authorizing any major payments or accepting any big customer orders. And I also told them that they should avoid telling any of the junior people what to do for a while, until they learned the ropes and knew what was going on.

"But now its been almost a year and they are still just doing the same old things. Last week Greg came to me to okay a disbursement check for $10,000. He's handled checks of that size several times and should know that he can handle them without me by now.

"And Kathy—about two weeks ago I gave her a new project to work on. It was a pretty big job, and so I expected her to get some of the junior people in to help. But I found out yesterday that she's trying to do the whole thing herself! And now it's going to be late, and I'm the one that's going to catch it. But don't worry—whatever flak I catch, she'll catch double!"

At about the same time this conversation was taking place, Greg and Kathy had already arrived at work and were commiserating over a cup of coffee in the employee lounge. "You know," Greg began, "I just don't know what she wants. Last week she got mad because I went in to get her authorization on a check. She acted as though I should have just gone ahead without her. I tried that about a month ago, but the controller's office sent it back. They said my signature wasn't on file to okay checks that large. I thought I'd do Sara a favor, so I got a signature authorization request, filled out my part of it, and put it on her desk. If only she'd finish filling it out and give her approval, I could okay checks without having to bother her. You know how disorganized she is, though. From the looks of her in-basket, she's at least a month behind. I'm sure she hasn't even seen that signature authorization request yet."

"I know exactly what you mean about her being disorganized," Kathy responded. "A couple of weeks ago she came running into my office and gave me a big project to do and said it needed to be done right away. From some of the dates in the files, though, I know it must have been on her desk at least three weeks before she gave it to me.

"She knows I'm up for promotion, and while I don't think she deliberately wants me to look bad, she sure doesn't want me to look too good, either. Anyway, I knew the project was important, so I plunged right in. I tried to get some help from the junior people, but that just didn't work out. The good ones all said that they

Communication and effective delegation

didn't have time unless Sara okayed their dropping what they were already working on, and the others would have done more harm than good anyway. The final report is due today, and it's not finished. I know Sara is going to catch it, and then she's going to pass it right on to me."

CASE
QUESTIONS

1. Can you identify the parts of the delegation process in this case?
2. What kinds of things might Sara, Greg, and Kathy all do to improve the situation?
3. How common do you think instances such as this are in organizations?

10

GETTING WORK DONE
IN ORGANIZATIONS

1. Discuss committees and work groups, and identify four kinds of committees and three kinds of work groups.

2. Distinguish between line and staff roles, discuss the functions and importance of each, and describe the nature of line–staff conflict.

3. Explain the staffing process and discuss several of its components.

4. Discuss job design and cite several alternatives to work specialization.

5. Describe traditional work schedules and suggest three alternative schedules now in use in some organizations.

6. Discuss organizational conflict, including its causes and consequences, and outline some techniques for managing it.

CHAPTER OUTLINE

Committees and work groups
Types of committees
Advantages and disadvantages of committees
Work groups

Line and staff positions
Differences between line and staff
Importance of line and staff roles
Line and staff conflict

Staffing the organization
Human resource planning
Recruiting
Selection and placement
Orientation
Compensation
Training and development
Performance appraisal

Designing jobs in organizations
Alternatives to work specialization
Current state of job design

Establishing work schedules
Traditional work schedules
Alternatives to traditional schedules

Managing organizational conflict
Primary causes of conflict
Consequences of conflict
Managing conflict

Summary of key points

OPENING INCIDENT

You are a manager at a major conglomerate comprised of about 9,000 products organized around approximately 435 product groups. After a bitter 3-year struggle, the board of directors has just named you CEO. One of the problems surrounding your company is how to maintain a high level of decentralization, which the company has long had, yet also to provide needed staff support for the operating units. For example, some of the smaller units can't afford to have a marketing manager, but there is no corporate marketing staff for them to call on. What would you do?

I n 1976 an employee at a Ford assembly plant in San Francisco described his job in very depressing terms. He walked slowly to the time clock each morning, relishing his last few moments of freedom. The job was dirty, boring, and routine, and the work was exhausting. Jobs in the automobile industry may still be quite dirty and difficult, but they are changing in subtle ways. Today some of the worst jobs are being performed by automated robots, and workers are being given an increased role in managing their own work. The basic structural components of United States automobile firms have not dramatically changed; what *has* changed is how they are getting work done.[1] This aspect of organizing is the subject of Chapter 10.

Chapter 9 described the basic building blocks of organizations: work specialization, departmentalization, delegation and decentralization, the span of management, and coordination. Now we begin to analyze how the various building blocks are combined into a total organizational system.

In this chapter, we focus on relatively short-term processes, many of which have almost a day-to-day flavor about them (hence the title "Getting Work Done in Organizations"). In Chapter 11 ("Organizational Design Processes"), we deal with longer-term considerations in assembling organizations. The topics we will address now include committees and work groups, line and staff positions, staffing processes, job design, work schedules, and the management of organizational conflict.

Committees and work groups

Almost everyone has heard the quip about the camel being a horse designed by a committee. In fact, committees are very common in most organizations,

1. See Ricky King, "Inside the Sanding Booth at Ford," in W. Clay Hamner, ed., *Organizational Shock* (New York: Wiley, 1980), pp. 201–208; and Charles G. Burck, "Can Detroit Catch Up?" *Fortune*, February 8, 1982, pp. 34–39.

and they offer an effective means for managing group decision making. In general, a *committee* can be defined as a group assembled to make a decision, submit a recommendation, conduct an investigation, or solve a problem.

Types of committees

The kinds of committees found in organizations include ad hoc committees, standing committees, task forces, and boards.

Ad hoc committees. An ad hoc committee is a committee created for a relatively narrow and short-run purpose, but that purpose may be extremely important to the organization. For example, an ad hoc committee might be appointed by a chief executive officer to evaluate a proposal to merge with another company. An ad hoc committee might also be created to deal with routine problems such as listing new-equipment needs, reviewing employee benefit packages, and so on.[2] When its purpose has been fulfilled, the committee is normally dissolved.

Standing committees. A standing committee, as the name implies, is a relatively permanent committee. The membership of a standing committee is long-term and stable. Some standing committees, such as budget review committees, deal with the same set of issues on a continuous basis. Others deal with a variety of problems. One special kind of standing committee is the executive committee, which is composed of top managers and is primarily concerned with strategy and policy. (Chapter 6 described the role executive committees play in developing plans.)

General Motors makes effective use of its executive committee by exploring how and why the company has or has not been successful at various activities. In addition, the committee reviews all of the company's top managers annually for possible promotion and replacement.[3]

Task forces. In many ways, a task force is like an ad hoc committee. It usually has a relatively narrow purpose and a limited time horizon. But it also has some unique characteristics. First, a task force is generally associated with the integration or coordination of activities between units. For example, we noted in Chapter 9 that task forces often function to integrate units that are highly interdependent. Second, the membership of a task force may change regularly as new skills and abilities are needed. In the early stages of new-product development, for example, more production and engineering people may be needed to develop technical specifications, cost estimates, and the like. Marketing people may become more important later, as promotion and advertising campaigns are planned.

2. See Joseph Allen and Bennet P. Lientz, *Effective Business Communication* (Santa Monica, Calif.: Goodyear, 1979), p. 122.

3. See Charles G. Burck, "How GM Turned Itself Around," *Fortune*, January 16, 1978, pp. 87–100.

Boards. Boards are a type of committee found in many organizations, especially public ones. Members of public boards may be elected, as are the members of school boards and hospital boards. Governmental boards, often called commissions, include the Federal Trade Commission and the Equal Employment Opportunity Commission.

Most private corporations have a board of directors elected by the stockholders to oversee and guide top management. P. Bruce Buchan has pointed out that a major factor in Japan's economic success has been a high degree of cooperation between management and the board of directors. In his opinion, such cooperation is often missing in American industry.[4]

Advantages and disadvantages of committees

The advantages and disadvantages of committees closely parallel those of group decision making in general. Those factors were discussed in Chapter 7, and we will summarize them only briefly here. The advantages of committee decisions over individual decisions include the availability of more information, increased acceptance of the committee's decision, solution, or recommendation, better communication, and (perhaps) improved accuracy of the decision. On the other hand, major disadvantages are that the deliberations of a committee can be quite lengthy and, therefore, costly, too much compromising may occur, one person may dominate the process, and there is some possibility of the members succumbing to groupthink.

Work groups

A great deal of work in organizations is done by various kinds of work groups: operative work groups, autonomous work groups, and teams.

Operative work groups. The operative work group is used when the nature of a particular job is such that a group can do it more efficiently than a set of individuals. For example, the maintenance of a 747 for TWA is best carried out by an operative work group. Each group member has individual responsibilities, and coordination is achieved via a common supervisor.

Autonomous work groups. The autonomous work group generally works more independently than an operative work group. The members may rotate jobs among themselves and are often rewarded for group performance rather than individual performance. Here the group leader is seen more as a facilitator than as a supervisor.[5] Organizations that have successfully used autonomous work groups include Volvo and General Foods.

4. See P. Bruce Buchan, "Boards of Directors: Adversaries or Advisers," *California Management Review,* Winter 1981, pp. 31–39.

5. See J. Richard Hackman, "Work Design," in J. Richard Hackman and J. Lloyd Suttle (eds.), *Improving Life at Work: Behavioral Science Approaches to Organizational Change* (Santa Monica, Calif.: Goodyear, 1977), p. 141.

Teams. The *team* brings together functional expertise from several areas to work on a single project. Basically, creating a team involves selecting representatives from appropriate departments (such as finance, marketing, and production) and assigning them to a particular project such as introducing a new product. Teams will be described in more detail in Chapter 11. Group activities and related behavioral processes will be explored in depth in Chapter 15 ("Groups and Group Processes").

Line and staff positions

Another approach to getting work done in organizations is through line and staff roles or positions. A *line position* is a position in the direct chain of command that is responsible for the achievement of an organization's goals. A *staff position,* on the other hand, is intended to provide expertise, advice, and support for line positions. These distinctions are illustrated in Figure 10.1. The president and the vice presidents for production, finance, and marketing are considered line managers; they occupy a position in the direct chain of command and contribute directly to the firm's goals. The assistant to the president and the assistant to the vice president of production hold personal staff positions; they assist the individual manager in a variety of activities. The legal advisor and the vice presidents of research and development (R&D) and personnel are called professional staff, because they have special skills and because they work with many departments rather than just one individual. The vice president of personnel, for example, would work with all of the other top managers to hire and train employees for their units.

Figure 10.1
Line and staff roles

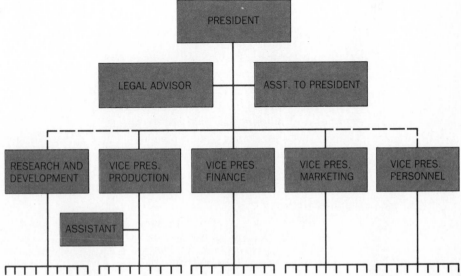

Differences between line and staff

The most obvious difference between line and staff is purpose: line's purpose is to work directly toward organizational goals, whereas staff advises and assists. But other distinctions exist as well.

One very important difference is authority. Line authority is generally thought of as the formal or legitimate authority created by the organizational hierarchy. Staff authority is less concrete and may take a variety of forms. One form is the authority simply to advise, but the line manager can always choose whether to seek or to avoid input from the staff. Even if staff advice is sought, the manager can choose to use it or ignore it. Another form of staff authority is called *compulsory advice;* in this case the line manager must at least listen to the advice but can still choose to heed it or ignore it. For example, the Pope is expected to listen to the advice of the Sacred College when dealing with church doctrine, but he may follow his own beliefs when making decisions.[6] Perhaps the most important form of staff authority is called *functional authority,* which is formal or legitimate authority over activities related to the staff member's specialty. In Figure 10.1 we termed the vice president of personnel a member of the professional staff. This individual is likely to have expertise in such special areas as Equal Employment Opportunity. When a legal question arises that pertains to hiring, this expert is likely to be given authority to make appropriate decisions. Conferring functional authority is probably the most effective way to use staff positions, because it allows the organization to take advantage of specialized expertise while also maintaining a chain of command.

Another distinction between line and staff in some organizations emerges in the demographic makeup of the individuals involved. Line managers tend to be older, to be less well educated, and to have risen through the ranks of the organization. Staff specialists are likely to be younger, to be better educated, and to have been hired directly into upper-level staff positions. As we shall see, such differences may be a major source of line–staff conflict.[7]

Importance of line and staff roles

The importance of line positions in an organization should be obvious. In business firms, production, marketing, and finance managers often play key roles in the overall chain of command. YMCA directors and ministers of churches are instrumental in their organizations. Hospital administrators play major roles in promoting effective health care.

The importance of staff positions may not be so obvious, but the expertise of staff managers is often just as important as that of line managers. One organization that makes very effective use of staff positions is TRW Inc., a major international conglomerate with activities ranging from the manufacture of

6. See James Mooney, *Principles of Organization* (New York: Harper & Row, 1947).

7. For more information on line and staff authority, see Louis A. Allen, "The Line-Staff Relationship," *Management Record,* 1955, pp. 346–349ff., and Vivian Nossiter, "A New Approach Toward Resolving the Line and Staff Dilemma," *Academy of Management Review,* January 1979, pp. 103–106.

auto parts to that of aerospace and industrial products. TRW has a human relations staff of 20 behavioral scientists working on ways to make jobs more productive for the firm and more satisfying for the employee. A staff of 92 other experts supports the financial activities of the firm. TRW's federal tax return alone fills four 2-inch binders and requires the equivalent of 2 employees working a full year to prepare.[8]

Line and staff conflict

For several reasons, conflict can arise between line and staff managers. We will describe the nature of this conflict here; later in the chapter we will consider conflict at a more general level.

Demographic factors. The suggestion that staff managers may be younger than line managers, better educated, more ambitious, better dressed, and more firmly allied with their profession than with their company is based on an early study by Melville Dalton.[9] Some of these factors have probably changed over the years, but staff managers are still likely to be highly educated and to relate more strongly to their professions than to the organization. Naturally these demographic factors are a possible source of conflict.

Threats to authority. Line managers may also perceive staff managers as threats to their own authority. This is likely to occur most often when staff managers are given functional authority. As a means of forestalling the possible erosion of their own authority, line managers may decide not to take advantage of staff expertise. Staff managers, in turn, complain that they are not being used effectively.

Dependence on knowledge. In other situations, line managers may become uncomfortable and frustrated when they grow too dependent on staff expertise and knowledge. The line managers may feel less important and resent the fact that they need the staff managers in order to do their own jobs. The problem is even more acute when the knowledge (and vocabulary) gap is so great that distrust results, simply because the line manager doesn't really understand what is going on.

Other causes of conflict. Other causes of line–staff conflict are usually a function of different perceptions. Line managers often see staff managers as overstepping their authority, embracing too narrow or idealistic a perspective, or stealing credit for the line managers' accomplishments. Staff managers, in turn, accuse line managers of not giving them enough authority and resisting new ideas.

8. See Richard Martin, "A Staff Manager's Job," *Wall Street Journal*, April 18, 1977, pp. 1, 23.
9. See Melville Dalton, "Conflicts Between Staff and Line Managerial Officers," *American Sociological Review*, June 1950, pp. 342–351.

Several methods of dealing with these and other forms of line–staff conflict have been suggested by Edward Schleh.[10]

Integration of activities. The activities of line and staff managers should be integrated. Rather than working on projects sequentially (as when staff managers make suggestions to line managers, who then decide what to do), line and staff managers should work together as a team.

Education. A major reason for line–staff conflict is that line managers may not fully understand staff roles. They need to be shown what staff experts can and cannot do.

Clear areas of responsibility. Line and staff roles should be clearly defined so that everyone knows the various areas of responsibility. By operating within their own defined positions, line and staff managers can then avoid stepping on each other's toes.

Accountability for results. Both line and staff should be accountable for the results of their activities. When a line manager does not make effective use of available staff expertise and makes a poor decision as a result, it should be brought to the manager's attention. When a staff manager provides inappropriate or incorrect advice or information, he or she should be informed of the results.

Staffing the organization

The heart of an organization is its people, its human resources, and one critical part of getting work done in an organization is attracting and retaining effective employees. This process is known as *staffing.* Later we will devote an entire chapter to the personnel process in general and to staffing in particular. Our intent at this point is simply to show how the basic elements of staffing fit into overall organizational design. These basic elements are shown in Figure 10.2.

Human resource planning

The logical starting point for most staffing activities is *human resource planning:* determination of an organization's future human resource needs.[11] Within this general framework, however, a variety of other activities must also take place. Job specifications and descriptions must be developed in an effort to achieve complete understanding of the jobs that already exist in the organization. A

---

10. See Edward C. Schleh, "Using Central Staff to Boost Line Initiative," *Management Review,* May 1976, pp. 17–23.

11. See Edwin L. Miller, Elmer H. Burack, and Maryann H. Albrecht, *Management of Human Resources* (Englewood Cliffs, N.J.: Prentice-Hall, 1980).

Figure 10.2
The staffing process

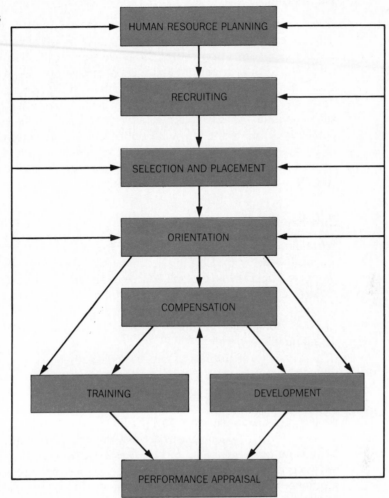

human resource inventory must be conducted to determine exactly what kinds of resources the firm presently has. The human resource plan must also be integrated with the organization's strategic plan. If the size of the organization is expected to diminish, plans must be made to eliminate existing personnel. If the organization is expected to grow, the human resource planner must forecast the internal demand for various kinds of people and the supply likely to be on hand. If a firm projects a need for 100 additional engineers in 1990 but also projects a small supply of qualified engineers in the work force, steps should be taken earlier than 1990 to begin filling the 100 positions. If a new plant is to be opened in 1992, the organization will probably assume that its need for unskilled labor can be filled on short notice just before the plant is opened. The position of plant manager, however, must be attended to well beforehand.

Recruiting

Once future human resource needs have been projected, the organization begins to recruit applicants, and the first step is usually to develop a pool of qualified applicants from which the organization can select appropriate personnel.[12] The form of *recruiting* that is most familiar to college students is campus interviews. Companies send representatives to colleges and universities to interview prospective managers and management trainees. Other forms of external recruiting include placing advertisements in newspapers and trade publications and listing jobs with public and private employment agencies. Recruits can often be found internally—among existing employees who want to advance within the organization. Many companies, such as Procter & Gamble and IBM, have a promotion-from-within policy.

Selection and placement

Selection is the process of choosing the most appropriate applicants from among those attracted by the organization's recruiting efforts.[13] The most appropriate applicant is the one whose skills and aspirations are closest to the requirements of the job and the opportunities it offers. We probably don't want to hire a high school drop-out for an important executive position, and we probably don't want to hire a scientist with a Ph.D. to perform an unskilled operating job.

A variety of techniques are used to gather information and to evaluate potential candidates. Application blanks are generally used to gather background data on the applicant. Interviews are held and tests are often administered. References are sometimes checked. For certain sensitive kinds of positions (for example, a job in security or with the FBI), polygraph tests may be used. Physical examinations are also commonly required.

More time, attention, and resources are devoted to hiring managers than to hiring operating employees. An executive candidate is often scrutinized by a number of other executives and perhaps even by the board of directors. The complete process may take weeks or even months. On the other hand, an operating employee may be hired after filling out an application and having a brief interview with a personnel manager.

Probably as much as any other area of management, recruitment and selection are subject to legislative and judicial restriction. The passage of Title VII of the Civil Rights Act of 1964 (amended in 1972) requires that organizations not discriminate on the basis of race, sex, religion, color, or national origin. Various executive orders have extended this philosophy by requiring all organizations that conduct business with the federal government to make special efforts to recruit, hire, and promote women and members of minority groups. Such efforts are organized as affirmative action programs. Other sig-

12. See John P. Wanous, *Organizational Entry: Recruitment, Selection, and Socialization of Newcomers* (Reading, Mass.: Addison-Wesley, 1980).

13. See Benjamin Schneider, *Staffing Organizations* (Santa Monica, Calif.: Goodyear, 1976).

nificant constraints on recruiting and selection include the Age Discrimination Act of 1967, the Vocational Rehabilitation Act of 1973 (amended in 1974), the Vietnam-Era Veteran's Readjustment Act of 1974, and various court decisions handed down over the last several years.

A notable example of an organization that suffered because of discrimination in hiring and promotion is American Telephone & Telegraph. Because of its illegal discrimination, AT&T was ordered by the courts to pay $15 million in back wages and to commit another $50 million annually for promotion and wage adjustments for women and members of minority groups.[14] Now, after twenty years, the equal employment opportunity and affirmative action concepts are firmly entrenched in the American employment system.[15]

Orientation

After new employees have been selected and hired to fill specific positions, they must be "oriented." At one level, *orientation* means explaining organizational procedures such as pay schedules, benefit options, and working hours. It also involves socializing the newcomer into the organizational system.[16] In some organizations, orientation is a brief introduction handled during the first few hours of the individual's first day. In other settings, elaborate orientation may take a number of days or weeks.

Compensation

Few people are willing to work for nothing. *Compensation* includes not only wages or salary but also a variety of benefits. Compensation levels are usually arrived at in some systematic way. Different means of job evaluation provide the manager with a framework for assigning dollar values (wages or salaries) to different jobs and for developing a range of wages or salaries for people with different amounts of experience or levels of proficiency.

Employee benefits are a significant element in compensation, often costing as much as 35 cents for each dollar of salary or wages. These benefits may include health, life, and dental insurance, retirement benefits, paid vacation, profit sharing, holiday and sick time, credit unions, options to purchase stock, and so forth.

Training and development

Another key element in effective human resource management is training and developing employees in order to enhance their value to the organization. Spe-

14. See Carol J. Loomis, "AT&T in the Throes of 'Equal Employment,' " *Fortune*, January 15, 1979, pp. 44–48ff.

15. See Daniel Seligman, "Affirmative Action Is Here to Stay," *Fortune*, April 19, 1982, pp. 145–162.

16. See Wanous, *Organizational Entry*.

cifically, training and development consists of "planned efforts by the organization to facilitate the learning of job-related behaviors by its employees."[17]

Training typically involves operating employees such as machine operators, sales clerks, and cash register operators. Much training takes place on the job, where the supervisor normally serves as the instructor. *Development,* on the other hand, usually refers to the education of managers. Because managers constitute a major part of an organization's human resource investment, it is not surprising that most organizations make at least some effort in management development. For example, the typical new management trainee at General Mills spends roughly three years learning the ropes before being promoted to product manager. The company's training program is regarded as one of the best in the country.[18] A survey by Desmond D. Martin and William J. Kearney found that almost three fourths of participating organizations employing 1,000 or more had formal management development programs.[19]

Performance appraisal

A final component of most staffing systems is performance appraisal. As the term suggests, *performance appraisal* involves evaluating some aspect of an employee's performance. Gary Latham and Kenneth Wexley define performance appraisal as any "decision that influences the status of employees regarding their retention, termination, promotion, transfer, salary increase or decrease, or admission into a training program."[20]

The personnel unit typically develops an organization's performance appraisal system. Common devices for performance appraisal include rating scales of various kinds, objective measures (for example, dollars of sales or units of output), and attendance (such as number of days absent or late for work). The line manager then administers the system.

A key purpose of appraisal is to enhance employee motivation: an employee who does a good job and is rewarded will probably continue to do a good job. Similarly, if a poor performer is not rewarded and understands why, he or she may try to do a better job in the future. Hence, as shown in Figure 10.2, performance appraisal activities should be related to compensation. Performance appraisal also affects the other phases of staffing. If most employees are doing a good job, the existing planning, recruiting, selection, orientation, compensation, and training and development activities are evidently effective. If many performance problems arise, however, one or more of the other staffing activities may require modification (more information about rewards and reward systems will be found in Chapter 13). To varying degrees, then, per-

17. See Kenneth N. Wexley and Gary P. Latham, *Developing and Training Human Resources in Organizations* (Glenview, Il.: Scott, Foresman, 1981), p. 3.

18. Ann M. Morrison, "The General Mills Brand of Managers," *Fortune,* January 12, 1981, pp. 98–107.

19. Desmond D. Martin and William J. Kearney, "The Behavioral Sciences in Management Development Programs," *Journal of Business,* May 1978, p. 28.

20. Gary P. Latham and Kenneth N. Wexley, *Increasing Productivity Through Performance Appraisal* (Reading, Mass.: Addison-Wesley, 1981).

formance appraisals influence subsequent human resource planning, recruiting, selection and placement, and orientation activities.

Designing jobs in organizations

After employees have been hired, what do they do? They go to work, performing a job that the organization has designed for them. At the beginning of this chapter, we described a 1976 job and hinted that a more recent version of that same job would be significantly improved. Originally, this person's job consisted of sitting in a sanding booth and sanding the body of each car as it rolled down the line. That same job may still exist today, but the employee probably has more say in how it is done and plays a larger role in defining it.

Job design is the specification of an employee's task-related activities. In our last chapter, we described the tendency for jobs to become increasingly narrow and specialized. This high degree of specialization may increase efficiency, but it is also likely to decrease satisfaction and motivation. Hence managers have learned to search for alternatives to work specialization, looking for ways to design jobs so as to keep employees satisfied and motivated to do their best.[21]

Alternatives to work specialization

Four common approaches to designing jobs in such a way so as to avoid the problems of extreme specialization are job rotation, job enlargement, job enrichment, and work redesign.

Job rotation. Job rotation involves systematically moving employees from one job to another. In a warehouse, a worker might unload trucks on Monday, carry in-coming inventory to storage on Tuesday, verify invoices on Wednesday, pull out-going inventory from storage on Thursday, and load trucks on Friday. A typical job rotation arrangement is shown in Figure 10.3. The jobs themselves do not change; rather, the worker moves from job to job.

Unfortunately, job rotation has not been very successful in enhancing employee motivation or satisfaction. Jobs that are amenable to rotation tend to be relatively standard and routine. A worker who is rotated to a "new" job may show increased interest at first, but this interest soon wanes. Although many companies (among them American Cyanamid, Baker International, Bethlehem Steel, Ford Motor Company, Prudential Insurance, TRW Inc., and Western Electric) have tried job rotation, it is most often used today as a training device to improve worker skills and flexibility.

Job enlargement. On the assumption that doing the same basic task over and over is an important cause of worker dissatisfaction, job enlargement

21. Much of the material in this section is based on Ricky W. Griffin, *Task Design—An Integrative Approach* (Glenview, Il.: Scott, Foresman, 1982).

Figure 10.3
Job rotation

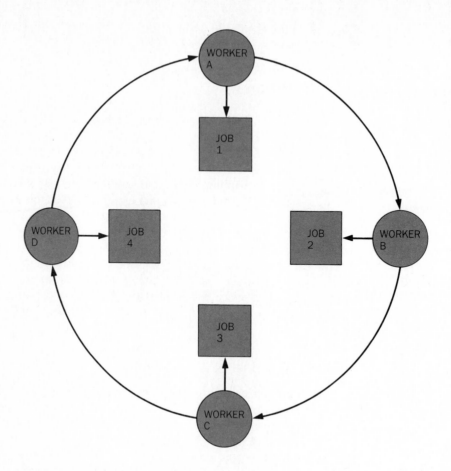

was developed to increase the number of tasks each worker performs. Job enlargement is illustrated in Figure 10.4. Before job enlargement, each worker had his or her own special task. Enlargement gives each worker more activities to perform by "stretching" the process.

Many organizations have adopted job enlargement as a means for improving employee motivation. Notable examples include IBM, Detroit Edison, American Telephone & Telegraph, the Colonial Life Insurance Company, the U.S. Civil Service, the Social Security Administration, and Maytag. At Maytag the assembly line for producing washing machine water pumps was systematically changed so that work that had originally been performed by six workers, who passed the work sequentially from one person to another, was performed by four workers, each of whom assembled a complete pump.[22] Although some benefits are associated with job enlargement, they tend to be offset by several disadvantages: (1) training costs rise, (2) unions have argued that pay should increase because the worker is doing more things, and (3) in many cases the work remains boring and routine even after job enlargement.

22. See M. D. Kilbridge, "Reduced Costs Through Job Enrichment: A Case," *The Journal of Business*, 1960, pp. 357–362.

Figure 10.4
Job enlargement

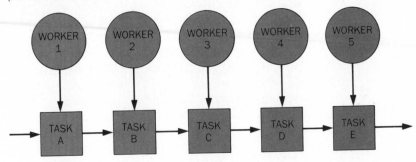

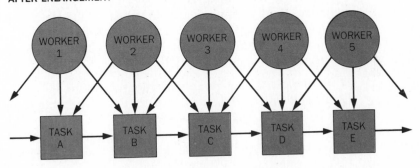

Source: Ricky W. Griffin, *Task Design—An Integrative Approach* (Glenview, Ill.: Scott, Foresman, 1982), p. 22. Used with permission.

Job enrichment. An even more comprehensive approach to designing jobs is through a technique known as job enrichment. *Job enrichment* is based on Frederick Herzberg's two-factor theory of motivation[23] which will be described in detail in Chapter 13. Herzberg has argued that, because job rotation and job enlargement do not provide the worker with any additional responsibility or control, they do not really enhance employee motivation. Job enrichment purports to increase both the number of tasks a worker does *and* the control the worker has over the job.

To accomplish this, a number of job changes are made. The manager removes some controls from the job, delegates more authority to employees, and structures the work in complete, natural units. These changes increase the subordinates' sense of responsibility. Another change suggested by Herzberg is to continually assign new and challenging tasks, thereby increasing the employees' opportunity for growth and advancement.

Robert Ford describes one interesting application of job enrichment at AT&T.[24] Prior to enrichment, eight typists in one service unit prepared cus-

23. See Frederick Herzberg, *Work and the Nature of Man* (Cleveland: World Press, 1966).

24. Robert Ford, "Job Enrichment Lessons From AT&T," *Harvard Business Review*, January–February 1973, pp. 96–106.

tomer service orders. Faced with low output and high turnover, management realized that the typists felt little responsibility to clients and received little feedback. The unit was changed so as to create a typing team. Typists were matched with designated service representatives, the task was changed from ten specific steps to three more general steps, and job titles were up-graded. As a result, the frequency of orders being processed versus awaiting processing increased from 27 percent to 90 percent, the need for messenger service was eliminated, accuracy improved, and turnover became practically nil.

Other organizations that employ job enrichment include Texas Instruments, IBM, and General Foods. Problems have been encountered, however. Analysis of a work system *before* enrichment is needed but seldom performed, and managers rarely deal with employee preferences when enriching jobs.

Work redesign. An alternative to work specialization that takes the work system and employee characteristics more into account is called work redesign. Work redesign is usually based on the job characteristics theory developed by Richard Hackman and Greg Oldham[25] (see Figure 10.5). As indicated in the figure, jobs can be diagnosed and improved along five core dimensions.

1. **Skill variety.** The number of things a person does in a job.
2. **Task identify.** The extent to which the worker does a complete or identifiable portion of the total job.
3. **Task significance.** The perceived importance of the task.
4. **Autonomy.** The degree of control the worker has over how the work is performed.
5. **Feedback.** The extent to which the worker knows how well the job is being performed.

The model predicts that, the higher on these dimensions a job is, the more employees will experience various desirable psychological states. Experiencing these states is expected to lead to high motivation, high-quality performance, high satisfaction, and low absenteeism and turnover.

Finally, an individual difference variable called growth-need strength is presumed to affect the overall process. People with a strong desire to grow, develop, and expand their capabilities are expected to respond as the model predicts; individuals with low growth-need strength are expected not to respond so strongly or consistently.

A large number of research studies have been conducted to test the usefulness of work redesign as an alternative to work specialization. The Southwestern Division of Prudential Insurance, for example, used work redesign in its claims division. Results included moderate declines in turnover and a small but measurable improvement in work quality. Some of the research findings have supported the theory while others have not. Although work redesign is the most promising contemporary approach to designing jobs, it is probably

25. J. Richard Hackman and Greg R. Oldham, *Work Redesign* (Reading, Mass.: Addison–Wesley, 1980). This section is based on Griffin, *Task Design.*

Figure 10.5
Work redesign

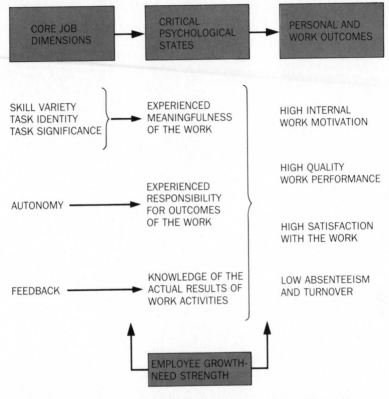

Source: J. R. Hackman and G. R. Oldham, "Motivation Through the Design of Work: Test of a Theory," *Organizational Behavior and Human Performance*, Vol. 16 (1976), pp. 250–279. Used with permission of Academic Press Inc.

not the final answer. Management must still look for new ways to optimize efficiency, productivity, motivation, and job satisfaction.

Current state of job design

Other approaches to designing jobs are also being used. Perhaps the most interesting is the concept of autonomous work groups, which was briefly introduced earlier.

Figure 10.6 shows how Volvo, the Swedish automobile manufacturer, has successfully used autonomous work groups in one of its plants. The part of the plant shown in the figure represents the work area of one such group, which performs all work within this wing. Note that the group has its own inventory area (stores), toilets, and changing rooms. The effect is much like working in a small machine shop rather than a big automobile plant.

The groups in the plant range in size from 15 to 25 members. Each group has a complete set of tasks, such as wiring or upholstery. The group members themselves determine who will perform each task. They can speed up or slow down the flow of work somewhat without disrupting the work of other

Figure 10.6
Autonomous work
groups at Volvo

Key:
1. Stores
2. Body buffers
3. Material intake by electric trucks
4. Preassembly
5. Materials
6. Bodies (on the left, stationary;
   on the right, moving)
7. Pause area
8. Toilets, etc.
9. Changing rooms

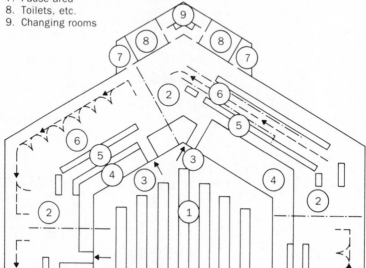

Source: Reprinted, by permission of the publisher, from "Job Redesign on the Assembly Line: Farewell to Blue-Collar Blues?" by William F. Dowling, p. 62, *Organizational Dynamics*, Autumn 1973. © 1973 AMACOM, a division of American Management Associations, New York. All rights reserved.

groups. The group receives frequent feedback on its productivity via computer display screens. Although the plant cost more to build than Volvo's conventional facilities, the company has witnessed an improvement in quality and decreased turnover and absenteeism.

Other issues currently surrounding job design include the exact nature of the relationship between job design and individual worker performance and the impact of automation on workers. This latter area promises to attract increasing managerial attention. In its manufacturing plants, Nissan Motor Corporation has pioneered the use of robots to weld body parts together, bolt on doors, and so forth. In offices, automated office systems are potentially important.

Establishing work schedules

After jobs have been properly designed, it is necessary to decide *when* people will work. This involves setting up *work schedules* for individuals, departments, and the whole organization.

Traditional work schedules

The usual work schedule in the United States is a 9:00–5:00 arrangement for Monday through Friday, with the weekend off. Many clerical and administrative jobs still follow this pattern. The hours between 8:00 or 9:00 A.M. and 5:00 P.M. (with an hour off for lunch) are considered "business hours," because all businesses are presumed to be in operation during those hours. Manufacturers and the construction trades may follow a 7:00 A.M. to 3:30 P.M. daily arrangement instead. Such a schedule results in 40 hours of work each week. In recent years, the 40-hour week has become the legal and cultural norm in the United States for a "full-time" job.

Many professionals, however, work far in excess of 40 hours per week, usually without benefit of extra compensation. They do this because they enjoy the work, want to accomplish a goal, or view the extra work as a means of gaining recognition and earning promotion. Other workers seek overtime work for the sake of extra pay. Furthermore, many organizations have regular work schedules that deviate from the 9:00–5:00 pattern. Manufacturers who operate more than one shift may have one set of employees who work 8:00 A.M.–4:00 P.M., another set of those who work 4:00 P.M.–12:00 midnight, and a third set of those who work 12:00 midnight–8:00 A.M. Many retailers are open evenings and weekends. Waitresses, police officers, fire fighters, hospital personnel, and airline employees also must regularly work outside the "normal" 9:00–5:00 day.

Organizations that set up extended work hours must constantly balance employees' schedules with peak demand for their time. In retailing, for example, Saturday is usually the biggest sales day and therefore the day when all sales personnel are needed. Yet Saturday is also a day that many employees want off in order to travel or spend the weekend with their families.

Of course, the normal 9:00–5:00 schedule also causes problems. Employees must often transact legitimate personal business (banking, dental and physician visits, automobile repairs, and so on) during the business day, so they may be late returning from lunch or simply have to take time off to attend to such matters. In either case, managers must shift other employees around, do the work themselves, hire a temporary employee, or otherwise make arrangements to keep output from suffering.

Alternatives to traditional schedules

To overcome these and related problems and to enhance employee motivation, organizations have recently begun to experiment with alternative work schedules, three of which are the compressed workweek, flexible work schedules, and job sharing.[26]

The compressed workweek. The compressed workweek is a work schedule in which the employee works 40 hours in fewer than 5 days. Usually

26. See Simcha Rosen, *Flexible Working Hours: An Innovation in the Quality of Work Life* (New York: McGraw-Hill, 1981).

the compressed workweek consists of four 10-hour days per week (some people refer to this as a 4/40 week). Although some organizations schedule all employees for the same four days, the typical arrangement is for work schedules to be staggered, with the organization remaining in operation other days as well.

The rationale for the compressed workweek is to allow the employee an extra day off (for personal business, leisure time at home, and so on) in hopes that absenteeism and tardiness will drop. However, fatigue at the end of the workday tends to increase, and managers have difficulty interacting with other organizations on a traditional schedule.

Organizations that have adopted the compressed workweek include John Hancock Insurance, Atlantic Richfield, R. J. Reynolds, and General Dynamics. In one interesting experiment, it was found that both satisfaction and performance initially increased after conversion to a 4/40 week but that both declined to the original level after two years.[27] While around 750,000 Americans are currently on a compressed workweek, companies are dropping these programs at a rate of 4 to 5 percent per year.[28]

Flexible work schedule. Compressed workweeks require employees to be at work during specified hours, but a flexible work schedule (or flexi-time) provides employees with more flexibility in *which* hours they work. Typically, organizations that use flexi-time divide the workday into two components: core time, when everyone must be present, and flexible time, when employees choose their own hours. Examples of three flexible work schedules are shown in Figure 10.7.

Schedule A might be adopted by the early riser, who would go to work at 6:00 A.M., take an hour for lunch sometime between 11:00 A.M. and 1:00 P.M., and be finished for the day at 3:00 P.M. A night owl might prefer schedule B: come in at 9:00 A.M., have an hour for lunch, and work until 6:00 P.M. Finally, a person who needs to run errands at lunch (or who has a big appetite!) might adopt schedule C. This person can come in at 7:00 A.M., take 2 hours for lunch from 11:00 A.M. to 1:00 P.M., and be finished at 5:00 P.M. Some organizations allow employees to select their own schedule but then require them to maintain it for a specified period of time; other organizations allow employees to vary their schedule daily.

Flexi-time gives employees the opportunity to balance their work life and their personal life. Many studies have shown that flexi-time often results in lower absenteeism and turnover and improved performance. On the negative side, more controls may be needed to monitor employee hours, and utility expenses may increase due to increased hours of operation. Control Data Corporation, Metropolitan Life, and several agencies of the United States govern-

27. John M. Ivancevich and Herbert C. Lyon, "The Shortend Workweek: A Field Experiment," *Journal of Applied Psychology*, Vol. 62, 1977, pp. 34–37.

28. See Allan R. Cohen and Herman Gadon, *Alternative Work Schedules: Integrating Individual and Organizational Needs* (Reading, Mass.: Addison–Wesley, 1978).

Figure 10.7
Flexible work schedules

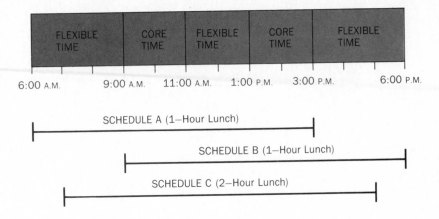

ment have adopted flexi-time. At present, about 400,000 organizations have some form of flexible work schedule, and the number seems to be increasing.[29]

Job sharing. Many people are familiar with job sharing because of its mention in the popular Dolly Parton–Jane Fonda movie *9 to 5*. Job sharing means that two (or possibly more) people literally share one job. The people sharing the job might be husband and wife, friends, or complete strangers. An example of job sharing might involve one person working from 8:00 A.M. to 12:30 P.M. and the other working from 12:30 P.M. to 5:00 P.M. Of course, if the job is complex, the two employees may need to spend some time communicating and coordinating their activities.

Individuals might prefer job sharing when they want more leisure time or more time with their families. Or a husband and wife might both want to pursue careers in a tight job market or along with raising a young family. The organization, in turn, is able to draw on a broader spectrum of talent and may be less dependent on one individual. If a person is sick, for example, the organization loses only a half day rather than a full day. One disadvantage is the need to maintain more personnel files and conduct more performance appraisals.

Job sharing is a relatively new technique, so there are no reliable estimates of how many people are currently involved. It appears, however, to be potentially valuable as an alternative work schedule.

Managing organizational conflict

Organizational conflict has both positive and negative implications for getting work done. *Conflict* might be defined as a disagreement between two or more individuals or groups. *Organizational conflict* results from disagreement be-

29. See Cohen and Gadon, *Alternative Work Schedules.*

tween individual employees, work groups, or departments. Conflict is coming under close scrutiny in many organizations. Union Carbide recently sent two hundred of its managers to a three-day workshop on conflict management. The managers engaged in a variety of exercises and discussions to learn who they were most likely to have conflict with and how they should try to resolve it.[30]

Primary causes of conflict

Many factors cause conflict in organizations. Some of these factors are the result of organizational design; others are individual or social in nature. (Line–staff conflict was discussed earlier in this chapter.)

Group interdependence. Chapter 9 described three forms of group interdependence: pooled, sequential, and reciprocal. Just as increased interdependence increases coordination problems, it also increases the potential for conflict. For example, recall that in sequential interdependence work is passed from one unit to another. Conflict may arise if the first group is turning out too much work (the second group will get behind), too little work (the second group can't meet its goals), or work of poor quality.

Differences in goals. Just like different people, different departments have different goals, and these goals may often be incompatible. A marketing goal of maximizing sales, achieved partially by offering a wide variety of sizes, shapes, colors, and models, may conflict with a production goal of minimizing costs, achieved partially by long production runs of a limited number of items. (For more information on goal differences and goal organization, see Chapter 4.)

Resources. Most organizations—especially universities, hospitals, government agencies, and businesses in depressed industries—do not have unlimited resources. Hence conflict may arise from competition for limited resources. In one New England town, the public works department and the library recently battled over funds from a federal construction grant.

Interpersonal dynamics. Conflict may also arise from interpersonal dynamics. Different people may perceive a situation from different points of view. New management trainees may resent having to learn routine administrative duties, whereas senior managers may believe it is necessary for them to learn the business from the ground up. Some people are extremely competitive, so conflict may arise when, say, two managers are vying for a promotion. Other people may resent someone simply because of the role he or she plays. For example, if a work group is very loyal to its boss, and if the boss gets fired or transferred, the group will probably react negatively to *any* new boss. And,

---

30. See "Teaching How to Cope with Workplace Conflicts," *Business Week*, February 18, 1980, pp. 136, 139.

of course, genuine personality conflicts may arise between individuals who, for purely personal reasons, cannot seem to work well together.

Consequences of conflict

Most people assume that conflict is "bad" because it connotes antagonism, hostility, unpleasantness, and dissension. Indeed, managers and management theorists have traditionally viewed conflict as a problem to be avoided.[31]

In recent years, we have come to recognize that, although conflict can be a major problem, certain kinds of conflict may actually be beneficial. Consider the example of two hospitals that disagree on how best to provide health care or two manufacturing plants that disagree over how to improve efficiency. As each hospital strives to demonstrate the value of its own approach, the community may realize an overall increase in the quality of health care available to its citizens. Or the manufacturer may discover numerous techniques for improving efficiency.

A general relationship between conflict and performance is suggested in Figure 10.8. If there is no conflict, complacency and stagnation may set in, and performance may suffer as a result. A moderate level of conflict can spark motivation, creativity, and initiative. But too much conflict can produce such undesirable results as hostility and lack of cooperation. The key is to find and

Figure 10.8
Organizational conflict and performance

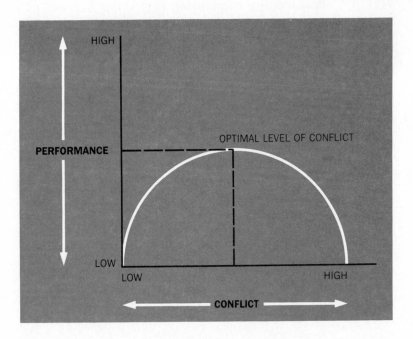

31. Stephen P. Robbins, *Managing Organizational Conflict* (Englewood Cliffs, N.J.: Prentice-Hall, 1974).

Table 10.1 Strategies for managing conflict

Stimulating conflict	Avoiding conflict	Resolving conflict
1. Encouraging competition 2. Bringing in outsiders 3. Changing established procedures	1. Expansion of resources 2. Managing interdependencies 3. Maintaining supraordinate goals 4. Managing interpersonal dynamics	1. Avoidance 2. Smoothing 3. Compromise 4. Confrontation

maintain the optimal level of conflict that fosters the highest level of performance.

Managing conflict

The management of organizational conflict can be aimed at avoiding conflict before it arises, resolving conflict if it does occur, or stimulating constructive kinds of conflict. Table 10.1 summarizes a number of strategies for managing conflict for these ends.

Encouraging competition. Quite often conflict may be stimulated by placing individuals or groups in competitive situations. Recall the number of "disagreements" you have observed between two football, baseball, basketball, or hockey teams! Managers can establish sales contests, incentive plans, bonuses, or other competitive stimuli to spark competition.

Bringing in outsiders. Some organizations have successfully brought in outsiders to shake things up in order to stimulate a certain level of conflict. For example, when Michael Blumenthal became chairman at Burroughs, he replaced one third of his top executives and introduced a number of far-reaching changes within the company. The results of these changes may or may not have been what he had in mind, but he believes he has laid a firm foundation for the company's future.[32]

Changing established procedures. By changing established procedures, especially procedures that have outlived their usefulness, a manager can stimulate conflict. For example, a new university president announced that all vacant staff positions could henceforth be filled only after written justification had received his approval. Most requests were okayed, but department heads had to think through their staffing needs and a few unnecessary positions were eliminated.

32. Bro Uttal, "The Blumenthal Revival at Burroughs," *Fortune,* October 5, 1981, pp. 128–136.

For the most part, these techniques are aimed at stimulating desirable kinds of conflict. Of course, it may also be necessary to avoid other kinds of conflict, and conflict avoidance strategies generally focus on eliminating or at least buffering the causes of conflict.

Expansion of resources. If scarce resources can be expanded, conflict will usually subside. Suppose a top manager receives two budget requests for $100,000 each. If she has only $180,000 to distribute, the stage is set for conflict. If both proposals are worthwhile, it may be possible for her to come up with the extra $20,000 from some other source and thereby avoid difficulty.

Managing interdependencies. Pooled, sequential, and reciprocal interdependencies can all dissolve into conflict, so the manager should use an appropriate technique for enhancing coordination and reducing the probability that conflict will arise. Techniques for coordination (described in Chapter 9) include making use of the managerial hierarchy, relying on rules and procedures, and enlisting liaison persons, task forces, and integrating departments.

Maintaining supraordinate goals. Differences in goals can also be a potential source of conflict. Managers can sometimes focus the employees' attention on higher-level, or supraordinate, goals as a way of eliminating lower-level conflict. When labor unions such as the United Auto Workers recognize that they must make wage concessions to ensure survival of the industry, they are considering a supraordinate goal. Their immediate goal may be higher wages for members, but they realize that without the automobile industry, their members wouldn't even have jobs.

Managing interpersonal dynamics. Another way to avoid conflict is through the management of interpersonal dynamics. A manager who has two valuable subordinates, one a chain smoker and the other a vehement anti-smoker, should avoid requiring them to work together in a confined space. In general, managers should try to match the personalities and work habits of employees in order to avoid conflict between individuals.

Regardless of everyone's best intentions, conflict is inevitable in any organization. If it is harming the firm, attempts must be made to resolve it. Four techniques managers can use to try to resolve conflict are avoidance, smoothing, compromise, and confrontation.

Avoidance. The avoidance approach is simply to ignore the conflict and hope it will go away. Some managers adopt avoidance because they are uncomfortable when dealing with conflict. Avoidance may sometimes be effective in the short run, but it does little to resolve long-run or acute conflict.

Smoothing. Smoothing is minimizing the conflict and telling everyone that things will "get better." In many cases, though, the conflict gets worse as people continue to think about it. Smoothing is generally not advisable.

Compromise. Compromise can work if it is used with care, but in most compromise situations someone wins and someone loses. Budget problems may be amenable to compromise because of their objective nature. Assume, for example, that additional resources are not available, there is $180,000 to divide, and each of two groups claims to need $100,000. If the manager believes that both projects warrant funding, she can allocate $90,000 to each, and the fact that the two groups have at least been treated equally may still the conflict.

Confrontation. This method of conflict resolution, which is also called interpersonal problem solving, involves bringing the parties together to confront the conflict. The parties discuss the nature of their conflict and attempt to reach an agreement or a solution. Confrontation obviously requires a reasonable degree of maturity on the part of the participants, and the manager must structure the situation carefully. If handled well, this approach can be an effective means of resolving conflict.

In addition to these techniques for resolving conflict, some of the techniques for avoiding conflict may also be used to resolve conflict that does arise. If conflict arises from incompatible personalities, the manager might transfer one or both parties to other units. If conflict stems from group interdependence, the manager might realize that he or she is using an inappropriate coordination technique and shift to another.

Summary of key points

Committees and work groups represent one means of getting work done in organizations. Ad hoc committees, standing committees, task forces, and boards are all examples of committees commonly found in many organizations. In general, the advantages and disadvantages of committees are the same as those that characterize group decision making. Three kinds of work groups found in many organizations are operative work groups, autonomous work groups, and teams.

A line role is a position in the direct chain of command, whereas a staff role is a position intended to provide expertise, advice, and support. Line managers generally have direct authority over a major unit; staff managers may serve as advisors and/or managers of units that are not directly related to the organization's mission. Both line and staff roles are extremely important to an organization's success. Conflict occasionally breaks out between line and staff managers because of demographic differences, threats to authority, line's dependence on staff knowledge, and other factors. Several techniques are available for dealing with this conflict.

Staffing the organization means attracting and retaining effective employees. Aspects of the staffing process include human resource planning, recruiting, selection and placement, orientation, compensation, training and development, and performance appraisal. Legal requirements influence several of these components, especially selection and placement, and compensation.

Designing jobs is another important part of getting work done in organizations. The traditional approach to job design was work specialization, but contemporary alternatives include job rotation, job enlargement, job enrichment, and work redesign. Each of these innovations represents an attempt to balance efficiency and productivity with employee satisfaction and motivation. At present some companies are using autonomous work groups, automation (such as robotics), and automated office systems in attempts to improve job design.

Establishing work schedules means determining when employees are to work. Traditional work schedules usually run from early morning to late afternoon (such as 9:00 A.M. to 5:00 P.M.) and total 40 hours per week, although many people (such as shift workers, police officers, hospital employees, and so on) work other kinds of schedules. Alternatives to these schedules include compressed workweeks, flexible work schedules, and job sharing.

Organizational conflict results from disagreement among individuals, work groups, and/or departments. Primary causes of conflict include group interdependence, differences in goals, scarce resources, and interpersonal dynamics. A total lack of conflict may result in stagnation and apathy, whereas a moderate level of conflict tends to spark initiative, creativity, and motivation. Of course, too much conflict can be quite harmful. Techniques for stimulating conflict include encouraging competition, bringing in outsiders, and changing established procedures. Useful methods for avoiding conflict include the expansion of resources, managing interdependencies, maintaining supraordinate goals, and managing interpersonal dynamics. Methods for resolving conflict after it occurs include avoidance, smoothing, compromise, and confrontation, as well as the methods that can be used to avoid conflict in the first place.

QUESTIONS FOR DISCUSSION

1. Think of a committee or work group you have dealt with. Was the experience pleasant or unpleasant? Was formation of that committee or work group an appropriate way to accomplish whatever objective was at issue? Why or why not?

2. Some companies have used a concept called the "plural executive," whereby a committee rather than an individual serves as chief executive. What are the pros and cons of this approach?

3. Are line positions or staff positions more important? Could an organization survive without either? If you were to accept a position as a staff manager, what could you do to avoid conflict with line managers?

4. Is line–staff conflict always dysfunctional? Why or why not?

5. We indicated that laws prohibit discrimination in hiring. How do these same restrictions affect other components of the staffing process, such as recruiting, compensation, and training and development?

6. Many companies have an employee called a personnel manager. Does this individual do all the things identified as components of staffing? If not, who else might be involved?

7. Think of the three most unpleasant jobs imaginable. How could they be improved? Will jobs like these always be necessary?

8. Assume you are a plant manager in an area characterized by very high unemployment. Your plant has several jobs that are physically demanding, dirty, boring, and degrading. A new robot has just been introduced that can do the work about as efficiently as a human. Would you buy some robots or keep the existing employees?

9. Can you identify other alternatives to traditional work schedules besides compressed workweeks, flexi-time, and job sharing? Will the traditional workweek always be the most common schedule? Why or why not?

10. "From the manager's perspective, a common-sense approach to make job sharing effective is to have a high level of work specialization." Defend or refute this statement.

11. Can you identify organizations that have had a high level of conflict but have also been eminently successful?

12. Some people have argued that very large organizations such as General Motors, Exxon, and IBM are generally immune to the effects of conflict. What reasoning leads to this statement? Do you agree or disagree with this line of reasoning?

C A S E   10.1

At the beginning of this chapter, you read an incident about the new CEO of a large conglomerate. The CEO was appointed after a bitter struggle among members of the board of directors. One problem facing the new boss was how to maintain decentralization while also providing increased staff services to the 400-plus units comprising the organization. The company being described was Beatrice Foods. The case that follows explains some of the things Beatrice has done and then raises some other issues for your consideration.

Decentralization or support services at Beatrice Foods?

Beatrice Foods Company is a Chicago-based conglomerate with annual sales of around $9 billion. All told, the firm produces and sells almost 9,000 products and is organized around approximately 435 product groups. Well-known brand names owned by Beatrice Foods include Samsonite luggage, Clark candy bars, and La Choy Chinese foods; popular regional lines are Eckrich meats and Meadow Gold dairy products. Other major units include the Coca-Cola Bottling Company of Los Angeles and a variety of industrial and chemical products.

For many years Beatrice Foods grew rapidly and posted impressive earnings by aggressively pursuing a deceptively simple strategy. First Beatrice would buy a small company, usually paying with its own stock, and then expand the new company's markets. Second, Beatrice practices decentralization to an extreme: the new company would usually be allowed to maintain its existing management team and proceed with its ongoing activities without intrusion from Beatrice. Following this strategy, Beatrice Foods grew rapidly but also evolved into a disjointed collection of relatively small operations with no unified purpose or direction.

When the company's chief executive, who was responsible for developing and executing this strategy, retired in 1976, conflict erupted over his successor. The out-going CEO succeeded in selecting a temporary replacement who was to serve for three years and then step aside for a new CEO being groomed for the position. However, these two men didn't get along and the future CEO resigned. The temporary replacement was then forced to retire when he turned 65 in 1979. Several members of the board of directors favored the current chief operating officer, James Dutt, while others advocated a young vice president. Dutt was eventually appointed CEO in late 1979. As a result, two board members (as well as the talented vice president) also resigned.

Dutt set to work attempting to chart a new direction for Beatrice Foods. Through 1982 he sold 56 companies, including Dannon Yogurt and Airstream trailers. He also continued to expand, however. For example, Dutt paid $580 million for Northwest Industries' beverage operation in early 1982.

Beyond the issue of strategy and direction, Beatrice Foods seems to have two major problems to deal with. Dutt acknowledges that the managers of the various product groups need to do a better job of introducing and marketing new products. As an incentive, he has established an award of $10,000 for the manager who launches the most successful new product each year. Unfortunately, given that some of these managers earn over $100,000 a year, the award may not be a powerful motivator.

An even more serious organizational problem involves the time-honored corporate policy of extreme decentralization and how to reconcile it with the need for increased staff support in some areas. For example, many of the companies within Beatrice Foods are too small to justify a full-time marketing manager. In similar situations in other conglomerates, the normal solution is to establish a corporate marketing staff to provide assistance. Beatrice, however, fears that such a unit would tend to centralize marketing activities at the corporate level. Instead, Beatrice has established satellite marketing staffs for certain product groups but not for others. The situation, some managers argue, is far from satisfactory.

A similar problem exists in Beatrice Foods's financial control activities. The company has a corporate controller with a small staff, but there is not an auditing staff large enough to closely monitor the activities of Beatrice's more than 400 companies. As a result, the company has no way to keep a running check on the accuracy of the financial information forwarded from the companies themselves to corporate headquarters.

CASE
QUESTIONS

1. On the basis of the information presented, how would you evaluate the performance of the board of directors of Beatrice Foods? What kinds of things may have prompted the conflict among board members? Was this conflict functional or dysfunctional?

2. Would it be possible for Beatrice Foods to expand its staff component and yet retain its present level of decentralization? If so, how? If not, which route should the company take?

3. Why do you think Beatrice Foods is so determined to maintain a small staff component?

4. What conclusions about staffing can you draw from the experiences of Beatrice Foods?

CASE
REFERENCES

"Beatrice Revamps." *Fortune*, March 21, 1983, p. 7.

"Beatrice to Narrow Its Base as Result of Recession's Impact on Non-Food Units." *Wall Street Journal*, February 12, 1981, p. 10.

Colvin, Geoffrey. "The Bigness Cult's Grip on Beatrice Foods." *Fortune,* September 20, 1982, pp. 122–129.

"Quiet Revolution." *Wall Street Journal,* July 21, 1980, p. 1.

C A S E   10.2

Sam Baker and Scott Lopez were embroiled in one of their typical discussions. "Now listen," roared Sam, "I don't need some wise-acre punk telling me how to run my shop. I know you studied this job enrichment jazz in college, but that stuff only works in your textbooks. And this ain't textbook, this is the real world."

"Go ahead," retorted Scott, "Keep parading your ignorance. You've been stuck here in this shop so long that you don't even realize that management has gotten out of the dark ages. You can't motivate people with a kick in the tail and an extra buck an hour every year. People want some say in their work. And they want a chance to pick up new skills. Ah, what's the use? You'll never learn."

Contrary to what a casual observer might think, Sam and Scott don't really dislike each other. In fact, they are good friends. Sam Baker is plant manager at Acme Manufacturing and Scott Lopez is his assistant. Sam has worked at Acme for thirty years and was promoted to plant manager five years ago. Scott graduated from college three years ago and was hired by Acme as the assistant plant manager. Sam and Scott quickly became good friends. They enjoy baiting one another, Sam about Scott's youth, lack of experience, and education, and Scott about Sam's age, stubbornness, and lack of education.

In recent months, Acme has been experiencing some labor problems. Turnover has increased, absenteeism is up, and plant supervisors have reported increases in employee complaints. For the last several days, Sam and Scott have been discussing possible solutions.

Job enrichment as a solution to labor problems

Sam thinks that the best solutions are to give the employees a raise and to crack down on absences and griping. The plant is scheduled for a 90-cent-per-hour cost-of-living raise in two months and Sam is fairly certain he could get it authorized early. He also wants to attack the problem of absenteeism. Company policy currently requires a doctor's verification for absences of three consecutive days or longer. Sam wants to require verification for any absence, regardless of length.

Scott, on the other hand, wants to use job enrichment, a job design strategy he studied in college. The company has budgeted $300,000 for a plant renovation beginning in the next quarter. Scott has investigated the equipment that can be purchased and has determined that, with only minor modifications, most of the jobs in the plant can be substantially improved. In particular, the workers could have more control over how they do their jobs and receive more accurate feedback about their performance. They could also perform more different kinds of activities.

Scott thinks that money isn't the problem at all. Instead, he thinks the workers are simply bored with their jobs. By enriching the jobs, Scott believes that Acme can make its employees feel more involved with their work and more motivated to stay with Acme. As Sam and Scott continued their discussion at a nearby tavern after work, Sam set the stage for the evening's discussion by remarking, "You know, kid, this job enrichment stuff might not be so bad by itself. But if I let you get away with this, next month you'll want to build a company country club on that vacant lot next door."

"Now that you mention it," Scott responded, "I have been thinking about that vacant lot. . . ."

CASE
QUESTIONS

1. Do you think job enrichment will work for Acme? Why or why not?
2. Discuss the relative merits of Scott's and Sam's proposals.
3. What else might account for Acme's problems? If Acme proceeds with a job enrichment program, can you think of any unexpected problems it might encounter?
4. How much conflict exists between Sam and Scott? Do you think it is dysfunctional or constructive?

11

ORGANIZATIONAL DESIGN PROCESSES

CHAPTER OBJECTIVES

1. Discuss the classical perspective on organization theory, and outline the strengths and weaknesses of the bureaucratic model.

2. Evaluate Likert's System 4 organization from a behavioral perspective, and explain the idea of a linking pin role.

3. Discuss and assess the impact of technology and organization size on organization design.

4. Relate environmental factors and information-processing needs to organization structure.

5. Discuss the steps involved in creating a matrix form of organization, and summarize its advantages and disadvantages.

6. Enumerate Mintzberg's five types of organizational design, and summarize the benefits of each.

7. Describe organization climate and its relationship to organization design.

321

OPENING INCIDENT

You are a manager at an electronics company that uses a matrix form of design (created by overlaying product centers onto functional departments). After achieving phenomenal growth during the 1970s, the company has recently fallen on hard times. One cause of the problem has been identified as your matrix design. Product managers are given the responsibility of designing, producing, and marketing products, but they do not have the authority to get functional departments to help as needed. What would you do?

American Can Company has recently begun to change a number of the components of its structure. The company is becoming more decentralized while also decreasing the size of its staff component. A committee of top-level managers has been established to coordinate divisional goals, and the span of management of the chief executive has been increased.[1] Hence American Can is actually creating a totally new organization design for itself. Such changes represent a major undertaking for any organization, and their effects are likely to be felt for many years.

This chapter represents the culmination of our discussion of the organizing process. If the basic building blocks discussed in Chapter 9 are analogous to the bricks and stones of a building, the techniques for getting work done described in Chapter 10 are somewhat like the mortar and cement used to hold the building blocks together. We can now focus on the complete system that consists of all the bricks and stones held together by the mortar and cement. This complete system is the design of the organization.

As defined in Chapter 9, *organization design* is concerned with the unique interrelationships among the components of an organization. The first section of this chapter summarizes the classical or historical perspective on organization design. We then discuss a behavioral approach to organization design that has its roots in the human relations school of management thought. The focus then shifts to contemporary views as we discuss several contingency or situational factors that affect organization design. After an in-depth analysis of the links between organization structure and strategy, we conclude with a brief description of an organization's internal environment, or climate.

As we discuss organization design processes throughout this chapter, remember that organizations are seldom if ever designed and then left intact. Indeed, most organizations change constantly as situations, people, and other factors vary. The processes of organization change will be discussed in the next chapter.

---

1. See Peter Nulty, "American Can's Big Shakeout," *Fortune*, August 24, 1981, pp. 74–80.

The classical perspective: Bureaucracy

Chapter 2 traced the history of management theory and noted the contributions to classical organization theory of such writers as Henri Fayol, Lyndall Urwick, and Chester Barnard. These contributions paralleled the growth of scientific management, which was popularized by Frederick Taylor. Another important classical organization theorist was a German sociologist named Max Weber, whose writings stimulated much research on organization structure and design.[2] Weber himself lived from 1864 to 1920 and worked as a professor, author, and consultant to the German government.[3]

The bureaucratic model

At the core of Weber's writings was the bureaucratic model of organization design. The Weberian perspective suggests that a *bureaucracy* is an organization structure based on a legitimate and formal system of authority. Many people associate bureaucracy with red tape, rigidity, and buck-passing. For example, how many times have you heard people refer to "the Federal bureaucracy" in a pejorative sense?

Weber, however, viewed a bureaucratic form of organization as logical, rational, and efficient. He offered the bureaucratic model as the normative framework to which all organizations should aspire, the "one best way" of doing things. According to Weber, the *ideal* bureaucracy exhibits five basic characteristics.

1. The organization should adopt a distinct division of labor, and each position should be filled by an expert.
2. The organization should develop a consistent set of abstract rules to ensure that task performance is uniform.
3. The organization should establish a hierarchy of positions or offices such that a chain of command from the top of the organization to the bottom is created.
4. Managers should conduct business in an impersonal way. Especially, they should maintain an appropriate social distance between themselves and their subordinates.
5. Employment and advancement in the organization should be based on technical expertise. As a corollary, employees should be protected from arbitrary dismissal. A high level of loyalty should therefore develop.

Perhaps the best examples of contemporary bureaucracies are government agencies and universities. Consider, for example, the steps you must go through and the forms you must fill out to apply for admission to college, request housing, register each semester, change majors, submit a degree plan, substitute a course, and file for graduation. The reason why this is necessary, of course, is that both the government and universities deal with large num-

2. Max Weber, *Theory of Social and Economic Organization*, A. M. Henderson and T. Parsons, trans. (London: Oxford University Press, 1921).

3. See Daniel Wren, *The Evolution of Management Thought*, 2nd ed. (New York: Wiley, 1979).

bers of people who must be treated equally and fairly. Hence rules, regulations, and standard operating procedures are necessary. (Of course, not all of Weber's suggestions are still appropriate. Fewer people would now be concerned about maintaining social distance between superiors and subordinates.)

Strengths and weaknesses

The bureaucratic model of organization has two primary strengths:

1. Several of the elements of the bureaucratic model (such as division of labor, reliance on rules, a hierarchy of authority, and employment based on expertise) may improve efficiency.
2. As noted earlier, the bureaucratic model was the catalyst for most later research and writing about organization design.

Unfortunately, the pursuit of an ideal bureaucracy also results in several disadvantages:

1. The bureaucracy tends to be inflexible and rigid.
2. Human and social processes within the bureaucracy are neglected.
3. The assumptions Weber made about loyalty and impersonal relations are unrealistic.

The bureaucratic model of organization design was an important milestone in the development of management theory. As environments became more complex, our understanding of behavioral processes more complete, and employees and managers more sophisticated, the bureaucratic model gave way to other perspectives.

The behavioral perspective: System 4

Just as the classical approach to organization design paralleled the development of scientific management, the human relations movement encouraged a behavioral approach to organization design. The best-known and most important behavioral approach is Likert's System 4.

Likert's System 4 organization

Rensis Likert, working at the University of Michigan, studied large numbers of organizations to determine what made some of them effective and others less so.[4] He found that organizations that hewed to the bureaucratic model tended to be less effective, whereas effective organizations paid more attention to developing work groups and were more concerned about behavioral and social processes. Likert described organizations in terms of eight key dimensions or processes: leadership processes, motivational processes, communication pro-

---

4. See Rensis Likert, *New Patterns in Management,* (New York: McGraw-Hill, 1961), and Rensis Likert, *The Human Organization* (New York: McGraw-Hill, 1967).

cesses, interaction processes, decision processes, goal-setting processes, control processes, and performance goals.

At one extreme, Likert identified a form of organization he called System 1. In many ways, a System 1 organization is similar to an ideal bureaucracy. In such an organization, motivational processes are assumed to be based on economic factors, and interaction processes are closed and restricted. That is, communication is relatively formal and primarily job-related. These and other characteristics of the System 1 organization are summarized in Table 11.1.

Table 11.1 System 1 and System 4 organizations

System 1 organization	System 4 organization
1. **Leadership process** includes no perceived confidence and trust. Subordinates do not feel free to discuss job problems with their superiors, who in turn do not solicit their ideas and opinions.	1. **Leadership process** includes perceived confidence and trust between superiors and subordinates in all matters. Subordinates feel free to discuss job problems with their superiors, who in turn solicit their ideas and opinions.
2. **Motivational process** taps only physical, security, and economic motives through the use of fear and sanctions. Unfavorable attitudes toward the organization prevail among employees.	2. **Motivational process** taps a full range of motives through participatory methods. Attitudes are favorable toward the organization and its goals.
3. **Communication process** is such that information flows downward and tends to be distorted, inaccurate, and viewed with suspicion by subordinates.	3. **Communication process** is such that information flows freely throughout the organization—upward, downward, and laterally. The information is accurate and undistorted.
4. **Interaction process** is closed and restricted; subordinates have little effect on departmental goals, methods, and activities.	4. **Interaction process** is open and extensive; both superiors and subordinates are able to affect departmental goals, methods, and activities.
5. **Decision process** occurs only at the top of the organization; it is relatively centralized.	5. **Decision process** occurs at all levels through group processes; it is relatively decentralized.
6. **Goal-setting process** located at the top of the organization, discourages group participation.	6. **Goal-setting process** encourages group participation in setting high, realistic objectives.
7. **Control process** is centralized and emphasizes fixing of blame for mistakes.	7. **Control process** is dispersed throughout the organization and emphasizes self-control and problem solving.
8. **Performance goals** are low and passively sought by managers who make no commitment to developing the human resources of the organization.	8. **Performance goals** are high and actively sought by superiors, who recognize the necessity for making a full commitment to developing, through training, the human resources of the organization.

Source: Adapted from Rensis Likert, *The Human Organization* (New York: McGraw-Hill, 1967), pp. 197–211. Used with permission.

Also summarized in this table are characteristics of Likert's other extreme form of organization design, called *System 4.* Note in particular that a System 4 organization uses a wide array of motivational processes and that its interaction processes are open and extensive. People communicate with each other in an unguarded way, everybody talks to everybody else, and so on. Other distinctions between System 1 and System 4 organizations are equally obvious. In between the System 1 and System 4 extremes lie the System 2 and System 3 organizations.

Likert argues that System 4 should be adopted by all organizations. He suggests that managers should emphasize supportive relationships, establish high performance goals, and practice group decision making to achieve the System 4 state.

Many organizations have attempted to adopt the System 4 design. In 1969 a GM plant in the Atlanta area was converted from a System 2 to a System 4 status. Over a period of three years, direct and indirect labor efficiency improved, as did tool breakage rates, scrap costs, and quality.[5]

The linking pin role

Another important contribution made by Likert and the behavioral perspective on organization design was the identification of *linking pin roles.* Every managerial position is linked to two groups of positions: a higher-level group of which the manager is a member and a lower-level group of which the manager is the head. Thus the manager can be viewed as a linking pin between levels of the organization (see Figure 11.1). This concept focuses attention on the role that managers at the middle levels of an organization play in coordinating and communicating the activities of higher-level and lower-level managers.

Strengths and weaknesses

The behavioral approach to organization design is characterized by one major strength and one major weakness. The major strength is its emphasis on behavioral processes in organizations. Whereas the classical perspective treated people like components of a large machine and minimized the importance of any one person, the behavioral model recognized the individual value of an organization's employees. Likert and his associates thus paved the way to a more humanistic perspective.

On the other hand, the behavioral approach to organization design, like the classical approach, was based on the premise that there is only one best way to design organizations. Researchers call this "one best way" view a universal approach. That is, the ideas are assumed to be universally true. (Thus the bureaucratic model is also universal in nature.) Subsequent research, however, has suggested that numerous situational factors or contingencies affect

5. See William F. Dowling, "At General Motors: System 4 Builds Performance and Profits," *Organizational Dynamics,* Winter 1975, pp. 23–28.

Figure 11.1
Linking pin roles

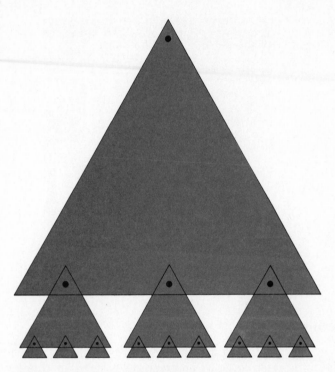

Source: Adapted from Rensis Likert, *The Human Organization* (New York: Mc-Graw-Hill, 1967), p. 50. Used with permission.

the design of any particular organization. What works for one organization may not work for another. Hence universal models like bureaucracy and System 4 have been largely supplanted by newer models that take these contingency factors into account. Drawing on our previous discussion of the contingency approach in Chapter 1, we can define the **contingency view of organization design** as the belief that the design that is appropriate for an organization depends on a variety of situational factors. Three of these factors are key variables inside the organization, key variables outside the organization, and the organization's strategy.

Internal contingency factors: Technology and size

Factors *internal* to the organization—those within its own boundaries—have a decided effect on various structural components (see Figure 11.2). Two important internal factors that may influence the design of an organization are the technology of the organization and its size.

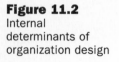

Figure 11.2
Internal
determinants of
organization design

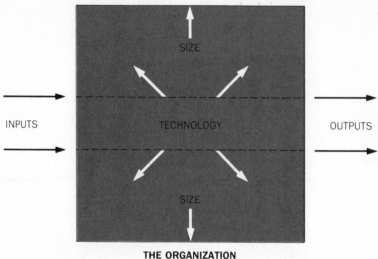

THE ORGANIZATION

Technology

Using systems theory as a framework, we will define *technology* as the conversion processes used by an organization in transforming inputs (such as materials or information) into outputs (such as products or services). Although most people visualize assembly lines and machinery when they think of technology, the term can also be applied to processing information, teaching students, and so forth.

Much of what we know about the link between technology and organization design we owe to the pioneering work of Joan Woodward.[6] In the early 1960s she led a team of researchers studying 100 manufacturing firms in southern England. They collected information about such things as the history of each organization, its manufacturing processes, its forms and procedures, and financial data. Woodward expected to find a relationship between the size of an organization and its structure, but no such relationship emerged, so she began to seek other explanations for differences in organization design.

This follow-up analysis led Woodward to classify the organizations according to their technology. Three basic forms of technology identified by Woodward are:

1. **Unit or small batch technology.** The product is custom-made to customer specifications or else produced in small quantities. Examples of organizations using this form of technology include a tailor shop (custom suits) and a printing shop (business cards and so on).

6. See Joan Woodward, *Industrial Organization: Theory and Practice* (London: Oxford University Press, 1965).

2. **Large batch or mass production technology.** The product is manufactured in assembly-line fashion by combining component parts into another part or finished product. Examples include automobile companies and washing machine companies.
3. **Continuous process technology.** The product is transformed from raw materials to a finished good by a series of machine or process transformations. The composition of the materials themselves is changed. Examples include petroleum refineries and chemical refineries.

These forms of technology are listed in order of increasing complexity. That is, large batch technology is presumed to be more complex than that which is used to produce small batches and less complex than that which is required for continuous processes. Woodward found that different forms of organization design were associated with each technology.

Table 11.2 summarizes the differences in structural components for each kind of technology. Note that, as technology becomes more complex, the number of levels of management increases (that is, the organization becomes taller). The executive (or top management) span of control also increases, and the relative size of the staff component grows. (In the small batch organizations, Woodward and her associates found one staff member for every eight line workers; in the continuous process organizations, they found one staff member for every two line workers.) However, the supervisory (or lower-level management) span of control first increases and then decreases as technology becomes more complex. This is attributable to the fact that much work in continuous process technologies is automated. Fewer workers are needed, but the skills necessary to do the job increase. These findings are consistent with our discussion of the span of management in Chapter 9: the more complex the job, the narrower the span should probably be.

At a more general level of analysis, Woodward found that the two extremes (unit or small batch, and continuous process) tended to be very similar to Likert's System 4 organization, whereas the middle-range organizations (large batch or mass production) were much more like bureaucracies. There

Table 11.2 Woodward's findings on technology and organization design

| Technology type | Structural component[a] | | | |
	Number of levels of management	Supervisory span of control	Executive span of control	Ratio of industrial workers (line) to staff workers
Unit or small batch	3	23	4	8:1
Large batch or mass production	4	48	7	5:1
Continuous process	6	15	10	2:1

[a]The numbers in the table are medians for the organizations in each group.

was also a higher level of specialization in the large batch and mass production organizations.[7]

Finally, she found that organizational success was related to the extent to which organizations followed the typical pattern. For example, note in Table 11.2 that the median executive span of control in large batch or mass production organizations was 7. Successful organizations employing that technology tended to have an executive span very close to 7. Less successful organizations of that kind tended to have an executive span considerably smaller or larger than 7.

Technology appears to play an important role in determining organization design. As future technologies become even more diverse and complex, managers should pay close attention to the relationship between technology and structure. But technology is not the only variable that can influence organization design. Another internal factor that affects organizations is size.

Size

Even though Woodward did not find a relationship between organization size and structure, other researchers and many managers have for years been intrigued by the implications of organization size. We have already noted (especially in Chapter 9) how organizations change as they become larger. For example, they tend to departmentalize by product rather than function.

Several different definitions of size could be developed, including those based on number of employees, total assets, or the scope of operations.[8] For our purposes, we will define organization *size* in terms of the total number of full-time or equivalent employees. (By equivalent, we mean that two part-time employees who work a combined 40-hour week are counted as one full-time employee.)

Interesting research on organization size and design was conducted by a team of researchers at the University of Aston in Birmingham, England.[9] These researchers felt that Woodward failed to find a size–structure relationship because almost all the organizations she studied were relatively small (three fourths of them had fewer than 500 employees). They decided to study a wider array of organizations to determine how size and technology both individually and jointly affect the design of an organization. None of the organizations in their sample had fewer than 250 employees, and 60 percent had over 500 employees.

The primary finding of the Aston studies was that technology did in fact influence structural variables in smaller firms, wherein all activities tended to be arranged around the organization's technology. In larger firms, however, wherein technology was not central to the organization, the strong technology–structure link broke down; other factors were more important.

7. See Joan Woodward, *Management and Technology, Problems of Progress Industry*, No. 3 (London: Her Majesty's Stationery Office, 1958).

8. See Daniel Robey, *Designing Organizations* (Homewood, Il.: Irwin, 1982).

9. See Derek S. Pugh and David J. Hickson, *Organization Structure in Its Context: The Aston Programme I* (Lexington, Mass.: D. C. Heath, 1976).

Figure 11.3
The relationship
between
organization size
and design

The following generalizations about organization size and design may be drawn from the Aston research and other studies:

1. The larger an organization becomes, the more job specialization is likely to be practiced.[10]
2. The larger an organization becomes, the more standard operating procedures, rules, and regulations are likely to be imposed.[11]
3. The larger an organization becomes, the more likely it is to become more decentralized.[12]

These key relationships are illustrated in Figure 11.3.

External contingency factors: Environment and information processing

In one sense, the only thing outside an organization is its environment, but there are a number of useful ways of approaching it. Chapter 3 devoted considerable attention to the external environment. Here we will first describe the general influence of the environment on organization design and then focus on information processing as a means of dealing with both environmental and technological concerns. These relationships are illustrated in Figure 11.4.

Environment

The first widely recognized contemporary formulation of the relationship between environment and organization design was provided by Tom Burns and G. M. Stalker.[13] Working in England just as Joan Woodward and the Aston

---

10. Peter Blau and Richard Schoenherr, *The Structure of Organizations* (New York: Basic Books, 1971).

11. Pugh and Hickson, *Organization Structure in Its Context.*

12. Blau and Schoenherr, *The Structure of Organizations.*

13. See Tom Burns and G. M. Stalker, *The Management of Innovation* (London:Tavistock, 1961).

Figure 11.4
External factors
influencing
organization design

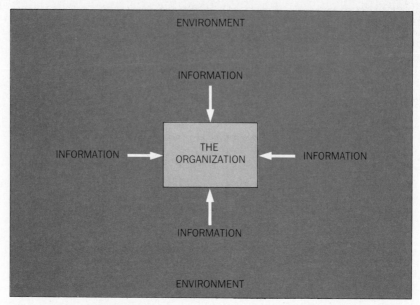

group did, these researchers identified two extreme forms of organization environments. A stable environment is one that remains relatively constant over time, whereas an unstable environment is subject to uncertainty and rapid change. Further, they found that organizations operating in stable environments tend to have a different kind of design from organizations operating in unstable environments. The two kinds of organization designs that emerged, summarized in Table 11.3, were called mechanistic and organic.

A *mechanistic design,* which is quite similar to the bureaucratic model, was generally associated with stable environments. Free from uncertainty, organizations could structure their activities in rather predictable ways via rules, specialized jobs, and centralized authority. Although no environment is completely stable, there are companies exhibiting the mechanistic design. They include Del Monte Corporation (the food industry is relatively placid) and Singer Company (few domestic competitors and a stable market).

An *organic design,* on the other hand, is useful in unstable and unpredictable environments. The constant change and uncertainty of such environments usually dictate a much higher level of fluidity and flexibility. Texas Instruments (rapid technological change) and Levi Strauss (constant change in consumer tastes) are both somewhat organic in design.

These concepts of Burns and Stalker were extended in the United States by Paul R. Lawrence and Jay W. Lorsch, two Harvard professors.[14] They agreed that environmental factors influence organization design but felt that

14. See Paul R. Lawrence and Jay W. Lorsch, *Organization and Environment* (Homewood, Ill.: Irwin, 1967).

Table 11.3 Mechanistic and organic organizations

Mechanistic	Organic
1. Tasks are highly fractionated and specialized; little regard paid to clarifying relationship between tasks and organizational objectives.	1. Tasks are more interdependent; emphasis on relevance of tasks and organizational objectives.
2. Tasks tend to remain rigidly defined unless altered formally by top management.	2. Tasks are continually adjusted and redefined through interaction of organizational members.
3. Specific role definition (rights, obligations, and technical methods prescribed for each member).	3. Generalized role definition (members accept general responsibility for task accomplishment beyond individual role definition).
4. Hierarchic structure of control, authority, and communication. Sanctions derive from employment contract between employee and organization.	4. Network structure of control, authority, and communication. Sanctions derive more from community of interest than from contractual relationship.
5. Information relevant to situation and operations of the organization formally assumed to rest with chief executive.	5. Leader not assumed to be omniscient; knowledge centers identified where located throughout organization.
6. Communication is primarily vertical between superior and subordinate.	6. Communication is both vertical and horizontal, depending upon where needed information resides.
7. Communications primarily take form of instructions and decisions issued by superiors, of information and requests for decisions supplied by inferiors.	7. Communications primarily take form of information and advice.
8. Insistence on loyalty to organization and obedience to superiors.	8. Commitment to organization's tasks and goals more highly valued than loyalty or obedience.
9. Importance and prestige attached to identification with organization and its members.	9. Importance and prestige attached to affiliations and expertise in external environment.

Source: Adapted from Tom Burns and G. M. Stalker, *The Management of Innovation* (London: Tavistock, 1961), pp. 119–122. Used with permission.

this influence probably varies between different units of the same organization. In fact, they hypothesized that each organizational unit or subsystem has its own unique environment and responds by developing unique attributes.

Lawrence and Lorsch suggested that organizations could be characterized along two primary dimensions. One of these dimensions, *differentiation,* is the extent to which the organization is broken down into subunits. A firm with many departments is highly differentiated; one with few departments has a low level of differentiation. The second dimension, *integration,* is the degree to which the various units must work together in a coordinated fashion. If each unit competes in a different market and has its own production facilities, little integration may be needed; if the units share resources and have a common sales staff, more integration will be required. Lawrence and Lorsch reasoned that the degree of differentiation and integration needed by an organization would depend on the stability of the environments its subunits faced.

To test this idea, they studied an effective firm and a less effective firm in each of three different levels of environmental stability. The organizations found to have the most stable environment were two container companies, whereas two plastics firms had the least stable environments. Two food companies were found to have a moderate level of environmental stability. As predicted, the plastics firms had the highest level of differentiation and the container companies the lowest level. *Further*, the effective organization within each environment had a higher level of integration than its less effective counterpart. Thus the more an organization can coordinate the activities of its subunits, the more effective it tends to be. A variety of techniques are available for achieving this desired level of integration (they were discussed in Chapter 9 as methods for coordinating organizational activities).

To conclude our discussion of Lawrence and Lorsch, we should recall their prediction involving subunits and their environments. Just as patterns of organization design vary according to environmental stability, they hypothesized, so does the design of each organizational subunit vary according to its unique environmental stability. If the production subsystem faces a relatively stable environment and the marketing subsystem a relatively unstable one, the two subsystems are likely to develop different structures. Probably the production department will be somewhat mechanistic (in response to a stable environment), while the marketing department will be more organic (because of the relatively unstable setting in which it operates).

Information processing

Because a major upshot of environmental instability, uncertainty, and turbulence is the profusion of important information in the environment, it makes sense to explore how the need to process that information affects organization design.

The noted organization theorist Jay Galbraith suggests that the primary consequence of environmental uncertainty or instability is that the organization must process more information.[15] He goes on to suggest four methods an organization can enlist in handling its information-processing needs. Two of those methods focus on reducing the need for information processing; the other two involve increasing the organization's capacity to process information.

Slack resources. One way to decrease information-processing needs is to create slack resources. Consider a wholesaler who ships merchandise to retailers across the United States. The information that affects an optimal inventory level includes forecasted demand for the products, existing retail

---

15. See Jay Galbraith, *Designing Complex Organizations* (Reading, Mass.: Addison-Wesley, 1973); and Jay Galbraith, *Organization Design* (Reading, Mass.: Addison-Wesley, 1977).

inventories, shipping time, frequency of reorders, and so forth. The wholesaler has a great deal of information to handle. If the wholesaler does not carry an inventory large enough to fill all the orders, he or she runs the risk of permanently losing retail customers to another wholesaler. The wholesaler could deal with this problem by increasing the size of the inventory until it is large enough to cover all orders at all times. Naturally, this amount of inventory is more than enough for ordinary demands, so the excess inventory becomes a slack resource, allowing the organization to be less concerned with forecasts, shipping times, and so on. Note that slack resources need not be physical in nature. Slack time can be built into a schedule, and contingency funds into a budget.

Of course, additional costs are associated with this technique. In terms of organization design, the effect of having slack resources depends on the nature of those resources. The wholesaler just described will need additional employees and managers to handle the new storage facilities. Such changes may also affect the planning staff and the budget department.

Self-contained tasks. Another way to reduce information-processing requirements is to create self-contained tasks. When an organization moves from functional departments to product departments, each new department becomes self-contained, with its own engineers, marketing staff, and so on. This works to reduce the need for information processing by reducing the number of demands on each specialist. Whenever a particular product group needs the expertise of a given staff specialist, it doesn't have to compete with another unit for that specialist's time. Of course, the organization loses the advantages of functional departmentalization.

Vertical information systems. Whereas the preceding two techniques decrease the need to process information, vertical information systems allow the organization to process more information. That is, the organization can create systems to transmit information more efficiently up and down the chain of command. These systems might range from electronic computers or data processing systems to clerical assistants who organize and summarize information. A system could be established whereby all information about changes in the price of raw materials would be entered automatically into a computer. Whenever a product manager needed to calculate current production costs for her or his products, she or he could obtain the information easily without going through the finance or purchasing department.

Lateral relationships. Another way to increase an organization's capacity to process information is to create lateral relationships. Basically, this involves using any of the coordination techniques described in Chapter 9 (liaison roles, task forces, teams, integrating departments). Then, when two interdependent units need to coordinate their activities by sharing information, the existence of a task force facilitates the process. Matrix design, which also involves lateral relationships, is much more comprehensive in scope and will be described in the next section.

As we have indicated, a major consequence of environmental uncertainty is the additional information-processing requirements that it imposes on the organization. Two methods for dealing with these requirements, slack resources and self-contained tasks, reduce the information-processing needs of the organization. Two other methods, vertical information systems and lateral relationships, increase the organization's capacity to process information.

The matrix design

A matrix goes far beyond simply establishing lateral relationships. Indeed, it involves creating a totally new kind of organization design. Essentially, a *matrix design* sets up a multiple-command system that includes not only a structure for multiple command but also related support mechanisms and an associated culture.[16] The hallmark of a matrix design is the presence of two or more intersecting lines of authority.

Creating a matrix

First of all, it is important to recognize that a matrix design is not always appropriate. The matrix form of organization design is most often used in one of three situations:[17]

1. **When there is outside pressure for a dual focus.** For example, external competition may dictate the sort of strong marketing thrust that is best spearheaded by a functional department, but the diversity of a company's products may argue for product departments.
2. **When large amounts of information need to be processed.** For example, creating lateral relations via a matrix is one effective way to increase the organization's capacity to process information.
3. **When there is pressure for shared resources.** For example, a company with ten product departments may have resources for only three marketing specialists. A matrix design would allow all the departments to share the company's scarce marketing resource.

If one or more of these conditions exist, a matrix design may be appropriate.

The easiest way to visualize a matrix design is to imagine product-based departments superimposed on an existing functional structure. Such an arrangement is shown in Figure 11.5. At the top of the organizational chart are functional units headed by vice presidents of engineering, production, finance, and marketing. Each of these managers has several subordinates.

Along the side of the organizational chart are a number of positions termed project manager. Each project manager heads a project group com-

16. See Stanley M. Davis and Paul R. Lawrence, *Matrix* (Reading, Mass.: Addison-Wesley, 1977).
17. See Harvey F. Koloday, "Managing in a Matrix," *Business Horizons*, March–April 1981, pp. 17–24.

Figure 11.5
A matrix
organization

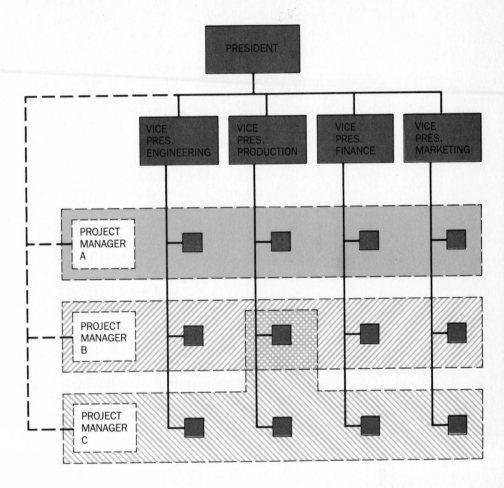

prised of representatives or workers from the functional departments. Now the multiple-command structure we referred to earlier becomes apparent: any given individual may report both to a functional superior and to one or more project managers.

The project groups, or teams, are assigned to designated projects or programs. For example, a company might want to develop a new product. Representatives are chosen from each functional area to work as a team on the new product. They also retain membership in the original functional group. At any given time, a person may be a member of several teams as well as a functional group.

Stanley M. Davis and Paul R. Lawrence have suggested that the organization design may go through four phases as it evolves into a matrix.[18] Phase I is the *traditional pyramid* of functional organization design. Phase II, the *temporary overlay*, involves creating teams for especially significant and impor-

18. See Davis and Lawrence, *Matrix*.

tant projects only. The *permanent overlay,* phase III, uses teams for many on-going activities. And phase IV, the *mature matrix,* is reached when the vertical and lateral lines of authority are brought into equilibrium and functional and project managers are accorded equal authority.

Many major organizations have adopted the matrix form of organization design. Notable among them are American Cyanamid, Monsanto, NCR Corporation (formerly National Cash Register), Chase Manhattan Bank, Prudential Insurance, General Motors, and several state and federal government agencies. On the other hand, some organizations such as Citibank and the Dutch firm, Philips, have adopted—and then dropped—the matrix design.

One firm that has enjoyed a great deal of success with the matrix is General Motors. In the mid-1970s, GM used project centers and teams to scale down all its products for the sake of fuel efficiency. Engineers were lent by all the divisions to staff the teams. GM credits the matrix design with reducing redundant activities and speeding up several technological breakthroughs.[19] (In terms of the Davis and Lawrence framework, GM was using a temporary overlay, or phase II, matrix.)

Advantages and disadvantages of the matrix

As is true of most contemporary management techniques, there are both advantages and disadvantages associated with the matrix form of organization design. In the appropriate circumstances, however, the advantages seem to outweigh the disadvantages. Six primary advantages of matrix designs have been observed.[20]

Flexibility. One of the truly significant advantages of a matrix is its flexibility. Teams can be created, redefined, and dissolved almost continuously, allowing the organization to cope readily with uncertainty, instability, and change.

Improved motivation and commitment. Because the teams in a matrix organization consist of specialists from different functional areas, each member assumes a major role in decision making. As a consequence, team members are likely to be highly motivated and committed to the organization.

Personal development. Employees in a matrix organization have considerable opportunity to learn new skills. This stems from their involvement in a variety of projects and from their interaction in the teams with experts from other areas.

Human resources. The matrix design also provides an efficient way for the organization to take full advantage of its human resources. Because the

19. See Charles G. Burck, "How GM Turned Itself Around," *Fortune,* January 16, 1978, pp. 87–100.

20. See Kenneth Knight, "Matrix Organization: A Review," *Journal of Management Studies,* May 1976, pp. 111–130.

same expert can be assigned to several different teams, unnecessary duplication of personnel is reduced.

Cooperation. Team members retain membership in their functional unit, so they can serve as a bridge between the functional unit and the team, enhancing cooperation.

Management planning. The matrix design gives top management a useful vehicle for decentralization. Once the day-to-day operations have been delegated, top management can devote more attention to such areas as long-range planning.

Even in the best of circumstances, however, three major problems associated with the matrix form of design can still be significant and should not be ignored.[21]

Power/authority confusion. Employees may be uncertain about whom they are supposed to report to, especially if they are simultaneously assigned to a functional manager and several project managers. What happens when their several bosses make conflicting demands on them? To complicate matters, some managers may see the matrix as a form of anarchy in which they are free to do anything they want. These problems can be minimized by explicitly defining all authority relationships.

Group problems. Another set of problems is associated with the dynamics of group behavior. As noted in earlier chapters, groups take longer to make decisions, may be dominated by a strong individual, and may compromise unnecessarily. They may also get bogged down in discussion and not focus on their primary objectives.

Costs. A matrix design is expensive because more managers and staff may be needed. More time may also be required for coordinating task-related activities.

Although significant disadvantages are associated with the matrix form of organization design, these disadvantages can probably be offset by the advantages. In the future, as environmental uncertainty continues to increase, more and more organizations will no doubt consider the matrix design because of its flexibility.

Strategy and organization design

Another contemporary approach to organization design is through the relationship between organization strategy and organization structure. This approach

21. See Davis and Lawrence, *Matrix.*

began with the work of Alfred D. Chandler in the early 1960s.[22] Chandler studied several large American organizations such as Du Pont, Sears, and General Motors over a period of several years. The primary conclusion he reached was that an organization's strategy tends to influence its structure. The impact is usually indirect: strategy indirectly determines such things as the organization's tasks, technology, and environments, and each of these influences the design of the organization.

More recently, Henry Mintzberg has provided additional insight into the relationship between strategy and organization design.[23] Like Chandler, he suggests that an organization's strategy determines its technology, environment, and tasks, which in turn affect design. But he goes on to suggest that its growth rate and distribution of power, which are other factors determined by strategy, also affect the design the organization adopts.

Mintzberg argues that organizations can be differentiated along three basic dimensions: (1) the prime coordinating mechanism, or the major approach used to coordinate organizational activities, (2) the key part of the organization, the part of the organization that plays the major role in determining its success or failure, and (3) the type of decentralization employed.[24] Each of these dimensions has several different aspects. The prime coordinating mechanisms are:

1. **Direct supervision.** One individual is responsible for the work of others.
2. **Standardization of work process.** The content of the work is specified or programmed.
3. **Standardization of skills.** The kind of training necessary to do the work is specified.
4. **Standardization of output.** The results of the work are specified.
5. **Mutual adjustment.** Work is coordinated through informal communication.

The key parts of an organization are:

1. **The strategic apex.** Top management and its support staff.
2. **The operative core.** The workers who actually carry out the organization's tasks.
3. **The middle line.** Middle and lower-level management.
4. **The technostructure.** Analysts such as industrial engineers, accountants, planners, and personnel managers.
5. **The support staff.** Units that provide support to the organization outside the operating work flow (for example, legal counsel, executive dining room staff, consultants, and so on).

22. See Alfred D. Chandler, Jr., *Strategy and Structure* (Cambridge, Mass.: MIT Press, 1962). See also Alfred D. Chandler, Jr., *The Visible Hand: The Managerial Revolution in America* (Cambridge, Mass.: Belknap Press, 1977).

23. See Henry Mintzberg, *The Structuring of Organizations* (Englewood Cliffs, N.J.: Prentice-Hall, 1979).

24. This material follows Henry Mintzberg, *The Structuring of Organizations: A Synthesis of the Research,* © 1979. Adapted by permission of Prentice-Hall, Inc., Englewood Cliffs, N.J.

The types of decentralization are:

1. **Vertical decentralization.** The distribution of power down the chain of command, or shared authority between superiors and their subordinates.
2. **Horizontal decentralization.** The extent to which nonmanagers (including staff) make decisions, or shared authority between line and staff.
3. **Selective decentralization.** The extent to which power over different kinds of decisions rests with different units within the organization.

Using the different forms of coordinating mechanisms, key parts, and levels of decentralization, Mintzberg proposes that the strategy an organization adopts and how far it has moved to fulfill that strategy result in five different forms of organization design. These forms are summarized in Table 11.4.

The simple structure

The *simple structure* uses direct supervision as its primary coordinating mechanism, has as its most important part its strategic apex, and employs vertical and horizontal centralization. Relatively small corporations controlled by aggressive entrepreneurs, new government departments, and medium-sized retail stores are all likely to exhibit a simple structure design. These organizations tend to be relatively young. The CEO (often the owner) retains much of the decision-making power. The organization is relatively flat and does not emphasize specialization.

The machine bureaucracy

The *machine bureaucracy* uses standardization of work processes as its prime coordinating mechanism, the technostructure is its most important part, and

Table 11.4 Mintzberg's five designs

Structural configuration	Prime coordinating mechanism	Key part of organization	Type of decentralization
Simple structure	Direct supervision	Strategic apex	Vertical and horizontal centralization
Machine bureaucracy	Standardization of work processes	Technostructure	Limited horizontal decentralization
Professional bureaucracy	Standardization of skills	Operating core	Vertical and horizontal decentralization
Divisionalized form	Standardization of outputs	Middle line	Limited vertical decentralization
Adhocracy	Mutual adjustment	Support staff	Selective decentralization

Source: Henry Mintzberg, *The Structuring of Organizations: A Synthesis of the Research,* © 1979, p. 301. Reprinted by permission of Prentice-Hall, Inc., Englewood Cliffs, N.J.

limited horizontal decentralization is established. Actually, the machine bureaucracy is quite similar to Burns and Stalker's mechanistic design.[25] Examples
include steel companies and automobile manufacturers. This kind of organization is generally mature in age, and its environment is usually stable and predictable. A high level of task specialization and a rigid pattern of authority are
also typical. Spans of management are likely to be narrow, and the organization will usually be tall.

The professional bureaucracy

The third form of organization design suggested by Mintzberg is the professional bureaucracy. Examples of this form of organization include universities,
general hospitals, and public accounting firms. The *professional bureaucracy*
uses standardization of skills as its prime coordinating mechanism, has the
operating core as its most important part, and practices both vertical and horizontal decentralization. It has relatively few middle managers. Further, like
some staff managers, its members tend to identify more with their professions
than with the organization. Coordination problems are common.

The divisionalized form

The *divisionalized form,* Mintzberg's fourth design, exhibits standardization of
output as its prime coordinating mechanism, the middle line as its most important part, and limited vertical decentralization. Most large organizations
(especially those with product-based departments) are likely to adopt this form.
Power is generally decentralized down to middle management—but no further. Hence each division itself is relatively centralized and tends to structure
itself as a machine bureaucracy. As might be expected, the primary reason for
an organization to adopt this kind of design is market diversity.

The adhocracy

The *adhocracy* uses mutual adjustment as a means of coordination, has as its
most important part the support staff, and maintains selective patterns of decentralization. Two examples of adhocracies are NASA and Boeing. In some
ways, the adhocracy is similar to the organic form of organization design; it
avoids specialization, formality, and unity of command. Even the term itself,
derived from "ad hoc," suggests a lack of formality.

Clearly, our understanding of the relationship between an organization's
strategy and its design is still in its infancy. However, the work begun by
Chandler and continued by Mintzberg has laid a reasonable foundation for
arguing that such a relationship exists. We can hope that understanding of this

---

25. See Burns and Stalker, *The Management of Innovation.*

important linkage will increase in the future. At present, managers should at least recognize that the strategy of the organization is very likely to have an impact on its overall design.

A final design factor: Climate

Climate was briefly introduced in Chapter 3 as the organization's internal environment. Now *organizational climate* can be defined as the perceptions that the members of an organization share about its general character and culture. Climate is important because it can significantly affect employee attitudes and behaviors.[26]

To illustrate the effects climate can have on an organization, consider what happened to Levi Strauss & Company. Several years ago, Levi's executives felt that the company had outgrown its 68-year-old building. Even though everyone enjoyed the casual atmosphere, more space was needed. In 1974 Levi's moved into a modern office building in downtown San Francisco, where its new headquarters spread over 12 floors in a skyscraper. It quickly became apparent, however, that the change was affecting the corporate culture, and people didn't like it. Executives felt isolated and other managers missed the informal chance meetings in the hall. Within a few years, Levi's moved out of the skyscraper and back into a building that fosters informality. For example, there is an adjacent park area where employees frequently converge for lunchtime conversation. Clearly, Levi's has a climate that is important to its employees.[27]

Climate determines the "feel" of the organization. Some organizations are viewed by their employees as cold, uncaring, harsh, impersonal, and formal. Others, like Levi's, are perceived as warm, caring, personal, and informal. In all probability, the design of the organization and its climate are highly interrelated.

A specialized, centralized organization with an overall design that is bureaucratic, System 1, mechanistic, or a machine bureaucracy is likely to be viewed by its employees as impersonal and formal. Alternatively, if tasks are not specialized and authority is decentralized, and if the overall design is closer to System 4, organic, or an adhocracy, the organization's climate will probably have a more positive effect on its members.

The same climate is not necessarily found throughout an entire organization. The marketing and sales department, for example, may function in a complex and uncertain environment. As a result of the company's adopting an organic design in order to interact more effectively with this environment, the

26. See Richard Steers, *Organizational Effectiveness* (Santa Monica, Calif.: Goodyear, 1977), p. 100.
27. See Gurney Breckenfeld, "The Odyssey of Levi Strauss," *Fortune*, March 22, 1982, pp. 110–124.

department's climate may lead to favorable employee attitudes. The production department, operating in a relatively stable and simple environment, may have a more mechanistic structure. As a consequence, employees may perceive their workplace as more rigid, harsh, and impersonal.

Summary of key points

The primary contribution of classical organization theory, Weber's bureaucratic model, focused on a formal system of authority. According to this view, the ideal organization design is characterized by division of labor, a consistent set of rules, a vertical chain of command, impersonal behavior, and advancement based on expertise. Though seldom appropriate in contemporary society, the bureaucratic model was an important milestone in the development of management theory.

An important behavioral perspective on organization design, Likert's System 4, grew from the human relations movement. The System 4 organization is the antithesis of the ideal bureaucracy (which Likert calls System 1). An important element in the System 4 view is the linking pin role relating upper and lower managers.

The contingency approach to organization design, based on the premise that appropriate organization design is a function of situational factors, first viewed technology and size as primary determinants of organization design. Technology does appear to affect organization design, especially in smaller organizations.

Two external determinants of organization design are environment and information-processing requirements. In general, the more unstable and complex the environment, the more organic (System 4) the design. The more stable and simple the environment, the more mechanistic (bureaucratic) the design. Successful organizations in highly uncertain environments tend to be highly differentiated and integrated. Those in stable environments are also integrated but less differentiated. Structural components, or departments, tend to adopt designs appropriate for their own environments. Information-processing requirements can be managed by reducing the need for information processing (by creating slack resources or self-contained tasks) or by increasing information-processing capabilities (by investing in vertical information systems or creating lateral relationships).

A contemporary organization design, the matrix, is created by superimposing a product-based structure on a functional structure. The hallmark of a matrix is a multiple-command system whereby employees simultaneously report to a functional manager and to one or more product managers. A number of advantages and disadvantages are associated with matrix designs.

Another contemporary view of organization design focuses on the link between strategy and design. On the basis of differences in three dimensions (the prime coordinating mechanism, the key part of the organization, and the type of decentralization employed), Henry Mintzberg has identified five forms of organization design that result from differences in strategy. These forms of design are the simple structure, the machine bureaucracy, the professional bureaucracy, the divisionalized form, and the adhocracy.

Climate, which is part of the internal environment of the organization, is one important result of an organization's design. Climate consists of the shared perceptions of employees about the organization's general character and culture. The design adopted by the organization is a primary determinant of organizational climate.

QUESTIONS FOR DISCUSSION

1. The bureaucratic model was one of the first attempts to define a type of organization design. Do you think it is still a relevant model? Why or why not?

2. The chapter discussed various strengths and weaknesses of the bureaucratic model. What improvements can you suggest to overcome the flaws and make the model more useful?

3. Likert developed eight dimensions for defining organizations. Do you think Likert's dimensions are valid determinants? Why or why not?

4. According to Likert, *all* organizations should use a System 4 design. Do you agree? Can you think of any exceptions that could benefit more from using a System 1, 2, or 3 design?

5. The chapter cited two internal factors that were likely to influence organization design. Can you think of any types of industries in which one of these factors would not be influential?

6. What other factors are valid internal determinants in contemporary businesses? Would they have been applicable to industry ten years ago?

7. With the growth of increasingly automated information systems, organizations are able to process larger and larger amounts of data. Do you think this trend will help or hinder companies' attempts to operate effectively in the context of their internal and external environments? Why?

8. The matrix design is generally considered the most advanced form of organization design, even though it violates a basic tenet of organization design. How does this design deal with dual authority?

9. "A misused matrix design is better than none at all." Do you agree with this statement? Why or why not?

10. Can you think of a way to combine various types of organization designs in a single firm? What factors would influence your decision?

11. The adhocracy approach to organization design embodies certain aspects of the matrix design. What makes it different? Would this approach work in situations wherein the matrix approach is currently being employed?

12. An organization's climate is in some ways like an individual's personality. Do you feel it is important for the employee's and the organization's personalities to match? Why or why not?

C A S E 11.1

At the beginning of this chapter, you read an incident about an electronics company with some shortcomings in its operating systems. In particular, the organization's matrix design has caused a number of problems because responsibility and authority haven't been appropriately matched. The company being described was Texas Instruments. The case that follows explains what TI plans to do and then raises some other issues for your consideration.

Until recent years, Texas Instruments Incorporated was a model of efficient and effective management. The Dallas-based company has become the largest manufacturer of semiconductors in the world, with annual sales in excess of $3 billion. TI's scheme for growth has focused on technological innovation, production efficiency, and high volume. By investing heavily in research and development, more often than not TI has been first in its industry with new breakthroughs. Next the company would determine how to produce the new products at the lowest possible cost. Finally, the combination of technological innovation and low costs allowed TI to develop enormous sales volumes, thus capturing increasingly large market shares.

In the early 1970s, the company adopted a three-pronged strategy. One prong would be continued growth in semiconductor chips for use internally and for sale to other manufacturers. Second came consumer electronics, including such items as calculators and electronic toys. Finally, the company would increase its emphasis on minicomputer systems. This strategy was quite successful for TI during the 1970s.

In 1981, however, profits dipped substantially and management realized that a number of operating systems were badly in need of an overhaul. Chief among these was the organization design used by the company.

For years Texas Instruments has employed a matrix design. Traditional functional departments such as engineering and design, production, and finance produce the full line of semiconductor chips for TI. Overlaying these departments have been a number of product-based units called PCCs (product–customer centers). Each PCC is created to carry out all the design, production, and marketing activities for new products.

In an effort to spark creativity, TI gave each PCC manager responsibility for profits and losses, but not the authority to tell functional managers what to do. It was thought that having to rely on persuasion to get things done would make managers more inclined to concentrate on products that were likely to be profitable.

Unfortunately, this arrangement led to a number of serious problems. For example, the PCC responsible for TI's line of digital watches needed a certain new kind of chip to compete effectively in the marketplace. The functional departments, however, did not

The evolving matrix structure at Texas Instruments

see a large enough market of their own for the chip and therefore refused to produce it! As a result, TI's line of digital watches bombed and was eventually dropped.

In overhauling the company's design, TI plans to cut the number of PCCs and use only relatively large ones in the future. The reasoning behind this change is that larger PCCs will be better able to negotiate with the functional departments on an equal footing. The company also intends to concentrate more on integrating and coordinating the activities and resources of the functional departments and the PCCs. Because the company plans to maintain its three-pronged strategy of semiconductor chips, consumer products, and minicomputers, however, the matrix form of organization must be preserved. TI management hopes that the improved balance between functional departments and PCCs, coupled with better coordination, will help bring things back in line.

There are two major barriers that stand in the way of a smooth transition and continued growth and prosperity. The first of these is TI's climate. One former employee has described the company as using management by fear. Managers are forced to set artificially high goals and are then driven to reach them. If a manager presents a report suggesting that a goal will not be met, he or she is often criticized or even ridiculed for not working harder or for making a mistake. Thus people are motivated to say what top management wants them to say and then to try to hide disappointing results.

The second barrier confronting TI involves centralization. Even though the company has grown to enormous size, management is reluctant to delegate authority. Middle and lower-level managers have little power, and almost all major decisions and policies emanate from the top of the organization and flow down.

CASE QUESTIONS

1. Why did TI's matrix fail? Do you think the modified version will be more successful?
2. What other kinds of designs might be appropriate for TI? Do you see any interrelationships between the company's strategy and its design?
3. In what ways could the company's climate affect the organizational design that emerges? Will these effects be positive or negative?
4. How has the company's stance on centralization affected its design? What further effects might be felt in the future?
5. If you were hired by TI as a consultant, what would you recommend that the company do to straighten itself out?

CASE REFERENCES

"Texas Instruments in Midlife." *Forbes*, March 15, 1982, pp. 64–65.

"Texas Instruments Unscrambling Matrix Management to Cope with Gridlock in Major Profit Centers." *Electronic News*, April 26, 1982, p. 1.

Uttal, Bro. "Texas Instruments Regroups." *Fortune*, August 9, 1982, pp. 40–45.

C A S E   11.2

Susan Gerloff called the meeting to order. She had just assumed the position of president of Chapter One, a regional chain of book stores. Chapter One had grown rapidly from one store, opened in a small Midwestern town ten years ago, to 47 stores located across a six-state region. The company was in no danger of failure, but it had been only marginally profitable for the last three years. Four months ago, Chapter One had been purchased by Walker Brothers, a national retailing group consisting of department stores, fashion accessory boutiques, and a growing chain of sporting goods outlets. Susan was appointed president of Chapter One about two months ago and has spent several weeks studying Chapter One's history. She has just convened a meeting of the company's three vice presidents and six regional managers to discuss the situation.

Choosing an organization design

Though the first seven Chapter One stores had been located in downtown shopping districts, all the remaining stores have been opened in shopping malls. A few stores have to compete with a Walden or B. Dalton outlet, but most are the only bookstore in the mall. Annual sales for each store average $260,000, about $20,000 of which is profit.

Susan has become convinced that one thing the organization needs is a new design. At present, the six regional managers have almost total control over the stores in their regions. They are in charge of negotiating leases, hiring store managers, advertising, and monitoring inventory. After summarizing her view of things, Susan throws the issue open for discussion.

"I couldn't agree with you more, Susan," responded one vice president. "We do need to change our structure. We need to decentralize. As things stand now, we hire professional managers to run our stores but don't give them any control. I say we should make them real managers, not just sales clerks with fancy titles."

"You're right when you say our structure needs changing," suggested another vice president, "but you're all wrong about how we should set it up. I don't think we even need professional managers. It seems to me that what we need to do is centralize even more. We're big enough now so that we need to expand our computer system anyway. Why, with a little more capacity, we could handle all inventory control here at headquarters. We could also go to a uniform advertising program, rather than letting each region handle its own. If we did all this, we could get by without a high-priced manager at each store."

"Aren't you both forgetting us?" put in one regional manager. "It sounds like you're trying to put us out of a job. If we go with plan A, the store managers do all the work. If we go with plan B, you do all the work here. I just can't buy the idea that you can manage 47 stores without some kind of regional or divisional structure. If you ask me, either path will lead to disaster."

"No one's trying to put you out of work," responded Susan. "We're just trying to do things better. And when I said we needed a new structure, I didn't necessarily mean fewer people or more people. I simply meant that I think we could do things more effectively if some parts of the company were rearranged."

CASE
QUESTIONS

1. What are the important contingency factors that could affect Chapter One's organization design?
2. What do you think of the existing design and the designs suggested by the two vice presidents?
3. Can you suggest a good design for Chapter One to consider?

12

ORGANIZATIONAL CHANGE AND DEVELOPMENT

CHAPTER OBJECTIVES

1. Discuss the nature of organizational change and compare planned change to reactive change.

2. Describe the process of change.

3. Explain performance appraisal and control systems as structural changes.

4. Summarize the technological approaches to change in terms of equipment, work, automation, and information-processing systems.

5. Discuss organizational approaches to personnel changes.

6. Relate different organizational activities to organization development.

7. Explain organizational decline and termination and the various procedural approaches to them.

CHAPTER OUTLINE

The nature of organizational change
Forces for change
Planned versus reactive change

The process of change
Steps in the change process
Resistance to change
Overcoming resistance to change

Structural approaches to change
Compensation systems
Performance appraisal systems
Control systems

Technological approaches to change
Change in equipment
Change in work processes
Change in work sequence
Change in information-processing systems
Automation

People approaches to change
Replacement of personnel
Selection
Training and development

Organization development
Diagnostic activities
Team building
Survey feedback
Education
Intergroup activities
Third-party peacemaking
Technostructural activities
Process consultation
Life and career planning
Coaching and counseling
Planning and goal setting
Grid OD
The effectiveness of OD

Organizational decline and termination
Causes of decline and termination
Approaches to decline
Approaches to termination

Summary of key points

OPENING INCIDENT

You have just been appointed CEO for the world's largest conglomerate. Your predecessor left an indelible mark on the company by sacrificing profits for growth, overseeing every phase of the company's operations, and delivering scathing indictments against anyone who failed to accomplish his goals. The company has become so complex that it is difficult to manage, and profit margins are still mediocre. What would you do?

Westinghouse Electric's construction group in Pittsburgh recently had all its typewriters removed. Secretaries now use computer terminals to transmit memos, edit correspondence, design charts, and store and recall information. Their bosses dictate to a communications center. In 1981 General Electric's new CEO rearranged that company's organization chart by introducing two new divisions to concentrate on high-growth and high-technology businesses. One of these new divisions brought together all of GE's electronics activities for the first time. During late 1979 and early 1981, the top 162 managers at Rockwell International attended a six-day seminar designed to improve their overall managerial effectiveness. Rockwell reports that one immediate payoff to the company has been improved strategic planning.[1]

What do the preceding examples have in common? All three of these companies have gone through a relatively significant organizational change. Westinghouse introduced a *technological* change made possible by breakthroughs in computer and word processing technologies. General Electric made a major *structural* change in its organization design by rearranging product groups into different divisions. And Rockwell attempted to change its *people* by improving the managerial ability of top executives.

Although the topic of change has been debated for decades, the publication of Alvin Toffler's popular book *Future Shock* probably did more than anything else to bring the concept of change as a way of life to center stage.[2] Toffler tells us that, if we divide the last 50,000 years into 800 lifetimes of 62 years each, we find that the human race spent 650 of those lifetimes in caves. Electric motors have been around for only 2 lifetimes. Most of the technology we take for granted has existed for a single lifetime or less.

Paralleling this increased awareness of social and technological change has been a great deal of concern about organizational change. Changes in any

---

1. See Jeremy Main, "Work Won't Be the Same Again," *Fortune*, June 28, 1982, pp. 58–65; Ann M. Morrison, "'Trying to Bring GE to Life," *Fortune*, January 25, 1982, pp. 50–57; and Jeremy Main, "The Executive Yearn to Learn," *Fortune*, May 3, 1982, pp. 234–248.

2. See Alvin Toffler, *Future Shock* (New York: Random House, 1970).

of the elements of the general environment (that is, the economic, international, political, technological, and sociocultural environments) or in the task environment (customers, competitors, associates, unions, regulators, and suppliers) may necessitate a change in the organization itself. Change may also be brought about internally by a new manager or by the new philosophy of an existing manager.

Chapter 12 probes organizational change and development in detail. We begin by describing the nature of organizational change. Then, after discussing the process of planned change, we focus on the three major areas of organizational change: structure, technology, and people. Organization development is then summarized. Finally, we explore a form of change that many managers hope to avoid: decline and possible termination.

The nature of organizational change

We will define *organizational change* as any alteration in one or more elements of the organization. Changes can be made in anything: work schedules, bases for departmentalization, span of management, overall organization design, or people themselves. It is also important to keep in mind that any change in an organization may have effects extending beyond the actual arena in which the change takes place. For example, a job enrichment program could require the purchase of new machinery that might in turn affect other processes in the work system.

Forces for change

As we have noted, forces for change may gather outside or inside the organization. The following sections examine these forces in more detail.

External forces. External forces for change derive from the organization's general and task environments. In the international dimension of the general environment, a foreign competitor (such as Sony) might introduce a new product, increase prices, decrease prices, change standards, or enter new markets, thus forcing domestic organizations (such as RCA and GE) to react. In the political dimension, new laws, court decisions, and regulations all affect organizations. The technological dimension may yield new production techniques that the organization needs to explore. The economic dimension is evident in inflation, the cost of living, and money supplies. The sociocultural dimension, reflecting societal values, determines what kinds of products or services will find a ready market.

Due to its proximity to the organization, the task environment is usually an even more powerful force for change. Competitors obviously influence an organization via their price structures and product lines. Customers determine what products can be sold at what prices. The organization must constantly be concerned with consumer tastes and preferences. Suppliers affect organizations by raising or lowering prices, changing product lines, or even severing trade relations with a company. Regulators can have dramatic effects on an organization. If OSHA rules that a particular production process is dangerous to workers, it can force the company to close down until higher safety standards are met. Unions are a force for change when they negotiate for higher wages, win a certification election, or go out on strike. Finally, associates can spur change as they add to or drain from the resource base of the parent company. For example, after Philip Morris purchased Miller Brewing Company, it pumped millions of dollars into advertising Miller beer.[3] Although the money was well spent and no negative side effects were felt, the fact remains that the money *could* have been used for other purposes.

Internal forces. A variety of forces inside the organization may also cause change. If top management revises the organization's goals, organizational change is likely to result. A decision by an electronics company to enter the home computer market or a decision to increase a 10-year product sales goal by 3 percent would occasion many organizational changes.

Other internal forces may actually be indirect reflections of external forces. As sociocultural values shift, for example, workers' attitudes toward their jobs may also shift and they may demand a change in working hours or working conditions. In such a case, even though the force is rooted in the external environment, the organization must respond directly to the internal pressure it generates.

Planned versus reactive change

Some organizational change is planned well in advance, whereas other change comes about as a reaction to unexpected events. *Planned change* is change that is designed and implemented in an orderly and timely fashion in anticipation of future events. *Reactive change,* on the other hand, is a piecemeal response to problems as they develop. Such a response may have to be hurried, so the potential for poorly conceived and poorly executed change increases. Planned change is almost always preferable to reactive change.

Ford's European operation has long recognized the importance of planned change. One of the few automobile companies currently making a profit in Europe, Ford has taken a proactive stance on change. Ford of Europe headed off the Japanese threat with relative ease and is presently moving full-speed-ahead with automation, the "just-in-time" inventory system, an upgrading of its work force, increased worker inspection of finished work, and a trimmed-down bureaucratic organization. Each of these activities represents a carefully planned change that is paying dividends: profits from Ford of Europe have helped overset major losses in Ford's domestic operations.[4]

Warner Communications provides a dramatic example of the negative consequences of reactive change. During the first half of 1982, sales of Atari home video systems and cartridges were reaping huge profits for Warner. When Pac-Man was introduced, Warner sat back and waited for even higher

---

3. See "Philip Morris Unit to Build a Brewery for $247 Million," *Wall Street Journal,* April 12, 1978.

4. See David Tinnin, "Ford Is on a Roll in Europe," *Fortune,* October 18, 1982, pp. 182–191.

profits. The timing of the pause was most unfortunate. Other sophisticated systems were introduced and licenses for other popular games were grabbed up by competitors. Warner was then put in the precarious position of having to react to these rapid changes with little time for careful thought. It is unlikely that the company will be able to recapture its dominant position in the video market.[5]

These points become even more telling in view of the frequency of organizational change. Most companies or divisions of large companies must implement some form of moderate change at least every year—and one or more major changes every four to five years.[6] Managers who sit back and respond only when they have to are likely to spend a lot of time hastily changing and rechanging things. A more effective approach is to anticipate forces urging change and plan ahead to deal with them.

Figure 12.1 summarizes the nature of organizational change. Represented in the figure are the forces for change and the distinction between planned and

Figure 12.1
The nature of organizational change

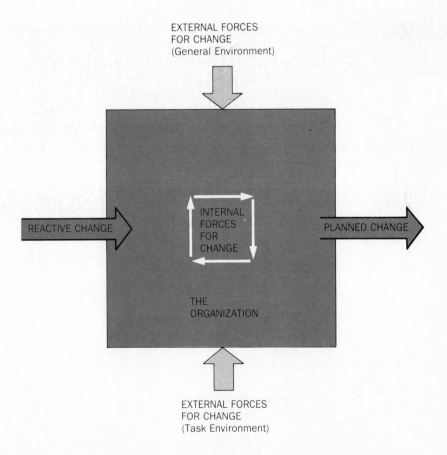

5. See Anne Pillsbury, "Warner's Fall from Grace," *Fortune*, January 10, 1983, pp. 82–83.

6. John P. Kotter and Leonard A. Schlesinger, "Choosing Strategies for Change," *Harvard Business Review*, March–April 1979, p. 106.

reactive change. Here reactive change emerges as the result of an environmental "push," whereas planned change anticipates this push. The next section outlines the general process of organizational change, with an emphasis on planned change.

The process of change

Understanding the process of change requires careful consideration of the steps in the change process, employee resistance to change, and how this resistance can be overcome.

Steps in the change process

A number of models or frameworks for change have been developed over the years. We will consider one theoretical approach and one more specific approach.

The Lewin model. Kurt Lewin, a noted organization theorist, suggested that every change requires three steps.[7] The first step is *unfreezing*, in which individuals who will be affected by the impending change are led to recognize why it is necessary. Next the *change* itself is implemented. Finally, *refreezing* involves reinforcing and supporting the change so that it becomes a part of the system. As valuable as Lewin's model is in pointing out the importance of planning the change, communicating its value, and reinforcing it after it has been made, this view lacks the specific details needed by an operating manager who must effect change.

An expanded change process. As the term suggests, this approach to change takes a more comprehensive view and is concerned with phases of change (see Table 12.1). The first step in the change process is recognizing the need for change. Recognition of the need for reactive change results from employee complaints, declines in performance indicators such as productivity or turnover, court injunctions, sales slumps, labor strikes, and similar events. In the case of planned change, recognition may simply be the manager's awareness that change in a certain area is inevitable. The manager may attempt to predict future conditions and then try to adapt the organization to those conditions. The immediate stimulus might be the results of a forecast indicating new market potential, the accumulation of cash surplus for possible investment, or an opportunity to achieve and capitalize on a key technological breakthrough.

The manager must then set goals for the proposed change. To maintain or increase market standing, to enter new markets, to restore employee mo-

7. Kurt Lewin, "Frontiers in Group Dynamics: Concept, Method, and Reality in Social Science," *Human Relations*, June 1947, pp. 5–41.

Table 12.1 Steps in the change process

1. Recognition of the need for change
2. Establishing goals for change
3. Diagnosis
4. Selection of change technique
5. Planning for implementation
6. Implementation
7. Evaluation and follow-up

rale, to reduce turnover, to settle a strike, to identify good investment opportunities—all are examples of possible goals for change.

Third, the manager must determine what has brought on the need for change. Turnover, for example, might be caused by any or all of the following factors: low pay, inferior working conditions, poor supervisors, better alternatives in the job market, and employee dissatisfaction about a variety of things. Turnover may be the immediate stimulus for change, but the manager must understand the causes of the turnover in order to make the right changes.

The next step is to select a change technique. If turnover is being caused by low pay, a new reward system may be needed. If the cause is poor supervision, human relations training for supervisors may be called for. (A variety of change techniques will be summarized later in this chapter.) Now implementation must be planned. Issues to consider here include the costs of the change, how the change will affect other areas of the organization, and the degree of employee participation appropriate for the situation. Assuming that the change is implemented as planned, the manager must then evaluate and follow up on the results of the change. If the change was intended to reduce turnover, the manager must check turnover after the change has been in effect for a while. If turnover is still too high, other changes may be necessary.

Resistance to change

In planning for change, managers must also take into account that for many reasons people may resist the change, regardless of how "necessary" it seems. When Westinghouse recently replaced all its typewriters with computer terminals and personal computers, most people responded favorably, but one manager resisted the change to the point where he began leaving work every day at noon! It was some time before he began staying in the office all day again.[8] There are a variety of reasons why people resist change.[9]

Uncertainty. Perhaps the biggest cause of employee resistance to change is uncertainty. In the face of impending change, employees are likely to become anxious and nervous. They may worry about their ability to meet the

8. See Jeremy Main, "Work Won't Be the Same Again," *Fortune,* June 28, 1982, pp. 58–65.
9. See Kotter and Schlesinger, "Choosing Strategies for Change."

new job demands, they may think their job security is threatened, or they may simply dislike ambiguity. Any of these elements can lead to substantial resistance to change.

Self-interests. Many impending changes threaten the self-interests of a particular manager or unit. For example, a major southwestern university had established an Office of University Research. The OUR coordinated efforts to attract external grants for the university and, in return, received most of the overhead generated by those grants. (Overhead refers to extra funds the university receives to cover office space, utilities, clerical assistance, and computing facilities.) When an engineering experiment station (funded by external grants) on campus aggressively began to establish research partnerships with other campus units, the OUR became concerned that overhead money would begin to be channeled through the experiment station. The university president ruled that any grant involving any personnel outside of the experiment station had to go through OUR, thus protecting the interests of that unit.

Different perceptions. A manager may recommend a plan for change on the basis of her or his own assessment of a situation. Others in the organization may resist this change because they don't agree with the manager's assessment or simply perceive the situation differently.

Feelings of loss. Some people resist change simply because of feelings of loss. Many changes involve altering work arrangements (as we shall see in later sections of this chapter), which may disrupt existing social networks. Social relationships are important to most people, and they will resist any change that might adversely affect those relationships. Other intangibles that are threatened by change include power, status, security, familiarity with existing procedures, and self-confidence.

Overcoming resistance to change

A manager shouldn't give up in the face of resistance to change when there are several useful strategies that can be applied to overcome it.[10]

Participation. Participation is generally considered the most effective technique for overcoming resistance to change. Employees who participate in planning and implementing a change are better able to understand the reasons for the change. Uncertainty is reduced and self-interests and social relationships may be less threatened. Having had an opportunity to express their own ideas and to assume the perspectives of others, such employees are more likely to accept the change gracefully.

The value of participation was shown in a classic study by Coch and French, who monitored the introduction of a change in production methods

10. See Kotter and Schlesinger, "Choosing Strategies for Change." See also Paul R. Lawrence, "How to Deal with Resistance to Change," *Harvard Business Review,* January–February 1969, pp. 4–12, and pp. 166–176.

Figure 12.2
Force-field analysis

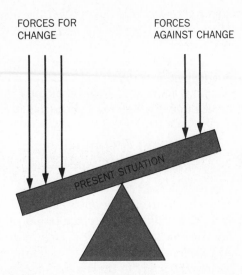

among four groups in a Virginia pajama factory.[11] In one group, the change was implemented with no worker participation. The results included no change in performance and a high level of turnover and hostility: 17 percent of this group quit within 40 days. Another group was allowed to send representatives to help plan the change. Efficiency increased somewhat and there was no turnover. Two other groups were allowed to participate fully in planning and implementing the change. The results for these two groups were significant improvements in productivity and a high level of morale and cooperation. More recently, 3 M Company (Minnesota Mining and Manufacturing) has found that employee participation in various areas of operation has resulted in savings of $10 million.[12]

Education and communication. Educating employees about the need for and the expected results of an impending change should reduce their resistance. And if open channels of communication are established and maintained, uncertainty can be minimized.

Facilitation. Introducing the change gradually can work wonders. Making only necessary changes, announcing those changes in advance, and allowing time for people to adjust to new ways of doing things can also help reduce resistance to change.

Force-field analysis. Although it sounds like something out of a science fiction movie, force-field analysis can help overcome resistance to change. Figure 12.2 shows the change situation according to force-field analysis. In any change situation, there are forces acting for and forces acting against the

11. Lester Coch and John R. P. French, Jr., "Overcoming Resistance to Change," *Human Relations*, August 1948, pp. 512–532.
12. See Charles K. Day, Jr., "Management's Mindless Mistakes," *Industry Week*, May 29, 1978, p. 42.

change. To facilitate the change, the manager must tip the balance so that the forces for the change outweigh those against the change (such as employee resistance). It is especially important to try to remove or at least minimize forces acting against the change. If a primary force pushing against the change is fear that a new work procedure will break up an existing work group, the manager might explore ways of keeping the group together. If such a solution can be found, one force acting against the change has been eliminated.

Structural approaches to change

Harold J. Leavitt has noted that there are three general approaches to organizational change: approaches aimed at structure, technology, or people.[13] A *structural change* is a change in any of the basic components of organization structure or in the organization's overall design. Most structural components and design dimensions have already been discussed, so we will note them again only briefly.[14] These areas of change are summarized in Table 12.2.

One kind of structural change addresses *decentralization*. Because of changes in environmental conditions or management philosophy an organization could move to become more or less decentralized. *Spans of management* could be changed by making them wider or narrower. The organization might also choose to change its present methods of *coordination*. *Job design* changes are becoming increasingly popular.[15] Any attempt to adopt job rotation, job enrichment, or work redesign represents a structural change in the organization. Changing *work schedules* by introducing a modified workweek, flexi-time, or job sharing would also fall in this category.

Major alterations in an organization's overall design are also part of a structural approach to change. Perhaps the most common case is the adoption of a *matrix design*; clearly, the process of superimposing a product design onto a functional design and the creation of work teams represent major structural changes. Other examples include a change from a *mechanistic* to an *organic* design and a move between any of *Mintzberg's five forms* of design, which were summarized in Chapter 11.[16]

Other areas of structural change include compensation systems, performance appraisal systems, and control systems.[17] Because we have not discussed them before, they will be treated in more depth here.

13. See Harold J. Leavitt, "Applied Organization Change in Industry: Structural, Technical, and Human Approaches," in W. W. Cooper, H. J. Leavitt, and M. W. Shelly, II., eds., *New Perspectives in Organization Research* (New York: Wiley, 1964), pp. 55–71.

14. For more information on structural change, see Michael Beer, *Organization Change and Development—A Systems View* (Santa Monica, Calif.: Goodyear, 1980), especially Chapter 10.

15. See Ricky W. Griffin, *Task Design—An Integrative Approach* (Glenview, Il.: Scott, Foresman, 1982).

16. See Henry Mintzberg, *The Structuring of Organizations* (Englewood Cliffs, N.J.: Prentice-Hall, 1979).

17. This discussion follows Beer, *Organization Change and Development—A Systems View* (Santa Monica, Calif.: Goodyear, 1980). Used with permission.

Table 12.2 Areas of structural change

Changes in structural components
Change in degree of decentralization
Change in span of management
Change in methods of coordination
Change in job design
Change in work schedule

Changes in overall organization design
Change between mechanistic and organic design
Change between simple structure, machine bureaucracy, professional bureaucracy,
    divisionalized form, and adhocracy
Change to (or from) a matrix design

Other structural changes
Change in reward systems
Change in performance appraisal systems
Change in control systems

Compensation systems

A compensation system is an arrangement for providing pay, benefits, promotions, and other rewards to organization members. The general purpose of
a compensation system should be to stimulate high performance while maintaining an equitable balance of rewards among employees. A variety of innovative compensation systems have become increasingly widespread in
organizations.

The Scanlon plan (named after a 1930s labor leader) is designed to reward
both management and labor for labor savings achieved via improved productivity. *Cafeteria benefits plans* allow employees to choose the benefit package best
suited to their own needs. *All-salary plans* do away with hourly wages and pay
all employees a fixed salary. *Open pay systems* give everyone in the organization
access to everyone else's salary information. *Reward system participation* involves
having the employees participate in the design and administration of the organization's reward system. For example, Romac Industries in Seattle allows
all employees to vote on pay raises for all other employees. Bonuses, profit-
sharing plans, and merit pay systems are also useful rewards.[18]

Performance appraisal systems

An organization's performance appraisal system consists of its procedures for
determining levels of performance within the organization. Such systems often

18. We will discuss reward systems in Chapter 13. See also Edward E. Lawler, III, *Pay and
Organization Development* (Reading, Mass. Addison-Wesley, 1981).

include supervisory evaluations using various kinds of rating scales; other systems use objective measures, such as number of units produced or dollar sales volume.

Management by objectives (MBO), discussed in Chapter 4, is also used in performance appraisal systems. Supervisor and subordinate collaborate in setting goals for the subordinate and, at the end of a specified time period, actual goal achievement is used as the basis for performance appraisal.

Any shift from one form of performance appraisal to another represents a structural organizational change, because performance appraisal is related to positions in the organization and to interrelationships among those positions.[19]

Control systems

A control system is a mechanism to ensure that the organization is making satisfactory progress toward its goals and is not deviating too much from acceptable standards. Chapters 17 through 19 are devoted to control. Various accounting systems, programs for monitoring investments and expenditures, and budgeting innovations such as zero-base budgeting are all contemporary control systems. Another way to exert control is to focus on minimizing work-related accidents. When Du Pont (which has achieved perhaps the lowest accident rate of all major manufacturers) implemented its control system, it was necessary to establish new safety-monitoring departments and to develop new procedures for encouraging safety and reporting accidents.[20] Again, introducing a new control system or changing from one type of control system to another often spells a structural change in the organization.[21]

Technological approaches to change

As we have defined it, the technology of an organization is the conversion process it uses to transform inputs into outputs. Because of the rapid rate of technological innovation in our society, *technological change* is becoming increasingly important to many organizations. Several areas wherein technological change is likely to be experienced are listed in Table 12.3.

Change in equipment

Perhaps the simplest form of technological change results from a change in equipment. To keep pace with competitors, many firms find it necessary to periodically replace existing machinery and equipment with newer models. In

19. For more information on performance appraisal systems, see Stephen J. Carroll and Craig E. Schneier, *Performance Appraisal and Review Systems* (Glenview, Ill.: Scott, Foresman, 1982).

20. See Jeremy Main, "When Accidents Don't Happen," *Fortune,* September 6, 1982, pp. 62–68.

21. For more information on organizational control systems, see Edward E. Lawler, III and John G. Rhode, *Information and Control in Organizations* (Santa Monica, Calif.: Goodyear, 1976).

Table 12.3 Areas of technological change

Equipment
Work processes
Work sequence
Information-processing systems
Automation

offset printing, for example, three separate machines were once needed for normal printing. One machine made the masters, one ran the copies, and a third did the collating. An initial refinement was to combine printing and collating, and now all three functions can be performed by one machine. This new machine reduces the time needed to complete printing jobs (due primarily to the fact that the operator has to adjust only one machine rather than three), so a printing shop that buys it gains a competitive advantage.

Change in work processes

A change in work processes often requires new and different equipment, but it also entails a change in work flow and job design.

In manufacturing industries, the major reason for changing a work process is to accommodate a change in the materials used to produce a finished product. Consider a firm that manufactures battery-operated flashlights. For many years flashlights were made of metal, but now most are made of plastic. A firm might decide to move from metal to plastic flashlights because of consumer preferences, raw materials costs, or other reasons. Table 12.4 summarizes the significant differences between these two kinds of work processing systems. Clearly the organization is undergoing a major technological change. As new raw materials and appropriate new production processes are developed, this form of technological change will probably become more pervasive.

Of course, work process changes may occur in service organizations as well as in manufacturing firms. As traditional male barber shops and female beauty parlors are replaced by hair salons catering to both sexes, for example, these hybrid organizations have to develop new methods for handling appointments and setting prices. It isn't just a matter of ordering a wider range of magazines for the waiting area!

Change in work sequence

A change in work sequence may or may not accompany a change in equipment or a change in work processes. Essentially, making a change in work sequence means altering the order (or sequence) of the work stations involved in a particular manufacturing process.

For example, a manufacturer might have two parallel assembly lines producing two similar sets of machine parts. The lines might converge at one

Table 12.4 Contrasting work processing systems for metal versus plastic flashlight casings

	Metal drawing	Plastic molding
Equipment	Punch press	Injection molding machine
Raw materials	Metal sheets	Plastic resin pellets
Tools	Die set—male or female	Split halves of a mold
Building	Heavy foundations to handle weight and impact	Ordinary floor
Manufacturing engineering	Mechanical, metal expertise	Plastics, hydraulics expertise
Maintenance	Mechanical, hydraulic	Mechanical, hydraulic
Operator	Heavier work, higher skill	Lighter work, lower skill
Supervisory skills	Managing male work force, scheduling	Mixed work force, machine troubleshooting, quality checking
Inventory	Sheet metal and work-in-process	Plastic powder and finished goods
Operations	May require several plus finishing	One
Scheduling	Potentially complex	Simple
Safety	Dangerous	Safer
Quality/precision	Depends on die and machine setup	Depends on molds, timing set into machine
Costs	Depends especially on die conditions and setup	Depends especially on short cycle and changeovers
Flexibility-product change	Die change necessary	Mold change necessary
Volume change	Add dies, machines, shifts or move to higher speed equipment	Add dies, machines, shifts; cycle limited
Potential for automation	Combine operations with transfer dies, install part location sensors, etc.; can be largely automatic	Largely automatic

Source: *Work in America: The Decade Ahead,* edited by Clark Kerr and Jerome M. Rosow, © 1979 by Litton Educational Publishing, Inc. Reprinted by permission of Van Nostrand Reinhold Company, Inc.

central quality control unit where tolerances are verified by inspectors. For any number of reasons, a manager might decide to change to periodic rather than final inspection. Under this arrangement, one or more inspection stations are established further up the line. Hence, rather than following an A–B–C–D–E–F–G–H–inspection sequence wherein a mistake won't be caught until the end, the plant could go to an A–B–C–D–inspection–E–F–G–H–inspection sequence to catch mistakes earlier.

Work sequence changes can be made in other than production settings. The processing of insurance claims could also follow this pattern. The sequence of logging claims, verifying claims, requesting checks, getting countersignatures, and mailing checks could be altered in several ways, such as combining steps 1 and 2 or routing the claims through one person while another handles checks.

Change in information-processing systems

A kind of technological change that has been especially important in recent years is change in information-processing systems. It is hard to find a major popular magazine that has not run an article on the computer invasion. Simultaneous advances in large mainframe computers, personal computers, and network tie-in systems have created vast potential for change in most workplaces. Recall how Westinghouse has replaced its typewriters with computer terminals.

The basic idea behind the adoption of computers in offices is the creation of an information-processing station for each employee. The person at each work station may manipulate ideas and drafts that are still in preliminary form, create, store, and retrieve documents, and distribute final copies. Although there are still some major obstacles to widespread adoption of such systems, it has been estimated that spending for electronic office equipment in the United States alone will increase from $3 billion in 1981 to more than $12 billion in 1986.[22]

Automation

Automation is the process of designing work such that it can be completely or almost completely performed by machines. As with information-processing systems, computers play a major role in the upsurge of automation.

The advent of automation has perhaps been most visible in the automobile industry. Nissan Motor's new U.S. light truck plant in Tennessee, for example, will deploy more than 200 computer-controlled robots. Robots have also been tested for such jobs as (1) inspecting the insides of pipes where humans can't enter, (2) cleaning and guarding facilities at night, (3) providing supplementary patient care in hospitals, (one robot has been developed to bring articles such as newspapers and fruit from a nearby cabinet to a patient in response to verbal commands), and (4) mining coal in hazardous areas. It has been estimated that the number of robots in use by business will grow to 8,000 in 1985 and may climb as high as 100,000 by 1990. Of course, the increased adoption of robots may have adverse effects, economically and psychologically, on the labor force. But it does seem that we are on the verge of an automation explosion, and successful managers must be prepared to deal with this significant form of technological change.[23]

People approaches to change

The third area of organizational change has to do with the human resources of the organization. A *people-focused change* might be concerned with changing

22. See Bro Uttal, "What's Detaining the Office of the Future," *Fortune*, May 3, 1982, pp. 176–196.

23. See Jeremy Main, "Work Won't Be the Same Again," *Fortune*, June 28, 1982, pp. 58–65; "Robots: Japan Takes the Lead," *Newsweek*, September 21, 1981, p. 92; and "The Speedup in Automation, *Business Week*, August 3, 1981, pp. 58–62.

Table 12.5 People approaches to change

Organization development
Replacement
Selection
Training and development

employee performance, skills, attitudes, perceptions, behaviors, or expectations. Changes in attitudes, perceptions, behaviors, and expectations are generally considered part of organization development, which is covered in the next section. At this point our discussion will focus somewhat more narrowly on efforts to upgrade employee skills and performance (see Table 12.5).

Replacement of personnel

There are many reasons why replacement of one or more employees may be desirable. A change in work processes may require that employees be able to operate new kinds of equipment. If no amount of training can increase the capabilities of an existing equipment operator, it may become necessary to replace the operator. Or a behavioral problem may arise that cannot be solved by any other means. Suppose that two or more employees simply aren't able to work together; one is a heavy smoker and the other a militant nonsmoker. It may be necessary to replace one (or both) of these individuals.

Of course, replacement is not limited to the operating ranks. Managers may allow their skills to become obsolete, or they may not be able to cope with a rapidly changing marketplace. The organization may find it necessary to replace such managers with others who are better able to satisfy the demands of the job.

Several different methods for dealing with "replaced" employees are available. Responding to their sense of social responsibility, managers sometimes try to find work for replaced employees with other companies, especially when the employee has logged many years of productive service. Early retirement is another option, and it is becoming increasingly popular. And, of course, the employee could simply be transferred to another job or department. In other cases, it may be necessary to simply terminate the employee and sever her or his relationship with the organization.

Selection

Another "people-focused" change strategy is selection, which takes a longer-term perspective than replacement. The idea is that the organization fine-tunes or upgrades its selection criteria so as to gradually achieve a significant change in its human resources. An organization may decide that henceforth it will hire only college graduates for its management training program. Assuming that a college degree has some validity as a predictor of managerial success, the overall quality of the organization's management group should gradually improve as the new managers enter the organization.

After a while, the organization might raise its standards again and hire only management trainees who hold an M.B.A. degree. Again assuming the validity of the degree, management quality should continue to rise. Finally, the criteria might be set at an M.B.A. plus five years of work experience. Of course, the organization must make sure that it really needs such a highly qualified (and hence more expensive) set of managers and that the new standards do not discriminate against women, blacks, or members of other minorities.

Training and development

A final technique for changing employee skills and performance is training and development. Whereas replacement and selection are concerned with replacing existing employees with new ones, training and development involve refining the skills and boosting the performance levels of existing employees. When a new piece of equipment is installed, it may well be possible to train an existing employee to operate it. Similarly, managerial skills can be developed and maintained to help managers keep pace with changes in their work environment.

Organization development

Jim Morrison has recently assumed the position of branch manager of a large urban bank. He is almost immediately struck by the degree of conflict and lack of cooperation among the branch employees. One of the first things Jim does in his new position is to engage the services of a consultant in an attempt to defuse conflict and increase cooperation among employees. The consultant uses a variety of behavioral science techniques in an effort to achieve these objectives. These kinds of activities are a part of organization development.

Organization development, or OD, is concerned with changing attitudes, perceptions, behaviors, and/or expectations. More precisely, OD can be defined as "an effort (1) *planned,* (2) *organization wide,* and (3) *managed* from the *top,* to (4) increase *organization effectiveness* and *health* through (5) *planned interventions* in the organization's 'process,' using *behavioral science* knowledge."[24] Hence, any attempt to use OD in an organization needs to be systematic, must be supported by top management, and should be broad in its application.

The theory and practice of OD are based on several very important assumptions: Employees have a desire to grow and develop. Employees have a strong need to be accepted by other group members. And the total organization and the way it is designed will influence individuals and groups within

24. Richard Beckhard, *Organization Development: Strategies and Models* (Reading, Mass.: Addison-Wesley, 1969), p. 9. Italics in original.

Table 12.6 Categories of organization development interventions

1. Diagnostic activities
2. Team building
3. Survey feedback
4. Education
5. Intergroup activities
6. Third-party peacemaking
7. Technostructural activities
8. Process consultation
9. Life and career planning
10. Coaching and counseling
11. Planning and goal setting
12. Grid OD

the organization. Some form of collaboration between managers and their employees is necessary to (1) take advantage of the skills and abilities of the employees and (2) eliminate aspects of the organization that retard employee growth, development, and group acceptance.

Wendell L. French and Cecil H. Bell, Jr., have identified twelve kinds of interventions or activities that are performed in the service of organization development.[25] These are listed in Table 12.6 and summarized in the following paragraphs.

Diagnostic activities

Just as a medical doctor examines a patient to diagnose her or his current condition, diagnostic OD activities analyze the current condition of an organization. Diagnostic techniques include such methods as questionnaires, opinion or attitude surveys, interviews, archival data, and meetings. The diagnosis may generate profiles of the organization's operating procedures, growth patterns, and problem areas.

Team building

Team-building activities are intended to enhance the effectiveness and satisfaction of individuals who work in groups, or teams. Project teams in a matrix organization are good candidates for these activities. An OD consultant might interview team members to determine how they feel about the group; then an

25. See Wendell L. French and Cecil H. Bell, Jr., *Organization Development: Behavioral Science Interventions for Organization Improvement,* 2nd ed. (Englewood Cliffs, N.J.: Prentice-Hall, 1978).

off-site meeting could be held to discuss the issues that surfaced and to iron out any problem areas or member concerns.

Survey feedback

In survey feedback each employee responds to a questionnaire intended to measure perceptions and attitudes (for example, satisfaction and supervisory style). The results of this survey are fed back to everyone involved, including the supervisor. Workshops are then conducted to evaluate results and suggest constructive changes.

Education

Educational activities focus on classroom training. Although such activities can obviously be used for technical or skill-related purposes, an OD educational activity typically focuses on "sensitivity skills." That is, it teaches people to be more considerate and understanding of the people they work with.

Intergroup activities

The focus of intergroup activities is on improving the interface between two or more groups. We noted in Chapter 9 that, as group interdependence increases, so do coordination difficulties. Intergroup OD activities are designed to promote cooperation or resolve conflict that may have arisen as a result of interdependence.

Third-party peacemaking

Another approach to resolving conflict is through third-party peacemaking, which can proceed on the individual, group, or organizational level. The third party, usually an OD consultant, uses a variety of mediation or negotiation techniques to resolve conflict.

Technostructural activities

Technostructural activities are concerned with the design of the organization and its technology. A structural change such as an increase in decentralization, a job design change such as a work redesign program, and technological change such as a change in work flow would all qualify as technostructural OD activities if they were approached from a collaborative perspective under the basic OD assumptions that were summarized earlier.

Process consultation

In process consultation an OD consultant observes groups in the organization to develop an understanding of their communication patterns, decision making and leadership processes, and methods of cooperation and conflict resolution. The consultant then provides feedback to the involved parties about the processes he or she has observed.

Life and career planning

Life and career planning helps employees formulate their personal goals and evaluate strategies for integrating these goals with the goals of the organization. Such activities could include specification of training needs, plotting a career map, and similar life-and career-related ideas.

Coaching and counseling

Coaching and counseling provide nonevaluative feedback to individuals. The purpose is to help people develop a better sense of how others see them and to help people learn behaviors that will assist others in achieving their work-related goals.

Planning and goal setting

More pragmatically oriented than many other interventions are activities designed to help managers improve their planning and goal setting. Emphasis still falls on the individual, however, in that the intent is to help individuals and groups integrate themselves better into the overall planning process.

Grid OD

The grid approach to OD is based on the Managerial Grid® developed by Robert Blake and Jane Mouton.[26] The Managerial Grid is a comprehensive program for evaluating leadership styles and then training managers to move toward an ideal style of behavior.

The Managerial Grid is shown in Figure 12.3. Here the horizontal axis represents concern for production, and the vertical axis represents concern for people. Note the five extremes of managerial behavior: the 1,1 manager who exhibits minimal concern for both production and people; the 9,1 manager who is highly concerned about production but exhibits little concern for people; the 1,9 manager who has the exact opposite concerns from the 9,1 manager; the 5,5 manager who maintains adequate concern for both people and production; and the 9,9 manager who exhibits maximum concern for both people and production.

According to Blake and Mouton, the ideal style of managerial behavior is 9,9. They have developed a six-phase program (seminar training, team build-

---

26. See Robert R. Blake and Jane S. Mouton, *The Managerial Grid* (Gulf Publishing Company, 1964). See also Robert R. Blake and Jane S. Mouton, *The New Managerial Grid* (Houston: Gulf Publishing, 1978).

Figure 12.3
The managerial grid

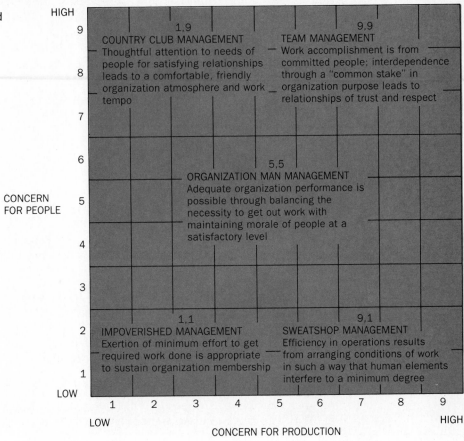

Source: From *The New Managerial Grid*, by Robert R. Blake and Jane Srygley Mouton (Houston: Gulf Publishing Company, Copyright © 1978), page 11. Reproduced by permission.

ing, intergroup interventions, organizational goal setting, goal attainment, and stabilization) to assist managers in achieving this style of behavior. Some people are critical of the Managerial Grid, but others have found it useful.

The effectiveness of OD

Given the diversity of activities encompassed by the term *organization development*, it is not surprising that managers report mixed results from various OD interventions. Organizations that actively practice OD include American Airlines, Texas Instruments, Federated Department Stores, Procter & Gamble, ITT, Polaroid, and B. F. Goodrich. B. F. Goodrich, for example, has trained sixty individuals in OD processes and techniques. These trained experts have subsequently become internal OD consultants to assist other managers in applying the techniques.[27] On the other hand, many other managers report that they have tried OD but then discarded it.[28]

OD will probably remain an important part of management theory and practice. Of course, there are no "sure things" when dealing with social systems such as organizations, and the effectiveness of many OD techniques is difficult to evaluate. Because all organizations are open systems interacting with their environments, an improvement in an organization may be attributable to an OD intervention—but it may also be attributable to changes in economic conditions, luck, or other factors.[29]

Organizational decline and termination

A different kind of organizational change is one that most managers hope to avoid. For many reasons organizations may begin to decline in size, sales, or assets and may eventually cease to exist. This decline and the possible demise of the firm are also facets of organizational change, and they are not uncommon.

1. In recent years, many large organizations have been terminated, including Braniff, W. T. Grant, the Atomic Energy Commission, Studebaker, and the World Football League.
2. Approximately half of all new businesses fail during their first year.
3. The early 1980s were characterized by major cutbacks and layoffs in many organizations.
4. Many organizations, such as Conoco and Kennecott, are purchased by other organizations (Conoco by Du Pont and Kennecott by Standard Oil of Ohio) and cease to exist as autonomous entities.

Table 12.7 summarizes the major causes of decline and termination and lists several ways in which the organization may respond.

Causes of decline and termination

A variety of factors may cause decline and potential termination, but poor management is certainly the most likely to be at fault. Poor management can include anything from choosing a bad location for a new business to over-investing in capital equipment to being too generous with customer credit. One could argue that all other causes of decline stem from poor management, but a few are only indirectly related and warrant specific note.

27. See Roger J. Howe, Mark G. Mindell, and Donna L. Simmons, "Introducing Innovation Through OD," *Management Review*, February 1978, pp. 52–56.

28. See "Is Organization Development Catching On? A Personnel Symposium," *Personnel*, November–December 1977, pp. 10–22.

29. For a recent discussion on the effectiveness of various OD techniques in different organizations, see John M. Nicholas, "The Comparative Impact of Organization Development Interventions on Hard Criteria Measures," *Academy of Management Review*, October 1982, pp. 531–542.

Table 12.7 Organizational decline and termination

Potential causes of decline and termination	Reactions to organizational decline	Forms of organizational termination
1. Poor management	1. Personnel cutbacks	1. Liquidation
2. Obsolescence	2. Cutbacks in physical assets	2. Merger
3. Competition	3. Financial cutbacks	3. Transformation
4. Economic conditions	4. Divestiture	
5. Regulation		

Obsolescence occurs when an organization's products or services are replaced by more desirable products or services. For example, the electronic calculator rendered the slide rule obsolete. Competitors may also be a cause of decline or termination. Economic conditions in general may hurt specific businesses; the housing industry is especially vulnerable and government regulation may also result in decline or termination. A city ordinance may close existing pornographic theaters, or a federal regulation may ban the major product of a chemical or drug company. Other factors can also plunge an organization into decline, but astute management can anticipate and deal with most of them.

Approaches to decline

Given the need to cut back, organizations have several strategies available to them. Personnel cutbacks can be accomplished through layoffs, transfers, attrition, early retirement, or release of employees. Volkswagen of America recently cut its work force three times within one year. The third cut, early in 1983, affected 1,500 employees.[30] Making cutbacks in physical assets may mean selling a manufacturing plant, a warehouse, a computer, an office building, or surplus inventory (at cost or below). Nestle sold its new U.S. headquarters to IBM before the building was even completed.[31] Financial cutbacks include reduction in operating budgets and freezes on hiring. Divestiture involves selling complete divisions or units to other organizations.

Approaches to termination

There are three primary approaches to termination. The most obvious one is to liquidate, closing down all phases of the organization, turning all assets into cash, and using them to pay creditors. Anything that remains is distributed to stockholders. A merger involves selling all or part of the organization to an-

30. See "VW of America to Lay Off 1,500 in Third Cutback," *Wall Street Journal,* January 10, 1983, p. 8.

31. See Robert Ball, "A 'Shopkeeper' Shakes Up Nestle," *Fortune,* December 27, 1982, pp. 103–106.

other firm. The new parent may have the resources and ability to get things back on track. Finally, the organization might attempt the most difficult form of termination, a transformation. A transformation is a change not just in the organization structure but (very often) from one kind of business to another. For example, the Mary Carter Paint Company is now Resorts International. Paint accounts for only a small part of the business; hotels and resort operations account for the lion's share.[32]

Summary of key points

Change in general, and organizational change in particular, have become increasingly important considerations for managers. Organizational change can be defined as any alteration in one or more elements of the organization. External forces for change may stem from any of the dimensions of the general environment (international, political, technological, economic, and sociocultural) or from the task environment (competitors, customers, suppliers, regulators, unions, and associates). Planned change tends to be a more effective strategy than reactive change.

At a general level, the change process should proceed through unfreezing, changing, and refreezing phases. At a more operational level, change should include recognition of a need for change, determination of the goals of the proposed change, diagnosis of the situation, selection of a change technique, implementation of the change, and a follow-up and evaluation of the effectiveness of the change. For a variety of reasons, people may resist change, and techniques are available for minimizing this resistance.

Structural approaches to change are aimed at any of the basic components of organization structure and/or at the organization's overall design. Examples of changes in structural components include changes in decentralization, span of management, coordination, job design, and work schedules. Design changes could involve a matrix design, organic or mechanistic designs, and/or Mintzberg's designs. Other structural changes focus on compensation systems, performance appraisal systems, and control systems.

Technological approaches to change are concerned with the actual process of transforming inputs into outputs. Examples include changes in equipment, changes in work processes, changes in work sequence, changes in information-processing systems, and automation.

Approaches to change in personnel are usually concerned with enhancing employee skills and performance. Useful techniques include replacement, selection, and training and development.

Organization development (OD) is a comprehensive set of approaches

---

32. For other recent perspectives on organizational decline and termination, see John R. Kimberly, Robert H. Miles, and associates, *The Organizational Life Cycle: Issues in the Creation, Transformation, and Decline of Organizations* (San Francisco: Jossey-Bass, 1980). For a discussion of how decline is managed in Japan, see Edward Boyer, "How Japan Manages Declining Industries," *Fortune,* January 10, 1983, pp. 58–63.

intended to improve attitudes, perceptions, behaviors, and/or expectations. The twelve categories of OD interventions are diagnosis, team building, survey feedback, education, intergroup activities, third-party peacemaking, techno-structural activities, process consultation, life and career planning, coaching and counseling, planning and goal-setting, and grid OD.

A final form of organizational change is decline and possible termination. Decline and termination may result from poor management, obsolescence, competition, adverse economic conditions, or government regulation. Techniques for coping with decline include personnel cutbacks, cutbacks in physical assets, financial cutbacks, and divestiture. Liquidation, merger, and transformation are termination techniques.

QUESTIONS FOR DISCUSSION

1. What kinds of events lead to organizational change? Classify each kind as a planned or a reactive change.
2. Could some of the reactive changes you cited in question 1 have been planned for ahead of time?
3. Give an example of organizational change, and outline the steps involved in making it.
4. Do any steps in the change process meet with more resistance than others? Could this vary with different organizations?
5. The text outlined three types of systems involved in structural approaches to change. How do these systems overlap? Give examples.
6. Change in equipment and automation affects nearly every type of industry. Give examples for the computer industry, the auto industry, and the consumer products industry.
7. Increases in automation and technology have endangered many unskilled-labor jobs. Do you agree or disagree with this statement?
8. You are the personnel manager of a large company that has just bought 7 machines to do the work of 100 employees. The union is very unhappy about this and is threatening court action. What can you do to satisfy the union *and* the company?
9. The chapter mentioned that some companies attempt to find other jobs for released employees. Do you think the company's social responsibility to its workers extends this far? Why or why not? Can you think of ways in which it is in the company's own interest to assist in such placement efforts?
10. As college graduates, you will be competing for jobs with other people with more experience, but possibly less education, than yourselves. Make notes for an interview in which you must convince a prospective employer that your extra four years of education will make you a more valuable employee than a high school graduate with four years of work experience.
11. The text listed various types of activities for organization development.

Which would be most beneficial to a new firm? Which to a more established one?

12. Break up into groups and design an educational seminar to help employees develop managerial skills. Design a survey to gauge worker response to the seminar.

13. Organizational take-overs can lead to wholesale employee replacement. What kind of services should the acquiring firm provide to workers whom it chooses not to retain?

14. The text cites three approaches to termination. Compare these approaches. In what type of situation would each work best?

C A S E   12.1

At the beginning of this chapter, you read a scenario about the world's largest conglomerate. The previous CEO had always sacrificed profits for growth, was involved in every phase of the company's operations, and was unmerciful when dealing with underlings who didn't perform up to expectations. At present, the company is perhaps overly complex and profits are weak. The company being described was ITT. The case that follows explains what ITT is doing and then raises some other issues for your consideration.

Organizational Change at ITT

Harold Geneen served as chief executive officer of ITT (International Telephone and Telegraph Corporation) for nineteen years. During that time, he wheeled and dealed the company into the world's largest conglomerate: 1981 sales exceeded $17 billion. Geneen had a passion for growth, and the companies he purchased ranged from Continental Baking (makers of such products as Wonder Bread and Twinkies) to Sheraton and Eason Oil.

During his tenure at ITT, Geneen built two reputations for himself. The first was as a consummate manager. At the same time, however, he was regarded as a tyrant. At a monthly three-day General Management Meeting in New York for the company's top 125 managers, Geneen often ridiculed any manager who presented disappointing results or was critical of his decisions. He also assembled a huge corporate staff for the express purpose of monitoring line management. A staff manager was generally believed to have the best chance of advancing her or his own career if he or she found fault with line management operations.

Despite Geneen's presumed skills as a manager, however, ITT has not always fared well on the bottom line. Though the company is one of the world's largest, its profits have typically been only mediocre and its stock price has never made it a particularly attractive investment.

Geneen stepped down from the top spot at ITT in 1977 and played a role in choosing his successor, Lyman Hamilton. Hamilton ran into problems with Geneen almost immediately and was sacked about 18 months later. (Geneen remained a powerful member of the board of directors.) Rand Araskog was then appointed CEO and has since launched ITT on a dramatically different course from that charted by Geneen. The most significant change initiated by Araskog was a major program of divestiture. By early 1982, some 40 companies had been sold. The goal of these divestitures is to streamline the organization and enable ITT to concentrate more on high-profit companies.

In a second major change, the General Management Meeting has been abolished in favor of a one-day-a-month meeting involving far fewer managers. Cutbacks in both the authority and the size of the corporate staff have also been implemented, and Araskog has eliminated a number of executive perquisites. During the Geneen years, ITT owned a fishing lodge in Maine, a hunting lodge in Georgia, a houseboat in Florida, and a Boeing 727. All are gone.

The company has changed a number of its financial procedures as well. Geneen was most interested in growth; Araskog emphasizes profits. Geneen saw no problem with the company's debt, whereas Araskog wants to substantially reduce it. And Araskog, unlike Geneen, is willing to give promising companies a reasonable period of time in which to prove themselves.

Surprisingly, these changes have met with little resistance within the company. Most executives applaud the divestitures, the elimination of the General Management Meeting, and the dismantling of the huge staff network. Of course, they would probably have preferred to keep the fishing lodge!

CASE QUESTIONS	**1.** Identify all the kinds of changes suggested by this case. Are they planned or reactive changes? **2.** Why do you think Araskog has encountered so little resistance? **3.** Could future changes meet with more resistance than those already completed? **4.** Is ITT an example of a declining organization?
CASE REFERENCES	Colvin, Geoffrey. "The De-Geneening of ITT.' *Fortune,* January 11, 1982, pp. 34–39. "Geneen Unsought." *Wall Street Journal,* July 8, 1981, p. 23. "ITT Reaches Geneen Accord." *New York Times,* December 13, 1979, p. D5.

C A S E 12.2

Bill Ferris and David Yates were discussing business problems one recent evening over a beer. Bill and David are old friends; they went to the same high school and still live in the same neighborhood. About ten years ago Bill quit his job at a local manufacturing plant and opened an automobile repair shop. After a few rocky months, the shop attracted a loyal following. During the ensuing years, the shop expanded twice and currently employs eight full-time mechanics. About four years ago, Bill purchased a vacant lot nextdoor to the repair shop and built a tire and battery store. That operation has also flourished.

Anticipating the need for organizational change

David's business, on the other hand, has not done nearly so well. About six years ago, David used an inheritance to buy a clothing store specializing in casual and work clothes for men. The store has been only marginally profitable and has edged perilously close to bankruptcy on two different occasions.

"You know," David remarked, "Sometimes I don't know if it's all worth it. Being your own boss has its advantages, but it also has its disadvantages. If I get through this latest crisis, it'll be a miracle. I just seem to go from one crisis to another."

"I know things get rough sometimes," remarked Bill, "but I've found that we can usually weather the storm. My business has hit some bumps along the way, too, but I haven't really had too many crises. Do you think it's just that we're in different businesses?"

"You've got me," David replied. "I can still remember the first time I almost went under. I bought in under an existing lease, but after a year the lease expired and I had to renegotiate. The landlord hiked the rent $300 a month and I just wasn't prepared for it.

"And then there was the plant closing. Sure, I knew the plant was scheduled to be shut down—it was all over the papers for months ahead. I just didn't think it would make that much difference. Man, was I surprised! Sales of my work clothes dropped by 30 percent. I'm still not up to the level I was before.

"Next there was the urban cowboy thing. All the other shops in town started selling blue jeans and cowboy hats. I admit I was a little late getting into that market, and I lost some of my best customers as a result. And just when I got a lot of that stuff in stock, the fad died out and I had to take a big markdown.

"But this latest thing may be the last straw. When the pharmacy next door went out of business last year, I thought about leasing it and expanding my store. I was thinking about putting in a line of women's casual clothes and shoes, but I just never got around to it. Then, just last month, I found out that a big national chain has picked up an option on that building. A lot of their stuff is going to compete directly with my store, and I won't be able to match their prices. I just don't know what I should do."

CASE
QUESTIONS

1. Can you identify examples of planned and reactive change in this case?

3. Describe how David Yates might have been better able to execute the steps in the change process.

3. What steps might David now take to cope with potential decline or termination of his business?

Leading

PART CONTENTS

13

MOTIVATING EMPLOYEES

1. Discuss the general nature of the motivational process and explain why motivation is important.

2. Outline the three historical perspectives on motivation.

3. Identify and explain the two major content perspectives on motivation.

4. Identify and explain the two major process perspectives on motivation.

5. Discuss the reinforcement perspective on motivation.

6. Describe how organizational reward systems relate to motivation, cite the characteristics of effective reward systems, and summarize six contemporary reward systems.

7. List and briefly describe four useful motivational techniques and programs.

OPENING INCIDENT

You are the founder and president of a rapidly growing computer company based in California's "Silicon Valley." Qualified employees are difficult to find and even more difficult to keep. Moreover, you are convinced that employees are a valuable human resource that should be nurtured. What kind of incentive techniques would you use to motivate your employees and also to allow them the opportunity to grow and develop?

Every morning at 8:00, Connie Mathers begins her workday as an administrative assistant for Ajax Enterprises. This particular morning, she pulls into the parking lot at 7:45 but sits in her car listening to the radio until almost eight because her job doesn't start until then. During the day, she does just about everything asked of her, but little more. When her phone rings at two minutes before noon, she doesn't answer it because she's afraid the conversation will cut into her lunch hour. Later in the afternoon, she submits a report to her boss on employee morale. She could have done a better job, but she knows her boss will be satisfied with the report as it is. Connie starts clearing her desk at five minutes before 5:00 so she'll be ready to leave on time. On the way to her car Connie remarks to a friend, "Another day, another dollar. Wait, make that $1.05. We got our annual cost-of-living raise today."

A few blocks away, Sherry McBride, an administrative assistant at Epic Incorporated, is still at her desk. Her boss wants a report on company productivity gains by the end of the week. She has the data to put something together now but wants to do an especially good job. In fact, she realizes that she may have to come in a little early tomorrow to wrap things up. At 5:45 she takes a phone call, even though the office is officially closed, and then heads home. She doesn't really mind the extra work. Last quarter, her boss got her an extra 5 percent merit pay increase. The extra money was nice, but she felt especially good because hers was the largest merit increase in the company.

Although Connie and Sherry may be similar in some ways, they are clearly quite different in one important dimension: their motivation to perform. Connie is barely motivated enough to get by, whereas Sherry is more concerned with doing a good job than with the hours she puts in.

This chapter begins a four-chapter section on behavioral processes in organizations. The third management function, leading, consists of managing these behavioral processes. In this chapter, we consider employee motivation. Chapter 14 is concerned with the leadership skills and practices of effective managers. Groups and group processes in organizations are explored in Chapter 15. And Chapter 16 focuses on communication in organizations.

The nature of motivation

Employee motivation is a major concern of most managers. How can employees be induced to see organizational goals as part of their own goal sets and to work hard to achieve them? *Motivation* is a cyclical process affecting the inner needs or drives that energize, channel, and maintain behavior.[1]

The motivation process begins with inner drives and needs that motivate the individual to work toward certain goals (see Figure 13.1), which the individual has chosen in the belief that they will satisfy the inner drives and needs. After attaining these goals, the individual consciously or unconsciously judges whether the effort has been worthwhile. To the extent that the individual perceives the effort as rewarding, the behavior of making the effort is reinforced and the individual will continue or repeat that kind of behavior. Reinforcement, or what happens as a result of behavior, affects other needs and drives as the process is repeated; hence its cyclical nature. These various concepts and processes are explored in more depth later in this chapter.

As we have indicated, employee motivation is of crucial concern to managers, mainly because of the role that employee motivation plays in performance. Basically, performance is determined by three things: ability, motivation, and environment. To perform effectively, one must know how to do the job (ability), must want to do the job (motivation), and must have the proper setting, materials, and tools to do the job (environment). If any of these factors is deficient or missing, effective performance is impossible. A manager can have the most highly qualified subordinate in the world and provide her or him with the best tools and equipment available, but effective performance will not result unless the subordinate is motivated to perform. Without moti-

Figure 13.1
The motivation
process

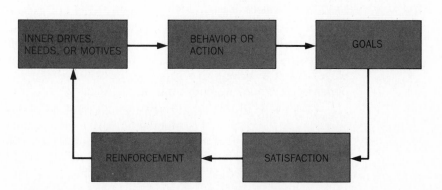

1. See Richard M. Steers and Lyman W. Porter, *Motivation and Work Behavior*, 2nd ed. (New York: McGraw-Hill, 1979), p. 6.

vation all employees would be like Connie Mathers. They would do the bare minimum necessary to get by, and nothing else.

Historical perspectives on motivation

To appreciate what we know (and don't know) about motivation, it is helpful to review previous thinking about this vital variable in the workplace. Motivation theory has evolved through three different philosophical views: the traditional approach, the human relations approach, and the human resource approach.[2]

The traditional approach

The traditional approach to understanding employee motivation is well represented by the work of Frederick Taylor.[3] As we noted in Chapter 2, Taylor made significant contributions to the scientific study of work and specialization in work, and he suggested the use of an incentive pay system. He believed that management knew more about the jobs being performed than the workers did, and he assumed that economic gain was the primary goal in the motivation process.

Other assumptions of the traditional approach were that work is inherently unpleasant for most people and that the money they earn is more important to employees than the nature of the job they are performing. Hence people could be expected to tolerate any kind of work if they were paid enough. Although the role of money as a motivating factor cannot be dismissed, proponents of the traditional approach took too narrow a view of the role of monetary compensation and failed to consider other motivational factors as well.

The human relations approach

The human relations approach (also summarized in Chapter 2) grew out of the work at Western Electric of Elton Mayo and his associates.[4] The human relationists emphasized the role of social processes in the workplace. Their basic assumptions were that employees want to feel useful and important, that employees want to belong to a social group, and that these needs are more important than money in motivating employees.

Proponents of the human relations approach advised managers to make

2. This section is based on Richard M. Steers and Lyman W. Porter, *Motivation and Work Behavior*, 2nd ed. (New York: McGraw-Hill, 1979). Used with permission.

3. Frederick W. Taylor, *Principles of Scientific Management* (New York: Harper and Brothers, 1911).

4. Elton Mayo, *The Social Problems of an Industrial Civilization* (Boston: Harvard University Press, 1945); and Fritz J. Roethlisberger and W. J. Dickson, *Management and the Worker* (Boston: Harvard University Press, 1939).

workers feel important, keep them informed, and allow them a modicum of self-direction and self-control in carrying out routine activities. This involvement and perceived importance were expected to satisfy workers' basic social needs and result in higher motivation to perform. However, the workers' involvement was merely tolerated by managers; it probably never occurred to them that the workers actually could make meaningful contributions. It was assumed that, even if employees were not making a tangible contribution to the organization, the mere fact that they thought they were would enhance motivation. For example, a manager might allow a work group to participate in making a decision, even though he or she had already determined what the decision would be. The symbolic gesture of seeming to allow participation was expected to enhance motivation, even though no real participation took place.

The human resource approach

The human resource approach to motivation carries the concepts of human needs and motivation one step further. Whereas the human relationists believed that the illusion of contribution and participation would enhance motivation, the human resource view holds that the contributions themselves are valuable. People are expected to want to contribute and to be able to make genuine contributions. Management's task is to encourage participation and to create a work environment that makes full use of the human resources available. This philosophy is reflected in current efforts in the automobile industry to increase employee participation in planning work and making decisions. It is assumed that the employees have real knowledge that the organization can use to enhance its own effectiveness.[5]

Content perspectives on motivation

Content perspectives on motivation deal with the beginning stage of the motivational process presented in Figure 13.1: drives, needs, or motives. More specifically, *content perspectives* are views on what factor or set of factors cause motivation. Labor leaders often argue that workers can be motivated by more pay, shorter working hours, and improved working conditions. And some behavioral scientists suggest that motivation can be enhanced by providing employees with more autonomy and greater responsibility. Both of these stances represent content views of motivation. The former asserts that motivation is a function of pay, working hours, and working conditions; the latter suggests that autonomy and responsibility are the causes of motivation. Two widely known content perspectives on motivation are the need hierarchy and the two-factor theory.

5. See Charles G. Burck, "Can Detroit Catch Up?" *Fortune*, February 8, 1982, pp. 34–39.

Figure 13.2
Maslow's need
hierarchy

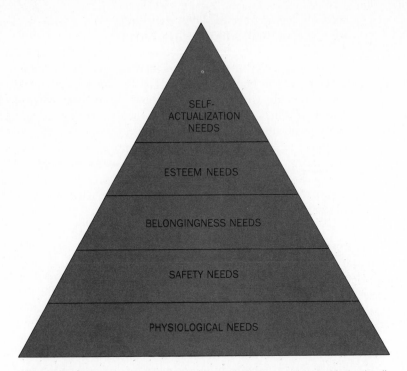

Source: Adapted from Abraham H. Maslow, "A Theory of Human Motivation,"
Psychological Review, Vol. 50, 1943, pp. 370–396. Copyright 1943 by the
American Psychological Association. Used with permission.

The need hierarchy

The concept of the ***need hierarchy*** was first advanced by Abraham Maslow in
the 1940s.[6] Maslow assumed that people are "wanting" animals who are motivated to satisfy various needs and that these needs are arranged in a hierarchy of importance.

As shown in Figure 13.2, there are five kinds of needs in Maslow's hierarchy. The *physiological needs* for such things as food, sex, and air represent
basic issues of survival and biological function. Next are the *safety needs* for a
secure physical and emotional environment. Examples include the desire for
adequate housing and clothing and the need to be free from worry about
money and job security.

Belongingness needs are related to social processes; they include the need
for love and affection and the need to be accepted by one's peers. *Esteem needs*
actually comprise two different sets of needs: the need for a positive self-image
and self-respect *and* the need for recognition and respect from others.

At the top of the hierarchy are what Maslow calls the *self-actualization*

6. See Abraham H. Maslow, "A Theory of Human Motivation," *Psychological Review*, Vol. 50,
1943, pp. 370–396; and Abraham H. Maslow, *Motivation and Personality* (New York: Harper &
Row, 1954).

needs. They involve realizing one's potential for continued growth. The focus of self-actualization needs is thus individual development.

Maslow suggests that the five need categories are arranged in order of importance, starting at the bottom of the hierarchy. That is, an individual is motivated first and foremost to satisfy physiological needs. As long as these needs remain unsatisfied, the individual is motivated only to fulfill them. When satisfaction of physiological needs is achieved, however, they cease to act as primary motivational factors and the individual moves "up" the hierarchy and becomes concerned with safety needs. This process continues until the individual reaches the self-actualization level.

In organizational settings, physiological needs are generally taken care of by adequate wages and the work environment itself, which provides restrooms, adequate lighting, comfortable temperatures, and ventilation.

Safety needs are satisfied for many people by job continuity (no layoffs), a grievance system (to protect against arbitrary supervisory actions), and an adequate insurance and retirement benefit package (for security against illness and provision of income in later life). Even today, however, depressed industries and general economic decline can put people out of work and restore the primacy of lower-level needs.

Belongingness needs are satisfied for most people by a combination of family and community relationships outside of work and friendships on the job. A manager can lend to the satisfaction of these needs by allowing social interaction and by making employees feel like part of a team or work group. The manager can also be sensitive to the probable effects (such as absenteeism or low performance) when an employee has family problems.

A manager can address esteem needs by providing such extrinsic symbols of accomplishment as job titles and spacious offices *as appropriate*. At a more intrinsic level, the manager can provide challenging job assignments and other opportunities for the employee to feel a sense of accomplishment.

The self-actualization needs are perhaps the most difficult for a manager to address. In fact, it can be argued that these needs must be met entirely from within the individual. But a manager can help by promoting a climate wherein self-actualization is possible. For instance, a manager could give employees a chance to participate in making decisions about their work and the opportunity to learn new things about their jobs and the organization.

Maslow's concept of the need hierarchy has a certain intuitive logic and has been accepted by many managers, but research has revealed certain shortcomings and defects in the theory. Some researchers have found that five levels of needs are not always present, and in other cases the order of the levels is not always the same as postulated by Maslow.[7]

In response to these and similar criticisms, Clayton Alderfer, a noted Yale scholar, has proposed an alternative hierarchy of needs called the ERG theory

7. See Mahmond A. Wahba and Lawrence G. Bridwell, "Maslow Reconsidered: A Review of Research on the Need Hierarchy Theory," *Organizational Behavior and Human Performance*, April 1976, pp. 212–240.

of motivation.[8] The letters E, R, and G stand for existence, relatedness, and growth. The *ERG theory* collapses the need hierarchy developed by Maslow into three levels. Existence needs correspond to the physiological and security needs of Maslow's hierarchy. Relatedness needs focus on how people relate to their social environment. In Maslow's hierarchy, they would encompass both the need to belong and the need to earn the esteem of others. Growth needs, the highest level, include the needs for self-esteem and self-actualization.

Although the ERG theory assumes that motivated behavior follows a hierarchy in somewhat the same fashion as suggested by Maslow, there are two important differences. First, the ERG theory suggests that more than one level of needs can cause motivation at the same time, so it acknowledges that people can be motivated by a desire for money (existence), friendship (relatedness), and the opportunity to learn new skills (growth) all at once.

Second, the ERG theory has what has been called a frustration-regression element that is missing from Maslow's need hierarchy. Maslow maintained that a need must be satisfied before an individual can progress to a higher level and that the individual then continues to function at that higher level until the new need is satisfied. The ERG theory suggests that, if needs remain unsatisfied at this higher level, the individual will become frustrated, regress to the lower level, and begin to pursue those things again. For example, a worker previously motivated by money (existence needs) may have just been awarded a pay raise sufficient to satisfy those needs. Suppose that he or she then attempts to establish more friendships in order to satisfy relatedness needs. If, for whatever reason, the employee finds that it is impossible to become better friends with others in the workplace, he or she eventually gets frustrated and regresses to being motivated to earn even more money.

The ERG theory is relatively new compared to Maslow's need hierarchy, but research suggests that it may be a more valid account of motivation in organizations.[9] Managers should not, of course, rely too heavily on any one particular perspective to guide their thinking about employee motivation. Perhaps the key insights to be gleaned from the need hierarchy view are that some needs may be more important than others and that people may change their behavior after any particular set of needs has been satisfied.

The two-factor theory

Another popular content perspective on motivation is the *two-factor theory* developed by Frederick Herzberg.[10] Herzberg developed his theory in the 1950s by interviewing 200 accountants and engineers in Pittsburgh. During the interviews, he asked them to recall occasions when they had been especially

8. Clayton P. Alderfer, *Existence, and Relatedness, and Growth* (New York: Free Press, 1972).

9. For example, see Clayton P. Alderfer, "An Empirical Test of a New Theory of Human Needs," *Organizational Behavior and Human Performance*, Vol. 4, 1969, pp. 142–175.

10. Frederick Herzberg, Bernard Mausner, and Barbara Snyderman, *The Motivation to Work* (New York: Wiley, 1959). See also Frederick Herzberg, "One More Time: How Do You Motivate Employees?" *Harvard Business Review*, January–February 1968, pp. 53–62.

satisfied with their work and highly motivated and occasions when they had been dissatisfied and unmotivated. Somewhat surprisingly, he found that entirely different sets of factors were associated with satisfaction and with dissatisfaction. That is, although "low pay" might well be described as causing dissatisfaction, "high pay" would not necessarily be named as a cause of satisfaction. Instead different factors, such as a recognition or accomplishment, were cited as satisfying.

This finding led Herzberg to conclude that the traditional model of job satisfaction was incomplete. As shown in Figure 13.3, the traditional view of satisfaction was that satisfaction and dissatisfaction were at opposite ends of a continuum. Employees might be satisfied, dissatisfied, or somewhere in between. But Herzberg's interviews had identified two *different* sets of factors: one ranging from satisfaction to no satisfaction and the other ranging from dissatisfaction to no dissatisfaction.

Table 13.1 lists the two sets of factors identified by Herzberg. Note that the factors influencing the satisfaction continuum are called *motivation factors* and that they are related specifically to the work *content*. The other set of factors (the ones causing dissatisfaction) Herzberg called *hygiene factors*; they are related to the work environment.

Herzberg then argues that there are two stages in the process of motivating employees. First the manager must ensure that the hygiene factors are adequate. That is, pay and security must be appropriate, working conditions must be safe, technical supervision must be acceptable, and the like. By providing these factors at an appropriate level, the manager does not stimulate motivation but merely assures that employees become "not dissatisfied." Much

Figure 13.3
Two views of job satisfaction

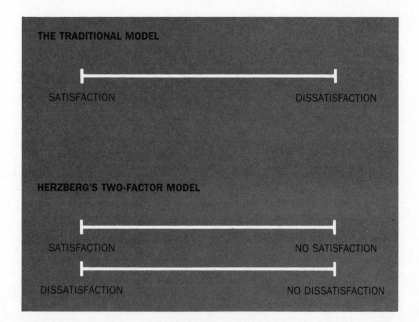

Table 13.1 Motivation and hygiene factors in the workplace

Motivation factors	Hygiene factors
Achievement	Supervisors
Recognition	Working conditions
The work itself	Interpersonal relationships
Responsibility	Pay and security
Advancement and growth	Company policy and administration

Source: Reprinted by permission of the *Harvard Business Review*. An exhibit from "One More Time: How Do You Motivate Employees?" by Frederick Herzberg (January–February, 1968). Copyright © 1968 by the President and Fellows of Harvard College; all rights reserved.

like Connie Mathers at the beginning of this chapter, employees whom managers attempt to "satisfy" via hygiene factors alone will do just enough to get by.

Managers should then proceed to stage two: they should give employees the opportunity to experience motivation factors such as achievement and recognition. The result is predicted to be a high level of satisfaction and motivation, such as that exhibited by Sherry McBride. Herzberg also goes a step further than most theorists and describes exactly how to use the two-factor theory. Specifically, he recommends job enrichment as discussed in Chapter 10. Jobs, he says, should be redesigned to provide higher levels of the motivation factors.

Although widely accepted by many managers, Herzberg's two-factor theory is not without its critics. One criticism is that the findings in Herzberg's initial interviews are subject to different explanations. Others charge that his sample was not representative of the general population and that subsequent research often failed to uphold the theory.[11] At the present time, Herzberg's theory is not held in high esteem by researchers in the field. The theory has had a major impact on managers, however, and has played a key role in increasing their awareness of motivation and its importance in the workplace.

Other important needs

The need hierarchy and the two-factor theory of motivation identify a number of individual needs and then attempt to arrange them in some kind of order of importance. Other content views of motivation have focused more on the important needs themselves without being concerned about ordering them. The three needs most often discussed are the needs for achievement, affiliation, and power.[12]

The *need for achievement,* the best known of the three, reflects the desire

11. See Robert J. House and Lawrence A. Wigdor, "Herzberg's Dual-Factor Theory of Job Satisfaction and Motivation: A Review of the Evidence and a Criticism," *Personnel Psychology,* Winter 1967, pp. 369–389; and Victor Vroom, *Work and Motivation* (New York: Wiley, 1964).

12. See David C. McClelland, *The Achieving Society* (Princeton, N.J.: Van Nostrand, 1961); and David C. McClelland, *Power: The Inner Experience* (New York: Irvington, 1975).

to accomplish a goal or task more effectively than in the past. Most of what we know about the need for achievement is based on the work of David Mc-Clelland, a psychologist at Harvard.[13] People with a high need for achievement are assumed to have (1) a desire to assume personal responsibility, (2) a tendency to set moderately difficult goals, (3) a need for specific and immediate feedback, and (4) a preoccupation with their task. McClelland argues that only about 10 percent of the U.S. population has a high need for achievement. Because such a need is assumed to be important for managerial success, he has devised a training program for increasing one's need for achievement. Some studies have found that people who complete this achievement training make more money and receive promotions faster than other managers.[14]

The need for affiliation is less well understood. Like Maslow's need for belongingness, the **need for affiliation** is a desire to have human companionship and acceptance. People with a strong need for affiliation are likely to prefer (and perform better in) a job that entails a lot of social interaction and offers opportunities to make friends.

The need for power has recently received considerable attention as an important managerial need. The **need for power** might be defined as the desire to be influential in a group and to control one's environment. Research has shown that people with a strong need for power are likely to be superior performers, have good attendance records, and occupy supervisory positions. One study found that all managers tend to have a stronger power motive than the general population and that successful managers tend to have stronger power motives than less successful managers.[15]

In summary, the major content perspectives on motivation focus on individual needs and drives. Maslow's need hierarchy, the ERG theory, the two-factor theory, and the needs for achievement, affiliation, and power all provide useful insights into factors that cause motivation. They relate specifically to the first step of the process shown in Figure 13.1.

What they do *not* do is shed much light on the *process* of motivation. That is, they don't explain why people might be motivated by one factor rather than another at a given level, or how people might go about trying to satisfy the different needs. These questions involve behaviors or actions, goals, and feelings of satisfaction—concepts that are addressed by various process perspectives on motivation.

Process perspectives on motivation

Process perspectives on motivation are concerned with how motivation occurs. That is, rather than attempting to identify or list motivational stimuli, process perspectives focus on how people choose various goals to work toward and

13. See McClelland, *The Achieving Society*.

14. See David McClelland, "That Urge to Achieve," *Think,* November–December 1966, p. 22.

15. See David McClelland and David H. Burnham, "Power Is the Great Motivator," *Harvard Business Review*, March–April 1976, pp. 100–110.

how they evaluate their satisfaction after they have attained these goals. Two of the more useful process perspectives on motivation are expectancy theory and equity theory.

Expectancy theory

The expectancy theory of motivation has many different forms and labels. We will describe it from a general perspective and in the form that is most easily understood. Basically, *expectancy theory* suggests that motivation depends on two things: how much we want something and how likely we think we are to get it. Assume for a moment that you are approaching graduation and are therefore looking for a job. You see in the want ads that Exxon is seeking a new vice president with a starting salary of $250,000 per year. Even though you might want the job, you probably don't apply because you realize that you have little chance of getting it. The next ad you see is for someone to scrape bubble gum from underneath theater seats. Starting salary: $4.00 an hour. Even though you realize that you could probably get the job, you don't apply because you don't want it. Then you see an ad for a management trainee for a big company with a starting salary of $22,000. You apply for this job because you want it *and* because you think you have a reasonable chance of getting it.

The formal expectancy framework as we now recognize it was developed by Victor Vroom.[16] The important assumptions of expectancy theory are as follows:

1. Behavior is determined by a combination of forces in the individual and forces in the environment.
2. People make decisions about their own behavior in organizations.
3. Different people have different types of needs, desires, and goals.
4. People make decisions among alternative plans of behavior based on their perceptions of the extent to which a given behavior will lead to desired outcomes.[17]

Figure 13.4 summarizes the basic expectancy model of employee motivation. The model suggests that motivation leads to effort and that effort, combined with employee ability and environmental factors, results in performance. Performance leads to various outcomes, each of which has an associated value. The value of an outcome to the individual is referred to as its valence. The most important parts of the expectancy model cannot be shown in the figure. They are the individual's expectation that effort will lead to high performance, that performance will lead to outcomes, and that each outcome will have some kind of value.

Consider the example of a young manager who strongly wants a pay raise (an outcome). If he or she perceives that a pay raise is likely to result

16. See Victor H. Vroom, *Work and Motivation* (New York: Wiley, 1964).

17. See David A. Nadler and Edward E. Lawler, III, ''Motivation: A Diagnostic Approach,'' in J. Richard Hackman, Edward E. Lawler, III, and Lyman W. Porter (eds.), *Perspectives on Behavior in Organizations,* 2nd ed. (New York: McGraw-Hill, 1983), pp. 67–78.

Figure 13.4
The expectancy
model of motivation

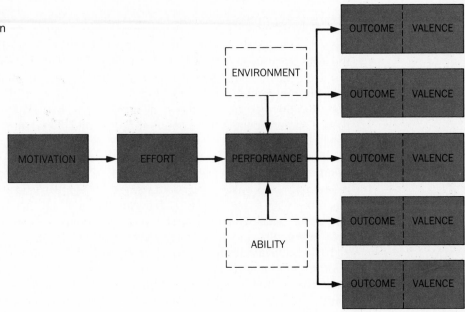

from high performance, and if he or she also believes that high performance is likely to follow effort, the manager will be motivated to exert effort.

Effort-to-performance expectancy. The effort-to-performance expectancy is the individual's perception of the probability that effort will lead to high performance. When the individual believes without question that "If I expend effort I will be a high performer," expectancy will be quite strong (close to 1.00). When the individual believes that "The effort I expend will have no bearing at all on the level of performance I attain," effort-to-performance expectancy is very weak (close to 0). The belief that "My effort has some effect on performance," signals moderate expectancy (somewhere between 0 and 1).

Performance-to-outcome expectancy. The performance-to-outcome expectancy is the individual's perception that performance will lead to a specific outcome. For example, the individual may believe that "If I am a high performer, I will definitely get a pay raise." Expectancy in this case is high (approaching 1.00). The individual who believes that "If I am a high performer, I may or may not get a promotion" exhibits moderate expectancy (between 1.00 and 0). When the individual believes that "Regardless of how I perform, I will not get praise because my boss never praises anyone," performance-to-outcome expectancy is low (close to 0).

Outcomes and valences. Finally, expectancy theory recognizes that an individual may experience a variety of outcomes or rewards in an organizational setting. A high performer may get (1) bigger pay raises, (2) faster promotions, and (3) more praise from the boss. On the other hand, he or she may also (4) be subject to more stress, and (5) incur resentment from co-workers.

Each of these outcomes has an associated value, or valence, which is simply an index of how much an individual desires a particular outcome. If the individual wants the outcome, its valence is positive; if the individual does not want the outcome, its valence is negative; if the individual is indifferent to the outcome, its valence is zero.

It is this part of expectancy theory that goes beyond the content perspectives. Different people have different needs, and they will try to satisfy these needs in different ways. For an employee who has a high need for achievement and a low need for affiliation, the pay raise and promotions cited above as outcomes of high performance might have positive valences, the praise and resentment zero valences, and the stress a negative valence. For a different employee with a low need for achievement and a high need for affiliation, the pay raise, promotions and praise might all have positive valences, whereas both resentment and stress could have negative valences.

For motivated behavior to occur, then, three conditions must be met. The effort-to-performance expectancy must be greater than zero (the individual must believe that, if effort is expended, high performance will result). The performance-to-outcome expectancy must be greater than zero (the individual must believe that, if high performance is achieved, certain outcomes will follow). And the sum of the valences for all relevant outcomes must be greater than zero. (One or more outcomes may have negative valences if they are more than offset by the positive valences of other outcomes. For example, the attractiveness of a pay raise, a promotion, and praise from the boss may outweigh the unattractiveness of more stress and resentment from co-workers). Expectancy theory maintains that, when all of these conditions are met, the individual is motivated to expend effort.

The Porter–Lawler extension. An interesting extension to expectancy theory has been proposed by Porter and Lawler.[18] You will recall from Chapter 2 that the human relationists assumed employee satisfaction causes good performance but that research has not borne out such a relationship. Porter and Lawler suggest that there may indeed be a relationship between satisfaction and performance, but that it goes in the opposite direction! That is, high performance leads to satisfaction.

Figure 13.5 summarizes Porter and Lawler's logic. Performance results in various outcomes, or rewards. Some of these rewards are extrinsic in nature (such as pay and promotions), whereas others are intrinsic (such as self-esteem and a feeling of accomplishment). The individual then evaluates the equity, or fairness, of the various rewards relative to the effort expended and the level of performance attained (we will learn more about equity decisions and equity theory later in this section). If the rewards are felt to be equitable, the individual is satisfied.

18. See Lyman W. Porter and Edward E. Lawler, III, *Managerial Attitudes and Performance* (Homewood, Il.: Dorsey Press, 1968).

Figure 13.5
The Porter–Lawler
extension of
expectancy theory

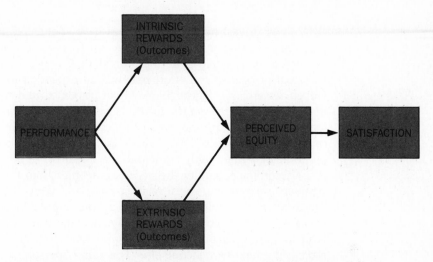

Source: Edward E. Lawler, III, and Lyman W. Porter, "The Effect of Performance on Job Satisfaction," *Industrial Relations*, October 1967, p. 23. Used with permission of the University of California.

Implications for managers. Expectancy theory can be useful for managers who are trying to improve the motivation of their subordinates. Nadler and Lawler suggest the following steps:

1. Figure out the outcomes each employee is likely to want.
2. Decide what kinds and levels of performance are needed to meet organizational goals.
3. Make sure that the desired levels of performance are attainable.
4. Link desired outcomes and desired performance.
5. Analyze the complete situation for conflicting expectancies.
6. Make sure the rewards are large enough.
7. Make sure the total system is equitable (fair to all).[19]

These issues will be explored in more detail later in this chapter when we discuss organizational reward systems.

Of course, expectancy theory has its limitations. Though the theory makes sense and has been generally supported by empirical research, it is quite difficult to apply.[20] To really use the complete theory in the workplace, it would be necessary to identify all the potential outcomes for each employee, to determine all relevant expectancies, and then to balance everything somehow to maximize employee motivation.

19. Nadler and Lawler, "Motivation: A Diagnostic Approach."

20. See Terence Mitchell, "Expectancy Models of Job Satisfaction, Occupational Preference, and Effort: A Theoretical, Methodological, and Empirical Appraisal," *Psychological Bulletin*, December 1974, pp. 1053–1077.

Equity theory

After inner drives, needs, and motives have stimulated the motivation process and the individual has chosen an action that she or he expects will lead to attainment of a certain goal, the individual assesses the fairness, or equity, of that goal in light of the effort that will be expended to reach it and the presumed reward (see Figure 13.1). Much of our current thinking on equity has been shaped by the *equity theory* developed by J. Stacey Adams, who contends that people are motivated to seek social equity in the rewards they receive for performance.[21] We can define *equity* at this point as the belief that one is being treated fairly relative to the treatment of others.

According to equity theory, the outcomes from the job include pay, recognition, promotions, social relationships, and intrinsic rewards. To get these rewards, the individual contributes various inputs to the job, such as time, experience, effort, education, and loyalty. Equity theory suggests that people tend to view their outcomes and inputs as a ratio and then to compare this ratio to the ratio of someone else. This other "person" may be someone in the work group or some sort of group average or composite. The process of comparison looks like this:

$$\frac{\text{Outcomes (self)}}{\text{Inputs (self)}} \overset{?}{=} \frac{\text{Outcomes (other)}}{\text{Inputs (other)}}$$

After arriving at these ratios in what is probably a nonquantitative and subjective way, the individual compares them. Comparing the two ratios is likewise imprecise, but the individual's attitudes are affected nonetheless. Three alternatives are possible: the individual may feel equitably rewarded, under-rewarded, or over-rewarded.

The individual will experience a state of equity if the two ratios are equal. This condition may also exist when the other person's outcomes are greater than the individual's own outcomes—provided that the other's inputs are also proportionately greater. Suppose that Mark has a high school education and earns only $10,000. He may still feel equitably treated relative to Jim, who earns $15,000, if Jim has a college education.

People who feel under-rewarded compared to someone else try to reduce the inequity. Ways of reducing inequity include (1) decreasing one's inputs by exerting less effort, (2) increasing one's outcomes by asking for a raise, (3) distorting the original ratios by rationalizing, (4) trying to get the other person to change his or her outcomes or inputs, (5) leaving the situation, and (6) changing the object of comparison.

An individual may also feel over-rewarded relative to the other person. This is not likely to be terribly disturbing to most people, but research suggests that some experience inequity under these conditions and are motivated to

21. J. Stacey Adams, "Toward an Understanding of Inequity," *Journal of Abnormal and Social Psychology*, November 1963, pp. 422–436. See also Richard T. Mowday, "Equity Theory Predictions of Behavior in Organizations," in Richard M. Steers and Lyman W. Porter (eds.), *Motivation and Work Behavior*, 2nd ed. (New York: McGraw-Hill, 1979).

reduce it.[22] Methods for reducing this kind of inequity include (1) increasing one's inputs by exerting more effort, (2) reducing one's outcomes by producing fewer units, if paid on a per-unit basis, (3) distorting the original ratios by rationalizing, and (4) trying to reduce the inputs or increase the outcomes of the other person.

Implications for managers. The single most important idea for managers to remember in this context is that, for rewards to motivate employees, the employees must perceive them as being equitable and fair. If the individual achieves various intrinsic and extrinsic rewards as a result of performance and regards these rewards as equitable, satisfaction will result.

A second implication of equity theory is that managers need to consider the nature of the "other" to whom the employee is comparing herself or himself. During the early 1980s, many engineering schools were having a hard time attracting and retaining qualified faculty members.[23] The reason? Engineers could make more money by working in industry. If a university administrator assumed that the engineering professor compared her or his situation to that of an English professor, the university would not know how to respond. But administrators who saw that the engineering professor's "comparison other" was an industry counterpart realized that higher salaries were needed.

On balance, the research support for equity theory is mixed. The concepts of equity and comparisons with others are certainly important for the manager to consider, but it is also apparent that managers should not rely only on this framework in attempting to manage employee motivation.[24]

Reinforcement perspectives on motivation

The final element of the motivational framework outlined in Figure 13.1 concerns reinforcement. As we have seen, content perspectives relate to the needs or motives that stimulate behavior, and process perspectives explain how people choose various behaviors to achieve goals and how they evaluate the equity of the rewards they get for attaining those goals. The reinforcement perspective on motivation explains the role of those rewards as they cause behavior to change or remain the same over time. Specifically, the *reinforcement theory* is based on the fairly simple assumption that behavior that results in rewarding consequences is likely to be repeated, whereas behavior that results in punishing consequences is less likely to be repeated. This approach to explaining

22. For a review, see Paul S. Goodman and Abraham Friedman, "An Examination of Adams's Theory of Inequity," *Administrative Science Quarterly*, September 1971, pp. 271–288.

23. See Jeremy Main, "Why Engineering Deans Worry a Lot," *Fortune*, January 11, 1982, pp. 84–90.

24. See Goodman and Friedman, "An Examination of Adams's Theory of Inequity."

behavior was originally tested on animals, but B. F. Skinner has been instrumental in demonstrating how it also applies to human behavior.[25]

Using the terminology of reinforcement theory, Figure 13.6 gives another view of the motivation process. The starting point is a stimulus. (This stimulus can be thought of as the needs or motives that trigger behavior.) The individual follows path 1 to a response. (The process of selecting and following this path is consistent with our earlier discussion of expectancy theory.) As a result of this response, the individual experiences various consequences (path 2). The value of those consequences affects future responses, as shown in path 3. If the consequences were pleasant or desirable, the individual will probably choose the same response (path 4) the next time he or she encounters the same stimulus. But if the original consequences were unpleasant or undesirable, a different response (path 5) is more likely.

Consider the case of an employee trying to get a pay raise. If he starts working harder and subsequently gets a raise, his behavior has been reinforced. The next time he wants a raise, he is likely to try working harder again. On the other hand, if his additional effort did not result in a pay raise, he is likely to try other behaviors (such as buttering up the boss or threatening to quit).

Decades of psychological research have revealed four major elements of reinforcement: positive reinforcement, avoidance, punishment, and extinction. Table 13.2 summarizes these primary elements of reinforcement theory.

Figure 13.6
The reinforcement
theory of motivation

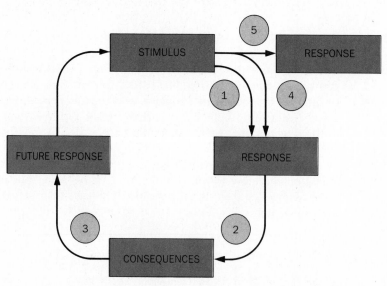

25. B. F. Skinner, *Beyond Freedom and Dignity* (New York: Knopf, 1971).

Table 13.2 Elements of reinforcement theory

Arrangement of the reinforcement contingencies	Schedules for applying reinforcement
1. **Positive reinforcement.** Strengthens behavior by providing a desirable consequence.	1. **Fixed interval.** Reinforcement applied at fixed time intervals, regardless of behavior.
2. **Avoidance.** Strengthens behavior by allowing escape from an undesirable consequence.	2. **Variable interval.** Reinforcement applied at variable time intervals, regardless of behavior.
3. **Punishment.** Weakens behavior by providing an undesirable consequence.	3. **Fixed ratio.** Reinforcement applied after a fixed number of behaviors, regardless of time.
4. **Extinction.** Weakens behavior by not providing a desirable consequence.	4. **Variable ratio.** Reinforcement applied after a variable number of behaviors, regardless of time.

Kinds of reinforcement

Two kinds of reinforcement strengthen or maintain behavior, whereas the other two weaken or decrease behavior. Positive reinforcement, a method of strengthening behavior, consists of providing a reward or a positive outcome after a desired behavior is performed. When a manager observes an employee working especially well and offers praise, the praise serves to positively reinforce the behavior of working well. Other positive reinforcers in organizations include pay raises, promotions, and awards.

The other method of strengthening desired behavior is through avoidance. An employee may come to work on time in order to avoid a reprimand. Here the employee is motivated to perform the behavior of punctuality in order to avoid an unpleasant consequence that is likely to follow tardiness.

Punishment is used by some managers to weaken undesired behaviors. When an employee is loafing, coming to work late, doing poor work, or interfering with the work of others, the manager might choose to reprimand, discipline, or fine the employee. The logic is that the unpleasant consequence will reduce the likelihood that the employee will choose that particular behavior again. Given the counterproductive side effects of punishment (such as resentment and hostility), it is often advisable to use the other kinds of reinforcement if at all possible.

Extinction can also be used to weaken behavior, especially behavior that has previously been rewarded. When an employee tells an off-color joke and the boss laughs, the laughter reinforces the behavior and the employee may continue to tell off-color jokes. By simply ignoring this behavior and not reinforcing it, the boss can cause the behavior to subside and eventually become "extinct."

Schedules of reinforcement

Various schedules of reinforcement are possible. The fixed-interval schedule provides reinforcement at fixed intervals, regardless of behavior. A good example of a fixed-interval schedule of reinforcement is the issuing of weekly or monthly paychecks. This method provides the least incentive for good work, because employees know they will be paid regularly regardless of their effort or lack of it.

A variable-interval schedule also uses time as the basis for reinforcement, but the time interval varies from one reinforcement to the next. This schedule is appropriate for praise or other rewards based on visits or inspections. When employees don't know when the boss is going to drop by, they tend to maintain a reasonably high level of effort all the time.

A fixed-ratio schedule gives reinforcement after a fixed number of behaviors, regardless of the time that elapses between behaviors. This results in an even higher level of effort. For example, if a department store sales clerk receives a $10 bonus for every fifth credit card application returned from her or his department, motivation will be high because each application gets the person closer to the next bonus.

The variable-ratio schedule, the most powerful schedule in terms of maintaining desired behaviors, varies the number of behaviors needed for each reinforcement. A supervisor who praises an employee for her or his second order, the seventh order after that, the ninth after that, then the fifth, and then the third is using a variable-ratio schedule. The employee is motivated to increase the frequency of the desired behavior because each performance increases the probability of receiving a reward. Of course, a variable-ratio schedule is difficult (if not impossible) to use for formal rewards such as pay because it would be too complicated to keep track of who was rewarded when.

Organizational reward systems and motivation

The theories of motivation that we have discussed so far are all useful frameworks for understanding how the employee initiates, channels, and maintains behavior. However, behavior is not entirely employee-directed. The organization also attempts to influence these motivational processes through its reward system. An organization's *reward system* consists of the formal and informal mechanisms by which employee performance is defined, evaluated, and rewarded. The primary rewards in most organizations are pay, promotions, benefits, and status symbols.

Rewards and attitudes

Though they are generally not a major determinant of job performance, employee attitudes such as satisfaction are nonetheless important. They contribute to (or discourage) absenteeism and also affect turnover, and they help establish the climate, or internal environment, of the organization.

Edward Lawler has advanced four major generalizations about employee attitudes toward rewards.[26] First, employee satisfaction is influenced by how much is received and how much the individual thinks should be received. Employee expectations thus play a key role. Second, employee satisfaction is affected by comparisons with what happens to others. This argument is closely related to equity theory. Third, employees often misperceive the rewards of others. This suggestion also has implications from equity theory. When an employee believes that someone else is making more money than that person really makes, the potential for dissatisfaction increases. Finally, overall job satisfaction is affected by how satisfied employees are with both the extrinsic and the intrinsic rewards they derive from their jobs. Drawing from the content theories and expectancy theory, this conclusion suggests that a variety of needs may cause behavior and that behavior may be channeled toward a variety of goals.

Rewards and behaviors

An organization's primary purpose in giving rewards is, of course, to influence employee behavior. Research has shown that extrinsic rewards affect employee satisfaction, which, in turn, plays a major role in determining whether an employee will remain on the job or seek a new one. Reward systems also influence patterns of attendance and absenteeism. And, if rewards are based on actual performance, employees tend to work harder in order to earn those rewards.

Rewards and motivation

Reward systems are clearly related to the expectancy theory of motivation. The effort-to-performance expectancy is strongly influenced by the performance appraisal that is often a part of the reward system. That is, an employee is likely to put forth more effort if he or she knows that performance will be measured and evaluated. The performance-to-outcome expectancy is clearly affected by the extent to which the employee believes that performance will be followed by rewards. Finally, as expectancy theory predicts, each reward or potential reward has a somewhat different value for each individual. One person may want a promotion more than benefits; someone else may want just the opposite.

Characteristics of effective reward systems

What are the elements of an effective reward system? Lawler has also identified four major characteristics. First, the reward system must meet the needs

---

26. This section draws heavily from Edward E. Lawler, III, *Pay and Organizational Development,* © 1981. Addison-Wesley, Reading, Mass., pp. 11–25, 61–75. Reprinted with permission. See also Edward E. Lawler, III, *Pay and Organizational Effectiveness: A Psychological View* (New York: McGraw-Hill, 1971); and Edward E. Lawler, III, "Reward Systems," in J. Richard Hackman and J. Lloyd Suttle (eds.), *Improving Life at Work: Behavioral Science Approaches to Organizational Change* (Santa Monica, Calif.: Goodyear, 1977), pp. 163–226.

of the individual for food, shelter, and other basic necessities.[27] These needs include the physiological and security needs identified by Maslow and Alderfer and the hygiene factors identified by Herzberg.

Next, the rewards should compare favorably with those offered by other organizations. Unfavorable comparisons with people in other settings could result in feelings of inequity. (Recall the case of the engineering professor comparing salaries with the engineer in an industrial position.[28])

Third, the distribution of rewards within the organization must also be equitable. When some employees feel underpaid compared to others in the organization, the probable results are low morale and poor performance. (People are more likely to compare their situation with that of others in their own organization than with that of outsiders, our engineering professor notwithstanding.)

Finally, the reward system must recognize that different people have different needs and choose different paths to satisfy those needs. Both content theories and expectancy theory contribute to this conclusion. Insofar as possible, a variety of rewards and a variety of methods for achieving them should be made available to employees.

Contemporary reward systems

Organizational reward systems have traditionally been one of two kinds: a fixed hourly or monthly rate or an incentive system. Fixed-rate systems are familiar to most people. Hourly employees are paid a specific wage (based on job demands, experience, and/or other factors) for each hour they work. Salaried employees receive a fixed sum of money on a weekly or monthly basis. Although some reductions may be made for absences, the amount is usually the same regardless of whether the individual works less than or more than a normal amount of time.

Incentive systems, on the other hand, attempt to reward employees in proportion to what they do. A piece-rate pay plan is a good example of an incentive system. In a factory manufacturing luggage, for example, each worker may be paid 20 cents for each handle and set of locks installed on a piece of luggage. Hence there is incentive for the employee to work hard: the more units produced, the higher the pay. Other useful incentive systems include sales commissions, merit rating plans, group incentives, and organization-wide plans such as the Scanlon plan and profit sharing.[29]

In addition to these techniques, organizations are also experimenting with other modifications to existing reward and compensation systems. Four especially interesting techniques are the all-salaried work force, skill-based job evaluation systems, lump-sum salary increases, and cafeteria benefits programs.[30]

27. See Lawler, "Reward Systems."
28. See Main, "Why Engineering Deans Worry a Lot."
29. See Lawler, "Reward Systems."
30. See Lawler, *Pay and Organizational Development.*

Members of all-salaried work forces (already existing in such organizations as Gillette, Dow Chemical, and IBM) do not punch time clocks, do not have their pay docked if they are late for work, and have reasonable leave programs. In other words, factory workers are accorded the benefits that office workers have enjoyed for many decades. Such a system reduces administrative and overhead costs and theoretically enhances motivation because employees are treated as mature and responsible adults.

Skill-based job evaluation systems focus on paying the individual rather than the job. Under a traditional arrangement, two workers doing the same job are paid the same rate, regardless of their skills. Under the new arrangement, people are advanced in pay grade for each new skill or set of skills they learn. School teachers often receive higher pay for increased training. General Foods and Texas Instruments have also experimented with this method and by and large have had favorable results.

Another innovative method for rewarding employees is through the use of lump-sum salary increases. Annual salary increases are normally spread across each pay period, but the new technique allows individuals the option of taking the entire increase in one lump-sum payment at the beginning of the year. Of course, the money is treated as an interest-free loan; if the employee resigns during the year the unearned portion must be repaid. Aetna Life and Casualty, Timex, and B. F. Goodrich have adopted lump-sum salary increases.

The cafeteria benefits program allows each employee to choose the mix of benefits and salary that is most appropriate for her or his particular circumstances. Consider the case of a dual-career married couple. If both employing organizations provide health insurance, the two employees really have more protection than they need, because they won't be "double-paid" for claims. A cafeteria plan would allow one partner to take more salary and/or a different benefit in lieu of the health insurance. Similarly, a single person without dependents can forgo life insurance in favor of other benefits. Cafeteria programs may also include other forms of insurance and time off from work. Due to the costs involved in administering such programs, organizations have been slow to adopt them. Firms that have tried cafeteria benefits plans, including American Can and TRW, report a fairly high level of employee acceptance and satisfaction with them.

Motivational techniques and programs

Offering various rewards is the most obvious way to apply motivation theories to organizational settings, but other techniques are also used to motivate employees. Four popular techniques are summarized in Table 13.3.

MBO and goal setting

MBO, which we discussed in Chapter 4, is a process of collaborative goal setting between a manager and a subordinate with the understanding that the degree of goal attainment by the subordinate will be a major factor in evaluat-

Table 13.3 Motivational techniques used by managers

1. **MBO.** Helps employees see how their efforts will lead to measurable results and how these results will lead to rewards. (See the discussion of expectancy theory.)
2. **Behavior modification.** Applies various kinds of reinforcement to employee performance. (See the discussion of reinforcement theory.)
3. **Modified workweek.** Gives employees more freedom to direct their own actions and to fulfill several needs simultaneously. (See the discussion of needs theory.)
4. **Work redesign.** Provides opportunities for employees to believe in and experience the intrinsic rewards of complex and challenging work. (See the discussion of needs theory and the Porter and Lawler extension of expectancy theory.)

ing and rewarding the subordinate's performance.[31] The role of MBO as a motivational technique is perhaps best seen from the standpoint of expectancy theory. By sitting down with a subordinate, jointly establishing goals for the subordinate, and agreeing that future rewards will be based on goal attainment, the manager is clarifying both the effort-to-performance expectancy and the performance-to-reward expectancy. Then, if the available rewards have a positive valence for the subordinate, he or she should be more motivated to work toward the goals that merit them.

Behavior modification

Behavior modification, or OB Mod (for organizational behavior modification), is a technique for applying the basic concepts of reinforcement theory in organizational settings.[32] An OB Mod program typically proceeds through five stages. First the manager specifies behaviors that are to be increased (such as producing more units) or decreased (such as coming to work late). Next these target behaviors are measured to establish a baseline against which the effectiveness of OB Mod will later be assessed. Then the manager analyzes the situation to ascertain what rewards subordinates value most and how best to tie these rewards to the target behaviors. Now action plans and strategies revolving around positive reinforcement, avoidance, punishment, and/or extinction are implemented in such a way that desired target behaviors have pleasant consequences and undesirable target behaviors have unpleasant consequences. Finally, the target behaviors are measured again to determine the value of the program.

---

31. See Peter Drucker, *The Practice of Management* (New York: Harper & Row, 1954). For a more applied discussion of MBO and its relevance for motivation, see Stephen J. Carroll and Henry L. Tosi, *Management by Objectives: Applications and Research* (New York: Macmillan, 1973).

32. See Fred Luthans and Robert Kreitner, *Organizational Behavior Modification* (Glenview, Il.: Scott, Foresman, 1975); and W. Clay Hamner and Ellen P. Hamner, "Behavior Modification on the Bottom Line," *Organizational Dynamics*, Spring 1976, pp. 2–21.

Although many organizations (such as Proctor & Gamble, Warner-Lambert, and Ford) have used OB Mod, the best-known application has been at Emery Air Freight. Management felt that the containers used to consolidate small shipments into fewer, larger ones were not being packed efficiently. Primarily through a system of self-recorded feedback, Emery increased container usage from 45 percent to 95 percent and saved over $3 million during the first 3 years of the program.[33]

Modified workweek

The modified workweek (the compressed workweek, flexible working hours, and job sharing) was discussed in Chapter 10. The primary motivational implications of the modified workweek are that it helps individuals satisfy higher-level needs and provides an opportunity to fulfill several needs simultaneously.

By allowing employees more independence in terms of when they come to work and when they leave, managers acknowledge and show "esteem" for the employees' ability to exercise self-control. It is hoped that employees will respond with higher levels of motivation. Modified workweeks give employees the opportunity to fulfill a variety of needs. Using either flexible working hours or job sharing, a person can contribute to the organization and still have time to attend school, for example, or to pursue similar developmental activities.

Work redesign

Work redesign is being used more and more as a motivational technique. Expectancy theory helps explain the role of work redesign in motivation.[34] The basic idea is that employees will improve their task performance if they believe that doing so will lead to intrinsic rewards. A number of studies have shown that improvements in the design of work do often result in higher levels of employee motivation.[35] One study at Texas Instruments found that work redesign resulted in decreased turnover and improved employee motivation.[36] Apparently work redesign, as well as MBO, behavior modification, and the modified workweek, can play an important role in the motivation of employees in organizations.

33. See "At Emery Air Freight: Positive Reinforcement Boosts Performance," *Organizational Dynamics*, Winter 1973, pp. 41–50.

34. See Ricky W. Griffin, *Task Design—An Integrative Approach* (Glenview, Il.: Scott, Foresman, 1982).

35. See also J. Richard Hackman and Greg R. Oldham, *Work Redesign* (Reading, Mass.: Addison-Wesley, 1980).

36. See Earl D. Weed, "Job Enrichment 'Cleans Up' at Texas Instruments," in J. R. Maher (ed.), *New Perspectives in Job Enrichment* (New York: Van Nostrand, 1971), pp. 55–77.

Summary of key points

The study of motivation deals with what energizes behavior, what directs or channels such behavior, and how this behavior is maintained. Motivation is an important consideration of managers because it, along with ability and environmental factors, determines individual performance.

According to the traditional view of motivation, people were motivated primarily to achieve economic gain. The human relations approach, on the other hand, suggested that people were motivated primarily by social needs and a desire to feel important. The human resource view assumes that people want to contribute to the success of the organization and that they have the potential to do so.

Content perspectives on motivation are concerned with what factor or factors cause motivation. Popular content theories include Maslow's need hierarchy, the ERG theory, and Herzberg's two-factor theory. The need hierarchy assumes that people are motivated by advancing up a hierarchy of needs as lower-level needs are satisfied. The two-factor theory suggests that job characteristics such as pay and working conditions (called hygiene factors) can cause dissatisfaction, but not satisfaction. Achievement and responsibility on the job (called motivation factors) are what cause satisfaction. Other important needs are the needs for achievement, affiliation, and power.

Process perspectives on motivation deal with how motivation occurs. Two popular process theories are the expectancy theory and equity theory. Expectancy theory suggests that people are motivated to perform if they believe that their effort will result in high performance, that this performance will lead to rewards, and that the positive aspects of the outcomes outweigh the negative aspects. Equity theory is based on the premise that people are motivated to achieve and maintain social equity. Employees are assumed to compare their outcome/input ratio to that of someone else. If they perceive inequity, they attempt to eliminate it.

Reinforcement perspectives on motivation focus on how motivation is maintained. The assumption here is that behavior that results in rewarding consequences is likely to be repeated, whereas behavior resulting in negative consequences is less likely to be repeated. Drawing heavily on learning theory, this view holds that reinforcement contingencies can be arranged in the form of positive reinforcement, avoidance, punishment, and extinction. Schedules of reinforcement include fixed-interval, variable-interval, fixed-ratio, and variable-ratio schedules.

Organizational reward systems are the primary mechanisms managers have for managing motivation. Properly designed systems can improve attitudes, motivation, and behaviors. Effective reward systems must provide sufficient rewards on an equitable basis at the individual level. Contemporary reward systems include fixed-rate systems, incentive systems, the all-salaried work force, skill-based job evaluation systems, lump-sum salary increases, and cafeteria benefits programs. In addition to reward systems, managers can use MBO and goal setting, behavior modification, modified workweeks, and work redesign to enhance employee motivation.

QUESTIONS FOR DISCUSSION

1. Motivation, ability, and environment have been described as the three determinants of performance. Is one of these factors more important than the others? Can you think of a situation in which one of these factors does *not* influence motivation?
2. Are any elements of the historical perspectives on motivation relevant today? Why or why not?
3. Compare and contrast the three historical perspectives on motivation (traditional, human relations, and human resource).
4. Compare and contrast the need hierarchy, the two-factor theory, and ERG theory. Can you think of any ways in which the theories are contradictory?
5. Herzberg's theory has been criticized on the grounds that it deals more with satisfaction than motivation. Do you think this is a valid criticism? In what ways are satisfaction and motivation likely to be related?
6. Some people have said that, although expectancy theory makes sense, it is too complex to actually use in organizations. Do you agree or disagree with this assertion?
7. Can you think of a situation wherein equity theory explains your own behavior? Consider the time you spend studying and the grades you receive compared to the time someone else puts in and the grades he or she gets.
8. If, as we have said, the fixed-interval schedule of reinforcement is least effective and the variable-ratio schedule is most effective, why do most organizations mete out their most powerful reinforcer, pay, on a fixed-interval schedule?
9. Offer situations besides the examples used in this chapter to illustrate positive reinforcement, avoidance, punishment, and extinction.
10. Consider a reward system with which you are familiar and evaluate it in terms of the four characteristics of effective reward systems summarized in this chapter.
11. Can you think of a new, radical, and perhaps revolutionary reward system that might further enhance employee motivation? Remember, though, that it must be feasible.
12. Three of the four specific motivational techniques covered in the last section were discussed in earlier chapters under different topics. Can you think of other things we have covered up to now that could be related to motivation?

C A S E   13.1

At the beginning of this chapter you read an incident about a rapidly growing computer company in northern California. You were asked what kinds of incentives might be used to motivate a valuable group of employees *and* to allow them the opportunity to grow and develop. The company being described was Tandem Computers. The case that follows explains what Tandem has done and then raises some other issues for your consideration.

Tandem Computers has been an enormously successful company. Founded in the mid-1970s by James Treybig, it already has annual sales over $300 million per year. The company projects sales of over $1 billion by 1985.

The foundation of Tandem Computers is a remarkable system called the Nonstop II. For companies like banks or hotels, a failure in a computer system, or even in one of its major components, can be disastrous. Records of banking transactions can be destroyed or an entire year's worth of hotel bookings lost when a system doesn't operate properly. The Nonstop II guards against these hazards by operating with two identical, parallel systems. That is, the system is essentially two computers in one. Under normal conditions the two computers share the work. If one fails, however, the other immediately takes over all operations. Various safeguards also protect all data that is stored in the machines.

Jim Treybig received an undergraduate degree in engineering and an MBA from Stanford. After several years with first Texas Instruments and then Hewlett-Packard, Treybig founded Tandem. Treybig has developed a unique approach to managing the people in his company, partly due to his own personal attitudes and partly due to competition from other firms for his employees.

Tandem is based in California's fabled "Silicon Valley," a stretch of high-tech electronics companies extending south from San Francisco. Competent and hard-working employees are hard to find—and even harder to keep. Treybig himself is a casual, relaxed manager who prefers to do things in an informal fashion. As a result of these two factors, Tandem uses a variety of techniques for keeping its employees and for motivating them to turn in their peak performance.

First, the company provides its employees with a very pleasant work environment. A basketball court, a jogging trail, and a swimming pool grace company headquarters. The company also sponsors a beer bust every Friday afternoon, throws lavish parties, and has sponsored such events as male beauty contests judged by the female employees. In addition, Tandem allows its employees to work flexible working hours.

Treybig also provides financial incentives. At a recent Halloween party, all employees were granted a 100-share stock option. On a more systematic basis, all employees periodically receive stock options. Employees who have been with the company since its inception have received options worth $100,000. And Tandem has a strong policy of promoting from within.

Perhaps the most powerful element in Tandem's motivational system, however, is the management philosophy of Treybig himself. The company makes sure that all employees have detailed, working knowledge of the company, its method of operation, and its five-year strategy. Because everyone knows the company so well, less supervision is needed and employees get deeply involved with their work. Further, because so many employees own stock in Tandem, they are vitally concerned with the price of that stock.

This commitment doesn't apply only to managers and engineers but to operating employees as well. One Tandem service technician insists that customers take his home phone number. He once took an emergency call at 2:30 A.M. and was on the customer's doorstep at 6:00 A.M.

Of course, Treybig and Tandem are not without their critics. Some people charge that the fervent, almost evangelical, dedication that Treybig inspires is not healthy. But most employees defend both the man and his methods. They speak in glowing terms of how they have grown at Tandem and how they have never been more satisfied with their work.

It will be difficult for Treybig to maintain such a highly dedicated and motivated work force. The rapid growth Tandem is now experiencing facilitates the autonomy and incentives currently provided. As the company gets larger, its growth rate must slow and a more formal structure will inevitably emerge. Monitoring changes at Tandem over the next few years should be a fascinating exercise for anyone interested in motivation.

CASE QUESTIONS

1. What aspects of this case can be explained by content, by process, and by reinforcement perspectives on motivation?

2. Evaluate Tandem Computers' reward system and explain why it works.

3. Would this approach to motivation work in all organizations? Why or why not?

4. How might Tandem adjust its reward system to fit a larger, more formal organization without sacrificing the key advantages of its present system?

CASE REFERENCES

"Beyond the Better Mousetrap (Tandem Computers Personnel Management Works Wonders)." *Forbes,* June 22, 1981, p. 58.

"Data Processing: What Makes Tandem Run." *Business Week,* July 14, 1980, p. 73.

Magnet, Myron. "Managing by Mystique at Tandem Computers." *Fortune,* June 28, 1982, pp. 84–91.

C A S E   13.2

Hudson Incorporated is a midwestern manufacturer of men's hats. Hudson was founded around 60 years ago by Adam Hudson and is presently owned and managed by his daughter Susan. The plant has a work force of around 300 full-time employees. In addition there are 23 managers and 42 sales representatives. The sales representatives work on commission and the managers are all salaried. The plant employees, all of whom belong to a union, are paid by the hour.

The hat industry has fallen on hard times in recent years. Few men wear dress hats these days, and Hudson has survived primarily by virtue of three big military contracts for supplying hats to the army and the navy. Hudson has struggled nonetheless, and is at present only marginally profitable.

In two months the existing labor contract expires and a new one will have to be negotiated. Hudson feels it simply cannot afford to increase hourly wages and still remain in business, but the union has indicated that it intends to take a hard line. Its members have not had a raise in two years, and their average pay rate is now almost $1.00 an hour below the industry average.

Susan Hudson and her personnel manager have recently been working long hours in an attempt to develop a proposal that will, on the one hand, allow the business to remain reasonably solvent and, on the other hand, satisfy union demands for increased pay. The basic components of the proposal are as follows:

1. The work force will be reduced from 300 to 250 employees.
2. The existing compensation system will be revamped to more clearly relate pay to performance. In particular, standards for each job will be developed. Producing at or below the standard established will pay 15 percent below the existing rate. Per-unit financial incentives will be added for each hat processed above that standard. The incentive system will be set up such that a 10 percent increase in output will pay the same as the present rate and further increases in output will pay progressively more.

In return for these changes, Hudson is prepared to offer two other major contract points.

1. The company will agree that no further cutbacks will be made in the size of the work force.
2. If company profits exceed $200,000 in any given year, 10 percent of all profits will be distributed back to the plant employees.

The union has seen a draft of the company's proposal and, though there are some reservations, it will probably be accepted. Union

representatives have also indicated that, if workers have not averaged at least a 20 percent wage increase at the end of the new
contract period, the new system must be scrapped.

CASE
QUESTIONS
1. What motivation theories and concepts can you identify in this case?
2. What kinds of motivational problems might Hudson encounter in the
future?

14

LEADERSHIP IN ORGANIZATIONS

1. Distinguish among power, influence, authority, and leadership, list the five kinds of power, and define leadership.

2. Explain the concept of leadership traits and comment on their validity.

3. Describe the leadership-behavior approach to leadership, identify the two most commonly discussed behaviors, and comment on the primary weakness of the behavioral approach.

4. Describe the rationale for situational models of leadership and fully discuss the contingency, path–goal, and Vroom–Yetton theories.

5. Explain the direction of causality as a perspective on leadership, and identify various substitutes for leadership.

6. Discuss the relationship of political behavior to power, explain why politics is so pervasive in organizations, and cite three ways of managing it.

CHAPTER OUTLINE

415

OPENING INCIDENT

You are somewhat of an elder statesman of management. After building a solid record of effective leadership and management in a variety of settings, you have just accepted your greatest challenge. Specifically, you have taken a position as CEO of a large, nationalized British firm that is losing $4 million a day. Productivity is low, morale is atrocious, and the company is in a shambles. How would you proceed?

Leadership is without doubt one of the most talked about, written about, and researched topics in the field of management.[1] Indeed, the process of leading is one of the four basic management functions around which this book is organized. Leadership is one of those elusive attributes that separate effective managers from less effective managers. Yet, for all of this, little is known about the leadership process.

Historians note the exemplary leadership of Washington, Roosevelt, and Churchill; Hitler and Jim Jones were equally effective in their own way. In the world of professional sports, Billy Martin has become a legend for taking mediocre baseball teams and turning them into winners—only to be fired after two or three seasons. Fred Silverman was extremely successful as head of first CBS and then ABC, yet NBC later fired him. In 1980 *Fortune* magazine enshrined Frederick Coolidge Crawford, a founder of TRW, in its Hall of Fame for Business Leadership, citing his belief in cooperation and communication. In the same issue, the magazine described the success of Harold Geneen at ITT, who set unrealistically high goals, drove his managers to meet them, and publicly humiliated those who failed.[2]

Despite a great deal of research on leadership, management theorists cannot explain these contradictions and inconsistencies. Then why devote an entire chapter to the topic? Because leadership is such an important part of the management process, it is better to know *something* about it than nothing at all.

In the first section, we define and describe the nature of leadership, including an analysis of power. The next three sections discuss trait, behavioral, and contingency theories of leadership. Finally, we examine some contemporary perspectives on leadership, including a discussion of politics and political behavior in organizations.

1. Bernard M. Bass, *Stogdill's Handbook of Leadership*, rev. ed. (Riverside, N.J.: Free Press, 1981).
2. Donald D. Holt, "The Hall of Fame for Business Leadership," *Fortune*, April 21, 1980, pp. 101–109; and Hugh D. Menzies, "The Ten Toughest Bosses," *Fortune*, April 21, 1980, pp. 62–73.

The nature of leadership

Leadership derives from power and is similar to, yet distinct from, management. After developing a definition of leadership, we will discuss these issues.

A definition of leadership

To develop a useful definition of leadership, we must first understand three related concepts: power, influence, and authority. *Power* is the potential ability to affect the behavior of others. As we shall see later, power is generally related to the control of valued or scarce resources. *Influence* exists when a person consciously or unconsciously exercises power to affect the behavior or attitudes of someone else. *Authority* is power created and granted by an organization. If the organizational chart specifies that Mary is the boss and Tom is the subordinate, Mary has authority over Tom. Of course, subordinates must acknowledge and accept the authority of their superior in order for it to have any real meaning. Within the context of the organization, Mary also has power and influence. Outside the organization, she might not have any power or influence over Tom at all.

Leadership, then, can be defined as the ability to influence others. Leaders have both power and influence. They may or may not have authority. Management and leadership may overlap to varying degrees—a point we will soon explain in more detail. First, however, we must explore the concept of power and see how it serves as a foundation for leadership.

Power and leadership

Power is the potential ability to affect the behavior of others. Note in particular the word *potential*. It suggests that one can have power without actually using it. For example, a football coach has the power to bench a player who is not performing up to par. The coach seldom has to actually use this power, because the players recognize that the power exists and work hard to keep their starting positions.

In organizational settings, there are usually five kinds of power: legitimate, reward, coercive, referent, and expert power.[3] These bases of power are summarized in Table 14.1. A manager may have one or more of these kinds of power.

Legitimate power. Legitimate power is power granted through the organizational hierarchy, so the power that occupying each position confers is part of the way that position is defined. A boss can tell a subordinate to do something, and, if the subordinate refuses, he or she can be reprimanded or even fired. Such outcomes stem from the boss's legitimate power as defined

3. John R. P. French and Bertram Raven, "The Bases of Social Power," in Dorwin Cartwright (ed.), *Studies in Social Power* (Ann Arbor, Mich.: University of Michigan Press, 1959), pp. 150–167.

Table 14.1 The five bases of power

1. **Legitimate power.** Power granted by the hierarchy.
2. **Reward power.** Power to give or withhold rewards.
3. **Coercive power.** Power to punish.
4. **Referent power.** Power through identification, initiation, or charisma.
5. **Expert power.** Power through information or expertise.

and vested in her or him by the organization. Legitimate power, then, is the same as authority. All managers have legitimate power over their subordinates. The mere possession of legitimate power, however, does not by itself make someone a leader. In many cases, subordinates follow only orders that are strictly within the letter of organizational rules and policies. If asked to do something outside their defined domain, they refuse or do a slipshod job. In such cases, the manager is exercising authority but not leadership.

Reward power. Reward power is the power to give or withhold rewards. Rewards that may be under the control of an individual manager include salary increases, bonuses, promotion recommendations, praise, recognition, and interesting job assignments. In general, the greater the number of rewards controlled by a manager and the more important the rewards are to subordinates, the greater the manager's reward power.

Coercive power. Coercive power is the power to force compliance via psychological, emotional, or physical threat. In some isolated settings, coercion can take the form of physical punishment. Examples include the military, prisons, and ship yards, where first-line supervisors occasionally strike or beat subordinates until they comply or as punishment for breaking rules and regulations. In most organizations, however, the available means of coercion are limited to verbal reprimands, written reprimands, disciplinary layoffs, fines, demotion, and termination. Some managers occasionally go so far as to use verbal abuse, humiliation, and psychological coercion in an attempt to manipulate subordinates. The former chairman of Beatrice Foods Company once told a subordinate that, if his wife and family got in the way of his working a twenty-four-hours-a-day, seven-days-a-week job, he should get rid of them.[4] The more punitive elements under a manager's control and the more important they are to subordinates, the more coercive power the manager possesses. On the other hand, the more a manager uses coercive power, the more likely he or she is to provoke resentment and hostility.

Referent power. Compared to legitimate, reward, and coercive power, which are relatively concrete and grounded in objective facets of organizational life, referent power is more abstract. It is based on identification, imitation, or charisma. That is, followers may react favorably to a leader because they identify in some way with the leader, who may be like them in personality, back-

4. Menzies, ''The Ten Toughest Bosses.''

ground, or attitudes. In other situations, followers might choose to imitate a leader with referent power by wearing the same kinds of clothes, working the same hours, or espousing the same management philosophy. Referent power may also take the form of charisma, an intangible attribute in the leader's personality that inspires loyalty and enthusiasm.

Expert power. Expert power is derived from information or expertise. A manager who knows how to deal with an eccentric but important customer, a scientist who is capable of achieving an important technical breakthrough that no other company has dreamed of, and a secretary who knows how to unravel bureaucratic red tape—all have expert power over anyone who needs that information. The more important the information and the fewer the people who have access to it, the greater the degree of expert power possessed by any one individual.

The uses of power

Gary Yukl has identified a variety of ways in which a manager can use power. Most of them depend on what kinds of power are available to the manager.[5]

Legitimate request. The legitimate request is based on legitimate power. It simply involves the manager requesting that the subordinate do something within the normal range of the job. The subordinate complies because he or she recognizes that the organization has given the manager the right to make the request. Most day-to-day interactions between manager and subordinate are of this type.

Instrumental compliance. This form of exchange is based primarily on reward power, and it bears out the reinforcement theory of motivation. Suppose that a manager asks a subordinate to do something outside the range of the subordinate's normal duties, such as working extra hours on the weekend, terminating a relationship with a long-standing buyer, or delivering bad news. The subordinate complies and, as a direct result, reaps praise and a bonus from the manager. The next time the subordinate is asked to perform a similar activity, that subordinate will recognize that compliance will be instrumental in her or his getting more rewards. Hence the basis of instrumental compliance is clarifying important performance–reward contingencies.

Coercion. As the term suggests, coercion rests on coercive power. When the manager suggests or implies that the subordinate will be punished, fired, or reprimanded if he or she does not do something, coercion is being practiced.

Rational persuasion. Rational persuasion occurs when the manager can convince the subordinate that compliance is in the subordinate's best interests. For example, a manager might argue that the subordinate should (or

---

5. Gary A. Yukl, *Leadership in Organizations* (Englewood Cliffs, N.J.: Prentice-Hall, 1981), pp. 10–17.

should not) accept a transfer because it would (or would not) be good for the subordinate's career. In some ways, rational persuasion is similar to reward power, except that the manager does not really control the reward. Elements of expert power are also present in that the manager may be seen as a knowledgeable person.

Personal identification. A manager who recognizes that he or she has referent power over a subordinate can shape the behavior of that subordinate by engaging in desired behaviors. That is, the manager consciously becomes a model for the subordinate and exploits personal identification.

Inspirational appeal. Sometimes a manager can induce someone to do something because it is consistent with a set of higher ideals or values. For example, a plea for loyalty represents an inspirational appeal. Referent power plays a role in determining the extent to which an inspirational appeal is successful, because its effectiveness depends at least in part on the persuasive abilities of the leader.

Information distortion. A dubious method of using power is through information distortion. The idea here is that the manager withholds or distorts information in order to influence subordinates' behavior. For example, if a manager has agreed to allow everyone to participate in choosing a new group member but subsequently finds one individual whom he or she really prefers, he or she might withhold some of the credentials of other qualified applicants so that the desired member is selected. This use of power is dangerous. Beyond the fact that it may be unethical, if subordinates find out the manager has deliberately misled them, they will lose their confidence and trust in that manager's leadership.

Management versus leadership

It is sometimes difficult to distinguish between management and leadership. Basically, management is founded on legitimate, reward, and coercive power. Followers comply with orders and directions but are not necessarily committed to them. Leadership may also draw on legitimate, reward, or coercive power, but it usually depends more on referent and expert power. Hence *a person may be either a manager or a leader without being the other*. In an organization, a manager may be able to use legitimate requests and coercion to get things done but may be drawing purely on his or her authority. This person is a manager but might not qualify as a leader. In other situations, someone with no authority at all may be able to use personal identification or inspirational appeal to influence people's behavior. This individual is a leader but may not be a manager.

From the standpoint of organizational effectiveness, it is clearly preferable to have managers who are also good leaders. This explains much of the preoccupation with leadership in both management theory and practice: organizations want to understand leadership so that they can increase the number of their people who are both managers and leaders.

Leadership traits

The first organized approach to studying leadership was to analyze the personality traits of strong leaders. The underlying assumption of the trait approach was that there existed some basic trait or set of traits that differentiated leaders from nonleaders. If those traits could be defined, potential leaders could be identified. It was thought that *leadership traits* might include intelligence, assertiveness, above-average height, good vocabulary, attractiveness, self-confidence, and similar attributes.[6]

During the first several decades of this century, literally hundreds of studies were conducted in an attempt to identify important leadership traits. For the most part, the results of these studies were disappointing. For every set of leaders who possess a common trait, a long list of exceptions was also found, and the list of suggested traits soon grew so long that it had little practical value. Alternative explanations usually existed even for those relationships that did appear valid. For example, it was observed that many leaders have good communication skills and are assertive. Rather than those traits being the cause of leadership, however, it might be that successful leaders begin to display those traits *after* they have achieved leadership positions.

Most researchers have given up trying to identify traits as predictors of leadership ability. However, many people still explicitly or implicitly adopt a trait orientation. For example, politicians are all too often elected on the basis of personal appearance, speaking ability, or an aura of self-confidence.

Leadership behaviors

Spurred on by their lack of success in identifying useful leadership traits, researchers soon began to investigate other variables, especially the behaviors or actions of leaders. The new hypothesis was that the behaviors of effective leaders were somehow different from the behaviors of less effective leaders, and the goal was to develop a fuller understanding of *leadership behaviors.*

The Michigan studies

Researchers at the University of Michigan, especially Rensis Likert, began studying leadership in the late 1940s.[7] Via extensive interviews with both leaders and followers (that is, managers and subordinates) the *Michigan studies* identified two basic forms of leader behavior.

1. **Job-centered leader behavior.** The leader practices close supervision so that performance can be closely monitored and controlled. The leader draws from legitimate, reward, and coercive bases of power. A leader who pays close attention to the work of subordinates, explains what to

6. See Bass, *Stogdill's Handbook of Leadership.*

7. See Rensis Likert, *New Patterns of Management* (New York: McGraw-Hill, 1961); and Rensis Likert, *The Human Organization* (New York: McGraw-Hill, 1967).

Figure 14.1
The University of
Michigan view of
leader behaviors

JOB-CENTERED
LEADER BEHAVIOR

EMPLOYEE-CENTERED
LEADER BEHAVIOR

do, and is primarily interested in performance is exhibiting job-centered behavior.

2. **Employee-centered leader behavior.** The leader demonstrates concern for the well-being of subordinates. In particular, the focus is on group formation and development and employee growth and participation. A leader who is interested in developing a cohesive work group and ensuring that employees are basically satisfied with their jobs can be described as employee-centered.

Figure 14.1 presents the early Michigan view of leader behavior. Note in particular that the two styles of leader behavior are presumed to be at opposite ends of a continuum. A leader may be either job-centered *or* employee-centered, but not both. Likert has suggested that employee-centered leader behavior generally tends to be more effective. We should also note the similarities between Likert's leadership research and his Systems 1 through 4 organization design (discussed in Chapter 11). Job-centered leader behavior is associated with the System 1 design, whereas employee-centered leader behavior is more consistent with the System 4 design. When Likert talks about moving organizations from System 1 to System 4, he is also advocating a transition from job-centered to employee-centered leader behavior.

The Ohio State studies

At about the same time that Likert was beginning his leadership work at Michigan, a group of researchers at Ohio State also began studying leadership.[8] The extensive questionnaire surveys conducted during the *Ohio State studies* suggested that there are two basic leader behaviors or styles.

1. **Initiating-structure behavior.** The leader organizes the work and defines for subordinates what each is supposed to do. The leader initiates the structure needed to perform the job. For example, if a leader summarizes the job for her or his subordinates, then breaks it down into steps, assigns various steps to each subordinate, and finally pulls everything back together in the end, he or she is initiating structure.

2. **Consideration behavior.** The leader shows concern for subordinates and attempts to establish a warm, friendly, and supportive climate. A leader

8. The Ohio State studies stimulated many articles, monographs, and books. A good overall reference is Ralph M. Stogdill and A. E. Coons (eds.), *Leader Behavior: Its Description and Measurement* (Columbus, Ohio: Bureau of Business Research, Ohio State University, 1957).

Figure 14.2
The Ohio State view
of leader behaviors

who is sensitive to an employee's feelings and who is legitimately concerned that employees be treated fairly and as human beings probably exhibits considerate behavior.

The job-centered and employee-centered behaviors identified at Michigan are similar to the initiating-structure and consideration behaviors recognized at Ohio State, but there are also significant differences. The most obvious difference is that the forms of leader behavior are not seen by the Ohio State researchers as being at opposite ends of a single continuum. Rather, they are assumed to be independent variables. A leader can exhibit varying levels of initiating structure and *at the same time* varying levels of consideration. Figure 14.2 shows the Ohio State view of leader behavior.

At first the Ohio State researchers thought that leaders who exhibit high levels of both behaviors tend to be more effective than other leaders. A study at International Harvester, however, suggested a more complicated pattern.[9] It found that employees of supervisors who ranked high on initiating structure were higher performers but that they expressed lower levels of satisfaction. Conversely, employees of supervisors who ranked high on consideration had lower performance ratings but also had fewer absences from work. Later research has isolated other variables that make consistent prediction difficult.

The Managerial Grid

In Chapter 12 we discussed an organization development technique called the *Managerial Grid*®.[10] We can now see that the basis of the Managerial Grid is two forms of leader behavior: concern for people (similar to employee-centered and consideration behaviors) and concern for production (similar to

9. Edwin A. Fleishman, E. F. Harris, and H. E. Burtt, *Leadership and Supervision in Industry* (Columbus, Ohio: Bureau of Educational Research, Ohio State University, 1955).

10. Robert R. Blake and Jane S. Mouton, *The Managerial Grid* (Houston: Gulf Publishing, 1964). See also Robert R. Blake and Jane S. Mouton, *The Versatile Manager: A Grid Profile* (Homewood, Il.: Dow Jones–Irwin, 1981).

job-centered and initiating-structure behaviors). By combining the two forms of behavior, the Managerial Grid offers a way to analyze leader behavior in ongoing organizations. Note that the Managerial Grid, like the Michigan and Ohio State frameworks, implies that there is one generally appropriate combination of leader behaviors—the 9,9 coordinates, or maximum concern for both people and production.

The personal behavior theories have played an important role in the development of contemporary thinking about leadership. In particular, they urge us not to be preoccupied with what leaders *are* (the trait approach) but to concentrate on what leaders *do* (their behaviors). Unfortunately, these theories fell prey to the problem of universalism along the way. When we are dealing with complex social systems composed of complex individuals, there are few if any consistently predictable relationships, and certainly there are no infallible formulas for success. Yet the personal behavior theorists tried to identify consistent relationships between leader behaviors and employee responses, in the hope of finding a dependable prescription for effective leadership. As we might expect, they often failed.

Other approaches to understanding leadership were needed. The catalyst for these new approaches was the realization that, although interpersonal and task-oriented dimensions might be useful ways to *describe* the behavior of leaders, they were not very useful for predicting or prescribing it. The next step in the evolution of leadership theory was the creation of situational models.

Situational approaches to leadership

The basic assumption of the situational models is that appropriate leader behavior varies from one situation to another. The goal of a *situational theory*, then, is to identify key situational factors and to specify how they interact to determine appropriate leader behavior. Several excellent examples of the situational nature of leadership stand out in the biography of former President Lyndon B. Johnson. During his stint in the U.S. Senate, Johnson had an uncanny knack for understanding every other senator's strengths, weaknesses, political aspirations, and self-image. He then tailored his interactions with each one to capitalize on his grasp of that person's make-up. As a result, he was soon designated Senate Democratic majority leader and ultimately inherited the White House.[11] Before discussing the three major situational theories, we should first note an important early model that laid the foundation for subsequent developments.

In 1958 Robert Tannenbaum and Warren H. Schmidt proposed a continuum of leader behavior in the decision-making process; their model is much like the original Michigan framework.[12] However, besides purely job-centered

11. Doris Kearns, *Lyndon Johnson and the American Dream* (New York: Harper & Row, 1976).

12. See Robert Tannenbaum and Warren H. Schmidt, ''How to Choose a Leadership Pattern,'' *Harvard Business Review*, March–April 1958, pp. 95–101.

behavior (or "boss-centered" behavior, as they termed it) and employee-centered behavior, they identified several intermediate possibilities a manager might consider. The range of possibilities, including both end points, is as follows:

1. The manager makes a decision and announces it to the group. This is the most authoritarian behavior.
2. The manager makes a decision and "sells" it to the group. This option offers subordinates a small degree of freedom—the freedom to at least try to reject the manager's decision.
3. The manager presents ideas and invites questions but retains the final word on the decision.
4. The manager presents a tentative decision subject to change.
5. The manager presents a problem, gets suggestions, and then makes the decision.
6. The manager sets relatively narrow limits and then asks the group to make the decision. That is, although the group makes the decision, the decision context is still defined by the manager.
7. The manager sets broad limits and then permits the group to function within those limits. This option offers subordinates the greatest amount of freedom in that they also define the decision context.

This continuum of behavior moves from the extreme of having the manager make the decision alone to the other extreme of having the employees make the decision with minimal guidance.

Each point on the continuum is influenced by factors relating manager, subordinates, and situation. Managerial factors include the manager's value system, confidence in subordinates, personal inclinations, and feelings of security. Subordinate factors include the subordinates' need for independence, readiness to assume responsibility, tolerance for ambiguity, interest in the problem, understanding of goals, knowledge, experience, and expectations. Situational factors that affect decision making include the type of organization, group effectiveness, the problem itself, and time pressures.

Although the Tannenbaum and Schmidt framework pointed out the importance of situational factors, it was simply descriptive. It remained for others to develop more comprehensive and integrated theories. In the following sections, we will describe the three most important and most widely accepted situational theories of leadership: the contingency theory, the path–goal theory, and the Vroom–Yetton model.

The contingency theory

The *contingency theory* of leadership was developed by Fred Fiedler.[13] Beginning with a leadership behavior approach, Fiedler identifies two styles of leadership, task-oriented (analogous to job-centered and initiating-structure behavior) and relationship-oriented (similar to employee-centered and

13. See Fred E. Fiedler, *A Theory of Leadership Effectiveness* (New York: McGraw-Hill, 1967).

consideration behavior). However, he goes beyond the leadership behavior approaches by arguing that the style of leader behavior is a reflection of the leader's personality and is basically constant for any person. That is, a leader is presumed to be task-oriented *or* relationship-oriented all of the time.

Fiedler measures leader style via a controversial questionnaire called the least preferred co-worker (LPC) measure. Each manager or leader is asked to describe the person with whom he or she is able to work least well, her or his LPC, by filling in a set of 16 scales anchored at each end by a positive or negative adjective. For example, three of the scales Fiedler uses in the LPC are:

Helpful	__	__	__	__	__	__	__	__	Frustrating
	8	7	6	5	4	3	2	1	
Tense	__	__	__	__	__	__	__	__	Relaxed
	1	2	3	4	5	6	7	8	
Boring	__	__	__	__	__	__	__	__	Interesting
	1	2	3	4	5	6	7	8	

The leader's LPC score is then calculated by adding up the numbers below the line checked on each scale.

Note in these three examples that the higher numbers are associated with the "good" words (helpful, relaxed, and interesting), whereas the "bad" words (frustrating, tense, and boring) have low point values. A high total score is assumed to reflect a relationship orientation and a low score a task orientation on the part of the leader.

We noted that the LPC measure is controversial; researchers disagree on its validity. Some of them question exactly what an LPC measure reflects and whether the score is an index of behavior, personality, or some other unknown factor.[14]

Favorableness of the situation. The underlying assumption of situational models of leadership is that appropriate leader behavior varies from one situation to another. According to Fiedler, the key situational factor is the favorableness of the situation from the leader's point of view. And this factor, in turn, is determined by three things: leader–member relations, task structure, and position power.

Leader–member relations refer to the nature of the relationship between the leader and the work group. If the leader and the group have a high degree of mutual trust, respect, and confidence, and if they like one another, relations are assumed to be good. If there is little trust, respect, or confidence, and if they do not like one another, relations are assumed to be bad. Good relations are assumed to be favorable and bad relations unfavorable.

14. For a recent critique, see Chester A. Schriesheim, B. D. Bannister, and W. H. Money, "Psychometric Properties of the LPC Scale: An Extension of Rice's Review," *Academy of Management Review*, April 1979, pp. 287–294. An earlier, more thorough review is George Graen, K. Alvares, J. B. Orris, and J. A. Martella, "A Contingency Model of Leadership Effectiveness: Antecedent and Evidential Results," *Psychological Bulletin*, Vol. 74, 1970, pp. 285–295.

Task structure refers to the degree to which the group's task is well defined. When the task is routine, easily understood, and unambiguous, and when the group has standard procedures and precedents to rely on, structure is assumed to be high. A task with low structure is the opposite: nonroutine, ambiguous, and complex, with no standard procedures or precedents. High structure results is a more favorable position for the leader; low structure is more unfavorable. For example, if task structure is low, the group won't know what to do and the leader will have to play a major role in guiding and directing its activities. If task structure is high, the leader won't have to get so involved and can devote time to other activities.

Position power is the power vested in the leader's position. If the leader has the power to assign work, reward and punish employees, and recommend them for promotion or demotion, position power is assumed to be strong. If the leader must get job assignments approved by someone else, does not administer rewards and punishment, and has no voice in promotions or demotions, position power is weak. From the leader's point of view, strong position power is clearly favorable and weak position power is unfavorable.

Favorableness and leader style. Fiedler and his associates have conducted numerous studies linking the favorableness of various situations to leader style and group effectiveness.[15] The results of these studies are shown in Figure 14.3.

To interpret the model, look first at the situational factors at the bottom of the figure. Note that good/bad leader–member relations, high/low task structure, and strong/weak position power can be combined to yield eight unique situations. For example, good relations, high structure, and strong position power (at the left of the continuum) are presumed to define the most favorable situation; poor relations, low structure, and weak power (at the right of the continuum) the least favorable situation; and other combinations intermediate levels of favorableness.

Above each situation is shown the form of leader behavior found to be most strongly associated with effective group performance in that situation. When the situation is such that relations are good, structure is high, and power is strong, Fiedler has found that a task-oriented leader is most effective. However, when relations are good but task structure is low and position power is weak, a relationship-oriented leader is predicted to be most effective. Note that a task-oriented leader is supposedly effective when the situation is very favorable *and* when the situation is very unfavorable. The relationship-oriented style is most effective under the intermediate conditions.

Flexibility of leader style. A final point about Fiedler's theory concerns his view of the inflexibility of leader style. Fiedler argues that, because leader behavior is presumed by his theory to be a personality trait, it is essentially

---

15. See Fiedler, *A Theory of Leadership Effectiveness*. See also Fred E. Fiedler and M. M. Chemers, *Leadership and Effective Management* (Glenview, Il.: Scott, Foresman, 1974).

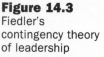

Figure 14.3
Fiedler's
contingency theory
of leadership

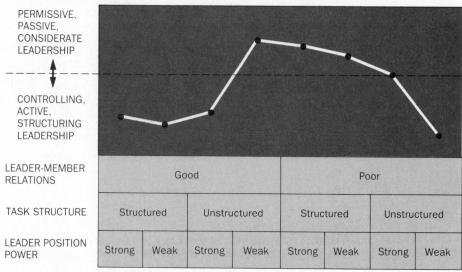

Source: Fred E. Fiedler, "The Effects of Leadership Training and Experience: A
Contingency Model Interpretation," *Administrative Science Quarterly*, December
1972, p. 455. Used with permission.

fixed and cannot be changed. That is, a leader cannot change her or his behavior to fit a particular situation. According to Fiedler, leaders are either task-oriented or relationship-oriented.

When a leader's style and the situation do not match, Fiedler argues that the situation should be changed to fit the leader's style.[16] For example, when leader–member relations are good, task structure low, and position power weak, the leader style most likely to be effective is relationship–oriented. If the leader is task–oriented, a mismatch exists. According to Fiedler, the elements of the situation should be made more congruent by structuring the task (by developing guidelines and procedures, for instance) and increasing power (by requesting additional authority or by other means).

Fiedler's contingency theory has been attacked on the grounds that it is not always supported by research, that his findings are subject to other interpretations, that the LPC measure lacks validity, and that his assumptions about the inflexibility of leader behavior are unrealistic.[17] On the other hand, Fiedler's theory was one of the first to adopt a situational perspective on leadership. It has helped many managers recognize the important situational factors they must contend with.

16. See Fred E. Fiedler, "Engineering the Job to Fit the Manager," *Harvard Business Review*, September–October 1965, pp. 115–122.
17. See Schriesheim et al., "Psychometric Properties of the LPC Scale"; Graen et al., "A Contingency Model of Leadership Effectiveness"; and J. Timothy McMahon, "The Contingency Theory: Logic and Method Revisited," *Personnel Psychology*, 1972, pp. 697–711.

The path–goal theory

The path–goal theory of leadership, which is associated most closely with Martin Evans and Robert House,[18] is a direct extension of the expectancy theory of motivation discussed in Chapter 13.[19] Recall that the primary components of expectancy theory included the likelihood of attaining various outcomes and the value associated with those outcomes. The *path–goal theory* of leadership suggests that the primary functions of a leader are to make valued or desired rewards available in the workplace and to clarify for the subordinate the kinds of behavior that will lead to goal accomplishment and valued rewards. That is, the leader should clarify the paths to goal attainment.

Leader behaviors. The current version of path–goal theory identifies four kinds of leader behavior.[20]

1. **Directive leader behavior.** Letting subordinates know what is expected of them, giving guidance and direction, and scheduling work (similar to initiating-structure and task-oriented behavior).
2. **Supportive leader behavior.** Being friendly and approachable, showing concern for subordinate welfare, and treating members as equals (similar to consideration and relationship-oriented behavior).
3. **Participative leader behavior.** Consulting subordinates, soliciting suggestions, and allowing participation in decision making.
4. **Achievement-oriented leader behavior.** Setting challenging goals, expecting subordinates to perform at high levels, encouraging them, and showing confidence in subordinates' abilities.

In contrast to Fiedler's theory, the path–goal theory assumes that leaders can change their style or behavior to meet the demands of a particular situation. For example, when encountering a new group of subordinates and a new project, a leader may be directive in establishing task structure and in outlining what has to be done. Next, he or she may adopt supportive behavior in an effort to foster group cohesiveness and a positive climate. As the group becomes more familiar with the task and as new problems are encountered, the leader may exhibit participative behavior. Finally, achievement-oriented behavior may be used to encourage continued high performance.

Situational factors. Like other situational theories of leadership, the path–goal theory suggests that appropriate leader style depends on situational factors. Two general categories of situational factors that receive special attention in path–goal theory are the personal characteristics of subordinates and the environmental characteristics of the workplace.

18. See Martin G. Evans, "The Effects of Supervisory Behavior on the Path–Goal Relationship," *Organizational Behavior and Human Performance*, May 1970, pp. 277–298; and Robert J. House and Terence R. Mitchell, "Path–Goal Theory of Leadership," *Journal of Contemporary Business*, Autumn 1974, pp. 81–98.

19. See Victor Vroom, *Work and Motivation* (New York: Wiley, 1964).

20. See House and Mitchell, "Path–Goal Theory of Leadership."

Two important personal characteristics are the subordinate's perception of her or his own ability and her or his locus of control. If people perceive that they are lacking in ability, they may prefer directive leadership in order to better understand path–goal relationships. If their perceptions of their ability are high, however, employees may resent directive leadership. Locus of control is a personality trait. People who have an internal locus of control believe that what happens to them is a function of their own efforts and behaviors. Those who have an external locus of control assume that fate or luck or "the system" determines what happens to them. A person with an internal locus of control may prefer participative leadership, whereas a person with an external locus of control may prefer directive leadership. Managers can do little or nothing to influence the personal characteristics of subordinates, but they can shape the environment to take advantage of these personal characteristics.

Environmental characteristics include factors outside the subordinate's control. Task structure is one such factor. When structure is high, directive leadership is less effective than when structure is low. Subordinates do not usually need their boss to continually tell them how to do an extremely routine job. The formal authority system is another important environmental characteristic. Again, the higher the degree of formality, the less directive leader behavior will be accepted by subordinates. The nature of the work group also affects appropriate leader behavior. When the work group provides the individual with social support and satisfaction, supportive leader behavior is less critical. On the other hand, when social support and satisfaction cannot be derived from the group, the individual may look to the leader for this support.

The basic path–goal framework as illustrated in Figure 14.4 shows that leader behaviors affect subordinate motivation to perform. Personal and environmental characteristics influence the nature of this relationship.

Figure 14.4
The path–goal
framework

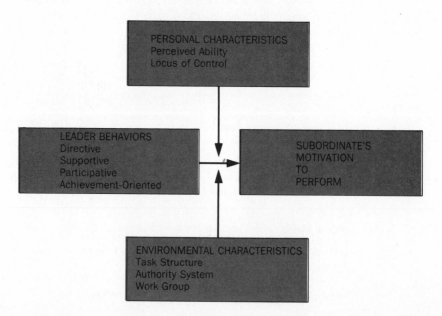

The path–goal theory of leadership is a dynamic and incomplete model at this time. The original intent was to state the theory in general terms so that a variety of interrelationships could be explored and the theory modified as a result of future research findings. Note, for example, that nothing is said about achievement-oriented leader behavior in the present version of the theory. Research that has been done suggests that the path–goal theory is a reasonably good description of the leadership process and that future investigations along these lines should enable us to discover more about the link between leadership and motivation.[21]

The Vroom–Yetton model

The final situational theory of leadership we will discuss is the *Vroom–Yetton model.*[22] This model is somewhat narrower than the other two situational theories. Drawing from the Tannenbaum and Schmidt framework summarized earlier,[23] this model focuses on how much participation subordinates should be allowed in various decision-making activities. More specifically, the model predicts what kinds of situations call for various degrees of group participation. The Vroom–Yetton model, then, sets norms or standards for including subordinates in decision making.

The Vroom–Yetton model argues that decision effectiveness is best gauged by the quality of the decision and by decision acceptance. Decision quality is the objective effect of the decision on employee performance. Decision acceptance is the extent to which employees accept and are committed to the decision. To maximize decision effectiveness, the Vroom–Yetton model suggests that managers adopt one of five decision-making styles, depending on the situation. As summarized in Table 14.2, there are two autocratic styles (AI and AII), two consultative styles (CI and CII), and one group style (GII).

In determining which style of decision making to adopt in a particular situation, Vroom and Yetton suggest that the manager be guided by the answers to a set of seven questions.

A. Is there a quality requirement in the situation? If so, the manager must seek an alternative that will provide the needed quality.

B. Does the manager have enough information to reach a high-quality decision? If not, some degree of employee input is clearly appropriate.

C. Is the situation structured? That is, can the manager identify the required information and determine how to get it?

D. Is acceptance of the decision by subordinates crucial for effective implementation? If so, subordinate input is very important.

---

21. See Chester Schriesheim and Steve Kerr, "Theories and Measures of Leadership: A Critical Appraisal of Current and Future Directives," in J. G. Hunt and C. C. Larson (eds.), *Leadership: The Cutting Edge* (Carbondale, Il.: Southern Illinois University Press, 1977).

22. See Victor H. Vroom and Philip H. Yetton, *Leadership and Decision Making* (Pittsburgh, Penn.: University of Pittsburgh Press, 1973).

23. See Tannenbaum and Schmidt, "How to Choose a Leadership Pattern."

Table 14.2 Decision styles in the Vroom–Yetton model

Decision style	Definition
AI	Manager makes the decision alone.
AII	Manager asks for information from subordinates but makes the decision alone. Subordinates may or may not be informed about what the situation is.
CI	Manager shares the situation with individual subordinates and asks for information and evaluation. Subordinates do not meet as a group, and the manager alone makes the decision.
CII	Manager and subordinates meet as a group to discuss the situation but the manager makes the decision.
GII	Manager and subordinates meet as a group to discuss the situation, and the group makes the decision.

A = autocratic; C = consultative; G = group

Source: Reprinted from *Leadership and Decision-Making* by Victor H. Vroom and Philip H. Yetton by permission of the University of Pittsburgh Press. © 1973 by the University of Pittsburgh Press.

E. If the manager makes the decision alone, will subordinates be likely to accept the decision? If not, more participation may be in order.

F. Do subordinates share the organizational goals that will be reached as a result of this decision?

G. If the preferred solution is reached, is conflict among subordinates likely?

A careful reading and analysis of these questions will show that some of them are clearly aimed at maintaining decision quality (especially questions A, B, and C), whereas the others (questions D, E, F, and G) focus on enhancing subordinate acceptance.

As a guide for answering and interpreting the results of each question, Vroom and Yetton have developed a flow chart for managers. This flow chart is reproduced in Figure 14.5. The manager first carefully analyzes her or his particular decision situation and then answers the seven questions "yes" or "no" in sequence. Each answer suggests a particular path along the flow chart. At the end of each path is a list of various decision styles appropriate for achieving both decision quality and decision acceptance in that particular situation.

For example, the manager may decide that there is a quality requirement and therefore proceed from A to B along the "yes" path. Next the manager might recognize that he or she does not have sufficient information and therefore move along the "no" path to question C. Similarly, a "no" to the structure question, a "yes" to the acceptance likelihood question, a "no" to the goal consequence question, and a "no" to the conflict question ultimately lead the manager to the CII decision style.

Some paths result in more than one appropriate style. In these instances, Vroom and Yetton suggest that the manager adopt the style that is least costly in money and time. To date, the Vroom–Yetton model has worked fairly well

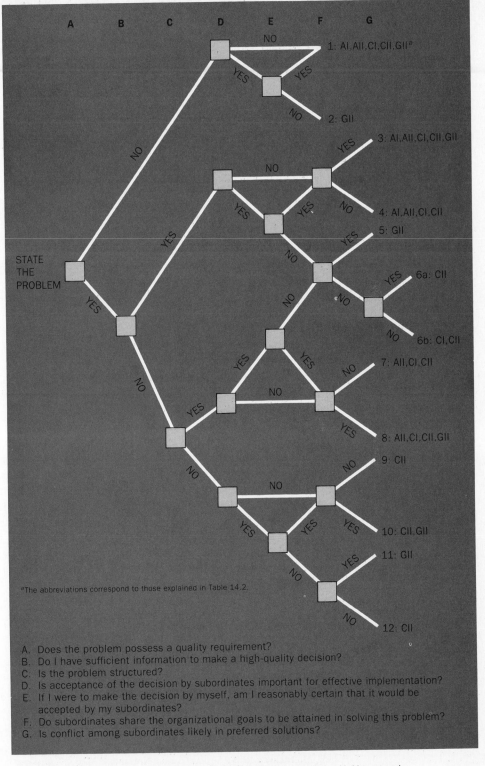

Figure 14.5
The Vroom–Yetton model

A   B   C   D   E   F   G

NO
1: AI,AII,CI,CII,GII[a]
YES   YES
NO
2: GII

YES
3: AI,AII,CI,CII,GII
NO
NO
4: AI,AII,CI,CII
YES   YES
5: GII
YES
NO

STATE
THE
PROBLEM
YES
6a: CII
NO
6b: CI,CII

YES   YES
NO
7: AII,CI,CII
NO   NO
YES
YES
8: AII,CI,CII,GII

NO
9: CII

NO   NO
10: CII,GII
YES   YES
YES

[a]The abbreviations correspond to those explained in Table 14.2.
YES
11: GII
NO   YES
NO
12: CII

A. Does the problem possess a quality requirement?
B. Do I have sufficient information to make a high-quality decision?
C. Is the problem structured?
D. Is acceptance of the decision by subordinates important for effective implementation?
E. If I were to make the decision by myself, am I reasonably certain that it would be
    accepted by my subordinates?
F. Do subordinates share the organizational goals to be attained in solving this problem?
G. Is conflict among subordinates likely in preferred solutions?

Source: Reprinted from *Leadership and Decision-Making* by Victor H. Vroom and
Philip W. Yetton by permission of the University of Pittsburgh Press. Copyright
© 1973 by the University of Pittsburgh Press.

in field studies. No normative model human behavior will ever be perfect, but the Vroom–Yetton model does seem to offer managers a useful technique for improving decision-making processes.[24]

Comparison of situational theories

To conclude our discussion of the situational theories of leadership, it seems appropriate to compare and, insofar as possible, integrate the various viewpoints. Such a comparison appears in Table 14.3. All three theories include task-oriented behavior, both the contingency theory and the path–goal theory include behaviors focusing on social considerations, and the path–goal theory and the Vroom–Yetton model both include participation. The path–goal theory includes achievement-oriented behavior. Not shown in the table but of some interest is the fact that Fiedler considers leadership styles to be personality traits. Both task- and relationship-oriented leader styles, in his view, are relatively inflexible.

Also shown in Table 14.3 are the situational variables associated with each theory. As indicated by the dotted lines, all three theories include task structure as an important factor. Though not closely related, leader position power in the contingency theory is somewhat similar to the authority system included in the path–goal theory.

Both the path–goal theory and the Vroom–Yetton model acknowledge the potential flexibility of leader style. This is in direct contrast to the contingency theory, which assumes that leader style is inflexible.

Finally, there is some overlap between the presumed consequences of appropriate leader behavior. Group performance, relevant to the contingency theory, is somewhat similar to decision quality as assessed by the Vroom–Yetton model. Subordinate motivation and satisfaction, predicted by the path–goal theory, are related to the Vroom–Yetton model's decision acceptance.

Overall, the different situational theories are more inconsistent than consistent with each other, but each approach has made meaningful contributions to the theory and practice of leader behavior. Taken together, the three theories reinforce our view that leadership in organizations is a complex process. Future research and/or unifying theories may build on these situational theories and partially dispel the mystery surrounding leadership.

Contemporary perspectives on leadership

Situational theories of leadership have been the focus of most theory building and research over the past ten years. Recently, however, other interesting and potentially useful perspectives have emerged. One of these probes the direc-

24. For recent evaluations and critiques of the Vroom–Yetton model, see R. H. George Field, "A Critique of the Vroom–Yetton Contingency Model of Leadership Behavior," *Academy of Management Review*, April 1979, pp. 249–268; Arthur G. Jago and Victor H. Vroom, "An Evaluation of Two Alternatives to the Vroom/Yetton Normative Model," *Academy of Management Journal*, June 1980, pp. 347–355; and Arthur G. Jago and Victor H. Vroom, "Some Differences in the Incidence and Evaluation of Participative Leader Behavior," *Journal of Applied Psychology*, December 1982, pp. 776–783.

Table 14.3 A comparison of situational theories of leadership

Basis of comparison	Situational theories		
	Contingency theory	Path–goal theory	Vroom–Yetton model
Leader behaviors or styles	Task-oriented – – – – – –Directive – – – – – –Autocratic (AI and AII)	Relationship-oriented – – –Supportive – – –Consultative (CI and CII)	Participative = = = – – –Group (GII)
		Achievement-oriented	
Situational variables	Favorableness of situation Leader–member relations Task structure– – – ⟍ Leader position power⟍ ⟍	Personal characteristics Ability Locus of control Environmental characteristics ⟍ –Task structure⟍ ⟍ –Authority system Work group	Quality requirement Information availability Situation structure Acceptance crucial Acceptance likely Shared goals Potential for conflict
Presumed flexibility of leader behavior	Inflexible	Flexible– – – – – – –Flexible	
Presumed consequences of leader behavior	Group performance⟍ ⟍ ⟍	Subordinate motivation – –Decision acceptance and satisfaction ⟍ Decision quality	

Factors linked with dotted lines are consistent.

tion of causality between leader behavior and subordinate responses; another involves the concept of substitutes for leadership.

The direction of causality

All of the trait approaches, leadership behavior approaches, and situational theories of leadership share one underlying assumption: the leader somehow does something that results in some kind of effectiveness. And all of these approaches fail to consider that the consequences of a leader's behavior may have implications for the future behavior of that leader. The attendant suggestion that subordinate behavior can influence leader behavior is an important part of this argument.[25]

To illustrate, consider two scenarios. Luke May is a leader of five men in a manufacturing plant. He practices task-oriented behavior. His men consistently produce at the highest level possible and, as a result, Luke's group wins a plant productivity award. It seems likely that, with the passage of time, Luke will become more relationship-oriented in response to his men's dedication and hard work. (Of course, he will probably also continue to be task-oriented.)

25. See Charles Greene, "Questions of Causation in the Path–Goal Theory of Leadership," *Academy of Management Journal*, March 1979, pp. 22–41.

Contrast this situation with the case of Jim Patterson. Jim supervises five men in the same plant. Jim has always been relationship-oriented, but his men have always been at the bottom of the plant in terms of productivity. He was recently "called on the carpet" and told that, if productivity did not improve, heads would roll. Jim is likely to become much more task-oriented in an effort to boost performance.

In each of these scenarios, it is obvious that the behavior of a leader's subordinates influenced the future behavior of that leader. This process becomes even more clear-cut when viewed from a reinforcement perspective[26] (as described in Chapter 13). The basic assumption of that perspective was that when behavior is followed by a desirable consequence it is likely to be repeated, but when it is followed by an undesirable consequence it is less likely to be repeated. If a leader practices a certain style of behavior and, as a result, achieves high levels of performance, motivation, and/or satisfaction, the behavior is likely to be repeated. If the leader's behavior results in unacceptable levels of performance, motivation, and/or satisfaction, he or she is likely to change it in the future. Luke May will probably continue his task-oriented behavior, but he will also become more relationship-oriented. Jim Patterson, on the other hand, is likely to change his behavior altogether.

Substitutes for leadership

The concept of *substitutes for leadership* has recently arisen in response to the fact that existing leadership models and theories do not account for situations in which leadership is not needed.[27] They simply try to specify what kind of leader behavior is appropriate. The substitute concepts, on the other hand, identify situations in which leader behaviors are neutralized by characteristics of the subordinate, the task, and the organization. For example, when a patient is delivered to a hospital emergency room, the personnel there do not wait to be told what to do by a leader. Nurses, doctors, and attendants all go into action without waiting for directive or supportive leader behavior from the emergency room supervisor.

Characteristics of the subordinate that may serve to neutralize leader behavior include ability, experience, need for independence, professional orientation, and indifference toward organizational rewards. For example, employees with a high level of ability and experience may not need to be told what to do. Similarly, a strong need for independence by the subordinate may render leader behavior ineffective.

Characteristics of the task that may substitute for leadership include routineness, the availability of feedback, and intrinsic satisfaction. When the job is routine and simple, the subordinate may not need direction. Or, when the task is challenging and otherwise intrinsically satisfying, the subordinate may not need or want social support from a leader.

26. See W. Clay Hammer and Ellen P. Hammer, "Behavior Modification on the Bottom Line," *Organizational Dynamics*, Spring 1976, pp. 2–21.

27. See Steven Kerr and John M. Jermier, "Substitutes for Leadership: Their Meaning and Measurement," *Organizational Behavior and Human Performance*, December 1978, pp. 375–403.

Finally, organizational characteristics that may serve as leadership substitutes include formalization, group cohesion, inflexibility, and a rigid reward structure. When policies and practices are formal and inflexible, for example, leadership may not be needed. Similarly, a rigid reward system may rob the leader's role of reward power, thereby decreasing the importance of the role.

Preliminary research has provided support for this concept of substitutes for leadership.[28] Along with the direction of causality, then, the concept of leader substitutes will probably attract more attention in the future.

Political behavior and politics

Although political behavior and politics in organizations may or may not be related to leadership per se, they are very clearly related to power and hence fit into our discussion. Jeffrey Pfeffer has recently defined *organizational politics* as the activities carried out in organizations to "acquire, develop, and use power and other resources to obtain one's preferred outcomes in a situation in which there is uncertainty or dissensus about choice."[29] Decisions ranging from the location of a manufacturing plant to the location of the company coffee pot are subject to political action. In any given situation, individuals may engage in political behavior to further their own ends, to protect themselves from others, to further goals they sincerely believe to be in the organization's best interests, or simply to acquire and exercise power. Power may be sought by individuals, by groups of individuals, or by groups of groups.

A recent survey provides some interesting insights into how political behavior is perceived in organizations.[30] Some 33 percent of the respondents (428 managers) felt that politics influenced salary decisions in their firms, and 28 percent felt that it influenced hiring decisions. The respondents also felt that the incidence of political behavior was greater at the upper levels of their organization and less at the lower levels. Well over half of the respondents felt that organizational politics was bad, unfair, unhealthy, and irrational. On the other hand, most suggested that successful executives have to be good politicians and that one has to be political to "get ahead."

How then does one deal with politics and political behavior? Two quite different approaches are to use organizational politics for one's own purposes and to minimize its potential for damaging the organization. An ambitious manager might use political behavior to get salary increases and promotions. At the same time, however, unbridled political behavior can do great harm to an organization. Some boards of directors spend months or even years squabbling over the choice of new top managers. During this time the organization may lose its sense of direction or fail to keep pace with its competitors.

---

28. See Kerr and Jermier, "Substitutes for Leadership."

29. Jeffrey Pfeffer, *Power in Organizations* (Marshfield, Mass.: Pitman Publishing, 1981), p. 7.

30. Victor Murray and Jeffrey Gandz, "Games Executives Play: Politics at Work," *Business Horizons*, December 1980, pp. 11–23. See also Jeffrey Gandz and Victor Murray, "The Experience of Workplace Politics," *Academy of Management Journal*, June 1980, pp. 237–251.

Using politics

The following suggestions and tactics for using politics were synthesized from previous theory and research by John Miner:[31]

1. Establish alliances with others, including peers, subordinates, and superiors.
2. Develop loyalty on the part of subordinates.
3. Do nothing to alienate or anger others.
4. Try not to be put in a position where you are dependent on an adversary.
5. Identify any weaknesses in your adversaries.

These and similar tactics might be interpreted as manipulative, but manipulation is a primary element in politics and political behavior. Indeed, two of the more popular business books in the 1960s and 1970s were *Management and Machiavelli* and *The Gamesman*.[32] The former tells how to use Machiavellian tactics to get ahead, and the latter describes a prototypical manager called the Gamesman. The Gamesman's primary goal is winning, and her or his primary motivation is competition and the desire to get ahead. Although these tactics and perspectives may be indicted on ethical grounds, the fact remains that they are part of organizational life. It is in one's best interest at least to be aware that they exist.

Managing political behavior

How can managers handle political behavior so that it doesn't do excessive damage? The following guidelines have been suggested:[33]

1. Be aware that, even if your actions are not politically motivated, others may assume that they are.
2. By providing subordinates with autonomy, responsibility, challenge, and feedback, you reduce the likelihood of political behavior on their part.
3. Avoid using power if you want to avoid charges of political motivation.
4. Get disagreements out in the open so that subordinates will have less opportunity for political behavior, using conflict for their own purposes.
5. Avoid covert activities. Behind-the-scenes activities reflect political intent even if none really exists.

Of course, these guidelines are a lot easier to list than they are to implement. The point is that the well-informed manager should not assume that political behavior does not exist or, worse yet, attempt to eliminate it by issuing orders or commands. Instead, the manager should recognize that political behavior exists in virtually all organizations and that it cannot be ignored or stamped out. It can, however, be managed in such a way that it will seldom

31. See John B. Miner, *The Management Process: Theory, Research, and Practice,* 2nd ed. (New York: Macmillan, 1978), pp. 179–180.

32. See Antony Jay, *Management and Machiavelli: An Inquiry into the Politics of Corporate Life* (New York: Holt, 1967); and Michael Maccoby, *The Gamesman* (New York: Simon and Schuster, 1976).

33. See Murray and Gandz, "Games Executives Play."

inflict serious damage on the organization. It may even play a useful role in some situations.

Summary of key points

Power is the potential ability to influence the behavior of others. Influence occurs when power is exercised; authority is power that is created and granted by an organizational hierarchy; and leadership is the ability to influence others. Leaders have both power and influence, but they may or may not have authority. The five kinds of power are legitimate, reward, coercive, referent, and expert power. Methods of using power include the legitimate request, instrumental compliance, coercion, rational persuasion, personal identification, inspirational appeal, and information distortion. Management and leadership differ in that the former derives most frequently from legitimate, reward, and coercive power, whereas the latter tends to build on referent and expert power also.

The trait approach to leadership assumed that some basic trait or set of traits differentiated leaders from nonleaders. The goal of the trait approach was to define those traits so that more effective leaders could be identified. Although research has failed to identify any valid leadership traits, some people still occasionally assume that traits such as appearance or dress suggest leadership ability.

The leadership behavior approach to leadership assumed that the behaviors of effective leaders was somehow different from the behavior of nonleaders. The goal was to identify those behaviors. Research at Michigan and Ohio State identified two basic forms of leadership behavior, one concentrating on work and performance (job-centered or initiating-structure behavior) and the other concentrating on employee welfare and support (employee-centered or consideration behavior). The Managerial Grid attempts to train managers to exhibit high levels of both forms of behavior. A shortcoming of the leadership behavior approach is the assumption that appropriate forms of leadership behavior are universally applicable.

Situational approaches to leadership recognize that appropriate forms of leadership behavior are *not* universally applicable and attempt to specify situations in which various behaviors are appropriate. The contingency theory suggests that a leader's behavior should be either task-oriented or relationship-oriented, depending on the favorableness of the situation. Favorableness, in turn, is based on leader–member relations, task structure, and the leader's position power. The theory also assumes that leaders cannot change their behaviors; if a mismatch exists, it is the situation that must be changed. The path–goal theory suggests that directive, supportive, participative, or achievement-oriented leader behaviors may be appropriate, depending on the personal characteristics of subordinates (ability and locus of control) and on environmental characteristics (task structure, formal authority system, and the work group). Finally, the Vroom–Yetton model maintains that leaders should vary the extent to which they allow subordinates to participate in making decisions as a function of seven situational factors. Both the path–goal theory and the Vroom–Yetton model assume that leader behavior is flexible. The three situational theories are not always consistent, but they are the most generally accepted approaches to leadership and have made valuable contributions to both theory and practice.

Two contemporary perspectives on leadership focus on the direction of causality (the behavior of followers may affect subsequent leader behaviors) and on substitutes for leadership. Substitutes for leadership are elements of the workplace that neutralize or render ineffective various leader behaviors. Examples include subordinate ability, task routineness, and formalization.

Political behavior in organizations takes a heavy toll on power. Individuals engage in political behavior for a variety of reasons, and a variety of techniques are available to those who choose to engage in political behavior. Managers can usually handle political behavior in such a way as to minimize its potential for harming the organization.

QUESTIONS FOR DISCUSSION

1. Can you think of situations in which a person has had either power, influence, authority, or leadership *without* having any of the other three? Which combination of these four concepts exists most often?

2. If you were a manager and had power and authority but were not perceived as a leader, could you function effectively? What could you do to improve things?

3. What contemporary leaders do you most admire? Do they have any traits in common?

4. What traits have you recently heard attributed to effective leaders? (*Hint:* They may include birth order and body shape!)

5. How is it possible for a manager to be both task-oriented *and* employee-oriented at the same time?

6. Can you think of other forms of leadership behaviors that we have not discussed?

7. Which of the situational theories do you think is most valid? Why?

8. Can you identify other variables besides those included in the three situational theories that might dictate appropriate leader behavior?

9. Do you agree or disagree with Fiedler about the inflexibility of leader behavior? What is your evidence?

10. Identify at least one situation you are familiar with wherein the behavior of subordinates caused the leader to change her or his behavior.

11. When all or most of the leadership substitutes are present, does the subordinate no longer need a boss? Why or why not?

12. Give examples of political behavior that have had "good" consequences and examples that have had "bad" consequences.

13. Do you agree or disagree with the assertion that political behavior is inevitable in organizations?

14. In the chapter it was stated that it is in one's best interest at least to be aware that political behavior may be going on in one's organization. Is this justification itself politically based? Why or why not?

C A S E   14.1

At the beginning of this chapter, you read an incident about a senior-level manager with an exemplary record. He had taken a position as head of a nationalized British firm that was losing $4 million a day. The manager being described was Ian MacGregor, the company British Steel Corporation. The case that follows describes what MacGregor has done and then raises some other issues for your consideration.

Saving British Steel Corporation

Ian MacGregor certainly qualifies as an exemplary manager. He won accolades for guiding Amax Corporation, a Connecticut mineral company, through ten years of successful expansion and growth. After retiring in 1977, he became a general partner in the international investment firm of Lazard Freres. Among his most notable accomplishments there was overseeing a number of financial maneuverings credited with saving the Jones & Laughlin Steel Company. In 1980 MacGregor was lured back into industry, taking on a job that would require not only managerial competence, but true leadership as well: saving British Steel Corporation.

After World War II the British steel industry struggled for many years, torn between conflicting ideologies. When the Labor party was in power, there was always the threat of nationalization, and even when the Conservative party had control, private investment lagged for fear that the Labor party would yet prevail. The threat became a reality when, in 1967, the British government took control of the country's 14 largest steel companies (all those capable of producing more than 475,000 tons of raw steel per year) and formed the government-owned and -controlled British Steel Corporation.

Unfortunately, government ownership and control meant that the company was not accountable to stockholders for efficiency, effectiveness, or profitability. Instead of attempting to integrate the fourteen companies into one smoothly functioning organization, the corporation embarked on a massive expansion program. Because steel companies in other countries were also expanding, British Steel was in trouble when demand for steel began to drop in the 1970s. By the time MacGregor was brought in, BSC was losing $4 million a day and had earned the dubious distinction of losing more money than any company in the world.

The situation MacGregor found was dismal to say the least. The work force was totally demoralized, productivity extremely low, and the staff much too large. A costly and bitter strike in 1980 had brought the company to its knees.

MacGregor's first actions focused on improving the morale of BSC's middle managers. He couldn't offer financial incentives, so he provided them with considerable independence and autonomy. For example, managers were given a choice of getting their raw materials from other units within BSC or buying them on the open market. This also motivated other managers within the company to be more efficient.

The new boss next decentralized labor questions so that is-sues surrounding job assignments and layoffs were all dealt with at the local level. At the same time, he made the kinds of hard decisions a leader must occasionally make, terminating 70,000 employees in an effort to trim excess personnel costs.

MacGregor then turned to improving efficiency and productiv-ity. To do this, he convinced labor leaders of the necessity to elim-inate featherbedding, to deploy personnel more efficiently, and to boost output per employee. Not only has he carried these pro-grams off, but he has also gotten most of the union labor leaders in his corner as a result. They realize that no one works if the company fails.

To increase sales, MacGregor has worked tirelessly to get more sales in the North Sea pipeline business. He has also tried to get Japanese producers to back off somewhat from pushing their steel in Great Britain. Finally, he has proposed that British and French investors finance a highway-railroad link between the two countries. Expectations are that BSC would be a major sup-plier for the project if it materializes.

Of course, MacGregor still faces major challenges. The gov-ernment has grown increasingly reluctant to cover BSC losses. La-bor officials are supportive now, but that could change if further cutbacks in personnel are needed. Finally, worldwide demand for steel must increase if BSC is to become a viable organization again.

CASE QUESTIONS

1. Can you identify examples of leadership and management in this case?
2. Which theory or theories of leadership best describe MacGregor's approach?
3. On the basis of information given in this case, would you say that Mac-Gregor is most effective as a leader, a manager, or both?
4. What bases of power did MacGregor use? Do you think he engaged in political behavior?

CASE REFERENCES

"British Steel: Moment of Truth." *New York Times,* January 16, 1981, p. 29.

"Help for British Steel." *Business Week,* March 9, 1981, p. 36.

Lubar, Robert. "An American Leads British Steel Back from the Brink." *Fortune,* Sep-tember 21, 1981, pp. 88–108.

"MacGregor's Mark," *Fortune,* January 10, 1983, p. 8.

"U.S. Complaint and Snow Hurt British Steel: Head Of Loss-Ridden Firm Plans to Hold Meeting with Leader of Union." *Wall Street Journal,* January 13, 1982, p. 27.

C A S E   14.2

Effective leadership styles

Anthony Giles and Brenda Roberts are both first-line supervisors at Eastern University on the Eastern seaboard. Anthony oversees a group of landscape crews. Each crew of five is responsible for mowing and edging a section of the university campus. Brenda works for the campus postal system. She coordinates the clerks and couriers who handle in-coming and out-going mail. Brenda is being considered for a promotion, while Anthony is in danger of being fired. In connection with each of these impending decisions, both Brenda and Anthony have been summoned to the office of the campus personnel director.

Brenda is scheduled for the first appointment. One of the reasons why she is being considered for a promotion, beyond the effectiveness of the postal system she coordinates, is the fact that she has demonstrated exemplary leadership characteristics. Her subordinates all recommend her highly, and postal employees have the lowest level of turnover and absenteeism of all the work groups on campus.

When asked why she has such a good working relationship with her subordinates, she identifies several contributing factors. "First and foremost," she begins, "I treat my subordinates like human beings. I show them that I care about their welfare and that I'll back them in a pinch. Of course, I also let them know that we have a job to do and that each of us has to contribute.

"I also do a lot of work at performance appraisal time. I make sure that each employee knows what he or she has to do to get a good evaluation and pay raise the next time around.

"Finally, it's also important to remember that you can't handle all situations the same way. On routine day-to-day stuff, I don't have to tell anybody what to do. When something new comes up, though, I step in and make sure everyone knows how to proceed."

When Anthony's turn came, a much different picture emerged. Absenteeism and turnover in his crew have been getting worse, several workers have recently filed grievances, and their work is sloppy. When asked what might be behind these problems, Anthony had no clear idea. "I'm not sure what's going on," he said. "I've always believed that you should treat everybody the same. I don't play favorites. I even go out of my way to make sure nobody gets the wrong idea. At lunch, I always eat with a guy from maintenance. Yes sir, I keep at arm's length from my people. And at pay raise time I make extra sure everyone gets equal treatment. They all get the same ratings and the same raise. And I'm really trying to keep the work quality up. I watch my people all the time, and I make sure I explain everything to them before they start a job."

CASE
QUESTIONS

1. Compare and contrast the leadership styles of Anthony and Brenda.

2. Which leadership theory best explains the effectiveness of Anthony and Brenda as leaders?

3. What might Anthony do to become a better leader?

15

GROUPS AND GROUP PROCESSES

1. Define the term *group* and identify three general types of groups.

2. Explain why people join groups, and trace the general stages of group development.

3. Discuss role dynamics, group norms, group cohesiveness, and informal leadership.

4. Explain the informal organization and its implications for managers.

5. Give guidelines for managing various kinds of groups in organizations.

CHAPTER OUTLINE

445

OPENING INCIDENT

Consider the following four men: one is a back-slapping salesman always looking for the spotlight. The second was once a rowdy party-goer but is now a born-again Christian married to the ex-wife of the first. The third man is a socialite who enjoys a good drink and is prone to frequent swearing. The fourth is a devoted family man who openly professes his Christian beliefs and his opposition to some of the ideas of the third. How well do you think these four men would function together as a group?

The president of a Houston-based company, part of a larger international firm headquartered in California, recently described a typical business day. The schedule he followed on that particular day was as follows:

8:00–8:15 A.M.	Arrive at work, review mail.
8:15–8:30 A.M.	Read *Wall Street Journal*.
8:30–9:15 A.M.	Meet with labor officials and plant managers to resolve minor labor disputes.
9:15–9:30 A.M.	Review internal report and dictate correspondence.
9:30–10:00 A.M.	Meet with two marketing executives to review advertising campaign.
10:00–12:00 A.M.	Meet with company executive committee to discuss strategy, budgetary issues, and the competition (this committee meets weekly).
12:00–1:15 P.M.	Lunch with the financial vice president and two executives from another subsidiary of the parent corporation. Primary topic of discussion is the Houston Oilers football team.
1:15–2:00 P.M.	Meet with personnel director and assistant about a recent OSHA inspection; establish a task force to investigate the problems identified and to suggest solutions.
2:00–3:00 P.M.	Conference call with four other company presidents.
3:30–4:15 P.M.	Meet with a group of sales representatives and the company purchasing agent.
4:15–5:30 P.M.	Work alone in office.
5:30–7:00 P.M.	Play racquetball at nearby athletic club with a friend.
7:00–8:00 P.M.	Dinner at home with wife and three children.
8:30–10:30 P.M.	Weekly bridge game with neighbors.

How did this executive spend his time? He spent most of it working and interacting with other people in various groups. This compressed daily schedule reveals twelve groups that he is either a member of or dealt with: labor officials, plant managers, marketing executives, executive committee, lunch group, personnel department, the OSHA task force, the corporation's company presidents, sales representatives, racquetball group, family, and bridge foursome.

We briefly introduced groups as a vehicle for getting work done in organizations back in Chapter 10. We will now explore the concepts of groups and group processes in more detail. After an initial overview of groups, including a definition, we will discuss two preliminary perspectives: the reasons why people join groups and the stages of group development. We will then explore several important characteristics of groups and describe how groups are used in organizations. After discussing informal groups and their role in organizations, we will conclude by suggesting guidelines for managing groups.

Groups and organizations

The existence of groups in organizations is a simple fact of life. Indeed, an organization itself could be approached as a group of groups. We must first establish what a group is, therefore, and then determine what kinds of groups there are in organizations.

Definition of a group

The list of definitions that have been developed is virtually endless. Groups have been defined in terms of perceptions, needs, motives, composition, and a variety of other characteristics. For our purposes, we will define a *group* as two or more people who interact regularly in order to accomplish a common purpose or goal.[1]

Note that there are three basic components of this definition. First, there must be at least two people involved for a group to exist. There can be no groups of one. On the other hand, when the size of a group increases to a certain point, usually around twenty members, it often ceases to be a group in its own right and formally or informally breaks up into smaller groups.

Second, the individuals must interact regularly in order to constitute a group. This interaction need not always follow the same pattern, but it must occur. The necessity for interaction is a primary reason for the upper limit on group size. When a group gets too large, it is difficult for members to interact with all other members. It is more comfortable to interact with only a few of the other members, facilitating the formation of a new, smaller group.

Finally, group members must have a common goal or purpose. This goal or purpose may range from preparing a new advertising campaign to informally sharing information to making important decisions to fulfilling social needs. A collection of five people riding an elevator is not a group. Even

1. Based on Linda N. Jewell and H. Joseph Reitz, *Group Effectiveness in Organizations* (Glenview, Il.: Scott, Foresman, 1981).

though more than two people are involved, and even though they share the same goal (moving from one floor to another), they do not interact regularly. By the same token, labor and management officials may interact regularly, but they probably don't have a common purpose. As we shall see, the goal or purpose of the group is a primary factor in distinguishing among different types of groups in organizations.

Types of groups

Chapter 10 identified several kinds of work groups: operative work groups, autonomous work groups, and teams, all of which are created by managers to accomplish specific things. In this chapter we will categorize groups along more general lines as functional groups, task groups, and informal or interest groups.[2]

Functional groups. A *functional group* is a group created by the organization to accomplish a number of organizational purposes with an indefinite time horizon. The production department of a manufacturing firm, the management department of a business school, and the nursing staff of a large hospital are all functional groups. Operative work groups, autonomous work groups, and standing committees are also functional groups. Each is created by the organization to serve a number of purposes specified by the organization. The production department in a manufacturing firm, for example, seeks to produce large numbers of products while allowing minimal waste and using human resources as efficiently as possible. It is assumed that the functional group will remain in existence after it attains its current objectives. (The goal of the business school's management department is to teach management, but this does not mean that the department will cease to exist at the end of the current semester.) Plant management, the marketing department, and the personnel department are other examples of functional groups.

Task groups. A *task group* is a group created by the organization to accomplish a relatively narrow range of purposes within a stated or implied time horizon. Ad hoc committees, task forces, teams, and your class are all task groups. The organization specifies group membership and assigns a relatively narrow set of goals, such as developing a new product, evaluating a proposed grievance procedure, or studying the field of management. The time horizon for accomplishing these purposes is either specified (your class ceases to exist at the end of the term) or implied (the project team will disband when the new product is developed). The country's fourteenth-largest bank, Marine Midland, recently used task groups to initiate a major organization design change. Eight task forces composed of 40 upper-level executives spent four months analyzing potential new markets and developing units to reach them. At the end of the four months, the change was complete and the executives

2. See Dorwin Cartwright and Alvin Zander (eds.), *Group Dynamics: Research and Theory*, 3rd ed. (New York: Harper & Row, 1968).

returned to their regular jobs.[3] The company president described at the beginning of this chapter appointed a task force to investigate some problems raised by OSHA and to suggest solutions.

Informal or interest groups. An *informal or interest group* is created by its members for purposes that may or may not be relevant to those of the organization, and it has an unspecified time horizon. The company president's lunch group is an informal group, whereas his bridge foursome is an interest group. Each member chooses to participate—rather than being told that he or she must do so. The activities of the group may or may not match the goals of the organization. At lunch, for example, a group of employees may be discussing how to improve productivity (relevant to and desired by the company), how to embezzle money (relevant to but not desired by the company), or local politics, the weather, and sports (not relevant to the company). Time considerations are usually not discussed. As long as the company president enjoys playing racquetball with his friend, he will probably continue to play. When it ceases to be pleasant, he will seek other company or a different activity. Further, even though the bridge schedule is relatively structured, the members of the foursome probably do not decide initially that they definitely will or will not play every Wednesday for the rest of their lives.

Informal groups can be a powerful organizational force with which managers must contend. For example, Robert Schrank describes how a group of employees at a furniture factory worked to subvert their boss's efforts to increase production. They all tacitly agreed to produce a reasonable amount of work but not to work too hard. One man kept a stockpile of completed work hidden as a back-up in case he ever got too far behind. In another example, workers in an automobile plant described how they engaged in planned sabotage, such as not welding critical spots, leaving out gaskets and seals, not tightening bolts, and putting soft drink bottles inside doors.[4] We will pay special attention to informal groups throughout this chapter.

Figure 15.1 reflects the pervasiveness of groups in organizations. The people inside the box shown as a solid line (as well as the other departments and the executive committee) make up a functional group. The people inside the box defined by a broken line constitute a task group. The group assigned to each of the three project managers is a task group. Finally, the area indicated by a broken line and dots represents an informal group composed of the legal advisor, a vice president, a project manager, and two subordinates. These people may socialize on weekends, fish or play bridge together, or simply chat around the water cooler. No doubt a large number of other informal groups are also present.

3. See Arthur M. Louis, "In Search of Style at the 'New Marine,' " *Fortune,* July 26, 1982, pp. 40–45.
4. See Robert Schrank, *Ten Thousand Working Days* (Cambridge, Mass.: The MIT Press, 1978); and Bill Watson, "Counter Planning on the Shop Floor," in Peter Frost, Vance Mitchell and Walter Nord (eds.), *Organizational Reality,* 2nd ed. (Glenview, Il.: Scott, Foresman, 1982), pp. 286–294.

Figure 15.1
Types of groups in
organizations

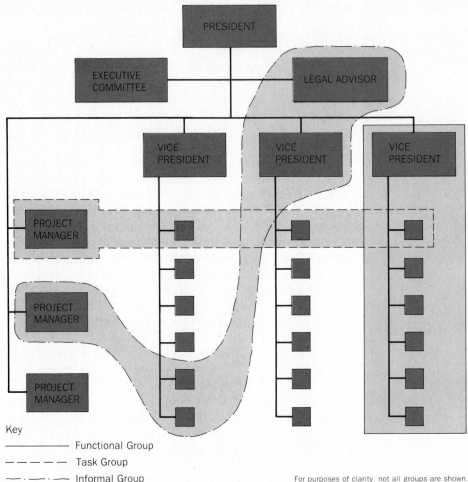

Key

——————— Functional Group

— — — — — Task Group

—·——·——·— Informal Group

For purposes of clarity, not all groups are shown.

Preliminary perspectives

To gain some initial insight into groups and group processes, let's look at what happens when a group is just getting started. First we will describe why people join groups and then examine the stages of group development.

Why people join groups

People join groups for a variety of reasons. They join functional groups simply because they join organizations. That is, people accept employment in order to earn money or to practice their chosen profession. Once inside the organization, they are assigned to jobs and roles and thus become members of functional groups. Usually, but not always, functional group membership precedes task group membership. People in existing functional groups are told, are asked, or volunteer to serve on ad hoc committees, task forces, and teams.

Table 15.1 Reasons for group formation

Interpersonal attraction
    Proximity, contact, and interaction
    Physical attractiveness
    Similarity
    Perceived ability of others
Group activities
Group goals
Group membership
Instrumental benefits

Source: Developed from Marvin E. Shaw, *Group Dynamics—The Psychology of Small Group Behavior*, 3rd ed. (New York: McGraw-Hill, 1981), pp. 81–97. Used with permission.

Why people join informal or interest groups is considerably of more interest. Because people choose whether or not to join such groups, their choices are related to motivation. Marvin E. Shaw has proposed several reasons, summarized in Table 15.1, why people elect to band together in groups.[5]

Interpersonal attraction. Perhaps the most obvious and logical reason why people choose to form groups is that they are attracted to each other. Many different factors contribute to interpersonal attraction. When people see a lot of each other, sheer proximity increases the likelihood that interpersonal attraction will develop. Physical features, especially as perceived by members of the opposite sex, can play a major role in interpersonal attraction. Attraction is also facilitated by similarity of attitudes, personality, or economic standing. Finally, the perceived usefulness of others affects interpersonal attraction. If you are an "A" student, do you seek out "D" students to study with? All of these factors lead in varying degrees to the interpersonal attraction that can result in the formation of an informal or interest group.

Group activities. Individuals may also be motivated to join an informal or interest group because the activities of the group appeal to them. Jogging, playing bridge, bowling, discussing poetry, playing war games, and flying model airplanes are all activities that some people enjoy. Many of them are more enjoyable to participate in as a member of a group, and most actually require more than one person. A person may join a bowling team not because of any noticeable attraction to other group members but simply because being a member of the group allows that person to participate in a pleasant activity. Of course, if the level of interpersonal attraction is very low, a person may choose to forego the activity rather than join the group.

Group goals. The goals of a group may also motivate people to join. The Sierra Club, which is dedicated to environmental conservation, is a good example of this kind of interest group. As another illustration, consider the

5. Marvin E. Shaw, *Group Dynamics—The Psychology of Small Group Behavior*, 3rd ed. (New York: McGraw-Hill, 1981).

groups that form to collect money for various charities. Members may or may not be personally attracted to the other fund raisers, and they probably don't enjoy the activity of knocking on doors to ask for money, but they join the group because they subscribe to its goal.

Group membership. A somewhat more abstract reason why people join groups is that the mere fact of being a member may be personally satisfying. It has been argued that the need for affiliation prompts people to seek the company of others and that fulfillment of this need seems to reduce their anxiety about being accepted and liked.[6] Others may satisfy their need for esteem by joining groups (such as fraternal organizations) that they admire or feel that other people admire.

Instrumental benefits. Another reason why people join groups is that group membership is sometimes seen as instrumental in providing other benefits to the individual. For example, it is fairly common for college students entering their senior year to join several professional clubs or associations. Why? Because listing such memberships on one's resumé is thought to enhance one's chances of getting a good job. Similarly, a manager might join a certain racquet club not because she is attracted to its members (although she might be) and not because of the opportunity to play tennis (although she may enjoy it). The club's goals are not relevant and her affiliation needs may be satisfied in other ways. However, she may feel that being a member of this club will lead to important and useful business contacts. The racquet club membership is instrumental in establishing those contacts. Membership in civic groups such as Kiwanis and Rotary may be solicited for similar reasons.

Stages of group development

After a group has been created, either by the organization or by group members, it spends a period of time developing. Imagine the differences between a collection of five people who have just been thrown together in a group and a group that has functioned like a well-oiled machine for years. Members of a new group are unfamiliar with how the others function and more tentative in their interactions. In a group with considerable experience, however, members are familiar with one another's strengths and weaknesses and more secure in their role in the group. To progress from the first state to the second, a group must go through certain stages of group development.

These stages do not necessarily follow neatly one after the other. Instead, they are phases through which the group evolves. The basic four-stage model of group development is presented in Figure 15.2.[7]

Forming. The first stage of development for a new group is a period of testing and dependence, or *forming.* The members of the group get acquainted

6. See Stanley Schachter, *The Psychology of Affiliation* (Stanford, Calif.: Stanford University Press, 1959).

7. See B. W. Tuckman, "Developmental Sequence in Small Groups," *Psychological Bulletin*, Vol. 63, 1965, pp. 383–399.

Figure 15.2
The stages of group
development

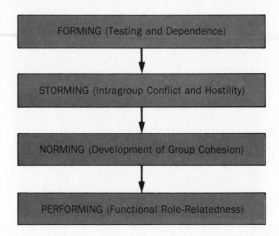

FORMING (Testing and Dependence)

STORMING (Intragroup Conflict and Hostility)

NORMING (Development of Group Cohesion)

PERFORMING (Functional Role-Relatedness)

and begin to test which interpersonal behaviors are acceptable and which are unacceptable to the other members of the group. The members are very dependent on others at this point to provide cues about what is acceptable. The basic ground rules for the group are established and a tentative group structure may emerge.

Storming. Intragroup conflict and hostility, or *storming,* is the second stage of group development. Now members of the group resist the structure that has begun to emerge. Each member wants to retain her or his individuality. There may be a general lack of unity, and patterns of interaction are uneven. At the same time, some members of the group may begin to exert themselves so as to become recognized as the group leader, or at least to play a major role in shaping the group's agenda.

Norming. The third stage is the development of group cohesion, or *norming* (both cohesion and norms will be discussed in detail later). During this stage each person begins to recognize and accept her or his role and to understand the roles of others. Members also begin to accept one another and to develop a sense of unity. But there may be temporary regressions to the storming stage. For example, the norming group might begin to accept one particular member as the leader. If this person later violated important norms and otherwise jeopardized his or her claim to leadership, conflict (storming) might re-emerge as the group rejected this leader and searched for another.

Performing. *Performing* is the final stage of group development, wherein the group really begins to focus on the problem at hand. The members enact the roles they have accepted, interaction occurs, and the efforts of the group are directed toward goal attainment. The basic structure of the group is no longer an issue but has become a mechanism for accomplishing the purposes of the group.

Although these stages do not occur as discrete steps with measurable starting and stopping points, they do reflect basic processes that groups pass

"This might be tougher than we planned on."

Drawing by Dean Vietor

through. Several models of group development have been proposed, but this one provides perhaps the clearest view of how a fully functioning group evolves from a loose collection of individuals.[8]

Basic group characteristics

As groups develop, they begin to take on important characteristics, four of which are role dynamics, norms, cohesiveness, and informal leadership.

Role dynamics

The word *role* is commonly used in a theatrical sense; in a play or movie, actors play roles. Roles in a group are quite similar. Some people are leaders, some do the work, some interface with other groups, and so on. Further, each of us has many group memberships and therefore plays multiple roles in work groups, classes, families, and social organizations.[9]

Perhaps the easiest way to introduce the concept of **role dynamics** is to describe a role episode (see Figure 15.3). The first step in the role episode, or process, is the *expected role*. The individual's expected role is what other members of the group expect the individual to do. The expected role then gets translated into the *sent role,* which consists of the messages and cues that group members use to communicate the expected role to the individual. The *perceived role* is what the individual perceives the sent role to mean. Finally, the *enacted role* is what the individual actually does in the role. And the enacted role, in turn, influences future expectations of the group.

8. For another interesting framework, see Warren Bennis and H. A. Shepard, "A Theory of Group Development," *Human Relations,* Summer 1963, pp. 414–457.

9. See David Katz and Robert L. Kahn, *The Social Psychology of Organizations,* 2nd ed. (New York: Wiley, 1978), pp. 187–221.

Figure 15.3
The role episode

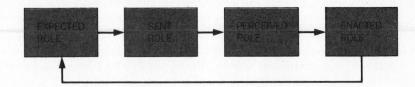

Consider the case of a new employee joining an existing work group. The group's manager and each member have their own expectations about what they want the newcomer to do. These expectations comprise the expected role, and they lose no time in transmitting cues about those expectations. (The newcomer may be expected to make the first pot of coffee each morning and deal with problem customers.) These cues are the sent role. The individual then perceives and processes these cues internally. (A cue that the newcomer makes the coffee may be received very clearly, whereas cues about problem customers may be more difficult to interpret.) These perceptions result in the perceived role. Finally, the newcomer actually enacts the role. (The person may not know how to make coffee but may be very effective in dealing with problem customers. Or vice versa.)

At each step of the process, distortions may creep in. The group members may choose the wrong messages or cues to send their expectations. The individual may not perceive these messages and cues correctly because of differing frames of reference and experiences. Or the enacted role may deviate from the expected role because the individual doesn't have the ability to carry out the role or chooses not to do so. The results of these various breakdowns in the role episode may include role ambiguity, role conflict, or role overload.

Role ambiguity. *Role ambiguity* arises when the sent role is unclear.[10] If your instructor tells you to write a term paper but refuses to provide more information, you will probably experience role ambiguity. You don't know what the topic is, how long the paper should be, what format to use, or when the paper is due.

In work settings, role ambiguity can stem from poor job descriptions, vague instructions from a supervisor, or unclear cues from co-workers. The result is likely to be a subordinate who doesn't know what to do. Obviously, role ambiguity can be a significant problem for both the individual who must contend with it and the organization that expects the employee to perform.

Role conflict. *Role conflict* occurs when the messages and cues comprising the sent role are clear but contradictory or mutually exclusive. A number of different forms of role conflict can occur.[11]

One common form is *inter-role conflict*, wherein a conflict arises between

10. See Katz and Kahn, *The Social Psychology of Organizations.*

11. See Robert L. Kahn, D. M. Wolfe, R. P. Quinn, J. D. Snoek, and R. A. Rosenthal, *Organizational Stress: Studies in Role Conflict and Role Ambiguity* (New York: Wiley, 1964).

roles. For example, if a person's boss says that to get ahead one must work overtime and on weekends, and the same person's spouse says that more time is needed at home with the family, conflict may result. In a matrix organization, inter-role conflict often arises between the roles one plays in different task groups as well as between task group roles and one's permanent role in a functional group.

Another form of role conflict is *intra-role conflict*. In this situation, the person gets conflicting demands from different sources within the context of the same role. A manager's boss may let it be known that the manager needs to put more pressure on subordinates to follow new work rules. At the same time, the manager's subordinates may indicate that they expect the manager to get the rules changed. Here the cues are in conflict, and the manager may be unsure about which course to follow.

Intra-sender conflict occurs when a single source sends clear but contradictory messages. If the boss says one morning that there can be no more overtime for the next month but after lunch tells someone to work late that same evening, intra-sender conflict is evident.

Person–role conflict results from a discrepancy between the role requirements and the individual's personal values, attitudes, and needs.[12] If a person is told to do something unethical or illegal, or if the work is distasteful (for example, firing a close friend), person–role conflict is likely.

Role conflict is of particular concern to managers. Research has shown that conflict may occur in a variety of situations and with a variety of adverse consequences, including stress, poor performance, and rapid turnover.[13]

Role overload. A final consequence of a poorly executed role episode is *role overload,* which occurs when expectations for the role exceed the individual's capabilities. When a manager gives an employee several major assignments at once while increasing the person's regular workload, the employee will probably experience role overload.

Implications. In a functional or task group, the manager can take steps to avoid role ambiguity, role conflict, and role overload. Having clear and reasonable expectations and sending clear and straightforward cues go a long way toward eliminating role ambiguity. Consistent expectations that take into account the employee's other roles and personal value system may minimize role conflict. And role overload can be avoided simply by recognizing the individual's capabilities and limits.

In friendship and interest groups, the role episode is likely to be less formal. Hence the possibility of role ambiguity, conflict, or overload may not be so great. On the other hand, if one or more of these problems do occur,

12. See Kahn et al., *Organizational Stress.*

13. See L. Roos and F. Starke, "Roles in Organizations," in William Starbuck and P. Nystrom (eds.), *Handbook of Organization Design* (Oxford, England: Oxford University Press, 1980). See also Kahn et al., *Organizational Stress;* and John M. Ivancevich and James M. Donnelly, Jr., "A Study of Role Clarity and Need for Clarity for These Occupational Groups," *Academy of Management Journal,* March 1974, pp. 28–36.

they may be more difficult for the individual to handle. This stems from the fact that roles in friendship and interest groups are less likely to be partially defined by a formal authority structure or written job descriptions. The individual cannot turn to these sources to clarify her or his role.

Group norms

A second major characteristic of groups is norms. *Norms* are standards of behavior that the group accepts for its members.[14] Most committees, for example, develop norms governing their discussions. If a person talks too much, he or she is perceived as doing so in order to make a good impression or to get her or his own way. Other members may not talk so much to this person, may not sit nearby, may glare at the person, and may otherwise "punish" the individual for violating the norm.

Norms, then, define the boundaries between acceptable and unacceptable behavior. Some groups develop norms that limit the upper bounds of behavior in order to "make life easier" for the group. In general, these norms are counter-productive. Examples: Don't make more than two comments in a committee discussion. Don't produce any more than you have to. Don't hurry to greet customers. Other groups may develop norms that limit the lower bounds of behavior. These norms tend to reflect motivation, commitment, and high performance. Examples: Don't come to committee meetings unless you've read the reports to be discussed. Produce as much as you can. Greet every customer with a smile.

Norm generalization. It is important to realize that the norms of one group cannot be generalized to another group. Some academic groups, for example, have a dress norm that suggests that male faculty members wear a coat and tie on teaching days. People who fail to observe this norm are "punished" by sarcastic remarks or even formal reprimands. In other departments the norm may be jeans and casual shirts, and the person unfortunate enough to wear a tie may be punished just as vehemently.

Even within the same work area, similar groups can develop different norms. One work group may strive to always produce above its assigned quota; another may maintain productivity just below its quota. The norm of one group may be to be friendly and cordial to its supervisor; that of another group may be to remain aloof and distant. The differences are due primarily to the composition of the groups.

Norm variation. Norms may sometimes dictate different roles for different group members. A very common norm is that the least senior member of a group is expected to perform unpleasant or trivial tasks for the rest of the group. These tasks might be to make the first pot of coffee in the morning (in

14. See J. E. McGrath, *Social Psychology: A Brief Introduction* (New York: Holt, 1964).

an office), to wait on customers who are known to be small tippers (in a restaurant), to deal with complaining customers (in a department store), or handle
the low-commission line of merchandise (in a sales department).

Another example of norm variation is that certain individuals, especially
informal leaders, may violate the norms with impunity in certain situations. If
the group is going to meet at 8:00, anyone arriving late will be chastised for
holding things up. Occasionally, however, the informal leader may arrive a
few minutes late. As long as it does not happen too often, and as long as the
leader is not too late, the group will probably not do anything. People with
expert power may also be allowed to violate norms. If a member of a student
study group happens to be a friend of the instructor, he or she may be accorded special privileges by the group.

Norm conformity. Norms have the power to force a certain degree of
conformity among group members. The power of norm conformity was first
demonstrated in a classic experiment by Solomon Asch.[15] Asch set up a situation wherein groups of people were asked to indicate which of three lines was
the same length as another line. Actually all the group members except one
were Asch's confederates; they only pretended to be subjects. When all the
confederates agreed on an answer that was obviously incorrect, the real subject
went along with the rest of the group more than one third of the time, even
when he or she had already decided on the correct answer!

Four basic sets of factors contribute to norm conformity.[16]

1. Factors associated with the group itself affect conformity. For example,
   some groups may exert more pressure than others.
2. The initial stimulus that prompts behavior can affect conformity. The
   more ambiguous the stimulus (for example, news that the group is going
   to be transferred to a newly created unit), the more pressure there is to
   conform.
3. Individual traits such as intelligence determine the individual's propen-
   sity to conform (for example, more intelligent people are often less susceptible to pressure to conform).
4. Situational factors such as group size and unanimity influence conformity.

When a person does not conform, several things happen. At first the
group may increase its communication with the deviant individual in order to
bring her or him back in line. If this does not work, communication may decline. Over time, the group may begin to exclude the individual from its activities and, in effect, ostracize the person. If the norm is especially powerful and
fraught with emotional overtones, physical coercion may even be used. People
who cross union picket lines are occasionally subjected to physical abuse.

15. See Solomon E. Asch, "Effects of Group Pressure Upon the Modification and Distortion of
Judgment," in H. Guetzkow (ed.), *Group, Leadership, and Men* (Pittsburgh, Penn.: Carnegie
Press, 1951), pp. 177–190.

16. See H. T. Reitan and M. E. Shaw, "Group Membership, Sex Composition of the Group,
and Continuity Behavior," *Journal of Social Psychology*, October 1964, pp. 45–51.

Group cohesiveness

A third group characteristic that is important to managers is group cohesiveness. *Cohesiveness* is the extent to which members are attracted to each other as individuals and to the group as a whole.[17] Of particular interest are the factors that increase and reduce cohesiveness and the consequences of group cohesiveness. The factors that increase group cohesiveness and the factors that reduce it are summarized in Table 15.2.

Factors that increase cohesiveness. Five factors apparently increase the level of cohesiveness in a group.[18] One of the strongest of these is intergroup competition. When two or more groups are in direct competition (for example, three sales groups competing for top sales honors or two football teams competing for a conference championship), each group is likely to become more cohesive. Second, just as personal attraction plays a role in causing a group to form, so too does attraction seem to enhance cohesiveness. Third, favorable evaluation of the entire group by outsiders can increase cohesiveness. Thus a group's winning a sales contest or a conference title or receiving recognition and praise from a superior will tend to increase its cohesiveness. Similarly, if all the members of the group agree on their goals, cohesiveness is likely to increase. And the more frequently members of the group interact with each other, the more likely the group is to become cohesive. A manager who wants to foster a high level of cohesiveness in a group might do well to establish some form of intergroup competition, assign members to the group who are likely to be attracted to one another, provide opportunities for success, establish goals that all members are likely to accept, and allow ample opportunity for interaction.

Factors that reduce cohesiveness. There are also five factors that are known to reduce group cohesiveness.[19] We noted earlier in this chapter that

Table 15.2 Factors that influence group cohesiveness

Factors that increase cohesiveness	Factors that reduce cohesiveness
Intergroup competition	Group size
Personal attraction	Disagreement on goals
Favorable evaluation	Intragroup competition
Agreement on goals	Domination
Interaction	Unpleasant experiences

17. See Jewell and Reitz, *Group Effectiveness in Organizations.*

18. Andrew Szilagyi and Marc Wallace, *Organizational Behavior and Performance,* 3rd ed. (Glenview, Il.: Scott, Foresman, 1983).

19. See Szilagyi and Wallace, *Organizational Behavior and Performance.*

size is an important element in groups and that, once size reaches a certain point (perhaps around twenty members), subgroups tend to emerge. In a similar fashion, cohesiveness tends to decline as group size increases beyond a certain point.[20] Second, when members of a group disagree on what the goals of the group should be, cohesiveness may decrease. When some members believe the group should maximize output and others think output should be restricted, cohesiveness declines. Third, intragroup competition reduces cohesiveness. When members are competing among themselves, they focus more on their own actions and behaviors than on those of the group. Fourth, domination by one or more persons in the group may cause overall cohesiveness to decline. Other members may feel that they aren't being given an opportunity to interact and contribute, and they may become less attracted to the group as a consequence. Finally, unpleasant experiences that result from group membership may reduce cohesiveness. A sales group that comes in last in a sales contest, an athletic team that sustains a long losing streak, and a work group reprimanded for poor-quality work may all become less cohesive as a result of their unpleasant experience.

Consequences of cohesiveness. In general, as groups become more cohesive their members tend to interact more frequently, conform more to group norms, and become more satisfied with the group.[21]

Cohesiveness may also influence group performance. However, these effects are likely to interact with the group's performance norms. (When a group tries to maintain high levels of performance, its performance norms are high; when it wants to do just enough to avoid penalties, its performance norms are low.) The manner in which a group's level of cohesiveness and its performance norms interact is shown in Figure 15.4.

When both cohesiveness and performance norms are high, high performance should result. This is because the group wants to perform at a high level (norms) and its members are committed to working together toward that end (cohesiveness). When performance norms are high and cohesiveness is low, performance will be moderate. Although the group wants to perform at a high level, its members aren't necessarily working together as a unit. When performance norms are low, performance will also be low, regardless of the level of group cohesiveness. The less desirable of these two situations is the low performance norm combined with high cohesiveness. In this case all group members fervently embrace the standard of restricting performance (due to the low performance norm) and the group is united in its efforts to maintain that standard (due to the high cohesiveness). If cohesiveness were low, the manager might be able to raise performance norms by establishing high goals and rewarding goal attainment, or by bringing in new group members who are high performers. But a highly cohesive group is likely to resist these interventions.

20. See Jewell and Reitz, *Group Effectiveness in Organizations.*
21. See Shaw, *Group Dynamics.*

Figure 15.4
The interaction between cohesiveness and performance norms

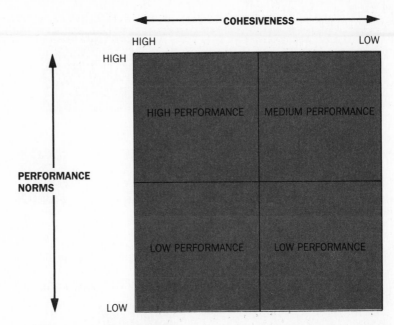

Source: From *Organizational Behavior and Performance*, 3rd edition, by Andrew D. Szilagyi and Marc J. Wallace, Jr. Copyright © 1983 Scott, Foresman and Company. Reprinted by permission.

Informal leadership

Most functional and task groups have a formal leader—that is, one appointed by the organization. Because friendship and interest groups are formed by the members themselves, however, any formal leader must be elected or designated by the members. Although some groups do designate such a leader (a softball team may elect a captain), many do not. Moreover, even when a formal leader is designated, the group may also look to others for leadership.

A formal leader is one appointed by the organization or officially chosen by the group itself. An informal leader is a person who engages in leadership activities but whose right to do so has not been formally recognized.

The formal and the informal leader in any group may be the same person, or they may be different people. Figure 15.5 shows these different possibilities in five-person groups. Group A has one person filling both roles, whereas Group B has both a formal leader and an informal leader.

Let's look at the difference between the roles played by formal and informal leaders. The two most common roles are that of task specialist, who concentrates on getting the job done, and that of maintenance specialist, who concentrates on bolstering morale and building cohesiveness. Most groups require both functions, even though it is difficult for one person to fill both roles successfully. If the formal leader *can* do both, an informal leader may not emerge. If the formal leader can fulfill one role but not the other, an informal

Figure 15.5
Informal and formal
leaders

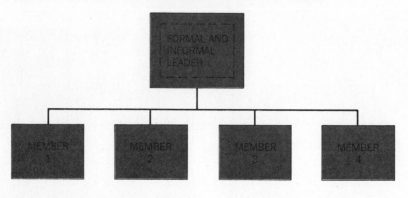

GROUP A: FORMAL AND INFORMAL LEADER IS THE SAME PERSON

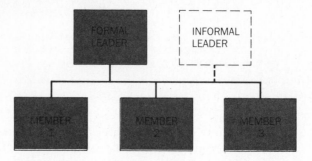

GROUP B: FORMAL AND INFORMAL LEADERS ARE DIFFERENT PEOPLE

leader often emerges to supplement the formal leader's functions. If the formal leader cannot fill either role, one or more informal leaders may emerge to carry out both sets of functions.

Is informal leadership desirable? In many cases informal leaders are quite powerful because they draw from referent or expert power. When they are working in the best interests of the organization, they can be a tremendous asset. Notable athletes such as Roger Staubach, Bart Starr, and Johnny Unitas are classic examples of informal leaders. On the other hand, when informal leaders work counter to the goals of the organization, they can cause significant difficulties. Such leaders may lower performance norms, instigate walk-outs or wildcat strikes, or otherwise disrupt the organization.

The informal organization

In virtually every organization of more than a few individuals, a shadow organization underlies the formal organization structure. Managers who hope to deal successfully with groups should be aware of the many facets of this informal organization.[22] James Patrick Wright provides many insights into the informal organization within General Motors. Promotions are often based on appearance, personality, and loyalty—as opposed to actual performance. Underlings are expected to ceremoniously pick up higher-level managers at the airport. When a GM executive checks into a hotel while traveling, local company officials make sure the room is stocked with the executive's preferred beverages and reading material. Finally, even though the name Vega was deemed inappropriate for Chevrolet's 1970s compact car on the basis of market research, the name was used nonetheless, because an upper manager liked it.[23]

The *informal organization* can be defined as the patterns of influence and behavior arising from friendship and interest groups in organizations. Although it is possible for the informal organization to follow the lines of the formal organization structure, it is more likely to deviate from it. (One important part of the informal organization, the grapevine, will be discussed in the next chapter.)

Perhaps the most useful way to analyze the effect of the informal organization is through Homans's model of groups.[24] Homans's model consists of four basic components (see Figure 15.6). First there are the background factors that influence group processes. As shown in the model, the major background factors are technology, job design, working conditions, managerial assumptions, leadership, rules, reward systems, the economic and social environment, and personal attributes of the various group members.

These contextual or background factors provide a framework for the group's required and given behavior. *Required activities* are those that are necessary for task performance. In an insurance claims department, required activities might be the processing and posting of all claims within 48 hours of receipt. *Required interactions* are the personal interactions needed to do the task. For the claims department, such interactions could flow from the processing clerk to the posting clerk to the disbursements clerk. *Required sentiments* are the feelings the organization believes are necessary to do the job. The insurance company might require that processing clerks be interested in paying all legitimate claims but that they not show sympathy toward claims that do not meet eligibility requirements. *Given sentiments* are those that individuals bring with them to the group.

The various required and given behaviors play a role in shaping the third component of Homans's model, emergent behavior, or the internal system of the group. *Emergent activities* are those activities that the group actually begins to perform. In the insurance claims department, the clerks, realizing that 48-hour turnaround is not always needed, may begin to let some claims slide an extra day. *Emergent interactions* are the interaction patterns that the group

22. See Robert F. Bales, *Interaction Process Analysis: A Method for the Study of Small Groups* (Reading, Mass.: Addison-Wesley, 1949).

23. See James Patrick Wright, *On a Clear Day You Can See General Motors* (New York: Wright Enterprises, 1979).

24. See George Homans, *The Human Group,* (New York: Harcourt, 1950).

Figure 15.6
Homans's model of
group behavior

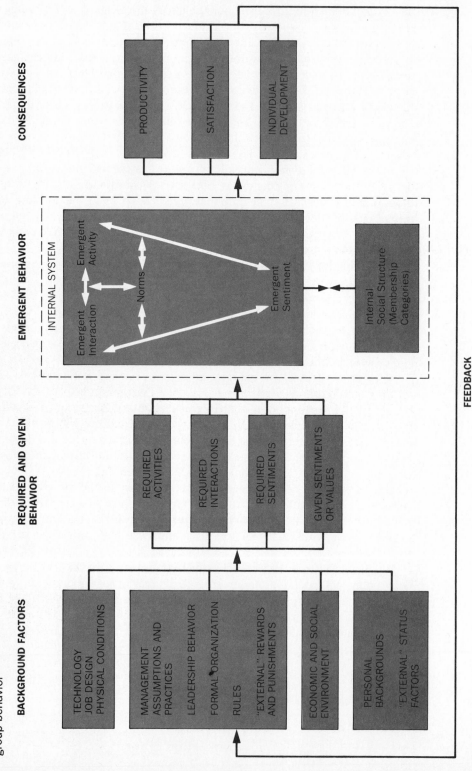

BACKGROUND FACTORS

REQUIRED AND GIVEN
BEHAVIOR

EMERGENT BEHAVIOR

CONSEQUENCES

FEEDBACK

Source: Paul R. Lawrence and John A. Seiler, *Organizational Behavior and Administration* (Homewood, Ill.: Richard D. Irwin, 1965), p. 158. Used with permission.

develops for itself. The posting clerk and the disbursements clerk might not get along, so another person might serve as a buffer between them by carrying the posted claims to the disbursements desk. *Emergent sentiments* are those the group deems appropriate. Group members might decide that families filing claims for having a baby are likely to be especially hard-pressed financially and therefore be more lenient in paying such claims. (Also relevant at this point is the internal social structure of the group. This structure defines the informal leader, high- and low-status members, and so on.)

Finally, as shown in Figure 15.6, the emergent behaviors have an effect on productivity, satisfaction, and individual development, and these factors affect background factors in subsequent group activities.

The real core of Homans's model is a point that deserves additional emphasis. Figure 15.7 diagrams the formal and informal processes within a work group. The solid boxes represent the required or formal processes: the activities, interactions, and sentiments required of the group. Suppose that an organization creates a group, assigns it a task (required activities), specifies formal interrelationships (required interactions), and assumes that group feelings will correspond to those of the organization (required sentiments).

What happens, though, is that an internal system begins to emerge from the group members themselves. These emergent processes are shown in Figure 15.7 as dashed boxes. Note that for some processes, such as required and emergent activities, the formal and emergent systems are likely to be the same. Other processes, such as required and emergent interactions, probably overlap to some extent. But such processes as required and emergent sentiments may be completely different. Here the manager must recognize that merely imposing a formal system on a group does not necessarily ensure that the group will function in accordance with it.

Figure 15.7
Required versus
emergent processes

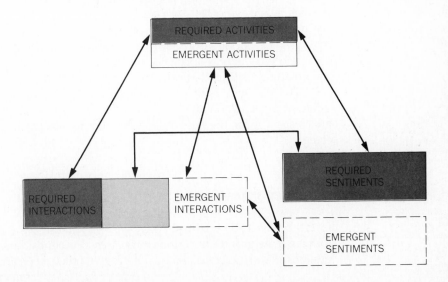

Reasons for the informal organization

At this point one might ask, "Why do informal groups and an informal organization emerge?" Many of the reasons were touched on earlier in our discussion of why people join groups. Those reasons involve interpersonal attraction, group activities, group goals, group membership, and instrumental benefits. In addition to these factors, there are a few other reasons why people participate in the informal organization.

Communication. Access to the informal communication network, or grapevine, is one reason why people join the informal organization. Information passes very rapidly (though not necessarily very accurately) through this network. Thus people who are "plugged in" feel they get inside information in a timely way.

Social satisfaction. Interacting with others and being accepted in an informal group provide social satisfaction for many people. They know they are being accepted for reasons above and beyond their formal organizational role, and they derive pleasure from belonging to the informal organization.

Balance and security. Finally, people participate in the informal organization because it offers balance and security. By balance, we mean that it may serve to counter tedious and routine work by providing social interaction. By security, we mean that the individual may derive comfort from knowing that he or she is supported and backed up by others in the informal organization.

Advantages and disadvantages

The informal organization has several advantages and several disadvantages. On the negative side, the informal organization may reinforce low performance norms, transmit damaging and/or inaccurate information, unite one set of employees against another, or undermine the formal authority system through the presence of informal leaders. In other situations, the informal organization may provide social satisfaction for employees that is missing in their formal jobs, reinforce high performance norms, supplement the formal activity system by providing dedicated informal leaders, or increase group cohesiveness.

The key point is that the manager must not ignore or try to eliminate the informal organization. It is important to recognize the informal organization and respect it for the power it has to accomplish positive as well as negative things.

Managing groups in organizations

In this final section of the chapter, we will summarize a number of guidelines for managing groups and group processes in organizations. Some of these suggestions pertain to specific kinds of groups; others refer to groups in general.

Managing task groups

Jay Galbraith has suggested six basic guidelines for designing task groups or teams for use in a matrix design.[25] These guidelines are as follows: (1) Most of the group members should be line managers who will be ultimately responsible for implementing the group's output. (2) The group should have access to all pertinent information. (3) Group members should have the power to command their departments to follow various courses of activities. (4) The influence system in the group should be based on expert power. (5) The task group should be integrated with relevant functional departments. (6) Group members should be chosen for both their technical expertise and their interpersonal skills.

Managing autonomous work groups

Similarly, J. Richard Hackman has made five suggestions for managing autonomous work groups.[26] (1) The group should probably have no more than fifteen members. (2) Sensitivity training and similar forms of organization development should be avoided. (3) The reward system should reward the entire group as opposed to individuals. (4) The group supervisor should serve more as coordinator and liaison than as decision maker. (5) The group should have the authority to plan, organize, and control its work.

Managing committees

It may be useful at this point to consider several guidelines for effective committee management.[27] According to Cyril O'Donnell, it is important to clearly define the goals of the committee, specify the committee's authority, start and stop meetings on schedule, maintain an agenda, appoint a formal leader, and hold the number of members to ten or fewer.

Other guidelines

In addition to these specific guidelines, a more general set of suggestions has been advanced for managing many different types of group situations.[28] These four general guidelines pertain directly to the basic group characteristics discussed earlier in this chapter. First, design the group in such a way as to minimize the potential for difficulties in role dynamics. Roles should be carefully

25. See Jay Galbraith, *Organization Design,* (Reading, Mass.: Addison-Wesley, 1977).

26. See J. Richard Hackman, "Work Design," in J. R. Hackman and J. Lloyd Suttle (eds.), *Improving Life at Work: Behavioral Science Approaches to Organizational Change* (Santa Monica, Calif.: Goodyear, 1977).

27. See Cyril O'Donnell, "Ground Rules for Using Committees," *Management Review,* October 1961, pp. 63–67.

28. See Ricky W. Griffin, *Task Design—An Integrative Approach,* (Glenview, Il.: Scott, Foresman, 1982).

defined unless there is clear reason to do otherwise (for example, one guideline for autonomous work groups is to allow workers to create their own roles). Second, design the group so as to foster high performance norms. For example, reward high group performance or assign highly productive individuals to the group. Third, facilitate and enhance group cohesiveness. This can be accomplished by encouraging interaction and avoiding intragroup competition. Finally, understand who the informal leaders are and what roles they play. An informal leader who does a good job in the maintenance role might be assigned to a group with a formal leader who is most concerned with the task role. Of course, the members of the informal organization must also be accounted for.

It should be clear that all these guidelines are only suggestions and not iron-clad rules. The effective manager will recognize their limitations as well as their strengths and use them as appropriate in particular situations.

Summary of key points

A group is two or more people who interact in order to accomplish a common purpose or goal. General kinds of groups in organizations are functional groups (created by the organization to accomplish a number of organizationally specified purposes with an indefinite time horizon), task groups (created by the organization to accomplish a relatively narrow range of organizationally specified purposes within a stated or implied time horizon), and informal or interest groups (created by the members for purposes that may or may not be consistent with those of an organization and having an unspecified time horizon).

People join functional or task groups in order to pursue a career. Their reasons for joining informal or interest groups include interpersonal attraction, group activities, group goals, the intangible rewards of group membership, and potential instrumental benefits. The stages of group development include testing and dependence (forming), intragroup conflict and hostility (storming), development of group cohesion (norming), and functional role-relatedness (performing).

Four important group characteristics are role dynamics, group norms, group cohesiveness, and informal leadership. The basic unit of analysis of role dynamics is the role episode, which consists of expected, sent, perceived, and enacted role behaviors. Within each role episode, there is potential for role ambiguity, role conflict and/or role overload. Group norms are standards of behavior for group members. Norms cannot always be generalized from one group to another. Some members of the group (such as informal leaders and/ or those with expert power) may not have to honor norms as rigidly as everyone else. A variety of factors influence norm conformity. Group cohesiveness is the extent to which members are attracted to each other and to the group as a whole. Several factors can increase or reduce group cohesiveness, but performance norms are especially important. Informal leaders are those leaders whom the group members themselves choose to follow. The formal leader and the informal leader may or may not be the same person. One may serve as a task specialist and the other as a maintenance specialist.

The informal organization consists of patterns of influence and behavior arising from friendship and interest groups in organizations. Homans's model is a useful framework for understanding the informal organization, especially required activities, interactions, and sentiments versus emergent activities, interactions, and sentiments. The manager must not ignore or try to eliminate the informal organization but should recognize it and respect what it can do.

Several sets of guidelines exist for managing various kinds of group situations. Some of these relate specifically to task groups, autonomous work groups, and committees; others pertain to more general group settings.

QUESTIONS FOR DISCUSSION

1. Is it possible for a group to be of more than one type at the same time? If so, under what circumstances? If not, why not?
2. How personal must the interaction be for a group to exist? For example, if two people never see one another but constantly exchange letters, memos, or telephone calls, can they be a group?
3. What groups do you belong to? What kinds of groups are they? Why did you join each?
4. Can you think of six groups you have participated in that progressed through the four stages of development? Can you think of an example of a group that did *not* evolve through the four stages?
5. Are role ambiguity, conflict, and overload always bad? Why or why not?
6. Identify the most relevant and important norms of a group with which you are familiar.
7. Suppose you have just been appointed the formal leader of a work group that has low performance norms and a high level of cohesiveness. What would you do?
8. How could you go about identifying the informal leader of a work group? Could there be more than one?
9. How does the formal organization work in your college or university? Can you think of situations in which the informal organization served "good" purposes? "Bad" purposes?
10. Using a group that you are familiar with and Homans's model, identify situations in which required activities, interactions, and/or sentiments were not the same as emergent activities, interactions, and/or sentiments.
11. Can you think of additional guidelines that might be useful in managing groups? Can you think of *exceptions* to the guidelines presented in the chapter?

C A S E   15.1

At the beginning of this chapter, you read an incident about four vastly different men. One is a born-again Christian and another a life-long Christian. A third is a rowdy party-goer and the fourth a back-slapping salesman. You were asked how they might function together as a group. The four men are the management team of the Dallas Cowboys, the most successful NFL team since its inception in 1960. The case that follows describes how they function together and then raises some other issues for your consideration.

The Dallas Cowboys are managed by a group of four men—Clint Murchison, Tex Schramm, Tom Landry, and Gil Brandt. These men function extremely well together as a management team, but it is difficult to imagine a more diverse foursome.

Perhaps the best known of the four men is Tom Landry, the only coach in the history of the organization. Landry is an extremely religious man who openly professes his faith in God. He has also been critical of the Dallas Cowboy Cheerleaders and the image they project. He has a reputation for being unemotional and has been described by some players as "plastic." In reality Landry is gracious, warm, and pleasant and a man of great conviction. He doesn't drink or use abusive language, nor has he sought to capitalize on his fame and success. He did not do his first television commercial, for example, until 1982, and only then a well-crafted and tasteful endorsement for American Express.

Gil Brandt is the Cowboys' vice president of personnel development. He is generally given credit for the Cowboys' success in scouting and evaluating the talent of college players. In many ways, Brandt is the antithesis of Landry. He is out-going and openly concerned with image and public relations. For example, he makes sure that the children of all major college football coaches receive a birthday card from the Cowboys every year and is always on the sidelines during the games for public relations purposes.

Clint Murchison, the owner of the Cowboys, is intelligent, articulate, and outgoing. The son of a Texas millionaire, Murchison has a Master's degree in theoretical mathematics from MIT. For many years, Murchison was somewhat rowdy. He indulged in wide-ranging social activities and enjoyed nothing more than a good drink. In 1975, however, he married Gil Brandt's ex-wife and has since become a born-again Christian.

Finally there is Tex Schramm, president and general manager of the Cowboys. Schramm is quite a showman, occasionally given to show-biz theatrics. For example, it was Schramm who created the Cowboy Cheerleaders. He still enjoys his alcohol and has been known to hurl unprintable epithets at game officials from the press box. Schramm is tightly wired into league headquarters; his association with NFL Commissioner Pete Rozelle dates back to the

The Dallas Cowboys' management team

early 1950s. Others around the league occasionally refer to him as the unofficial commissioner.

Given such diverse backgrounds, how have these four created and maintained one of the most successful operations in the history of organized sports? The key is probably the fact that each man has a well-defined role. On day one, for example, Schramm and Murchison specified in writing that Schramm would hire all coaches and that the head coach would have complete control over the players.

In order to develop and maintain a sophisticated management information system, Murchison started his own computer company, and the application of computer technology to sports has become a Cowboy trademark. It is still Landry, though, who maintains final authority over personnel decisions. Landry is often described as the glue that holds the organization together and the leader who maintains its direction and focus.

While Landry provides leadership, Schramm handles the flair. In addition to creating the Cowboy Cheerleaders, he has hustled so much national exposure for the team that the Cowboys have become known as "America's Team." Schramm created the Cowboy newsletter, which currently circulates to over 100,000 readers.

The effectiveness of the Cowboy organization can be easily measured both on and off the field. Since 1966 the team has always won more games than it has lost. During that same period, Dallas has failed to make the play-offs only one time. Overall, the team has had the highest percentage of victories in the entire league since it came into existence in 1960.

Off the playing field, the Cowboys are also a profitable business enterprise. Twenty-four percent of all NFL-authorized products have the Dallas trademark. All in all, the Dallas Cowboys are a well managed and effective business organization. Of course, inasmuch as three of the four men in charge are about 60 years of age, the management group cannot remain together indefinitely.

CASE
QUESTIONS

1. Can you apply the concepts of role dynamics, performance norms, cohesiveness, and informal leadership to the Cowboys' management team?
2. Which member of the organization is most crucial to its success? Why?
3. What situational characteristics contribute most to the success of the Cowboys?
4. Are any elements of the informal organization relevant to the Dallas Cowboys?

CASE
REFERENCES

Johnson, William. "There Are No Holes at the Top." *Sports Illustrated,* September 1, 1982, pp. 160–168.

Steadman, John. "Cowboys' Stars Start at the Top." *The Sporting News,* January 9, 1982.

C A S E   15.2

Ted Lofton was aghast. He had just completed his first inspection of the plant and had seen so many problems he didn't know where to begin. This was Ted's first major management position and he knew that his future with the company depended on how he handled this job. The East Hampton plant had a reputation in the company as a real trouble spot. He knew that if he could get things straightened out, he would be on his way.

And suddenly, Ted knew just where to begin. As he toured the plant, the most shocking scene had been in Section C. There were five older women down there who had turned the place into a living room. Whereas everyone else had worked at tables arranged in neat rows, these five had their tables arranged in a circle. They had put down a carpet and even hung some pictures on the wall. They had stashed a small refrigerator off to one side and kept a radio playing music. Ted didn't understand why they needed the radio, though. They talked incessantly and couldn't possibly have heard anything. And, Ted was sure, the talking and other distractions were surely hurting productivity. Yes, Ted thought, that's where I'll start.

Late that evening, after everyone else had gone, Ted sent a maintenance crew down to Section C. He had them unplug the radio and refrigerator and set them in a corner. The carpet was rolled up, the pictures taken off the wall, and the work tables arranged in a neat straight line.

The next morning, Ted fully expected the women to come storming into his office, and he was prepared to deal with them. He was surprised, however, when they simply sat down and went to work. He was equally surprised to find three days later that output from Section C was down 75 percent. He immediately raced to the floor to find out how the women were cutting back, but he couldn't find any evidence that they were working at anything but maximum efficiency.

Ted next went back to his office and did something he realized he should have done much earlier. He looked at the performance records of the five women. Three pieces of information were especially enlightening. The women had worked together in the same section for over fifteen years, and they consistently produced at a rate of 70 to 80 percent above the standard established for their jobs. Finally, their supervisor had noted several times in their files that they were all very dedicated and committed employees.

As much as he hated to admit it, Ted had to face the fact that he had made a serious error. After a couple of hours of building up his nerve, Ted walked down to Section C. He apologized for what he had done and helped the women rearrange their work area

Productivity and group dynamics

the way it was before. The next day, he was pleased to find that productivity was once again up to its previous high level.

CASE
QUESTIONS

1. Can you characterize the work group in Section C both before and after the changes Ted made?
2. At what stage of development was the work group in Section C?
3. How would you assess Ted's potential as a manager?
4. How many of the key terms and concepts discussed in this chapter are illustrated here?

16

COMMUNICATION IN ORGANIZATIONS

CHAPTER OBJECTIVES

1. Describe the basic communication process and relate communication to the manager's job.

2. Describe how perception and attitudes can influence communication.

3. Identify three forms of interpersonal communication and discuss their strengths and weaknesses.

4. Identify four forms of organizational communication and discuss how each can be made more effective.

5. Discuss the major barriers to effective communication and how they can be overcome.

6. Explain how the informal communication network works and how managers should react to it.

7. Briefly describe the emerging impact of electronic communication.

475

476

OPENING INCIDENT

You are a top manager at a foreign office of a major bank. Recently you have discovered that the bank is maintaining one set of records in a management information system for external disclosure and a second system for internal use. The internal system handles a number of illegal transactions by which the bank is evading taxes. How would you try to communicate your discovery to other managers?

A typical day for a manager includes most of the following activities: desk work, attending scheduled meetings, telephone calls, reading correspondence, answering correspondence, attending unscheduled meetings, and tours.[1] Most of these activities involve communication. In fact, managers usually spend well over half of their time involved in some form of communication. Communication always involves two or more people, so behavioral processes such as motivation, leadership, and group dynamics as well as perception and attitudes all come into play.

This chapter first relates communication to the manager's job, especially to the management function of leading. Then we describe how perceptions and attitudes affect communication. Interpersonal communication and organizational communication are the next topics. Then, after discussing the barriers to effective communication and several ways to overcome them, we analyze informal communication processes. Finally, the emerging importance of electronic communication is briefly summarized.

Communication and the manager's job

Imagine three shipwreck survivors stranded on separate islands. The first is yelling for help although he has no radio and there is no one around for 1,000 miles. The second is talking through a radio that, unfortunately, got a little wet during the wreck. A passing airplane picks up some of the noise he is transmitting but can't understand the coordinates he is repeating. The third survivor has just successfully transmitted his location to a nearby ship (his radio didn't get wet). The ship informs him that a rescue plane is on the way. What do these three individuals have in common? They are all stranded on an island. But the differences among them are more striking: each is engaged in a different communication process.

1. See Henry Mintzberg, *The Nature of Managerial Work* (New York: Harper & Row, 1973).

A definition of communication

Communication can be defined as the process of transmitting information from one person to another. Did any of our three shipwreck survivors communicate? Clearly the last did and the first did not, but how about the second? He communicated in that he transmitted information and information was received. The problem, of course, was that the message transmitted and the message received were not the same. The words he spoke were turned into static and noise. *Effective communication* is the process of sending a message in such a way that the message received is close in meaning to the message intended. Although the second survivor engaged in communication, he did not engage in effective communication.

In our definition of communication, we see that three conditions are necessary for communication to take place. First, there must be at least two people involved. The relationship between these two people can vary significantly, of course, in terms of proximity, intensity, and time. Two managers having a discussion in an office engage in communication. So do a student reading a book written five hundred years ago and the Renaissance philosopher who wrote it. Of course, many more than two people can be involved in communication. Second, there must be information to be communicated. And third, some attempt must be made to transmit this information.

Expanding further, our definition of effective communication incorporates the ideas of meaning and consistency of meaning. Meaning is that which the individual who initiates the communication process wishes to convey. In effective communication, the meaning is transmitted in such a manner that the receiving person understands it. For example, consider the following messages:

1. It will be cold today
2. Ceteris paribus
3. Shucking and jiving
4. Xngp boczjk

Most of you understand the meaning of the first statement. Probably fewer of you understand the second and third statements; the second is a Latin phrase and the third is street talk. None of you understands the fourth phrase, because it's written in a secret code your author developed as a child.

The communication model

We are now ready to look at an expanded model of how communication occurs (see Figure 16.1).[2] One-way communication (or communication from one person to another) involves five steps: meaning, encoding, transmission, decoding, and meaning. In the case of two-way communication (involving interaction between people), the three steps of encoding, transmission, and decoding are repeated as the second person responds to the first.

The process begins when one person (a sender) initiates a communication

2. This model draws from a variety of sources, including Otis W. Baskin and Craig E. Aronoff, *Interpersonal Communication in Organizations*, (Santa Monica, Calif.: Goodyear, 1980); and Terence R. Mitchell, *People in Organizations*, 2nd ed. (New York: McGraw-Hill, 1982).

Figure 16.1
A communication
model

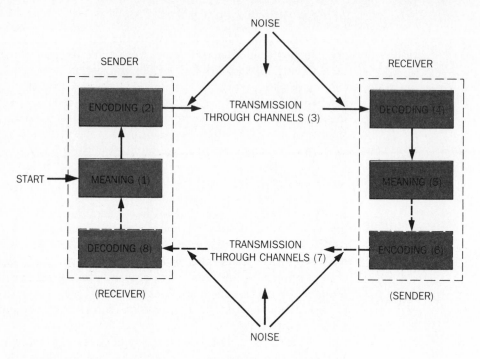

The numbers in parentheses indicate the sequence in which the steps take place.

exchange. This person has decided that a fact, idea, opinion, or similar concept needs to be transmitted to someone else. This fact, idea, or opinion has meaning to the sender, whether it be simple and concrete or complex and abstract. Thus *meaning* is the first step in the communication process.

The next step is to *encode* the meaning into a form appropriate to the situation. This encoding might take the form of words, facial expressions, gestures, or even artistic expressions and physical actions. For example, a few of the many alternatives for encoding the simple thought "I don't like you" are

1. "I don't like you."
2. "Go away!"
3. "For some unknown reason that I don't understand, you are simply not the kind of person I enjoy being with."
4. "You really turn me off."
5. "I have a disaffinity for you."
6. Sticking out one's tongue at the other person.

Obviously, the selection of an appropriate form for encoding the meaning is one point in the process where problems can arise.

After the message has been encoded, it is *transmitted* through the appropriate channel. The channel by which this present encoded message is being transmitted to you is the printed page. Other common channels include face-to-face discussion, the air waves (usually one-way communication) and telephone lines. Transmission is step 3 of the communication process.

Next the message is received and *decoded* by one or more other people via such senses as eyesight and hearing. And after the message is received, it must be translated into *meaning* relevant to the receiver.

In many cases, this meaning prompts a response, and the cycle is continued when the new message is sent by the same steps back to the original sender (steps 6, 7, and 8). As suggested in Figure 16.1, "noise" may disrupt the process after it is transmitted but before it is received. Noise can literally *be* noise, such as someone coughing, a truck driving by, or two other people talking close at hand. It can also include such disruptions as a letter being lost in the mail, a telephone line going dead, or one of the individuals being called away before the communication process is completed.

The role of communication in management

At the beginning of this chapter we noted the variety of activities that comprise the manager's day. Meetings, telephone calls, and correspondence are all a necessary part of every manager's job, and all clearly involve communication. As a starting point for understanding the importance of communication in management, consider the variety of roles managers must fill.

The managerial roles observed by Henry Mintzberg (and discussed in Chapter 1) involve a great deal of communication.[3] The *interpersonal roles* involve interacting with supervisors, subordinates, peers, and others outside the organization. The *decisional roles* require that managers seek out information to use in making decisions and then communicate those decisions to others. The *informational roles* obviously involve communication; they focus specifically on acquiring and disseminating information.

Communication also relates directly to the basic management functions of planning, organizing, leading, and controlling. Environmental scanning, integrating, planning time horizons, and decision making, for example, all necessitate communication. Delegation, coordination, and organization change and development also entail communication. Developing reward systems and interacting with subordinates as a part of the leading function would be impossible without some form of communication. And communication is essential to establishing standards, monitoring performance, and taking corrective actions as a part of control.

Behavioral processes that affect communication

By definition, communication involves more than one person, so we would expect emotional and psychological differences between people to affect the communication process. When Mike enthusiastically describes his new pay raise to Deborah, her response depends in part on her own situation. She may

---

3. See Mintzberg, *The Nature of Managerial Work.*

respond in a variety of ways, depending on whether she got a similar raise, no raise at all, or a cut in pay. The behavioral processes that probably have the most impact on communication are perception and attitudes.

Perception and communication

Perception can be defined as the processes an individual uses to receive information from the environment. Hence perception exploits the five senses of hearing, seeing, feeling, tasting, and smelling. In terms of communication, perception plays a major role in receiving the message transmitted from the sender (step 3 in Figure 16.1) and in decoding it (step 4 in Figure 16.1).[4]

Each of us is constantly bombarded with information from our environment. Everywhere we turn we encounter information—so much information that we cannot handle it all. To illustrate, answer the following questions:

1. What color shirt was the last person you saw wearing?
2. What was the last song you heard on the radio?
3. Exactly how much did you pay for the tank of gas you most recently purchased?
4. When you were last watching television, how many commercials did you see?

Most people cannot answer all four of these simple questions, even though we all regularly see and hear the things they ask about. For managers, this humdrum barrage of information takes the form of sales forecasts, economic indexes, memos, letters, reports, phone calls, and conversations.

As shown in Figure 16.2, perception acts as a filter for us. It screens out information that is trivial or that we don't want to know about. Perception helps us *select* and *organize* information from the environment.

Selection. Selection, or selective perception, is the process of screening out information we are uncomfortable with or just don't want to bother about. People who buy a new car tend to be more aware of advertising for that car, because it reassures them that they made a wise decision, and to be less aware of advertising for other kinds of cars, because it insinuates that they made a mistake.

In an early study of selective perception, a group of executives read a case study about a steel company and then were asked to identify the company's major problems. Almost all the executives identified a problem deriving from their own area of expertise. For example, five out of six sales managers said the company's major problem was in sales, and four out of five production managers identified production problems. These executives filtered out information that dealt with other areas and focused almost exclusively on the information most relevant to their own jobs.[5]

4. For a general overview of perception, see E. E. Jones and R. E. Nisbett, *The Actor and the Observer: Divergent Perceptions of the Causes of Behavior* (Morristown, N.J.: General Learning Press, 1971).

5. See D. C. Dearborn and H. A. Simon, "Selective Perception: A Note on the Departmental Identification of Executives," *Sociometry*, Vol. 21, 1958, p. 143.

Figure 16.2
Basic perceptual
processes

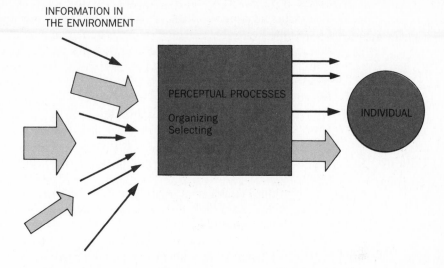

INFORMATION IN
THE ENVIRONMENT

PERCEPTUAL PROCESSES

Organizing
Selecting

INDIVIDUAL

Organization. As the information from our environment is being selected and filtered, it is also being organized. Organization is the process of
categorizing, grouping, and filling in information in a systematic fashion. The
primary means of categorizing information is stereotyping. Whereas stereotyping by race or sex is not a good idea, other forms of stereotyping can be helpful. If we are looking for a person with good public relations skills, we may be
able to categorize people into acceptable or unacceptable groups with relative
ease. Of course, we must be sure that we do not exclude qualified people
through such a simplistic approach.

We also organize information by grouping it into categories. As managers
approach their daily schedule, they may respond to all telephone messages,
then turn to letters and memos, and finally attend meetings and conferences.
After information has been organized, there is also a tendency to fill in gaps to
make it more meaningful. When a personnel manager receives three resigna-
tions in one week from the same department, he or she may "fill in the gap"
by assuming a problem exists in that department.

Attitudes and communication

A second important behavioral process that can affect communication is the
attitudes of the people involved. An *attitude* is a person's predisposition to
respond in a favorable or unfavorable way to an object (in this sense, an object
can be a person or an idea as well as a physical object). All of us harbor attitudes toward our jobs, other people, movies, sports teams, and just about
everything else we come into contact with.[6]

Most theorists agree that attitudes have three basic components. The

6. See Martin Fishbein and I. Ajzen, *Belief, Attitude, and Behavior: An Introduction to Theory and
Research* (Reading, Mass.: Addison-Wesley, 1975).

emotional component is the individual's feelings about the object. That is, it reflects whether a person likes or dislikes the object and how central this like or dislike is to her or his personal value system. You may like one of your classes, dislike another, and be indifferent toward a third. If the class that you dislike is an elective, your dislike for it may not worry you very much. If it is the first course you have taken in your major, however, your attitude may cause you considerably more concern.

The *knowledge component* of an attitude is the beliefs and information the person has about the object. You may dislike a class because it requires too much time, has a poor textbook, and is taught by an unsympathetic instructor. Some or all of this information might not be true, but it still represents your beliefs.

The third component of an attitude is *behavioral intention*. Because of how we feel about the object and what we think we know about it, we develop intentions of how we expect to behave. The student who dislikes a course may resolve to drop it at mid-term—or even to consider changing majors. In the statement "I don't like that new seafood restaurant because I got some bad shrimp there—I'll never eat there again," the behavioral intention is reflected at the end ("I don't like . . ." is the emotional part of the attitude; "I got some . . ." represents the knowledge component). Circumstances often change, of course, and we are forced to change our behavioral intentions accordingly. Your favorite date, for example, might insist on eating at the seafood restaurant.

To see how attitudes influence communication, examine the memo shown in Figure 16.3. This memo is from a secretary to the three managers he or she works for. Note in particular that the secretary is asking for time off and soliciting a nomination for an award.

Suppose that Mr. Jones has a very favorable attitude toward the secretary, Ms. Smith has an extremely negative attitude toward the secretary, and Mr. Williams has just started working for the company. The responses from Jones and Smith might be similar to those given in

Figure 16.3
Memo from
secretary to bosses

Memorandum

TO Mr. Jones, Ms. Smith, and   FROM B. Carter   DATE April 9, 1985
    Mr. Williams
SUBJECT

I would like to request three days off next week. As you know, my mother is quite ill
and I would like to visit her. Since I have used up my allotment of sick days this
year, the personnel department has indicated that I need your okay. Someone from the
steno pool can cover my desk.

By the way, nominations for the secretary of the year award are due next week. I believe
I am as deserving of this award as anyone else in the company. If any or all of you would
care to nominate me, the forms are in my top desk drawer.

Figure 16.4
Memos from bosses
to secretary

Memorandum

TO   B. Carter   FROM   Mr. Jones   DATE   April 10, 1985

SUBJECT

Of course it's all right for you to visit your mother next week. Please give her my best
wishes. I also agree that you should be considered for secretary of the year. I'll
prepare the nomination myself and turn it in.

Memorandum

TO   B. Carter   FROM   Ms. Smith   DATE   April 10, 1985

SUBJECT

You probably don't think anyone would have the nerve to deny your request to visit your
"sick mother." I'll grant permission, provided you bring a letter from her doctor describing the severity of her illness. I'm also notifying the personnel department that any
further absences will result in your termination.

It's also presumptuous of you to ask us to nominate you for the secretary of the year award.
Even if anyone felt you deserved it, no one would be around to type the nomination.

Figure 16.4. It is clear that their respective positive and negative attitudes
affected how they interpreted and responded to the memo from the secretary.
Because Williams is new, he probably hasn't formed an opinion and may turn
to Jones or Smith for suggestions on how to respond. His choice of which
colleague to query will play a role in the early stages of his own attitude
formation.

Attitudes are closely related to both the decoding (step 4) and the meaning (step 5) stages of the communication model given in Figure 16.1. They
also influence the receiver's responses. Attitudes interact with perception
within the communication process. In the previous example, Smith selectively
did not perceive that a temporary replacement would be filling in for Carter
and could type the nomination for secretary of the year. Attitudes, then,
help determine what information people selectively perceive and how they
organize it.

Interpersonal communication

Interpersonal communication, as the term suggests, is concerned with communication between people, especially small numbers of people. Later we will
discuss communication in a broader organizational context. Our focus here is

on oral, written, and nonverbal communication between small numbers of people in an organization.

Oral communication

Oral communication involves face-to-face conversation, group discussions, telephone calls, and other situations in which the sender uses the spoken word to communicate. Mintzberg demonstrated the importance of oral communication when he found that most managers spend between 50 and 90 percent of their time talking to people.[7] There are several reasons why oral communication is so prevalent. The primary advantage of this form of communication is that it allows prompt feedback in the form of verbal questions or agreement, facial expressions, and gestures (we will discuss nonverbal communication later). Oral communication is easy (all one needs to do is talk), and it can be done with little preparation (though careful preparation is advisable in certain situations). One doesn't need a pencil and paper, typewriter, or other equipment. In a recent survey, 55 percent of the executives sampled felt that their own written communication skills were fair or poor, so they chose oral communication to avoid embarrassment![8]

However, oral communication also has its drawbacks. It may suffer from problems of inaccuracy as the speaker chooses the wrong words to convey her or his meaning or leaves out pertinent details, as noise disrupts the process, or as the receiver forgets part or all of the message. In a two-way discussion, there is seldom time for a thoughtful, considered response or for introducing many new facts. And there is no permanent record of what has been said.

Written communication

"Putting it in writing" can solve many of the problems inherent in oral communication. Nevertheless, and perhaps surprisingly, **written communication** does not occur as frequently as one might imagine, nor is it a mode of communication much respected by managers. Only 13 percent of the mail received by managers is of immediate use to them.[9] And over 80 percent of the managers who responded to the survey mentioned earlier indicated that the written communication they received was of fair or poor quality.[10]

The biggest single drawback of written communication is that it slows feedback. When one manager sends another manager a letter, it must be written or dictated, typed, mailed, received, routed, opened, and read. If there is a misunderstanding, it may take several days for it to be recognized, let alone rectified. A phone call could settle the whole matter in just a few minutes.

Of course, written communication also has its advantages. The two big-

7. See Mintzberg, *The Nature of Managerial Work*.

8. See Walter Kiechel, III, "The Big Presentation," *Fortune*, July 26, 1982, pp. 98–100.

9. See Mintzberg, *The Nature of Managerial Work*.

10. See Kiechel, "The Big Presentation."

gest advantages are that written communication is often quite accurate and that it provides a permanent record of the communication. The sender can take the time to collect and assimilate the information and can draft and revise it before it is transmitted. The receiver can take the time to read through it carefully and can refer to it repeatedly, as needed. For these reasons, written communication is generally preferable when important details are involved. There are also times when it is important to one or both parties to have a written record available as "evidence" of exactly what took place.

Nonverbal communication

A powerful but little-understood form of interpersonal communication in organizations is *nonverbal communication:* any communication exchange that does not use words or that uses verbalization to carry more meaning than the strict definition of the words themselves. Facial expressions, body movements, physical contact, sneers, and gestures may all be used. One study of nonverbal communication has suggested that as much as 55 percent of the content of a message is transmitted via facial expression and body posture and that another 38 percent derives from inflection and tone. The words themselves account for only 7 percent of the content of the message.[11] It is safe to assume, of course, that these percentages vary considerably in different situations.

Michael B. McCaskey has identified three important kinds of nonverbal communication practiced by managers: images, settings, and body language.[12] *Images* in this connection are the kinds of words people elect to use. "Damn the torpedoes, full speed ahead" and "Even though there are some potential hazards, we should proceed with this course of action" may convey the same meaning. Yet the person who uses the first expression may be perceived as a maverick, a courageous hero, an individualist, or a reckless and foolhardy adventurer. The person who uses the second expression, on the other hand, might be described as aggressive, forceful, diligent, or narrow-minded and resistant to change. In short, our choice of words conveys much more than just the strict meaning of the words we choose.

The *setting* for communication also plays a major role in nonverbal communication. Boundaries, familiarity, the home turf, and other elements of the setting are all important. Much has been written, for example, about the symbols of power in organizations.[13] The size and location of one's office, the kinds of furniture in the office, and the accessibility of the person in the office all communicate useful information.

Suppose, for example, that Nick Warburton, recently promoted to purchasing manager, is considering three alternative office layouts (see Figure 16.5). Each includes a desk, a manager's chair, and a visitor's chair. By choosing

11. See Albert Mehrabian, *Non-Verbal Communication* (Chicago: Aldine, 1972).

12. See Michael B. McCaskey, "The Hidden Messages Managers Send," *Harvard Business Review*, November–December 1979, pp. 135–148.

13. See, for example, Michael Korda, *Power! How to Get It, How to Use It* (New York: Random House, 1975).

Figure 16.5
Nonverbal
communication and
office arrangement

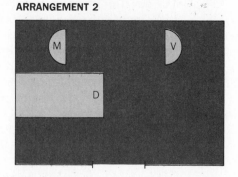

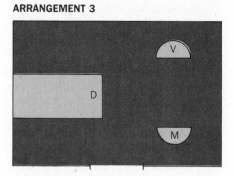

Key:
M = Manager
V = Visitor
D = Desk

arrangement 1, Nick would be indicating that he is in control and has more power than the visitor. How? By keeping the desk (a symbol of status and authority) between them. In effect he would be saying, "I'm behind the desk and you're in front of it, and we both know what *that* means."

In arrangement 2, Nick would be sending a different message. By positioning the visitor so that the desk was no longer between them, he would be giving up some power—yet he would still be behind the desk. He would be saying, "I'm willing to remove this barrier, but it's still right there if I need it."

Finally, in arrangement 3, Nick would have given up the barrier completely. He would position himself and the visitor so that they were on an equal footing with no barrier between them. In effect he would be saying, "I don't need this barrier; I'm willing to accept you on my level." Each of these three layouts, then, conveys a different message about the manager.

A third form of nonverbal communication is body language. The distance we stand from someone as we speak, for example, has meaning. The English and Germans stand farther apart than Americans when talking, whereas the Arabs, Japanese, and Mexicans stand closer together.[14] Positioning oneself closer than customary may signal familiarity or aggression. (Consider the confusion that can result when individuals who are unaware of their different customs regarding distance during conversation try to communicate with each other!) Eye contact is another effective means of nonverbal communication. Depending on the situation, prolonged eye contact might suggest either hostility or romantic interest. Other kinds of body language include movement, pauses in speech, and mode of dress.

Organizational communication

Unlike interpersonal communication, organizational communication involves broad patterns of communication and (usually) large numbers of people. In this section we will discuss four aspects of organizational communication: communication networks, vertical communication, horizontal communication, and management information systems.

Communication networks

A *communication network* is a recurring pattern of communication processes among members of a group. Researchers studying group dynamics have discovered several typical networks in groups numbering three, four, and five members.[15]

Representative networks among members of five-member groups are shown in Figure 16.6. In the wheel, all communication flows through one central person who is probably the group's formal or informal leader. In a sense this is the most centralized network, because one person receives and disseminates all information. The Y is slightly less centralized: two persons are close to the center. The chain begins to offer a more even flow of information among members, although there are two people (the ones at each end) who interact

14. See Edward J. Hall, *The Hidden Dimension* (New York: Doubleday, 1966).

15. See A. Bavelas, "Communication Patterns in Task-Oriented Groups," *Journal of the Acoustical Society of America*, Vol. 22, 1950, pp. 725–730; and Jerry Wofford, Edwin Gerloff, and Robert Cummins, *Organizational Communication*, (New York: McGraw-Hill, 1977).

Figure 16.6
Types of
communication
networks

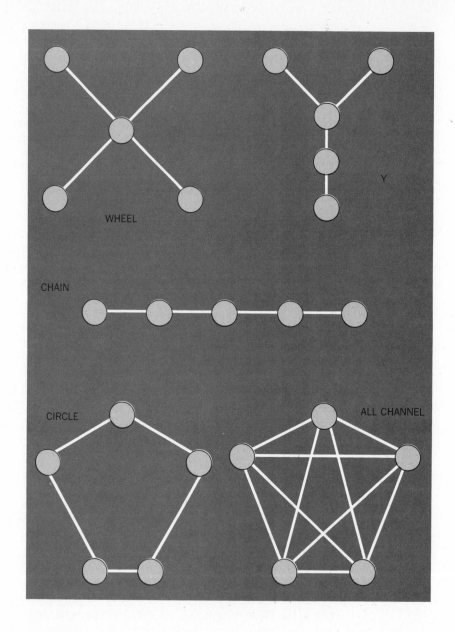

with only one other person. This path is closed in the circle pattern. Finally, the all-channel network allows a free flow of information among all group members. This network is the most decentralized; everyone participates equally, and the group's leader, if there is one, is not likely to have excessive power.

Research that has been conducted on networks suggests some interesting connections between the network and group performance. For example, when the group's task is relatively simple and routine, the more centralized networks tend to perform with greater efficiency and accuracy. The dominant leader facilitates performance in this structure by coordinating information flow. When the group is logging in-coming invoices and distributing them for payment, one centralized leader can coordinate things efficiently. When the task is complex and nonroutine, such as making a major decision about organizational strategy, decentralized networks tend to be more effective. This is because open channels of communication permit more interaction and a more efficient sharing of relevant information. Managers should recognize the effects of communication networks on group and organizational performance and should try to structure such networks accordingly.

Vertical communication

An earlier section of this chapter described an exchange of memos between a secretary and a group of managers. This pattern of communication is vertical in nature, because it flows between a subordinate and a manager. *Vertical communication* may involve only two people, or it may flow among several different levels in the organization. And it may flow both up and down the organization.

Upward communication. Upward communication includes oral, written, and nonverbal messages from subordinates to superiors. Typically, this flow is from a subordinate to her or his direct superior, then to that person's direct superior, and so on up through the hierarchy. Occasionally, however, a message might by-pass a particular superior. Research has shown that the by-passed superior may feel resentful and hostile when this happens.[16]

Other studies have shown quite clearly that upward communication is more subject to distortion than downward communication. Subordinates are prone to withholding or distorting information that makes them look bad. The greater the degree of difference in status between superior and subordinate and the greater the degree of distrust, the more likely the subordinate is to suppress or distort information.

Downward communication. Downward communication occurs when information flows down the hierarchy from superiors to subordinates. The superior may be assigning jobs or passing along needed information. In some cases the manager may transmit so much information that subordinates suffer from role overload. In other situations the manager may fail to pass on important information, and as a result subordinates cannot do their jobs effectively. The solution is to transmit just the right amount of information— neither too much nor too little. Such a balance is often difficult to achieve. In a later section of this chapter we will discuss several ways to improve communication.

16. See M. M. Bird, "Gains and Losses from an Open Line Program as Perceived by By-passed Managers: A Case Study," *Academy of Management Journal*, Vol. 16, 1973, pp. 325–329.

Horizontal communication

Whereas vertical communication involves a superior and a subordinate, *horizontal communication* involves colleagues and peers. For example, the production manager might communicate to the marketing manager that inventory levels are running low and that projected delivery dates should be extended by two weeks. Horizontal communication probably occurs more among managers than among non-managers.

Communication among peers and colleagues serves a number of purposes. First, it facilitates coordination among interdependent units. If unit A provides input for unit B (sequential interdependence), the supervisor of unit A might let the supervisor of unit B know in advance when the anticipated workload for the next day is going to be especially light or heavy so that he or she can plan accordingly. Horizontal communication can also be used for joint problem-solving, as when two plant managers of a large manufacturing firm get together to work out ways to improve productivity. Finally, horizontal communication plays a major role in matrix designs and in committees with representatives drawn from several departments.

Management information systems

The concept of management information systems, or MIS, was briefly introduced in Chapter 2 as a contribution of quantitative management theory. At this point we will describe MIS in more detail. A *management information system* (MIS) is a system designed to provide information to managers; hence it is a mechanism for managing the communication process in an organization.

Creating an MIS. Figure 16.7 shows how an MIS is created and used by managers.[17] The first step in creating an MIS is to develop an information bank, which is simply a compilation of useful information. This bank should include all relevant historical data as well as data about the organization's current situation. Some of the data needed for the information system are already available; the rest may have to be developed. The exact composition of the information bank depends on the organization's needs, but it should usually include financial data and information on marketing, procedures and operations, personnel, planning, and control. Sophisticated computer systems may also include simulation and modeling packages.

As the information is gathered, it must be stored in such a way that it can be managed (updated or deleted), processed (combined or manipulated), and then retrieved as needed. In most cases, especially in larger organizations,

---

17. For more information on these processes, see Walter J. Kennevan, "Management Information Systems," *Data Management*, September 1970, pp. 62–64; Paul M. Cheney and Norman R. Lyons, "MIS Update," *Data Management*, October 1980, pp. 26–32; and Charles R. Litecky, "Corporate Strategy and MIS Planning," *Journal of Systems Management*, January 1981, pp. 36–39.

Figure 16.7
Creating and using
an MIS

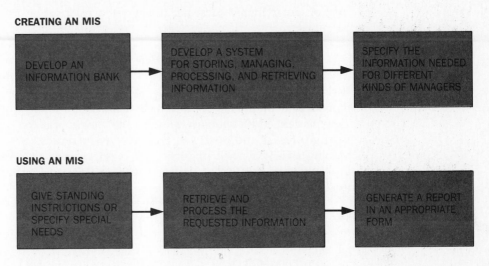

the MIS is computerized, but it is possible to have an MIS without using a computer.

Finally, the system needs to "know" what kinds of information different managers need, in what form, and how often. A sales representative may need a brief report each day describing his sales activity, the district sales manager may need a report describing the entire district's sales every week, and the vice president of marketing may need a comprehensive report on a monthly basis. The system should be able to provide "special request" reports as well as routine reports.

Using the MIS. Part 2 of Figure 16.7 shows how an established MIS is used. First the system needs to be told what to do. Standing instructions, or data parameters, are sufficient for routine reports. For "special request" situations, however, individual computer commands are necessary. The district sales manager, for example, might occasionally request daily sales summaries, or the vice president of marketing might ask for a simulation of the effects of raising prices 4 percent.

Next the system retrieves and processes the information requested. For the district sales manager's request, the system can simply locate the daily summaries that have already been prepared for the sales representatives. The request from the vice president of marketing will involve engaging a simulation model, plugging in a 4 percent price increase, and computing the probable outcomes.

The information is then reported in a form appropriate for the manager and the request. This form is typically a computer print-out or video display, though clerical labor is obviously needed when the system is not computerized. The information reported by the system may be discarded after use, or it

may be programmed back into the system's information bank for possible re-
trieval later.

The Daft and MacIntosh MIS model. Richard L. Daft and Norman B.
MacIntosh have recently developed a very interesting and useful approach for
designing and using an MIS.[18] The basis of their approach is the technology of
individual departments or units within an organization. Technology, in their
view, is defined by two key variables: the variety of tasks involved in the conversion process and how well that conversion process is understood. By describing variety as low or high, and by describing task knowledge as well
understood or not well understood, they developed four different MIS styles
(see Table 16.1).

Departments characterized by low variety and low task knowledge are
said to have craft technology. Examples of *craft technology* include buying fu-
tures, cooking, manufacturing fine glassware, and performing many managge-
rial activities. Daft and MacIntosh suggest that such departments need a

Table 16.1 Features of the Daft–MacIntosh MIS model

Kind of technology	Variety of tasks	Task knowledge	Appropriate MIS	Typical examples
Craft technology	Low	Not well understood	Cursory—limited and superficial information for routine decision making	Buying futures Cooking Manufacturing glassware
Research technology	High	Not well understood	Diffuse—broad coverage of a wide range of topics; marked by ambiguity; information often used in a slow, deliberate manner	Strategy formulation Research and development
Technical–professional technology	High	Well understood	Elaborate—large amounts of precise and detailed information; information often used in a slow, deliberate manner	Law Accounting Engineering
Programmable technology	Low	Well understood	Concise—precise information in small to moderate quantities for quick decisions	Airline reservation systems Bank card verification systems

18. See Richard L. Daft and Norman B. MacIntosh, "A New Approach to Design and Use of
Management Information," *California Management Review*, Fall 1978, pp. 82–92.

cursory MIS: one providing small amounts of information, often superficial and not precise or detailed, that is used in casual but decisive ways.

When task knowledge is low but variety is high, *research technology* exists. Examples of research technology include strategy formulation and research and development activities. The suggested form of MIS, a diffuse MIS, must handle large amounts of information covering a wide range of subjects. This information is usually poorly defined and ambiguous and is often used in a slow and deliberate manner.

Departments or units exhibiting high variety and high task knowledge are described as having a *technical–professional technology*. Law, accounting, and engineering are examples of this kind of technology. The elaborate MIS needed for this situation must be capable of handling large amounts of precise and detailed information. The information itself, however, is often used in a slow and deliberate fashion.

Programmable technology exists when variety is low but task knowledge is high. Examples include airline reservation systems and bank card verification systems. The MIS, called a concise MIS, provides precise and unambiguous information in small to moderate quantities for quick and decisive use.

Daft and MacIntosh provide several guidelines for setting up and using an MIS.[19]

1. An MIS should be designed to fit the technology of the department or unit, rather than the personal characteristics of individual managers.
2. MIS designers should not over-systematize by rushing in to develop large, data-based systems for departments or units that don't really need that kind of system.
3. MIS designers should not, on the other hand, under-systematize when large, data-based systems *are* needed.
4. Because technologies vary within organizations, a uniform, company-wide MIS will probably not be successful.
5. Managers should be cautious about transferring an MIS from one organization to another.
6. Top management work is poorly understood. The relevance of this fact for MIS design is that the MIS should not try to provide top managers with large quantities of objective data. Personally obtained information is more useful at that level of the organization.
7. Information system design requires a flexible approach in order to transfer the system to the department where it will be used.

To illustrate how several of these guidelines apply, consider a company like Corning Glass Works. Corning would be likely to need a cursory MIS for its glassware manufacturing activities, a diffuse MIS for its strategic planners, an elaborate MIS for its legal and accounting units, and a concise MIS for its customer order processing unit. Such an approach would include designing an

---

19. See Daft and MacIntosh, "A New Approach to Design and Use of Management Information," pp. 88–90.

MIS for each unit, varying the MIS within the organization, and maintaining a reasonable degree of flexibility.

Managing the communication process

Given the obvious importance of communication in organizations, it is vital for managers to understand how best to manage the communication process. By this, we mean that managers should understand how to maximize the potential benefits of communication and minimize the potential problems. We will begin our discussion by considering what factors might disrupt effective communication and how to deal with them.

Barriers to communication

Several factors may disrupt the communication process or serve as barriers to effective communication.[20] As shown in Table 16.2, they may be divided into four classes: attributes of the sender, attributes of the receiver, interactions between attributes of both sender and receiver, and environmental factors.

Attributes of the sender. Several attributes of the sender may disrupt effective communication. One common problem is conflicting or inconsistent signals. Another is lack of credibility.

Table 16.2 Barriers to effective communication

Attributes of the sender
Conflicting or inconsistent signals
Credibility

Attributes of the receiver
Poor listening habits
Predispositions

Interactions between attributes of both sender and receiver
Semantics problems
Status differences
Power differences
Different perceptions

Environmental factors
Noise
Overload

20. See Wofford, Gerloff, and Cummins, *Organizational Communication*. See also James L. Gibson, John M. Ivancevich, and James H. Donnelly, Jr., *Organizations*, 4th ed. (Plano, Texas: BPI, 1982), Chapter 14.

A manager is sending conflicting signals when he says on Monday that things should be done one way but then prescribes an entirely different procedure on Wednesday. Inconsistent signals are being sent when a manager announces that she has an "open door" policy and wants her subordinates to drop by whenever it's convenient—but then keeps her door closed and becomes irritated whenever someone stops by.

Credibility problems arise when the sender is not considered a reliable source of information. He or she may not be trusted or may not be perceived as knowledgeable about the subject at hand. When a politician is caught withholding information or when a manager makes a series of bad decisions, the extent to which they will be listened to and believed thereafter diminishes. In extreme cases, people may talk about something they obviously know little or nothing about.

Attributes of the receiver. Two attributes of the receiver that may impede effective communication are poor listening habits and the predisposition to think in a certain set way.

Some people are poor listeners. When someone is talking to them they may be daydreaming, looking around, reading, or listening to another conversation. Because they are not concentrating on what is being said, they may not comprehend part or all of the message. And they may actually think that they really are paying attention, only to realize later that they can't remember parts of the conversation.

Receivers may also bring certain predispositions to the communication process. They may already have their minds made up, firmly set in a certain way. Consider the case of a management leader and a labor leader meeting to discuss a new contract. Both may be so certain the other wants a strike that they may not pay full attention to what their counterpart across the table is saying.

Interactions. Sometimes problems develop because attributes of the sender conflict with those of the receiver. That is, communication is disrupted by the interaction of sender and receiver attributes. Four of these interactions involve semantics problems, status differences, power differences, and perceptual differences.

Semantics problems arise when words have different meanings for different people. Words and phrases such as *profit, increased productivity, retained earnings,* and *return on investment* may have positive meanings for managers but less positive (or even negative) meanings for labor.

Communication problems may arise when people of different status try to communicate with each other. The company president may not pay much attention to a suggestion from an operating employee, thinking something like, "How can someone at that level help me run my business?" Or, when the president goes out to inspect a new plant, workers may be reluctant to offer suggestions because of their lower status.

Power differences can also disrupt communication. The marketing vice president may have more power than the personnel vice president, for example, and consequently may not pay much attention to a staffing report submitted by personnel.

If people perceive a situation differently, they may also have difficulty communicating with one another. When two managers observe that a third manager has not spent much time in her office lately, one may believe that she has been to several important meetings while the other may think she is "hiding out." If they need to talk about her in some official capacity, problems may arise because one has a positive impression and the other a negative one.

Environmental factors. Environmental factors may also disrupt effective communication. As mentioned earlier, noise may affect communication in many ways. Similarly, overload may be a problem when the receiver is being sent more information than he or she can effectively handle. When the manager gives a subordinate many jobs to work on simultaneously and then constantly bombards the subordinate with additional information, overload may result.

Improving communication effectiveness

Considering how many factors can disrupt communication, it is fortunate that we can resort to several techniques for improving communication effectiveness.[21] As shown in Table 16.3, these techniques may be used by the sender, the receiver, or both.

Techniques for the sender. As much as possible, the sender should bear in mind four elements that can improve communication effectiveness: feedback, awareness, credibility, and empathy.

Feedback, perhaps the most important of these, is facilitated by two-way communication. Two-way communication allows the receiver to ask questions, request clarification, and express opinions that let the sender know whether he or she has been understood. In general, the more complicated the message, the more useful two-way communication is.[22]

Second, the sender should be aware of the meanings that different receivers might attach to various words. When addressing stockholders, use the word *profit* liberally. When addressing labor officials, it might be better to emphasize other terms.

Third, the sender should try to maintain credibility. One can accomplish this by not pretending to be an expert when one is not, by "doing one's homework" and checking facts, and by otherwise being as accurate and honest as possible.

Finally, the sender should be sensitive to the receiver's perspective and try to empathize with the receiver. When a manager must tell a subordinate that she has not been recommended for a promotion, he or she should recog-

21. See Wofford, Gerloff, and Cummings, *Organizational Communication.* See also Joseph Allen and Bennet P. Lientz, *Effective Business Communication,* (Santa Monica, Calif.: Goodyear, 1979).

22. See Leonard R. Sayles and George Strauss, *Human Behavior in Organizations,* (Englewood Cliffs, N.J.: Prentice-Hall, 1966).

Table 16.3 Improving communication effectiveness

For the sender
  Encourage two-way communication
  Be aware of language and meaning
  Maintain credibility
  Be sensitive to receiver's perspective

For the receiver
  Listen
  Be sensitive to sender's perspective

For both sender and receiver
  Follow up
  Regulate information flow
  Understand the richness of channels

nize that the subordinate will be frustrated and unhappy. The content of the message and its method of delivery should be chosen accordingly.

Techniques for the receiver. Two techniques for receiving messages more effectively are to be a better listener and to be sensitive to the sender's perspective.

Being an effective listener involves a variety of things: not interrupting, putting the speaker at ease, showing that you are interested, not getting distracted, being patient, and asking questions.[23] Effective listening is felt to be so important that some companies, like the Sperry Corporation, have established training programs to help their managers become better listeners. Sperry's program involves having managers participate in a variety of seminars and exercises to improve their listening skills.[24]

Being sensitive to the sender's perspective involves trying to appreciate the sender's position and to understand why he or she might be sending a particular message. When a subordinate receives bad news from a manager, the subordinate is likely to react with abruptness and hostility at first. After a period of time, the mature subordinate will regain composure and the hostility will subside.

Techniques for both sender and receiver. Three useful techniques can enhance communication effectiveness for both the sender and the receiver: following up, regulating information flow, and understanding the richness of different channels.

Following up simply involves checking at a later time to be sure that the message has been received and understood. After a manager mails a report to

23. See Keith Davis, *Human Behavior at Work,* 6th ed. (New York: McGraw-Hill, 1981).

24. See "Developing Listening Skills at Sperry Corporation," *Management Review,* April 1980, p. 40.

a colleague, she or he might call a few days later to make sure it has arrived. If the answer is yes, the manager might ask whether there are any questions about it. Of course, carrying this practice to an extreme can become a problem in itself.

Regulating information flow means that the sender or receiver takes steps to ensure that overload doesn't occur. For the sender, this could mean not passing too much information through the system at one time. For the receiver, it might be necessary to call attention to the fact that she or he is being asked to do too many things at once. Many managers limit the influx of information by periodically weeding out the list of journals and routine reports they receive; or they may train a secretary to screen phone calls and visitors.

Both parties should understand the richness associated with different media. When a manager is going to lay off a subordinate temporarily, the message should probably be delivered in person. A face-to-face channel gives the manager an opportunity to explain the situation and answer questions. When the purpose of the message is to grant a pay increase, however, written communication may be appropriate because it can be more objective and precise. The manager could then follow up the written notice with personal congratulations.

The informal communication network

The concept of the informal communication network, commonly referred to as the grapevine, was briefly introduced in Chapter 15 in our discussion of the informal organization. The *grapevine* is simply the informal communication network among people in an organization. Grapevines are found in all organizations except the very smallest, but they don't always follow the same patterns, nor do they necessarily coincide with formal channels of authority and communication.

Figure 16.8 illustrates several important characteristics of grapevines. Note that message 1 starts one level below the top of the organization and flows from one person to another across the second and third levels of the organization, with the final recipient sending it down to a still lower level (not shown in the figure). Message 2 begins at the third level but follows a more complicated path as it flows through all three of the top levels of the organization and is eventually transmitted outside to another organization. Message 3 follows the most complicated path of all. It comes into the organization from outside, travels through all three levels, and is transmitted to more than one person at a time.

Note in Figure 16.8 that some people receive all three messages, that some receive only two messages, and that one manager does not receive any of them. Note also that some people transmit the message to only one other person, whereas others tell more than one person. And some people receive the same message from more than one source. Finally, note that this communication network seldom follows formal paths; some messages travel up, some down, some laterally, and still others diagonally.

Figure 16.8
The informal
communication
network

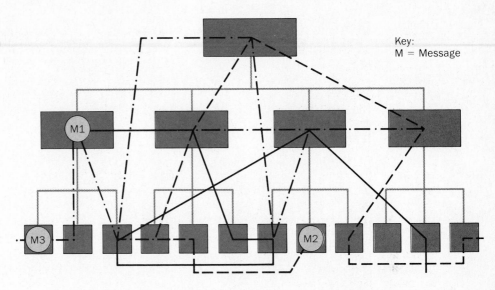

Key:
M = Message

Keith Davis has identified four basic kinds of grapevines.[25] As shown in
Figure 16.9, the least common grapevine is the probability chain. In this situation, people simply pass on messages to others on a random basis. This chain
is likely to emerge when the information is of only passing interest and not
really very important to anybody. The possibility of a manager in another organization changing jobs might be transmitted through a probability chain. The
gossip chain occurs when one person spreads the message to as many others
as possible. This chain is likely to carry personal information about such matters as divorces, births, and love affairs. Also of intermediate frequency is the
single-strand chain, wherein one person passes the information to only one
other person. Accuracy of information suffers the most in this chain. The most
common grapevine pattern is the cluster chain. In this situation, one person
passes the information to a selected few individuals, some of whom continue
to pass it to a few other individuals while the others keep it to themselves.

There is some disagreement about how accurate the information carried
by the grapevine is. Some researchers have suggested that as much as 75 percent of the information in the grapevine is accurate; others have found that
over half of the information is incorrect and another 16 percent distorted.[26]

The manager has some control over the accuracy of information in the
grapevine. By maintaining open communication channels and responding vig-
orously to inaccurate information, she or he can help minimize the damage the

25. See Keith Davis, "Management Communication and the Grapevine," *Harvard Business Review*, September–October 1953, pp. 43–49; and Keith Davis, "Cut Those Rumors Down to
Size," *Supervisory Management*, June 1975, pp. 2–6.

26. See Keith Davis, *Human Behavior at Work*, 6th ed. (New York: McGraw-Hill, 1981); and
Robert Hershey, "The Grapevine . . . Here to Stay But Not Beyond Control," *Personnel*, January 1966, pp. 62–66.

Figure 16.9
Grapevine chains

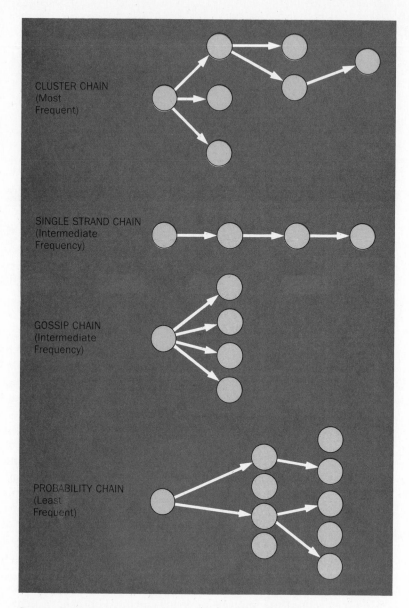

CLUSTER CHAIN
(Most
Frequent)

SINGLE STRAND CHAIN
(Intermediate
Frequency)

GOSSIP CHAIN
(Intermediate
Frequency)

PROBABILITY CHAIN
(Least
Frequent)

Source: Reprinted by permission of the *Harvard Business Review*. An exhibit from "Management Communication and the Grapevine" by Keith Davis (September–October 1953). Copyright © 1953 by the President and Fellows of Harvard College; all rights reserved.

grapevine can do. Attempts to eliminate the grapevine are fruitless, so it is fortunate that the grapevine can actually be an asset. By learning who the key people in the grapevine are, for example, the manager can partially control the information they receive and use the grapevine to sound out employee reactions to new ideas such as a change in personnel policies or benefit packages. The manager can also get valuable information via the grapevine and use it to improve decision making.

A final aspect of the grapevine is the rumor network that extends beyond the organization's boundaries (recall that, in Figure 16.8, one of the messages originated outside the organization and another was ultimately transmitted to the outside). Many of these rumors stop after being received by one or two people, but others spread to many people. And, of course, they may also be started by someone outside the organization.

Rumors about impending mergers, acquisitions, or liquidations may affect stock prices and credit ratings. Even more damaging are rumors that undermine the public's faith in an organization. McDonald's spent a year combating a false rumor that the company was using red worms in its hamburgers to increase their protein content, and Squibb had to spend $100,000 to convince the public that there was no truth to the rumor that its new Bubble Yum contained spider eggs.[27] Some organizations have gone so far as to hire consultants or establish clinics or hot-line numbers to squelch false rumors.

Electronic communication

In recent years, we have seen a veritable explosion in electronic communication. Computers, copying machines, and sophisticated electronic typewriters have begun to change how managers receive, process, and transmit information to others.

For example, it is now possible to have teleconferences in which managers stay at their own locations (such as offices in different cities) but are all seen on television monitors as they "meet." A manager in New York can type a letter or memorandum into a terminal, push a few buttons, and have it printed out in San Francisco. Highly detailed information can be retrieved with ease from large computer data banks.

Chapter 12 described how managers may one day have professional work stations with all sorts of communications equipment for managing the increasingly complex and rapidly changing information that has become a part of the manager's job.[28] Some managers resist such innovations, but the widespread use of automated information systems and other forms of electronic communication is probably inevitable. Consider how the manuscript that became this book was developed. The first three chapters were typed on a conventional

27. See Roy Rowan, "Where Did *That* Rumor Come From?" *Fortune*, August 13, 1979, pp. 130–137.
28. See Bro Uttal, "Xerox Xooms Toward the Office of the Future," *Fortune*, May 18, 1981, pp. 44–52.

electric typewriter. Errors were corrected and changes made by using correction fluid and by cutting, pasting, and retyping. The bulk of the book was typed with a word processor. Corrections were made and sections added, deleted, and reordered by pushing a few buttons. And the last few chapters were "typed" with a computer. The "manuscript" was proofread and corrected on the electronic display screen of a computer terminal before it was ever printed on paper.

Summary of key points

Communication is the process of transmitting information from one person to another. Effective communication results when the message received is close in meaning to the message intended. The communication process consists of a sender encoding meaning and transmitting it to one or more receivers, who receive the message and decode it into meaning. In two-way communication the process continues with the roles reversed. Noise can disrupt any part of the overall process. Communication is a major part of the manager's job. It is crucial in each of the managerial roles as well as in the managerial functions of planning, organizing, leading, and controlling.

Two behavioral processes that affect communication are perception and attitudes. Perception consists of the processes individuals use to receive information for the environment. Selection and organization are important elements of perception. Attitudes are a person's predispositions to respond in a favorable or unfavorable way to an object. The important components of attitudes are emotions, knowledge, and behavioral intentions.

Interpersonal communication focuses on communication among a small number of people. Two important forms of interpersonal communication, oral and written, both offer unique advantages and disadvantages. Nonverbal communication includes facial expressions, body movement, physical contact, gestures, and inflection and tone.

Organizational communication entails broader patterns of communication and may involve larger numbers of people. Communication networks are recurring patterns of communication among members of a group. Vertical communication between superiors and subordinates may flow upward or downward, although two-way communication is generally preferable. Horizontal communication involves peers and colleagues at the same level in the organization. Management information systems (MIS) are systems designed to provide information to managers. The Daft and MacIntosh MIS model suggests that the appropriate design of an MIS varies by department as a function of departmental technology.

Managing the communication process necessitates recognizing the barriers to effective communication and understanding how to overcome them. Common barriers can be classified as attributes of the sender, attributes of the receiver, interactions between sender and receiver attributes, and environmental factors. It is possible for both sender and receiver to learn and practice effective techniques for improving communication.

The grapevine is the informal communication network among people in an organization. Grapevines do not necessarily follow formal lines of communication and authority. The four basic kinds of grapevines are the probability chain, the gossip chain, the single-strand chain, and the cluster chain. Some information on the grapevine may be accurate, while other information may be distorted and inaccurate. Managers should recognize that, instead of trying to eliminate the grapevine (which is probably impossible), they should learn to use it themselves. Sometimes managers must also contend with rumors circulating among the general public.

Electronic communications, represented by computers, copying machines, word processing systems, and the like, will certainly have a profound effect on managerial and organizational communication in the years to come.

QUESTIONS FOR DISCUSSION

1. Can you think of any managerial activities that do *not* involve communication?
2. Using the communication model described in the chapter, analyze and diagram a communication exchange between you and your instructor.
3. Can you give examples of how perception and attitudes have influenced communications between you and someone else?
4. Describe how a manager can combine oral, written, and nonverbal communication into an effective communication system.
5. Can you identify five examples of nonverbal communication that you have recently observed?
6. How are the communication networks we have discussed related to group cohesiveness, norms, and role dynamics?
7. How could your college or university apply the Daft and MacIntosh MIS model?
8. Have you recently encountered any of the communication barriers discussed in the chapter? Are there other such barriers you can think of?
9. Match each of the techniques for improving communication effectiveness with the barriers it would most directly overcome. Can you think of other helpful techniques?
10. How does the grapevine work at your school? Is the information it carries generally accurate or inaccurate?
11. What risks do managers run when they attempt to use the grapevine for their own purposes?
12. Can you speculate about even more innovative electronic communication devices that might be developed in the years ahead? Why do you think some managers resist these innovations? What could be done to minimize their resistance?

C A S E   16.1

At the beginning of this chapter, you read an incident about a top manager at a foreign office of a major bank. The manager has discovered a second management information system being used for handling illegal banking transactions that were intended to evade taxes. You were asked how you would communicate your discovery. The bank being described was Citicorp, the manager David Edwards. The case that follows describes what Edwards did and how Citicorp responded. Then it raises some other issues for your consideration.

Citicorp, a New York-based financial corporation, is the largest foreign exchange dealer in the world. By actively and aggressively buying and selling currency, Citicorp has been able to fortify its top position in the international currency market and to reap huge profits. For example, currency trading contributes about 30 percent of Citicorp's pretax income. Unfortunately, it now appears that some of these profits may be a result of tax evasion and violations of international currency-trading regulations.

A number of complicated techniques were apparently used by Citicorp, but the core of the transgressions was a procedure known as "parking." Parking involves illegally transferring foreign exchange positions between countries in order to reduce taxes. For example, the Citicorp branch in Paris could instruct the Citicorp branch in the Bahamas to buy $5 million worth of French francs on the open market and then to sell them back to the Paris branch at a 3 percent higher rate. This transaction would net $150,000 in profits for the Bahamas branch. Because taxes are considerably lower in the Bahamas than in France, the overall sequence of transactions would result in higher profits for Citicorp. Profits in the Bahamas would not be taxed heavily, and the losses posted in Paris would help lower the tax bill there.

For obvious reasons, Citicorp needed to maintain records showing both the "public" transactions (for example, the profits in the Bahamas and the losses in Paris) and the "private" ones as well (for example, the true performance of each unit). To accomplish this, the company implemented not one but two management information systems. The first was used to handle the public transactions. Hence it reflected the profits and losses being reported for tax purposes and was used to report to bank examiners. The other system, called the Management Profit Report (or MPR), was strictly confidential. It dealt with the actual performance of the company, and its existence was kept secret from bank examiners.

These circumstances became publicly known through the efforts of David Edwards. Edwards joined Citicorp in 1972 and quickly rose to a senior management position at the company's Paris branch. Edwards soon began to suspect that the head foreign exchange trader, Jean Pierre DeLaet, was conducting unau-

Misuse of information systems at Citicorp

thorized and perhaps illegal off-the-record transactions. In 1975 Edwards reported his suspicions to his boss, Chuck Young. Young seemed indifferent and suggested that Edwards forget the whole thing, but Edwards believed that higher-level management was unaware of what was going on and would eventually thank him if he could set the record straight.

Ultimately, Edwards found that parking was a widespread practice across several of Citicorp's European offices. This finding served to strengthen his resolve to make sure top management understood what was going on. Several heated discussions with Young led nowhere. Conversations with the senior vice president for foreign exchange and the chief foreign exchange auditor were also fruitless. In fact, the auditor wrote to a vice president in New York suggesting that Edwards be fired (the auditor was at that very time devising a plan to make parking harder to detect).

Edwards next talked to George Vojta, executive vice president of the International Banking Group. By this time, Vojta had heard all about David Edwards and promised to straighten things out. Nothing came of this, however, and Vojta was eventually replaced by Thomas Theobald. Edwards sent Theobald a long letter describing what was going on—the result was a reprimand from Theobald for putting his allegations in writing.

Finally Edwards attempted to reach the top of the organization. He prepared a 106-page report summarizing everything he knew. This report was mailed to nine members of Citicorp's board of directors in early 1978. Shortly thereafter, Edwards received a letter from Theobald terminating his employment with Citicorp.

Eventually the French government discovered 24 illegal foreign exchange deals handled by DeLaet in 1976 and 1977. Back taxes and fines totaled $1.1 million. As a result of similar inquiries, Citicorp had to pay $5.7 million in back taxes in Switzerland and another $3.7 million in Germany. DeLaet was forced to leave the bank in 1979.

CASE QUESTIONS

1. Can you suggest legitimate circumstances in which a company might establish two (or more) management information systems?

2. How might the grapevine have led to David Edwards's downfall?

3. Could Edwards have handled this situation better? Could he have combined written and verbal communication in a more effective way?

4. If you ever find yourself in Edwards's position, what will you do?

CASE REFERENCES

"Citibank Says Probes on Foreign Exchange Include Studies Abroad." *Wall Street Journal,* January 19, 1979, p. 23.

"Close Encounters: Was Law Firm's Study of Citibank's Dealings Abroad a Whitewash?" *Wall Street Journal,* September 14, 1982, p. 1.

Rowan, Roy. "The Maverick Who Yelled Foul at Citibank." *Fortune,* January 10, 1983, pp. 46–56.

C A S E   16.2

The following series of events took place recently at the head-quarters of Stafford Airlines, a rapidly growing regional airline based in the Northwest. It's no secret that Paul Stafford, president and chief stockholder of the company, wants to sell his interest in the company but remain on as president. He has outlined two strategies, one of them selling the business outright and the other attempting to merge with an existing airline. Stafford has carefully drafted a confidential report summarizing the pros and cons of each strategy and asked a trusted vice president, Sam Benjamin, to make a recommendation. Benjamin has recommended a merger. His secretary, Bill McDonald, has just typed a memo sum-marizing that recommendation and has gone to the employee lounge to get a cup of coffee. There he meets Terri Kennedy, the secretary to another vice president.

"Terri," Bill whispers, "I've got some real hot news. We're going to merge with another airline! They hope there won't be any personnel cutbacks, but we've got to be prepared to present a united front on this."

Dave Reck, an office courier, overhears a part of this conver-sation and excitedly relays it to his boss, Barbara Stuart. "Yes, that's just what McDonald's secretary said," he concludes, "We're going to merge with United Airlines, but there won't be any person-nel cutbacks."

Barbara Stuart immediately writes a memo to Clyde Martin, Stafford Airline's personnel director. In it she expresses enthusi-asm for the impending merger with United and adds that she hopes the company will make good on its promise to retain per-sonnel. After all, with the current level of unemployment in Amer-ica, it would be criminal to terminate any more employees.

The next day Stuart's secretary types the memo. As she proofreads it, Everett Monroe, the office snoop, walks by. He hes-itates as he passes behind her just long enough to skim the memo. He immediately rushes into the office of Martha Ginzberg and yells, "I can't believe Stafford could do this. We're selling out to American Airlines, and there's going to be a massive personnel cutback."

Meanwhile, the memo from Stuart arrives at the office of Clyde Martin. Martin's secretary opens the envelope, but before he can read it Martin comes out to pick up the mail. The secretary does, however, see a few words in the memo and later in the day tells a friend, "I don't know what kind of trouble he's in. I just know it has something to do with not making good on a promise and that it's a criminal offense!"

And so the news traveled. Three days later, Stafford (who had incidentally decided to sell the business outright rather than merge with another airline) began to receive a number of unusual phone calls and letters. Three people expressed righteous indig-

Communication through the grapevine

nation at his cavalier firing of two hundred faithful employees. Two expressed pleasure and one displeasure at the impending merger with United, one was pleased about the merger with American, and two thought that Delta was a wise choice. The fact that the company was moving its corporate headquarters from Seattle to Miami disturbed one employee. Finally, he received a fifty dollar contribution to his legal fund from one faithful employee, along with a note pledging undying loyalty to his president. Stafford, by this time, was quite confused.

CASE
QUESTIONS

1. Can you explain what happened at Stafford Airlines?
2. What should Paul Stafford do to straighten things out?
3. How realistic or unrealistic do you think this scenario is?

PART 5

The Controlling Process

PART CONTENTS

17

THE NATURE OF ORGANIZATIONAL CONTROL

CHAPTER OBJECTIVES

1. Define control, discuss its focus and importance, and explain the link between planning and controlling.

2. Explain cybernetic control, describe three different approaches to the timing of control, and justify the need for multiple control systems.

3. Summarize the steps in the control process.

4. Cite several steps a manager can take to make control more effective.

5. Explain why some employees resist control and how this resistance can be overcome.

6. Discuss the job of controller.

7. Explain how a manager can consider organizational factors in choosing what kind of control to adopt.

OPENING INCIDENT

You are a manager at an art auction house. The company has always operated under the assumption that art prices will escalate indefinitely. A former chief executive has established a framework by which staff experts have almost total freedom, including unlimited expense accounts, to travel the world looking for collections for sale. They can expand their own staffs at will and can negotiate commission arrangements with clients on their own. The company has now reached the size where such autonomy may become a problem. For example, it has just posted its first loss since World War II. How would you proceed?

Conrail is a regional railroad serving the northeastern and midwestern United States. During the late 1970s and early 1980s, Conrail management made several important changes. Excess track was eliminated to reduce maintenance costs. One seventh of Conrail's lines, which had been producing only 1.6 percent of the company's operating revenues, were abandoned. And the labor force was pared from over 100,000 to only 60,000 employees.[1]

Each of these activities was a part of Conrail's control process. Control is the last of the four basic management functions to be discussed in this book, and this chapter is the first of three devoted to it. We will begin by discussing the nature of organizational control. Following an overview, we will describe the kinds of control systems that organizations may adopt, the means of implementing a control system, resistance to control, the position of controller, and a framework to help management choose an appropriate control strategy. Chapter 18 summarizes a number of useful control techniques and methods. And in Chapter 19 we will discuss organizational effectiveness, performance, and productivity.

An overview of control

Organizational control can be defined as the regulation of organizational activity in such a way as to facilitate goal attainment. For example, an organization might determine that, if desired profit levels are to be maintained, its manufacturing costs must not exceed $5.00 per unit. A system would then be established to provide on-going cost information to management. If costs rose above $5.00, some action would be taken (raising productivity quotas, changing suppliers in order to buy less expensive materials, or recycling defective products) to get costs back in line. In this example, the desired levels of profitability

1. See "Conrail Starts to Look Like an Outfit Someone Might Buy," *Fortune*, August 23, 1982, p. 7.

reflect the organization's goals, whereas the management of production costs is the regulation of activities required to attain those goals. Conrail's elimination of excess track, abandonment of low-revenue-producing track, and reduction in labor force were all regulating activities intended to advance the goal of profitability.

The focus of control

Organizational control can focus on almost any organizational activity or set of activities. One useful way to classify it is in terms of the organization's four basic kinds of inputs: financial, physical, human, and information resources (see Figure 17.1). The management process itself involves efficiently and effectively combining these resources into appropriate outputs.

Control of physical resources includes inventory management (stocking neither too few nor too many units in inventory), quality control (maintaining appropriate levels of output quality), and equipment control (having the proper kinds of buildings, office equipment, and so on). Control of human resources includes proper selection and placement activities, training and development, performance appraisal, and compensation levels. The control of information resources involves such things as accurate sales and marketing forecasting, adequate environmental analysis, public relations, production scheduling, and economic forecasting.

Figure 17.1
The focus of
organizational
control

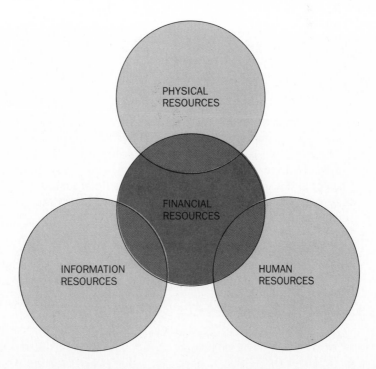

Note in Figure 17.1 that financial resources are shown at the center. This is because financial resources, beyond being organizational resources in their own right, are related to all the other resources. Pure financial control does exist: an example is ensuring that the organization always has enough cash on hand to meet its obligations but that it does not have excess cash lying around in a checking account. But financial control extends to the other three kinds of resources as well: too much inventory is bad because of storage costs, poor selection of personnel is bad because of termination and rehiring expenses, inaccurate sales forecasts are bad because of disruptions in cash flows and other financial effects. Financial issues, then, tend to pervade most control-related activities.

The importance of control

Some people feel that organizational control is a negative force—necessary, perhaps, but unpleasant. Others view it as constructive, regulating and shaping the ongoing activities of the organization in much the same way that river banks channel the waters of a river. Without effective control systems, an organization could flounder and veer off course. Viewing control as a positive element in the organization, we can identify three major reasons why it is necessary.

Changing circumstances. In today's complex and turbulent environment, all organizations must contend with change.[2] If managers could establish goals and achieve them instantaneously, control would not be needed. But between the time when a goal is established and the time when it is reached, many things can happen in the organization and its environments to disrupt movement toward the goal—or even to change the goal itself.

A properly designed control system can help managers anticipate, monitor, and respond to changing circumstances. In general, the longer the time horizon of organizational goals, the more important it is to have adequate control. A university administrator might have forecasted a 3 percent enrollment increase for each of the next 4 years. After 1 year, however, the control system may indicate that enrollment is up 8 percent and that applications for the following year are coming in at an even faster pace. The administrator may then decide to raise admissions standards (to slow growth) or to hire additional faculty and acquire more classroom space (to accommodate more students). In any case, the control system helped the administrator recognize that adjustments of some kind were needed.

Compounding of errors. Another factor underlying the importance of control is the process of error compounding. Often, small mistakes and errors do not seriously damage the health of an organization. With the passage of time, however, small errors may accumulate and become very serious. For example, when a purchasing agent fails to negotiate an industry standard

2. See Peter F. Drucker, *Managing in Turbulent Times* (New York: Harper & Row, 1980).

2 percent discount on raw materials, the impact of this error on the firm's initial order of $100,000 is relatively small (only $2,000). But after several orders totaling, say, $5,000,000, the firm will have spent $100,000 unnecessarily (the size of its initial order). Control can help managers catch errors before they compound.

Organizational complexity. A third reason for control is the complexity of modern organizations. When a firm purchases only one raw material, produces but one product, has a simple structure, and enjoys constant demand for its product, its manager can probably maintain control with a notepad and pencil. But in an organization that produces many products from myriad raw materials, has a large market area and a complicated organization structure, and operates in a competitive environment, it is difficult (if not impossible) to maintain adequate control without an elaborate control system. In the early 1970s, the Transamerica conglomerate fell on hard times because it failed to monitor the activities of all its subsidiaries. In effect it lost control. Each subsidiary was charting its own course, and none was attempting to coordinate its activities with those of the others. A major control system was developed and implemented in order to get the conglomerate back on track.[3]

The link between planning and controlling

Chapter 5 described how RCA has established a corporate strategy revolving around NBC, C.I.T. Financial, RCA Electronics, and other units; a business strategy for each unit; and a functional strategy for areas within each unit. At the same time, RCA also established control systems to monitor financial performance, sales growth, and the like.[4] As we shall see, planning and controlling should be closely related. The link between them is illustrated in Figure 17.2. As indicated in Chapter 1, planning is usually the first part of the management process. Then the organizing and leading functions get the actual work of the organization done, and the controlling function is directly tied back into planning.[5]

For example, management may plan to increase market share by 2 percent each of the next 7 years. At the end of year 1, as expected, market share has increased 2 percent. This performance, as measured by the control system, tells management that it should continue with the existing plan. In year 2, however, market share has increased only 1 percent. This tells management that some adjustment is needed to steer the firm back toward its desired rate of growth. Finally, at the end of year 3, the control system might reveal that the firm is exceeding its projected 2 percent growth rate by so much that a new plan is called for.

3. See Peter J. Schuyten, "United Artists's Script Calls for Divorce," *Fortune*, January 16, 1978, pp. 130–137.

4. See A. F. Ehrbar, "Splitting up RCA," *Fortune*, March 22, 1982, pp. 62–76.

5. See J. M. Horovitz, "Strategic Control: A New Task for Top Management," *Long Range Planning*, June 1979, pp. 28–37.

Figure 17.2
The link between
planning and
controlling

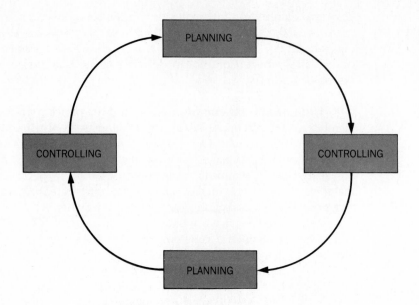

Hence the organization continuously cycles back and forth between planning and controlling. The manager makes plans and then uses the control system to monitor progress toward fulfillment of these plans. The control system, in turn, tells the manager that things are going as they should (the current plan should be maintained), that things are not going as they should (the current plan should be modified), or that the situation has changed (a new plan should be drafted). We will explore the planning-controlling link in more detail later in the chapter.

Types of control

What kinds of control or control systems are available for managers to use? In this section we describe a variety of perspectives on this question. Chapter 18 will discuss specific control techniques that may be used in some or all of these types of control.

Cybernetic control

When your body needs nourishment it "tells" you to eat, and when it has received enough nourishment it "tells" you to stop eating. That which is being controlled (intake of food) is monitored and managed by a self-regulating mechanism (the stomach). This kind of control is called cybernetic. More specifically, we can define *cybernetic control* as the type of control that monitors and manages a process by means of a self-regulating mechanism.

An organization might set up a similar system to monitor and manage its inventory of a certain raw material. A computerized ordering system might order the material until inventory reaches a certain level. Then, until inventory falls back below a certain level, no more orders are issued. In effect the system controls itself.

Noncybernetic control, on the other hand, requires an external monitoring system. Consider a firm that manufactures products only when it receives an order (the production of a Boeing 767, for example). It would be foolish for the company to maintain large stockpiles of inventory that might not be needed for months or years. Instead, the necessary materials are ordered in response to each order. The inventory system in this case does not monitor and manage itself; it is controlled by an external agent such as a purchasing manager.

Timing of control

An organization can introduce control at one or more of three general points: before, during, or after the transformation processes.[6] Using systems theory as a framework, let's consider a small bicycle repair shop. It may specify parts of a certain quality when it places its orders, and it may inspect those parts when they arrive. By doing so, it is controlling inputs (preliminary control). The manager of the shop may also stroll around and keep an eye on the work while repairs are being made; this screening control is exercised during the transformation process. Finally, all bicycles are tested before they are released to customers, and the shop guarantees all work for thirty days; these efforts control outputs (post-action control). Figure 17.3 shows how control can focus on the inputs to the transformation process, on the transformation itself, or on its outputs.

Preliminary control. *Preliminary control* (also called steering control or feedforward control) concentrates on inputs to the system early in the overall process (see Figure 17.3). Preliminary control attempts to monitor the quality and/or quantity of financial, physical, human, and information resources *before* they become a part of the system.[7]

Procter & Gamble hires only college graduates for its management training program. In this way it controls the quality of its human resource inputs. When Sears orders merchandise to be manufactured under its own brand name, it specifies rigid standards of quality, thereby controlling material inputs. Similarly, organizations often take steps to control financial and information resources as they enter the system.

Screening control. *Screening control* (also called yes/no control or concurrent control) takes place during the actual transformation process. Screening control relies heavily on feedback processes, so screening controls are much like cybernetic controls.

---

6. See William H. Newman, *Constructive Control* (Englewood Cliffs, N.J.: Prentice-Hall, 1975).

7. See Harold Koontz and Robert W. Bradspies, "Managing Through Feedforward Control," *Business Horizons*, June 1972, pp. 25–36.

Figure 17.3
The timing of
control

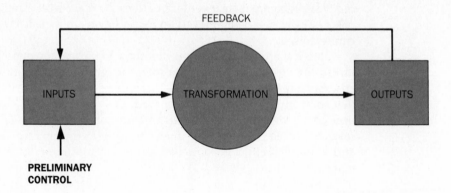

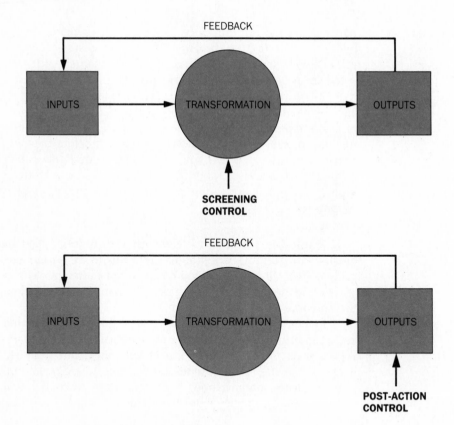

Suppose a manager of a manufacturing plant establishes a number of checkpoints along the assembly line so that, as the product moves along, it is periodically checked to make sure that all of the components that have been assembled up to that point are working. This is screening control, because the product is being controlled during the transformation process itself.

One of the reasons for the strength of Japanese auto makers during the late 1970s and early 1980s was the intimate involvement of their operating employees in screening control. In a Detroit plant, inspection is typically performed after the car is fully assembled. Japanese factories, however, are set up so that each worker plays the role of inspector and will not pass on a part that is defective.[8] This is screening control because it occurs during the actual transformation of the product. Because they are widely applicable and useful in identifying the cause of problems, screening controls tend to be used more often than other forms of control.

Post-action control. *Post-action control* focuses on the outputs of the organization after the transformation process is complete. Detroit's inspecting automobiles after they are assembled is an example of post-action control.

In other situations, post-action control may be more useful than in the case of automobiles. Because an automobile is a complex machine consisting of thousands of parts and subsystems, it makes more sense to use screening control. For a simpler product, such as a light bulb or a flashlight battery, it is probably more economical to wait and check the finished product.

Although post-action control is generally not so useful as preliminary or screening control, it is effective in two important ways. It provides management with information for future planning. For example, when a quality check of finished goods indicates an unacceptably high defective rate, the manager knows that he or she must ferret out the causes and take steps to correct them. Post-action control also provides a basis for rewarding employees. Recognizing that an employee has exceeded her or his sales goals by a wide margin, for example, may alert the manager that a bonus or promotion is in order.[9]

Multiple control systems

Most organizations need multiple control systems. The complex organization cannot usually adopt just one preliminary, screening, or post-action control technique and expect it to be effective. It is generally best to develop several control systems.

One organization can establish several preliminary control systems to deal with each category of resources it employs. That is, various preliminary controls can be established for raw material quality, personnel selection, and so on. The firm may then create a number of screening controls to monitor each phase of the transformation process. For example, several inspection points could be established for work in process. Finally, several post-action

8. See Charles G. Burck, "Can Detroit Catch Up?" *Fortune*, February 8, 1982, pp. 24–39.
9. See Newman, *Constructive Control*.

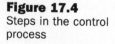

Figure 17.4
Steps in the control process

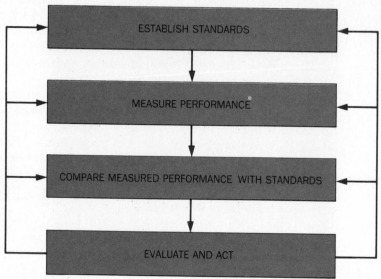

controls can be used to reward employees and to provide feedback relevant to future planning. That is, final product inspection and financial rewards might also be appropriate. Some of these controls and control systems may be cybernetic and others noncybernetic.

Steps in the control process

Regardless of the type or number of control systems an organization needs, there are four general steps in any control process.[10] (See Figure 17.4.)

Establishing standards

The first step in the control process is the establishment of standards. A *standard* is a target against which subsequent performance is to be measured. Standards for a fast-food restaurant like McDonald's might include the following:

1. A minimum of 95 percent of all customers will be greeted within 3 minutes of their arrival.
2. Precooked hamburgers will not sit in the warmer more than 5 minutes before they are served to customers.
3. All empty tables will be cleared within 5 minutes after they have been vacated.

---

10. For other perspectives on how to establish control systems, see Newman, *Constructive Control;* and Edward E. Lawler, III, and John G. Rhode, *Information and Control in Organizations* (Pacific Palisades, Calif.: Goodyear, 1976).

As much as possible, standards established for control purposes should be derived from the organization's goals. Like objectives, they should be expressed along a time dimension and should have a specific target. Note that standard 1 for a fast-food restaurant has a time limit of 3 minutes and an objective target of 95 percent of all customers. In standard 2, the objective target is implied: "all" pre-cooked hamburgers.

On a broader level, control standards reflect organizational strategy. A control standard for a retailer might be to increase its annual sales volume by 25 percent within 5 years. A hospital might aim to increase its patient recovery rate to 98 percent within 6 years. A university might adopt a standard of graduating 80 percent of its student athletes within 5 years of their initial enrollment by the year 1990. In short, control standards can be as narrow or as broad as the level of activity to which they apply.

A final aspect of establishing standards is to decide which performance indicators are relevant. When a new product is introduced, its manufacturer should have some idea in advance whether the first month's sales will accurately indicate long-term growth or whether sales will take a while to gather momentum. Similarly, when a retailer adopts a standard of increasing sales by 12 percent next year, management should have some idea whether to expect even growth of 1 percent per month, or 2 percent for the first 10 months and 10 percent during the Christmas season. If the former, a 1 percent increase during the first six months is cause for alarm; if the latter, a 1 percent increase by July is probably okay.

Measuring performance

The second step in the control process is measuring performance. In this context, performance refers to that which we are attempting to control. The measurement of performance is a constant, ongoing activity for most organizations, and for control to be effective, relevant performance measures must be valid.

When a manager is concerned with controlling sales, daily, weekly, or monthly sales figures represent actual performance. For a production manager, performance may be expressed in terms of unit cost. For employees, performance may be measured in terms of quality or quantity of output.

For many jobs, however, measuring performance is not easy. A research and development scientist may spend years working on a single project before achieving a major breakthrough. A manager who takes over a business that is on the brink of failure may need months or even years to turn things around. Nevertheless, some performance indicators can usually be developed. The scientist's progress, for example, can be partially assessed by peer review. The crucial point is to recognize that valid performance measurement, however challenging, is necessary to maintain effective control.[11]

11. For a good discussion of performance evaluation of employees, see Stephen J. Carroll and Craig E. Schneier, *Performance Appraisal and Review Systems* (Glenview, Il.: Scott, Foresman, 1982).

Comparing performance against standards

The third step in the control process is to compare measured performance against the standards developed in step 1. Performance may be higher, lower, or the same as the standard. The issue is how much leeway is permissible before remedial action is taken.

In some cases comparison is easy. Each product manager at General Electric has a goal of being either number 1 or number 2 in her or his market. It is relatively simple to determine whether this standard has been met.[12]

In other settings, comparisons are less clear-cut. Assume that each of three sales managers has a goal of increasing sales by 10 percent during the year. At the end of the year, one manager has increased sales by 9.9 percent, another by 9.3 percent, and the third by 8.7 percent. How do we decide whether each one has met the goal? For the most part, this is a management decision that must be based on many relevant factors, including the absolute dollar amounts involved and any mitigating circumstances. That is, although none of the three attained the precise goal of 10 percent, one was only a small fraction off. Another may have met with unexpected competition from a new company. These and other relevant factors must be considered.

For screening control systems, it is important that comparisons between performance and standards be made frequently. The rationale for using screening control in the first place is to enable managers to correct problems early in the transformation process before errors begin to compound. Hence sophisticated feedback systems may be necessary to provide promptly the information management needs to make comparisons.

Evaluation and action

The final step in the control process is to evaluate performance (via the comparisons made in step 3) and then take appropriate action. This evaluation draws heavily on a manager's analytic and diagnostic skills, which were discussed in Chapter 1. After evaluation, one of three actions is usually appropriate.

Maintain the status quo. One response is to do nothing, or maintain the status quo. This action is generally appropriate when performance more or less measures up to the standard. If the standard for cost reductions this year is 4 percent and we have achieved a reduction of 3.99 percent, we are clearly on the right track.

Correct the deviation. It is more likely that some action will be needed to correct a deviation from the standard. If the cost-reduction standard is 4 percent and we have thus far managed only a 1 percent reduction, something must be done to get us back on track. We may need to motivate our employees to work harder or to supply them with new machinery.

12. See Ann M. Morrison, "Trying to Bring GE to Life," *Fortune*, January 25, 1982, pp. 50–57.

In some situations, we may be doing better than anticipated but still need to correct this "problem." For example, when Coleco introduced its video game system in late 1982, demand was far greater than expected, and many people who wanted to buy the system for Christmas were unable to do so. Some retailers and customers may have been unhappy because the new system was heavily advertised but not available in adequate supplies.

Change standards. A final response to the outcome of comparing performance to standards is to change the standards. The standard may have been too high or too low to begin with. This is apparent if large numbers of employees exceed the standard by a wide margin or if no one ever meets the standard.

In other situations, a standard that was perfectly good when it was set may need to be adjusted because circumstances have changed. A sales-increase standard of 10 percent may have to be modified when a new competitor breaks on the scene. Given new market conditions, the old standard of 10 percent is no longer realistic.

Making control effective

Managers can do a great deal to improve the effectiveness of their control systems. The five most important steps that managers can take are to integrate control with planning and to make sure that controls are flexible, accurate, timely, and objective.[13]

Integrating control and planning

To further illustrate the relationship between planning and controlling, consider the business practices of 3M, the Minnesota company that produces products ranging from Scotch-brand tape to sandpaper to x-ray film. A basic aspect of 3 M's strategy is to emphasize innovation and new-product development. Consequently, one of 3 M's goals is that 25 percent of company sales must derive from products that did not exist five years before. To counterbalance this, top management also reviews each product every year. Products that are not yielding an acceptable return on investment may be dropped.[14] The emphasis on innovation is an element of strategy, the annual review of existing products an element of control.

The most important factor in effectively integrating planning and control is to account for control as plans are developed. Figure 17.5 shows one way in which this can be done.

13. See William G. Ouchi, "The Transmission of Control Through Organizational Hierarchy," *Academy of Management Journal*, June 1978, pp. 173–192; and Cortlandt Cammann and David A. Nadler, "Fit Control Systems to Your Managerial Style," *Harvard Business Review*, January–February, 1976, pp. 65–72.

14. See Lee Smith, "The Lures and Limits of Innovation," *Fortune*, October 20, 1980, pp. 84–94.

Figure 17.5
Integrating planning
and control

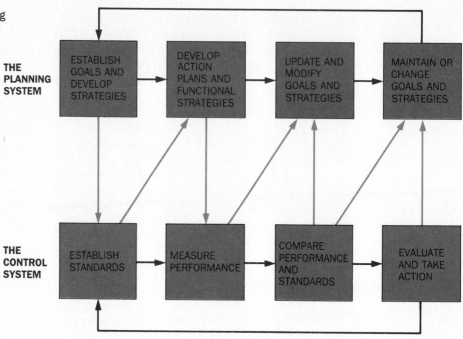

The top of the figure draws on two earlier figures (Figure 4.1, The planning framework, and Figure 6.4, Integrating planning time frames). Note also that this is a simplified representation of the planning function. The four control stages are the same as those illustrated in Figure 17.4.

The first step in the planning system is establishing goals and developing strategy. This leads to the second step in planning (developing action plans and functional strategies) and also to the first step in the control system (establishing standards). The standards established for control purposes also play a role in determining action plans and functional strategies.

The action plans and functional strategies, in turn, figure significantly in performance measurement. Existing action plans, functional strategies, measured performance, and comparisons of performance with standards then affect the updating and modification of future plans. Finally, decisions about whether to maintain or change goals and strategy are affected by previous modifications and updates, by comparisons between standards and performance, and by evaluations and actions taken within the control system.

At the beginning of the process, planning plays a major role in shaping the control system. By the end of the process, however, the later stages of control exert a primary influence on planning. A careful integration of planning and control can improve the effectiveness of both sets of activities.[15]

15. See Horovitz, "Strategic Control: A New Task for Top Management."

Flexibility

Another characteristic of an effective control system is *flexibility*. That is, the control system itself must be flexible enough to accommodate change.[16]

Consider an organization whose diverse product line requires 75 different raw materials. The company's inventory control system must be able to manage and monitor current levels of inventory for all 75 materials. When a change in the product line changes the number of raw materials needed, or when the required quantities of any of the existing materials change, the control system should be able to accommodate the revised requirements. Designing and implementing a new control system would be an unnecessary expense.

Another example of control system flexibility is found in a university setting, where student registration is often computerized. When a course's enrollment reaches a specified upper limit, no additional students are allowed in. Yet graduating seniors and perhaps other students with work or class conflicts may simply *have* to take the course. A flexible control system would allow these students to be added manually to the class enrollment.

Accuracy

Control systems must also be accurate. This seems obvious enough, but it is surprising how many managers base decisions on inaccurate information. Sales representatives in the field may hedge their sales estimates to make themselves look better. Production managers may hide costs to meet their targets. Personnel managers may overestimate their minority recruiting prospects to meet affirmative action goals. In each case the information received by higher management is inaccurate. And, denied accurate measurement and reporting of performance, higher management may take inappropriate action.

If sales estimates are artificially high, a manager might either cut advertising (thinking it is no longer needed) or increase advertising (to further build momentum). In either case the action may not be appropriate. Similarly, having been fed artificially low production costs, a manager who is unaware of the hidden costs may quote a sales price much lower than desirable. Or a personnel executive may speak out publicly on the effectiveness of the company's minority recruiting, only to find out later that these prospects have been overestimated. The *accuracy* of control systems goes a long way to prevent such damaging outcomes.

Timeliness

Another characteristic of an effective control system is that it provides information in a timely way. *Timeliness* doesn't necessarily mean speed; it simply means as often as is suitable for that which is being controlled. In a retail store, sales results are usually needed daily so that cash flow can be managed, ad-

16. See Peter F. Drucker, *Management: Tasks, Practices, Responsibilities* (New York: Harper & Row, 1974).

vertising and promotion adjusted, and so on. Physical inventory counts, however, may be taken only quarterly or even annually. When a new product comes on the market, managers may need frequent sales reports to gauge public acceptance. For older, more established products, sales reports are needed less often.

In general, the more uncertain the situation, the more frequently information is needed, and the more predictable the situation, the less often information is needed.

Objectivity

Insofar as possible, the information provided by the control system should be objective. Consider a personnel manager who is responsible for control of his organization's human resources. He asks two plant managers to submit reports summarizing their respective plants' human resource situations. One manager notes that morale at his plant is "okay," that grievances are "about where they should be," and that turnover is "under control." The other reports that absenteeism at her plant is running at 4 percent, that 16 grievances have been filed this year (compared to 24 last year), and that turnover is 12 percent. Which manager's report is more useful?

Of course, *objectivity* isn't everything, and managers need to look beyond the numbers when making decisions. When a sales representative is posting impressive sales increases every month, or when a production manager is cutting costs consistently, upper-level managers should be pleased. However, one way to increase sales is to offer unauthorized discounts, make unrealistic guarantees about product performance, or promise earlier delivery dates. And costs can be cut by decreasing quality or putting unreasonable pressure on employees. For many reasons, these techniques may not be as desirable as others. The control system ideally provides objective information to the manager for evaluation and action, but the manager must take appropriate precautions in interpreting it.

Resistance to control

As useful and effective as properly designed control systems are, many people resist control for a variety of reasons. Earlier in this chapter we noted that Transamerica dramatically increased its controls to monitor its subsidiaries better.[17] One subsidiary, United Artists, was angered and embittered by those controls, however, and eventually left the parent company. This section explores why employees resist control and then suggests some ways to overcome this resistance.

17. See Schuyten, "United Artists' Script Calls for Divorce."

Table 17.1 Resistance to control

Why employees resist control	Techniques for overcoming resistance to control
Overcontrol	Create effective control
Incorrect focus	Participation
Rewarding inefficiency	MBO
Accountability	Checks and balances

Why employees resist control

The reasons why employees often resist control are summarized in Table 17.1. The following paragraphs explore each of those reasons in more detail.

Overcontrol. Occasionally, organizations make the mistake of overcontrol: they try to control too many things.[18] This becomes especially problematic when the controls pertain directly to employee behavior. If an organization tells its employees when to come to work, where to park, when to have morning coffee, when to go to lunch, when to return, when to have afternoon coffee, and when to leave for the day, it is exerting considerable control over their daily activities. Yet many organizations find it necessary to impose these rules. Troubles arise when additional, gratuitous controls are added. If a company also tells its employees how to dress, what they can and cannot put on their desks, and how to wear their hair, employees are likely to feel overcontrolled. The point is that, if controls are perceived as excessive, employees resist them.

Inappropriate focus. Another reason for resistance is that the focus of the control system may be inappropriate. The control system may be too narrow, or it may focus too much on quantifiable variables and leave no room for analysis or interpretation. A sales standard that encourages high-pressure tactics to maximize short-run sales may do so at the expense of goodwill from long-term customers. Such a standard is too narrow. A university reward system that encourages faculty members to publish large numbers of articles but fails to consider the quality of the work is also inappropriately focused.[19]

Rewarding inefficiency. Imagine two operating departments that are approaching the end of the fiscal year. One department expects to have $5,000 of its budget left over; the second is already $3,000 in the red. As a result,

18. For a thorough discussion of the behavioral implications of control, see Lawler and Rhode, *Information and Control in Organizations.*

19. See Newman, *Constructive Control.*

department 1 is likely to have its budget cut for the next year ("They had money left, so they obviously got too much to begin with") and department 2 is likely to get a budget increase ("They obviously haven't been getting enough money"). Thus department 1 is punished for being efficient and department 2 is rewarded for being inefficient. (No wonder departments commonly hasten to deplete their budgets as the end of the year approaches!) People naturally resist this kind of control, because the rewards and punishments associated with spending and conserving are unfair. Budgeting processes are examined in detail in Chapter 18.[20]

Accountability. Another reason why some people resist control is that effective control systems create accountability. That is, when people have the responsibility to do something, effective controls allow managers to determine whether or not they successfully discharge that responsibility. If standards are properly set and performance accurately measured, managers not only know when problems arise but also know which departments and even which individuals are responsible. Some people, especially those who are not doing a good job, do not want to be answerable for their mistakes and therefore resist control.

Overcoming resistance to control

Fortunately, several techniques can help managers overcome resistance to control. A number of them are summarized in Table 17.1.

Create effective controls. Perhaps the best way to overcome resistance to control is to create effective control to begin with. If control systems are properly integrated with an organization's planning system and if the controls are flexible, accurate, timely, and objective, the organization should not fall victim to the problems of overcontrol, incorrect focus, or rewarding inefficiency. And those employees who fear accountability most will perhaps be held accountable for their poor performance.

Participation. In Chapter 12 we noted that participation can help overcome resistance to change. By the same token, when employees are involved with planning and implementing the control system, they are less likely to resist it. For instance, employee participation at the Chevrolet Gear Axle plant in Detroit has resulted in increased employee concern for quality and a greater commitment to meeting standards.[21]

20. See Jay Lorsch, James Baughman, James Reece, and Henry Mintzberg, *Understanding Management* (New York: Harper & Row, 1978), Chapter 7.
21. See Charles G. Burck, "What Happens When Workers Manage Themselves," *Fortune*, July 27, 1981, pp. 62–69.

MBO. Management by objectives, or MBO (discussed in Chapter 4), can also overcome employee resistance to control.[22] When MBO is used properly, employees help establish their own goals or standards. They also know in advance that their rewards will be based on the extent to which they achieve and maintain those goals and standards. MBO, then, is a vehicle for facilitating the integration of planning and control.[23]

Checks and balances. Another way to overcome employee resistance to control is to maintain a system of checks and balances. Suppose a production manager argues that he or she failed to meet a certain cost standard because of increased prices of raw materials. If the inventory control system is properly designed, it should clearly support or refute the production manager's explanation. Suppose that an employee who has been fired for excessive absences argues that she or he has not been absent "for a long time." The personnel control system should have records on the matter. In brief, multiple standards and information systems provide checks and balances for control. Resistance declines because this system of checks and balances serves to protect employees as well as management. For example, if the production manager's argument about the rising cost of raw materials is supported by the inventory control records, he or she will not be held solely accountable for failing to meet the cost standard.

Control and the controller

All managers are involved in the control process to one extent or another. That is, all managers help establish standards, measure performance, compare that performance against the established standards, and take appropriate action. One manager in particular, however, the *controller*, is most closely associated with the control function (some organizations also use the title comptroller). The controller is responsible for helping line managers with their control activities, coordinating the organization's overall control system, and gathering and assimilating relevant information.[24]

Most medium-sized and large organizations (including businesses, universities, and hospitals) have a controller. Many businesses that use a divisionalized form of organization design have several controllers: one for the corporation and one for each division.[25]

In recent years, the position of controller has taken on added importance

22. See Fred Luthans and Jerry L. Sellentin, "MBO in Hospitals: A Step Toward Accountability," *Personnel Administration*, October, 1976, pp. 42–45.

23. See also Drucker, *Management: Tasks, Practices, Responsibilities.*

24. See David Anderson and Leon Schmidt, *Practical Controllership* (Homewood, Il.: Irwin, 1961).

25. See Vijay Sathe, "Who Should Control Division Controllers?" *Harvard Business Review*, September–October, 1978, pp. 99-104.

Figure 17.6
The position of
controller in a
divisionalized
corporation

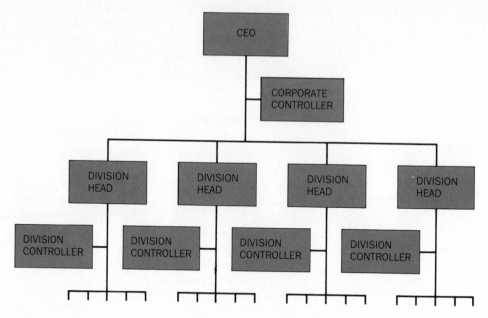

in many organizations. Companies have become more interested in improving their profit margins than in simply increasing sales. During the 1960s and early 1970s, when the economy was expanding, many companies borrowed extensively to keep pace. As economic growth began to slow in the late 1970s, controllers and their expertise in managing these steep debt levels came to be highly valued. Controllers now play an important role in planning and decision making, as well as in helping all managers improve their own control activities.

The increased importance of the controller is reflected in the large number of controllers who now head major U.S. corporations. The chief executive officers of Cooper Industries, Singer, FMC Corporation, CPC International, General Motors, Pfizer, and Fruehauf are all former controllers.[26]

The increased importance of the controller's position also occasions certain problems. Figure 17.6 shows the partial organization chart of a company with several divisions. As noted earlier, many companies of this sort have a corporate controller and a number of division controllers. ITT has just such an arrangement. The problem is how to coordinate the activities of all the controllers. Some argue that the division controllers should be responsible to the division heads, whereas others believe that they should report to the corporate controller. In a survey of several major corporations, Vijay Sathe found that both arrangements are common.[27] The deciding factor seems to be the relative

26. See "The Controller—Inflation Gives Him More Clout with Management," *Business Week*, August 15, 1977, pp. 85-87, 90, 95.
27. See Sathe, "Who Should Control Division Controllers?"

independence of the divisions. When divisional considerations outweigh corporate considerations, the division controller reports to the division head; when the considerations are reversed, the corporate controller has authority; when divisional and corporate considerations are roughly equal, both corporate controller and division head have authority over the division controller.

Choosing a style of control

How should a manager go about developing a control strategy? An approach suggested by Cortlandt Cammann and David A. Nadler has proved useful.[28] In their view, four basic sets of factors determine the appropriate kind of control system: managerial style, organizational style, performance measures, and employee desire to participate.

Table 17.2 suggests four questions about these factors that managers can ask themselves. Managerial styles are presumed to be either participative (consulting with subordinates) or directive. Organizational style, which is a composite of climate, structure, and reward systems, can be participative (participative decision making throughout the organization) or nonparticipative (centralized, with few people participating in the decision making process). Performance measures are classified as accurate (reliable, valid, and truly reflective of performance) or relatively inaccurate. Finally, employees are assumed to have either considerable desire to participate in decision making or little desire to participate.

The answers to these questions indicate the form of control a manager should adopt (see the decision tree shown in Figure 17.7). The manager answers each of the questions in Table 17.2 and follows the appropriate path. For example, if the manager's style is participative, the organization's style is participative, and the employees want to participate (the top path through the diagram), a control strategy that depends on internal motivation will probably work well. Note that not all paths (including the one we just traced) involve all four questions. This is because, if managers and organizations are participative and employees desire to participate, an internal motivation strategy is appropriate regardless of the accuracy of performance measures.

An internal motivation strategy is one of two basic strategies proposed by Cammann and Nadler. This strategy would attempt to provide employees with such intrinsic rewards as feelings of accomplishment, well-being, responsibility, growth, and achievement. Hence the organization might adopt job enrichment or modified work weeks. The other basic strategy would be to emphasize an external motivation strategy, offering extrinsic rewards such as pay and status symbols.

Because most organizations require multiple control systems, this model is not for organizations as a whole but for individual managers within an

28. See Cammann and Nadler, "Fit Control Systems to Your Managerial Style."

Table 17.2 Useful questions to ask when choosing a control strategy

1. **In general, what kind of managerial style do I have?**

   Participative. I frequently consult my subordinates on decisions, encourage them to disagree with my opinion, share information with them, and let them make decisions whenever possible.

   Directive. I usually take most of the responsibility for and make most of the major decisions, pass on only the most necessary job-relevant information, and provide detailed and close direction for my subordinates.

2. **In general, what kind of climate, structure, and reward system does my organization have?**

   Participative. Employees at all levels of the organization are used to participate in decisions and influence the course of events. Managers are clearly rewarded for developing employees' skills and decision making capacity.

   Non-participative. Most important decisions are made by a few people at the top of the organization. Managers are not rewarded for developing employee competence or encouraging employees to participate in decision making.

3. **How accurate and reliable are the measures of key areas of subordinate performance?**

   Accurate. Measures are reliable, all major aspects of performance can be adequately measured, changes in measures accurately reflect changes in performance, measures cannot be easily sabotaged or faked by subordinates.

   Inaccurate. Not all important aspects of performance can be measured, measures often don't pick up on important changes in performance, good performance cannot be adequately defined in terms of the measures, measures can be easily sabotaged.

4. **Do my subordinates desire to participate and respond well to opportunities to take responsibility for decision making and performance?**

   High desire to participate. Employees are eager to participate in decisions, can make a contribution to decision making, and want to take more responsibility.

   Low desire to participate. Employees do not want to be involved in many decisions, don't want additional responsibility, and have little to contribute to decisions being made.

Source: Reprinted by permission of the *Harvard Business Review*. An exhibit from "Fit Control Systems to Your Management Style" by Cortlandt Cammann and David A. Nadler (January–February 1976). Copyright © 1976 by the President and Fellows of Harvard College; all rights reserved.

Figure 17.7
Selecting a control strategy

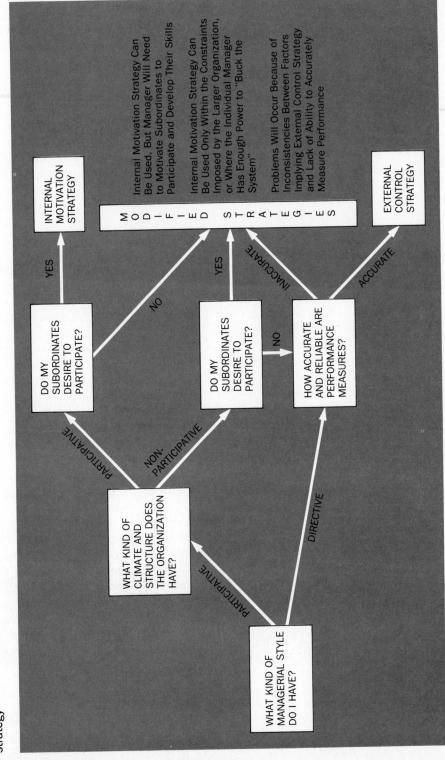

Source: Reprinted by permission of the *Harvard Business Review*. An exhibit from "Fit Control Systems to Your Management Style" by Cortlandt Cammann and David A. Nadler (January–February 1976). Copyright © 1976 by the President and Fellows of Harvard College;

organization. Finally, we should note that this contingency model of control has not been scientifically tested. It does, however, have intuitive appeal and appears to provide useful insights and guidance for practicing managers.[29]

Summary of key points

Control is one of the four basic managerial functions. Organizational control is the regulation of organizational activities in such a way as to facilitate goal attainment. Organizational control can focus on almost any organizational activity or set of activities. In general, control is directed toward financial, physical, information, and human resources. Organizational control is important because of changing conditions, the possibility of compounding errors, and the complexity of organizations. Planning and controlling are intimately related.

Cybernetic control is the type of control that monitors and manages a process via a self-regulating mechanism. Noncybernetic control depends on an external monitoring system. In terms of timing, control may occur before, during, or after the transformation process. Preliminary control focuses on inputs to the system. Screening control, perhaps the most effective kind, concentrates on the transformation process itself. And post-action control focuses on outputs; it provides information for future planning and for rewarding employees. Most organizations need multiple control systems.

Four basic steps are involved in the control process. Standards of expected performance must be established—standards that are derived from goals, reflect organizational strategy, and identify relevant performance indicators. The second step is to measure actual performance, making sure that performance measures are valid. Then measured performance should be compared against the standards. Finally, the manager must evaluate the results of this comparison and take appropriate action, which may consist of maintaining the status quo, correcting a deviation from the standard, or changing the standard.

One way to increase the effectiveness of control is to ensure that planning and control are fully integrated. The control system should also be flexible, accurate, timely, and as objective as possible.

Many employees resist organizational control. They do so because of overcontrol, inappropriate focus of control, rewards for inefficiency, and fear of accountability. Managers can help overcome their resistance by concentrating on the things that improve the effectiveness of control. In addition, they can allow employee participation, use MBO, and establish a system of checks and balances.

29. Other useful perspectives on designing control systems have been presented by William G. Ouchi, "A Conceptual Framework for the Design of Organizational Control Mechanisms," *Management Science*, September 1979, pp. 833–848; and Eric Flamholtz, "Organizational Control Systems as a Managerial Tool," *California Management Review*, Winter 1979, pp. 50–58.

The position of controller is a role created specifically to manage the control process. Because of economic pressures, the job of controller has recently taken on added importance. One issue confronting large organizations is whether division controllers should report to their division heads or to the corporate controller.

Control strategy can focus on either internal motivation or external motivation, depending on the situation. Four situational factors that help determine the appropriate control strategy are managerial style, organizational style, the accuracy of performance measures, and employee desire to participate.

QUESTIONS FOR DISCUSSION

1. Is it possible to exercise control in a closed system? Why or why not?
2. How is the controlling process related to the organizing and leading functions?
3. Using your university or business as background, provide examples of cybernetic, noncybernetic, preliminary, screening, and post-action controls.
4. How can a manager ensure that multiple control systems fit together effectively?
5. Which of the steps in control is most likely to spark employee resistance and anger?
6. At which step of the control process is there the greatest potential for mistakes? Why?
7. Can you think of additional techniques for making control more effective?
8. Identify settings wherein objective control is *not* desirable.
9. What controls that instructors use are most resisted by students?
10. What could an instructor do to overcome this resistance?
11. Does your university or business have a controller? If so, find out how the position fits into the organization's design. If not, why do you think such a position has not been created?
12. Aside from the situational factors suggested by Cammann and Nadler, are there other factors that a manager should consider when choosing a control strategy?

C A S E   17.1

At the beginning of this chapter, you read an incident about an art auction house. The company has been operating under the assumption of constant growth. Staff experts have been given total autonomy for their operations but have not been responsible for bottom-line results. The company has just posted its first loss since World War II. The company being described was Sotheby's. The case that follows describes what Sotheby's has done and then raises some other issues for your consideration.

Sotheby Parke Bernet Group, commonly known as Sotheby's, is the world's largest art auction house. The company was created in 1744 and became the first English auction house to expand into the United States when it opened a branch office in New York in the early 1960s.

Much of the credit for Sotheby's success belongs to Peter Wilson, who served as the company's chairman from 1958 until his retirement in 1979. He was able to combine the strategic vision of a management pioneer with the taste and credentials of an art connoisseur. Under his leadership, Sotheby's was praised for taking a businesslike and dynamic approach to the world of art marketing. In 1981 the company reported sales of $651 million, almost half of which was generated in the United States.

Wilson was also an acknowledged expert in the art world. The staff of an art auction house typically consists of specialists who locate collections, appraise them, and then catalog them for sale. Such specialists are usually more interested in the aesthetic nature of their work than in profit margins and overhead expenses. Yet, rather than seeing Wilson as an autocratic administrator, they saw him as a peer. Wilson also continually reinforced his position by locating prize collections himself.

As difficult as it is to fault Wilson as a manager, it must be admitted that he took a casual approach to the business side of things. His basic operating assumption was that art prices would continue escalating indefinitely, with only occasional rough spots. Wilson also drew no clear lines of authority and was reluctant to impose any kind of financial control.

One example of how Wilson practiced management can be drawn from his staff art experts and how they were allowed to operate. Basically, they were given unlimited expense accounts to travel the globe in search of art treasures for auction. The staff experts could also expand their own units "as needed," and Sotheby's worldwide staff increased from 1,050 to 1,560 between 1977 and 1979. Further, each staff member was given the authority to negotiate commissions with sellers, to waive commissions, and even to pay transportation charges for some sellers.

Another example of Wilson's loss of control is found in Sotheby's rapid expansion program and how it was financed. The com-

The need for control at Sotheby's

pany's auction house in New York was located on Madison Avenue, in the center of the art district. In 1978, however, Sotheby's invested $8.4 million of borrowed funds in another auction house several blocks away on York Avenue. Other major expenses included $6 million for a new building in London, $4 million for another British auction company, and $1.5 million for a computer system. All told, Sotheby's debt reached $37.5 million; interest payments in 1981 alone equaled 15 percent of the company's pre-tax profits.

After Wilson's retirement in 1979, his cousin Lord Westmoreland became chairman. After announcing that the company might report a loss for the first time since World War II, Westmoreland also stepped down in early 1982.

The top management team charged with replacing Westmoreland quickly realized that radical intervention was needed to revitalize the company and to bring operations back under control. The most dramatic move has been to close down Sotheby's Madison Avenue auction house as well as its Los Angeles house. All United States operations are now consolidated at the York Avenue gallery. Worldwide staff has been cut by 20 percent and further reductions are likely. Commissions have been raised to 15 percent. Finally, some auctions are being conducted with a little less pomp and ceremony. Overall, however, the company still has a way to go before it recovers its previous glamour and fiscal well-being.

CASE QUESTIONS

1. Explain why and how Sotheby's problems arose. Is it true that an increase in size should always be accompanied by increased control?
2. What types of control is Sotheby's now using? Can you describe the steps involved in creating a potential control system for the company?
3. What are the similarities and differences between control for a company like Sotheby's and control for a company like Exxon or Ford?
4. How could Sotheby's better integrate planning and control?

CASE REFERENCES

Kinkead, Gwen. "Sotheby's Lost Art: Management." *Fortune*, May 31, 1982, pp. 123–129.

Mahon, Gigi. "Chips Off the Old Block." *Barron's*, June 14, 1982, pp. 24, 55, 72.

"Sotheby's Sees Loss, Changes Management." *Wall Street Journal*, April 9, 1982, p. 27.

C A S E 17.2

Greg Jackson was at a loss for words. He had just received his plant's end-of-the-year operating statistics and they weren't what he had expected. Greg was appointed plant manager about 16 months ago. One of the first things he did was to establish a number of operating goals for the coming year. In particular, he was concerned with the plant's high scrappage rate and its excessive overtime for employees. While they were not really a problem, he was also interested in finding ways to cut freight costs.

Accordingly, Greg had established goals intended to achieve improvements in each of those areas. His goal for scrappage was to reduce it from last year's level of 15 percent to 10 percent of total raw material costs. Overtime costs were to be cut from $110,000 to $60,000. Finally, Greg wanted to cut freight costs by 3 percent. After establishing these goals, Greg had communicated them to other members of the plant management team and had suggested a variety of techniques they might use to reach the goals he had established for them.

At year's end, however, the results were somewhat less than overwhelming. Scrappage was higher than last year, with a yearly average of 16 percent of raw material costs. Overtime had been cut, but only to $90,000. And freight costs were at the same level as before.

The first thing Greg did was talk to the production manager about the scrappage. She had no idea what might have happened. She argued that she had been putting more pressure on the workers to cut scrappage and really thought that they had been bringing it down.

In a later conversation, the personnel manager also expressed surprise at the year-end report. He indicated that he had taken a harder line on approving overtime and that he had approved it only when the production people said it was absolutely necessary.

The transportation manager, by contrast, was not surprised at the lack of change in freight costs. He noted that he had always been diligent about trying to hold down costs and that most freight charges were fixed. He further asserted that rate increases planned by several carriers would probably increase freight costs by 3 or 4 percent for the coming year.

Having talked to each manager individually, Greg called them all together for a meeting. During the meeting he really took a hard line. He told the production manager that scrappage rates had to come down to 10 percent. Overtime was still a big problem, and the new target was to be $70,000. Greg concluded by announcing that, even if freight rates went up, the company had to hold the line at the present level. He concluded the meeting by

Control systems for goal attainment

noting that he would be very much interested in seeing the company's operating statistics next year.

CASE
QUESTIONS

1. What kinds of things are not being done properly at this company?
2. How successful is the company likely to be next year?
3. What kind of control system should this company use?

18

CONTROL TECHNIQUES AND METHODS

1. Describe the budgeting process and various types of budgets, differentiate between fixed and variable components of budgets, summarize zero-base budgeting, and discuss the pros and cons of budgeting.

2. Identify and describe several other financial control techniques.

3. Describe operations control, discuss its four basic elements, and list the major techniques of operations control.

4. Describe personnel control and briefly summarize its major techniques.

5. Describe marketing control and briefly summarize its major techniques.

Budgetary control
The budgeting process
Types of budgets
Fixed and variable budgets
Zero-base budgeting
Strengths and weaknesses of budgeting

Other financial control techniques
Financial analysis
Financial audits

Operations control
Operations design
Operations planning
Quality control
Inventory control
Operations control techniques

Personnel control
Performance appraisal
Personnel ratios

Marketing control
Test marketing
Marketing ratios

Summary of key points

OPENING INCIDENT

You have just been hired as chief executive officer for a cosmetics firm. You come from an organization that practices tight control over all areas of operations. Arriving at your new company, you discover that little or no control is exercised. Managers, for example, have no five-year plans and seem to operate on a day-to-day basis. How would you proceed?

As part of the planning process, organizations allocate financial resources to various organizational units such as divisions or departments. From the standpoint of control, top management is interested in the extent to which those units make use of their financial resources in a fashion that is both efficient and effective. This interest reflects the control function of the manager's job. How are the financial resources controlled? Generally the organization uses a specific control technique called a budget. Budgets are just one of several control techniques discussed in this chapter.

Chapter 17 explored basic concepts in organizational control. In this chapter, we describe specific techniques for managing the control process. We first discuss budgets and budgetary control. Next we treat other financial control techniques and methods. Subsequent sections describe operations control, marketing control, and personnel control.

Some of these techniques and methods overlap with our earlier discussion (in Chapter 8) of quantitative tools for planning. This is to be expected, given the close connection between planning and control. When we discuss techniques that have already been described, we will simply note how they can also be used for control without rehearsing their quantitative aspects. Techniques and methods introduced here for the first time are examined in more detail.

Budgetary control

Budgeting involves expressing a set of planned activities for the coming time period in dollar or other quantitative terms.[1] Organizations may establish budgets for subunits, departments, divisions, or the whole organization. The usual time period for a budget is one year, although breakdowns of budgets

---

1. See Jay W. Lorsch, James P. Baughman, James Reece, and Henry Mintzberg, *Understanding Management* (New York: Harper & Row, 1978), pp. 187–188.

by the quarter or month are also common. Budgets are generally expressed in financial terms, but they may occasionally be in terms of units of output, time, or other quantifiable factors.

Budgets are the foundation of most control systems.[2] Because of their quantitative nature, they provide yardsticks for measuring performance and facilitate comparisons across departments, between levels in the organization, and from one time period to another.

In particular, budgets serve four primary purposes. They help managers coordinate resources and projects. (This stems from their use of a common denominator, usually dollars.) They help define the standards needed in all control systems. They provide clear and unambiguous guidelines about the organization's resources and expectations. And they facilitate performance evaluations of managers and units.[3]

The budgeting process

Budgets have traditionally been developed by top management and the controller and then imposed on lower-level managers.[4] Although some organizations still follow this pattern, many contemporary organizations now allow lower-level managers to participate in the process. The course of a typical budget preparation process is illustrated in Figure 18.1.

In step 1, the heads of the operating units submit their budget requests to the division heads. These operating unit heads might be department managers in a wholesaling firm or program directors in a social service agency. The division heads might include plant managers, regional sales managers, or college deans.

The division head takes the various budget requests from the operating unit heads and integrates and consolidates them into one overall division budget request (step 2). Overlapping and/or inconsistent requests are corrected at this stage. In a college budget, 2 department heads might each request 5 new typewriters at a cost of $1,000 each. The dean might be aware that the typewriter manufacturer grants a 10 percent discount on orders of 10 typewriters, so she or he would request $9,000 rather than $10,000 for the 10 typewriters. Similarly, if a regional sales manager sees that a certain sales manager's request assumes a 15 percent increase in product price whereas another assumes a 12 percent increase, he or she would resolve the inconsistency. A great deal of interaction between managers usually takes place as the division head works to integrate and coordinate the budgetary needs of the various departments.

In step 3, division budget requests are forwarded to a budget committee. The budget committee itself, shown as step 4, is comprised of top managers with line authority. In businesses, the committee members are likely to be vice presidents. As shown in the figure, budget requests from several divisions are

2. See Robert N. Anthony and John Dearden, *Management Control Systems*, 4th ed. (Homewood, Il.: Irwin, 1980).

3. See Lorsch et al., *Understanding Management*.

4. See Anthony and Dearden, *Management Control Systems*.

Figure 18.1
The budgeting
process

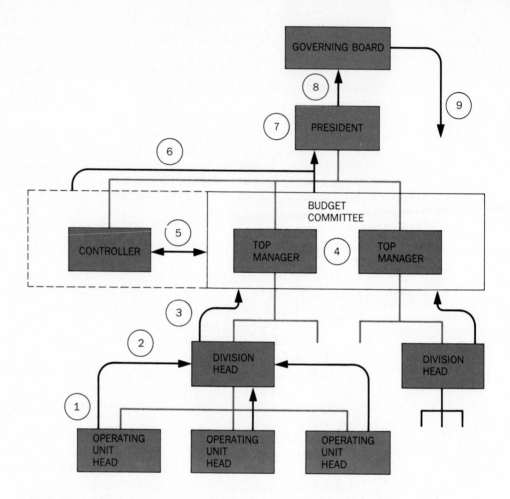

reviewed at this stage and, once again, overlapping and inconsistencies are corrected. A university's business college and its speech department might both request funds to develop a new course in business communication. Campus administrators would have to eliminate this duplication. Similarly, the news and the entertainment divisions of a television network might both request funds for a news magazine show like *20/20* or *Good Morning, America*. Again, the budget committee would resolve this overlap.

Step 5 of the process involves interaction between the budget committee and the controller. This interaction can take a variety of forms. The budgets could all pass from the committee to the controller for further evaluation and approval. Or the controller could be a member of the budget committee. Or the controller might evaluate the budget requests before they ever go to the budget committee.

In step 6, the final budget is sent to the president or CEO for approval. After undergoing his or her scrutiny (step 7), it may be passed on to the board of directors or other governing board for review (step 8). Final budgets are then communicated back to the divisions and operating units. Of course, as budget requests pass through these various stages, it is almost certain that some changes will be made. The budget the unit ultimately has available may be more than, less than, or the same as what it initially requested.

The budgetary process has been described here in very general terms, and endless variations are possible. Many organizations, for example, have budget departments that assist managers in preparing and evaluating budget requests. Occasionally, top management provides initial guidelines on what resources are available, so that lower-level managers will have some sense of what it is realistic to ask for. Mechanisms are also needed for revising budgets during their term if that should prove necessary. If demand for a firm's products were to jump unexpectedly, a plant manager should be able to request additional funds to pay for the overtime labor needed to meet this demand.

This "bottom-up" approach to budgeting is often advocated because it has two primary strengths. First, individual unit managers are likely to be more familiar than anyone else with their own needs and requirements. They can call attention to special situations that top management may not be aware of and will probably include all the important elements in developing their own budgets. Second, managers are more likely to "live with" and try to meet a budget if they had a hand in developing it.[5]

Types of budgets

Up to this point, we have talked about budgets in a general or global sense. In practice, however, most organizations have a number of different kinds of budgets: financial, operating, and nonmonetary. These are summarized in Table 18.1.

Financial budgets. Financial budgets detail where the organization expects to get its cash for the coming time period and how it plans to spend it. Usual sources of cash include sales revenue, loans, the sale of assets, and the issuance of new stock. Common uses of cash are to pay expenses, repay debt, purchase new assets, and pay dividends to stockholders.

One type of financial budget, the *cash-flow budget*, breaks down incoming and outgoing cash into monthly, weekly, or even daily periods so that the organization can make sure it is able to meet its current obligations. In a small business, for example, if the owner has a $10,000 payroll and a $1,000 utility bill due on the last day of every month, he or she must make sure that there is sufficient cash on hand to meet these obligations.

Another type of financial budget, the *capital expenditures budget*, concentrates on major assets such as a new plant, machinery or land. Companies often acquire such resources by borrowing significant amounts (through long-term loans or bonds), so the capital expenditures budget is quite important. All organizations, even mammoth firms like Exxon and General Electric, pay close attention to these budgets because of the large investment usually associated with capital expenditures.

5. See Selwin W. Becker and David Green, Jr., "Budgeting and Employee Behavior," *Journal of Business*, October 1962, pp. 392–402.

Table 18.1 Types of budgets

Financial budgets. Focus on incoming and outgoing cash.	**Cash-flow budget.** Focuses on short-run and current financial obligations. **Capital expenditures budget.** Focuses on major assets such as plant, equipment, and property. **Balance sheet budget.** Focuses on what the organization's balance sheet will look like if all other budgets are met.
Operating budgets. Express planned operations in financial terms.	**Sales or revenue budget.** Focuses on anticipated income from normal operations. **Expense budget.** Focuses on anticipated expenses. **Profit budget.** Focuses on projected differences between sales or revenues and expenses.
Nonmonetary budgets. Are expressed in terms that are not financial.	

The *balance sheet budget* forecasts what the organization's balance sheet will look like if all other budgets are met. Hence it serves as an overall control framework to ensure that other budgets mesh properly and will yield results that are in the best interests of the organization.

Operating budgets. A second major category of budgets includes operating budgets. An *operating budget* is an expression of the organization's planned operations in financial terms. That is, an operating budget outlines what the organization will consume and what it will produce.

A *sales or revenue budget* focuses on income the organization expects to receive from normal operations. If a firm expects to sell 1,000,000 products at $10 each, its sales budget is $10,000,000. For a government organization, the revenue budget might specify the anticipated influx of tax dollars. Sales or revenue budgets are vitally important because they help the manager understand what the future financial position of the organization will be.

An *expense budget* outlines the anticipated expenses of the organization in the coming time period. If a manager has a telephone expense budget of $12,000 a year, for example, he or she knows that the unit can spend about $1,000 a month on telephone calls. The expense budget also points out upcoming expenses so that the manager can better prepare for them.

A *profit budget* focuses on anticipated differences between sales or revenues and expenses. If budgeted sales are $1,000,000 and budgeted expenses are $700,000, the manager has a profit budget of $300,000. If budgeted sales and expenses are too close together, the profit budget may not be acceptable because the resultant profit is too small. In this case, steps may be needed to increase the sales budget (such as cutting prices or raising sales quotas) or to cut the expense budget (such as reducing inventory costs or improving scrappage rates).

Nonmonetary budgets. A *nonmonetary budget* is simply a budget expressed in terms that are not financial. They may include units of output, hours of direct labor, machine hours, or square-foot allocations. Nonmonetary budgets are generally used at the lower levels of an organization because they are especially helpful to managers at that level. For example, a plant manager can probably schedule work more effectively knowing that he or she has 8,000 labor hours to allocate in a week, rather than $76,451 in wages.

Fixed and variable budgets

Regardless of their purpose, most budgets must account for three kinds of costs: fixed, variable, and semivariable.[6] *Fixed costs* are expenses that the organization incurs whether it is in operation or not. A retailer may pay a fixed monthly rent regardless of how many days the store is open. Other fixed costs may include property taxes, minimum utility bills, and some salaries.

Variable costs are costs that vary according to the scope of operations. The best example of a variable cost is raw materials used in production. If $2 worth of material is used per unit, costs for 10 units are $20, costs for 40 units are $80, and so on. Other variable costs include travel expenses, sales taxes, and utility expenses above base rates.

Semivariable costs vary as well, but in a less direct fashion. Advertising varies according to season and competition. Other major semivariable costs include direct labor, equipment and plant repairs and maintenance, and so forth.

When developing a budget, managers must accurately account for all three categories of costs. Fixed costs are usually the easiest to deal with. Rent, for example, is almost always governed by a lease and cannot change until the lease expires. Variable costs can often be forecasted—but with less precision—from projected operations. Semivariable costs are the most difficult to predict because they are likely to vary, but not in direct relation to operations. For these costs, the manager must often rely on experience and judgment. Some forecasting techniques are also useful for estimating semivariable costs.[7]

Zero-base budgeting

Zero-base budgeting, or ZBB, was pioneered at Texas Instruments in 1970 and popularized by President Jimmy Carter when he used it in the federal government in the late 1970s.[8]

The basic idea underlying ZBB is quite simple. Under a conventional budgeting system, yearly budgets are based on the previous year's budget, and the manager concentrates on justifying any additional funding that may be

6. See Glenn A. Welsch, *Budgeting: Profit Planning and Control,* 4th ed. (Englewood Cliffs, N.J.: Prentice-Hall, 1976).

7. See Anthony and Dearden, *Management Control Systems;* and Welsch, *Budgeting: Profit Planning and Control.*

8. See Peter A. Pyhrr, "Zero-Base Budgeting," *Harvard Business Review,* November–December 1970, pp. 111–121.

needed. The existing budget is considered a given, and debate centers on the merits of the proposed changes. Under a ZBB system, however, each budgeting unit begins with a clean slate each year. The entire budget must be justified, rather than merely the adjustments to an existing budget.

The first step in ZBB is to break down the activities of the organization into decision packages. Each package represents an activity or set of activities and specifies its costs and benefits and the consequences of nonapproval. Decision packages are then ranked in order of importance. Finally, funds are allocated to each decision package according to its relative rank. The higher the rank, the greater the probability of full funding; the lower the rank, the more likely the activity is to be dropped or only partially funded.

In a relatively short period of time, ZBB has been adopted by a variety of organizations, including Xerox Corporation, Ford, Westinghouse, Playboy, and many federal and state agencies. Ford attributes millions of dollars in savings to zero-base budgeting and Xerox enjoyed a substantial boost in profits following a shift to ZBB.[9]

The primary advantage of ZBB is that it helps maintain vitality by constantly assessing and questioning existing programs. It also facilitates the development of new programs. On the other hand, the process of continual justification necessitates more paperwork, and managers may resort to inflating the importance of their programs to maintain funding. ZBB will probably be used more widely in the future as a technique for organizational control.[10]

Strengths and weaknesses of budgeting

Budgets offer a number of advantages, but they have potential drawbacks as well. Both are summarized in Table 18.2.

On the plus side, budgets facilitate effective control. By placing dollar values on operations, managers can monitor operations better and pinpoint problem areas. Second, budgets facilitate coordination and communication between departments. In a sense, unit budgets are like pieces of a puzzle that fit together to yield an overall framework. By expressing diverse activities in terms of a common denominator (dollars), different units can better communicate with one another. Budgets also help maintain records of organizational performance. Finally, budgets are a natural complement to planning. The link between planning and control was examined in earlier chapters. As managers first plan and then develop control systems, budgets are often a natural next step.[11]

On the other hand, some managers apply budgets too rigidly. They fail to acknowledge that changing circumstances may justify budget adjustments.

9. See "What It Means to Build a Budget from Zero," *Business Week*, April 18, 1977, p. 160.

10. For recent reviews, see Mark W. Dirsmith and Stephen F. Jablonsky, "Zero-Base Budgeting as a Management Technique and Political Strategy," *Academy of Management Review*, October 1979, pp. 555–565; and Stanton C. Lindquist and K. Bryant Mills, "Whatever Happened to Zero-Base Budgeting?" *Management Planning*, January–February 1981, pp. 31–35.

Table 18.2 Strengths and weaknesses of budgeting

Strengths	Weaknesses
1. Budgets facilitate effective control.	1. Budgets may be used too rigidly.
2. Budgets facilitate coordination and communication.	2. Budgets may be time-consuming.
3. Budgets facilitate record keeping.	3. Budgets may limit innovation and change.
4. Budgets are a natural complement to planning.	

Moreover, the process of developing budgets can be very time-consuming. This is especially true when organizations adopt ZBB. Finally, budgets may limit innovation and change. When all available funds are allocated to specific operating budgets, it may be impossible to get additional funds to take advantage of an unexpected opportunity.[12]

In summary, budgets are an important element of an organization's control system. It is difficult to imagine an organization functioning without proper budgetary procedures. Some drawbacks exist, but paying careful attention to the development and use of budgets generally provides managers with an effective tool for executing the control function.

Other financial control techniques

Although budgets are the most common method of financial control, other techniques are also used. One of these techniques involves financial ratios, and another is the financial audit.

Financial analysis

Managers can learn a great deal by performing a *financial analysis*, or analyzing various ratios of the components of an organization's financial profile. These components are drawn from the balance sheet and/or income statement. The *balance sheet* presents the assets and liabilities of the organization at a particular point in time. The *income statement* presents revenues and expenses over a period of time. An example of each of these financial reports is shown in Tables 18.3 and 18.4.

Note that the balance sheet (Table 18.3) is divided into current assets (assets that are relatively liquid, or easily convertible into cash), fixed assets

11. See V. Bruce Irvine, "Budgeting: Functional Analysis and Behavioral Implications," *Cost and Management*, March–April 1970, pp. 6–16.

12. See Henry L. Tosi, Jr., "The Human Effects of Budgeting Systems on Management," *MSU Business Topics*, Autumn 1974, pp. 53–63.

Table 18.3 A balance sheet for Fast-Stop Grocery

Fast-Stop Grocery, Inc.
Balance Sheet
December 31, 1984

Current assets		Current liabilities	
Cash	$ 5,000	Accounts payable	$ 30,000
Accounts receivable	5,000	Accrued expenses	10,000
Inventory	70,000	Long-term liabilities	75,000
	80,000		115,000
Fixed assets		Stockholders' equity	
Land	30,000	Common stock	100,000
Building and equipment	200,000	Retained earnings	95,000
	230,000		195,000
Total current and fixed assets	$310,000	Total liabilities and equity	$310,000

(assets that are longer-term in nature and less liquid), current liabilities (debts and other obligations that must be paid in the near future), long-term liabilities (payable over an extended period of time), and stockholders' equity (the owners' claim against the assets). The sum of all current and fixed assets must equal the sum of all liabilities and equity.

Whereas the balance sheet reflects a snapshot profile of an organization's financial position, the income statement (Table 18.4) captures performance over a period of time. In general, the income statement adds up all income to the organization and then subtracts all expenses, debts, and liabilities. The "bottom line" of the statement represents net income, or profit. Information from the balance sheet and income statements are used in computing the important financial ratios.[13]

Liquidity ratios. Several *liquidity ratios* are used to learn how liquid the organization's assets are. The most common of these, the *current ratio*, is current assets divided by current liabilities. For Fast-Stop Grocery, this is 80,000 ÷ 40,000, or 2. This ratio of 2:1 is generally regarded as normal. It indicates how many dollars of liquid assets are available for each dollar of current liability. Creditors consider the current ratio a good index of an organization's ability to pay its bills on time.

Debt ratios. *Debt ratios* reflect long-term ability to meet financial obligations. The most common expression of the debt ratio is total liabilities di-

13. See J. Fred Weston and Eugene F. Brigham, *Managerial Finance,* 7th ed. (Hinsdale, Il.: Dryden Press, 1981).

Table 18.4 An income statement for Fast-Stop Grocery

Fast-Stop Grocery, Inc.
Income Statement
For the year ended December 31, 1984

Gross sales		403,000
Less returns	3,000	
Net sales		400,000
Less expenses and cost of sales		
Expenses	60,000	
Depreciation	20,000	
Cost of goods sold	<u>200,000</u>	<u>280,000</u>
Operating profit		120,000
Other income		10,000
Interest expense	15,000	
Taxable income		<u>115,000</u>
Less taxes	55,000	
Net income		<u>60,000</u>

vided by total assets. Hence the debt ratio for Fast-Stop Grocery is 115,000 ÷ 310,000, or .37. This indicates that the company has approximately 37 cents in liabilities for every dollar of its assets. The higher this ratio, the poorer credit risk the organization is perceived to be. If management were to ask for a loan of $30,000, for example, the bank would recognize that, even if the store were to go out of business, there would still be enough money left to repay the loan after all other debts were paid.

Return on assets. A third important financial ratio is return on assets, or ROA. ROA is the percentage return to investors on each dollar of assets. It serves as a yardstick for investors and managers to gauge which of several investment opportunities is most profitable. The common formula for ROA is

$$\frac{\text{Net income}}{\text{Total assets}} = \text{ROA}$$

For Fast-Stop Grocery, net income is $60,000 and there are $310,000 in total assets. Hence ROA is

$$\frac{60,000}{310,000} = .19$$

For each dollar invested by Fast-Stop Grocery, the company realizes $1.19, a return of 19 percent per year. This would compare quite favorably with many other investments; a 12 percent savings account, for example, would earn only 12 cents for each dollar invested.

Other ratios. Liquidity ratios, debt ratios, and return on assets are widely used forms of financial analysis. The other frequently used ratio is return on investment, or ROI. ROI is determined by dividing owner's equity into net income. This ratio represents the return to the invester from each dollar of equity.

Other ratios are also of interest to managers and investors. *Coverage ratios* help in estimating the organization's ability to cover interest expenses on borrowed capital. *Operating ratios* focus on functional areas rather than on the total organization. For example, inventory turnover (cost of goods sold divided by average daily inventory) reflects how efficiently the organization is forecasting sales and ordering merchandise. *Profitability ratios* reflect the relative effectiveness of an organization. For example, profits of $5 million are quite good on sales of $20 million but are poor if sales were $100 million.

Break-even analysis. Another form of financial analysis is *break-even analysis.* We discussed break-even analysis earlier, in Chapter 8, as a technique for finding the point at which a project will cover its costs, or break even. Our reason for discussing it in Chapter 8 was that it is often used to make an initial decision on whether to proceed with a project. Break-even analysis is also pertinent to control, because further analyses may be necessary as conditions change. For example, an initial break-even analysis may have indicated that sales of 100,000 units would be needed for a division to break even. Midway through the project, however, material costs could rise, anticipated demand could change, or standard prices for the product could drop. Any or all of these changes would change the break-even point. Hence break-even analysis can be used initially for decision-making purposes and later for control.

Financial audits

Whereas most control techniques also have other purposes, audits are used almost exclusively for control. Audits are independent appraisals of an organization's accounting, financial, and operational systems. The two major forms of *financial audits* are the external audit and the internal audit.[14]

External audits. External audits are financial audits conducted by experts who are not employees of the organization. External audits are typically concerned with the extent to which the organization's accounting procedures and financial statements are compiled in an objective and verifiable fashion. Certified public accountants (CPAs) are usually engaged for this purpose. Their main objective is not to prepare financial documents and reports but to verify the methods by which those documents and reports have been prepared by financial managers and accountants within the organization.

External audits are almost always extremely thorough. In some cases, auditors even count physical inventory to verify that it agrees with what is shown on the balance sheet. The reason for this precision is that auditors who

14. See Arthur W. Holmes and Wayne S. Overmeyer, *Basic Auditing,* 5th ed. (Homewood, Il.: Irwin, 1976).

make mistakes are subject to loss of reputation and even may have their license revoked. External audits are so important that publicly held corporations are required by law to have external audits on a regular basis, as assurance to investors that the corporations' financial reports are reliable.

Internal audits. Whereas external audits are conducted by external accountants, an *internal audit* is handled by employees of the organization. Its primary objective is the same as that of an external audit: to verify the accuracy of financial and accounting procedures used by the organization. Internal audits also focus on the efficiency and appropriateness of the financial and accounting procedures. In some cases, an accounting system may be technically correct but inefficient. Both external and internal audits verify the accuracy of reports, but only the internal audit is concerned with efficiency.

Large organizations such as Exxon, General Motors, and AT&T have internal auditing staffs. These staffs spend all their time conducting audits of different divisions and functional areas of the organization. Smaller organizations may assign accountants to an internal audit group on a temporary or rotating basis.

Because the staff members who conduct them are permanently on the organization's payroll, internal audits tend to be more expensive. However, employees may be more familiar with the organization and can point out other aspects of the accounting system besides its technical correctness. External auditors may be more objective and have more specialized skills. They are also generally less expensive than a full-time auditing staff.

Operations control

Control techniques and methods are an essential part of operations. Whereas financial control deals with monetary resources, **operations control** is concerned with the processes the organization uses to transform inputs into outputs. For manufacturing organizations, the technology of the assembly line or similar conversion process is used in operations, but even service organizations have an operations component.[15] The four primary elements of operations management control are operations design, operations planning, quality control, and inventory control. Useful techniques for operations control include PERT, linear programming, queuing theory, and break-even analysis. (We will discuss operations management in more detail in Chapter 20.)

Operations design

Operations design, which is a part of operations control, is concerned with how work-related facilities (such as machines and jobs) are designed, arranged, and coordinated. Figure 18.2 shows the general sequence of activities in designing operations processes.

15. See Everett E. Adam, Jr. and Ronald J. Ebert, *Production and Operations Management: Concepts, Models and Behavior,* 2nd ed. (Englewood Cliffs, N.J.: Prentice-Hall, 1982).

Figure 18.2
Operations design

Planning products or services. First the organization must plan and design its products and/or services. In a general sense, these decisions are a part of the organization's mission, as discussed in Chapter 5. When General Motors decided to pursue profits in the automobile industry, it explicitly made a decision to build cars. Product/service planning for General Motors, therefore, would involve planning what models to build, how they will look, and so on.

Planning capacity. After an organization decides what to make or do, it must decide on the level of its operations: how many units will be needed or what level of service it should try to provide. For example, one restaurant might decide to have fifteen tables available for dining. More than likely, the owner would plan on providing a high-quality dining experience with all the amenities. Another restaurant might have one hundred tables and focus on specialized menu items at economical prices. Deciding whether to serve fifteen or one hundred parties, then, is an issue of capacity. In like manner, manufacturers must plan in advance for the capacity of various kinds of facilities.

Planning technology. Manufacturing technology generally depends on planned capacity.[16] For example, an airplane manufacturer like Boeing does not set up assembly lines to make 747's. Because so few units are made, it is more efficient to produce them one at a time. When General Electric makes clock radios, however, mass production is more feasible.

Planning facility location. The organization then determines where to build its facility. A dry cleaner might look for a site in a small shopping center adjacent to a residential area, whereas a manufacturer might build a plant in a small rural community close to a railroad.[17]

Planning facility design and layout. The next step in operations design is to design the facility and plan its layout. What will it look like, and how will work move through the facility as it undergoes the transformation process? A manufacturer must decide whether work will pass from one machine to another in sequence (like an assembly line) or machines will be grouped together by function.

Planning and designing jobs. Finally, jobs within the facility must be planned and designed. Chapter 10 discussed job design from a motivational perspective, but in an operations design, the focus is more on efficiency. The manager of a fast-food restaurant must decide whether the person taking an order should also fill it, or one person should take the order and ring up the sale while someone else fills it.[18]

Operations planning

A second important element of operations control is *operations planning:* the process of determining what materials and services are necessary to do the work of the organization in an effective way. Consider a contractor who is about to begin construction on a new house. One of the basic materials needed will be 2 × 4 studs for framing the walls. Obviously the contractor doesn't order them one at a time, nor is it likely that he will need several thousand. Instead the contractor determines in advance how many studs will be required. Similarly, if the studs are delivered too early they may get stolen or scattered, but construction is delayed if they are delivered too late. The process of deter-

16. See Richard B. Chase and Nicholas J. Aquilano, *Production and Operations Management: A Life Cycle Approach*, 3rd ed. (Homewood, Il.: Irwin, 1981).

17. See Chase and Aquilano, *Production and Operations Management*, for a detailed discussion of site selection.

18. See Louis E. Davis and James C. Taylor (eds.), *Design of Jobs*, 2nd ed. (Santa Monica, Calif.: Goodyear, 1979).

PART FIVE THE CONTROLLING PROCESS

556

mining how many studs to buy and when to have them delivered is an operations planning issue.

In recent years, attention has focused on a relatively new approach to this activity called materials requirements planning (MRP).[19] An MRP system is shown in Figure 18.3.

Specification of materials and parts. The first step in an MRP system is to specify the materials and parts needed for production and operations. These materials and parts are generally listed in a document called a bill of materials (BOM). The BOM for a pizza parlor might include flour, tomato paste, cheese, various toppings, and soft drink syrup. For a complex product like a computer, automobile, or airplane, the BOM may list thousands of parts.

Determination of inventory. The next step in an MRP system is to determine existing inventory on hand; the organization obviously doesn't want to order more materials than it needs. We will discuss inventory control in more detail later in this chapter.

Establishment of schedules. The manager using an MRP system then establishes ordering and delivery schedules for materials and parts that are still needed. A fast-food restaurant like McDonald's gets daily delivery of perisha-

Figure 18.3
A materials
requirements
planning (MRP)
system

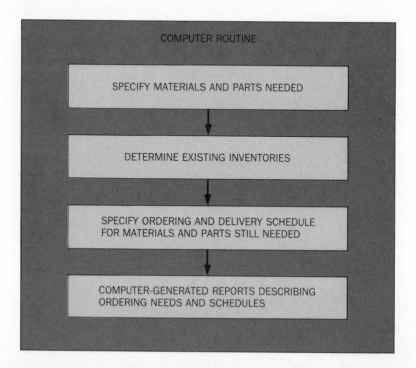

19. See Joseph Orlicky, *Materials Requirements Planning* (New York: McGraw-Hill, 1975).

bles such as hamburger buns from a local supplier. Delivery time for an advanced guidance system for a fighter plane, on the other hand, may be months or years.

One of the great assets of an MRP system is its ability to juggle different delivery schedules and lead times effectively. When hundreds of parts are needed in vastly different quantities, and delivery times range from a day to several months, coordination is difficult or impossible for individual managers. An MRP system can arrange things so that parts and materials are ordered in such a way as to arrive on schedule.

Computer-generated reports. The ordering of parts and materials is usually initiated by a series of computer-generated reports. When a plant needs 1,000 units of raw material A per month, there are 3,000 units in inventory, and delivery time is 2 months, a computer-generated report will tell the manager when it is time to reorder. In sophisticated systems, the computer may even be programmed to place the order automatically.

Computer routine. Throughout our discussion, we have assumed that the MRP system is some form of computer routine. In smaller organizations it is possible to use a manual MRP system, but in complex situations a computer routine is generally needed.

Quality control

A third important element of operations control is quality control. *Quality control* is the maintenance of appropriate levels of quality for an organization's products or services. The importance of quality has been underscored in recent years by the rapid influx of products from other countries, especially Japan. In contrast to popular thinking several years ago, it is now commonly assumed that Japanese products are superior in quality to their American counterparts.

Quality control begins at the strategic level.[20] Organizations such as Volvo, Maytag, F.A.O. Schwarz, Neiman-Marcus, Yale University, and Mercedes-Benz have all made strategic decisions to portray themselves as producing and/or selling high-quality products and services—at rather high prices. Honda, Sears, the Arrow Company, Toys "Я" Us, local community colleges, and McDonald's also promote quality, but quality at an affordable price. Hence Neiman-Marcus may carry only designer clothes and all-wood furniture at premium prices, whereas Sears carries its own brand of clothes and furniture made of wood, wood veneers, and plastics at considerably lower prices. In both cases, quality is influenced by strategic decisions.

Quality control also comes into play at the tactical or operational level.[21] Here the quality criteria include process (Will the product last as long as it should?), safety (Does the product conform to safety standards?), function

20. See Chase and Aquilano, *Production and Operations Management.*
21. See Chase and Aquilano, *Production and Operations Management.*

(Does the product work as it should?), and esthetics (Is the product esthetically pleasing?).[22]

A number of techniques and approaches can be used for quality control. *Acceptance sampling* involves sampling finished goods to ensure that quality standards have been met. The key to effective acceptance sampling is determining what percentage of the products should be tested (for example, 2, 5, or 25 out of 100). This decision is especially important when the test renders the product useless (for example, flash cubes, wine, and collapsible steering wheels).

In-process sampling involves assessing the products during production so that needed changes can be made. The painting department of a furniture company may periodically check the lead content of the paint it is using. By so doing, the company can adjust the level of lead as necessary to conform to safety standards. The advantage of in-process sampling is that it allows the detection of problems before they accumulate.

Inventory control

The last major element of operations control is inventory control. When a firm maintains a level of inventory that is too low, frequent shortages result, sales may be lost, and customers will complain. On the other hand, when inventory levels are too high, the organization pays large storage costs and ties up capital unnecessarily. Another factor is that frequent re-ordering results in higher administrative and transportation costs. **Inventory control** is the management of inventory levels so that shortage, carrying, and ordering costs are optimized.

The traditional approach to inventory control revolved around the concept of economic order quantity, or EOQ. EOQ determines mathematically how much inventory should be ordered to optimize the factors we have cited above. The EOQ formula is:

$$EOQ = \sqrt{\frac{2RS}{C}}$$

where R = yearly requirement of what is being ordered

S = procurement or set-up costs

C = carrying costs per unit

If we use 4,500 units per year, if set-up costs are $20, and if carrying costs are $.50 per unit, then

$$EOQ = \sqrt{\frac{2 \times 4500 \times 20}{.5}} = \sqrt{360,000} = 600$$

Each order, then, should be for 600 units.

In recent years, newer and more complex approaches to inventory control have been developed. MRP (described in the previous section) has inventory

---

22. See Harold E. Fearon, William A. Ruch, Patrick G. Decker, Ross R. Reck, Vincent G. Renter, and C. David Wieters, *Fundamentals of Production/Operations Management* (St. Paul, Minn.: West, 1979).

control as a major component. One estimate is that improved inventory control resulting primarily from MRP could save this country's 500 largest industrial firms $15 billion a year; for the average company, operating income could be expected to improve by 11 percent.[23]

Another recent innovation in inventory control has been borrowed from the Japanese by U.S. automobile companies. Historically, firms like Ford and General Motors have carried large raw materials and parts inventories. The Japanese approach, called "just-in-time," involves having parts and materials arrive just as they are needed. Obviously this requires that production schedules be established far in advance and that suppliers coordinate deliveries with the firm's production schedule. The results of this system are impressive: a U.S. plant producing 1,000 cars a day and using a conventional inventory system requires 2 million square feet, but a Japanese plant with the same production capability requires only 1 million square feet. The U.S. firm carries $775 in inventory for each car produced, whereas the Japanese firm carries only $150 per car. Clearly this inventory system has considerable appeal.[24]

Operations control techniques

Although a variety of management science models, tools, and techniques are appropriate for operations control, four in particular are used most often. These four techniques were discussed in Chapter 8 and are summarized in Table 18.5.

Table 18.5 Operations control techniques

PERT (Program evaluation and review technique)
A network technique for diagraming and interrelating various activities associated with a project. The control function of a PERT analysis is to control time and/or costs for a project.

Linear programming
An approach to determining simultaneous solutions to a set of linear equations representing objectives and constraints. The control function of linear programming is to optimize the objectives.

Break-even analysis
A technique for determining the number of units that must be sold to cover fixed and variable costs. The control function of break-even analysis is to determine whether costs have yet been recovered on a project.

Queuing theory
An approach to the management of time spent waiting in lines. The purpose of queuing theory for control is to determine the optimal number of waiting lines necessary to balance the costs of maintaining enough lines against the costs of losing customers due to offering an inadequate number of lines.

23. See Lewis Beman, "A Big Payoff from Inventory Control," *Fortune*, July 27, 1981, pp. 76–80.
24. See Charles G. Burck, "Can Detroit Catch Up?" *Fortune*, February 8, 1982, pp. 34–39.

Both time and costs can be effectively monitored with PERT. Linear programming helps the manager maximize objectives such as sales or output that are subject to known constraints. Although break-even analysis is primarily a technique for financial control, it also helps production and operating managers determine the number of units that have to be produced and sold in order to cover costs. Finally, queuing theory helps organize and control waiting lines in a way that optimizes costs and waiting time.

Personnel control

Most control efforts concentrate on budgeting, finance, or operations, but managers also try to control other areas in a systematic way. One of these areas is personnel. Essentially, *personnel control* focuses on the organization's human resources. The two primary means of personnel control are performance appraisal and the analysis of key personnel ratios.

Performance appraisal

Performance appraisal (which was briefly introduced in Chapter 10 and will be discussed in more detail in Chapter 21) is concerned with evaluating the performance of employees and managers within an organization.[25] For control purposes, performance appraisal helps the manager monitor the performance of individuals and groups, compare these observed performance levels against some standard, and correct any problems.

The process of performance appraisal is shown in Figure 18.4. Each step leads logically to the next, as we will see as we trace through a typical industrial job as an example. Assume that a manufacturer introduces a new line of machinery and therefore needs to establish a performance appraisal framework for the machine operators.

First a job analysis is conducted to determine the components of the job and their relative importance. For the machine operator, these components might be adjusting machine settings, making parts, and inspecting them for quality.

Performance criteria, then, would include ability to set the machine, manufacture the parts, and inspect the finished products. Valid measures could include making spot checks of machine settings, counting the number of units produced, and conducting occasional follow-up inspections to verify quality.

Establishing performance standards would involve setting the desired levels of actual performance. For our machine operator, these could be 98 percent accurate machine settings, 40 units of production per hour, and a quality acceptance rate of 93 percent. Actual performance is then measured. Finally,

25. See Gary P. Latham and Kenneth N. Wexley, *Increasing Productivity Through Performance Appraisal* (Reading, Mass.: Addison-Wesley, 1981); and Stephen Carroll and Craig Schneier, *Performance Appraisal and Review Systems* (Glenview, Il.: Scott, Foresman, 1982).

Figure 18.4
The performance
appraisal process

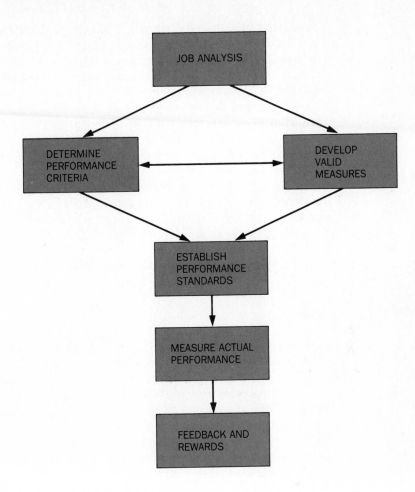

the manager provides feedback to the individual and administers whatever rewards (or takes whatever corrective actions) are appropriate.

Performance appraisal is easier for some jobs than others. Managers' jobs, for example, are often more ambiguous than those of operating employees. Determining performance criteria, establishing performance standards, and measuring actual performance in such jobs is more difficult and challenging.

Personnel ratios

Another aspect of personnel control focuses on *personnel ratios.*[26] One common ratio is employee turnover, which may be defined as the average percentage of an organization's work force that leaves and must be replaced over

26. See Wendell L. French, *The Personnel Management Process,* 5th ed. (Boston: Houghton Mifflin, 1982).

a period of time (usually one year). Some organizations, such as fast-food restaurants like McDonald's and Burger King, have turnover ratios of nearly 100
percent, whereas others' ratios are considerably less. If a manager notes a significant increase in the turnover ratio, or if the organization's ratio is above the
industry average, personnel practices may need to be changed.

Absenteeism is the percentage of an organization's work force that is absent from work over a given time period (usually one day). Ratios may range
from 3 or 4 percent to as high as 20 or 30 percent. For some organizations,
absenteeism is a special problem on Mondays and Fridays, as employees try
to stretch their weekends.

Managers may also monitor *work force composition ratios* to guard against
discrimination. For example, if a firm's surrounding labor market is composed
of 45 percent female and 20 percent minority workers, its own labor force
should reflect approximately the same distribution. If only 20 percent of its
workers are female and only 5 percent are minority workers, the firm's selection system might be regarded as discriminatory.

Marketing control

The year Kodak introduced its new line of disc cameras, eight million were
sold to retailers. The same year, General Foods introduced a new line of frozen
snacks called Pudding Pops, and they immediately began selling at an annual
$100 million rate. Why were these products both so successful? A primary
reason is that Kodak and General Foods carefully controlled their introductions
by first investing heavily in research and development and then doing a good
job of test marketing.[27] *Marketing control,* a vital element of the control function, concentrates on an organization's marketing activities. Test marketing is
an important part of marketing control, and marketing ratios are also useful.[28]

Test marketing

When an organization introduces a new product or service, or when it begins
a new advertising campaign, it runs a substantial risk if it plunges in without
knowing how the public will react. *Test marketing* in advance is often used to
control these new marketing activities.

Suppose Burger King plans to introduce a new kind of sandwich in its
restaurants. It would be quite costly to buy the necessary new equipment for
all its kitchens, train employees to make the sandwich, and advertise it nationally. If the public fails to accept the sandwich, Burger King has lost its entire
investment and suffered embarrassment besides.

These risks can be minimized by test marketing. One method would be
to select a small area of the country where Burger King plans to sell the sandwich. If it is successful there, it is introduced nationally; if it fails, it is with-

27. See "Products of the Year," *Fortune,* December 27, 1982, pp. 42–45.
28. See William M. Pride and O. C. Ferrell, *Marketing—Basic Concepts and Decisions,* 3rd ed.
(Boston: Houghton Mifflin, 1983).

drawn and the relatively low test marketing costs written off. In other situations, consumer panels may be established to try out new ideas or react to commercials. There are many variations on test marketing, but they all have the same aim: testing new products on a relatively small scale in order to minimize potential loss to the organization.

Marketing ratios

Certain *marketing ratios* are also useful control techniques, especially market share. *Market share* is defined as the percentage of the total market for a product that is controlled by one particular company's product. If the total market is 1,000,000 units per year and if one organization sells 100,000 units in that market, its market share is 10 percent. Substantial changes in market share can be of great concern to managers.

Another useful ratio is *profit margin on sales.* This ratio, calculated by dividing net income by sales, is a measure of profitability in relation to sales. For example, sales of $1 million and net income (or profits) of $100,000 for a particular product (a ratio of 10 percent) compare unfavorably with sales of only $500,000 and profits of $100,000 (a ratio of 20 percent). This ratio helps managers identify those products that yield the highest profit margins as opposed to just the highest sales.

Summary of key points

Budgetary control involves expressing a set of planned activities for a coming time period in dollar or other quantitative terms. Budgets, the foundation of most control systems, may be established for subunits, departments, divisions, or the entire organization. The normal time period for a budget is one year, though quarterly or monthly budgets are also frequently used.

Many organizations allow subordinates to participate in the budgeting process. Common types of budgets include financial budgets (such as cashflow, capital expenditure, and balance sheet budgets), operating budgets (such as sales or revenue, expense, and profit budgets), and nonmonetary budgets. Most budgets account for fixed, variable, and semivariable costs. A recent, innovative method for developing budgets called zero-base budgeting requires that each budget be developed and justified "from scratch" every year. Budgets have many advantages and are generally necessary, but there are risks associated with their use.

Although budgets are the cornerstone of financial control systems, other techniques are also common. Financial analysis involves monitoring the income statement and balance sheet and computing various financial ratios. Common types of ratios are liquidity ratios, debt ratios, return on assets, and return on investments. Break-even analysis is used for both planning and financial control. Financial audits, which may be external or internal, verify the accuracy and appropriateness of an organization's accounting, financial, and operational systems.

Operations control monitors the transformation process the organization uses to convert inputs into outputs. The four primary elements of operations control are operations design, operations planning, quality control, and inventory control. Operations design is concerned with how physical facilities are designed, arranged, and coordinated. Production and operations planning focuses on acquiring the materials and services necessary to do the work of the organization. (A recent innovation in this area is materials requirements planning, or MRP.) Quality control involves maintaining appropriate levels of quality for an organization's products. Inventory control has as its objective the optimization of shortage, carrying, and ordering costs. Four useful techniques for operations control are PERT, linear programming, break-even analysis, and queuing theory.

Personnel control centers on an organization's human resources. Common techniques include performance appraisals and various ratios expressing turnover, absenteeism, and work force composition.

Marketing control takes many forms. Test marketing and computing ratios such as market share and profit margin on sales are fairly common.

QUESTIONS FOR DISCUSSION

1. Do you think organizations could function without budgets? Why or why not?
2. Why do you think some managers resist zero-base budgeting? Describe how it might be used in your university or organization.
3. In what ways do you think financial managers and accountants are similar to other kinds of managers? In what ways are they different?
4. What are the hazards of using ratio analysis to assess an organization's fiscal well-being? Do the advantages of ratio analysis offset them?
5. Operations control is obviously important to manufacturers. Explain how it is also relevant to a pizza parlor, an airline, and a university.
6. Which of the four elements of operations control do you think is most important? Are some more important in some settings than in others?
7. Why do you think the area of personnel control is less developed than financial control and production and operations control?
8. Can you think of other aspects of an organization's work force that might be amenable to control?
9. What other elements or components of marketing might be amenable to control?
10. Are financial, operations, personnel, and marketing control independent, or are they interrelated? Explain.

C A S E 18.1

At the beginning of this chapter, you read an incident about the new chief executive officer for a cosmetics company. His former organization practiced tight control. The new firm, however, has

Control techniques at Revlon

virtually no control systems in place. The company being described was Revlon. The case that follows describes what the new CEO, Michel Bergerac, chose to do and then raises some other issues for your consideration.

Revlon, Inc., was founded by Charles Revson. Using a $300 nail enamel operation as a cornerstone, he transformed the company into a $600 million cosmetics business. When Revson discovered he had terminal cancer in 1974, he took two steps that were destined to change the shape of the company. First, he established a goal of entering the scientific health care industry. Second, he hired Michel Bergerac as his replacement. At the time, Bergerac headed ITT's European operations. To persuade him to leave ITT, Revson gave Bergerac a multimillion-dollar contract.

Revson died in 1975 and Bergerac took over. He immediately began to execute Revson's strategy in the health-care industry through a series of acquisitions. The goal underlying each of the acquisitions has been one of the following: to develop a large business in unregulated health care markets, to develop a business in ethical pharmaceuticals, or to develop channels of distribution for both types of products.

Bergerac also instituted a tight control system throughout all of Revlon's operations. For example, he was shocked to discover that Revlon had no plans for as short a period as five years. Now every part of the company has its own annual budget. The head of each department reports on its budget every month. At the beginning of each monthly report, the manager is expected to raise red flags about any trouble spots.

The new boss also insists on the monthly management meetings he himself was subjected to at ITT. Operating managers sit on one side of the table, Bergerac and his staff on the other. Each operating manager defends his or her business in front of all the rest. A video screen in the room displays the financial data for each business as it is described. A number of important ratios are always of particular interest to Bergerac. He focuses especially on return on sales, return on assets, and manufacturing costs. Other areas of control that he emphasizes include human resources, accounts receivable, and cost improvements.

For the remainder of the 1970s, Revlon scored triumph after triumph. Sales, growing at a compound annual rate of 24 percent, reached $2.2 billion in 1980. The rate of return on stockholders' equity increased from 16.5 percent to 20.1 percent. The cosmetics segment of Revlon introduced such successful new products as Charlie and Jontue. The health care business fared even better: sales increased from $197 million in 1974 to $1.1 billion in 1981. In 1979 *Fortune* declared Revlon one of ten American Business Triumphs of the 1970s.

As the company moved into the 1980s, however, problems began to arise. In 1982 Revlon posted the first earnings decline in its history. Sales have leveled off, and the company's stock price has dropped. A number of factors have been cited as causes for this change in company performance.

First, the domestic cosmetics business has leveled off dramatically. Second, the company's expertise in marketing glamourous perfumes has not always translated easily into marketing expensive health care equipment. Sales from new acquisitions have not been as strong as originally anticipated. For example, Continuous Curve Contact Lenses, a company manufacturing extended-wear contacts, has not lived up to expectations. The European recession in the early 1980s also hurt the company badly.

Finally, Revlon blundered in several areas of international marketing. Sales representatives were too aggressive in West Germany. In Japan, the company offended retailers and confused customers by initially selling only in prestigious stores and then rushing lower-priced products into larger-volume discount outlets.

Bergerac seems to feel, however, that the company can get back on the right track. The overseas operations are being overhauled, and cosmetics sales may be starting to pick up again. A wide array of new products and product lines is under development. And Revlon believes that the millions of dollars spent on research and development and acquisitions in the health care industry will soon begin to pay off.

CASE
QUESTIONS

1. Which kinds of control techniques has Bergerac emphasized at Revlon? Which kinds may have been neglected?
2. Is it possible that too much control may have been imposed at Revlon?
3. What changes might be appropriate for Revlon's control system?
4. How do you think other managers may have reacted to Bergerac's ideas when he first came to Revlon?

CASE
REFERENCES

Morrison, Ann. "Revlon's Surprising New Face." *Fortune,* November 2, 1981, pp. 72–80.
"The Other Side of Revlon." *Forbes,* August 18, 1980, p. 130.
"Revlon: A Painful Case of Slow Growth and Fading Glamour." *Business Week,* April 12, 1982, pp. 116–119.
Rowan, Roy. "Business Triumphs of the Seventies." *Fortune,* December 31, 1979, pp. 30–34.

C A S E   18.2

Ross Insurance Company is a moderate-sized regional insurance company specializing in life, health, and automobile insurance. Ross currently has $75,000,000 of life insurance in force. Though some individual health policies are written, Ross specializes in group health policies for school districts and small- to medium-sized businesses. Auto insurance is the largest of the three areas and contributes over half of the company's total profits each year.

Edward Carlson has recently been hired as president of Ross Insurance. Over the past several years, Ross has grown somewhat

**Developing a
comprehensive
control design**

stagnant. Growth and profits have leveled off, and stockholder return on investment has been averaging only 5 to 6 percent. When the former president retired, the board of directors saw an opportunity to turn things around and, after a national search, decided on Carlson as the new president. At the time of his hiring, Carlson was a vice president at one of the country's largest insurance companies and had over twenty years of experience in the industry.

It didn't take Carlson long to identify some of the major problems at Ross. Most of them seemed to stem from a lack of adequate control. Perhaps most significant, there was no integration of the budgeting process across the three major divisions. Each division prepared its own budget and submitted it to the president. The president, in turn, made whatever changes he deemed necessary and then sent the budgets back down the line.

Compounding this problem was the fact that each unit was free to use whatever budgeting approach it chose. Life insurance used a cash-flow budget, whereas health and auto insurance did not. Health used a revenue budget as the basis for its budgetary requests, whereas life used an expense budget and auto a profit budget. Auto also used a human resource budget; life and health did not.

Control problems did not stop with the budgeting process, however. Even though the company's size warranted it, there was no internal auditing staff. Ross had used a large CPA firm for its annual financial audit, but that was the only time its financial control procedures were ever examined.

There were also deficiencies in both the personnel and marketing control systems. Though all three units seemed to have high absenteeism and turnover, they had taken no steps to monitor these difficulties over time or to control them. Further, although the company maintained detailed records of its own policies, it had poor estimates of how competitors were doing. Hence Ross did not know its own market share or how it was faring in relation to other regional firms.

Carlson decided that his first order of business should be to develop and install a comprehensive control system for Ross Insurance. Such a system, he reasoned, would help both himself and other managers to develop a clearer perspective on where the company stood and how it could become more effective in the future.

CASE
QUESTIONS

1. Can you develop a control system for Ross?
2. Might Carlson be overlooking other areas in need of greater control, such as operations?
3. What kinds of problems might Carlson encounter in implementing plans based on his decision?

19

ORGANIZATIONAL EFFECTIVENESS, PERFORMANCE, AND PRODUCTIVITY

CHAPTER OBJECTIVES

1. Define and explain the importance of effectiveness, performance, and productivity.

2. Summarize various approaches to the study of effectiveness, describe how effectiveness is assessed, and relate effectiveness to control.

3. Describe organizational performance and discuss two methods for assessing it.

4. Discuss productivity trends, identify factors behind those trends, and suggest methods for enhancing productivity.

5. Summarize a framework for integrating effectiveness, performance, and productivity.

The importance of effectiveness, performance, and productivity

Organizational effectiveness
Approaches to the study of effectiveness
Assessing organizational effectiveness
Effectiveness and control

Organizational performance
Management audits
Human resource accounting

Productivity in organizations
Productivity trends
Improving productivity

An effectiveness—performance—productivity framework

Summary of key points

OPENING INCIDENT

You are a manager at an organization characterized by extreme "ups and downs." The company grew rapidly until the mid-1970s and then floundered. A new CEO came on board in 1977 and seemed to have things straightened out. For example, he implemented a productivity program that resulted in numerous improvements. However, he left in 1980 and the company stalled again. At present the company is charting a new path for itself, emphasizing an aggressive marketing strategy. How would you characterize the performance of the company?

T his chapter is the last of three dealing with the control function of management. Chapter 17 described the general nature of organizational control, and Chapter 18 summarized a variety of specific control techniques. In this chapter we describe a set of issues that are at some points broader than the control function and at other points narrower. In particular, we will deal with organizational effectiveness, performance, and productivity. The first section compares and points up the importance of these three basic issues. Later sections discuss each of them in more detail.

The importance of effectiveness, performance, and productivity

Most people would probably agree that effectiveness, performance, and productivity are important to organizations. For this assertion to have meaning, however, we must recognize why they are important. Let us begin by defining our terms.

Chapter 1 suggested that effectiveness meant doing the right things. A more complete definition is that *organizational effectiveness* is the extent to which an organization optimizes its goals set over an extended period of time.

Recall from Chapter 4 that organizations have four basic kinds of goals: financial, participant, environmental, and survival goals. Organizations can seldom (if ever) maximize all of them simultaneously, because goals are often contradictory and inconsistent. An effective organization is one that can optimize its goal set over time.

To illustrate the concept of effectiveness, recall the case discussion of Tandem Computers (at the end of Chapter 13). Tandem is very profitable and efficient (financial goals). The company has an innovative system for motivating employees and takes an interest in their personal lives (participant goals). Tandem has good relations with both customers and suppliers and has achieved an enviable record of sales growth (environmental goals). Finally, Tandem seems to be laying a firm foundation for its future growth and prosperity by emphasizing research and development and growth (survival goals).[1] Hence, although survival must by definition have an indefinite time horizon, Tandem seems to be doing a reasonably good job of optimizing its goals.

Whereas organizational effectiveness is a broad, general concept, performance has more of a mid-range flavor. We define *organizational performance* as the way in which an organization tries to be effective. Suppose a manager is attempting to achieve a 20 percent return on investment (a financial goal) and to build up a highly satisfied and committed work force (a participant goal). The first year, the manager pays very high wages, provides extra employee benefits, and does not exercise close supervision. Employee satisfaction goes up, but return on investment goes down because of higher expenses. The next year, the manager reacts to the low return on investment by cutting labor costs to the bone. The result is a higher return on investment, but employee satisfaction and commitment drop off. This manager is trying to be effective by optimizing different kinds of goals but is going about it the wrong way. Organizational performance, then, involves the methods an organization or manager chooses to pursue effectiveness.

Finally, *productivity* is the level of output of goods and services achieved by the resources of an organization. For example, it has been estimated that Japanese automobile manufacturers have been able to produce a car for around $2,000 less than GM, Ford, or Chrysler. Hence the Japanese are more productive; they are producing a comparable product (output) for less money (a resource).[2] In general, most people think of the work of individual employees when they discuss productivity. However, goods and services can also be produced through other organizational resources such as dollars invested, capital equipment, and information.[3]

When an organization does not have a high level of productivity, it tends to be less efficient and less attractive to investors. Reasonable levels of performance are needed for the organization to maintain its resources and to continue operating smoothly. Finally, effectiveness has an impact not only on profits but also on the very survival of the organization.[4]

Figure 19.1 shows how productivity, performance, and effectiveness are interrelated on a general level. Of the three concepts, productivity is the narrowest in scope, with a relatively short time horizon. Its basic thrust is on what is produced, but it doesn't account for how appropriate those goods and services might be. (An organization might be very productive but be producing

1. See Myron Magnet, "Managing by Mystique at Tandem Computers," *Fortune*, June 28, 1982, pp. 84–91.

2. See Charles Burck, "Can Detroit Catch Up?" *Fortune*, February 8, 1982, pp. 34–39.

3. See John W. Kendrick, *Understanding Productivity: An Introduction to the Dynamics of Productivity Change* (Baltimore, Md.: Johns Hopkins, 1977).

4. For a discussion of the role of survival and organizational effectiveness, see James L. Gibson, John M. Ivancevich, and James H. Donnelly, Jr., *Organizations—Behavior, Structure, Processes*, 4th ed., (Dallas, Texas: Business Publications, 1982).

Figure 19.1
The interrelation-
ship between
productivity,
performance, and
effectiveness

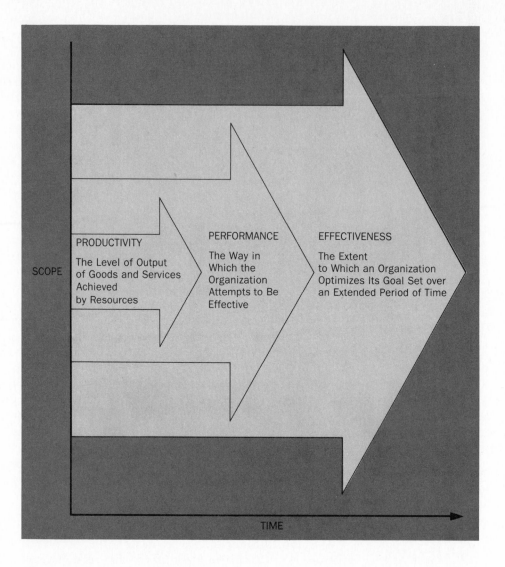

the wrong things.) Performance is at an intermediate level in both scope and time horizon. It is partially but not completely determined by productivity. Performance, in turn, is a partial determinant of effectiveness. Organizational effectiveness, as shown in the figure, has a broad scope and an extended time horizon. It takes the large view.

Overall, then, we are interested in a process that relates productivity to performance and performance to effectiveness. The three major sections that follow develop these concepts in more detail. At the end we tie them together again and demonstrate how they are related to the control function of management.

Organizational effectiveness

Over the years, management theorists and researchers have pondered the concept of organizational effectiveness. The reasons for this concern stem from the importance of effectiveness and the feeling that an overall understanding of effectiveness could assist managers, investors, researchers, and others concerned with organizations.

Approaches to the study of effectiveness

Theorists and researchers have developed four basic models of effectiveness (see Table 19.1). These models provide diverse perspectives on organizational effectiveness.

Systems resource approach. The systems resource approach to organizational effectiveness focuses on inputs—that is, on the extent to which the organization can acquire the resources it needs.[5] A manufacturer that can get raw materials during a shortage, a college of engineering that can hire qualified faculty despite competition from industry, a firm that can borrow at reasonable interest rates, and an organization that is doing a good job of monitoring its environments are all effective from the systems resource perspective. That is, they are acquiring the material, human, financial, and information resources they need to compete successfully in the marketplace.

Interestingly, this perspective attributes effectiveness to organizations that exhibit low performance or productivity, so long as they are able to acquire needed resources. Although Chrysler made dozens of tactical and strategic errors during the 1960s and 1970s, for example, it could be argued that its ability to acquire hundreds of millions of dollars in government loan guarantees was nevertheless a mark of effectiveness.[6]

Table 19.1 Models of organizational effectiveness

1. **Systems resource approach.** An effective organization is one that can acquire the resources it needs.
2. **Goal approach.** An effective organization is one that achieves its goals.
3. **Internal functioning approach.** An effective organization is one that operates smoothly and efficiently, without strain.
4. **Strategic constituencies approach.** An effective organization is one that satisfies the demands and expectations of the groups that have a strong interest in the organization.

5. See E. Yuchtman and S. Seashore, "A System Resource Approach to Organizational Effectiveness," *American Sociological Review*, Vol. 32, 1967, pp. 891–903.
6. See Irwin Ross, "Chrysler on the Brink," *Fortune*, February 9, 1981, pp. 38–42.

Goal approach. The goal approach to effectiveness focuses on the organization's outputs—that is, on the degree of goal attainment achieved by the organization.[7] When a firm establishes a goal of increasing sales next year by 10 percent and then achieves that increase, the goal approach maintains that the organization is effective.

As we have seen, financial and participant goals often conflict with one another. Short-term financial goals may also be inconsistent with costs associated with survival, such as research and development. The key is optimization. Trade-offs among the various goals of the organization are necessary to achieve balanced performance.

Internal functioning approach. A third approach to organizational effectiveness, the internal functioning approach, deals more narrowly with the internal mechanisms of the organization. It focuses on minimizing strain, integrating individuals and the organization, and conducting smooth and efficient operations.[8] An organization that focuses primarily on maintaining employee satisfaction and morale, minimizing conflict, and being efficient subscribes to this view. Whereas the systems resource perspective deals with inputs and the goal approach deals with outputs, the internal functioning approach concentrates on transformation processes. An effective organization is assumed to be one that operates smoothly and efficiently, without strain.

Strategic constituencies approach. The strategic constituencies approach to organizational effectiveness focuses on the groups that have a stake in the organization.[9] The strategic constituencies of Ford Motor Company, for example, include its suppliers (steel companies, tire companies, and so on), lenders (stockholders and banks), participants (employees and managers), customers, and others who are influenced by the company. In this view, effectiveness is the extent to which the organization satisfies the demands and expectations of all these groups. As in the goal approach, trade-offs are essential.

Using systems theory as a frame of reference, Figure 19.2 compares the four different approaches to studying organizational effectiveness. The systems resource approach focuses on inputs, the goal approach on outputs, and the internal functioning approach on transformation processes. The strategic constituencies approach is most closely related to feedback processes. It is through feedback that the organization learns how well it has met the demands and expectations of its strategic constituencies.

When we discussed systems theory and contingency theory in Chapter 2, we noted their value as integrating frameworks for the classical, behavioral,

---

7. See Richard Steers, *Organizational Effectiveness—A Behavioral View* (Santa Monica, Calif.: Goodyear, 1977).

8. See B. S. Georgopoules and A. S. Tannenbaum, "The Study of Organizational Effectiveness," *American Sociological Review*, Vol. 22, 1957, pp. 534–540.

9. See Robert H. Miles, *Macro Organizational Behavior* (Santa Monica, Calif.: Goodyear, 1980), Chapter 12.

Figure 19.2
Approaches to the
study of
organizational
effectiveness

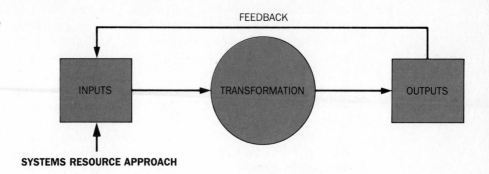

SYSTEMS RESOURCE APPROACH

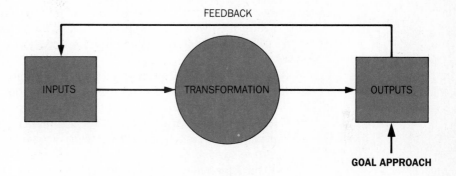

GOAL APPROACH

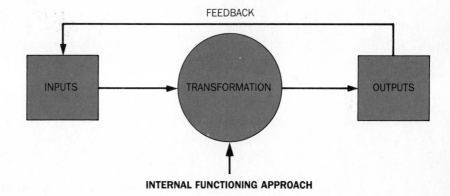

INTERNAL FUNCTIONING APPROACH

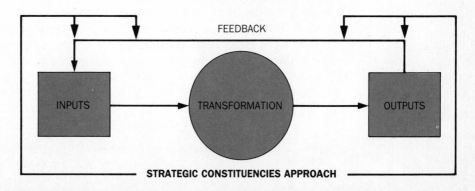

STRATEGIC CONSTITUENCIES APPROACH

and quantitative schools of management thought. We can also use them to tie together the four general perspectives of organizational effectiveness.

This unifying model is shown in Figure 19.3. At its core is the organizational system, with its inputs, transformations, outputs, and feedback. Surrounding the core are the four kinds of organizational goals: financial goals, environmental goals, participant goals, and survival goals. Each kind of goal may relate to any part of the system. For example, participant goals may include acquiring high-quality human resources (inputs), using those human resources effectively (transformation), having those human resources make a positive impact on society (outputs), and receiving information from the environment that the impact of the organization's human resources has, in fact, been positive (feedback).

Note also that the four kinds of goals are interrelated in the figure. They are shown in this way because the goals must be jointly optimized rather than individually maximized. Managers must balance goals from all the various categories.

Contingency theory also comes into play in evaluating effectiveness. At all times, managers must consider situational factors. In times of economic recession, for example, the manager must juggle financial goals (for example, remaining solvent), environmental goals (maintaining market share and supplier contacts), and participant goals (laying off employees when necessary) in an attempt to survive. Some managers may decide to terminate employees and cut back on advertising in order to maintain a positive cash flow. For other managers, a better approach might be to hold on to highly trained employees, maintain the advertising budget, and allow financial ratios to deteriorate somewhat. The appropriate course of action in any given situation depends on many factors, including financial strength, the economic outlook, top management values and attitudes, and organizational strategy.

Assessing organizational effectiveness

For a model of organizational effectiveness to have value, managers must be able to use it. One practical approach is for them to ask themselves a set of questions that focus on the criteria of effectiveness.[10] Several such questions follow.

1. Are the organization's financial, participant, environmental, and survival goals fully understood? The organization must know where it intends to go before it can hope to monitor its effectiveness. Major goals from each of the four categories must be understood and fully developed. Boeing, for example, should clearly specify its goals in the areas of efficiency and return on investment (financial goals), market share and adaptability (environmental goal), employee satisfaction and turnover (participant goals), and expectations for survival.

10. These questions are drawn from the work of Richard Steers, ''When Is an Organization Effective?'' *Organizational Dynamics*, Autumn 1976, pp. 50–63; and Kim Cameron, ''Critical Questions in Assessing Organizational Effectiveness,'' *Organizational Dynamics*, Autumn 1980, pp. 66–80.

Figure 19.3
A model of organizational effectiveness

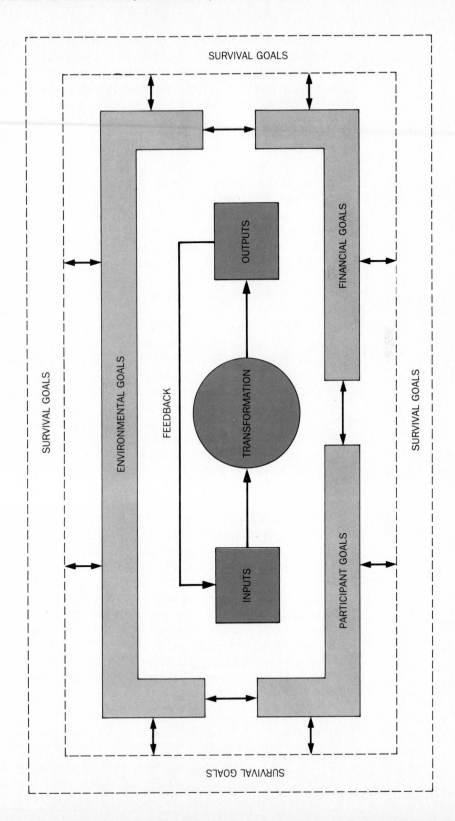

2. Are the interrelationships among the various goals understood? As stated earlier, our approach to effectiveness emphasizes goal optimization: a balance of goal achievement that is appropriate to the situation. Hence managers must recognize which goals are interrelated and how changes in one area can affect other areas. Electronics firms such as Wang and Westinghouse must invest heavily in research and development if they are to maintain competitive positions in the marketplace. R&D costs, however, detract from profitability because they are charged against earnings. A manager for one of these organizations would need to recognize that profits (a financial goal) and research and development aimed at new product breakthroughs (a survival goal) must be continuously counterbalanced.

3. Is the proper time frame established for all goals? Issues regarding goals and time frames were discussed in Chapter 4. In assessing effectiveness, managers must recognize how different kinds of goals are related to different time horizons and how these different time horizons affect the optimization process. Wang and Westinghouse's current investments in research and development may result in lower current profits, but they may also lead to greater profits in the future. That is, money invested in research and development today is likely to pay off in the future as new products and services resulting from that R&D are introduced into the marketplace.

4. Is the organization monitoring and evaluating environmental conditions? To be effective, organizations must also attempt to achieve and maintain congruence with their environments. That is, the organization's operations and outputs should be consistent with what the environments of the organization expect it to do and to produce. For example, most electronics firms have increased their emphasis on computers and computer systems in recent years. Such a firm that does *not* move into computers may be out of synch with its environments and may ultimately falter. Over time, three basic patterns of congruence/incongruence between organizations and their environments may evolve.

First, the organization and its environments may maintain a high level of congruence. McDonald's is a good example. McDonald's restaurants have always been and probably always will be family-oriented restaurants emphasizing a consistent product at low prices. Second, the organization may change its environmental congruence in an effort to expand and/or shift to different markets. Philip Morris's acquisition of Miller Brewing and Seven-Up reflect an organization in a turbulent and troubling environment (tobacco) diversifying into new markets and environments (beer and soft drinks). Finally, the organization may allow incongruence to develop by failing to monitor and react appropriately to changing environmental conditions. Slide rule manufacturers, for example, were caught napping by the advent of electronic hand-held calculators.[11]

11. See John Clark, *Business Today—Successes and Failures* (New York: Random House, 1979), for discussions of several organizations that maintained various levels of congruence/incongruence with their environments.

© ROTHCO

"What we need is a brand new idea that has been thoroughly tested."
Drawing © Ross/Rothco.

Effectiveness and control

In relating effectiveness specifically to control, managers might use these four basic questions for evaluating effectiveness as a control framework for management strategy and planning. A manager who can answer "yes" to all four questions in a control context can demonstrate that the organization: (1) knows what its goals are, (2) knows how these goals are interrelated, (3) knows the time frames for the goals, and (4) knows the extent of organization–environmental congruence. In all probability, the organization is exercising effective control.

The manager who must answer "no" to one or more of these questions has identified a substantial problem area. For example, if the answer to question 2 is no, the manager can take appropriate steps to learn how the organization's goals are interrelated. Getting that "no" answer itself represents a degree of control, and the process of correcting the situation should improve the organization's strategy and plans.

Organizational performance

Organizational performance is the way in which an organization tries to be effective. We should recognize that organizations can choose different paths to a goal, yet both can be effective. This concept is called *equifinality*, a component of systems theory.[12] General Motors and Toyota, for instance, may adopt different strategies and structures, but both can still be high-performing companies. Moreover, the contingency approach to management (Chapter 2) suggests that different actions may be called for in different situations.

Dow Chemical and Du Pont show how different approaches and perspectives can still result in high performance and, ultimately, organizational effectiveness. Dow is a global organization, whereas Du Pont derives 70 percent of its sales from the domestic market. Du Pont avoids borrowing capital; Dow borrows heavily. Du Pont is generally slower in reacting to environmental shifts, whereas Dow responds quickly. In spite of these differences, both companies are among the top ten chemical producers in the world.[13]

High performance reveals that the organization has chosen its approaches wisely. Managers and organizations employ several techniques for monitoring their performance. Two of these techniques are management audits and human resource accounting.

Management audits

Just as financial audits (discussed in Chapter 18) are checks of an organization's financial and accounting procedures, a management audit is a check of an organization's management procedures. Specifically, a *management audit* is a complete review and evaluation of the organization's total set of activities from a management perspective.[14]

Management audits are typically conducted by trained professionals from outside the organization. One frequently used management audit program was developed by Jackson Martindell of the American Institute of Management, or AIM.[15] The AIM program collects data about an organization via a number of techniques, including a standardized questionnaire, interviews with members of the organization, interviews with selected members of the organizations in the task environment, and scrutiny of published information.

The data are used to assess ten vital dimensions of organizational performance. As shown in Figure 19.4, these dimensions are corporate structure, health of earnings, research and development, economic function, executive effectiveness, service to stockholders, effectiveness of the board of directors, fiscal policies, sales vigor, and production efficiency. The organization is assigned a rating along each dimension. The maximum potential rating for executive effectiveness is 2,400, whereas health of earnings has a maximum potential score of 600. Out of a potential maximum of 10,000 points, the AIM defines an excellent level of organizational performance as a score of 7,500 or higher.

12. See Fremont E. Kast and James E. Rosenzweig, "General Systems Theory: Applications for Organization and Management," *Academy of Management Journal*, December 1972, pp. 447–465.

13. See Lee Smith, "Dow Versus Du Pont: Rival Formulas for Leadership," *Fortune*, September 10, 1979, pp. 74–84.

14. See William L. Campfield, "Auditing Management Performance," *Financial Executive*, January 1971, pp. 24-34.

15. See Jackson Martindell, *The Appraisal of Management* (New York: Harper & Row, 1962).

Figure 19.4
The AIM management audit of organizational performance

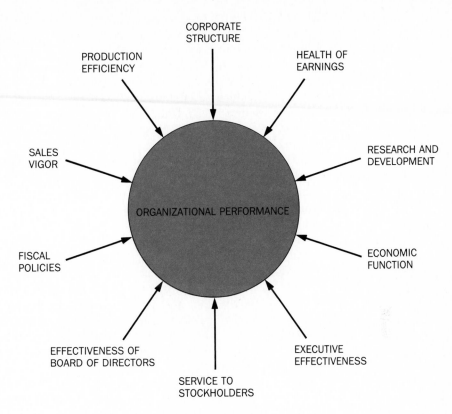

After the management audit is complete, the auditing team submits a report to management. It is then left up to company management to take any action deemed appropriate. If the company's structure got a poor rating, reorganization might be indicated. If research and development were given a low score, management might adopt guidelines for channeling more funds into R&D activities. Similar actions could be pursued for each component of the audit results.

Because a management audit takes a considerable amount of time and involves subjective evaluations as well as objective appraisals, some companies have been reluctant to adopt the management audit as a means of assessing and controlling performance. It is unlikely that the management audit will ever become as widely used and recognized as the financial audit, but it does have the potential for helping managers control organizational performance on a periodic basis.

Human resource accounting

Another means of measuring and controlling organizational performance is *human resource accounting*. HRA was developed to fill a void in traditional accounting techniques. Consider a small manufacturer whose balance sheet lists assets of equipment, a plant, inventory, patents, furniture, cash, and so on. But what about its plant manager, with his thirty-odd years of experience? What about its new sales director, a highly sought-after Harvard M.B.A.? And what about the company's personnel director, a woman with detailed knowledge of federal legislation and how it affects small manufacturers? Each of these three individuals is an extremely valuable asset, yet none of them appears on the balance sheet. Traditional accounting techniques simply offer no mechanism for computing and reporting the value of an organization's human resources.

Much of the pioneering work in HRA was done by Rensis Likert and his associates, who asserted that the cost of replacing an organization's human resources would exceed three times its annual payroll, or roughly twenty times its annual earnings.[16]

Human resources can be assessed along two dimensions: the dollar value of the individual and the extent to which her or his contributions are internal or external. These perspectives are shown in Figure 19.5.

The dollar value of an individual can be expressed in one of two ways. *Replacement costs* are the costs that the company would incur in replacing the individual: hiring, training, and termination costs. The other way to place a dollar value on individuals is to estimate their *contributions* to the organization. A sales representative who averages $100,000 in sales per month is contributing more to the organization that one who averages only $50,000 per month. (Of course, other factors might mitigate this conclusion.)

Human resources can also be viewed as being oriented internally or externally. Employees whose jobs are oriented toward the organization itself represent *internal assets*. Individual aptitudes, skills, and experience pertinent for such jobs are internally oriented. Similarly, individual leadership ability, decision-making ability, and administrative efficiency are also internally oriented. The externally oriented assets that employees represent focus more on the individual in relation to the environment. For example, individual abilities to relate effectively to customers, suppliers, unions, government officials, and stockholders are important *external assets*.

Also included in Figure 19.5 are examples of the kinds of employees who are likely to be emphasized in HRA from the perspectives of orientation and dollar value. A skilled machinist, for example, who has been trained to operate a complicated piece of equipment might be approached in terms of an internal orientation and replacement costs. A baseball player who attracts a national following would be more appropriately viewed from an external orientation and in terms of the value of his contributions to the organization. When the California Angels signed Reggie Jackson in 1982, they clearly recognized his value along these dimensions: they included a clause in his contract that stipulated a cash bonus for every ticket sold in excess of 2.4 million for the season. Of course, any person could be evaluated from any of these perspectives. The

---

16. See Rensis Likert, *The Human Organization* (New York: McGraw-Hill, 1967); and Rensis Likert, "Human Organizational Measurements: Key to Financial Success," *Michigan Business Review*, May 1971, pp. 1–5.

Figure 19.5
Human resource
accounting

DOLLAR VALUE OF INDIVIDUAL

REPLACEMENT COST   VALUE OF CONTRIBUTIONS

INTERNAL

1. SKILLED MACHINIST 2. ADMINISTRATOR WHO EFFICIENTLY OVER-SEES OPERATIONS	1. MANAGER WHO UN-SELFISHLY DEVOTES TIME TO HELPING OTHERS 2. SECRETARY WHO FACILITATES BOSS'S PER-FORMANCE
1. TECHNICIAN FAMILIAR WITH ELECTRONIC BREAKTHROUGHS 2. SKILLED PUBLIC RELATIONS SPECIALIST	1. SALES REPRESENTA-TIVE WITH HIGH SALES 2. BASEBALL PLAYER WHO ATTRACTS A NATIONAL FOLLOWING

ORIENTATION

EXTERNAL

The instances within the matrix are examples.

distinction is based on how the individual contributes to the organization and on whether the person plays a key role in dealing with the environment.

Human resource accounting is relatively new, and many problems are associated with it, especially problems of measurement. Managers are becoming more aware of it, however, and it may be more widely used in the future. At present its primary value is to reinforce the idea that an organization's human resources are as valuable as (if not more valuable than) the financial assets listed on company balance sheets.

Before leaving the subject of performance, we should identify the connections between HRA, management audits, and individual performance appraisal. Performance appraisal could be used to rank organizational participants to facilitate HRA. Similarly, the appraisal of individual managers in an organization could be a useful component of a broader, more comprehensive audit. Performance appraisal is discussed in more depth in Chapter 21.

Productivity in organizations

As defined earlier in this chapter, productivity is the level of output of goods and services achieved by the resources of an organization. Measures of productivity can be used to compare people to one another, to compare organizations, or to track one organization over time.

Within a manufacturing plant, one worker may produce 90 units per day, 4 of which are defective. Another worker may produce 93 units per day with only 2 defective. Assuming that all other dimensions of performance (such as attendance) are equal, we can conclude that the latter worker is more productive than the former.

At the organizational level, we might consider the teller operations of two large banks. At bank A, tellers process 26.4 customers per hour. Tellers at bank B process only 24.2 customers per hour. The tellers at bank A, therefore, are more productive than their counterparts at bank B.

Finally, productivity measures help monitor the performance of an organization over time. A department store, for example, may generate $100 in annual sales for each square foot of floor space. If this rate of sales per square foot increases over time (after adjustments for inflation), we can conclude that the organization is becoming more productive; a decline in sales per square foot indicates a decline in productivity.

Productivity trends

In recent years, the rate of productivity growth in the United States has fallen considerably behind that in other countries—a trend that has received considerable attention.[17] Labor productivity, defined as output per hour for all persons in the private business sector, increased at a rate of 3.2 percent per year from 1947 to 1966. From 1966 to 1976, however, the rate of growth in productivity was only 1.6 percent per year. From 1976 to 1981 the growth rate fell even more, to only 0.7 percent.[18]

Table 19.2 summarizes productivity growth rates for selected industries during these years. Clearly, many industries have suffered dramatic declines in their rates of productivity growth. Note, for example, the changes in areas that affect many of our day-to-day activities: bakery products, sugar, petroleum refining, footwear, and utilities.

These trends become even more alarming when they are compared with progress in other countries. Figure 19.6 presents actual output (per capita gross national product) and productivity growth (in manufacturing organizations only) for the period 1960–1980 in the United States, Japan, West Germany, and France. Two things are evident immediately. First, the absolute level of production for United States workers is higher than for workers in other countries. This is the case not only for the four countries featured in Figure 19.6, but also for every other country in the world. But at the same time, these countries have sharply increased their rates of productivity gain and are narrowing the gap between themselves and the United States. Many factors have combined to slow the rate of growth in the United States relative to that in other coun-

17. For example, see "The Productivity Pinch," *Time*, August 17, 1979, p. 36; and "Productivity Debate Is Clouded by Problem of Measuring Its Lag," *Wall Street Journal*, October 13, 1980, p. 1.

18. See Jerome A. Mark, "Productivity Trends and Prospects," in Clark Kerr and Jerome M. Rosow (eds.), *Work in America—The Decade Ahead* (New York: Van Nostrand, 1979), pp. 188–203; and John W. Kendrick, "The Coming Rebound in Productivity," *Fortune*, June 28, 1982, pp. 25–28.

Table 19.2 Annual productivity increases for selected industries

Industry	1947–1966	1966–1976
Coal mining	6.6	−3.5
Canning and preserving	2.7	3.2
Bakery products	2.0	1.8
Sugar	4.6	1.5
Tobacco products	3.7	1.7
Petroleum refining	4.2	2.3
Footwear	1.9	0.4
Steel	1.7	1.8
Metal cans	2.5	1.7
Air transportation	7.9	4.4
Gas and electric utilities	7.3	3.6

Source: U.S. Bureau of Labor Statistics.

tries.[19] However, no one has been able to prove which factors are most important; much of the discussion has been conjecture.

Changes in the work force. Over the past several years, a number of major changes have occurred in the American work force. For one thing, after World War II more and more of the general population went to college, and early gains in productivity were attributable to higher levels of education. Now, as the proportion of workers with higher education has leveled off, productivity gains have also tended to level off. Another factor is that the work force has absorbed many new and inexperienced employees during the last decade, as women and younger workers have thronged into the ranks of the employed. Until they gain experience, these employees are likely to be less productive.

Change in industrial composition. Shifts in industrial composition sometimes move large numbers of workers from one industry to another that is more productive. Such a change would, of course, affect the productivity growth rate. Many workers moved from farm work to nonagricultural jobs in the fifties and early sixties. Because farming jobs had relatively low levels of productivity at that time, many of those people found themselves in more productive lines of work. Most of this shift was over by 1966, however. In the

19. See Mark, "Productivity Trends and Prospects"; Burton G. Malkiel, "Productivity—The Problem Behind the Headlines," *Harvard Business Review*, May–June 1979; and "Many Businesses Blame Governmental Policies for Productivity Lag," *Wall Street Journal*, October 28, 1980, pp. 1, 22.

Figure 19.6
Production and
productivity trends

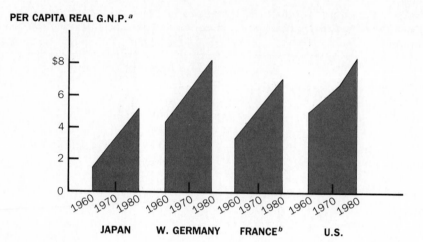

PER CAPITA REAL G.N.P.[a]

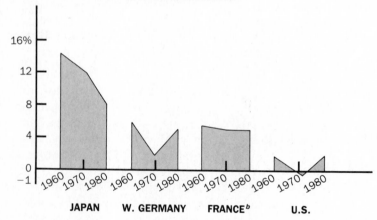

PERCENT PRODUCTIVITY GROWTH IN MANUFACTURING

[a]In thousands of 1975 dollars.
[b]Gross Domestic Product.

Source: Adapted from Lester C. Thurow, "Other Countries are as Smart as We Are," *New York Times*, April 5, 1981. © 1981 by the New York Times Company. Reprinted by permission.

years since then, the number of farm workers has remained about the same. Productivity may have been influenced first by the change in industrial composition and then later by increased stability in industrial composition.

Change in capital/labor ratio. A third factor affecting productivity is change in the capital/labor ratio. This ratio reflects the extent to which an organization invests in capital (new equipment, technology, and so on) rather than labor (for example, more employees). During the past decade, business has not invested so much in capital equipment as it did in the previous period. Workers have not been getting as much new equipment as before, and productivity growth has suffered.

Decrease in research-and-development spending. Another factor contributing to declining productivity growth rates has been reduced spending on research and development. In 1964 industry, government, and universities spent a sum equivalent to 3 percent of the gross national product (GNP) on research and development. This figure dropped to 2.3 percent of the GNP by 1980.[20] It follows that fewer scientific and technological breakthroughs are likely to be achieved. These breakthroughs often play a major role in improving productivity, so a decline in the number of breakthroughs almost by definition has an adverse effect on productivity growth.

Governmental regulation. Increases in governmental regulation are often cited as a cause of productivity problems. During the last several years, we have seen the birth of the Occupational Safety and Health Administration (OSHA), the Food and Drug Administration (FDA), the Environmental Protection Agency (EPA), and similar governmental agencies. Although these agencies play an important role, they also limit what a business can do and they require many time-consuming reports. Goodyear Tire & Rubber Company recently generated 345,000 pages of computer reports weighing 3,200 pounds to comply with one new OSHA regulation. Further, it costs Goodyear $35.5 million each year to comply with the regulations of 6 federal agencies, and it takes 34 employee-years annually just to fill out the required reports.[21]

Improving productivity

Given the troubling trends in productivity growth, it is not surprising that managers in the United States have focused renewed attention on improving productivity. Table 19.3 summarizes some of the more widely suggested ways of spurring productivity growth.

Table 19.3 Methods for enhancing productivity growth

1. Increase investment in research and development.
2. Place more emphasis on manufacturing.
3. Change incentives for working.
4. Increase cooperation between labor and management.
5. Increase employee participation.
6. Tighten existing controls.
7. Change government policies.

20. See Malkiel, "Productivity—The Problem Behind the Headlines."
21. See "Many Businesses Blame Governmental Policies for Productivity Lag."

Stimulate research and development. Almost everyone is agreed that the country as a whole should spend more on research and development.[22] Federal tax bills passed in 1978 were designed to provide this stimulation via extended investment tax credits and a reduced corporate tax rate. Of course, it will take several years for these bills to have any real impact on research and development.

Place more emphasis on manufacturing. During the first several decades of this century, as mass production technology and the assembly line came into their heyday, the manufacturing process was the dominant concern of most businesses. Then, during the 1960s, manufacturing gave way to marketing, finance, and other areas. It was felt that production technology had reached its zenith and that further profits could only be attained via other functions. Recently, however, it has been suggested that basic manufacturing processes might hold the key to improved efficiency and productivity. Companies that have recently adopted a stronger manufacturing orientation include S. C. Johnson & Son (producer of Johnson's Wax), IBM, and TRW. S. C. Johnson & Son, for example, weighed several alternatives when it expanded into industrial products and personal-care products. Its solution was to reserve its large plant in Racine, Wisconsin, for producing high-volume products like Raid and to concentrate new-product activities in smaller satellite plants where production techniques could be easily modified as old products were dropped and new ones added.[23]

Change incentives for working. A third strategy for improving productivity involves changing employee incentives, especially in governmental and other not-for-profit organizations.[24] In many job settings, employees are paid for their time rather than their efforts or output. All an employee has to do is to show up for work, do the minimum necessary to get by, and then go home. The resulting paycheck may have little or no relationship to what the employee actually produced. Changing this practice is difficult, especially in white-collar or professional jobs where it is hard to quantify output. It is also difficult in government, where there is no bottom-line profit or loss. (Indeed, the rewards there often go to those who can justify expanding their staff or getting a bigger budget.) Although some state and local governments, such as those of Phoenix, San Francisco, and North Carolina, have been successful at changing incentives for work, such efforts in other areas are just getting started (see Chapter 13 for a discussion of reward systems). Potentially useful incentives include financial bonuses, awards, promotions, and other forms of recognition.

Increase labor–management cooperation. Another approach to improving productivity is to increase cooperation between labor and manage-

22. See Malkiel, ''Productivity—The Problem Behind the Headlines.''
23. See Robert Lubar, ''Rediscovering the Factory,'' *Fortune*, July 13, 1981, pp. 52–64.
24. See Jeremy Main, ''Why Government Works Dumb,'' *Fortune*, August 20, 1981, pp. 146–158.

ment.[25] Traditionally the two groups have been on opposite sides of the fence on most issues, but the United Auto Workers, the United Steelworkers of America, the United Rubber Workers, and several other unions have now formally or informally decided to work more closely with management to simultaneously improve productivity and enhance the quality of working life for their members. In St. Louis, cooperation between management and construction trade unions has boosted productivity 10 to 15 percent. One luxury hotel was recently completed there at an approximate cost of $71,000 per room; a comparable hotel in other areas would have cost $80,000 to $85,000 per room. The city's new convention center was completed three months early and at $864,000 less than the projected cost. These and similar successes in St. Louis have all been attributed to increased productivity stemming from labor–management cooperation.[26]

Increase employee participation. A popular proposal for improving productivity is to increase employee participation in decision making and problem solving. Although participative management has been advocated for decades, it has recently enjoyed renewed attention because of its importance in Japanese management techniques, especially Theory Z (see Chapter 2) and quality circles. A *quality circle* is a group of employees who meet periodically to discuss problems regarding quality, output, and similar issues. Organizations that use quality circles include General Foods, General Motors, Polaroid, and Procter & Gamble. At GM, for example, quality circles helped employees at that company's Chevrolet Gear & Axle plant in Detroit to improve both the nature of their jobs and their level of output.[27]

Tighten existing controls. Another way to improve productivity is to tighten existing controls so as to eliminate inefficiencies and increase individual output. Under a new productivity program at Revlon, for example, the prevailing opinion is that, when a manager asks for more people, he or she will probably be told to get the job done with fewer rather than more employees![28] This strategy can be dangerous if carried to an extreme and is probably useful only for short periods of time. If everyone is subjected to increased pressure for extended periods of time, morale suffers and employees may leave the organization.

Change government policies. A final way to improve productivity is to change government policies.[29] Decreased regulation would free organizations from the burden of generating reports and paperwork that tie up em-

25. See Charles G. Burck, "What's in It for the Unions?" *Fortune*, August 24, 1981, pp. 88–92.

26. See Irwin Ross, "The New Work Spirit in St. Louis," *Fortune*, November 16, 1981, pp. 92–106.

27. See Charles G. Burck, "What Happens When Workers Manage Themselves," *Fortune*, July 27, 1981, pp. 62–69.

28. See Ann M. Morrison, "Revlon's Surprising New Face," *Fortune*, November 2, 1981, pp. 72–80.

29. See Malkiel, "Productivity—The Problem Behind the Headlines."

ployees and limit productivity. Tax credits for capital investment would spark spending for new plants and equipment. Fiscal and monetary policies aimed at reducing inflation would also facilitate long-term investment and increased spending on research and development.

These seven approaches are the most commonly endorsed methods for improving productivity in the United States. Other techniques have been greeted with a variety of reactions. For example, there has recently been an upsurge in the number of productivity seminars offered by consultants. Some people find these seminars useful, but others feel they are a waste of time.[30]

The noted productivity expert John W. Kendrick has predicted that productivity growth rates in the 1980s should be around 2.3 percent. This prediction is based on projected increases in capital investment and research and development, other economic indicators, and historical trends.[31] If it comes to pass, it will be a considerable improvement over the 1973–1981 growth rate of 0.7 percent, but it will still be below that of other industrial nations.

An effectiveness–performance–productivity framework

Earlier in this chapter we presented an introductory framework that related effectiveness, performance, and productivity. Having discussed these concepts in detail, we are now ready to develop a more detailed model (see Figure 19.7).

The first step in this process is to determine the organization's goal set. As we discussed in Chapter 4, organizations typically establish financial goals (such as a target rate of return or a certain increase in productivity), environmental goals (such as growth or market share) and participant goals (such as lower turnover or employee satisfaction). Survival is generally an implied goal.

The organization then attempts to achieve these goals in an optimal fashion. That is, it tries to balance goals that are by nature contradictory and inconsistent. As Figure 19.7 shows, goals are pursued through the basic management functions of planning and decision making, organizing, leading, and controlling. We noted earlier that these functions are not discrete, sequential activities but interacting dimensions of the typical manager's job.

As a result, the organization achieves certain levels of performance and productivity. Performance reflects the ways in which the organization attempts to be effective. Productivity represents the level of outputs achieved by the resources of the organization.

At some point, management should assess the extent to which the organization is effective. The framework diagrammed in Figure 19.7 suggests that one method for assessing effectiveness is to ask the four basic questions framed earlier in this chapter. Those questions focus on whether the goals of the organization are understood, whether interrelationships among these goals are known, whether proper time frames for the goals have been established, and

30. See "Productivity Seminars Grow But Draw Fire," *Wall Street Journal*, June 17, 1982, pp. 27, 31.

31. See John W. Kendrick, "The Coming Rebound in Productivity," *Fortune*, June 28, 1982, pp. 25–28.

Figure 19.7
An effectiveness-performance-productivity framework

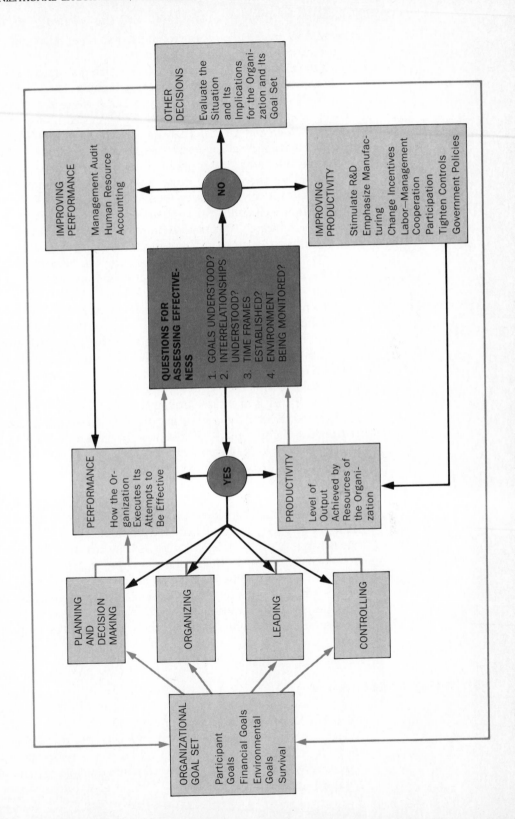

whether the organization's environments are being adequately monitored and evaluated.

If the organization can answer yes to each question, it is evidently achieving an appropriate level of effectiveness (assuming, of course, that proper goals were established to begin with!). If this is the case, the organization can proceed on course with its existing goal set or modify those goals to meet new and different circumstances. This process directly affects both the basic managerial functions and subsequent levels of performance and productivity.

If the answer to one or more of the questions for assessing effectiveness is no, however, the manager must evaluate the situation and take appropriate action. If a "no" answer has performance consequences, several actions are possible. Two techniques we discussed are the management audit and human resource accounting. A management audit can answer several questions about the organization (such as probing executive effectiveness and production efficiency), whereas human resource accounting can help the organization determine the distribution pattern of strengths and weaknesses among its human resources.

If a negative assessment of effectiveness indicates problems with productivity, different kinds of action may be needed. They include investing in research and development, emphasizing manufacturing, changing incentives for employees, enhancing cooperation with labor, increasing employee participation, tightening controls, and attempting to change government policies.

Finally, a "no" answer to a question about effectiveness may reveal other problems. If this is the case, managers must evaluate the seriousness of the problem and its implications for the organization and its goal set. Appropriate changes can then be made. If the error is a failure to monitor the prices of a small, relatively insignificant competitor, the organization may choose to do nothing. But if the organization's very survival is in danger, a drastic overhaul of the goal set may be necessary.

In this section we have presented a framework interrelating organizational effectiveness, performance, and productivity. The primary value of this framework is its potential usefulness as a technique for overall organizational control. Many of the control methods and techniques discussed in Chapter 17 and 18 pertain only to parts of the organization, such as the financial, production, personnel, or marketing dimensions. This framework, however, encompasses the total organization. As such, it can help managers monitor all of their activities and successfully carry out the control function at the organizational level.

Summary of key points

Effectiveness, performance, and productivity are all important concepts for managers and organizations. Organizational effectiveness is the extent to which an organization is able to optimize its goal set over an extended period of time. Organizational performance reflects how an organization executes its attempts to be effective. Productivity is the level of output of goals and services achieved by the resources of an organization. Effectiveness is the broadest of these concepts in scope and has the longest time horizon. Productivity is the narrowest and has the shortest time horizon.

Four basic approaches to the study of effectiveness are the systems resource approach (the extent to which resources can be acquired), the goal approach (the extent to which the organization achieves its goals), the internal functioning approach (the extent to which the organization operates with minimal stress and strain), and the strategic constituencies approach (the extent to which the organization satisfies interested parties). One useful model of effectiveness, combining these four approaches with systems and contingency theories, focuses on goal optimization. The four basic questions we suggested are helpful to managers in assessing organizational effectiveness. Effectiveness is related to control in that these basic questions help managers stay on course in achieving their goals and executing their strategic plans.

Two useful techniques for facilitating organizational performance are the management audit and human resource accounting. A management audit is a complete review and evaluation of an organization's total set of activities from a management perspective. Human resource accounting attempts to assign a dollar value of an organization's human resources.

Although the level of productivity per worker in the United States is higher than that in any other country, our rate of growth in productivity has fallen considerably behind that of other industrial countries such as Japan, West Germany, and France. This situation is attributable to changes in the work force, changes in industrial composition, change in capital/labor ratios, declines in research-and-development spending, and increased governmental regulation. Suggestions for improving productivity growth rates are to stimulate research and development, increase emphasis on manufacturing, add incentives for working, increase labor–management cooperation, boost employee participation, tighten existing controls, and change government policies.

One helpful process for integrating effectiveness, performance, and productivity flows from the goal set through the management functions and performance and productivity to the assessment of effectiveness. And of course, decisions stemming from that assessment have implications for subsequent management activities.

QUESTIONS FOR DISCUSSION

1. Is it possible to achieve a high level of effectiveness, performance, or productivity and yet be deficient in the other two? How about achieving a high level on two factors but not on the other?
2. Which comes first: effectiveness, performance, or productivity?
3. What are the strengths and weaknesses of each of the basic models of effectiveness? Can you think of kinds of organizations that are especially appropriate and kinds that are inappropriate for analysis by each model or approach?
4. Are there other useful questions for assessing organizational effectiveness? (See pages 576–578.)

5. How would you go about conducting a management audit of your university or company?
6. What do you think is the future of human resource accounting?
7. How serious a problem do you think our declining rate of growth in productivity is?
8. Do you think productivity is the main reason for the dramatic in-roads made here by Japanese products? What other factors could contribute to this pattern?
9. Suggest other ways in which effectiveness, performance, and productivity could be interrelated. That is, develop your own framework to integrate the three concepts.
10. Can you think of an organization that can be described and analyzed in terms of the integrative framework at the end of the chapter?

C A S E   19.1

At the beginning of this chapter, you read an incident about an organization characterized by extreme ups and downs: the company performed well during some periods but floundered during others. You were asked how you would characterize the company's performance. The company being described was Burger King. The case that follows provides additional information about Burger King's performance and then raises some other issues for your consideration.

Burger King's erratic performance

In the twenty-plus years of its existence, Burger King Corporation has been on a roller coaster of ups and downs. In 1959 two Florida entrepreneurs named James McLamore and David Edgerton decided to expand their five hamburger restaurants into a national chain of franchised outlets. By 1967 there were 274 Burger Kings in operation. In that year, McLamore and Edgerton sold out to the Pillsbury Company for $1 million.

In 1982 there were approximately 2,700 Burger King restaurants open. A fairly small number of these restaurants are owned and operated by Burger King. Another group is operated by independent franchises on land or in buildings owned by Pillsbury. About half of all the units have no direct ties to Pillsbury except the basic franchise agreement.

For several years Burger King stumbled along, succeeding almost in spite of itself. One franchisee, itself incorporated as Chart House, Inc., began opening so many restaurants that it soon had the power to ignore many of Pillsbury's operating guidelines. In fact, Chart House even tried to buy Burger King from Pillsbury in 1972. Pillsbury eventually won the battle with Chart House, but strained relations with some franchises still persist.

This three-pronged arrangement has typically been less successful than the approach used by McDonald's. McDonald's has always exercised much greater control over its franchises. Today it owns or leases almost all of the land and buildings used by its nearly 6,000 restaurants.

In an effort to more closely match the success of McDonald's, Burger King hired that company's third-ranking executive to spearhead its own operations in 1977. The new boss, Donald Smith, did an outstanding job by any standard. He installed many of McDonald's cooking procedures, such as that used for French fries, in the Burger King restaurants. He successfully redirected advertising toward children. He also smoothed franchise relations.

Perhaps Smith's greatest contribution to Burger King, however, is the company's productivity improvement program. The program has made a number of substantial contributions. Time-and-motion studies have been used to measure and refine the movements of prototypical Burger King employees. By changing the location of the bell hose in drive-through windows, the program lowered transaction time by thirty seconds per car. French fry machines have been computerized so that they automatically increase volume of output at peak periods. In some restaurants, as the cashier is ringing up a customer's order, it is already being relayed to the kitchen on television monitors. As an incentive to further progress, store managers who develop useful techniques for improving productivity are given cash awards.

Productivity has also been emphasized at the corporate level. Site evaluation reports that used to take two weeks can now be generated in a day. Designs for new stores can be produced in two weeks instead of six.

Overall, the changes implemented by Smith made Burger King a formidable member of the fast-food industry. From 1977 through 1980, sales per restaurant at Burger King grew faster than at McDonald's. Unfortunately for Burger King, however, Smith left in 1980 to head up Pizza Hut, and the company began to flounder once again. Sales skidded and profits slipped.

In 1982 a new chief executive began once again to try to reverse Burger King's fortunes. The focus now is on aggression. The core of this aggressive strategy is comparative advertising. One advertising campaign, for example, focused on claims that Burger King's products beat McDonald's and Wendy's products in consumer taste tests. The company has also changed its advertising thrust again, focusing on adults rather than children.

Additional cost-cutting programs have attempted to cut down premium giveaways, curtail new products, and further enhance franchise relations. Burger King estimates that it will take from three to five years for these new efforts to bear fruit.

CASE
QUESTIONS

1. How would you evaluate Burger King's productivity program? What parts of it might be applicable to other businesses?
2. To what extent does Burger King's experience with Donald Smith underscore the value of human resource accounting?

3. On the basis of your own observations and experiences, which fast-food chains are more effective and which are less effective?

4. Of the three concepts of effectiveness, performance, and productivity, which is most applicable to a parent company like Pillsbury, to a business like Burger King, and to a single Burger King restaurant?

CASE
REFERENCES

"Burger King Steps Up War with McDonald's." *New York Times,* October 21, 1982, p. 44.

"Pillsbury's Burger King Brass is Certain Recipe for Growth Is Spelled: Aggressive." *Wall Street Journal,* October 1982, p. 14.

Meadows, Edward. "How Three Companies Increased Their Productivity." *Fortune,* March 10, 1980, pp. 92–101.

Smith, Lee. "Burger King Puts Down Its Dukes." *Fortune,* June 16, 1980, pp. 90–98.

C A S E 19.2

Rita Jameson has a dilemma. Her grandmother recently passed away and left her quite a lot of money, but there is one stipulation attached to her inheritance: she must use it to invest in a business that will provide her with a long-term return. For the last four months, Rita has been investigating various alternatives. She has narrowed her choices down to buying one of two companies, but each of these has its own peculiar strengths and weaknesses.

One potential investment is Apex Computer Systems. ACS has a history of being in the right place at the right time. The company got its start by purchasing electronic components from other manufacturers and assembling them into pocket calculators and by writing software systems for companies with large mainframes from IBM and similar big companies. The company got out of calculators just as the prices started to plunge.

It next went into consulting with companies to help them determine exactly what kinds of systems they need. It also assisted clients in purchasing and installing computer systems, and it was still doing quite well with its software business.

ACS anticipated the advent of personal computers with remarkable precision. It was one of the first companies to market an inexpensive personal computer and was also at the forefront of personal computer software. ACS recently began providing training programs and seminars for people who purchase ACS personal computers.

Unfortunately, while ACS always seemed to do the right things, it somehow didn't always do them well. For example, its return on investment has consistently been 3 to 4 percent below the industry average. Further, its personal computer is providing a profit margin of only $100 per unit. The price of the computer is competitive, but the production costs of the machine appear to be too high.

The other investment alternative Rita is considering is Eagle

Comparative effectiveness, performance, and productivity

Audio. Unlike ACS, Eagle has a history of making bad decisions but surviving because of the high levels of efficiency the company has always maintained. For example, Eagle pushed heavily into eight-track tape systems just as most consumers were moving to cassettes. The company survived by dumping its huge inventory of eight-track tape players at bargain-basement prices. Because the company was producing high-quality units at low cost, it was able to slash retail prices by 40 percent and still break even.

Eagle's next mistake was investing heavily in quadrophonic home stereo systems. Even though it appeared at the time that this was a wise move, the market for quadrophonic stereo never materialized—and again the company had to dump inventory. This time, however, Eagle was able to squeeze out a small profit.

At present, Eagle is exploring a number of alternatives. One future area of growth might be television stereo systems. Another could be improved audio systems for movie theaters and interoffice communication networks. A final alternative Eagle is considering is a proposal for developing stereo systems for airline passengers.

CASE QUESTIONS

1. On the basis of the information presented, evaluate the apparent effectiveness, performance, and productivity of Apex Computer Systems and of Eagle Audio.
2. Which company would you recommend that Rita Jameson buy? Why?
3. Assuming that Rita has decided to buy ACS, what would you suggest she do to improve the company (consistent with the stipulation of her grandmother's will)? What if she has decided to purchase Eagle?

Management in Special Contexts

PART CONTENTS

20

OPERATIONS
MANAGEMENT

CHAPTER OBJECTIVES

1. Discuss the nature of operations management, including its role in providing economic utility, its relationship to conversion processes, and its challenges.

2. Describe the link between planning and operations management, including planning for operations and operational planning.

3. Identify relationships between the organizing process and operations management, including structural arrangements for operations, the division of work, and change and operations.

4. Discuss the control function of management and explain how it is related to operations management, especially to control differences between capital-intensive and labor-intensive technologies and to areas of operations control.

601

OPENING INCIDENT

American industry has traditionally achieved high levels of efficiency through mass-production assembly lines. Recent breakthroughs in manufacturing involve automation and the use of flexible manufacturing systems. It is now possible to efficiently produce a wider array of products with smaller inventory than before. Many Japanese companies have adopted these concepts and used them to bolster their positions in the world economy. How do you think American companies might react?

Every ongoing organization offers products in the form of physical goods or services to its clientele and customers. A company like Shell Oil provides gasoline for consumers. Steak and Ale offers the convenience of prepared meals in a nice setting. Your university's products include the education you are receiving. A local barber shop provides a service. *Operations management* refers to the set of organizational activities that organizations engage in to create their products and services.

These activities were at one time generally called "production management," and many people still use this term today. To other people, however, production seems to focus too narrowly on manufacturing. When managers began to expand their view of production to include services and other intangible products, the phrase "production and operations management" evolved. This term is still frequently used, but "operations management" is rapidly becoming the generally accepted phrase.

Managers of every organization, whether large or small, public or private, need to be familiar with operations management and how it dovetails with the many other functions and activities that characterize organizations. This chapter explores key operations concepts and responsibilities, major problems that arise, and the decisions that are central in the life of the operations manager.

The operations management process

Operations and economic utility

The operations function is directly involved in creating products. In an economic sense it provides utility of one type or another, depending on the nature of the product. If the product is a physical good, such as a motorcycle, operations management provides primarily *form* utility by combining many dissimilar inputs (sheet metal, rubber, paint, combustion engines, and human

Figure 20.1
The operations
management
conversion process

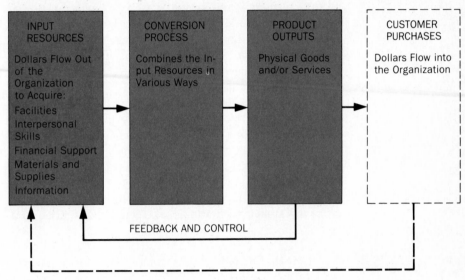

craftsmanship) to produce the desired physical form. The inputs are converted from their incoming forms into a new physical output; this typifies operations management in manufacturing organizations.

By contrast, the operations management activities of a commercial airline create a service product featuring *time* and *place* utility. The airline transports passengers and freight according to agreed-on departure and arrival places and times.

Other service operations, such as beer distributorships and retail merchandisers, provide primarily *place* and *possession* utility by bringing together the item and the customer. Although the organizations in these examples produce different kinds of products, their operations processes share many important features, which we will discuss next.

Operations and conversion processes

Operations management, as a conversion process, can be visualized as consisting of the elements shown as solid lines in Figure 20.1. Obviously this framework is derived from systems theory.[1] Let's examine the inputs, conversion processes, outputs, and feedback and control cycle depicted in the figure from an operations perspective.

Product outputs. The primary driving force of operations management is the desired end product(s). Operations managers and operative employees must have a clear and precise definition of the product(s), including the key

1. See Fremont E. Kast and James E. Rosenzweig, "General Systems Theory: Applications for Organization and Management," *Academy of Management Journal*, December 1972, pp. 447–465.

product attributes, the important quality characteristics, and quality standards for each attribute. They also need to know how many of each product are needed at what times to meet customer demand. In other words, operations employees need a clear picture of what they are trying to accomplish in their day-to-day activities.

Conversion process. What activities have to be performed to create the desired product? How do we describe the nature of these activities and how they differ from one setting to another? Conversion processes may involve any of several different types of technologies, and technologies vary widely. Petroleum processing in a refinery operation utilizes a continuous-process technology; automobile manufacturers employ primarily a mass-production technology; an aircraft manufacturer uses unit or small-batch technology.[2] You are probably familiar with additional examples of fundamentally different technologies.

Inputs. Operations management relies on receiving resources from other parts of the organization and from the outer environment. Operations cannot occur for very long without sustained support in the form of inputs to the organizational system. Some of these resources are more or less permanent, such as buildings and land devoted to production, whereas others are transient resources that are consumed fully on a day-to-day basis, such as raw materials and office supplies.

Feedback and control. Operations management systems are directed toward achieving goals. Once operations goals are established, controls help the system conform to standards of efficiency and effectiveness. Managers obtain information for evaluating system performance by monitoring various stages of the conversion process, the inputs, and the product outputs. Recall, for example, our discussion in Chapter 17 of preliminary, screening, and post-action controls. As we noted then, the control system must provide timely information so that appropriate actions can be taken. Deviations from standards are a prime basis for changing the inputs, the conversion process, or even the product or service design.

Operations as a management challenge

This brief background is enough to suggest some of the responsibilities of operations managers. The problems they face revolve around the *acquisition* and *utilization* of resources for conversion. Some familiar operations activities and roles include purchasing, production forecasting, work flow and process analysis, job design, inventory control, production scheduling, quality control supervision, and manufacturing management. These activities and roles seek to achieve balance and consistency among the three elements: inputs, conversion

---

2. See Joan Woodward, *Industrial Organizations: Theory and Practice* (London: Oxford University Press, 1965). See also Chapter 11 in this book.

process, and outputs. These elements, in turn, must be balanced and consistent with the other functions of the overall organization. Therefore each organization has different expectations of its operations function, and the operations function in one organization has different capabilities from that in another.

Product output specifications that cannot be achieved in one conversion process may perhaps be easily met in another. The capability of the process, then, must match the output goals. A mismatch requires a change of goals, product, or conversion process. When a firm has a goal of producing 100,000 units of an extremely high-quality stereo system, but has the capacity to produce only 75,000 units, three alternatives are available. The firm could decide to produce only 75,000 units (a change of goals), to lower product quality so that stereos could be produced faster (a change of product), or to increase plant capacity (a change of conversion process). Similarly, input resources must be consistent with and supportive of the conversion process and its product output goals.

What amounts and types of resources must be obtained—and when—to fuel the conversion process in its drive toward attaining output goals? These issues are part of the challenge facing the operations manager. We will see more detailed issues emerge as we examine decisions that arise in operations planning.

Chapter 18 briefly discussed the elements of operations control, including operations design, operations planning, quality control, and inventory control. Some of these same topics are reiterated in the section that follows, but they are covered in considerably more depth and from a broader perspective.

Planning and operations management

The proper outputs flowing from the conversion process indicate that the operations function is effective. Such success is usually not an accident, or at least *sustained* success is not. To maintain successful operations we must remember that transactions extend well beyond the operations activities. In Figure 20.1, for example, the dotted lines show the completion of the monetary resource cycle, emphasizing that consumed outputs create the monetary resources that sustain operations and all other activities of the organization. In other words, products must be sold. Because the available monetary resources are limited, managers try to allocate them in a rational manner among all the organization's activities, including the operations function, by developing plans.

The importance of operations for organizational planning

As discussed in Chapters 4, 5, and 6, the goals, strategies, and plans of the overall organization set the tone for subunit operations goals, strategies, and plans. But the flow of influence runs both ways; subunit capabilities and potential strengths and weaknesses are taken into consideration when overall plans are developed in the first place.

Operations management should always support overall organizational goals. Different overall goals dictate different types of operations designs. For example, if an overriding goal is to promote high quality of the finished product, the operations function must be arranged in such a way as to provide workers with the time and tools necessary to do high-quality work, and frequent quality control checks may be necessary. If the focus is on mass production with a lower level of quality, a different design will be required. Various target markets must be matched with different product designs and competitive strategies to capitalize on specific market opportunities.[3] The broad character of the operations function must be in harmony with the organization's overall goals, strategies, and plans.

As an extended example, consider the different competitive strategies of two computer companies and the effect of these strategies on operations.

Digitgro Corporation is a specialty company that manufactures and distributes a mid-range computer system for industrial organizations. Digitgro produces four minor variations on its basic model, and its operations function emphasizes special expertise and technical competence within this narrow product line. The computers are produced in one manufacturing facility. Digitgro's competitive strategy stresses high product reliability and low product selling price. It is able to maintain low prices because of its low unit production costs. Product sales are handled externally—that is, sales responsibilities are subcontracted to independent representatives specializing in industrial sales throughout the United States.

American Better Computer Systems' (ABC's) goal, on the other hand, is to become the dominant name in computer systems and related technology during the next decade. Its diverse product line includes micro, mid-range, and mainframe computer hardware systems, as well as a complete line of computer software (program) packages for use in the home, office, or factory.

ABC's microcomputer production facility has several assembly lines that are changed periodically for production runs of the many different micro models. One assembly line, an excess capacity line, is currently unused; it exists so that production can begin quickly on new micro models that might emerge at any time from ABC's large research and development department. ABC has additional separate production facilities for manufacturing its mid-range and mainframe computers.

ABC's competitive strategy emphasizes a highly trained and extensive marketing service orientation, coupled with state-of-the-art product development that keeps the product line one jump ahead of competition in the industry.

Consider the contrasts (Table 20.1) in the operations orientation of these two companies and why these differences exist. Digitgro's emphasis on a low-cost operation is consistent with its strategic product-pricing posture. The company has carved out a narrow market niche that it will exploit via its production competence and efficiency with one product. It avoids the heavy bur-

---

3. See Roger A. More, "Why Industrial Product Strategic Planning Fails," *Business Quarterly*, May 1982, pp. 54–60.

Table 20.1 Contrast of strategy and operations in two computer companies

	ABC	Digitgro
Overall strategy	Product innovation Marketing strength Comprehensive systems services	Low product selling price and unit cost High product reliability Specialized production expertise
Operations emphasis	Short production runs for each of many products Frequent production line changeovers High inventories of diverse component parts Excess capacity for flexibility to meet short-notice opportunities Ability to adapt production technology to new products as old ones phase out	Long, economical production runs of one product Few production line changeovers Constant production technology Premium placed on cost control and production efficiency

den of additional research-and-development costs, of maintaining excess capacity, and of making changes in the production process to accommodate new products. The facilities, employee skills, and management systems at Digitgro are all geared to being good at producing one product efficiently. Accordingly, when top management periodically updates its one-year and three-year overall plans, it does so fully recognizing the nature of the company's operations function, its strengths, and its limitations. Management is using the operations function as a competitive weapon, an asset, in the company's overall strategy.[4]

ABC's operations function is considerably different, as it should be, because it serves a different purpose in the overall organization from Digitgro's operations function. ABC's marketing and R&D functions are the keys to organizational success, and the operations function is designed to respond to and support these other functions. Low-cost production is not a primary goal. Indeed, high-cost production activities will be adopted intentionally and gladly if marketing effectiveness is enhanced with a new-product introduction that is first to reach the marketplace. Marketing and product innovation goals have higher priority than production efficiency in ABC's overall plans and strategies. These two companies illustrate that plans for the operations function must mesh with and are dependent on the broader planning framework of the overall organization.

4. See Wickham Skinner, "Manufacturing—Missing Link in Corporate Strategy," *Harvard Business Review,* May–June 1969, pp. 136–145. See also Wickham Skinner, "The Focused Factory," *Harvard Business Review,* May–June 1974, pp. 113–121.

Planning for operations: Design decisions

At its most basic level, planning for operations involves the design or redesign of the operations subsystem. Overall design goals are guided by higher organizational goals, and the operations manager will then encounter several distinct operations decision areas in which design choices must be made. As shown in Figure 20.2, the decision areas are interrelated. Choices in any one area, such as designing an operations control system, must be consistent with choices in all the other areas, such as the types of interpersonal skills adopted in the operations system. Furthermore, each choice involves trade-offs; each alternative has both good and undesirable features that the manager must weigh. Obviously, operations design is a complicated set of decisions involving many

Figure 20.2
Major decision areas in operations system design

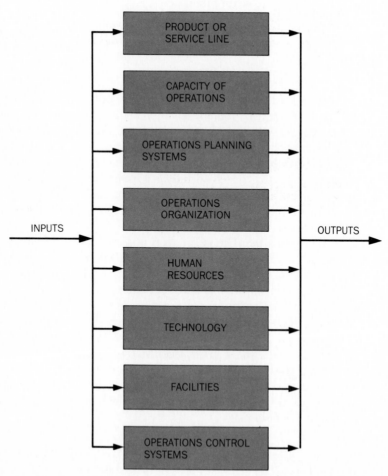

Table 20.2 Capacity measures used in different organizations

Physical goods producers	Capacity measure (output)
Steel company	Tons of steel
Concrete company	Cubic yards of concrete
Agricultural/grower	Bushels of wheat

Service producers	Capacity measure (input)
University	Number of faculty members
Architecture/design	Number of each professional specialty
Hospital	Number of beds

considerations. Let us briefly consider each of these decision areas—some in slightly more detail than others.[5]

Product line. It is usually a combination of corporate, business, and marketing functional strategies in an organization that defines general product specifications, but the operations function then develops the detailed product specifications.[6] For example, RCA's decision to develop and market its video-disc player aimed at a certain segment of the consumer market clearly reflects both business and marketing perspectives. However, the operations system was then put in the position of specifying the components needed, their tolerance levels, and so on.[7]

Proposed new products or changes in existing products may have high market potential, but their production may not be feasible within the existing operations system. Therefore the operations manager is usually involved in the organization's product line decisions. He or she might supply information relevant to the technological feasibility of new product proposals, identify the capital costs involved in modifying the operations system to build the new product, suggest alternative product designs that are more cost-effective or that make production feasible in the existing operations system, or provide production cost information for setting the selling price of the new product.

Capacity. The operations capacity decision involves choosing the amount of conversion capacity appropriate for the organization. Although the operating capacity for firms that produce physical goods is usually expressed in terms of output, service organizations often express capacity in terms of *input* re-

5. For a comprehensive discussion of operations design considerations, see Everett E. Adam, Jr., and Ronald J. Ebert, *Production and Operations Management: Concepts, Models, and Behavior,* 2nd ed. (Englewood Cliffs, N.J.: Prentice-Hall, 1982).

6. See Charles W. Hofer and Dan Schendel, *Strategy Formulation: Analytical Concepts* (St. Paul, Minn.: West, 1978).

7. See Edward Meadows, "The Slippery Market for Videodiscs, *Fortune,* November 2, 1981, pp. 82–88.

sources. Some examples of capacity measures for selected organizations are shown in Table 20.2.

The capacity decision is truly high-risk, because of the uncertainties of future product demand and the large monetary stakes involved. If we want sufficient capacity to meet market demand, we must make some estimates. The long-range forecasting techniques discussed in Chapter 8 provide these estimates of future demand, which help determine the size of the operations function—its capacity. We can build capacity that exceeds our needs and requires resource commitments (capital investment) that may never be recovered. Or we can build a facility with a smaller capacity than expected demand; doing so may result in lost market opportunities, but it may also free capital resources for use elsewhere in the organization. These kinds of trade-offs are inherent in making the capacity decision.

Technology. The operations technology in producing physical goods can vary along a continuum from highly labor-intensive to highly capital-intensive. A home cleaning service and a football team are highly labor-intensive. It is people who do the work. An automated plant, however, is highly capital-intensive. Expensive machinery does the work. The degree of mechanization and automation chosen by an organization has significant impact on output quality, production costs, labor and management skills required, and operations flexibility in a strategic sense.

Although the technologies of most service organizations continue to be highly labor-intensive, relatively more capital-intensive options have evolved. Especially with increasing applications of computers, such traditionally labor-intensive professional services such as medicine, law, and education and other service industries such as commercial banking have adopted new, more capital-intensive technologies for creating and delivering their products.[8]

Facilities. How many production facilities are appropriate, and where should they be located? It all depends. In our earlier example, American Better Computer Systems chose to produce micro, mid-range, and mainframe computers in separate facilities. Why wasn't one large facility chosen instead? Company management believed that the three highly dissimilar production processes would create unnecessary congestion and confusion if grouped together.

The *location* of facilities must also be determined. Operations managers face the dilemma of whether to locate facilities near sources of supply (input resources) or near product markets (ease of output disposal). This decision affects the capital cost of construction, the future costs of operations, and the reliability of service to customers.

The choice of physical configuration, or the *layout*, of facilities is closely related to the previous decisions on product or service line, capacity, and op-

---

8. Some of the difficulties arising from technological changes in service industries are identified in Donald G. Long and Paul S. Nadler, "Technology versus Tradition," *The Banker's Magazine*, May–June 1982, pp. 22–28.

Figure 20.3
Two layout
concepts

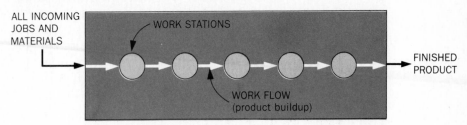

PRODUCT LAYOUT

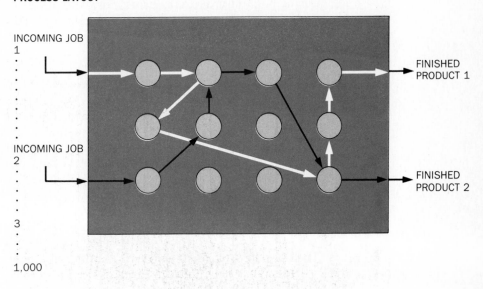

PROCESS LAYOUT

erations technology.[9] Two entirely different layout alternatives, shown in Figure 20.3, help demonstrate the importance of the layout decision.

A *product layout* is appropriate when large quantities of a single product are needed. It makes sense to custom design a straight-line flow of work for this one product, in which a special task is performed at each work station as each unit flows through. Most large-scale assembly lines use this format.

Process layouts are used in operations settings that create a variety of products. Auto repair shops and health care clinics are good examples; each automobile and each individual is a separate "product." Only the general

9. The consumer-oriented facilities designs in service organizations are discussed in Carolyn U. Lambert, "Environment Design: The Food-Service Manager's Role," *The Cornell Hotel and Restaurant Administration Quarterly*, May 1981, pp. 62–68.

nature of each job is known in advance. Detailed product specifications cannot be known until the customer's arrival. The needs of each incoming job are diagnosed as it enters the operations system, and the job is routed through the unique sequence of work stations needed to create the desired finished product. In a process layout, each type of conversion process (or technology) is centralized in a single work station or department. All welding is done in one designated shop location, and any auto that requires welding is moved to that area. This is in contrast to the product layout, in which several different work stations may perform welding operations if the product buildup sequence so dictates.

Human resources. Decisions about the types and amounts of human skills—labor, managerial, professional/technical—must be consistent with the technology and the other decision areas. Similarly, methods chosen for selecting, training, and rewarding employees must be compatible with choices made in the other areas. These human resource decisions are closely related to location decisions, because the availability of different skills varies widely in different geographic regions.[10]

Operations planning, organizing, and controlling. We have already considered the interrelationship of long-range strategic planning and the design of the operations function. In addition, operations managers must choose an operational planning process to achieve smooth day-to-day utilization of resources. A good operations planning process in one environment may be ineffective or even highly disruptive in another. We will discuss short-run and intermediate operations planning processes in a later section.

There are many different ways to subdivide overall operations activities and, subsequently, to establish links among the subunits to achieve unified, coordinated performance. These organizing choices are also discussed in a later section.

The operations function, perhaps more than any other part of the organization, has emphasized systematic methods for controlling activities. These are discussed in our section on controlling and operations management.

A composite design example. The decisions made in each of the eight areas shown in Figure 20.2 mesh to create a unique operations environment for each organization. For example, Table 20.3 summarizes major differences between two operations functions for an air conditioner manufacturer. The production function that creates residential air conditioners is separate from the division that produces commercial air conditioners. The reasons for this separation are elaborated in our later discussion of organizing for operations.

The operations designs for the two kinds of air conditioners are well suited to their respective strategic roles. Any attempt to transpose one design into the other situation would result in an organizational mismatch and overall

10. See Thomas H. Patten, Jr., *Manpower Planning and the Development of Human Resources* (New York: Wiley, 1971).

Table 20.3 Operations designs for two kinds of air conditioners

	Residential air conditioners	Commercial air conditioners
Product	Standardized, high-volume product; stable product specifications.	Variable product specifications to customer order; low unit volume, high product variety.
Capacity	Output capability matched exactly to expected market demand.	Excess equipment capacity to enable rapid service after each customer order is received.
Technology	Capital-intensive, mechanized, and automated; highly specialized equipment and processes; high degree of job specialization and division of labor.	Balanced capital and human resources; general-purpose equipment and processes; high job diversity.
Facilities	Three large physical plants; geographically dispersed to be near regional distribution centers; product (assembly line) layout.	One large plant; central geographic location near large population with skilled human resources; process-oriented layout.
Human resources	Unskilled and semiskilled production work force; specialized production supervision emphasizing employee training and performance control; highly skilled equipment and maintenance technicians; specialized production planning and control personnel.	Highly skilled production work force with flexibility and initiative to perform diverse tasks independently; production supervision emphasizes planning and coordination among diverse irregular production activities; liaison sales engineers.
Operations planning	High reliance on market forecasts of product demand; finished goods produced in advance of market demand; work force fluctuations (hiring/laying off) normally occur throughout the year; raw materials and components purchased in large quantities before scheduled production.	Highly coordinated with field sales engineers; materials and components procured as needed for individual job orders; stable work force to safeguard valued labor skill.
Operations organizing	Residential division organized on geographic basis; three plant managers report to divisional vice president; close coordination among plant activities achieved by centralized planning and control.	New orders centralized with divisional vice president; commercial division organized on the basis of manufacturing process; centralized assigning of priorities to jobs and scheduling of work centers; highly decentralized shop floor assignments.
Operations controlling	Specialized staffs for inspection and quality control, inventory control, work measurement and methods analysis, and product and process analysis; emphasis on efficiency and cost control.	Emphasis on control of job flow, comparing current job progress with promised delivery date to minimize delays and excess work-in-process inventories; quality assurance resides in professional norms and pride of craftspeople.

inefficiency. When the final system design is implemented, the operations function is in place and ready for use. Then operational planning is undertaken.

Operational planning

The operations manager determines how facilities and resources will be used productively in an ongoing concern. The emphasis should be on producing output that will satisfy customer demand and organizational goals. *Operational planning* usually involves the following steps:

1. Selecting a planning time horizon
2. Estimating product demand that is expected during that time
3. Comparing productive capability with demand requirements
4. Developing ways to adjust any capability/demand mismatches

The specifics of operational planning vary in different settings. We will illustrate the process for a manufacturing facility that produces two similar models of hand-held calculators for mass-market consumption.

Step 1: Selecting a planning horizon. This company uses a twelve-month planning horizon, with the old plan updated and extended at the end of each month. It was found that longer planning horizons are wasted effort because of distant uncertainties. Shorter planning horizons are wasteful too because, if followed too closely, they result in expensive over-reactions to month-to-month variations in demand.

Step 2: Estimating demand. The monthly demand for each kind of calculator for each of the next twelve months is estimated by a time-series forecasting model. These continuously updated short-range forecasts are recorded graphically in Figure 20.4.

Figure 20.4
Forecasts of monthly demand for two calculators

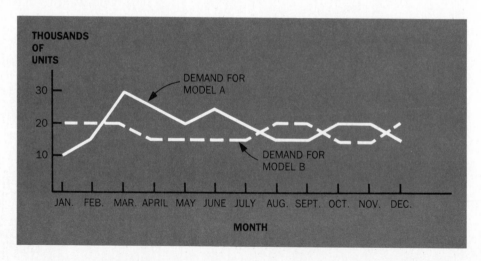

Step 3: Comparing capacity with demand. Normal production capacity of the facility is 33,000 units. Because the two existing models are so similar in their production processing, they are treated as equivalent products for planning purposes. Total forecasted demand, then, is the sum of the demand for model A and the demand for model B.

Graphs of total monthly demand and of capacity (see Figure 20.5) reveal that normal operating capacity is insufficient for meeting demand, especially in each of the next few months. Over the entire twelve months, total demand is expected to exceed normal capacity by 44,000 units.

Step 4: Adjusting capacity to demand. This company knows from experience that several adjustment options are possible. More production employees can be hired and trained, for example, to raise capacity capabilities. The company is reluctant to do this, however, because of the high costs of recruitment, selection, and training, as well as potential community ill will if a demand downturn should require layoffs in the near future. Another option is the use of temporary employees obtained through a local agency, but this course of action has created dissatisfaction among permanent employees in the past.

Another alternative is to subcontract some portion of the work load to another manufacturer, thereby gaining a temporary increase in capacity. Finally, overtime operations, involving premium pay to permanent employees, can provide the temporary capacity needed to meet anticipated demand.

Figure 20.5
A comparison of demand and capacity for calculators

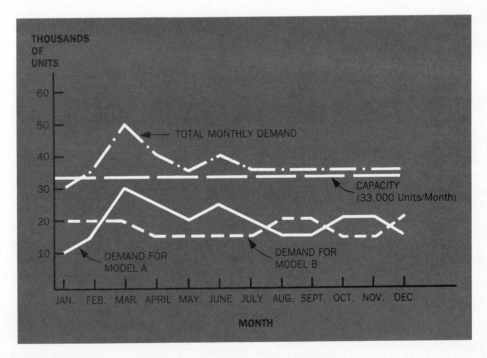

Overtime also offers the advantage of temporary extra pay to employees who want it.

Each adjustment option must be evaluated using managerial judgment, assisted by quantitative models such as linear programming (see Chapter 8). After comparing costs and effectiveness, management develops a specific overall production plan. The plan specifies how many units of each kind of calculator will be produced by whom in each month.

Subsidiary plans. After the overall operational plan is developed, management uses it as a guide for the more detailed planning efforts that now begin. Plans must be developed for procuring materials and components from suppliers. Arrangements are made to advertise, select, and train employees where needed. The timing of production line change-overs for the two products is planned in such a way as to minimize disruption and congestion in the facility. Inventory managers plan storage space for needed materials. Marketing personnel have a clearer picture of upcoming product availability, enabling them to give customers more accurate estimates of delivery dates. Finance personnel develop detailed schedules of working-capital needs and cash flows for payroll outlays, payments for purchases, and receivables from sales.

Clearly, operations planning is an important process for achieving coordination and effectiveness in the overall organization and among the various subunits within the operations system.[11] Equally important are the organizing activities we discuss next.

Organizing and operations management

Modern managers need to be familiar with the ways in which the operations function fits into the overall organization. How is the operations function itself organized? How is it structured, and how does it perform its tasks? These questions are addressed in the following sections. An extended example shows several bases for the division of work (departmentalization), illustrates operations line activities and areas of staff specialization, and outlines some current issues that suggest changes in operations subsystems.

Structural arrangements for operations management

The position of operations in the organization depends, of course, on its overall role and on how managers want it to interact with all of the organization's other activities. Different industries exhibit various structural configurations, depending on the basis on which the organization divides its work. Although a functional organizing principle (based on essential functions such as marketing, production, and finance, as discussed in Chapter 9) makes it easy to identify the operations subsystems, most organizations aren't structured so simply.

11. The integrative role of operations planning and control systems is discussed in Roland Van Dierdonck and Jeffrey G. Miller, "Designing Production Planning and Control Systems," *Journal of Operations Management*, Vol. 1, No. 1, 1980, pp. 37–46.

Instead, they are organized on the basis of some combination of product, function, customer, and location. The organization depicted in Figure 20.6 illustrates such a structure for the air conditioner manufacturer we discussed earlier.

At the vice presidential level, responsibilities are divided on a functional basis (finance, marketing, personnel, operations) and, for operations, on a customer basis (residential and commercial). Recall that in Table 20.3 the two operations divisions had dissimilar design characteristics. Two entirely different orientations are essential for competing successfully in these two target markets. Therefore the two operations divisions are autonomous units, and their activities are formally coordinated with the other divisions only at the presidential level. Informal relationships are indicated by dotted lines in Figure 20.6.

Beneath the vice presidential level, we begin to see substantial differences between the two operations structures. The Residential Operations Division has more central authority and formal procedures, generally, than the Commercial Operations Division. The Residential Operations Division has three production plants established on a geographic basis to assure rapid, inexpensive delivery to regional distribution centers.

Centralization of staff activities at the divisional level confers advantages of cost efficiency, extensive staff expertise, and coordination across the three manufacturing plants. All three plants use identical conversion processes to create the same standardized product, so all product design and process design is also centralized at the divisional level. Sales forecasts generated by marketing people are used by the divisional production planning staff to create coordinated production plans for all plants. If product design or quality standards change, all plants adopt the changes in a coordinated, consistent manner, ensuring uniform product reliability.

Each regional manufacturing plant is organized on a process basis: metal fabrication, components subassembly, and final assembly. The plant manager also has three other responsibilities—plant engineering, inventory control, and purchasing—which are assigned to specialized staff members. Other staff activities exist, but authority for these is not decentralized to the plants. Instead they are jointly coordinated with and through their corresponding functions at the vice presidential level. Overall personnel policies and practices, for example, are established at the corporate level and implemented through the plant personnel staff. Similarly, product quality standards are centrally coordinated because uniform product quality at all plants is vital in the marketplace. The organizational structure for the Residential Operations Division appropriately emphasizes cost control, quality control, and volume control of operations.[12]

The Commercial Operations Division carries out all its operations activities at one facility. Because each commercial customer's needs are unique, the product design engineers work closely with the sales staff to determine product specifications and product price for each customer. This system emphasizes individual product design and manufacturing flexibility. After the design and

12. See William J. Abernathy and Robert H. Hayes, "Managing Our Way to Economic Decline," *Harvard Business Review*, July–August 1980, pp. 67–77.

Figure 20.6
The organization
chart for a
manufacturer of air
conditioners

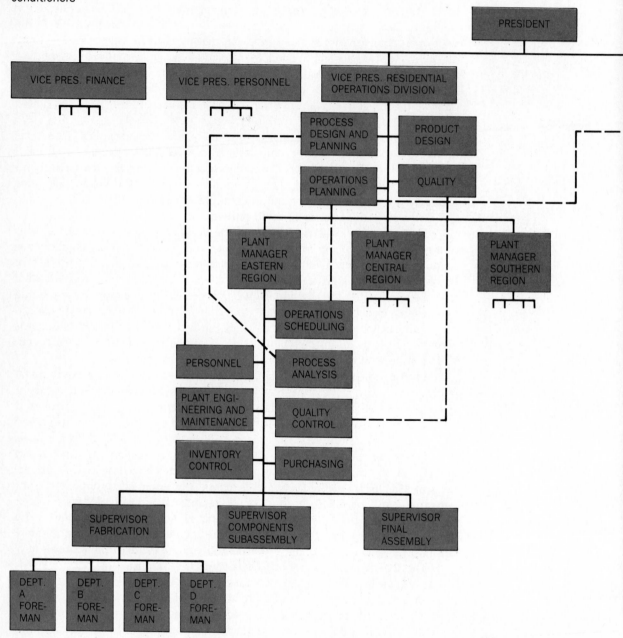

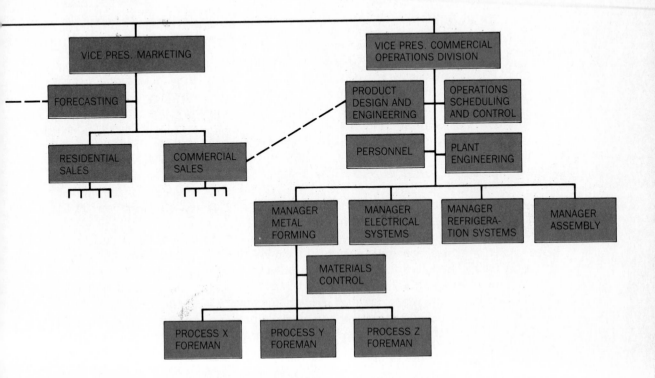

production requirements are determined, the production scheduling staff sets target delivery dates in light of current and planned work loads. Qualitative forecasting techniques that rely on the judgment of both sales and engineering staffs are used to anticipate work loads. (For example, the sales-force-composition method of sales forecasting that we discussed in Chapter 8 might be appropriate.) Once new orders are received, the updated schedule is disseminated to the operations managers involved.

Authority for operations decisions in the commercial division is decentralized to permit quick reactions to changing conditions. Having received updated production schedules and future production plans, each manager determines when, how, and by whom the work will be done to meet scheduled delivery commitments. Each manager has a materials control specialist to determine materials requirements for each job and to coordinate job flows with the other processing departments. Quality control is not a formal process in this division; acceptable quality is attributable to the skills and professional norms of the experienced work force.

This example of the air conditioner manufacturer shows why different operations structures are used in dissimilar organizations. It also shows that different bases for dividing the operations work can be used within a single organization. Choices involving the degree of centralization, the delegation of authority, and the creation of specialized staff cannot be made by any hard and fast rules; rather they must be shaped by overall strategy considerations.

Re-examining the division of work in organizing

Organizing for operations involves individuals in their various roles and relationships, but methods once used to define these roles and relationships may become obsolete as value systems change in society. In manufacturing settings especially, sophisticated techniques have evolved for dividing the total amount of work into individual jobs.[13] Historically, job analysis, refinement of work methods, and time-and-motion study were all applied to "scientifically" determine job content. American productivity flourished with the widespread application of such techniques. Since the 1970s, however, we have witnessed a decline in American productivity and serious probing for the reasons for this decline.[14] Many observers are concerned about our prospects for the future.[15] The production excellence that was the forte of United States industry in the 1950s and 1960s continues to wane significantly.

More recently the mixed results of applying newer techniques such as job enlargement, job enrichment, and job rotation suggest caution in adopting them. These techniques don't always lead to higher productivity. The suitability of each method of job design depends on many elements—individual, organizational, technological, and environmental.[16]

For most organizations, no single approach to job design is clearly best, yet operations managers are always under pressure to improve performance somehow. The managerial response to such pressure is often a compulsive eagerness to grasp at methods that have succeeded for others. Japanese management practices are among the ideas recently embraced by harassed managers. But vast differences in cultural values suggest that simplistic attempts to foist Japanese practices onto American organizations may lead to even further frustration. A careful and reasoned evaluation of Japanese methods may reveal only limited benefits in new settings.[17] Meanwhile, the ambiguity of job design remains a management dilemma. Operations managers will continue to be confronted with trade-offs among efficiency, worker satisfaction, control, and

13. For a recent update, see Gene Bylinsky, "The Race to the Automatic Factory," *Fortune*, February 21, 1983, pp. 52–64.

14. See Y. K. Shetty, "Key Elements of Productivity Improvement Programs," *Business Horizons*, March–April 1982, pp. 15–22.

15. See William G. Scott and David K. Hart, *Organizational America* (Boston: Houghton Mifflin, 1979). For a more optimistic outlook, see John W. Kendrick, "The Coming Rebound in Productivity," *Fortune*, June 28, 1982, pp. 25–28. See also Chapter 19 in this book.

16. Job design was discussed in Chapter 10. For more information, see Ricky W. Griffin, *Task Design—An Integrative Approach* (Glenview, Il.: Scott, Foresman, 1982).

17. Japanese management practices are discussed in William S. Anderson, "Japan Could Teach Us a Thing or Two," *The Kansas City Star*, February 21, 1982, p. 14 F. See also Frank M. Gryna, Jr., *Quality Circles: A Team Approach to Problem Solving* (New York: AMACOM, 1981).

participation as they organize and reorganize to keep pace with a changing environment.

Change and operations management

Changes, unexpected ones as well as planned changes, are normal in organizations and occur frequently. Although some changes are made voluntarily, others are virtually imposed on organizations. Product line and technology decisions must be periodically re-evaluated.[18] When consumer tastes change, products and the processes used to make them must change accordingly. When new materials and manufacturing processes that have competitive implications are invented, such as computer-aided manufacturing, change must be considered.[19] One way of preparing for orderly change is to be aware of the characteristics of changes. Chief among these are the wide-ranging effects of change throughout the organization. A change in marketing, for example, often affects operations, as one organization learned the hard way.

In the early 1960s a major company in the home appliance industry experienced seasonal sales dips each year. Its marketing division successfully conducted a special promotional campaign and consumer demand surged upward. The overall effort was a failure, however, because of poor communication between marketing and operations and poor handling of the increased demand. Only the usual numbers of appliances were available; no extras had been produced to meet the new, higher level of demand. Furthermore, components and materials suppliers were totally unprepared to provide the large rush-order requests they suddenly received as the appliance company tried to pull off its hasty recovery. High production costs ensued when overtime operations were used to catch up with sales orders.

Just as changes elsewhere affect operations, changes in operations have an impact on the other parts of the organization. An operations decision to change inventory policy, for example, by increasing the size of raw materials ordering quantities, has the direct effect of raising the level of accounts payable and, thus, the requirements for cash flow and working capital (finance department concerns). It may also necessitate new contracts with raw materials supliers (a purchasing department concern). Similarly, a planned increase in production rate imposes new demands on the personnel department; new human resources may have to be sought, selected, trained, and integrated into the company to raise production levels.

Changes within operations most obviously affect the other operations activities or subunits. The interrelationships among the eight decision areas shown in Figure 20.2 are important to remember when dealing with changes in the operations environment. A decision to plan production in a more centralized way, for example, might include some reorganizing to create a special planning staff, and authority relationships may be changed. This decision

18. See Kevin F. McCrohan and Jay M. Finkelman, "Social Character and the New Automobile Industry," *California Management Review,* Fall 1981, pp. 58–68.

19. See Donald Gerwin, "Do's and Don'ts of Computerized Manufacturing," *Harvard Business Review,* March–April 1982, pp. 107–116.

might also lead to hiring staff experts and even to a general change in managerial orientation.

An awareness of these inherent links between different areas of operations decisions should alert us to the fact that change takes time. Inevitably, the *transition* has some important consequences that are easily overlooked or unanticipated. This happened to a well-known producer of quality cutlery when the company decided to enter the mass-consumer, lower-price cutlery market. It anticipated that the conversion of its production processes would take six to nine months, but it actually experienced two years' delay and nearly fatal cost consequences. The product change involved changes in the old production processes, in work methods, and in quality specifications. The highly skilled production employees resented and resisted these changes and, at one point, went out on strike. Eventually the company made the changes it wanted, but the unanticipated delays and employee dissatisfaction had a significant impact on the entire organization.

Changes in all of the operations decision areas should be expected from time to time. When contemplating possible changes, it is important to consider the time and cost involved in achieving each alternative. Then the desired changes can be incorporated into the planning process so that orderly, predictable transitions unfold.[20]

Controlling and operations management

Operations management exists to serve purposes defined by its goals, which derive from the higher goals and strategy of the parent organization. Operations activities and performance should be evaluated and modified in the context of those broader purposes. One way of achieving this organizational control over the operations function is to coordinate it with the other functions. A large company, for example, may establish a consumer products division that mass-produces and distributes a product line; the operations function could be set up organizationally as an autonomous profit center for purposes of organizational control. The division is responsible for attaining profitability. This is appropriate when the manufacturing division is given the authority to determine not only the costs of creating the product, but also the product price and the marketing programs.

In terms of overall organizational control, the division should be accountable only for those activities in which it has decision-making authority. It would be inappropriate to make operations accountable for profitability in an organization with a marketing-dominated competitive strategy. Misplaced accountability results in ineffective organizational control, to say nothing of a lot of bad feeling. Depending on the strategic role of operations, then, operations managers are accountable for different kinds of results.

Within operations, managerial control ensures that resources and activi-

20. For a general discussion of organizational change, see Michael Beer, *Organization Change and Development—A Systems View* (Santa Monica, Calif.: Goodyear, 1980). For a recent discussion of operations change, see Jeremy Main, "Work Won't Be the Same Again," *Fortune*, June 28, 1982, pp. 58–65. See also Chapter 12 in this book.

ties achieve primary goals such as a high percentage of on-time deliveries, low unit production cost, or high product reliability. Controlling operations involves monitoring and adjusting the inputs, outputs, and conversion processes in the operations subsystem, as we saw in Figure 20.1. A key question is which of the many system subcomponents should be emphasized. The answer is that the control system should focus on the elements that are most crucial to goal attainment. For example, if product quality is a key concern, the firm might adopt a screening control system to monitor the product as it is being created. If quantity is a more pressing issue, a post-action system might be used to identify defects at the end of the system without disrupting the manufacturing process itself. Obviously the particular conversion technology used will have a major effect on the design of the control system.[21]

Controlling capital-intensive and labor-intensive technologies

In capital-intensive operations such as oil refining and steel manufacturing, a substantial amount of control is achieved through design and engineering. Intricate, special-purpose facilities and equipment are engineered to perform precisely specified activities repetitively. The technology is geared intensively to a narrow, relatively stable product line. The reliability and quality of the products that are produced stem largely from the precision of the equipment; quality is designed and engineered into the manufacturing process. As a result, control adjustment of these processes may be infrequent and it requires high technical competence. So do the elaborate procedures and equipment that are designed to monitor critical stages of the process. Accordingly, highly technical staffs are maintained to provide this control expertise.

Labor-intensive operations introduce entirely different types of control complexities. Many control problems and variations in processes cannot be anticipated, nor can we economically design our way around them. Plumbing services, auto repair services, and job shop manufacturing firms exhibit very dissimilar complexities in operations control. When product specifications are unpredictable, most operations control occurs during and after resource conversion. That is, the emphasis is on screening and post-action control. Some degree of indirect control is achieved before conversion by carefully selecting inputs such as reliable component suppliers, proven materials, and skilled employees. Still, direct product and process control is exerted by human intervention during the conversion process.

Effective control in labor-intensive systems is often a matter of managerial judgment and experience with the capabilities of the particular operations processes and employees.[22] Skilled employees, even the best ones, perform variably from day to day, so operations control in labor-intensive operations requires managerial skill in interpersonal relations and motivation. The first-line manager or supervisor, who is aware of employee capabilities and

21. See William H. Newman, *Constructive Control* (Englewood Cliffs, N.J.: Prentice-Hall, 1975).

22. The role of judgment in decisions is discussed in "Decisions, Decisions, Decisions," *Dun's Review*, May 1981, pp. 98–101.

limitations, needs to consider control standards in making work assignments and designing job content.

In general, operational control in labor-intensive systems is less formal than in capital-intensive systems and more directly dependent on interpersonal skills.

Areas of operations control

The areas of most frequent concern in operations control are costs, inventory, schedules, and quality. *Cost control* typically involves payment for labor services and materials consumed in the course of operations. Process analysis and work measurement are often used to determine standard requirements for materials and labor. Actual use of materials and labor is periodically compared with standards to detect variances, as discussed in Chapter 18. Significant variances call for management control action.

Inventory control, also called *materials control,* is essential for effective operations management. Inventories are an investment and, when organizational products and goals change, corresponding changes must be made in the kinds and purposes of inventories. The four basic kinds of inventories are raw materials, work-in-process, finished-goods, and in-transit inventories. As shown in Table 20.4, the sources of control over these inventories are as different as their purposes. Work-in-process inventories, for example, occur when products are partially completed and need further processing. Shop managers, by their decisions on how to sequence the jobs awaiting further buildup, determine the amounts of these inventories and hence the related costs that are incurred. By contrast, the quantities and costs of finished-goods inventories are under the control of the overall production scheduling system, which is determined by higher-level planning decisions. In-transit inventories are controlled by the transportation/distribution system. Each of these areas has goals for in-

Table 20.4 Inventory types, purposes, and sources of control

Type	Purpose	Source of control
Raw materials	Provides the materials needed to make the product.	Purchasing models and systems.
Work in process	Enables overall production to be divided into stages of manageable size.	Shop floor control systems.
Finished goods	Provides ready supply of products upon customer demand and enables long, efficient production runs.	High-level production scheduling systems in conjunction with marketing.
In-transit (pipeline)	Distributes products to customers.	Transportation/distribution control systems.

ventory cost and quantity. Inventories should be monitored and action taken to correct significant deviations from the path toward these goals. Techniques for inventory control were discussed in Chapter 18.

Scheduling control involves having the right things arriving and departing at the right times. When raw materials arrive too soon, the organization has resources sitting idle and the materials themselves may spoil, shrink, or otherwise lose value. And when materials arrive late, production is delayed. PERT (Chapter 8) and MRP (Chapter 18) are both useful techniques for planning and controlling operations schedules.

Quality control, or *quality assurance,* begins with product and performance specifications. Quality control systems then inspect (monitor), either continuously or intermittently, the incoming raw materials and components, intermediate stages of product buildup, machine process settings, and final products. Statistical procedures and models are commonly used to assist in these control efforts. Statistical sampling helps monitor the quality of incoming materials, for example. Similarly, statistical control charts help monitor the process outputs that are deemed most critical.

We should also note that quality control is as appropriate for service organizations as for companies that manufacture a product. A restaurant must make sure that food is properly prepared and served. A barber shop wants its customers to like their haircuts. A university usually takes steps to ensure that instructors are doing an adequate job of classroom instruction. A dry cleaner typically inspects garments after they have been cleaned and pressed.

All control activities are geared toward identifying discrepancies between what is actually happening and what is desired in the operations subsystem. Control is achieved when actions are taken to identify and correct the sources of discrepancy, so that desired performance is achieved.

Summary of key points

Operations management is the set of organizational activities that organizations use in creating their products and services. Operations management creates products that provide form, time, place, and/or possession utility, depending on the physical good or service the company produces. Resource inputs are converted through a processing technology that transforms the inputs into the desired outputs, guided by information feedback and control procedures.

The specific direction, emphasis, and capabilities of any particular operations function are unique to its organizational setting and are designed to achieve special strategic objectives. Accordingly, the operations management is planned, organized, and controlled with those strategic objectives in mind. In operations planning, design decisions must be made about product or service line, capability, technology, facilities (number, location, layout), human resources, and operational planning, organizing, and controlling.

Organizing for operations requires that decisions be made on the basis of the division of work, clarification of line and staff activities, and adjustment of structural relationships to various environments and technologies.

Operations control subsystems vary from setting to setting, depending on the organization's strategic goals and on the type of conversion technology used. In capital-intensive technologies, control is typically achieved through design and engineering. For labor-intensive conversion processes, control is usually achieved through interpersonal and motivational skills. Operations systems generally seek to control costs, schedules, inventory (materials), and product quality. Finally, all of these planning, organizing, and controlling activities for operations must be blended with those of other functions in the organization.

QUESTIONS FOR DISCUSSION

1. What are the primary distinctions between "management" and "operations management?"
2. Identify areas of operations management in a manufacturer, a local pizza parlor, an automobile repair shop, and a university.
3. Is operations management most closely linked to corporate, business, or functional strategies?
4. How is contingency planning related to operations management?
5. Sketch simple organization charts for firms departmentalized by function, by product, by location, and by customer. Identify the location of operations management in each. Do the same for a matrix organization design.
6. Can you explain how technological, structural, and personnel changes might each affect, and be affected by, a change in the operations management subsystem of an organization?
7. How might the basic elements of leading (that is, motivation, leading, groups, and communication) relate to operations management? Why do you think a separate section in this chapter was not devoted to these linkages?
8. How are the concepts of effectiveness, performance, and productivity related to operations management?
9. What kinds of budgets might be most relevant to an operations manager?
10. Can you relate the four areas of operations control (costs, inventory, schedules, and quality) to a hospital? To a local hamburger joint?
11. What can marketing and financial managers learn from operations managers?

CASE 20.1

At the beginning of this chapter, you read a scenario about breakthroughs in automation and flexible manufacturing systems. It was noted that these techniques improve efficiency and reduce inventory needs. It was also noted that many Japanese firms use these concepts effectively. You were asked how American industry might

The use of FMS at John Deere

respond. The case that follows discusses the techniques in more detail, describes how one American company, John Deere, has used them, and then raises some other issues for your consideration.

Jules Verne may once have envisioned a manufacturing plant without people, a plant capable of turning out products day in and day out without human intervention. Such a plant may never actually exist, but recent breakthroughs in manufacturing technology have clearly moved things in that direction. The breakthroughs began with isolated uses of robotics and numerical control machines operated by computer tapes.

Most recently, the concept of flexible manufacturing systems, or FMS, has emerged as the latest innovation in automation. A flexible manufacturing system consists of three basic sets of components. Computer-controlled machines process metal, plastic, or wooden parts. Then sophisticated robots handle the parts, putting them into the machines and taking them out. Next automated carts and parts bins carry the parts from one work station to another. An elaborate electronic control system, using state-of-the-art computer technology, coordinates all the activities and keeps the manufacturing system operating smoothly.

The basic objectives of FMS are two-fold. First, the system is concerned with using equipment more efficiently. Some experts estimate that parts sit idle over 90 percent of the time in a traditional job shop. If parts can be made to move through the system with less idle time, overall efficiency and productivity should increase.

More significantly, FMS allows manufacturers increased flexibility in designing work systems. A traditional assembly line requires that machines and work stations be developed in a relatively fixed sequential fashion. To achieve maximum efficiency, a firm had to produce a large number of units. This stemmed from the relatively rigid arrangement—changing the work system meant major adjustments. An FMS, however, allows manufacturers the option of efficiently producing smaller batches and rearranging work system components with relative ease.

The adoption of the FMS approach is credited as one reason why Japanese automobile manufacturers have enjoyed tremendous success over the last several years. Other Japanese companies that have adopted the FMS concept include Panasonic, Mitsubishi, and Yamazaki Machinery Works. At one Yamazaki plant, 12 workers comprise the day shift and only a guard is present at night. Using conventional technology, a plant would need 215 workers, 4 times as many machines, and 3 months to produce what that Yamazaki plant turns out in only 3 days. Another Yamazaki plant is even more advanced. The entire manufacturing system can be operated by telephone. The plant can produce $230 million worth of machine tools a year, but it can also cut back to an $80-million-a-year output without laying off any workers!

To date, few United States companies have been aggressive in adopting the FMS concept. Perhaps the most notable exception is John Deere. John Deere Company recently invested $500 million in its mammoth tractor assembly complex in Waterloo, Iowa. Most of the materials handling at the complex is controlled by computers.

Each component part is automatically assigned to a specific tractor as it is produced. Next the chassis and engine arrive from other plants. All the parts are then pulled and transported to the assembly line just as they are needed. By using a version of the just-in-time inventory system, Deere has cut inventory needs in some areas by as much as 50 percent.

The company is also able to build a tractor in half the time it needed before, and Deere's new-found flexibility has increased its ability to react to changes in the marketplace. For example, the company has broadened its product line in order to compete with a wider array of farm equipment manufacturers. Deere is also attempting to gain a foothold in heavy construction equipment (such as bulldozers and graders) against established companies like J. I. Case and Caterpillar Tractor Company.

Other American firms have been reluctant to follow Deere's lead, and in 1983 there were only 30 fully developed FMS operations in the United States. At that same time, one Japanese firm (Toyoda Machine Tool Company) had more than 30 such systems itself.

CASE QUESTIONS

1. Why have American firms been so reluctant to adopt the FMS concept?
2. Is FMS applicable to industries other than manufacturing? Could it be used in service organizations?
3. Identify the potential risks and payoffs that John Deere must have contemplated in making its decision to adopt FMS.

CASE REFERENCES

Bettner, Jill, with Gross, Lisa. "Planting Deep and Wide at John Deere," *Forbes,* March 14, 1983, pp. 119–122.

Burck, Charles G. "Can Detroit Catch Up?" *Fortune,* February 8, 1982, pp. 34–39.

Bylinsky, Gene. "The Race to the Automatic Factory." *Fortune,* February 21, 1983, pp. 52–64.

McCann, Michael K. "Flexible Manufacturing—Another Step Towards the Automated Plant." *Automotive Industries,* November 1981, pp. 61–63.

C A S E 20.2

Allied Food Services is a West Coast restaurant company. AFS operates two chains of restaurants and is considering adding a third. One existing chain is Duke Burger, 92 restaurants competing with McDonald's, Burger King, and Wendy's. Duke Burger sells several kinds of sandwiches, French fries, ice cream, and soft drinks. Its primary product, the Duke, is a 6-ounce hamburger with all the trimmings.

Duke Burger restaurants are laid out in the same way as most McDonald's outlets. Customers walk up to any of several or-

Operations design in fast-food chains

der stations and place their order. The attendant takes their money and fills the order from precooked food on a warming rack. Behind the rack, cooks prepare food and keep the rack filled. A supervisor keeps track of current product levels and instructs the cooks on what to prepare.

All Duke Burger restaurants are company-owned and -operated. All supplies (cups, drinks, hamburger wrappers, and so on) are bought from one company and shipped to the restaurants from a central warehouse. Frozen meat patties and other food materials are also bought from suppliers and distributed to the restaurants as needed. Buns, however, are bought locally and delivered to each restaurant daily.

The Duke Burger chain has been quite profitable for AFS, and in 1983 Duke Burger contributed 80 percent of AFS's profits. The other AFS chain, however, has been less successful. This chain, Beef & Brew, is a franchised steak restaurant operation intended to compete with Steak and Ale. There are now 46 Beef & Brew restaurants in operation.

Each Beef & Brew is independently owned. Franchisees pay AFS 8 percent of their sales; AFS provides advertising and general management guidance. Each Beef & Brew owner buys her or his own supplies and food from local distributors. Furthermore, although each restaurant is expected to provide a common core of traditional steaks, individual units can supplement their menus with seafood, pork, lamb, or other items.

The Beef & Brew chain has been only marginally profitable for AFS. Ten franchises have folded in the past two years. The remaining units appear to be relatively strong, however, and if the profit picture can be improved, the chain should still be able to become an important part of AFS.

At present AFS is considering the purchase of a chain of pizza parlors, Fun-Time Pizza. Fun-Time consists of 64 restaurants that compete with Pizza Hut and Pizza Inn. All units are company-owned. At the Fun-Time restaurant, customers walk in and order their pizza and drinks at a counter. They are given their drinks at that time. The pizza is brought to their table when it is cooked. Customers pay as they leave.

AFS believes Fun-Time Pizza holds a lot of promise for the future. It has been projected, for example, that the current market area could support at least 40 more outlets. And operations people who have been working with Duke Burger believe that they can improve on the layout and work flow of the Fun-Time Pizza restaurants.

CASE
QUESTIONS

1. What are the similarities and differences in operations among Duke Burger, Beef & Brew, and Fun-Time Pizza?

2. How might AFS be restructured after the acquisition of Fun-Time to improve its operations?

3. What similarities and differences in planning, organizing, and controlling do these three chains exhibit?

21

PERSONNEL MANAGEMENT AND THE STAFFING PROCESS

CHAPTER OBJECTIVES

1. Discuss the importance of the personnel function in organizations and describe the legal environment of personnel.

2. Briefly explain the concept of job analysis.

3. Describe the process of human resource planning.

4. Discuss how organizations go about recruiting prospective new employees.

5. Explain the process of selecting new employees.

6. Discuss the process of developing and evaluating a training program.

7. Describe several methods of performance appraisal.

8. Explain how wage rates are set.

9. Describe how a union is formed and how a labor contract is negotiated and administered.

OPENING INCIDENT

Consider the CEOs of two major conglomerates. One's company has been a mediocre performer at best. For example, over a recent 5-year period, the company's stock price declined by 12 percent. The other company clearly outperformed the first, and its stock price rose by 147 percent during the same time interval. To what kinds of rewards should these two CEOs be entitled?

H uman resources are absolutely critical for effective organizational functioning. We have already discussed some aspects of managing people, such as communication, leadership, and motivation. In this chapter we turn more specifically to the procurement and maintenance of human resources in organizations. Procuring human resources, or *staffing,* includes planning for the future employment needs of the organization and taking steps to meet these needs via recruiting and selection, promotion, layoff, transfer, and early retirement. Maintaining the human resources of an organization involves the on-going process of dealing with present employees, including training and development, performance appraisal, compensation and benefits, management–union relations, and safety and health. *Job analysis* provides information that personnel managers need to perform many of their staffing and maintenance functions. All these activities occur within the increasingly complex legal environment of personnel, as shown in Figure 21.1.

The importance of personnel management has grown dramatically in the last two decades. Organizations are coming to realize that the effectiveness of their personnel function has a substantial impact on the "bottom line" performance of the firm.[1] For instance, poor personnel planning can result in spurts of hiring followed by layoffs, which are costly in terms of unemployment compensation payments, training expenses, and morale. Haphazard compensation systems do not attract, keep, and motivate good employees, and outmoded recruitment practices can lay the firm open to expensive and embarrassing discrimination lawsuits.

Organizations with more than two hundred employees usually have a personnel manager and a personnel department charged with overseeing these activities. However, responsibility for personnel activities is invariably *shared*

1. See Herbert E. Meyer, "Personnel Directors Are the New Corporate Heroes," *Fortune,* February 1976, pp. 84ff.

Figure 21.1
Human resource
management

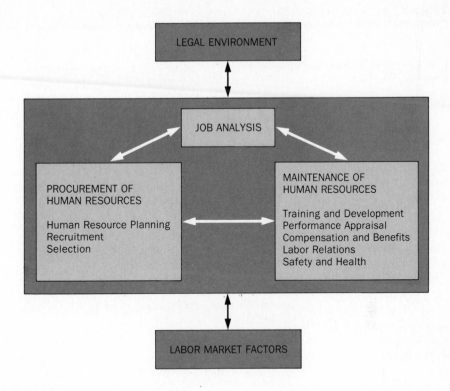

between the personnel department and line managers (see Table 21.1). For instance, the personnel department may recruit and do initial screening of candidates, but the final selection is usually made by managers in the department where the new employee will work. Similarly, although the personnel department may establish performance appraisal policies and procedures, the actual evaluating and coaching of employees is done by their immediate superiors. Thus every manager is involved and needs to understand the basics of personnel management. To provide such understanding is the goal of this chapter.

We will discuss each of the major personnel activities involved in procuring and maintaining a qualified work force. First, however, we will consider the legal environment of personnel. Recent federal legislation has had a tremendous impact on the practice of personnel management.

The legal environment of personnel management

Many laws regulate different aspects of employee–employer relations, especially in the areas of equal employment opportunity, compensation and benefits, labor relations, and occupational safety and health.

Table 21.1 Shared responsibility for human resource management

	Personnel professionals	Other managers
Planning	Initiate planning; select or develop planning techniques; gather information; help make forecasts; participate in planning programs; implement programs.	Provide information and expert judgment; help make forecasts; help plan programs; help implement programs.
Recruiting and selection	Select recruiting methods; conduct recruiting and initial screening; refer candidates to appropriate departments for further interviewing; test candidates when appropriate; validate selection procedures; ensure equal opportunity and keep EEO records.	May serve as campus recruiters; conduct interviews with candidates; make final hiring decision.
Training and development	Oversee orientation of new employees; identify training needs; plan and carry out training programs; evaluate training effectiveness.	Orient new employees to their jobs; conduct on-the-job training; help identify training needs and recommend employees for training; provide data used to evaluate training.
Compensation and benefits	Initiate and oversee job evaluation; set up wage structure and pay policies; administer benefit plan.	May serve on job evaluation committees; recommend employees for raises.
Performance appraisal	Design appraisal system; train other managers to use system; assure that appraisals are carried out at appropriate intervals; maintain employee performance records.	May participate in design of appraisal system; conduct appraisals of subordinates; conduct feedback and goal setting sessions with subordinates.
Labor relations	Gather information in preparation for negotiation; participate in negotiation; oversee implementation of the contract; may participate in grievance procedure.	Manage in such a way as to make unions unnecessary; conduct self properly during an organizing campaign; aid in negotiations; live within the contract on a daily basis; handle grievances at first step or two.

Equal employment opportunity and affirmative action

Title VII. Several laws forbid unfair discrimination by employers, but the most important is Title VII of the Civil Rights Act of 1964. Title VII forbids discrimination on the basis of sex, race, color, religion, or national origin in all areas of the employment relationship, including hiring, layoff, discharge, discipline, compensation, access to training, and promotion. As amended, Title VII applies to all private employers with 15 or more employees, to state and local governments, and to educational institutions, labor unions, and employment agencies. The intent of Title VII is to ensure that employment decisions are made on the basis of an individual's qualifications for a particular job, rather than sex, race, religion, or national origin. The effect of the law has been to curtail such practices as refusing to promote blacks into management, failing to hire men as telephone operators and flight attendants, and refusing to hire women as construction workers.

Less overt forms of discrimination have also been curbed. For instance, the use of employment tests that whites pass at a higher rate than blacks is forbidden *unless* the employer can document that the test is a valid predictor of job performance. Similarly, many height and weight standards (at least 5 ft 7 in. and 150 lb) for police officers and fire fighters have been eliminated because they excluded a disproportionate number of female, hispanic, and Asian applicants and could seldom be proved necessary for success as a police officer or fire fighter. Such practices are assumed to have an "adverse impact" on minorities and/or women when such individuals pass the selection standard at a rate less than 80 percent of the pass rate for majority group members. Practices that have an adverse impact on protected groups can be used only when there is solid evidence that they are *valid*—that they effectively identify individuals who are better able than others to do the job. The Equal Employment Opportunity Commission and several other federal agencies concerned with discrimination have recently published the "Uniform Guidelines on Employee Selection Procedures," which detail how to properly establish validity and comply with the law.[2]

Age Discrimination in Employment Act. The Age Discrimination in Employment Act was passed in 1967 and amended in 1978. It applies to basically the same types of employers and situations as Title VII but outlaws discrimination against people aged 40 through 69. Individuals cannot be forced to retire before age 70 except for documented health- or performance-related reasons. People under the age of 40 who are discriminated against because of being too young have no protection under this federal law, though some states have broader age discrimination acts that may provide relief.

Both the Age Discrimination Act and Title VII require passive nondiscrimination or equal employment opportunity. Employers are not required to seek out and hire large numbers of older employees or minority group

2. See Equal Employment Opportunity Commission, "Uniform Guidelines on Employee Selection Procedures," *Federal Register*, August 25, 1978, pp. 38290–38315.

members, but they must treat fairly all who apply.[3] However, there are some regulations that require employers to go one step further: to actively seek, hire, and advance particular classes of individuals. We will discuss these next.

Executive orders. A series of executive orders issued in the last twenty years requires employers holding government contracts to engage in *affirmative action.* This means intentionally seeking and hiring qualified or qualifiable employees from race/sex/ethnic groups that are "underutilized" or under-represented in the organization. Ideally, an employer's work force should reflect the race/sex/ethnic makeup of the relevant labor market. If 15 percent of the carpenters in the area where a company is located are black, then approximately 15 percent of the carpenters it employs should also be black. Employers with federal contracts over $50,000 per year must have a written Affirmative Action Plan that spells out employment goals for each underutilized group and the company's plans for meeting these goals. The latter might include recruiting at largely minority schools or making special efforts to attract women into apprenticeship programs. Employers with government contracts are also required to act affirmatively in hiring Vietnam era veterans and qualified handicapped individuals.

Compensation and benefits

A number of important state and federal laws also regulate the payment of wages and the provision of benefits to employees.

Fair Labor Standards Act. The wage law with the widest impact is the Fair Labor Standards Act, which was passed in 1938 and has been amended frequently since then. Among many other provisions, this law sets the "minimum wage" and requires payment of overtime rates for work in excess of forty hours per week. Not all employees are covered. Salaried professional, executive, and administrative employees are "exempt" from the minimum hourly wage and overtime provisions.[4]

Equal Pay Act. Another law with implications for compensation is the Equal Pay Act of 1963, which requires that men and women be paid the same amount for doing the same jobs, assuming the jobs demand equal skill, effort, and responsibility and are performed under the same working conditions. For instance, it is against the law to pay male chemistry teachers more than female chemistry teachers merely because of sex or assumed "head of household" status. Attempts to circumvent the law by having different job titles and pay rates for males and females who perform essentially the same work (she is the "head secretary," he the "office manager") are also illegal. However, it is per-

3. See Daniel Seligman, "How 'Equal Opportunity' Turned into Employment Quotas," *Fortune,* March 1973, pp. 160–186.

4. See Thomas H. Patten, Jr., *Pay: Employee Compensation and Incentive Plans* (New York: Free Press, 1977).

fectly reasonable to base an individual's pay on her or his seniority, performance, or qualifications, even if this results in a particular man and woman being paid different amounts for doing the same job. Although a number of cases have been filed under the Equal Pay Act, it is a bit redundant because Title VII also covers pay discrimination on the basis of sex.

Laws about benefits. The provision of benefits is also regulated in some ways by state and federal law. Certain benefits are mandatory, such as unemployment compensation for employees who are laid off and worker's compensation for employees who are injured on the job. Employers who provide a pension plan for their employees are subject to the Employee Retirement Income Security Act of 1974 (ERISA). This law sets standards for pension plans and provides federal insurance if pension funds go bankrupt. The primary goals of ERISA are to ensure that employees get the pension benefits due them when they retire and that they do not lose accrued benefits if they change employers.[5] However, the law does not require every employer to have a pension plan.

Labor relations laws

Union activities and management behavior toward unions constitute another heavily regulated personnel area. Before the 1930s, federal laws generally inhibited unionization, and unions were often prosecuted as "conspiracies in restraint of trade."[6] However, during the New Deal Era, new laws affirmed the right of unions to exist and the obligation of management to bargain collectively with them. There are two major labor laws that every manager should know about.

National Labor Relations Act. The National Labor Relations Act (Wagner Act), passed in 1935, set up a procedure by which employees can vote whether to have a union. If they vote for a union, management is required to bargain collectively with the union. The Wagner Act lists certain "unfair labor practices": things management may not do because they hinder the right of employees to unionize. Unfair labor practices include such actions as firing or otherwise punishing employees known to be pro-union, threatening or bribing employees to vote against the union, attempting to dominate the union, and sending spies to union meetings. The National Labor Relations Board was established by the Wagner Act to enforce the provisions of the Act.

Labor–Management Relations Act. Following a series of severe strikes in 1946, the Labor–Management Relations Act (Taft–Hartley Act) was passed in 1947 to limit union power. First, the law lists unfair labor practices

---

5. See James Ledvinka, *Federal Regulation of Personnel and Human Resources Management* (Boston: Kent, 1982).

6. See Benjamin J. Taylor and Fred Witney, *Labor Relations Law,* 3rd ed. (Englewood Cliffs, N.J.: Prentice-Hall, 1979).

by unions, such as refusing to bargain in good faith, harassing both union members and nonmembers, and charging excessive dues and fees. Second, it gives management more rights to speak out against the union during an organizing campaign, though management must still be careful not to threaten employees. Finally, the Taft–Hartley Act contains the National Emergency Strike provision. This allows the President of the United States to obtain a court injunction to prevent or end a strike that endangers the national health and safety. The injunction is good for up to 80 days; it is hoped that the strike can be settled during this time.

Taken together, these laws balance the power of unions and management. Employees are entitled to be represented by a properly constituted union, whereas management retains the right to make nonemployee-related business decisions without interference.

Health and safety

Both state and federal laws promote safety in the workplace. For instance, workers' compensation laws indirectly encourage safety by requiring employers with poor safety records to pay higher premiums. The Occupational Safety and Health Act of 1970 (OSHA) directly mandates the provision of safe working conditions. OSHA is undoubtedly the most influential occupational safety law and merits further discussion.

Occupational Safety and Health Act. OSHA requires that employers (1) provide employees "employment and a place of employment which are free from recognized hazards that are causing or are likely to cause death or serious physical harm" and (2) obey the safety and health standards established by the Occupational Safety and Health Administration. *Safety standards* are intended to prevent accidents such as falling off a scaffolding or being injured by a moving piece of machinery. Occupational *health standards* are concerned with preventing occupational disease due to long-term exposure to hazards such as excessive noise, carcinogenic chemicals, or other contaminants. For instance, there are standards that limit the concentration of cotton dust in the air, because this contaminant has been associated with lung disease in textile workers.

OSHA standards are enforced by OSHA inspections, which are conducted when an employee files a complaint of unsafe conditions or when a serious accident occurs. Spot inspections of plants in especially hazardous industries are also made. Employers who fail to meet OSHA standards may be fined.[7]

Having discussed the legal environment of personnel management, we now turn to a topic-by-topic discussion of the major personnel activities identified in Figure 21.1. Job analysis is discussed first because this information-

7. Ledvinka, *Federal Regulation,* Chapters 8 and 9.

gathering process contributes to many of the other personnel activities that are explored later.

Job analysis

Job analysis is a systematized procedure for collecting and recording information about jobs. A job analysis is usually made up of two parts: a job description and a job specification. The *job description* includes a list of the duties the job entails, the working conditions under which the job is performed, and the tools, materials, and equipment used on the job. The *job specification* is a list of the skills (typing), abilities (manual dexterity), and other credentials (college degree, chauffeur license) needed to perform the duties of the job. There are many methods of collecting and presenting job analysis data, from simple "homemade" forms to standardized and computer-scored questionnaires. The interested reader is referred to a recent book by McCormick for further details.[8]

Job analysis information is used in many personnel activities. For instance, it is necessary to know about job content and job requirements in order to develop appropriate selection methods and job-relevant performance appraisal systems and to set equitable compensation rates across jobs. Job analysis information is used in the development of training programs and also in human resource planning, our next topic of discussion.

Human resource planning

Human resource planning is forecasting the organization's future needs for employees of various sorts, forecasting the availability of such employees, and then planning programs to meet unfilled needs so that the organization will have the right number and kind of employees when they are needed. More and more organizations are implementing human resource planning systems. "Top management has begun to recognize that a significant lead time exists between the recognition of a need for the right person and having that person in place. Without a functioning human resources forecasting procedure, a firm stands little chance of operating efficiently or effectively."[9] Short-range planning (one to two years) to guide immediate recruiting needs is most common, but mid- and long-range planning (up to ten years) can also be helpful, especially for managerial and technical jobs. When we foresee a need for many more middle managers in seven years' time, we had better begin right away to locate and develop individuals with management potential.

There are many techniques available for forecasting human resource de-

8. For more information on job analysis methods, see Ernest J. McCormick, *Job Analysis: Methods and Applications* (New York: AMACOM, 1979).

9. See Norman Scarborough and Thomas W. Zimmerer, "Human Resources Forecasting: Why and Where to Begin," *Personnel Administrator*, May 1982, pp. 55–61.

Table 21.2 Predicted demand for air conditioner assemblers

Predicted sales of air conditioner units		150,000 units
Direct labor hours to assemble one unit (based on past data)	×	20 hours
Total direct labor hours	=	3,000,000
Hours worked per year per assembler (48[a] weeks/year × 40 hours/week)	÷	1,920
Number of full-time assemblers needed	=	1,562

[a]Assume 4 weeks per year lost due to vacation, holidays, and sick leave.

mands and supplies. Some complex, computerized models are best suited to large organizations or can be used when extensive data from past years are available. Some methods work best under stable conditions, whereas others can help us predict and deal with a turbulent environment. A few of these methods are described in the paragraphs that follow.[10]

Forecasting demand

To forecast the organization's future demand for employees, the first thing one needs is information, such as staffing levels for previous years, predicted future sales, organizational plans (such as entering new businesses or closing old plants), and economic trends. One also needs to decide which jobs to plan for—all jobs in the organization, only managerial jobs, or only jobs that have presented staffing difficulties in the past.

When a good sales forecast is available, a simple method of forecasting is to work backward to derive human resource needs, as shown in Table 21.2. In this example, the number of predicted sales (in units) is multiplied by average labor hours per unit to obtain the total number of labor hours needed. The number of labor hours is converted into an estimate of the number of employees needed by dividing by the average number of hours worked per employee per year. To get demand figures for jobs that are further removed from direct production, staffing ratios from past years can be used. Perhaps the firm in Table 21.2 has had 1.5 office workers for every 10 production workers. If so, it could predict that about 234 office workers will be needed. However, if the office workers are going to switch from manual typewriters to word processors next year, the estimate can be revised downward in view of the expected increase in productivity per worker.

Much more complicated quantitative models for predicting staffing demands are sometimes used, including multiple regression and computer simulation of the organization. Another popular method is to use the expert

10. See James W. Walker, *Human Resource Planning* (New York: McGraw-Hill, 1980). See also Elmer H. Burack and Nicholas J. Mathys, *Human Resource Planning: A Pragmatic Approach to Manpower Staffing and Development* (Lake Forest: Brace-Park Press, 1980).

Table 21.3 Predicted internal supply of air conditioner assemblers

Present number of assemblers	1244
Minus average number lost per year to voluntary turnover (10%)[a]	−124
Minus average number lost per year to firing (1.5%)[a]	−19
Minus average number expected to retire (3%)[a]	−37
Minus average number promoted or transferred per year (6%)[a]	−75
Equals predicted internal supply	980

[a]Percents based on past several years of data for this job.

judgments of knowledgeable individuals inside and outside the organization to arrive at a forecast. Sometimes the Delphi technique (described in Chapter 7) is used to help the experts reach consensus.

Forecasting supply

The task of forecasting the supply of labor is really two tasks: forecasting the internal supply, or the number and type of employees who will be in the firm at some future date, and forecasting the external supply, or the number and type of people who will be available for hiring in the labor market at large. Several mathematical models are available for forecasting internal supply. The simplest approach merely adjusts present staffing levels for anticipated turnover and promotions. On the basis of past data, for example, one might make the predictions shown in Table 21.3 about the number of air conditioner assemblers who will still be employed in that job next year. More sophisticated models apply this kind of procedure simultaneously to all jobs in the organization and can predict conditions more than one year in advance. Union Oil Company has a very complex forecasting system for keeping tabs on the present and future distributions of professionals and managers.[11] Their system can spot areas wherein there will eventually be too many qualified professionals competing for too few promotions or, conversely, too few good people available to fill important positions.

Thus far we have talked about forecasting in the aggregate. For instance, we have predicted that we will have 989 assemblers left next year. Exactly who these 989 are is of no real concern. However, at the higher levels of the organization, we need to plan for specific people and positions. The technique most commonly used is the *replacement chart*, which lists each important managerial position, who occupies it now, how long he or she will probably stay in it before moving on, and who (by name) is now qualified or soon will be qualified to move into the position. This allows ample time to plan developmental experiences for individuals identified as potential successors to critical managerial jobs.

11. See W. E. Bright, "How One Company Manages Its Human Resources," *Harvard Business Review,* January–February 1976, pp. 81–93.

To facilitate both planning and the identification of individuals for current transfer or promotion, some organizations have an employee information system, or *skills inventory*. Such systems are often computerized, containing information on each employee's education, skills, work experience, and career aspirations.[12] Such a system could quickly locate all the employees in a large organization who are ostensibly qualified to fill a position requiring, for instance, a degree in chemical engineering, three years of experience in an oil refinery, and fluency in Spanish.

Forecasting the external supply of labor is a different problem altogether. How does one predict how many electrical engineers will be seeking work in Georgia three years from now? Planners must rely on information from outside sources, like state employment commissions, government reports, and figures supplied by colleges on the number of students in major fields, to get an idea of the future availability of labor.

Planning programs

After comparing future demand and future internal supply, managers charged with personnel planning can make plans to deal with predicted shortfalls or overstaffing. If a shortfall is predicted, new employees can be hired from outside, present employees retrained and transferred into the understaffed area, individuals approaching retirement tempted to stay on by additional benefits, or labor-saving/productivity-enhancing systems installed. If overstaffing is expected to be a problem, the main options are transferring the extra employees, not replacing individuals who quit, encouraging early retirement, and laying people off.

Recruitment

Recruitment is the process of attracting individuals to apply for the jobs that are open. The goal is to attract *qualified* candidates, not merely large numbers of candidates.[13] Attracting too few candidates is obviously a problem, because those who must make the final choice either will not be able to be very selective or will have to leave openings unfilled. On the other hand, attracting far too many candidates is also undesirable. Evaluating candidates is quite costly and time-consuming (particularly when individual testing or interviews are used).

Internal recruiting

There are two types of recruiting—internal and external. Internal recruiting means considering your present employees as candidates for openings. A pol-

---

12. See Richard A. Kaumeyer, Jr., *Planning and Using Skills Inventory Systems* (New York: Van Nostrand, 1979).

13. See Van M. Evans, "Recruitment Advertising in the 80s," *Personnel Administrator*, December 1978, pp. 21–23.

icy of promotion from within can help build morale and keep high-quality employees from leaving the firm. In unionized companies, the procedures for notifying employees of internal job change opportunities are usually spelled out in the contract. This is often called the "job posting and bidding" method. For higher-level positions, a skills inventory system may be used to identify internal candidates, and/or superiors may be asked to recommend individuals who should be considered.

One disadvantage of internal recruiting is the "ripple effect." When a present employee moves to a different post, someone else must be found to take her or his job. If this replacement was already an employee, then her or his now-vacant job must also be filled. In one organization, 545 job movements were necessary as a result of filling 195 initial openings.[14] Although this gives many employees a chance to move up, it also increases training costs and other problems associated with inexperienced incumbents.

External recruiting

External recruiting means attracting individuals outside the organization to apply for positions with the firm. A number of methods are available, such as advertising, campus recruiting, use of public or private employment agencies or executive search firms, union hiring halls, referrals by present employees, and hiring "walk-ons" or "gate-hires" (people who show up without being solicited). It is important to select the most appropriate methods. For instance, one would probably not go to the state employment commission to find a nuclear physicist, but one would use it to find blue-collar workers. Private employment agencies can be a good source of clerical and technical employees, and executive search firms specialize in locating top management talent. Newspaper ads are often used because they reach a very wide audience and thus allow minorities "equal opportunity" to find out about and apply for job openings.

In selecting a recruiting method, both costs and results must be considered. Newspaper ads are quite inexpensive compared to executive search firms or campus recruiting. The results of various methods may also differ and can be measured as the quality or quantity of applicants generated by the recruiting method. For instance, a bank in New York City investigated the quality of tellers hired through each of seven recruiting methods. They found that three of the methods they had been using (newspaper advertising, major private employment agency, and other agencies) produced tellers who were more likely to quit than those produced by the other recruiting methods (rehiring former employees, acting on referrals from high schools or present employees, and hiring walk-ins). Analyses showed that the bank could save over $50,000 per year in hiring and training costs by using only the four most effective recruiting methods.[15]

14. See Burack and Mathys, *Human Resource Planning.*

15. See Martin F. Gannon, "Sources of Referral and Employee Turnover," *Journal of Applied Psychology*, June 1971, pp. 226–228.

Selection

Once recruiting methods have attracted a pool of applicants, the next step is to select whom to hire. The intent of the *selection* process is to gather information from applicants that will predict their job success and then to hire the candidate(s) predicted to be most successful. Information about candidates can be collected in many ways, including application blanks, tests, interviews, and reference checks. The process of proving that any of these selection devices is really predictive of future job performance is called *validation.* Recall that any selection device that has an adverse impact on members of minority groups or other "protected classes" such as females *must* be validated. However, *all* selection devices *should* be validated, because it is a waste of time and money to use a selection device without being certain that it helps pinpoint the best candidates.

Validation

There are two basic approaches to validation. The first is *statistical validation* or *empirical validation*, which involves collecting the scores of employees or applicants on the device to be validated and correlating these scores with actual job performance. A statistically significant correlation means that the selection device is a valid predictor of job performance. For instance, to the extent that

"Now then, Mr. Lawson, are you honest? Sincere? Highly self-motivated? Assertive? Can you put up with a lot of nonsense? Are you willing to play ball our way and handle petty office jealousies and be overlooked for pay raises and promotions. . . ."

©1983 Henry R. Martin

SAT scores are correlated with college grades, then the SAT would be a valid selection device for admission to college.

The second major validation method is called *content validation*. To apply this method, one uses logic and a thorough study of the job to establish that the selection device (usually a work-sample test) measures the exact skills needed for successful job performance. For example, if a job requires a great deal of typing of tables and figures, a typing test involving this kind of material is content-valid for the job. The most critical part of content validation is a careful job analysis, showing exactly what duties are to be performed. The test is then developed to measure the applicant's ability to do those duties.

Application blanks

Often the first step in selection is to have the candidate fill out an application blank. These forms have changed as a result of equal employment opportunity legislation. Few application blanks these days ask for sex, race, marital status, number of children, native tongue, religion, age, or a photograph; this kind of information could obviously be used to discriminate among candidates illegally. Application blank data are generally used informally to decide whether a candidate merits further evaluation, and interviewers use application blanks to familiarize themselves with candidates before interviewing them.

Application blanks can also be statistically weighted and can be quite good predictors of job success.[16] Weighting procedures can be used only when there are large numbers of current employees in a job. The weighting procedure consists of identifying items on which successful employees tended to answer differently from unsuccessful employees at the time of hire.[17] A brief example of a weighting procedure is given in Table 21.4. Responses are weighted positively or negatively according to how well they characterize successful versus unsuccessful employees. Responses that characterize good and poor employees equally well are given a weight of zero.

Tests

Tests are also used to select employees. Tests of ability, skill, aptitude, or knowledge that is relevant to the particular job are usually the best predictors, whereas tests of general intelligence or personality are seldom found to be valid for employee selection. If tests are used, of course, they should be validated and should be administered and scored in a very consistent fashion. That is, all candidates should be given the same directions, should be allowed the same amount of time, and should experience the same testing environment (temperature, lighting, distractions). If properly validated, tests can be very helpful in selection.

16. See James J. Asher, "The Biographical Item: Can It Be Improved?" *Personnel Psychology*, Summer 1972, pp. 251–269.

17. See George W. England, *Development and Use of Weighted Application Blanks*, rev. ed. (Minneapolis Minn.: University of Minnesota Industrial Relations Center, 1971).

Table 21.4 Weighting application blank items

Item	Response	Percent of successful employees	–	Percent of unsuccessful employees	=	Percent difference	Weight[a]
How many years of experience have you had in sales?	No experience	10%		32%		–22%	–2
	1 year	15		35		–20	–2
	1–2 years	25		25		0	0
	3–5 years	50 ___ 100%		8 ___ 100%		42	+4
Are you a citizen of the United States?	yes	95%		95%		0%	0
	no	5 ___ 100%		5 ___ 100%		0	0
Why did you leave your last job?	Fired	10%		40%		–30%	–3
	Laid off	40		40		0	0
	Seek better opportunity	40		10		+30	+3
	Other reason	10 ___ 100%		10 ___ 100%		0	0

[a]Percent differences can be divided by 10 and rounded to the nearest whole number to yield weights that are easier to use for hand scoring of application blanks. Note that items that successful and unsuccessful employees answer similarly are given a weight of zero.

Interviews

The interview is a very popular selection device. Besides evaluating the applicant, the interviewer can tell the applicant about the company. Unfortunately, interviews are often rather poor predictors of job success. There are many reasons for this, most of them stemming from biases inherent in the way people perceive and judge others on first meeting.[18] Interview validity can be improved by training interviewers to be aware of potential biases and by changing the format of the interview. In general, somewhat structured interviews are better than completely unstructured ones. In a structured interview, questions are written down in advance and all interviewers follow the same question list with each candidate they interview. This procedure is helpful for two reasons. It introduces consistency into the interview procedure, and the questions can be carefully screened and refined so that they are all relevant to job ability and are not discriminatory. Table 21.5 gives an outline of what a structured interview might contain. When interviewing managerial or professional candidates, a somewhat less structured approach can be used. That is, question areas and information-gathering objectives are still planned by the inter-

18. See Neal Schmitt, "Social and Situational Determinants of Interview Decisions: Implications for the Employment Interview," *Personnel Psychology*, Spring 1976, pp. 79–102.

Table 21.5 Format for a structured interview

1. Greet the applicant, state the purpose of the interview, and mention that you'll be taking notes during the interview.

2. Ask yes–no questions about unchangeable aspects of the job. For instance:

   Are you willing to work nights? Overtime?
   Do you have a Red Cross life-saving certificate?
   Do you have or can you get a chauffeur's license?

   Ask only about *absolute* prerequisites here. If the employee cannot meet these requirements, tactfully terminate the interview.

3. If you have an application blank, you should already have read through it to avoid asking redundant questions. At this point, ask questions designed to fill in any gaps left in the application blank. For example, "I notice that you didn't list a reason for leaving your last job. Can you tell me the reason?"

4. Tell the candidate about the job and the organization. Candidates won't be able to assess their interest in the job or to answer your questions about why they are qualified unless they know something about the job.

5. Ask structured oral questions. This is the heart of the interview. Lay out many questions ahead of time in the areas of work history, education and training, career goals, performance on earlier jobs, absenteeism and tardiness record, expected salary and benefits, and so on. Avoid any questions that are not relevant to job ability. Take notes on the answers, or you may forget half of what the candidate tells you!

6. Give the applicant a chance to ask questions or tell you about any qualifications you might have missed.

7. Tell the applicant what happens next and when he or she can expect to hear from you. Say goodbye.

8. Review your notes and rate the applicant on scales prepared ahead of time, being careful to avoid biases.

Source: Adapted from E. L. Levine, *The Joy of Interviewing* (Tempe, Ariz.: Personnel Services Organization, 1976). Used with permission.

viewer in advance, but the specific questions that are asked vary with the candidate's background.[19]

Assessment centers

The assessment center is a selection tool that is rapidly gaining in popularity. Assessment centers are used primarily to select managers and are particularly good for selecting present employees for promotion into management. The ***assessment center*** is a content-valid simulation of key parts of the managerial job. A typical center lasts two to three days, with groups of six to twelve assessees participating in a variety of managerial exercises. Most assessment

19. See Thomas L. Moffatt, *Selection Interviewing for Managers* (New York: Harper & Row, 1979) for guidance on how to conduct a semistructured interview.

centers include an "in-basket test" of individual decision making and group exercises to assess interpersonal skill. Centers may also include an interview, public speaking, and standardized ability tests. Candidates are assessed by several trained observers, usually managers several levels above the job for which the candidates are being considered. Assessment centers are quite valid if properly designed and are fair to members of minority groups and women.[20]

Training and development

After an individual is chosen for hiring or promotion, the next step is often some form of training. In personnel management, the term *training* usually refers to teaching lower-level or technical employees how to do their present jobs. *Development* refers to teaching managers and professionals the skills needed for both present and future jobs.[21]

Assessment of training needs

It is extremely important first to determine whether a *need* for training or development exists and then to plan an appropriate program if it is needed. For instance, if people who don't know welding are hired to be welders, the company obviously needs a training program on how to weld (or could change its selection standards to hire only those who already have this skill). On the other hand, when a group of office workers is performing poorly, training may or may not be the answer. The problem could be motivation, aging equipment, poor supervision, inefficient work design, or a deficiency of skills and knowledge. Only the last could be remedied by training the office workers.

If, after careful investigation, the problem does seem to require training, one should carefully assess the present level of skill and knowledge and then define the desired level of skill and knowledge in concrete, measurable form. An example is "Trainees will be able to type from handwritten copy at 60 words per minute with no more than one error per page." After the training is completed, you can assess trainee performance against the objectives you set up prior to training. Training programs should always be evaluated, because they are costly and should be modified or discontinued if they are not effective.

Training methods

A wide variety of training methods is available (see Table 21.6). Selection of a particular method depends on many considerations, but perhaps the most im-

20. See Ann Howard, "An Assessment of Assessment Centers," *Academy of Management Journal,* March 1974, pp. 115–134. See also J. R. Huck and D. W. Bray, "Management Assessment Center Evaluations and Subsequent Job Performance of White and Black Females," *Personnel Psychology,* Spring 1976, pp. 13–30.

21. See Gary Dessler, *Personnel Management* 2nd ed. (Reston, Va.: Reston Publishing, 1981), Chapters 7 and 15.

Table 21.6 Training and development methods

Method	Comments
Assigned readings	Readings may or may not be specially prepared for training purposes.
Behavior modeling training	Use of a videotaped model displaying the correct behavior, then trainee role playing and discussion of the correct behavior. Used extensively for supervisor training in human relations.
Business simulation	Both paper simulations (such as in-basket exercises) and computer-based business "games" are used to teach management skills.
Case discussion	Real or fictitious cases or incidents are discussed in small groups.
Conference	Small-group discussion of selected topics, usually with the trainer as leader.
Lecture	Oral presentation of material by the trainer, with limited or no audience participation.
On-the-job	Ranges from no instruction, to casual coaching by more experienced employees, to carefully structured explanation, demonstration, and supervised practice by a qualified trainer.
Programmed instruction	Self-paced method using text followed by questions and answers. Expensive to develop.
Role playing	Trainees act out roles with other trainees, such as "boss giving performance appraisal" and "subordinate reacting to appraisal" to gain experience in human relations.
Sensitivity training	Also called T-group and laboratory training, this is an intensive experience in a small group, wherein individuals give each other feedback and try out new behaviors. It is said to promote trust, open communication, and understanding of group dynamics.
Vestibule training	Supervised practice on manual tasks in a separate work area where the emphasis is on safety, learning, and feedback rather than productivity.

portant is training *content*. When the training content is factual material (such as company rules or how to fill out forms), then assigned reading, programmed learning, and lecture methods work well. However, when the content is human relations or group decision making, firms must obviously use a method that allows interpersonal contact, such as role playing or case discussion groups. When a physical skill is to be learned, methods allowing practice and actual use of tools and materials are needed, as in on-the-job training or vestibule training. Other considerations in selecting a training method are cost, time, number of trainees, and whether the training is to be done by in-house talent or contracted to an outside training firm.

Evaluation of training

As we have said, training should always be evaluated. There are two basic kinds of evaluation measures: those collected in or at the end of training and actual performance measures collected when the trainee is back on the job. The former are easier to get but the latter are more important. Trainees may say they enjoyed the training and learned a lot, but the true test is whether their job performance is better after their training than before.

Performance appraisal and feedback

When employees are trained and settled into their jobs, one of the next concerns is performance appraisal. There are many reasons to evaluate employee performance. One reason is for personnel research, such as validating selection devices and assessing the impact of training programs. A second reason is administrative: to aid in making decisions about pay raises, promotions, and training. And another reason is to provide feedback to employees to help them improve their present performance and plan future careers. Because performance evaluations often help determine wages and promotions, they should be fair and nondiscriminatory—that is, *valid*—just like any other selection device. In the case of appraisals, content validation is used to show that the appraisal system accurately measures performance on important job elements and does not measure traits or behavior that are irrelevant to job performance.[22]

Objective methods

Numerous appraisal methods are available, and they may be divided into those that are objective versus those that are judgmental. Objective methods include counts of output, scrap rate, dollar volume of sales, number of claims processed, and so on. Objective performance measures may be contaminated by "opportunity bias" if some individuals have a better chance to perform than others. For instance, a door-to-door Bible salesperson in Lincoln, Nebraska, would probably outsell a salesperson of equal diligence and ability in Tehran, Iran! It is often possible to adjust raw performance figures for the effect of opportunity bias and thereby to arrive at figures that accurately represent each individual's performance.

Another type of objective measure is the special performance test in which each employee is assessed under standardized conditions.[23] This kind of appraisal eliminates opportunity bias. For example, one telephone company

22. See William H. Holley and Hubert S. Field, "Performance Appraisal and the Law," *Labor Law Journal*, July 1975, pp. 423–451.

23. See Patricia C. Smith, "Behavior, Results, and Organizational Effectiveness: The Problem of Criteria," in M. D. Dunnette, M.D. (ed.), *The Handbook of Industrial and Organizational Psychology* (Chicago: Rand McNally, 1976).

has a series of prerecorded calls that operators in a test booth answer. The operators are graded on speed, accuracy, and courtesy in handling the calls. Performance tests measure ability but do not measure the extent to which one is motivated to use that ability on a daily basis. (A high-ability person may be a lazy performer except when being tested.) Therefore, special performance tests must be supplemented by other appraisal methods to provide a complete picture of performance.

Judgmental methods

By far the most common way to measure performance is through judgmental methods, which include ranking and rating techniques. Ranking is comparing employees directly to each other and ordering them from best to worst, usually on the basis of "overall performance." Ranking has a number of drawbacks. First, it is difficult to do in large groups, because the individuals in the middle of the distribution may be hard to distinguish from one another accurately. Second, there are unequal intervals between ranks. Number one is better than number two, but is he or she better by a lot or just a little? This kind of information is not conveyed by ranks. Third, comparison *between* work groups is impossible with ranking. Each group has a person ranked first, but which first is best?

The final criticism of ranking is that it is a global technique. The whole employee is being assessed at once as to overall goodness/badness compared to others. This is a bit simple-minded in that each employee certainly has both good and bad points. In addition, you never know what subjective criteria each evaluator used in arriving at a global judgment. One evaluator may consider quantity of performance above all else, whereas another may attend more to quality or cooperativeness. Furthermore, rankings (and global ratings) do not provide useful information for feedback. To be told that one is ranked third is not nearly so helpful as to be told that the quality of one's work is outstanding, its quantity is satisfactory, one's punctuality could use improvement, and one's paperwork is seriously deficient.

Rating differs from ranking in that it compares each employee to a fixed standard rather than to other employees. The *rating scale* provides the standard. Table 21.7 gives examples of graphical rating scales. Such scales are very common; they consist of a characteristic or performance dimension to be rated followed by a scale on which to make the rating. The scale at the top of Table 21.7 is an example of a poor scale; the characteristic to be rated and the anchors, or definitions of scale points, are extremely vague. The second scale is better; the clearer definitions help different raters use the scales consistently. In constructing graphical rating scales, it is extremely important to select performance dimensions that are relevant to job performance. As a rule, personality traits such as "honesty," "loyalty," and "creativity" should *not* be rated. Job behaviors and results should be the focus instead.

The Behaviorally Anchored Rating Scale (BARS) is a recently developed rating method that has been well researched but not yet widely adopted. This method calls on two (or more) groups of supervisors of the job to construct the

Table 21.7 Bad and better graphical rating scales

Initiative

1 Very poor	2	3 Average	4	5 Very good

Initiative—Extent to which employee is willing to act independently and without instruction when the need arises.

1 Never does anything without instruction.	2 Completes routine work on own, always seeks help for exceptions to routine.	3 Handles simple but nonroutine matters with little or no help.	4 Acts independently in all but the most nonroutine situations.	5 Handles all situations without help.

---

scales. They first identify relevant performance dimensions and then generate anchors: specific, observable behaviors typical of each performance level. An example of a behaviorally anchored rating scale for the dimension "supervising sales personnel" is given in Table 21.8. The other scales in this set, which was developed for the job of department manager in a chain of retail stores, include "handling customer complaints," "meeting day-to-day deadlines," "merchandise ordering," "planning special promotions," "using company systems and following through on administrative operations," "communicating relevant information," and "diagnosing and alleviating special department problems." BARS is potentially a good rating method because it requires that proper care be taken in constructing the scales. It is also costly, because a number of supervisors have to spend time constructing the scales.

Judgmental errors

In any kind of rating or ranking system, judgmental errors or biases can occur. One common problem is *recency error*, the tendency to base judgments on the subordinate's most recent performance, which is most easily recalled. Often a rating or ranking is intended to evaluate performance over an entire time period, such as six months or a year, so the recency error does introduce error into the judgment. Other errors include overuse of one part of the scale, being either too lenient or too severe, or giving nearly everyone a rating of "average." *Halo error* is allowing your assessment of an employee on one dimension to "spread" to your ratings of that employee on other dimensions. For instance, if a ratee is outstanding on quality of output, a rater might tend to give her or him higher marks than deserved on other dimensions.

Table 21.8 Behaviorally anchored rating scale for the dimension "supervising sales personnel"

9 ———

——— 8

——— 7

——— 6

5 ———

——— 4

3 ———

——— 2

1 ———

Could be expected to conduct a full day's clinic with two new sales personnel and thereby develop them into top sales people in the department.

Could be expected to give his sales personnel confidence and a strong sense of responsibility by delegating many important jobs to them.

Could be expected never to fail to conduct training meetings with his people weekly at a scheduled hour and to convey to them exactly what he expects.

Could be expected to exhibit courtesy and respect toward his sales personnel.

Could be expected to remind sales personnel to wait on customers instead of conversing with each other.

Could be expected to be rather critical of store standards in front of his own people, thereby risking their developing poor attitudes.

Could be expected to tell an individual to come in anyway even though she/he called in to say she/he was ill.

Could be expected to go back on a promise to an individual whom he had told could transfer back into previous department if she/he didn't like the new one.

Could be expected to make promises to an individual about his/her salary being based on department sales even when he knew such a practice was against company policy.

Source: J. P. Campbell, M. D. Dunnette, R. D. Arvey, and L. V. Hellervik, "The Development and Evaluation of Behaviorally Based Rating Scales," *Journal of Applied Psychology*, February 1973, pp. 15–22. Copyright 1973 by the American Psychological Association. Reprinted by permission of the author.

Additional errors can occur due to race, sex, or age discrimination, either intentionally or unintentionally.[24]

Feedback

Many appraisal systems include the final step of giving feedback to subordinates on their performance. This is accomplished in a private meeting between
superior and subordinate, and the discussion of past performance is usually
followed by planning for improvement in the future. However, feedback interviews are not easy to conduct. Superiors are uncomfortable with the task, especially if feedback is negative and subordinates are disappointed by what they
hear. Proper training of superiors can help them conduct more effective feedback interviews.

Compensation and benefits

Setting wage rates

A good compensation system can help attract qualified applicants, retain present employees, and stimulate high performance at a cost that is reasonable for
one's industry and geographic area. However, many compensation systems do
not succeed in meeting all these goals. To set up a successful system, three
major kinds of decisions must be made.

Wage level decision. The wage level decision is a management policy
decision about whether the firm wants to pay above, at, or below the going
rate for labor in the industry or the geographic area. Most firms choose to pay
near the average; those that cannot afford more pay below average. Large,
successful firms may like to cultivate the image of being "wage leaders" by
intentionally paying more than average and thus attracting and keeping high-
quality employees. The level of unemployment also affects wage levels: pay
declines when labor is plentiful (high unemployment) and increases when labor is scarce (low unemployment).[25]

Once the wage level decision is made, outside information is needed to
help set actual wage rates. Pay administrators need to know what the maximum, minimum, and average wages are for particular jobs in the appropriate
labor market. This information is collected by means of a *wage survey*. Area
wage surveys can be conducted by individual firms or by local personnel or

24. See William J. Bigoness, "Effect of Applicant's Sex, Race, and Performance on Employers'
Performance Ratings: Some Additional Findings," *Journal of Applied Psychology,* February 1976,
pp. 80–84. See also V. F. Nieva and B. A. Gutek, "Sex Effects on Evaluation," *Academy of
Management Review,* April 1980, pp. 267–276.

25. Allan N. Nash and Stephen J. Carroll, *The Management of Compensation* (Monterey, Calif.:
Brooks Cole, 1975).

Table 21.9 A simple point system for job evaluation

Compensable factors	Points associated with degrees of the factors				
	Very little	Low	Moderate	High	Very high[a]
Education	20	40	60	80	100
Responsibility	20	40	70	110	160
Skill	20	40	60	80	100
Physical demand	10	20	30	45	60

[a]The job evaluation committee that constructed this system believed that responsibility should be the most heavily weighted factor and physical demand the least. That is why the maximum points for these factors are different.

business associations. Professional and industry associations often conduct regional or nationwide surveys and make the results available to employers.

Survey data, however, do not provide enough information for making all wage decisions. First, it is unlikely that survey data will be available for every single job in an organization. Second, paying average or above-average rates based on survey data creates *external equity* (your employees feel fairly paid relative to others in the community, industry, or profession doing the same work) but does not address the issue of *internal equity*, the perception that different jobs within the firm are fairly paid relative to each other.[26] A common situation creating internal inequity arises when production workers earn as much as or more than their supervisors. This can happen when the former are on incentive plans or put in a lot of overtime, while supervisors on fixed salaries are "exempt" from the overtime pay requirement of the Fair Labor Standards Act. The set of pay differentials among different jobs within an organization is called the wage structure.

Wage structure decision. Wage structures are usually set up through a procedure called *job evaluation,* which attempts to assess the worth of each job relative to other jobs. Job evaluation is usually done by a committee made up of several managers and a few nonmanagerial employees. The simplest method is merely to rank jobs from those that should be paid the most (president) to those that should be paid the least (mail clerk, janitor). In a small firm with few jobs, this method is quick and practical, but medium-sized and large firms with many job titles require a more sophisticated approach. The most popular is known as the *point method.* To use this method, the committee first selects "compensable factors," or aspects of jobs that should affect how much pay each job warrants, and sets up scales like those given in Table 21.9. Examples of compensable factors might include amount of formal education required, physical demands, working conditions and hazards, amount of responsibility, and degree of skill. Jobs requiring more education would then be assigned more points on the education factor than jobs requiring less

26. See Patten, *Pay: Employee Compensation and Incentive Plans.*

Table 21.10 Applying the point system to three jobs

Compensable factors	Job		
	Secretary II	Office manager	Janitor
Education	Moderate = 60	High = 80	Very low = 20
Responsibility	Low = 40	Moderate = 70	Low = 40
Skill	High = 80	Moderate = 60	Low = 40
Physical demand	Low = 20	Low = 20	High = 45
Total Points	200	230	145

The job analysis committee carefully reviews the content of each job and decides what degree of each factor best describes the job.

education. Jobs performed under unpleasant or dangerous working conditions would be assigned more points on this factor than safe, comfortable jobs. Each job is carefully studied and evaluated on each factor, and then all the points assigned to each job are added up (see Table 21.10). A job assigned 400 points would be paid better than a job assigned 300 points. Using such a system, it is easy to explain to your employees why one job pays more than another and thus to enhance perceptions of internal equity.[27]

The next step is setting actual wage rates on the basis of a combination of survey data and the wage structure that results from job evaluation. Often jobs with similar numbers of points are grouped together into wage grades for ease of administration. For instance, if one has nine jobs with point totals between 375 and 400, it makes sense to group them in a single wage grade with the same pay rate.

Individual wage decision. Now there is only one decision left to make—the individual wage decision. This concerns how much to pay each employee on a particular job. The easiest decision is to pay a single rate for each wage grade, say $5.10 per hour for the grade including jobs with 375 to 400 points. All individuals on jobs in this grade would be paid this rate. More typically, however, a range of rates is associated with each wage grade. The range for the grade may be $4.85 to $5.39 per hour, with different employees earning different rates within the range. You then need a system for setting individual rates. This may be done on the basis of *seniority* (enter the job at $4.85, for example, and increase 5 cents per hour every 6 months on the job), on the basis of *initial qualifications* (inexperienced people start at $4.85, more experienced at a higher rate), or on the basis of merit (raises above the entering rate are given for good performance). Combinations of these bases may also be used.

27. See Nash and Carroll, *The Management of Compensation*, Chapter 6. See also J. L. Otis and R. H. Leukart, *Job Evaluation* (Englewood Cliffs, N.J.: Prentice-Hall, 1954) for a fuller description of job evaluation.

Pay and motivation

We said earlier that pay, when properly administered, could help attract and keep employees and could stimulate high performance. Pay level probably has the biggest impact on attracting and keeping employees. If you are a wage leader, you should not lack for applicants, and present employees hesitate to change employers because they would probably have to take a pay cut. Thus high wages encourage membership in an organization, but they do not automatically spell high performance. To do this, pay must be contingent on performance, so that improved performance leads to higher pay. One pay system that can do this is merit pay—whereby larger raises are given to better performers. Unfortunately, installing a "merit" system does not automatically improve performance. For the system to be effective, employees must believe that their performance will be evaluated fairly and accurately and that the differences in pay for differences in performance will be sizable.[28] For instance, would you work extra hard all year long if it meant getting an 11 percent raise compared to a 10 percent raise? A 15 percent raise compared to a 5 percent raise?

Other systems also link performance to pay. For managers and executives, bonuses of up to 50 percent or more of their base yearly salary may be offered for good individual and corporate performance. Salespeople are often paid commissions based on sales performance, and production workers may be placed on incentive or piece-rate systems. Group incentives pay employees on the basis of work-group productivity rather than individual productivity and can be quite effective when the group is not too large and teamwork is required to do the job. Profit sharing returns a percentage of the whole organization's profit to each employee. But suppose you are one of thousands of employees of General Electric. How likely is it that your improved performance will increase corporate profits enough to affect your profit-sharing check? As you can see, profit sharing would not usually spur employees on to high performance, but it does help attract and keep employees, at least during profitable years.

Benefits

It is estimated that companies spend an amount equal to 36.6 percent of their cash payroll on employee benefits, sometimes called fringe benefits. Thus an average individual who is paid $18,000 per year would get about $6,588 more per year in benefits.[29] These benefits come in several forms, including pay for time not worked, insurance benefits, retirement benefits, and employee services.[30] Pay for time not worked includes sick leave, vacations, holidays, and

28. See Nathan B. Winstanley, "Are Merit Increases Really Effective?" *Personnel Administrator*, April 1982, pp. 37–41. See also Michael Seitzinger, "Planning Supervisor/Subordinate Pay Differentials," *Personnel Administrator*, February 1983, pp. 74–77.

29. See U.S. Chamber of Commerce, *Employee Benefits 1979* (Washington, D.C.: U.S. Government Printing Office, 1980).

30. See Dessler, *Personnel Management*, Chapter 11.

unemployment compensation. Insurance benefits often include life and health insurance for the employee and her or his dependents. Some organizations pay the entire cost of insurance, others share the cost with employees, and still others negotiate group rates but let employees pay the full cost. Workers' compensation is a legally required insurance benefit that provides medical care and disability income for employees injured on the job. Social Security is a government pension plan to which both employers and employees contribute. Many employers also provide a private pension plan to which they and/or their employees contribute. Employee service benefits include such things as credit unions, tuition reimbursement, and recreational opportunities.

A good benefit plan may help encourage membership in an organization, but it seldom stimulates high performance because benefits are tied to membership—and perhaps to rank or salary—rather than to performance. To get a good return on their benefit dollars, companies should shop carefully, avoid redundant coverage, and provide only those benefits that their employees want. Too, benefit programs should be communicated to employees in plain English so that they can use the benefits appropriately and appreciate what the company is providing.

Some organizations have instituted "cafeteria benefit plans," whereby some basic coverage is provided for all employees, but employees are then allowed to choose which additional benefits they want (up to a cost limit based on salary). An employee with five children might choose medical and dental coverage for dependents, a single employee might prefer more vacation time, and an older employee might elect increased pension benefits. Such a flexible system would be expected to encourage continued membership in the organization and perhaps to help the company attract new employees.

Labor relations

Labor relations is a term used to refer to dealings with employees when they are represented by an employee association (union). Recall that nonmanagement employees have the legal right to organize and bargain collectively with management. In this section we discuss how unions are formed, the process of collective bargaining, and how collective bargaining contracts are enforced via the grievance procedure.

Forming a union

For a new local union to be formed, several things must occur. First, employees must become interested in having a union. Nonemployees who are professional organizers employed by a national union (like the Teamsters) may generate interest by making speeches and distributing literature outside the workplace. Inside, employees who want a union will try to convince other workers.

The second step is to collect signatures of employees on *authorization cards*. These cards state that the signer authorizes the union to represent her or him. Thirty percent of the employees in the potential bargaining unit must sign these cards to show the National Labor Relations Board (NLRB) that there is sufficient interest to justify holding an election. Before the election the *bargaining unit* must be defined. The bargaining unit consists of all employees who will be eligible to vote in the election and to join the union and/or be represented by the union if one is formed. The bargaining unit must be a logical grouping of employees, such as "all nonmanagement employees at the XYZ plant in Sunnytown" or "all clerical employees at the university."

The election is supervised by an NLRB representative and is conducted by secret ballot. If a simple majority of those voting (not of all those eligible to vote) votes for the union, then the union is certified as the official representative of the bargaining unit.[31] The new union then organizes itself by officially signing up members and electing officers and will soon be ready to negotiate the first contract.

Management usually prefers that employees not be unionized, because unions limit management's freedom in many areas. So management usually wages its own campaign to convince employees to vote against the union. It is at this point that "unfair labor practices" are often committed. For instance, management cannot interrogate employees about their feelings toward unions and cannot discriminate in hiring, firing, or layoffs on the basis of participation in union activities. It is also an unfair labor practice to promise to give employees a raise (or any other benefit) if the union is defeated.[32]

Experts agree that the best way to avoid unionization is to practice good employee relations all the time—not just when threatened by an election. Providing absolutely fair treatment with clear standards in the areas of pay, promotion, layoff, and discipline; having a complaint or appeal system for individuals who feel unfairly treated; and avoiding any kind of favoritism will help make employees feel that a union is unnecessary.[33]

Collective bargaining

The intent of collective bargaining is to write and agree on a contract between management and the union that is satisfactory to both parties. The contract contains agreements about "wages, hours, and other conditions of employment," including promotion, layoff, discipline, benefits, methods of allocating overtime, vacations, rest periods, and the grievance procedure. The union will want to have a "union security clause" that helps assure the union's continued existence by requiring new employees to join the union or contribute to its support or requiring present members to remain members. Management will want to include a "management rights clause" in the contract, which says that management retains the right to make unilateral decisions in all areas except those specified in the contract. A "no strike clause" is usually included, stating

31. See Taylor and Witney, *Labor Relations Law,* Chapter 12, for more details on how unions are formed.

32. See Alfred T. DeMaria, *The Supervisor's Handbook On Maintaining Nonunion Status* (New York: Executive Enterprises Publications Company, 1974).

33. See DeMaria, *The Supervisor's Handbook.* See also Matthew Goodfellow, "How to Lose an NLRB Election," *Personnel Administrator,* September 1976, pp. 40–44; and James Rand, "Preventive Maintenance Techniques for Staying Union-Free, *Personnel Journal,* June 1980, pp. 497–508.

that the union will not strike during the term of the contract (usually three years). The union (unless it is a union of federal, state, or municipal workers) is still free to strike before the contract is approved or after it expires if a new one has not been agreed on.

The process of bargaining may go on for weeks or months, with management and union representatives meeting to make proposals and counterproposals. The resulting agreement must be ratified by the union membership. If it is not approved, the union may strike to put pressure on management, or it may choose not to strike and simply continue negotiating until a more acceptable agreement is reached.

Grievance procedures

The grievance procedure is the means by which the contract is enforced. Most of what is in a contract concerns how management will treat employees, so when employees feel that they have not been treated fairly under the contract, they file a grievance to correct the problem. For instance, if the contract says that the most senior person will be given the first chance to work overtime, but a supervisor offers the overtime to a less senior employee first, the more senior employee can file a grievance.

The first step in a grievance procedure is for the aggrieved employee to discuss the alleged contract violation with her or his immediate superior. Often the grievance is resolved at this stage. However, if the employee still believes that he or she is being mistreated, the grievance can be appealed to the next step, perhaps to the foreman. The union steward may help an aggrieved employee present her or his case. If the foreman's decision is also unsatisfactory to the employee, additional appeals to successively higher management are made, until finally all in-company steps are exhausted. The final step is to submit the grievance to binding arbitration. An *arbitrator* is a labor law expert who is paid jointly by the union and management. The arbitrator studies the contract, hears both sides of the case, and renders a decision that must be obeyed by both parties. The grievance system for resolving disputes about contract enforcement prevents any need to strike during the term of the contract.

Discipline

Many grievances arise from disciplinary actions. The contract usually says that management may discipline an employee "for just cause." However, perceptions of what is "just cause" and what is fair punishment may differ between management and employees. For instance, an employee in a meat packing plant was given a three-day suspension without pay for throwing a piece of bologna at another worker. He filed a grievance stating that the punishment was excessive for such minor horseplay and that he was really aiming the bologna at a trash can. The company replied that there were closer trash cans and that the employee he threw the bologna at was working at an operating slicing machine. Thus the horseplay had been potentially dangerous. Further, employees had recently been warned that they would be punished for throwing meat. The arbitrator ruled in favor of the company, concluding that the suspension was justified.[34]

In order to avoid this kind of problem, rules should be clearly spelled out and communicated to employees. Penalties should also be made known and should "fit the crime." Most discipline systems use "progressive penalties"— the more often the violation is repeated, the more serious the penalty. For instance, a first incident of tardiness might occasion only a reminder, the second a stern warning, the third a written warning in the employee's file, and the fourth a short suspension. Some violations, such as fighting, stealing from the employer, and sabotage, obviously call for a much more severe initial penalty. Do you think it would be fair to fire an employee for a first offense of listening to a radio on the job? Probably not on most jobs, but in the plant where this rule exists, employees are monitoring a very expensive continuous-process chemical unit on which many of the warning signs are auditory and could be drowned out by a radio. Therefore, the rule is reasonable if it has been clearly communicated to all employees.

Summary of key points

Personnel management is concerned with acquiring and maintaining the human resources needed by an organization. Personnel management includes a number of specific activities, many of which are now regulated by law. For instance, employers may not discriminate in any of their actions because of employee or applicant color, race, sex, religion, national origin, or age (between 40 and 69). Employees with government contracts must take affirmative action to hire classes of individuals that are shown to be underrepresented in their current work force. Additional federal laws set the minimum wage, regulate pensions, and require adherence to occupational safety and health standards. Finally, employee and employer rights and obligations with regard to union activities are specified by law.

Job analysis is a critical information-gathering step in many personnel activities. Job analyses typically include both job descriptions and job specifications.

Human resource planning consists of forecasting the organization's future need for employees, forecasting the availability of employees both within and outside the organization, and planning programs to assure that the proper number and type of employees will be available when needed.

Recruiting and selection are the processes by which job applicants are attracted, assessed, and hired. Methods for assessing applicants include tests, interviews, application blanks, and assessment centers. Any method used for selection should be properly validated.

Training and development are necessary to enable employees to perform their present jobs well and to prepare for future jobs. Steps in training include

34. See "Working with People," from the Bureau of National Affairs, *Bulletin to Management,* as reprinted in Mary Green Miner and John B. Miner, *Policy Issues in Contemporary Personnel and Industrial Relations* (New York: Macmillan, 1977), pp. 421–435.

assessing training needs, planning and conducting the training program via an appropriate training method, and then evaluating the effectiveness of the training program.

Performance appraisals are important for determining training needs, pay raises, and promotions and for providing helpful feedback to employees. Both objective and judgmental methods of appraisal can be applied, and a good system usually includes several methods. The validity of appraisal information is always a concern, because it is difficult to accurately evaluate the many aspects of a person's job performance.

Compensation and benefit administration is also an important personnel management task. Compensation rates must be fair compared both to other jobs within the organization and to the same or similar jobs in other organizations in the labor market. Properly designed incentive or merit pay systems can encourage high performance, and a good benefit program can help attract and retain employees.

Finally, if a majority of a company's nonmanagement employees so desire, they have the right to be represented by a union. Management must engage in collective bargaining with the union in an effort to agree on a contract. While the contract is in effect, employees do not strike but use the grievance system to settle disputes with management.

QUESTIONS FOR DISCUSSION

1. What are the differences between equal employment opportunity and affirmative action? Do you think that "reverse discrimination" against white males exists as a result of the affirmative action requirement?
2. The laws recognize and protect the right of employees to form a union if they wish. Do you agree with this policy? Why or why not?
3. Why is job analysis central to so many personnel activities?
4. Discuss the pros and cons of internal and external recruiting. Think about the external recruiting methods listed in the chapter. Which methods would be most appropriate for recruiting an automobile mechanic in your city? Which methods would be best for recruiting a university president?
5. How do you know whether a selection test is valid? What are the possible consequences of using invalid selection devices? Why do you suppose assessment centers are such good predictors of managerial success?
6. What training methods would you use to teach a group of sixteen-year-olds to drive? Why would you use these methods? How could you evaluate the effectiveness of your training program?
7. How are wage rates set? From the company's point of view, what are the advantages and disadvantages of being a "wage leader"? What would you do if your job evaluation system showed that a job is worth $4.00 per hour but other employers in the community were paying $6.00 per hour?
8. If you were an hourly employee, would you want to belong to a union? What protections and services do unions provide for their members?

C A S E   21.1

At the beginning of this chapter, you read a scenario about two CEOs. One's company had clearly outperformed the other. You were asked about the kinds of rewards the two CEOs should get. The company with poor performance is International Telephone and Telegraph, the other Raytheon. The case that follows tells what compensation each CEO does receive and then raises some other issues for your consideration.

The performance-reward link at the top of the organization.

Operating employees are typically paid either by the hour (or other unit of time) or according to what is produced. Lower- and middle-level managers are often paid a salary. For both kinds of employees, the general goal is to establish some kind of compensation system that rewards desirable performance. That is, people who do a good job are presumed to get greater rewards than people who do not do such a good job.

At the level of top management, however, compensation systems often bear little relation to performance. Consider, for example, the performance and rewards for these two CEOs in the early 1980s. For the 5-year period ending in 1981, ITT averaged an 11 percent average return on stockholders' equity, experienced an average growth rate in earnings per share of only 3.5 percent, and suffered a 12 percent decline in the price of its common stock. ITT's CEO, Rand Araskog, received total compensation in 1981 of $1,150,000.

The CEO of another conglomerate, Raytheon, lead his company to higher levels of performance but earned a comparatively small reward. For the same period of time, Raytheon achieved an average return on stockholders' equity of 20.7 percent, an annual growth rate in earnings per share of 24.1 percent, and an increase in stock price of 147 percent. Yet Thomas Phillips, the head of Raytheon, received only $635,000 in 1981 compensation. This is obviously not an insignificant amount, but it is clear that the link between performance and reward is not so well defined in the executive ranks as at lower levels of the organization.

Some attempts are made to reward executives for exemplary performance via bonuses, but often these bonuses are more facade than true incentive. Sears recently established an incentive plan for executives in which bonuses are paid if the company's return on equity ranks at or above the median of the bottom third of the industry. That is, Sears executives receive bonuses if the company ranks as low as the seventeenth percentile in the industry.

Another part of the compensation package available only to top managers is what is commonly referred to as the "golden parachute." Essentially, a golden parachute is a special employment contract whereby an executive receives a generous severance package if control of her or his firm changes hands. At present, around 15 percent of this country's largest companies make parachutes available to executives. There were close to 2,000 mergers and acquisitions in 1982 alone, so it is likely that this concept will be even more sought-after by executives in the future.

The rationale behind the parachute concept is that it allows managers to work in the best interests of stockholders, even if doing so means they may lose their own jobs. For example, when Exxon initiated action to buy Reliance Electric, it meant that Reliance stockholders would benefit greatly. When talks began, the stock was selling at around $35 a share. Reliance's CEO negotiated an offer from Exxon of $72 a share and then fought federal intervention that threatened the acquisition. Because he had a golden parachute, he was able to take an aggressive approach to bargaining that worked in the best interests of stockholders. He had financial security in the event that the acquisition cost him his job.

Even so, a golden parachute can be a costly proposition for stockholders. When Bendix was merging with Martin Marietta and Allied Technology, the CEO of Bendix, William Agee, negotiated an attractive parachute for himself. When, in 1983, he was not appointed CEO of the new company, he left. Under the terms of his parachute agreement, Agee will receive total compensation of $4 million.

CASE
QUESTIONS

1. Why do you think the performance—reward link is different at the top of an organization from that at other levels?
2. Why are bonuses paid to executives? Do you think they act as an incentive to good performance?
3. Should golden parachutes be made available for operating employees? Why or why not?

CASE
REFERENCES

"Bill Agee Pulls the Golden Rip Cord." *Newsweek*, February 21, 1983, p. 64.

Loomis, Carol J. "The Madness of Executive Compensation." *Fortune*, July 12, 1982, pp. 47–52.

Morrison, Ann M. "Those Executive Bailout Deals." *Fortune*, December 13, 1982, pp. 82–87.

Smith, William J. "Executive Compensation After ERTA," *Personnel Administrator*, February 1983, pp. 63–65.

C A S E 21.2

Brooke Robertson doesn't know where to start. She has just accepted a position as personnel director for Big State Industries and has found the place in a shambles. Big State is a southern manufacturing company whose primary products are fabricated steel parts used in the automobile industry. Big State has two

Problems in personnel management

plants, one in Houston and the other in New Orleans. Each plant employs about 250 full-time workers.

When Brooke accepted the job, she knew she was taking on a real challenge. Big State has gone through four personnel directors in the last two years. When the last one quit over four months ago, Big State's president was so angry at personnel managers in general that he didn't fill the position until now. Brooke had been working as assistant personnel manager for another manufacturer for the last six years and welcomed the challenge.

She has just spent the last five days sorting through several months of letters, memos, reports, and other documents. She has made a list of several trouble spots in need of attention and is now deciding which to tackle first. The primary problems that Brooke has identified are:

1. **Recruiting and selection.** Big State has no approach to systematic recruiting and selection. The Houston plant is badly deficient in its number of black employees, and she herself is the only woman manager in the company. Applicants for operating jobs are given a manual dexterity test that is not really applicable to the job, and references are never checked.
2. **Employee safety.** The New Orleans plant has been tagged with five OSHA violations during the last two years. Four months ago, the plant was given six months to correct several major hazards. To date, nothing has been done.
3. **Employee training.** Big State provides no training for its employees. Because it hires only experienced personnel, the company assumes that training is not needed. First-line supervisors usually attend an annual two-day seminar on human relations sponsored by a local university. Again, Brooke is the first person with a college degree to be hired by the company.
4. **Labor relations.** The existing labor contract expires in three months. The union has indicated that its demands will include a 24 percent pay hike, two additional holidays per year, and an improved retirement plan. Even though contract talks are scheduled to open in four weeks, no background work has been done to determine how the company should respond.

Besides being unsure which problem to attack first, Brooke is unsure how best to approach the company president. She knows he hates government regulation and is also not too thrilled with labor unions. If she presents these problems to him, he will undoubtedly go into a tirade about the government forcing him to hire unqualified people and telling him how to run his company. He will have even fewer kind things to say about the union.

CASE
QUESTIONS

1. In what order should Brooke and Big State attack these problems?
2. How should Brooke present them to the company president?
3. Why do you think there has been such dramatic turnover among personnel directors at Big State?

22

ENTREPRENEURSHIP AND SMALL BUSINESS MANAGEMENT

CHAPTER OBJECTIVES

1. Describe the role and the place of small business in our economy.

2. Discuss how managing a small business differs from managing a big business.

3. Relate the planning function to small business.

4. Relate the organizing function to small business.

5. Relate the leading function to small business.

6. Relate the controlling function to small business.

CHAPTER OUTLINE

OPENING INCIDENT

You are a college student about to graduate with a degree in botany. For the past three and a half years you have managed the community's largest nursery. Presumably you could keep this position after you graduate, but you don't really think you would be happy working for someone else for the rest of your life. What would you do?

Today small business is riding the crest of a tidal wave of popularity, enjoying more esteem and prestige than ever before. Politicians and journalists alike now praise the achievements and opportunities of small business— and for good reason. So vital is small business that few if any parts of our economy could work without its steady stream of products and services. And just as vitally, small business is at the cutting edge of technological breakthroughs. For example, the personal computer revolution was triggered by two inventive men in their mid-twenties, Steven Jobs and Stephen Wozniak. It was they who founded the Apple Computer Company in 1976, with themselves as the sole employees, and Wozniak later designed the Apple II computer. In seven short years, Apple grew from scratch to sales of more than $1 billion a year.[1]

To succeed in small business, men and women must generally exhibit managerial skills and styles that differ sharply from those of their counterparts in big business. To help us grasp the uniqueness of small business, its problems, and its opportunities, this chapter will describe the role and place of small business in our economy and then relate to small business the major managerial functions of planning, organizing, leading, and controlling.

The role and place of small business in our economy

Definitions of small business

Definitions of *small business* differ widely. Even agencies within the federal government differ, as do Chambers of Commerce and even small business groups. The most widely quoted definitions are those of the *U.S. Small Business Administration* (SBA). Created in 1953 by the U.S. Congress,

---

1. See "Cover Story: Machine of the Year," *Time*, January 3, 1983, pp. 14–39.

Table 22.1 SBA standards of smallness for selected industries

Manufacturers	Employing fewer than
Aircraft	1,500 persons
Calculating machines	1,000
Household vacuum cleaners	750
Men's and boys' clothes	500
Macaroni and spaghetti	250

Retailers	Earning sales of less than
Mail order houses	$7.5 million a year
Grocery stores	7.5
Automobile agencies	6.5
Variety stores	3.0
Radio and television stores	2.5

Wholesalers	Earning sales of less than
Paints and varnishes	$22.0 million a year
Tires and tubes	22.0
Groceries	14.5
Sporting goods	14.5

Source: "SBA Rules and Regulations," *The Code of Federal Regulations* (Washington, D.C.: U.S. Government Printing Office, October 5, 1978), Section 121.3–10.

the SBA has a twofold purpose: to improve the managerial skills of small-businesspersons, and to help them to borrow money.

For small-businesspersons seeking its help, the SBA has drafted definitions to fit virtually every industry. A partial list appears in Table 22.1. Note that some definitions really cover medium-sized businesses. For example, an aircraft manufacturer with 1,500 employees probably boasts sales of more than $100 million a year. Few people would view such a business as small. Nor are the SBA's definitions hard and fast; they may be relaxed in exceptional cases. For example, in 1966 the SBA classified American Motors Corporation as a small business to enable the company to bid on defense contracts. At the time, American Motors posted sales of $991 million and employed 32,000 persons. The SBA justified its judgment by applying a seldom-used test of smallness—namely, that a business qualifies as small if it does not dominate its industry. Because it served just 1 percent of the total domestic automotive market, American Motors passed that "smallness" test easily.[2]

Other tests of smallness differ markedly from those of the SBA. For example, a business qualifies as small if it employs fewer than 500 people, according to both the U.S. Department of Commerce and the U.S. Chamber of Commerce, or fewer than 250 people, according to Small Business United, a

2. Nicholas C. Siropolis, *Small Business Management: A Guide to Entrepreneurship* (Boston: Houghton Mifflin, 1982), p. 7.

national network of small business organizations dedicated to legislative action at the federal level.

The vitality of small business

There are roughly 15 million businesses in the United States. This total includes part-time businesses as well as farms and franchises. Of these 15 million businesses, more than 99 percent are small—even if we define a business as small if it employs fewer than 100 persons. Clearly, small business is a vital force in our economy. Further evidence of its vitality is the fact that small business employs 58 percent of the nation's work force.[3]

Financial performance. In sheer numbers, then, small business far outstrips big business. But how well is it doing financially? Is it keeping pace with big business, falling behind, or moving ahead?

Although these questions are hard to answer with any degree of precision, the evidence suggests that small business outdoes big business. Some proof appears in Figure 22.1. Note that, *on the average*, small manufacturers earn a higher return on owners' equity than do big manufacturers. The two main reasons why small manufacturers do better are (1) in many manufacturing industries, small business can respond more rapidly and at less cost than big business to the quickening rate of change in products and services, processes and markets, and (2) small business has become more attractive to talented, individualistic men and women.

Similar data for nonmanufacturing industries such as retailing, services, and wholesaling are not yet available, but it seems likely that small businesses in those industries are also doing well financially, and for the same reasons.

Innovation. In recent years, much attention has been focused on the fact that big business has been expanding its dominance of the nation's economy. Yet much of the potential of free enterprise and innovation lies elsewhere, in the host of small-businesspersons who help push back the frontiers of knowledge.

In fact, major inventions are as likely to come from either individuals or small businesses as from big businesses, according to both the U.S. Department of Commerce and the U.S. Office of Management and Budget.[4] For example, small businesses or individuals invented the personal computer, the transistor radio, the photocopying machine, the jet engine, and the instant photograph. Their ingenuity also gave us the pocket calculator, power steering, the automatic transmission, air conditioning, and even the 19¢ ball-point pen.

Clearly, we are all better off for the presence in our economy of millions of small businesses. Their resourcefulness and ingenuity have spawned new

---

3. See U.S. Small Business Administration, *Facts About Small Business* (Washington, D.C.: U.S. Government Printing Office, 1980), p. 3.

4. See U.S. House of Representatives Committee on Small Business, *Future of Small Business in America* (Washington, D.C.: U.S. Government Printing Office, August 1979), p. 7.

Figure 22.1
A comparison of financial performance between big and small manufacturers

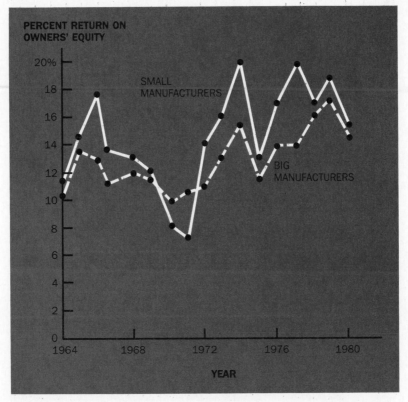

Source: Federal Trade Commission, *Quarterly Financial Reports for Manufacturing Corporations* (Washington, D.C.: U.S. Government Printing Office, 1964–1980), Table 5.

industries and contributed a great many innovative ideas and technological breakthroughs.

Job creation. Still another proof of its vitality is the fact that small business, not big business, creates most new jobs. In one study, David L. Birch found that, between 1969 and 1976, small businesses with 20 or fewer employees created 66 percent of all new jobs in the nation (in New England alone, such businesses created 99 percent of all new jobs), but that middle-sized and big businesses created few new jobs.

These statistics are significant, based as they are on data drawn from 5.6 million businesses. In Birch's words, "It appears that the smaller corporations . . . are aggressively seeking out new opportunities, while the larger ones are primarily redistributing their operations."[5]

In another study the U.S. Department of Commerce found that small,

5. See David L. Birch, *The Job Generation Process* (Cambridge, Mass.: MIT Program on Neighborhood and Regional Change, 1979), p. 8.

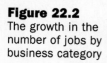

Figure 22.2
The growth in the
number of jobs by
business category

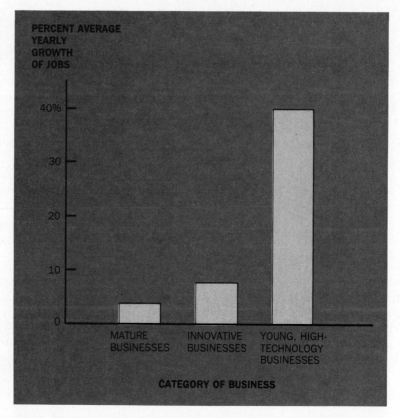

Source: U.S. Department of Commerce, *Recommendations for Creating Jobs Through the Success of Small, Innovative Businesses* (Washington, D.C.: U.S. Government Printing Office, March 1980), p. 88.

young, high-technology businesses created new jobs at a much faster rate than larger, older businesses. High-technology businesses (especially those in chemistry and electronics) require employees with a high degree of scientific or engineering knowledge. Their ability to create jobs quickly is illustrated in Figure 22.2.

New business formation. Yet another measure of the vitality of small business is the record number of businesses formed each year since 1960. New incorporations hit the 500,000 mark for the first time in 1979.[6] This total is more than triple the total in 1960. Of course, some of these new corporations represent mature businesses that were born as either sole proprietorships or partnerships and only recently incorporated.

Although it is impossible to pin down the precise number of small businesses formed each year, there undeniably is a boom in new businesses. The main reasons for this boom are threefold:

6. See Alfred L. Malabre, Jr., "Tracking a Trend," *Wall Street Journal,* March 12, 1980, p. 40.

1. **The desire to be one's own boss.** According to a recent Gallup poll, roughly half of all men and women in the country prefer to work for themselves rather than for somebody else.[7]
2. **The accelerated pace of innovation and new knowledge, creating opportunities for new businesses.** One example is the microcomputer industry, which has spawned hundreds of computer hardware manufacturers and thousands of software firms.
3. **A political and economic climate highly conducive to the formation of small businesses.** In 1980 President Jimmy Carter held the first White House Conference on Small Business. Bringing together 1,683 delegates from all 50 states, this conference might never have happened but for the newly widespread belief that small business is a seedbed for new jobs and innovation, productivity, and growth.[8]

The dark side of small business

Job creation and innovation, financial performance and opportunity, then, make up the bright side of small business. In contrast, the dark side reflects problems that are unique to small business. One grim fact is that many small businesses die in their infancy. Of the 500,000 to 600,000 new businesses born each year, only half live as long as 18 months and only 1 in 5 lives as long as 10 years.[9]

Perhaps the chief reason for so high a death rate is ease of entry. That is, it often is easier for people to go into business for themselves than to go out and find an employer. For example, if a person wants to launch a computer programming firm, no law stops her or him from doing it. The person may have ten years of experience in computer programming or none at all. He or she may do an exhaustive or a slipshod job of researching the markets. He or she may be financially well off or penniless. Regardless of the qualifications, freedom of opportunity guarantees the right to launch one's own computer programming firm. But freedom of opportunity guarantees us not only the right to succeed but also the right to fail. And failure to recognize this reality often causes hardship and financial loss.

Surface reasons for failure. Although ease of entry may be the root cause of much small business failure, Dun & Bradstreet identifies bad management as the overwhelming reason for failure. They have found that businesses fail for this very reason year after year. Listed in Table 22.2, and presented

7. See *The Gallup Report* (Princeton, N.J.: The Gallup Organization, July 1979), p. 1.

8. See the White House Commission on Small Business, *Report to the President: American Small Business Economy, Agenda for Action* (Washington, D.C.: U.S. Government Printing Office, April 1980), p. 9.

9. These statistics are "rough estimates" made by Dun & Bradstreet in 1969 as reported in the *Wall Street Journal* on April 10, 1969. These estimates probably still hold true today (per author's communication with Dun & Bradstreet, Inc., New York, March 1983). "For New Small-Firm Owners, Reality Plans Tend to Differ," *Wall Street Journal*, June 28, 1982, p. 15.

Table 22.2 Causes of business failures

Percentage of business failures	Cause of failure	Explanation
44%	Incompetence	Lack of fitness to run the business—physical, moral, or intellectual.
17	Lack of managerial experience	Little, if any, experience managing employees and other resources before going into business.
16	Unbalanced experience	Not well-rounded in marketing, finance, purchasing, and production.
15	Inexperience in line	Little, if any, experience in the product or service before going into business.
1	Neglect	Too little attention to the business, due to bad habits, poor health, or marital difficulties.
1	Fraud or disaster	Fraud: misleading name, false financial statements, premeditated overbuy, or irregular disposal of assets. Disaster: fire, flood, burglary, employees' fraud, or strike (some disasters could have been provided against through insurance).
6 / 100%	Unknown	

Source: Nicholas C. Siropolis, *Small Business Management: A Guide to Entrepreneurship,* 2nd ed. (Boston: Houghton Mifflin, 1982) p. 14. Copyright © 1982 by Houghton Mifflin Company. The first two columns are from *The Business Failure Record* (New York: Dun & Bradstreet, Inc., 1981), p. 12. Used with permission.

graphically in Figure 22.3, the reasons for failure point to bad management. Note that 92 percent fail for such specific reasons as:

1. Heavy operating expenses or slow-paying customers
2. A poor location or competitive weaknesses
3. Inventory difficulties or excessive fixed assets

All of these reasons add up to bad management. However, imposing as these statistics may be, the fact remains that ease of entry is the root cause of failure, with bad management merely the surface reason.

Other perspectives on failure. Although widely accepted as fact, the failure rates we have described may be open to question. For example, Albert Shapero argues:

> The fact is that no one knows the startup rate or the failure rate. In fact, we don't even know what "failure" means. Do we mean bankruptcy? But many people go out of business without declaring bankruptcy, working like hell to settle every debt even though they have to close the doors of their business.
>
> Others close because their owners reach retirement age and have no one to turn the company over to. Still others shut down because they're bored. Are these businesses failures?

Figure 22.3
Surface reasons why
businesses fail

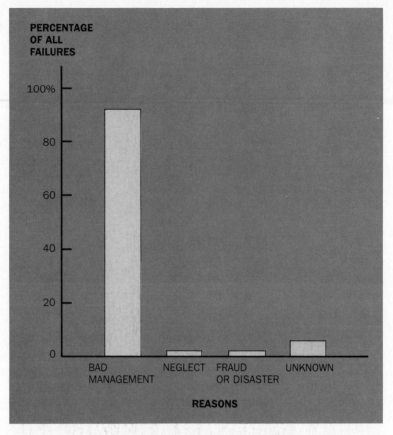

Source: *The Business Failure Record* (New York: Dun & Bradstreet, 1981), p. 12.
By permission of Dun & Bradstreet Credit Services a company of The Dun &
Bradstreet Corporation.

And is failure really failure? Many heroes of business failed at least once.
Henry Ford failed twice. Maybe trying and failing is a better business education than going to a business school that has little concern with small
business. . . .[10]

Minorities and women in small business. Historically, minorities and
women have always played a disproportionately small role in small business.
Although they have made some progress, minorities and women have a long
way to go before they participate in small business to the extent to which they
are represented in the general population. For example, blacks own only
1.7 percent of the nation's 15 million businesses even though they make up
11 percent of the total population. Moreover, their businesses account for less
than one tenth of 1 percent of the total yearly sales volume in the nation.[11]

10. See Albert Shapero, "Numbers That Lie," *Inc.*, May 1981, p. 16.
11. See "Business," *Black Enterprise*, February 1980, p. 55.

Further, women own only 5.0 percent of the nation's businesses even though they make up 51 percent of the total population. Like blacks, they account for less than one tenth of 1 percent of the total yearly sales volume.[12]

Statistics for Hispanics and Native Americans also show that their share of the business world is meager. To help close the gap, many government agencies, both local and federal, have joined with local communities to boost the number of minority small businesses. For example, through its Minority Enterprise Program, the SBA tries to match sound business opportunities with minority persons desirous of becoming small-businesspersons. The SBA then works closely with the minority person, often helping with market analyses and financial statements. Occasionally the SBA also helps the minority entrepreneur to prepare a business plan.

Management of small business

Until just a few years ago, it was the conventional wisdom among managers and researchers that management principles were no respecters of size. For example, the *Harvard Business Review* recently admitted that this view, which it had long held to be true, was false:

> We used to say that most of our articles are as applicable to small as to large companies, implying that management is management and that the proprietors of small companies should not be distracted by the trees from a vision of the forest.
>
> The managers of smaller companies are not persuaded. The environment in which they work is so disorderly, undermanned, cash poor, creative, perilous, and improvisatory that the recommendations of staff specialists seem irrelevant. The consultant and staff experts from a large company become perfectionists as soon as they put pen to paper.
>
> The small-businessperson looks for simplicity and economy and wants his problem broken down into its life and death components. As two of our former contributors . . . summarized what has been our view in recent years, "A small business is not a little big business." However much it needs management, a small company should not be *run* as if it were a large corporation.[13]

In contrast to their counterparts in big business, managers of small business generally must be able to handle a wider variety of problems and situations. They often must be their own troubleshooter, lawyer, planner, bookkeeper, financier, systems analyst, salesperson, marketing researcher, board of directors, purchasing agent, and even clerk–typist. In short, they often have no recourse but to stand alone.

One person who failed because he ignored this reality about smaller busi-

---

12. See U.S. Department of Commerce, *Selected Characteristics of Women-Owned Businesses* (Washington, D.C.: U.S. Government Printing Office, October 1980), p. 1.

13. See Kenneth R. Andrews, "Letter from the Editor," *Harvard Business Review*, January–February 1983, p. 1.

nesses was John Z. De Lorean. A former top executive with General Motors, in 1979 De Lorean founded the ill-fated De Lorean Motor Company to make sports cars. It failed three years later because De Lorean had not realized the role GM's organization had played in his success there. De Lorean had experts at GM to handle many of the operational details of marketing, manufacturing, finance, and so forth. In his own company, he did not have these experts to call on.[14]

Clearly, then, managing a small business well is a far different thing from managing a big business well. What kinds of managerial skills do small-businesspersons need? And how should they best apply such skills? These and related questions will be discussed in the following sections.

Planning the small business

Planning plays a pivotal part in how well a small-businessperson does business, yet perhaps no other function is ignored more than planning. Many small-businesspersons see planning as a function best done only by giant corporations such as General Motors or IBM.

One reason for this attitude is that small-businesspersons tend to have more technical skills than analytical, conceptual or diagnostic skills. Manufacturing requires technical skills, as do selling and purchasing. Planning, on the other hand, requires conceptual, analytical, and diagnostic skills that tend to intimidate small-businesspersons. It is not a tangible activity, so they tend to ignore it. And, in so doing, they often undermine the potential success of their venture before even starting the business.

In any case, let us now look at planning for the small business from two viewpoints: before start-up and after start-up.

Planning before start-up

To bring their ideas for a product or service to fruition, small-businesspersons must do a thorough job of planning. They may think: Why should I spend my time drawing up a *business plan?* The answer is simply that they cannot afford not to. An increasingly complex economy such as ours demands such planning.

At one time, it was possible to succeed in business simply through long hours and hard work. While long hours and hard work may still be important, increasingly complex technology, markets, and other environmental factors necessitate paying more attention to planning.[15]

The very act of preparing a business plan forces small-businesspersons to crystallize their thinking on what they must do to launch their business successfully—from the moment they decide to go into business for themselves

14. See Craig R. Waters, "John De Lorean and the Icarus Factor," *Inc.*, April 1983, p. 35.

15. See U.S. Small Business Administration, "Business Plan for Small Manufacturers," *Management Aid No. 218* (Washington, D.C.: U.S. Government Printing Office, 1973), p. 3.

through the moment they open for business. In essence, the business plan forces them to develop their business on paper before investing time and money in a business that may have little chance of success.

The idea of a business plan is hardly new. Big business has been engaged in planning for years. What *is* new is the growing use of business plans by small-businesspersons, mostly because creditors and investors whom they approach for money demand such a plan. These outside pressures are healthy because a business plan makes small-businesspersons better appreciate what it may take to succeed, and because a business plan gives investors and creditors better information on which to decide whether to help finance the small business.

What should the business plan cover? To begin with, it should match the small-businessperson's abilities with the requirements for a particular product or service. And it should define strategies for such activities as production and marketing, legal aspects and organization, and accounting and finance. It should answer such questions as:

1. What do I want and what am I capable of doing? What are my strengths?
2. What are the most workable ways of achieving my goals?
3. What can I expect in the future?

Some idea of the complexity of planning a new business may be gleaned from Figure 22.4.[16] This figure shows how the key steps in launching a new business are related. Note that the business plan really consists of a set of specific activities having to do with such things as marketing research and marketing mix, location, and production.

Of these activities, perhaps none is more pivotal than marketing research, which may be defined as the systematic and intensive study of all those facts, opinions, and judgments that bear on the successful marketing of a product or service—in short, fact finding. Clearly, the more small-businesspersons know about their markets, the greater their chances of creating customers at a profit. It is also largely through marketing research that small-businesspersons may establish how best to serve their customers uniquely. It often takes being different to be better than competitors in the marketplace.

Note also in Figure 22.4 that small-businesspersons cannot forecast their sales revenues without first researching their markets. In fact, the sales forecast is one of the most important elements in the business plan. Without such a forecast, for example, it would be all but impossible to estimate intelligently the size of a plant, store, or office. Nor would it be possible to determine how much inventory to carry or how many employees to hire.

Another important activity is the financial plan, which translates all other activities into dollars. Generally, the financial plan is made up of these statements:

---

16. See Siropolis, *Small Business Management: A Guide to Entrepreneurship*, pp. 137–150.

Figure 22.4
A flow diagram showing how the steps in the business plan relate

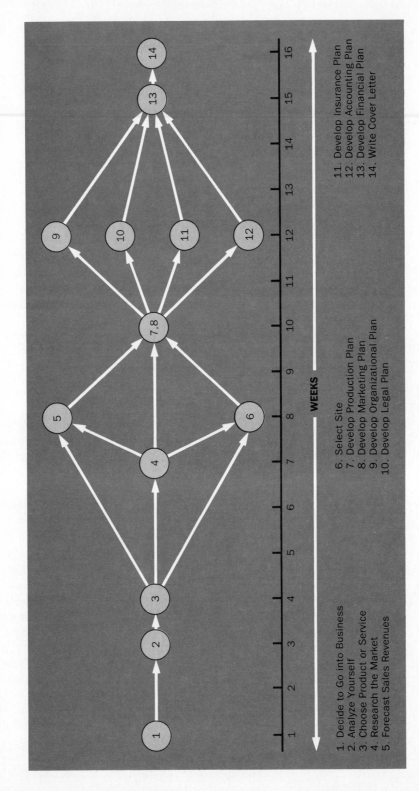

WEEKS

1. Decide to Go into Business
2. Analyze Yourself
3. Choose Product or Service
4. Research the Market
5. Forecast Sales Revenues
6. Select Site
7. Develop Production Plan
8. Develop Marketing Plan
9. Develop Organizational Plan
10. Develop Legal Plan
11. Develop Insurance Plan
12. Develop Accounting Plan
13. Develop Financial Plan
14. Write Cover Letter

Source: Nicholas C. Siropolis, *Small Business Management: A Guide to Entrepreneurship*, 2nd ed. (Boston: Houghton Mifflin, 1982), p. 141. Copyright © 1982 by Houghton Mifflin Company. Used with permission.

1. A cash budget
2. An income statement
3. Balance sheets
4. A break-even chart

The most important of these statements is the cash budget, because it tells small-businesspersons how much money they need *before* they open for business, and how much money they need *after* they open for business.

Planning after start-up

As vital as planning is before start-up, it is equally vital after start-up. Most small-businesspersons want their business to grow. Often, however, growth occurs erratically because they forget an important lesson they learned before launching their business—that planning helps to keep their business on track.

Some small-businesspersons contribute to their own failure by not continuing to plan their progress and assuming that planning takes place only before, not after, the birth of their business. This failure to continue planning is often the reason why so many small businesses grow erratically, stand still, or go under.

Many small businesses exhibit the pattern of growth shown in Figure 22.5. It is in the *acceptance stage* that small-businesspersons generally struggle to break even. Often, however, they are so close to their business that they

Figure 22.5
Stages in the growth of a business

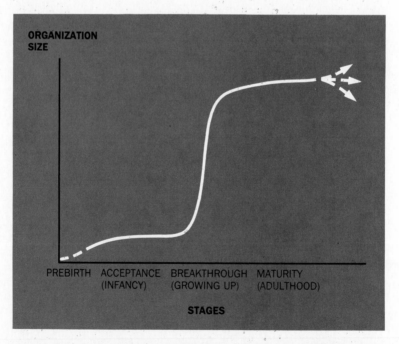

Source: Adapted from Nicholas C. Siropolis, *Small Business Management: A Guide to Entrepreneurship,* 2nd ed. (Boston: Houghton Mifflin, 1982), p. 318. Copyright © 1982 by Houghton Mifflin Company. Used with permission.

can spot obstacles and act quickly to remove them. For example, without some contracts in hand, a small-businessperson who leases factory space to make vinegar expects the first few months to be lean. It will probably take some time to "debug" the vinegar-making equipment and to ensure it makes vinegar that meets uniformly the quality standards of prospective customers; to make vinegar with negligible waste and at low cost; and to convince prospective customers, especially food chains, to buy the vinegar, generally on a trial basis. Meanwhile, with sales limping along, the cash drain becomes severe as bills and wages must be paid. There is little relief until the marketplace begins to accept the vinegar. Then, and only then, do cash inflows begin to match and finally overtake cash outflows—perhaps months after start-up.

Next follows the *breakthrough stage.* Until now, the rate of growth has been slow—so slow that it often passes unnoticed. But in the breakthrough stage, growth is so fast that small-businesspersons often fail to keep up with it. Caught unprepared, they often blunder. Sales revenues continue to spiral upward as problems begin to surface that cry out for attention. For example, problems may arise with

1. **Cash flow.** Will we have the cash when it comes time to pay our bills?
2. **Production.** Are we keeping our costs down in ways that are consistent with making a high-quality product?
3. **Quality.** Are we handling customer complaints by guaranteeing uniformly high quality?
4. **Delivery.** Are we delivering promptly on all customer orders?

At the same time, competition may become more severe. In the face of all these pressures, small-businesspersons often react rather than respond. They apply ill-conceived solutions to problems. For example, if sales begin to level off or slip, they may add such specialists as an accountant, a quality control analyst, or a customer services representative to relieve the problem.

As a result, costs go up momentarily, squeezing profits further. Meanwhile, small-businesspersons try to regain the flexibility they lost shortly after breakthrough, and the cycle of growth begins to repeat itself as they pass through the *maturity stage.*

The best way to head off the problems of growth is to continue updating the business plan. For example, continuing to update their financial plan can equip small-businesspersons better to head off cash-flow problems. Here the cash budget is especially useful, because it will alert them to future shortages in cash.

Organizing the small business

Given the high level of environmental uncertainty that exists today, few small-businesspersons have the skills needed to succeed on their own. Until World War II they worked in a world of few regulations, few taxes, few big competitors, few records, and no computers, but simplicity has since given way to complexity. Major corporations such as AT&T and Du Pont employ thousands of specialists. Du Pont, for example, has more than 600 marketing researchers, most of whom have at least a Master's degree. Such expert help is, of course, beyond the reach of most small-businesspersons, so they often have no choice but to stand alone.

Clearly small-businesspersons need help to survive and grow, and they must identify what kinds of help they need. To do so, they need to plan their organization before they launch their business and they need to continue updating their plan as the business grows. Yet despite the need for it, organizing is ignored by many (if not most) small-businesspersons. They fail to see how powerful a managerial function it really is. They ignore the fact that organizing carries their business, embodies its goals, and shapes all its personal and operating relations.

Defining skill needs

With limited resources, small-businesspersons have no recourse but to define their organization in terms of skills rather than in terms of persons. Usually they cannot afford to hire a full-time accountant or a full-time marketing researcher. Even so, they must plan their organization as though they *could* afford such specialists. Only by going through such a procedure can they assure

Table 22.3 Identifying skill needs

Step number	Description of step	Skill needed	Expert best suited to meet need	
			Entrepreneur	Other
1	Decide to go into business	Knowledge of self	✓	
2	Analyze yourself		✓	
3	Pick product or service		✓	
4	Research the market	Knowledge of marketing research		Marketing researcher
5	Forecast sales revenues			Marketing researcher
6	Select site			Marketing researcher
7	Develop production plan	Knowledge of chemical engineering	✓	
8	Develop marketing plan	Knowledge of marketing		Advertising account executive
9	Develop organizational plan	Knowledge of skill needs	✓	
10	Develop legal plan	Knowledge of law		Lawyer
11	Develop insurance plan	Knowledge of insurance		Insurance agent
12	Develop accounting plan	Knowledge of accounting		Accountant
13	Develop financial plan	Knowledge of finance		Loan officer
14	Write cover letter	Knowledge of venture	✓	

Source: Nicholas C. Siropolis, *Small Business Management: A Guide to Entrepreneurship,* 2nd ed. (Boston: Houghton Mifflin, 1982) p. 255. Copyright © 1982 by Houghton Mifflin Company. Used with permission.

Figure 22.6
Types of help
available to small-
businesspersons

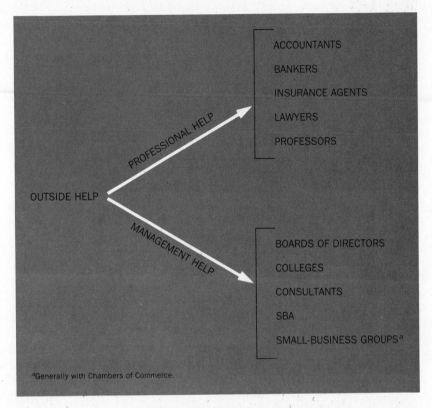

Source: Nicholas C. Siropolis, *Small Business Management: A Guide to Entrepreneurship*, 2nd ed. (Boston: Houghton Mifflin, 1982), p. 261. Copyright © 1982 by Houghton Mifflin Company. Used with permission.

themselves that needed skills have not been overlooked.

For example, if a chemical engineer were about to go into plastics manufacturing, he might begin defining his organization by asking himself, "What skills do I need to earn a net profit of $10,000 on sales of $200,000 by the end of my first year in business?" Let us assume that the chemical engineer has just invented a new process to make Fiberglas-reinforced plastic for sports cars like the Corvette. This process is faster and cheaper than the present one. Ready to exploit his invention, the chemical engineer must now define the specific skills needed to make his business a reality. A good place to begin is with the business plan we described earlier. Following the plan's outline in Figure 22.4, he might analyze the skills needed for the business via a skill needs assessment as shown in Table 22.3.[17] Note in the table that the engineer himself is best qualified to complete six of the steps shown. For the rest, he recognizes that he must rely on outside experts. Such help may come from a variety of sources, as suggested in Figure 22.6.

As shown in Figure 22.6, small-businesspersons like the chemical

17. *Ibid.*, pp. 253–255.

engineer in our example need outside professional help from accountants, bankers, lawyers, and insurance agents. We will say more later about the outside management help available, often at *no* cost, to the small-businessperson.

Job descriptions

The manager also needs to establish *job descriptions* that spell out who does what, who has what authority, and who reports to whom. Job descriptions spare small-businesspersons the problems associated with people not knowing exactly what their job involves, whom they report to, and so on.[18]

Organization charts

Many large organizations find themselves too large and complex to adequately chart all their positions and interrelationships. Such a chart, however, can be very useful for a small business. The small business manager should recognize, though, that such charts have their limitations. Although they symbolize how a small-businessperson plans to get out the work, they often *impress* more than they *express*. Few small businesses run precisely the way their organization charts indicate. In a growing business, for example, they may soon become dated. Or unpredictable events may change the course of a small-businessperson's plans. For these reasons and others, small-businesspersons often update their organization charts at least once a year.

Perhaps the chief value of an *organization chart* is that the very act of putting one together forces small-businesspersons to crystallize their thinking beforehand on what work must be done to make their business profitable, and how the work should be done.

Without such forethought, organization charts may have little value. Organization charts are also limited in that they cannot show how all the jobs within a small business are related. To try to do so would result in a chart with solid and broken lines criss-crossing the page in undecipherable confusion. A good organization chart is a simple one that highlights only those jobs and lines of authority that are crucial to the goals of the small business. An organization chart must communicate if it is to be effective.

Management help

Another aspect of organizing in the small business is the identification of sources of assistance. Since the 1950s, the idea that small businesses need management assistance has become increasingly widespread. Table 22.4 lists the many sources of management help now offered at little or no cost to small-businesspersons, either before or after they go into business for themselves. Different services are available to small-businesspersons who go into a high-technology business and to those who go into a low-technology business, because of the depth of management sophistication needed to launch a high-technology business such as microcomputer manufacture.

18. See Marvin Bower, *The Will to Manage* (New York: McGraw-Hill, 1966), p. 153.

Table 22.4 Sources of help for small business

Management help offered by	Where available	For small-businesspersons			
		Before they go into a business whose technology is		After they go into a business whose technology is	
		High	Low	High	Low
U.S. Small Business Administration					
Counseling by:					
Staff	N				✓
Service Corps of Retired Executives	N				✓
Active Corps of Executives	N				✓
Small Business Institutes	N			✓	✓
Small Business Development Centers	S	✓	✓	✓	✓
Prebusiness workshops	N		✓		
Nonaccredited courses and seminars	N				✓
Publications	N		✓		✓
U.S. Department of Commerce					
Seminars and workshops	N			✓	✓
Publications	N	✓	✓	✓	✓
Other federal agencies (example: IRS[a])					
Seminars and workshops	N				✓
Publications	N				✓
State, county, and local governments					
Counseling	S				✓
Seminars and workshops	S				✓
Publications	S				✓
Local development corporations and the like					
Counseling	N				✓
Seminars and workshops	N				✓
Universities					
Accredited courses	S	✓	✓	✓	✓
Nonaccredited courses and seminars	S				✓
Publications	S	✓	✓	✓	✓
Counseling	S				
Community colleges					
Accredited courses	S				✓
Nonaccredited courses and seminars	N				✓
Counseling	S				✓

[a]U.S. Internal Revenue Service.   N = Nationally   S = Some parts of nation

(continued)

Table 22.4 Sources of help for small business, *cont.*

Management help offered by	Where available	For small-businesspersons			
		Before they go into a business whose technology is		After they go into a business whose technology is	
		High	Low	High	Low
Small-business groups (example: NFIB[b])					
Seminars and workshops	S				
Counseling	S				√
Publications	N				√
					√
Large corporations (example: Bank of America)					
Publications	N		√		√
Counseling	S				√
Trade associations					
Publications	N			√	√
Seminars and workshops	N			√	√

[b]National Federation of Independent Business. S = Some parts of nation   N = Nationally

Source: Nicholas C. Siropolis, *Small Business Management: A Guide to Entrepreneurship,* 2nd ed. (Boston: Houghton Mifflin, 1982), p. 265. Copyright © 1982 by Houghton Mifflin Company. Used with permission.

Note that Table 22.4 covers not only federal help but also help from such other sources as community colleges and universities, Chambers of Commerce, and organizations made up of small businesses. Heading the list is the SBA. Since it was founded in 1953, the SBA has helped hundreds of thousands of small businesses.

Most small-businesspersons have the mistaken view that all the SBA does is lend money or guarantee repayment of loans made by commercial banks. Even *more* important, however, are the SBA's efforts to help them manage better. Any small-businessperson can spend money; the SBA's programs help them to spend it wisely. As one small-business expert puts it:

> No small business ever failed because of a lack of funds. The supply of funds and the availability of cash to meet obligations is merely a thermometer that measures the wisdom and discipline with which the small-businessperson has committed his funds. When and if he runs clean out of working cash, his thermometer reading is zero. It indicates his inability to live within his means.[19]

Though it is an exaggeration, the foregoing comment underscores the cardinal importance of management skills in any business, big or small. What

19. See Louis L. Allen, *Starting and Succeeding in Your Own Small Business* (New York: Grosset & Dunlap, 1968), p. 28.

counts most is the small-businessperson's skill in managing resources, of which money is only one. The SBA offers small-businesspersons four major management assistance programs:

SCORE (Service Corps of Retired Executives)
ACE (Active Corps of Executives)
SBI (Small Business Institute)
SBDC (Small Business Development Center)

All four programs offer management help *at no charge* to the small-businessperson. Under the SCORE program, the SBA tries to match the expert to the need. If a small-businessperson needs, say, a marketing plan and does not know how to put one together, the SBA pulls from its list of SCORE counselors someone with marketing knowledge and experience to help the small-businessperson.

The SBI program taps the talents available at colleges and universities. This program involves not only professors of business administration but also students working for advanced degrees. Under a professor's guidance, such students work with small-businesspersons to help solve their management problems.

Leading the small business

Small-businesspersons must also provide effective leadership if they are to succeed. It is part of leadership to help employees satisfy their own personal goals and at the same time enable them to work easily and productively. There are several things that managers can do along these lines.

First, small-businesspersons must want to help their employees become achievers. Some do not, holding fast to the idea that employees do not care about deriving satisfaction from their jobs. This attitude can cause such problems as absenteeism and high turnover, shoddy workmanship, and a decline in the employees' motivation to work.

Small-businesspersons are also very much like athletic coaches in many ways. Just as coaches must be close to their players to be effective as leaders, so must small-businesspersons be close to their employees. Topflight coaches generally have teams that win consistently, mostly because they know their jobs and have a knack for communicating that knowledge to their players.

Players see their assignments clearly because their coach helps them understand what is expected of them.
Players know how to carry out their assignments because their coach has meticulously laid out the game plan and the plays to use against the competition.
Players carry out their assignments with precision because their coach has created an atmosphere of fairness, confidence, and camaraderie, which generates the will to win.

Creating such a work atmosphere is difficult. No two players, or employees, are exactly alike. What appeals to one may repel another. Because all employees are unique and complex, small-businesspersons must understand their needs in order to help them do their best.

Third, small-businesspersons, as leaders, can help employees achieve status and gain a better opinion of themselves and their jobs. They may do so in a variety of ways, which include sharing decision-making responsibilities with employees, giving employees greater responsibility as soon as they are ready for it, taking employees' ideas and suggestions to heart, and judging employees rigorously on merit and rewarding them accordingly.

Small-businesspersons who follow these suggestions are more likely to succeed than those who do not. And, by building up their employees' self-image and improving their status, small-businesspersons are likely to grow as leaders themselves.

Of all the traits small-businesspersons must possess if they are to be effective leaders, perhaps none is so vital as the pursuit of excellence day in and day out. The small-businessperson must set the tone that helps motivate employees to excel. As noted by the famed football coach Vince Lombardi, "You don't try to win some of the time. You don't try to do things right some of the time. You do them right all of the time."[20]

Excellence usually emerges in the context of high employer expectations. If small-businesspersons expect excellence from employees, it often occurs. If not, it rarely occurs. Only highly motivated employees are likely to make and sell superior products that cause customers to develop loyalty to the business.

Small-businesspersons generally want their employees to be loyal to the business too, and some believe their employees should be blindly loyal to them. They expect employees to stick by them through good times and bad, regardless of how the employees are treated. Such unthinking loyalty, however, weakens rather than strengthens a small business. True loyalty means working up to one's capabilities and doing the best one can in the pursuit of excellence. In essence, then, true loyalty is loyalty to the job, not to the small-businessperson.

Controlling the small business

Discussion of this managerial function will bring us full circle. Without control, the other three managerial functions—planning, organizing, and leading—lose meaning, for only by practicing control can small-businesspersons tell how effective the other three functions are.

It is never enough just to set goals and then organize and lead to meet those goals. Small-businesspersons must also measure their progress at frequent intervals. To do that, they need information that tells them whether their goals are being met. Yet, despite its cardinal importance, control tends to be ignored by many small-businesspersons. One reason may be their dis-

---

20. From a film produced by the U.S. Small Business Administration, *The Habit of Winning*, 1972.

comfort with numbers, and to many, control is a function practiced only by big business.

With this attitude, it is hardly surprising that so many small-businesspersons find themselves in trouble from the start. They fail to see that control is simply the process by which they may assure themselves that their actions, as well as those of their employees, conform to plans and policies. Especially vital in such a process is accounting information, which may be useful in the following ways:

As a means of communication, helping to inform employees of the actions that the small-businessperson wishes them to take.

As a means of motivation, helping to motivate employees in such a way that they will do what the small-businessperson wants them to do.

As a means of checking up, helping the small-businessperson to assess how well the employees are doing their jobs. Such an appraisal of performance may result in salary increases, promotion, reassignment, or corrective action of various kinds.[21]

Thus the key element of the control process is the information that allows small-businesspersons to compare actual performance with planned performance. This information allows them to measure not only their performance but also the propriety of their goals and actions—and, if need be, to adjust them.

To illustrate the importance of control to the small business, consider the example of one small contracting firm. Elling Brothers Mechanical Contractors specializes in the design and installation of piping systems. After moving into the installation of custom and made-to-order systems, the company realized that tighter control was needed. On one job alone, Elling had lost $250,000 on small cost overruns that escalated and snowballed over the course of a 15-month job. Following a set of guidelines developed by a consultant, Elling implemented a new control system that saved the company. In 1981 Elling recorded pretax profits of 6 percent on sales of $12.2 million.[22]

Budgeting

This is perhaps the most vital control tool for a small business. It is the budget that translates operating plans into dollar terms or other quantitative measures. To see how the budget helps small-businesspersons control their operations better, let us go through an extended example.

A Buick dealer, Georgia Qua, expresses her new-car sales in units, as shown in Table 22.5. This unit budget is used by her sales manager to control the performance of salespeople. Here, units and not dollars have real meaning to sales representatives, but at the sales manager's level, dollars assume importance as a control. To meet his unit goal of 2,000 new-car sales a year, the sales manager might over-react and tell his salespeople to sell at a discount or

21. See Robert N. Anthony and James S. Reece, *Accounting* (Homewood, Il.: Irwin, 1979), p. 5.
22. See Matthew Berke, "Elling Bros. Got Costs Under Control," *Inc.*, January 1982, pp. 45–50.

Table 22.5 New-car sales budget (in units)

Model	Quarter				Total
	First	Second	Third	Fourth	
Small	200	300	300	200	1,000
Medium	100	150	150	100	500
Large	100	150	150	100	500
	400	600	600	400	2,000

Source: Nicholas C. Siropolis, *Small Business Management: A Guide to Entrepreneurship,* 2nd ed. (Boston: Houghton Mifflin, 1982) p. 326. Copyright © 1982 by Houghton Mifflin Company. Used with permission.

Table 22.6 New-car sales budget (net of trade-in)

Model	Quarter				Total
	First	Second	Third	Fourth	
Small	$ 600,000	$ 900,000	$ 900,000	$ 600,000	$3,000,000
Medium	450,000	675,000	675,000	450,000	2,250,000
Large	600,000	900,000	900,000	600,000	3,000,000
	$1,650,000	$2,475,000	$2,475,000	$1,650,000	$8,250,000

Source: Nicholas C. Siropolis, *Small Business Management: A Guide to Entrepreneurship,* 2nd ed. (Boston: Houghton Mifflin, 1982) p. 326. Copyright © 1982 by Houghton Mifflin Company. Used with permission.

accept trade-ins that erode profit margins. To avoid that problem, Qua prepares another budget, this one translating units into dollars (see Table 22.6). This control system is still incomplete, because the sales manager may overspend in his efforts to reach his unit goal of 2,000 new-car sales a year. So Qua prepares a third budget, this one dealing with selling expenses (see Table 22.7). Armed with these three budgets, Qua is now prepared to control the performance of her new-car sales department. By providing them with the information they need to make sound decisions, these budgets also encourage the sales manager and his salespeople to do their best. And these budgets enable Qua to evaluate the performance of her sales manager, and her sales manager to evaluate the performance of his sales force.[23]

Productivity

Many small businesses have begun to turn to automation and robotics to boost output per employee, especially in manufacturing. A Connecticut die casting plant, for example, installed 7 robots and achieved a 30 percent increase in productivity.[24]

23. Siropolis, *Small Business Management: A Guide to Entrepreneurship,* pp. 325–326.
24. See Craig R. Waters, "There's a Robot in Your Future," *Inc.,* June 1982, pp. 64–74.

Table 22.7 New-car selling expense budget

Item	Quarter				Total
	First	**Second**	**Third**	**Fourth**	**Total**
Salaries	$100,000	$100,000	$100,000	$100,000	$400,000
Commissions	50,000	75,000	75,000	50,000	250,000
Advertising	10,000	20,000	30,000	20,000	80,000
Telephone	500	500	500	500	2,000
Total	$160,500	$195,500	$205,500	$170,500	$732,000

Source: Nicholas C. Siropolis, *Small Business Management: A Guide to Entrepreneurship,* 2nd ed. (Boston: Houghton Mifflin, 1982) p. 327. Copyright © 1982 by Houghton Mifflin Company. Used with permission.

Of course, given the cost of robots (now about $50,000 each), small-businesspersons should be sure of what they are doing before investing heavily in automation. But a small business that, by whatever means, achieves a reasonable level of productivity increases its chances of surviving the early, critical years and building a pattern of long-term growth.

Summary of key points

Of the nation's 15 million businesses, 99 percent qualify as small, even if we define a small business as one that employs fewer than 100 persons. Small business is at the center of modern society, touching all our lives. Few if any parts of our economy could run without its endless flow of products and services. Equally important, its ingenuity sparks invention and innovation.

To a degree not generally recognized, managing a small business differs sharply from managing a big business. One major difference is that, in order to succeed, small-businesspersons must possess a broad spectrum of skills ranging from production to marketing to finance. Unlike their counterparts in big business, who often have hundreds of professional specialists at their disposal, small-businesspersons generally have no choice but to stand alone.

Small-businesspersons who ignore the planning function lay the foundation for their own failure even before launching their business. Preparation of a business plan is critical to the success of any small business, both before and after start-up.

With limited resources, small-businesspersons must plan their organization in terms of skills rather than persons. Usually they cannot afford to hire a full-time accountant or a full-time marketing researcher. Even so, they must plan their organization as though they could afford them; only then can they assure themselves that needed skills and talents have not been overlooked.

Small-businesspersons must provide effective leadership if they are to succeed. Without such leadership they are unlikely to attract and retain talented employees, who may prefer the excitement of a small but growing business to a big business that offers a host of fringe benefits and greater job security.

Only through practicing the managerial function of control may small-businesspersons give meaning to the managerial functions of planning, organizing, and leading. It is the means by which they can assure themselves that their actions, as well as those of employees, conform to their plans and policies.

QUESTIONS FOR DISCUSSION

1. On the basis of your own observations, is small business thriving or declining? Justify your answer.
2. Why do so many small businesses fail in the first few years of their existence? Explain fully.
3. Should all men and women be screened before they go into business for themselves? Why or why not?
4. How does managing a small business differ from managing a big business? Give examples.
5. Why is the business plan as vital to investors and creditors as it is to small-businesspersons?
6. How does planning after start-up of a business differ from planning before start-up?
7. How does organizing for a small business differ from organizing for a big business?
8. How helpful are organization charts? Explain fully.
9. Which is more important to the small-businessperson, management help or financial help? Explain fully.
10. If you were a small-businessperson, how would you compete for top-notch talent if you could not afford to pay the same wages and salaries that large corporations can pay?
11. Comment on the following statement made by a small-businessperson: "We really need to take a hard look at behavior in our shop. Our workers are totally unmotivated. So nothing gets done when it should or in the way that it should be done."
12. In your opinion, why do small-businesspersons often fail to plan, organize, lead, and control in the ways suggested in the chapter?
13. Is budgeting a planning tool, a control tool, or both? Explain fully.

CASE 22.1

At the beginning of this chapter you read a scenario about a college student approaching graduation with a degree in botany. For the past three and a half years, he has managed a local garden shop. He could keep this position but doesn't really think he wants

Elements of success in starting up Bill's Garden Center

to work for someone else. The student being described was a real person, Bill Oglevee. The case that follows explains what Bill did and then raises some other issues for your consideration.

Bill Oglevee moved to Bryan, Texas, in 1969 and enrolled in Texas A&M University. After exploring the fields of chemistry and mathematics, Bill eventually decided to major in botany. Because his father and uncle were involved in the florist industry and his cousin was a major plant grower and supplier, the plant sciences had an understandable appeal to Bill. He subsequently took the job of manager of Hardy Gardens, the area's largest nursery.

During his three and a half years there, Bill acquired an appreciation for the nursery business, developed good working relationships with the major suppliers, and decided that this was the field he would enjoy working in for the rest of his life. He also decided, however, that he wanted his own nursery, rather than simply working for someone else.

When he graduated in 1975, Bill set things in motion to establish his own nursery. The main barrier was financial but, working through a local bank, he was able to obtain a $20,000 loan from the SBA. In December 1975, he found a site for his business. The building was a gas station that had failed during the energy crunch. It was located along Texas Avenue, the major thoroughfare connecting Bryan and its neighboring city, College Station. Moreover, the location was far from North Bryan, which was experiencing serious economic decline, and close to the rapidly growing College Station. On the negative side, Bill had to work within the physical constraints of a building that was designed to serve as a gas station and had limited parking space.

Then an unexpected snag developed. Bill wanted to be open by February in order to take advantage of the spring planting season. The SBA, however, indicated that they could not get his funds to him until July. Fortunately, his father was able to provide a bridge loan, and Bill's Garden Center opened in February 1976.

Almost from day one, Bill's Garden Center was a success. The winter months are bad for garden centers, and during the first couple of years the nursery's financial reserves were just about depleted. Spring sales grew each year, however, and the company was on firm footing by the third year. By 1981 Bill's Garden Center was a solid success with annual sales in excess of $450,000.

Also from day one, Bill knew he wanted to eventually open another garden center. The new center would be designed from the ground up and would be a true "state-of-the-art" nursery. Bill estimated that he needed $400,000 for his new center. He obtained these funds from a local bank in 1982 and purchased 1.5 acres of land in South College Station on Texas Avenue. This location, he reasoned, was in the center of a growing residential area, was easily accessible, and was large enough to satisfy the projected needs of the business.

He also made a strategic decision to develop and maintain a different image for the new center. The name chosen was Sunset

Gardens. By differentiating between the centers, Bill felt that he would enable each to handle its own unique product lines, establish its own pricing structure, and run its own promotions without confusing the public. In particular, Sunset Gardens would carry a more expensive selection of plants to appeal to the more affluent residents in its market area. The new center would also have a separate landscaping service.

Ground was broken for Sunset Gardens in early 1983, with the grand opening set for September. Bill's Garden Center was performing at an annual sales level of around $700,000 and Bill predicted that the two nurseries combined would have sales in excess of $1.5 million in 1984.

CASE
QUESTIONS

1. Why do you think Bill Oglevee has been so successful in the nursery business?
2. What threats do you see that might hurt Bill's operations in the future?
3. Discuss the advantages and disadvantages of developing a new image for Sunset Gardens and differentiating it from Bill's Garden Center.

CASE
REFERENCE

Personal communication with Bill Oglevee.

C A S E 22.2

Jeffrey Brooks has a dilemma. At the age of 26, he had resigned from a lucrative management position and opened a small men's clothing store. After a couple of difficult years, the business flourished. Jeffrey eventually opened three more clothing stores and then sold the company for a handsome profit. But three months of boredom convinced him that he wasn't ready to retire. He took a management position with a big company but again realized that he wanted to be his own boss. Using the remaining profits from the sale of his clothing stores, he struck out on his own once again. This time he decided to open a construction firm.

The business got off to a decent start but soon floundered. Jeffrey quickly came to the conclusion that, although he was a good manager, he knew little about the technical side of things. He entered into an agreement with Paul Hansen, his general foreman, whereby Hansen became a partner in the company. Brooks was to provide general management expertise while Hansen attended to the operating side. After five years of this arrangement, Brooks and Hansen began to quarrel over how the company should be managed. Brooks sold out to Hansen and, at the age of 45, retired again.

An entrepreneur's successive ventures

Shortly after his forty-seventh birthday, Jeffrey decided that his retirement had been premature. He was again restless and wanted to get back into business. This time he decided to open a restaurant.

The town in which Jeffrey lives is a medium-sized community dominated by a large state university. (The success of his first business was partially attributable to the fact that he attracted the student business, and his construction firm did much of its work for the university.) For the restaurant venture, however, Jeffrey saw an opportunity to move away from the university. He recognized that all the restaurants around town were planned to appeal to the university community, so he reasoned that there existed a sizable demand for a quality restaurant designed to attract nonuniversity patrons. He purchased a building across town from the university and, six months later, opened an adult-oriented restaurant featuring steaks and fresh seafood. The restaurant was a tremendous success from the very first. Brooks attracted a large and loyal following.

By the time he was 56, Brooks had put away enough money to assure his comfort and security for the rest of his life. Further, he has just received a very attractive offer from another party to buy the restaurant. Jeffrey has two weeks to make a decision about whether to accept the offer.

CASE
QUESTIONS

1. Should Brooks sell the restaurant? Why or why not?

2. Why has Brooks been so successful with his various enterprises?

23

MANAGING IN THE INTERNATIONAL SECTOR

CHAPTER OBJECTIVES

1. Describe the nature of international management, including the levels of international involvement.

2. Discuss how the economic, political, and cultural dimensions of the environment are particularly relevant to international management.

3. Identify key elements in the decision to go international, international strategic planning, and international action planning.

4. Cite factors that influence international organization design and describe the three general design alternatives.

5. Discuss leading in the international sector, especially how it is affected by the social structure, and explain the implications for leadership, motivation, and communication.

6. Describe key areas of international control and discuss the applicability of various control techniques to international settings.

697

OPENING INCIDENT

You are a manager of a large U.S. company that wants to increase its market share in Japan. However, the Japanese market is controlled by one state-owned firm. This firm controls all new-product introductions, advertising, and distribution and helps establish the prices for your products. Current prices are considerably higher than those charged for its own products. As a result, your company has been unable to compete effectively. How would you proceed?

Nestle Enterprises, one of the 50 largest companies in existence, employs 146,000 people and has 300 plants scattered throughout the world. About 41 percent of Nestle's sales come from Europe, 19 percent from North America, 19 percent from Latin America, 14 percent from Asia, and 5 percent from Africa. Takeda Chemical, the largest Japanese drugmaker, does most of its business within the boundaries of its home country. Overseas sales account for just 7 percent of Takeda's total revenues and the company is only now beginning to emphasize international operations. Finally, any domestic Chevrolet dealership does all its business within the confines of the United States but must still compete with Toyota, Mazda, and Volkswagen dealerships. To varying degrees, each of these companies is affected by the international dimension of its general environment. Nestle is truly a multinational firm. Takeda is an organization just moving into the international arena. The Chevrolet dealer is a domestic firm whose products compete with those of foreign manufacturers.[1]

International management is not just domestic management on a grander scale. The complications of different languages, customs, laws, natural resources, and people's expectations add markedly to the complexity of international management. Despite differences of both degree and kind, we can nonetheless make effective use of general management principles in studying international management.

Throughout this book, we have attempted to integrate international management concepts and examples, as appropriate, with other major areas of interest. In this chapter we bring things together in one in-depth discussion. First we describe the nature of international management. Next the environment of international management is explored. Subsequent sections focus on the four managerial functions of planning, organizing, leading, and controlling and how they are related to international management.

---

1. See Robert Ball, "A 'Shopkeeper' Shakes Up Nestle," *Fortune,* December 27, 1982, pp. 103–106; and "Taproots—Takeda's U.S. Moves," *Fortune,* July 12, 1982, p. 11.

The nature of international management

Much of our knowledge of international management comes from research focused on American multinational firms.[2] International activity is far from a purely American phenomenon, of course. Multinationals are based in the United Kingdom (such as Unilever Ltd.), Germany (Siemens AG), the Netherlands (Royal Dutch/Shell), and many other countries. Increasingly, effective studies of multinationalism from other than U.S. perspectives are enriching our knowledge.[3]

Furthermore, in recent years we in the United States have increasingly found ourselves the "host country" (that is, we are the "foreign" location of the multinational company's plant or sales office). Sometimes foreign multinationals establish a manufacturing facility in the United States; Volkswagen recently did this. Sometimes they buy out all or part of a U.S. firm, as did Matsushita of Japan when it bought Motorola's color TV operations. In recent years some U.S. firms have formed joint ventures or become merger partners with stronger foreign firms, as when Renault acquired 46 percent of American Motors Corporation and B.A.T. Industries 80 percent of Marshall Field.

International management can be viewed from a number of perspectives. The Egyptian personnel manager of an American-owned plant in Cairo is involved in international management, as is the American manager of a Japanese-owned factory in Texas. For ease of presentation, however, we will approach the subject largely through the eyes of top management in the home country (principally the United States). Viewed from the top, international management consists of:

1. Relating the organization to its relevant task and general environment dimensions.
2. Planning strategy and operations on as large a scale as feasible, unfettered by national boundaries.
3. Organizing effectively in light of the inherent strengths and weaknesses of different country divisions.
4. Leading people of diverse nationalities in reaching corporate objectives as well as furthering their own ends.
5. Controlling activities that are widely separated in time and place and occur under dramatically different conditions.

Levels of international involvement

As shown in Figure 23.1, there are several different levels of involvement in international operations, ranging from the purely domestic company to immense multinational corporations that rival the size and power of nation–states.

2. For example, see Stanley M. Davis (ed.), *Managing and Organizing Multinational Corporations* (New York: Pergamon, 1978).

3. See Anant R. Neghandi, *Quest for Survival and Growth: A Comparative Study of American, European, and Japanese Multinationals* (New York: Praeger, 1970).

Figure 23.1
Degrees of
international
involvement

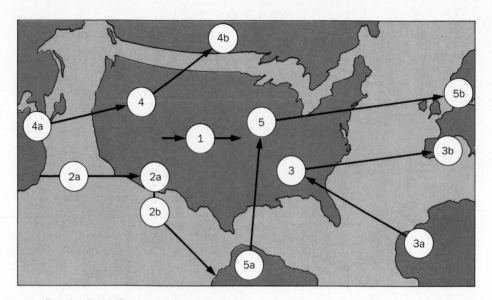

Firm 1.   Purely Domestic Company
Firm 2a. Importer
Firm 2b. Exporter
Firm 3a. Firm with Foreign Purchasing Branch
Firm 3b. Firm with Foreign Sales Branch
Firm 4a. Firm with Extraction, Processing, or Manufacturing Branch or Subsidiary
          Overseas, Primarily to Supply Home Market
Firm 4b. Firm with Processing or Manufacturing Branch or Subsidiary Overseas,
          Primarily Selling to Host Country or Region
Firm 5.   Firm with Foreign Joint-Venture Partners, to Supply Either Home or Host
          Country Markets

Purely domestic companies. This kind of company buys all its inputs in its own country and sells all its outputs within the country. It may feel the influence of international activities but plays no direct international role. For example, it may require an imported raw material, but it buys the material from a domestic supplier who has assumed the risk of importing it. It may also compete with foreign manufacturers.

Importing and exporting companies. These firms engage in international trade, but they are not really involved in international management. At most, they may send a representative overseas from time to time to call on foreign contacts. If they do more, such as establishing offices abroad, they become like the type 3 firms.

Firms with foreign purchasing and sales branches. These firms undertake the first truly international management tasks. They own resources abroad and they accept responsibility for employees. Even if they lease their offices, furniture, and equipment, they retain ownership of their own products (rather than selling them, say, through consignment).

Firms with processing or manufacturing operations in a foreign country. These firms represent a typical international management situation, and we will focus closely on them in this chapter. Firestone established rubber plantations in Liberia in 1926 to assure a supply of rubber for Akron-made (and largely U.S.-marketed) tires. Similarly, U.S. electronics firms set up assembly plants in Taiwan to supply radios for the U.S. market. In both of these examples, the firms did not regard the foreign country ("host" country) as a possible market for their products, but other type 4 firms both process and sell their products in the host country. For example, Volkswagen of America, a West German firm, built an assembly plant in Virginia to make cars to sell in the United States.

Firms with foreign joint venture partners. The objectives of these firms are often similar to those of type 4 firms, but they choose to set up international joint ventures, or "partnerships," with foreign organizations. Sometimes these arrangements are forced on the parent firm by host-country governments, but they are also undertaken as a means of decentralizing an otherwise huge and unwieldy organization that seeks greater efficiency and effectiveness.

Any firm at level 3, 4, or 5 is called a *multinational.* Because of their large size and substantial economic power, firms such as Exxon, General Motors, and ITT are sometimes compared with nation–states, but such comparisons are usually more damaging than helpful for understanding international management.[4] Large multinationals doubtless have great economic power, but they have that power only as long as they continue to please their host countries and their worldwide customers.

Growth of multinationalism

Any list of the world's largest corporations contains a high percentage of firms with substantial foreign assets, foreign revenue, and profits earned abroad. As recently reported in *Forbes,*[5] the 100 largest U.S. multinationals (ranked by foreign revenues) had $590 billion in foreign assets: 40 percent of their total assets. On these assets, they earned $29 billion in foreign operating profits: 37 percent of their total operating profits of $78 billion. Figure 23.2, which summarizes the status of the 100 largest U.S. multinationals, clearly indicates the extent of U.S. private investment beyond its own borders.

It is also interesting to note the decline of American dominance in the international management arena. In 1963, 67 of the world's 100 largest

4. See Richard J. Barnet and Ronald E. Muller, *Global Reach—The Power of the Multinational Corporations* (New York: Simon and Schuster, 1974).

5. "Spotlight on International Business," *Forbes,* July 5, 1982, pp. 126–128.

Figure 23.2
Aggregate revenues
and assets of the
U.S.' one hundred
largest
multinationals

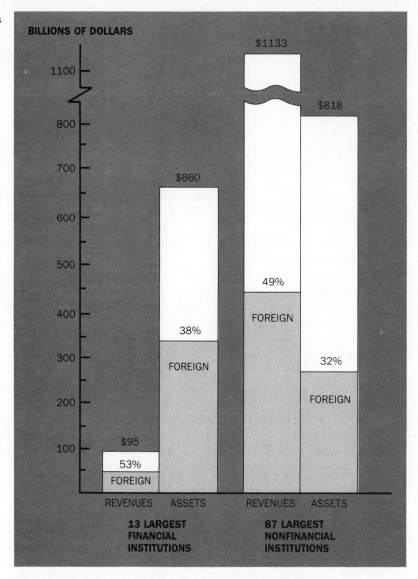

Source: *Forbes*, July 5, 1982, pp. 126–128.

industrial corporations were U.S. firms. By 1971 this number had declined to
58; by 1979 a further decline to 47 was observed. In 1979 the other 53 largest
companies were based in Germany (13), France (11), the United Kingdom and
Japan (7 each), and a number of other countries (15).[6]

Multinational organizations have often been criticized for their actions or
failures to act. For example, Citicorp was recently fined for conducting illegal

6. See "The International Scene," *The Week in Review* (New York: Deloitte, Haskins, & Sells),
May 1, 1981, p. 1.

banking transactions between countries, and Nestle has been charged with unethical promotional techniques in its marketing of infant formula in under-developed Third World countries.[7]

Often, however, the criticism seems to be based only on the size and power of multinationals—on their capacity to inflict harm rather than on their having actually done so. It is inevitable that controversy should swirl about such convenient targets. And the governments of host countries have legitimate concerns about how multinationals conduct their affairs. We hope to show that international management can be not only profitable but responsible and responsive as well. We begin by exploring the environment of international management.

The environment of international management

For convenience of expression and study, we will discuss the environment of international management under three broad headings: economic, political, and cultural. Naturally these three facets of the environment are interrelated. For example, an American multinational manager trying to understand the issues in the British rail strikes of 1982 would find an economic issue (attempts by management to change work rules by introducing "flexible rostering" to replace "fixed eight-hour days") to begin with. The "fixed eight-hour day" went back to 1919, when the rail unions forced rail management to make good on a British government promise (a political issue) made to them in order to gain strike-free cooperation during World War I. But the heat of the 1982 dispute, many would say, arose from a basic mistrust by working people of management's motives in pressing for a change in work rules. That mistrust went so far back in history that it seemed almost a cultural matter related to the separation of the classes in England.

Most analysis of environments should take place at the level of the nation–state. But smaller subdivisions are occasionally relevant. For example, one might wish to compare Northern Ireland, Scotland, or Wales with the Midlands of England for their relative attractiveness as plant sites to serve the United Kingdom market. Each is a part of the U.K., yet they offer different patterns of economic, political, and cultural inducements and disadvantages.

Economic environment

When a firm analyzes the economic environment of a possible host country, it is likely to consider the following:

1. Population and its composition and trends
2. Geographic size and material resources
3. Total and per capita wealth
4. Foreign exchange balance

7. See Roy Rowan, "The Maverick Who Yelled Foul at Citibank," *Fortune*, January 10, 1983, pp. 46–56; and Ball, "A 'Shopkeeper' Shakes Up Nestle."

5. Existing "infrastructure," such as power, transportation, and communications networks and the network of financial institutions
6. Annual total and per capita output of goods and services
7. Competition (for the industry of interest)

Population and income figures for major industrial countries are easily available in government reports. The U.S. Department of Commerce regularly publishes an *Overseas Business Report* summarizing population, total GNP, GNP per capita, total imports, and imports from the United States for most countries. Interpreting such data for developed countries is reasonably straightforward. For less-developed countries (LDCs), however, interpretation of economic data may be more difficult.

Populations, for example, differ in several ways. A rapidly growing population, such as that of Colombia, has a far larger proportion of its population under 15 years of age than does a slow-growth country like Canada. In 1970 both of these countries had about 20 million people. But Canada had 9 million in the labor force and Colombia had only 6.5 million. Such differences can have profound effects on both labor supply and marketing.

Per capita income statistics must also be interpreted carefully. The international manager needs to go beyond per capita averages, which are often very low in developing countries, to discover how many households have incomes above a certain level. This level differs, of course, for different products. Far more people can afford ballpoint pens than Rolls Royces. For example, India's per capita income average is less than $200 per year. If India's nearly 700 million people *each* had an income of only $200 per year, there would be no market for anything but the most basic food, clothing, and shelter. But because India has considerable diversity in income, it represents a substantial market for many manufactured items. Traveling through India, one sees transistor radios and bicycles throughout the cities and towns. In fact, because of India's immense population, even the tiny percentage who possess great wealth represent a significant market for expensive luxury goods.

The importance of *infrastructure* also cannot be overemphasized. In the West, we expect our power, transportation, and communication systems to work without fail most of the time. In many LDCs, however, these systems are far from complete and interruptions of service due to technical difficulties are frequent. Power failures may occur several times a day. Having to light candles toward the end of a dinner party may seem a bit romantic. Losing a batch of chemicals because the power failed at a critical point is quite another matter. Other facets of infrastructure include modern financial institutions, the educational system, and the myriad of support organizations from iron foundries to town zoning councils and public accounting firms. Where these are not available, the multinational firm must supply them. It is not unusual for a company building a factory near a previously underdeveloped raw materials source in an LDC to have to build an entire township, including housing, schools, hospital, and sometimes even extensive garden areas, in order to attract a sufficient work force.

The mechanism of economic control also affects virtually all of the firm's activities. We are used to a largely *market economy* in the United States, and we complain vehemently when the government interferes, as with wage and price controls. Some foreign countries, especially those behind the Iron Curtain, operate as *command economies.* Central governments control what is made, where it is shipped, and at what price it is sold. Although there is an emerging literature about dealing with the command economies, and these countries may become more important as trade partners in the future, by far the most important areas of the world for today's managers are the other countries with market economies and the very large number of countries, including nearly all the LDCs, with *mixed economies.*[8]

There are two major differences between market and mixed economies. First is the balance between public and private enterprise. Mixed economies tend to reserve a large portion of industry to "public sector companies" or "parastatals," including mail, telephone, radio, television, electric utilities, railroads, munitions, and basic industries such as steel and heavy machinery. Many have nationalized much of the financial sector as well.

The second major facet of a mixed economy is formal planning of economic development. Many mixed economies have published plans indicating the use of scarce resources for several years ahead. Although American managers bridle at these interventions of government into what they view as the rightful preserves of management, these plans often prove extremely useful to people who learn the ropes. A government that restricts entry into an industry by issuing only one or two licenses may provide a protected market for several years to the companies that are fortunate enough to receive those early licenses. In such circumstances a modest amount of price control may not seem too high a price to pay.

Political environment

The most important aspects of the political environment are the degree of law and order, the ruling government's attitude toward private enterprise in general and foreign direct investment in particular, and the relative stability of the current government.[9] All these elements affect the firm's future prospects. Because we have grown used to the political environment of the United States, we are likely to make hasty assumptions about other countries—either that things are "about the same" or that they are "entirely different." Neither assumption is warranted without careful study.

Extreme changes in political climate are infrequent among governmental systems that have been in existence for a generation or so. The best sociological and anthropological opinion is that political systems are not at all haphazard but, rather, embody the people's expectations. Those who hold power do so because they are granted such status by the cultures of which they are a part. Political power persists only when it is accorded legitimacy by the masses of the people. Studying a nation's history is very important in helping a manager

8. See Raymond Vernon and Louis T. Wells, Jr., *Manager in the International Economy,* 4th ed. (Englewood Cliffs, N.J.: Prentice-Hall, 1981).

9. See Michael Z. Brooke and H. Lee Remmers, *International Management and Business Policy* (Boston: Houghton Mifflin, 1978), Chapter 15.

decide whether a particular political situation is likely to remain stable. Where a change seems probable, it is important to ask whether the new order is likely to be substantially different in its treatment of foreign enterprises.

Unfortunately, LDCs, which offer emerging opportunity for international enterprise, have had such a short political history that they are hard to "read." And many former colonies, especially in Africa, consist of previously unrelated or even warring clans or tribes.

Some of the most obvious differences among political situations stem from professed ideologies. The notable separations are between communism and democracy. A government that professes to follow an identified ideology often makes the task of predicting its future actions somewhat easier.

In summary, an international firm must analyze and try to predict the political situation in a projected target country. Where the risk seems too great, the uncommitted firm can often afford to wait and see what happens. Once a firm has invested directly in a country, however, change in the political climate must simply be weathered.

Cultural environment

Culture is the most pervasive, and in many cases the most difficult, environment for the foreigner to understand.[10] Different value systems and different theories of cause and effect can be especially troublesome. Even so broad a matter as corporate purpose can be affected by differing value systems. Consider value system differences in the United States and India. It is generally accepted here that U.S. firms seek a profit above other goals; some level of profit is regarded as necessary for survival. By contrast, Indian culture, with its emphasis on the extended family, seems to look on private enterprises first as a means of providing jobs for as many male family members as possible, and only secondarily as a means of providing profits to the shareholders.

Overlooking cultural differences can be dangerous. Slaughtering and meat packing facilities were established some years ago on the edge of territory roamed by the Masai, a race of cattle breeders and herders in East Africa. No one had grasped that the Masai value their cattle as tangible evidence of wealth, in and of themselves, and not primarily because they could be sold for money. Far too few cattle were offered for sale, and the ones that were offered were usually in poor condition. The venture failed because its managers did not anticipate a basic difference in value systems.

Another source of confusion between cultures is different views of cause and effect. In order for a plan to gain support in Japan or India, consensus of all those involved may be required. In India this consensus may be almost automatic in support of a program sponsored by the head of the extended family—and impossible to arrive at over his opposition. In Japan a system of forwarding reports and recommendations up through the managerial hierarchy brings any disagreements to the surface. The decision process is not complete until any such disagreements have been worked out. Neither of these pro-

10. See Brooke and Remmers, *International Management and Business Policy,* Chapter 16.

cesses is familiar to most American managers, although in recent years foreign branches of U.S. firms have adjusted their style to permit more rank-and-file participation.

In the same vein, cultures differ in their opinions on the relative efficiency of reward and punishment as motivators for improved performance, the relative importance of monetary and nonmonetary rewards, and the most effective means of communication (oral, written, or nonverbal). As noted in Chapter 16, the English and Germans stand farther apart than Americans when talking, whereas the Arabs, Japanese, and Mexicans stand closer together.

Planning in the international context

Planning for international business is similar to planning for domestic business activities—but with added dimensions. Strategic planning must take into account both added commercial opportunities and the objectives of the host nation. Operational planning must be adjusted for greater distances, time differences, movement of goods and funds through several political jurisdictions, and cultural complexities.

When a company forms international joint ventures, the interests of the foreign partners must also be incorporated into strategic and operational plans. How will profits and losses be divided with the foreign partners, and how will the partnership affect taxes? This section considers these added dimensions of planning in the international context.

Figure 23.3 illustrates the decisions and processes associated with planning and international management. In most cases, international planning goes through three basic phases: the decision to enter international business, strategic planning, and action planning. Each phase requires that a number of decisions be made.

The decision to go international

An organization can make the decision to go international for a variety of reasons. The three most common reasons are cost, opportunity, and threat. By cost, we mean that the organization may be able to buy or manufacture products in other countries at a lower cost than is possible in its home country. For example, Atari recently closed its home computer operation in California and moved operations to Hong Kong and Taiwan. Atari was already involved in international business, but this specific move was made so that the company could cut labor costs and remain competitive.[11]

A second reason for going international is to take advantage of opportunities in other countries. Manufacturers of luxury goods have found new buyers in the oil-rich Middle East. Japanese automobile companies entered the

11. See "Atari to Idle 1,700 at California Site, Move Jobs to Asia," *Wall Street Journal*, February 23, 1983, p. 2.

Figure 23.3
Planning in the
international context

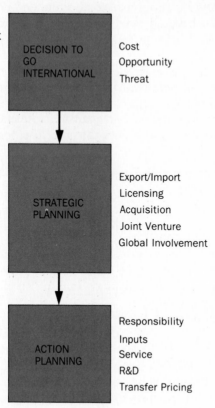

DECISION TO GO INTERNATIONAL

Cost
Opportunity
Threat

STRATEGIC PLANNING

Export/Import
Licensing
Acquisition
Joint Venture
Global Involvement

ACTION PLANNING

Responsibility
Inputs
Service
R&D
Transfer Pricing

U.S. market because they saw a demand for fuel-efficient cars that was not being met by GM, Ford, or Chrysler.

Finally, an organization may develop an international thrust because of competitive threats. We noted in Chapter 5 that, as an industry becomes international, firms within that industry may have to enter foreign markets to survive.[12]

International strategies

Regardless of the rationale for going international, organizations typically follow one or more of five basic strategies: exporting/importing, licensing, direct investment in branches or subsidiaries, joint ventures, and global involvement.[13]

12. See Thomas M. Hart, Michael E. Porter, Eileen Rudder, and Eric Vogt, "Global Industries: New Rules for the Competitive Game," Graduate School of Business Administration, Harvard University, Working Paper, HBS 80–53.

13. See Y. N. Chang and Filemon Campo-Flores, *Business Policy and Strategy* (Santa Monica, Calif.: Goodyear, 1980), Chapter 17.

Exporting/importing. Exporting and/or importing is typically an organization's initial foray into international business. On the export side, the organization may want to maintain its production facilities in one country and simply sell finished products in other countries. Export management companies, agents, or other intermediaries may be used to handle these activities.

Similar arrangements could be made for imports. A manufacturer could import materials or component parts from other countries. A retailer might contract with a foreign manufacturer to produce products under the retailer's own brand name.

Licensing. Licensing is a slightly more complicated form of international business. In licensing, a company allows another company to use its brand name, trademark, or technology. In return, the licensee pays a royalty, usually based on sales. One particularly fruitful avenue for licensing opens up when the product is moving toward obsolescence in the home country. The company may be able to extend the revenue stream of the product by licensing it in underdeveloped countries.

Direct investment. The establishment of a branch or subsidiary in a foreign country is called direct investment. Often this action is taken unilaterally, establishing an entirely new organization in the host country, by acquiring an operating site, building a factory and sales force, and so forth. In other instances, expanding companies have entered new countries by acquiring existing foreign companies or facilities. The strategy of acquisition involves purchasing production facilities or even entire companies in other countries. For the acquiring firm, this provides an intact facility with operating systems, personnel, and distribution networks already in place. Of course, some or all elements of the acquisition may be in need of modernization. In recent years, foreign companies have frequently adopted this strategy in entering the United States market. For example, Nestle entered the U.S. frozen food industry by acquiring Stouffer's.[14]

Joint ventures. Joint ventures involve two or more companies in different countries collaborating on a new enterprise. Strategic planning for international joint ventures is very complex. Such planning typically arises at two major points in the joint venture's history.

The first point is the critical negotiation of the joint venture agreement, which includes a target performance for the venture. During this negotiation the multinational parent corporation naturally acts in its own best interest.[15] Any host-country national interests must be represented by the local partners to the joint venture and backed up by the government if licenses are required. The agreement covers production and sales targets and limitations, resource

14. See Ball, ''A 'Shopkeeper' Shakes Up Nestle.''
15. See John I. Reynolds, *Indian–American Joint Ventures: Business Policy Relationships* (Washington: University Press of America, 1978).

commitments by both parties, and other general expectations over the first few years of the venture.

The second point for strategic planning for a joint venture occurs as the venture reaches its initial objectives and is ready to expand, diversify, or change direction. At this point a venture that is profitable enough to cover its own capital needs or that can borrow in the host country is likely to be treated much as a wholly owned subsidiary would be. When the venture needs an infusion of additional capital, the plan may necessitate a full renegotiation of the agreement.

Global involvement. The most integrated and comprehensive level of international strategy is global strategy. Most large multinationals (such as Exxon, Boeing, Unilever, Fiat, Siemens, Tenneco, and Nestle) operate at this level. Each has manufacturing facilities and generates a large portion of its sales outside its home country. A potentially usual framework for this approach to international business is the idea of global strategies summarized in Chapter 5.[16]

Action planning

Regardless of the type of international strategy adopted by a firm, a number of action-planning issues must still be confronted. The balance between centralized and decentralized decision making as a part of this action planning is often critical in international management.

The argument for decentralization rests on the overseas manager's superior knowledge of local conditions and closer contact with sources of relevant information. The argument for centralized planning is that only the head office has enough information to coordinate what may be conflicting plans. In practice, overseas profit centers that are doing well are likely to be given substantial responsibility for operational planning, and overseas centers that have trouble meeting targets are usually more subject to head-office planning.

Aside from the issue of the degree of decentralization for action planning in international business, four other important issues arise. They are inputs, market servicing, research and development, and transfer pricing.

Input sources. Where should each subsidiary get its inputs, including capital, raw and semifinished materials, and human resources? Choices must be made among host-country sources, the home country (including the parent company itself), and other countries. The choice of sources of borrowed funds is heavily influenced by availability, exchange-rate risks, and relative interest rates, as well as the regulations of the host government. Choice of materials frequently involves a trade-off between host-government requirements for the use of local materials and price–quality considerations. Human resource planning will be discussed more fully under organization issues later in the chapter.

---

16. See Hout et al., "Global Industries."

Market servicing. Which factories and other facilities should serve which markets? Choices in the short and medium term are influenced by factory capacities, shipping distances and costs, language and cultural similarities, national tariffs, and tax implications. Some major multinationals with truly global interests of enormous scale, such as IBM, consider decisions of input sourcing and market servicing as part of a package designed, as far as practicable, to "balance payments" for the corporation. Besides limiting the company's exposure to sudden changes in monetary exchange rates, such actions help satisfy each nation's concern about the impact of IBM's sales (or purchases) on its economy.

Some nations, particularly those having foreign exchange difficulties, are very suspicious of any real or apparent limitations on the right of branch plants within their borders to export to other parts of the world. Where a license to open a factory is required, as is the case in India, the multinational may be obliged to guarantee that its local (Indian) plant will be allowed to compete for exports throughout whatever region the product might ordinarily be shipped.

Research and development. Where the multinational should do its R&D is often a touchy planning question. Most multinationals conduct their most sensitive basic research in their home countries, because they find it less expensive to centralize this function at headquarters. Some truly global firms, however, establish many research units overseas. In some industries, notably pharmaceuticals, the overseas environment for developing and testing products is actually superior to that in the United States. The criteria for choosing an R&D site are the local availability of skilled people, the attitudes of home and host governments toward the projected kind of R&D, the cost of the operation in relation to expected results, and the firm's ability to control the expected product improvements. It is widely believed that an R&D group must be of a certain minimum size in order to be effective; a shortage of scientifically educated people in many LDCs has meant that few multinationals have located R&D efforts there. This has proved to be a sore point in some instances when LDC host countries have been disappointed in the amount of R&D located within their boundaries. In recent years, the trend has been to disperse such facilities throughout the developed world.

Transfer pricing. Whenever products, components, or services change hands between subsidiaries of a company, a transfer price must be set. This issue is sometimes troublesome when the transactions occur across national borders. Suspicion often arises on the part of governments that multinationals "rig" transfer prices to avoid taxation. Theoretically, there is substantial scope for misrepresentation in this area because of the large amounts of intracompany international trade.[17]

On the other hand, good business reasons tend to restrict abuses of transfer prices. For most multinationals the maintenance of good relations with the

17. See G. K. Helleiner, *Intra-Firm Trade and the Developing Countries* (New York: Macmillan, 1981).

host country outweighs any gains that might be realized from artificial transfer prices. Where market prices can be determined or simulated in some way, this is a frequent choice for setting a transfer price. We will say more about transfer pricing in later sections on profit centers and motivation.

Organizing in the international context

Organizing, the second important managerial function, is also important for international management. Figure 23.4 identifies the major factors that affect the organizing function for businesses operating in more than one country.

Factors influencing international designs

One key factor influencing the design of a multinational business is the corporate strategy adopted by the firm. As summarized earlier, organizations may adopt exporting/importing, licensing, direct investment, joint ventures, or global involvement. At the first extreme, a small staff or perhaps even one person could handle limited exporting or importing activities. At the other extreme, full-scale global involvement dictates that a large portion of the organization's design account for international activities.

By *market mix* we mean the nature of the countries being served by the multinational business. If a company is competing in the United States, England, France, West Germany, and Japan, the mix of markets is relatively similar in terms of infrastructure, economic environment, and so forth. If the mix includes the United States, India, South Africa, and Peru, however, much less similarity exists. Hence different forms of organization design may be needed in these two situations.

Figure 23.4
International factors that influence the organizing function

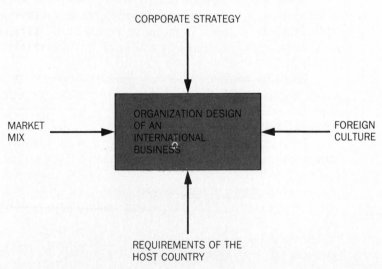

The culture of each foreign country must also be considered. People in different countries are motivated by different factors and subscribe to different beliefs about the role and importance of work in their lives. Structural components such as job design and work schedules may vary from one country to another.

Finally, host countries may also impose on companies certain requirements that influence their structure. For example, some countries require that domestic ownership of a business must exceed 50 percent.

Forming a corporation that includes this level of local participation brings a host-country board of directors into the overseas structure. The possible loss of control in joint ventures is one reason why some large multinationals avoid direct investment in countries that insist on local participation. For example, IBM withdrew from India in the late 1970s when the Indian government demanded more local control over the management of IBM's subsidiaries.

Even when international operations are wholly owned by the parent company, the host government's regulations and strong public opinion may spur the hiring of host-country nationals for management positions. This has at least an indirect effect on organization structure, because international movements of host-country nationals are far more rare than such movements of home-country managers. Fairly complete subsidiary organizations, from CEO right down through all the relevant functional managers, seem most consistent with full host-country management.

Organization design and international management

In response to these and other factors, a variety of organization designs may be appropriate. One recent study has suggested, however, that many such designs roughly fall into one of three major categories.[18] Figure 23.5 suggests how these three designs might look.

Divisional form of design. Under the *divisional form of organization design,* a separate department or division is established to handle international activities. That division, in turn, may be organized along functional, product, or location lines. The rest of the organization may also exhibit a variety of bases of departmentalization.

This approach is often used by organizations in the early stages of international involvement. In terms of strategy, firms using importing or exporting, licensing, or direct investment strategies in a small number of countries might adopt this form of design.

Levi Strauss uses the divisional form for its international activities. One major division within Levi's is Levi Strauss International. Within this division, units are based in Europe, Canada, Latin America, and the Asia/Pacific region. Each of these units, in turn, is organized by product.[19]

---

18. See William H. Davidson and Philippe Haspeslagh, "Shaping a Global Product Organization," *Harvard Business Review,* July–August 1982, pp. 125–132.

19. See "Levi's Problems Finding a Fit," *New York Times,* November 8, 1980, pp. 20, 32.

Figure 23.5
International
organization design

DIVISIONAL FORM OF DESIGN

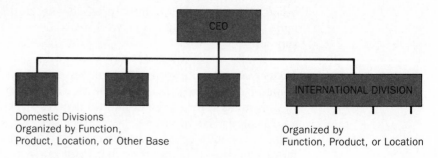

Domestic Divisions
Organized by Function,
Product, Location, or Other Base

Organized by
Function, Product, or Location

GLOBAL PRODUCT DESIGN

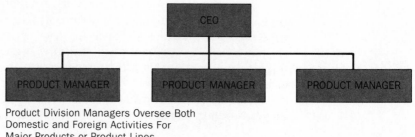

Product Division Managers Oversee Both
Domestic and Foreign Activities For
Major Products or Product Lines

GLOBAL MATRIX DESIGN

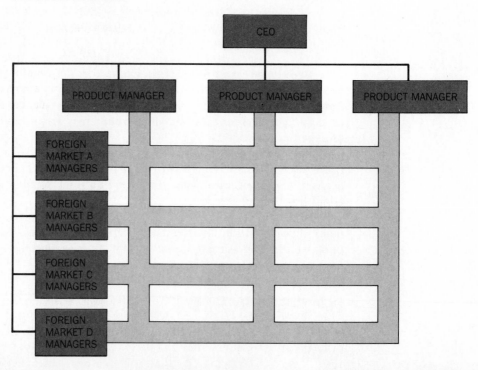

Global product design. The *global product design,* also shown in Figure 23.5 is sometimes adopted by firms as their level of international involvement increases. For example, an organization that is heavily committed to both a strong domestic base and widespread international activity might use this approach.

Basically, the global product design is used in the same way as the product approach to departmentalization discussed in Chapter 9. Senior executives oversee all the activities associated with products or product lines. Within each product division, the firm might have domestic and foreign production facilities, sales staffs, and so on. The rationale for this form of design is typically that it is efficient and groups activities around product lines in a logical fashion. Firms that have used this structure include International Harvester, Ford, and Union Carbide.

Global matrix design. The *global matrix design* may also be used by companies that are heavily involved in international business, particularly those adopting a strategy of global involvement. Recall from Chapter 11 that a conventional matrix is formed by superimposing product units onto functional units. As Figure 23.5 shows, a global matrix overlays location units onto product units.

Typically, the product managers and the location managers share responsibility. The primary advantage of this design is that it facilitates the transfer of resources between foreign operations. Managers in each foreign market can draw on the functional expertise housed within each relevant product group and can also use those product units to facilitate exchanges from one market to another.

As we noted earlier, these three designs represent general categories. No two firms have the same design, and these three designs are not pure forms in the sense that organizations adopt them exactly as drawn. They do, however, capture the major features of many international organization designs.

Leading in the international sector

The elements that make international management most different from domestic management are the relationships between middle management, supervisors, and workers. Although an expatriate manager is rarely assigned as a supervisor, he or she must be sensitive to the different expectations of both supervisors and workers in foreign cultures.

Cultural differences show up first in the actions of individuals, which often reflect the broad social groupings to which they belong. Such patterns, in turn, influence patterns of leadership, motivation, and communication in the workplace. We begin, therefore, by looking at these broad social groupings.

The effect of social structure on international management

Many dimensions of the social structure have greater influence on the workplace in foreign countries than in the United States. Clan or tribe affiliation, for

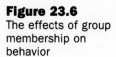

Figure 23.6
The effects of group
membership on
behavior

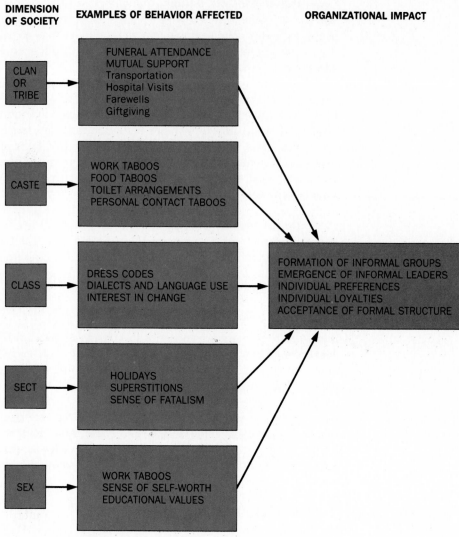

example, can be an important factor in many African countries, and vestiges of the caste system persist in India. Figure 23.6 lists five such dimensions of the social structure: clan or tribe, caste, class, sect, and sex. Each of these has an impact on certain kinds of behavior, examples of which are shown in the middle column. General effects on the workplace are shown to the right.

The influence of weekly and annual holidays (for example, Sunday, Christmas, and Yom Kippur) is well understood and accepted in the United States. But the American manager in the Middle East may have to deal with Moslem workers whose weekend includes Friday and whose major annual holy days not only vary from year to year (as does Easter) but also are subject to local interpretation. A work force that includes several sects with different holy days, in a foreign country where absences disrupt operations, at best compounds scheduling difficulties. At worst it causes frequent shortfalls in production.

Casteism, to take a different example, dies hard in India, despite laws abolishing it.[20] The various taboos that separate those who were previously stigmatized as "untouchables" from caste Hindus still influence management's ability to fill certain jobs. Job rotation to enrich experience is also hindered. Fortunately for modern industry, Hinduism does not assign new jobs, such as "computer programmer," to particular castes.

Whatever the cultural influences on individual behavior in the workplace, managers can expect to see the results in patterns of informal group formation and leadership; in individual preferences regarding task structure, supervisory style, and working conditions; in the degree of loyalty to the organization; and in the extent to which the formal structure is accepted.

Unionism in the international context

In many foreign countries, unions are as much political organizations as economic, and dealing with them is quite different from dealing with the economic unions in the United States.

In the United Kingdom, New Zealand, and Australia, the Labour party is politically potent whether it is in or out of power at the moment, and unions gain strength from their identification with that party. In August 1982 four unions in the U.K. announced a one-day strike to halt publication of newspapers, not because of any current grievance against the newspapers but in support of health service workers. Despite a court injunction against the newspaper unions' strike, the head of one union group was quoted as saying, "If this is the first shot in the war, then so be it. It is not only the health workers. It would be one in the eye for the Tory Government, because we are challenging the new industrial relations laws."[21] Although total days lost to strikes are not necessarily greater when the union considers itself a political organization, bargaining has a much different flavor.

On the outer fringes of industrial actions are outbreaks of violence. Violence is not unknown in the United States, of course. Union workers of Iowa Beef Packers recently attacked "scabs" hired by the company to keep a factory working through a strike. In India workers sometimes besiege managers in their offices for days or weeks until their demands are met. Managers have even been siezed as hostages, as were three Swedish managers in Bolivia in 1982. Some of this violence suggests the early days of unionism in the United States and can be expected to decline as unionism matures. Some of it may persist, however, because blue-collar workers in many countries see no hope of ever crossing over into supervision or management. Under such conditions it is no wonder that industrial bargaining has become the battle line between economic classes.

20. See Reynolds, *Indian–American Joint Ventures.*
21. "NHS Workers Ask Print Unions Not to Strike," *The Times,* August 10, 1982, p. 1.

Leadership

American managers often feel quite uncomfortable with the status accorded the managerial class in some countries. If they try to "act naturally" or informally in relationships with subordinates, they are likely to be misunderstood. Far from ingratiating themselves, American managers who move too quickly to a back-slapping, first-name basis with employees lose status and informal influence, leaving themselves only formal power to fall back on.

Of course, is it not necessary to throw out hard-won insights into effective leadership. What is needed is a change in habits and practices, not a disregard for subordinates as responsible human beings. The changes called for involve formality, patience, distance, and obligation. In any unfamiliar culture the American manager would do well to meet superiors and subordinates alike somewhat more formally than in the United States. Informality may well be misconstrued as weakness or as an effort to manipulate others.

Patience is another quality valued in managers. Americans are often perceived as the most impatient people in the world, and many cultures regard impatience as unseemly. Raising one's voice or insisting on instant action may lead to loss of respect. In many developing countries, an American's patience is constantly tried by systems that don't work well, from banking to telephones. The manager who lets frustration over the inefficiency of systems spill into personal relationships is less effective than one who stays calm. The social distance between superior and subordinate is almost universally greater elsewhere than in the United States. The expatriate manager is generally expected to maintain this distance by upholding formality in the workplace and by avoiding familiarity in after-hours activities.

Almost paradoxically, the *obligations* of leadership are often more compelling overseas than at home. Subordinates expect their managers to respond to personal needs at a level that would be considered paternal in the extreme in the United States. To become comfortable with the role of "padrone," as this is called in Latin America, is sometimes difficult for an American manager.

Despite the difficulties of leadership in a foreign setting, there are outstanding instances of companies (among them IBM, Hewlett-Packard, and Caterpillar Tractor) that have successfully transplanted their "company code of conduct" into a wide variety of international contexts. It is also true that many successful multinationals have an inherent style of leadership that makes their "codes" widely acceptable among other cultures. Furthermore, careful selection and training of managers, subordinates, and workers in these successful companies help them avoid the difficulties we have discussed.

Motivation

In many underdeveloped countries, workers are still preoccupied largely with wages and fundamentals such as housing.[22] The reasons are simple: few work-

22. See Geert Hofstede, "Motivation, Leadership, and Organization: Do American Theories Apply Abroad?" *Organizational Dynamics,* Summer 1980, pp. 42–63.

ers have enough. Newer concepts such as job enlargement or enrichment rarely need to be considered, except where they contribute directly to increased output. Even "old-fashioned" direct incentives such as piecework pay often prove very successful in raising output. A textile factory in socialist Ethiopia recently raised output in its spinning section enough to avoid purchasing new machines by establishing group incentives. The same caveats apply here as in using such systems elsewhere. Managers cannot continue indefinitely to raise output targets without raising total compensation, changing methods of work and supervision, or adding labor-saving equipment.

In more developed countries, the same kinds of motives and motivation processes hold as apply in the United States. Sweden has been a pioneer in the use of job design to enhance motivation.[23] Recent research also suggests that Chinese workers may be motivated by a variety of both intrinsic and extrinsic factors.[24] The manager must develop a thorough understanding of the relevant motivational factors when designing reward systems in other countries.

Communication

When the manager and the workers speak different languages, everyone is aware that the language barrier poses a special problem. Unusual efforts must be made to avoid misunderstandings and convey subtleties of thought. Even within a common language, differences of usage and nuance may create problems. And whatever the language, we are likely to find differences in the use of body language and humor as we move from one culture to another.

Edward J. Hall called our attention to the oft-hidden world of *body language,* the unspoken messages indicated by the way we stand and/or sit or hold our arms.[25] Within our own culture we are often quite skilled in "getting the message" from such silent communications. But gestures vary in meaning from culture to culture. For example, each culture seems to develop its own "comfort range" for the proper distance between people talking to one another. A distance that seems entirely proper to an Egyptian or Iranian may feel uncomfortably close to an American.

Humor, within its own culture, helps smooth difficult transitions and emphasize important points. But it seldom translates well between cultures and should be avoided in international communications. At best it will usually be misunderstood; at worst it may inflict unintended harm.

Misunderstanding, despite the best of intentions, is nonetheless a continuing problem in international communications. The best solution, of course, is bilingual managers. The next best thing is learning the other's language. After a while one develops a sixth sense of when someone has misunderstood in

23. See *Scandinavian Review,* June 1977, for several articles on Swedish job reforms.

24. See Rosalie L. Tung, "Patterns of Motivation in Chinese Industrial Enterprises," *Academy of Management Review,* July 1981, pp. 481–489.

25. Edward J. Hall, *The Hidden Dimension* (New York: Doubleday, 1966).

face-to-face communication. Then paraphrasing the message may clear matters up. When letters or cables are misunderstood, however, it often takes a long time to sort things out.

Controlling in the international sector

Controlling, the fourth managerial function, is also important for effective international management. When control systems are not properly established, major problems may result. For example, Nestle lost over $100 million in Argentina in 1980, partly because its control system did not provide timely feedback to corporate headquarters in Switzerland.[26]

Areas of international control

One kind of management that is most frequently controlled from the home office is the management of funds. It is often company policy that the local manager must keep cash and accounts receivable at a minimum in order to reduce currency risk. The home office may also tell a branch when and where to borrow (to control repayment in certain kinds of funds), and it may control transfers of funds between branches. All these are techniques to hedge against foreign-exchange risks. There is no way to avoid such risks altogether, but most multinationals feel that the central financial office is best equipped to control funds.

Figure 23.7 summarizes several other key areas of control that are of interest to the international manager. In at least two important areas, control of international operations is quite different from control of domestic operations. Bribery is almost a way of life among government officials in some countries, and several U.S. multinationals have been heavily involved. Largely due to public indignation in the United States, however, this practice is now subject to greater legal control than it was a few years ago. The other important difference in international operations is that materials and supplies cost more than labor in many foreign countries.

As a result of several well-publicized incidents, bribery seems to be on the wane today. Whatever may have been normal practice in the past, no American multinational today can afford the adverse publicity and loss of U.S. government business, in addition to the legal penalty, resulting from being caught in a bribery scandal. Uniformly, therefore, company rules now forbid bribery. Overseas managers may even be required to sign annual statements that they have not bribed and know of no bribery on behalf of the company. Internal audits of the accounts of overseas branches focus closely on current assets and liabilities to make sure that no illegal payments are concealed, because such payments would be an embarrassment if exposed during external, independent audits.

26. See Ball, "A 'Shopkeeper' Shakes Up Nestle."

Figure 23.7
Areas of
international control

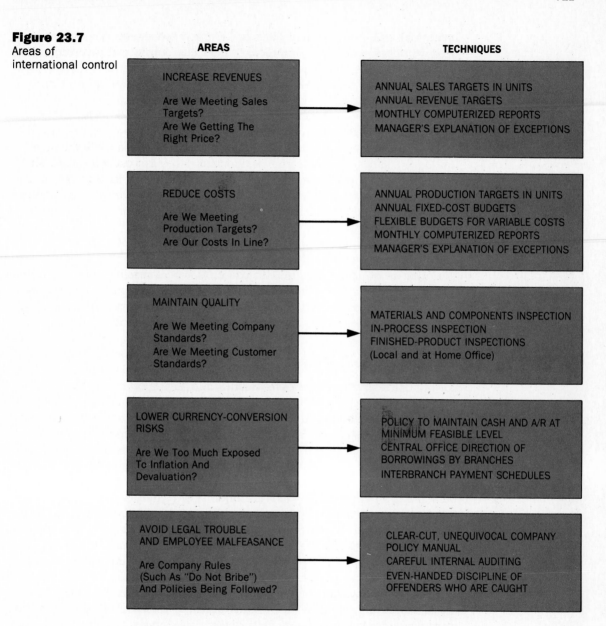

AREAS

INCREASE REVENUES

Are We Meeting Sales
Targets?
Are We Getting The
Right Price?

REDUCE COSTS

Are We Meeting
Production Targets?
Are Our Costs In Line?

MAINTAIN QUALITY

Are We Meeting Company
Standards?
Are We Meeting Customer
Standards?

LOWER CURRENCY-CONVERSION
RISKS

Are We Too Much Exposed
To Inflation And
Devaluation?

AVOID LEGAL TROUBLE
AND EMPLOYEE MALFEASANCE

Are Company Rules
(Such As "Do Not Bribe")
And Policies Being Followed?

TECHNIQUES

ANNUAL SALES TARGETS IN UNITS
ANNUAL REVENUE TARGETS
MONTHLY COMPUTERIZED REPORTS
MANAGER'S EXPLANATION OF EXCEPTIONS

ANNUAL PRODUCTION TARGETS IN UNITS
ANNUAL FIXED-COST BUDGETS
FLEXIBLE BUDGETS FOR VARIABLE COSTS
MONTHLY COMPUTERIZED REPORTS
MANAGER'S EXPLANATION OF EXCEPTIONS

MATERIALS AND COMPONENTS INSPECTION
IN-PROCESS INSPECTION
FINISHED-PRODUCT INSPECTIONS
(Local and at Home Office)

POLICY TO MAINTAIN CASH AND A/R AT
MINIMUM FEASIBLE LEVEL
CENTRAL OFFICE DIRECTION OF
BORROWINGS BY BRANCHES
INTERBRANCH PAYMENT SCHEDULES

CLEAR-CUT, UNEQUIVOCAL COMPANY
POLICY MANUAL
CAREFUL INTERNAL AUDITING
EVEN-HANDED DISCIPLINE OF
OFFENDERS WHO ARE CAUGHT

Some multinationals are involved in such large transactions that winning or losing a single bid can make the difference between a large profit and a large loss for the year. Under such circumstances, in countries where the receiver of a bribe is unlikely to be penalized if found out, some bidders are very likely to offer payments "under the table." Faced by such competition from companies based in other countries, some U.S. multinationals offer their products through independent local commission agents and expressly refuse to inquire into the expenses these agents incur in promoting sales. (It should be noted that using a local agent often makes good sense even when there is no need for bribes; it would be improper to infer that bribery was involved merely from the presence of an agent in the channel.) Some American multinationals sell directly, refuse to bribe, and rely on their products' quality and price to win their share of the business. Many foreign governments are happy to see bribery reduced by multinationals who observe the new U.S. laws.

Multinationals need to be aware of the effect of wage versus materials costs on their operations. In countries where wages are much lower than in the United States, materials and components typically cost more than labor. Furthermore, it is often very difficult to lay workers off or let them go permanently. These facts combine to focus day-to-day control more on reducing waste and scrap than on curtailing direct labor costs. Labor is treated more as a fixed than a variable cost.

Quality control is related to the high cost of materials. An Indian joint venture partner once said that his American partner "gives me the guts to say, 'No. That's not good enough.'" In countries where materials are scarce and expensive, it is very tempting to save on waste by allowing substandard products to pass inspection. The design of control systems to prevent waste and scrap thus goes along with a willingness to say "no" to a substandard article.[27]

Key control techniques

For hundreds of years, control techniques in overseas operations have been a combination of delegating limited authority to an expatriate manager and of making a complete post-audit of accounts and activities. Today's situation is different in degree but not in kind. It is still the local managers who must make sure that subordinates and workers achieve the desired results, and it is still the people in the head office who must assure themselves that the overseas manager is competent and honest.

Today's overseas managers are often host-country or third-country nationals. This fact, along with the availability of telecommunications and computers, has made it tempting to home-office managers to try to control overseas branches from the center. The best-managed companies do not centralize in this way, although there is a recurring complaint among overseas managers that "they want to know every time I sneeze."

Control today starts with setting up profit centers when possible. If transfer prices are important to an overseas unit and must be set arbitrarily, the manager is more likely to head a cost center. Sales targets in units and revenue targets in monetary terms are identified, often through MBO procedures. Production targets in units and cost budgets in monetary terms are developed. These targets and budgets then become the basis of comparison for frequent progress reports designed to identify adverse trends before they get out of hand. The best control systems are designed to give the overseas manager detailed reports, abstracts of which are sent to headquarters; the local manag-

27. For a recent discussion of foreign manufacturing techniques and their use in the United States, see Richard J. Schonberger, "The Transfer of Japanese Manufacturing Management Approaches to U.S. Industry," *Academy of Management Review*, July 1982, pp. 479–487.

er's explanation of exceptions and description of remedial actions must usually accompany or closely follow the routine reports. When things are going well, the overseas manager enjoys considerable autonomy. When things are going badly, people from headquarters begin to drop in. Computers and jet aircraft have tended to "shorten the leash" on overseas managers whose operations get out of control.

We have pointed out that labor overseas is more of a fixed than a variable cost. For a number of American multinationals (IBM and Hewlett-Packard, for example) this is true around the world. They, like many Japanese companies, have a policy of not letting people go once they are past the probationary period. For all multinationals this is true in certain countries, such as India, where it is extremely difficult to let workers go.

Multinationals' quality control systems have two facets. The first is systematic testing at all stages of production to be sure that no material or component is processed further once a defect is discovered. The second is final product testing. Often the in-process inspection system is automated even when the final assembly is by hand. IBM's CRT console assembly plant in Scotland has a computerized inspection station for incoming computer chips and subcontracted circuit-board assemblies. After the consoles have been assembled, human operators check them in use after they have been held for several hours at an elevated temperature. The computerized inspection means that no defective component is installed. The inspection in use checks on the quality of final assembly.

Branches are often expected to send samples of hard-to-inspect finished products back to the home office or to independent laboratories for testing. This is particularly the case in international joint ventures where the multinational has a minority interest.

This chapter has probed the environment of international business and suggested how the functions of planning, organizing, leading, and controlling apply to international managers. However, no single chapter can capture the scope and complexity of international management. Given our shrinking globe and the accelerating movement toward multinational operations, managers will increasingly need to develop and refine their understanding of the international sector and how it is related to their own unique situations.

Summary of key points

International management is not just domestic management on a bigger geographic scale. Different languages, customs, laws, resources, and expectations combine to make international management a complex challenge for business.

The scope of international management can range from overseeing a global network of plants or sales units to competing with foreign manufacturers for domestic consumer dollars. International management involves relating the organization to its environments and entails planning, organizing, leading, and controlling. Several levels of international involvement can be identified, and multinationalism has grown rapidly over the past several years.

Whereas the task and general environments of international management are similar in concept to those of domestic firms, the economic, political, and cultural dimensions take on added importance and complexity.

International planning goes through three basic phases: the decision to enter international business, strategic planning, and action planning. The decision to enter international business could be prompted by costs, opportunity, or threat. There are several alternative international strategies: exporting/importing, licensing, acquisitions, joint ventures, and global involvement. Key action-planning issues include the appropriate level of decentralization, input sources, market servicing, research and development, and transfer pricing.

Factors that influence the organization design of international organizations include corporate strategy, market mix, the culture of each foreign country, and host-country requirements. The three general design alternatives are the divisionalized form, the global product design, and the global matrix design.

The social structure of a particular culture greatly affects the leading function in international management. Unionism also varies greatly across countries. The activities associated with leadership, motivation, and communication should all be handled with care in international situations.

Controlling is important for effective international management. Primary areas of international control include the management of funds, bribery, and the costs of materials and supplies. International control is often based on profit or cost centers. Many financial ratios and other control techniques that are used in domestic operations are also useful in the international setting.

QUESTIONS FOR DISCUSSION

1. To what extent is international management relevant to non-business organizations?
2. What kinds of businesses or industries are most and least likely to be affected by foreign companies in the future?
3. Which dimensions of a firm's task environment are likely to be most important?
4. What are the key similarities and differences in the environment-organization interactions for domestic and international organizations?
5. How might the concepts of corporate, business, and functional strategies be applied to international settings?
6. Can you apply the adaptation model and the BCG matrix approaches to strategy to international business?
7. What kinds of coordination techniques might be most and least useful to international organizations?
8. What key areas of organization change and development might be most relevant to international businesses?
9. Can you identify other cultural factors beyond those cited in the chapter that could affect the leading function?
10. If you were an American manager just put in charge of a work force of 150 Italian employees, what leading activities would you be most concerned with at first?

11. How might cultural factors influence the kinds of control used by an organization?

12. What kinds of control techniques might be most and least useful to international organizations?

C A S E   23.1

At the beginning of this chapter, you read a scenario about a company that wants to increase its market share in Japan. The state-owned Japanese monopoly, however, tightly controls entry into the market and sets selling prices. Consequently your company has not done well in Japan. The company being described could be R. J. Reynolds or Philip Morris. The case that follows describes the Japanese trade restrictions in more detail, summarizes what American companies are attempting to do, and then raises some other issues for your consideration.

For years, United States tobacco producers such as R. J. Reynolds and Philip Morris have been trying to gain a foothold in the Japanese cigarette market. Japan could potentially be the largest overseas customer for these companies. Japanese consumers have shown a marked preference for American tobacco, and U.S. tobacco companies estimate that, under the right circumstances, they could export merchandise valued at $1.5 billion each year to Japan. A number of barriers, however, have limited entry into this lucrative market.

The Japanese market is controlled by Nihon Sembai Kosha, a state-owned company that prefers to translate its name into English as Japanese Tobacco and Salt Public Corporation (Japanese Monopoly Public Corporation is the literal translation). Sembai Kosha is the country's only cigarette manufacturer and controls all cigarette distribution.

Unlike many Japanese firms, Sembai Kosha is surprisingly inefficient. The company needs 27 factories to turn out half the number of cigarettes produced in 13 U.S. plants. Productivity per worker has been estimated at only 40 percent of that of American tobacco workers. Yet the company has almost total power to restrict the activities of foreign competitors.

For example, new brands of cigarettes must be test-marketed in 60 scattered retail outlets. Test marketing is allowed only once a year, and new brands must surpass certain sales goals to eventually be allowed to go into full distribution.

Advertising is limited according to past Japanese sales. As a result, each American firm can spend only $660,000 a year on advertising, while Sembai Kosha can spend $70 million. Further restrictions require that a brand can no longer be advertised after it has been on the market for three years.

Sembai Kosha also controls all distribution channels within Japan. Retailers must order all their cigarettes, both domestic and foreign, through the state monopoly. American cigarettes must be

Barriers to international competition in Japan

ordered and paid for weeks in advance yet are delivered only once a month. Japanese brands are usually delivered every week and on a C.O.D. basis. The most popular American brand in Japan, Lark, is often out of stock in many retail outlets, even though Philip Morris regularly provides Sembai Kosha with a three-month supply. Sembai Kosha sales representatives also discourage retailers from displaying American promotional materials.

Perhaps most frustrating for the American companies is the Japanese pricing structure. Until recently, U.S. companies did not know what the Japanese tariff structure was. They were simply told what the retail price of their cigarettes would be, and this price was substantially higher than the price charged for Japanese products.

In 1980 pressure from Washington forced the Japanese to lower tariffs and reveal their formula. In a series of swift moves, the Japanese imposed a 90 percent tariff, generously cut it to 35 percent, and then tacked on a 56.5 percent retail tax. Consequently the price of cigarettes went up rather than down.

The U.S. manufacturers have continued to battle, however. They first formed an export association to fight for better market access (Japanese companies have successfully used this strategy in the past when dealing with the United States). They have also teamed up with another Japanese firm, Mitsubishi, to more effectively promote their products. Finally, President Reagan was convinced to exert more pressure on the Japanese to ease trade restrictions, and the Japanese government agreed in 1983 to make real cuts in the import tariffs charged to the American tobacco companies. Of course, this may or may not come to pass.

CASE QUESTIONS

1. What other kinds of actions might American companies adopt to increase their market share in Japan?

2. Do you think these same problems would exist if Sembai Kosha were not state-owned?

3. Do you believe a government has the right and/or the responsibility to protect domestic imports from foreign competition?

4. What economic, political, and cultural differences between the Japanese and American markets might be inferred from this case?

CASE REFERENCE

Kraar, Louis. "Japan Blows Smoke About U.S. Cigarettes." *Fortune,* February 21, 1983, pp. 99–111.

C A S E   23.2

Today's Business News is a successful U.S. business newspaper that was established in 1973 to compete with the *Wall Street Journal.* TBS has achieved success by differentiating itself in sev-

Strategic planning in an international market

eral important ways. First, TBS is published and distributed only in major U.S. cities. The paper is not mailed but is distributed directly by courier (for corporations buying 50 or more copies of each issue) and through vending machines and newsstands. Third, the paper carries less financial news than WSJ but instead provides more in-depth coverage of major business transactions and governmental activities.

Staff writers begin preparing copy for the next day's edition shortly after noon. Articles are written and edited throughout the afternoon. A skeleton staff works through the night and early morning updating articles and covering late-breaking stories. An inventory of general interest articles is kept for filler. The paper goes to press at 11:00 A.M. and is ready by 1:00 P.M. TBS has offices in the 25 largest U.S. cities. Each issue is about 75 percent "core" material and about 25 percent material that is unique to the city in which it is printed.

TBS was recently purchased by a large multinational firm, and a new CEO, Jack Danielson, was placed in charge. Danielson has spent the last two months preparing an ambitious strategic plan for dramatically expanding TBS. In particular, Danielson wants to turn TBS into an international business newspaper. A major part of this expansion would involve three special editions of TBS for Latin America (including Mexico, Central America, Brazil, and other major countries in South America), Europe (including Great Britain, France, West Germany, and Italy), and Southeast Asia (including Japan, Hong Kong, and Taiwan). Danielson envisions that each edition would be prepared in the same manner as the U.S. editions.

A second part of Danielson's plan for TBS involves distribution of different editions across markets. For example, he believes that Japanese managers would have an interest in reading the U.S. editions of TBS. His plan, then, calls for distributing each of the four editions in the same way the U.S. edition is presently distributed and then distributing the same edition to the other three markets on a one-day-delayed basis.

Danielson also sees several barriers that TBS will have to overcome to succeed in this expansion. First, printing facilities in Latin America tend to be technologically inferior to those found in the United States. Second, distribution demands in Europe will be complicated by the large number of national boundaries involved. Third, the cost of distributing editions to other markets is such that the day-old issues will be sold at twice the retail price. Still, Danielson believes in his strategy and is now trying to sell his proposal to the TBS board of directors.

CASE
QUESTIONS

1. If you were a member of the board, what questions would you raise?
2. Do you think Danielson's plans will succeed? Why or why not?
3. What other problems might TBS encounter if Danielson gets his way?

NAME INDEX

SUBJECT INDEX